# THE LOEB CLASSICAL LIBRARY

FOUNDED BY JAMES LOEB

EDITED BY

## G. P. GOOLD

# THEOPHRASTUS
## CHARACTERS

# HERODAS
## MIMES

# CERCIDAS AND THE CHOLIAMBIC POETS

LCL 225

# THEOPHRASTUS
## CHARACTERS

# HERODAS
## MIMES

# CERCIDAS AND THE CHOLIAMBIC POETS

EDITED AND TRANSLATED BY

JEFFREY RUSTEN,

I. C. CUNNINGHAM, AND A. D. KNOX

HARVARD UNIVERSITY PRESS

CAMBRIDGE, MASSACHUSETTS

LONDON, ENGLAND

1993

First published 1929
Reprinted 1946, 1953, 1961, 1967
Second Edition (with new text and
translation of Theophrastus and Herodas) 1993

*Library of Congress Cataloging-in-Publication Data*

Theophrastus. [Characters.   English & Greek]
Characters / Theophrastus. Mimes / Herodas. Cercidas and
the Choliambic poets. — 2nd ed. / edited and translated
by Jeffrey Rusten, Ian C. Cunningham, A.D. Knox.
p.   cm. — (Loeb classical library : 225)
Includes bibliographical references.
ISBN 0–674–99244–X
1.  Character sketches.   2.  Greek literature—Translations
into English.   3.  Cynics (Greek philosophy)—Poetry.
4.  Pantomimes.   I.  Rusten, Jeffrey S.
II.  Cunningham, Ian C.   III.  Knox, A. D. (Alfred Dillwyn)
IV.  Herodas.  Mimiambi.  English & Greek.
V.  Cercidas and the Choliambic poets.  English & Greek.
VI.  Title.  VII.  Series.
PA4449.E5C5   1992          91–45098
888′.0108—dc20      CIP

*Typeset by Chiron, Inc, Cambridge, Massachusetts.*
*Printed in Great Britain by St Edmundsbury Press Ltd,*
*Bury St Edmunds, Suffolk, on acid-free paper.*
*Bound by Hunter & Foulis Ltd, Edinburgh, Scotland.*

# CONTENTS

# PREFACE

Theophrastus' *Characters* is a pleasant little book for the casual reader, but an enormously difficult one for the scholar; I would guess that most of its editors, even the likes of Casaubon, Korais, Immisch and company, and Diels, have begun their work with relish and confidence, but concluded with an apologetic feeling that there was much more to be done. I am certainly no exception. The manuscript tradition of the work is perhaps the most corrupt among classical Greek authors, almost every other sentence requiring some emendation. To produce a text that can be translated and read requires adopting more conjectures than a proper critical edition might normally allow. Such a full edition — and a repertory of conjectures — is very much needed, but not to be sought here: my notes on the Greek text are normally restricted to recording conjectures by modern scholars, and are thus very limited; manuscript readings are reported at all only in these cases, and are usually taken from Immisch's 1923 Teubner edition, which I judged to be most accurate.

Many allusions in the *Characters* to the daily life of Athens require explanation; so when necessary I have not hesitated to annotate the translation more (on 16, "Superstition," *much* more) than may be customary for a Loeb volume. My translations of the individual titles were chosen to suit the descriptions ("Griping," "Sponging," "Chiseling") rather than to render a single Greek word; but the Additional Notes give an account of each trait's literal meaning, and its treatment in ancient literature.

For the section numbers within each character I follow the standard numeration (Steinmetz, Navarre, Immisch), rather than Diels' Oxford Classical Text.

For advice and suggestions I owe thanks to many more than I could name. But I cannot pass over Peter Bing, who lent me his notes from what must have been fascinating lectures on the *Characters* by the late Konrad Gaiser; William Fortenbaugh, not only for the splendid new edition of the fragments of Theophrastus but also for comments and hints on the Introduction; Rudolf Kassel, who introduced me to the dissertation on the *Characters* by Markus Stein, who in turn generously allowed me to use it in advance of publication and made countless acute corrections of my own work; and, especially, Zeph Stewart, for many hours of careful reading of my results, and painstaking criticism combined with unfailing encouragement.

This edition of Theophrastus and that of Herodas by I. C. Cunningham replace those in the original Loeb volume (1929) by J. M. Edmonds and A. D. Knox respectively. The rest of that volume — Knox's edition and translation of Hipponax, Cercidas, and the other Choliambic poets — is reprinted here without change. For subsequent work on Hipponax see M. L. West, *Iambi et elegi graeci* vol. I (2nd ed. Oxford 1989) and E. Degani, *Hipponax* (Bibliotheca Teubneriana, 2nd ed. Leipzig 1991). For Cercidas see Enrico Livrea, *Studi cercidei* (Papyrologische Texte und Abhandlungen 37, Bonn 1986); a new edition of Cercidas by Livrea and F. W. Williams is in preparation.

Ithaca, New York                                Jeffrey Rusten
August 1992

# THEOPHRASTUS

## *CHARACTERS*

EDITED AND TRANSLATED BY
JEFFREY RUSTEN

# INTRODUCTION

THEOPHRASTUS' range of interests almost matched that of his teacher Aristotle, from great works on botany,[1] studies on winds, weather, and many other topics in natural science, to logic and metaphysics, rhetoric and poetics, politics and ethics.[2] He would doubtless be astonished to learn that he is best remembered today for a little book only marginal to these studies and preserved only in a mutilated, perhaps abbreviated, form. Yet his *Characters* became a paradigm in European literature, and in the seventeenth and eighteenth centuries found dozens of translators and imitators in England, France, and Germany.

Before turning to its relatively recent influence, however, we must first look at its author's career, the character of the book itself, and its affinities with ancient ethical, comic, and rhetorical writings,

---

[1] *Inquiry into Plants*, ed. and tr. A. Hort (2 vols., Loeb Classical Library, 1916); *De Causis Plantarum*, ed. and tr. B. Einarson and G. K. K. Link (3 vols., Loeb Classical Library, 1976–1990).

[2] See the bibliography in Wehrli, "Der Peripatos" 475–6. (For abbreviations and works cited by author or short title only see the Bibliography.)

as well as several difficult (perhaps insoluble) problems: how the book came into being, why the text is in such lamentable condition, and to what extent the method and substance of this book can be reconciled with what we know of the philosopher Theophrastus himself.

## THEOPHRASTUS

Theophrastus was born in Eresus, on the island of Lesbos, ca. 370 B.C. He may have studied philosophy earlier, but at least by the age of 25 he began to work with Aristotle, who after the death of Plato had left Athens for the patronage of Hermias at Assos, a town near Theophrastus' home.[3] Hermias was executed by the Persians in 341; the young man followed his master first to Macedonia and the court of Philip, then joined him on his return to Athens after 334, where he was recognized as Aristotle's preeminent student and designated successor.

Theophrastus' residence in Athens coincided with a turbulent period in its political history,[4] some

[3] For speculations on this period see Konrad Gaiser, *Theophrast in Assos* (Abhandlungen der Heidelberger Akademie der Wissenschaften, 1985.3). See in general the sketch of the lives of Aristotle (by H. Flashar) and Theophrastus in Wehrli, "Der Peripatos" 230–234, 477, and Theophr. fr., Introd. pp. 1–2.

[4] See W. S. Ferguson, *Hellenistic Athens* (London 1911) chapters 1–3, Claude Mossé, *Athens in Decline* (London 1973) chapter 5.

of which is mirrored in the *Characters*. Despite the power of Macedonia, the city remained democratic, under the leadership of Lycurgus, until his death in 324.[5] The subsequent death of Alexander himself threw all into confusion, beginning with the Athenian uprising against Alexander's regent Antipater in 322 (when Aristotle himself withdrew again from Athens, leaving his school behind, and died in Euboea). Athens' defeat by Antipater led to a new oligarchic constitution under the Athenian conservative Phocion, with a limitation on the number of citizens.[6] But then Antipater's death (319) produced a further struggle among his heirs, and the remnants of Alexander's family, for control of Greece: his designated successor Polyperchon, in partnership with Alexander's half-brother Philip III Arridaios, proclaimed the autonomy of all Greek states in exchange for their support. Democratic forces in Athens rallied to him, and Phocion was executed. But Polyperchon's power waned, and in 317 Antipater's son Cassander assumed control of Athens, which he placed under the control of Demetrius of Phaleron, a student of Aristotle and staunch supporter of Theophrastus. Demetrius fled to Egypt in 307, and Theophrastus was driven for a year into exile;[7] but after his return he remained

[5] F. Mitchel, "Lykourgan Athens, 388–322," *Semple Lectures*, series 2 (Cincinnati 1970).

[6] L. A. Trittle, *Phocion the Good* (London 1988).

[7] Through a decree against non-Athenian heads of schools, moved by a certain Sophocles of Sounion. J. P.

firmly established as the head of the most popular philosophical school in Athens until his death ca. 285 B.C.

## STYLE, STRUCTURE, AND SETTING OF THE CHARACTERS

As preserved in the medieval manuscripts, the *Characters* consist of: a *Table of Contents* and a *Preface* explaining the genesis and purpose of the whole collection; and *thirty chapters*, each with:

1) *Title*: a single-word personality trait, always ending in -ια;

2) *Definition* in abstract terms of this quality;

3) *Description*, the longest part of each chapter, introduced with the formula "the X man is the sort who . . .," and continuing in a series of infinitives giving characteristic actions.

4) *Epilogue* (in some cases) in a more rhetorical style, with moralizing generalizations.

It is certain that two of these elements — the preface and the epilogues — are not by Theophrastus himself, being later (perhaps much later) additions to the text. Of the definitions, one (the first) is certainly a later addition, and several others which seem irrelevant to the descriptions they introduce,

---

Lynch, *Aristotle's School* (Berkeley 1972) 103–104, Theophr. fr 1.38; cf. Alexis *PCG* fr. 99 with bibliography.

or seem to be taken from other sources, are probably interpolations as well. (For the reasons behind these assumptions, see pages 30–32 below.)

What remains at the heart of the work are the descriptions, which are priceless for several reasons. First, because of their style. Theophrastus was a master of Greek rhetoric both in theory and practice — he received his name ("the divine speaker") from it, being originally called Tyrtamus (fr. 5A-6) — but here he disregards its constraints: there is no avoidance of hiatus, no logical or rhetorical figures or structures. An introductory formula "X is the sort who . . ." (τοιοῦτός τις, οἷος . . . ) leads to an infinitive containing the characteristic act — usually qualified by a series of participles giving the circumstances — followed by another participle and infinitive, and then another and another (sometimes interrupted with δεινὸς καί . . . "he is also apt to . . .") until the description ends. Not all scholars have found this style pleasing, and the attempt to account for its singularity has led to theories that it springs from lecture notes or a personal sketchbook, or even that it is the work of an excerptor, or a forgery utterly unrelated to Theophrastus; the only certain conclusion is that it is unique in Greek literature.[8]

Second, the setting is anything but timeless or

[8] Critics of its monotony include R. Porson and H. Sauppe (see Gomperz 5), but most others have been more generous: see especially Pasquali, "Sui carratteri" 47–56.

idealizing, being unmistakably the Athens of the last few decades of the fourth century B.C., whose customs, institutions, and prejudices form the backdrop of every character's actions. Only the fragments of contemporary Athenian comedies offer an equal insight into the city's daily life, and no work of ancient Greek literature can be dated so precisely from its historical allusions alone.

Finally, the descriptions are equally distinctive as literary portraiture.[9] They are never generalizations, but catalogues of vivid detail (some indeed so distinctive that they are difficult to interpret). We learn, for example, the exact words of the obsequious man, the boor, or the babbler, which gods the superstitious man placates on which days, how the chiseler avoids school fees, how the rumor-monger or the garrulous man finds an audience and the ungenerous man avoids one, which market vendors the shameless man franchises, how much he makes each day, and where he carries his earnings.

## DATE OF THE *CHARACTERS*

Numerous allusions in the *Characters* themselves indicate with considerable precision when it was

[9] For the background see Ivo Bruns, *Das literarische Porträt der Griechen im fünften und vierten Jahrhundert* (Berlin 1896); comparisons between Theophrastus and the portraiture of Lysippus in T. B. L. Webster, *Art and Literature in Fourth Century Athens* (London 1956) 124–133.

composed.[10] The most important clue is in the gossip spread by the rumor-monger in *Character* 8: he claims that Polyperchon and "the king" have defeated and captured Cassander, and that the current Athenian leadership is worried. This suits best the situation in Athens in late 319, when a decree of the new regent Polyperchon had encouraged Athens to restore its democracy, and Cassander appeared weak;[11] in that case the king will have been Philip Arridaios, and the worried Athenian leader, Phocion.[12]

The historical situation of *Character* 8 was first noted by Cichorius, who assumed that the whole work should be dated to 319; although different characters may well have different dramatic dates, and the various sketches may have been composed over a period of years,[13] it does seem that other

[10] On dating see C. Cichorius, Introduction to the edition of the Leipzig Philological Society, lvii–lxii; A. Boegehold, "The Date of Theophrastus' *Characters*," *Transactions of the American Philological Association* 90 (1959) 15–19; Stein, *Definition und Schilderung*.

[11] Plutarch, *Phocion* 32.1, Diodorus 18.55–56.

[12] There are other, less plausible candidates for "the king" in the years 317–310: Alexander IV, or Heracles, in which case the nervous current ruler of Athens will be Demetrius of Phaleron; a detailed review of the possibilities in Stein, *Definition und Schilderung*.

[13] Particularly since 319 was a year of constant crisis in Athens; the attempted prosecution of Theophrastus by the democrat Hagnonides (Diog. Laert. 5.37) may belong to this year also (Boegehold [above n. 10] 17).

chronological indications are consistent with 319 as well: thus *Character* 23 assumes that the famine at Athens and the campaigns of Alexander are over, but that Antipater is still alive and in Macedon, which points to 326–3, 322–1, or 319. There is mention of liturgies (23.6, 26.6), which were abolished by Demetrius of Phaleron (317–307) and not reinstated thereafter. The complaints of the authoritarian in *Character* 26 seem to have been composed under a democracy (as do the democratic sentiments of the patron of scoundrels, 29.5), but the fact that commissioners are being elected (26.2) rather than chosen by lot (cf. Arist., *Constitution of Athens* 56.4) suggests a date after 322.[14]

There are other features of the *Characters* which link them to anecdotal evidence on the life and students of Theophrastus. They dressed rather well, and had a reputation for living high;[15] thus there are four varieties of stinginess, but none of extravagance (see the Additional Notes on *Character* 9). His elegant manners and sophistication were well known, and thus we have a large number of types who lack social graces or make themselves foolish in society (see Additional Notes on *Character* 4). Theophrastus discussed sacrifice at length (fr. 584A–585), and he constantly employs it to illus-

[14] See Boegehold (above n. 10) 18, and Stein, *Definition und Schilderung*.

[15] Stein, *Definition und Schilderung* cites Teles fr. 30 Hense, Theophr. fr. 12, 23, Lycon fr. 7, 8, 14 Wehrli.

trate his types (9.2, 12.11, 15.5, 16 *passim*, 17.2, 21.7, 21.11, 22.4, 27.5); his father was a fuller, a trade with which his characters often have dealings (18.6, 22.8, 30.10; for the prominence of this craft in *De Causis Plantarum* see Einarson and Link, Introd., viii note a).

## THE *CHARACTERS* AND ANCIENT LITERATURE[16]

### *Ethics*

The meanings of ancient Greek χαρακτήρ are derived from an original sense of an *inscribing* (χαράσσειν) onto a surface: the *imprint* on a coin, the *form* of a letter, often the *style* of an author for rhetorical analysis.[17] "Character" in the modern sense is *not* one of its meanings—the Greek word for "character" is usually ἦθος[18]—and if it were not firmly established, Theophrastus' title might better be rendered "traits." Basic to his whole enterprise is the notion that individual good or bad traits of character may be isolated and studied separately, a notion formulated most memorably by his teacher

[16] For the concept in general see the survey in C. B. R. Pelling (ed.), *Characterization and Individuality in Greek Literature* (Oxford 1990).

[17] See A. Koerte, "ΧΑΡΑΚΤΗΡ," *Hermes* 64 (1928) 69–86.

[18] For examples of the various Greek terms for character see O. Thimme, Φύσις, τρόπος, ἦθος (Diss. Göttingen, 1935).

11

Aristotle in the *Nicomachean Ethics* Book 2:[19] for
each range of emotion (fear, anger) or sphere of
action (wealth, honor), Aristotle defines moral virtue and vice (ἀρετὴ καὶ κακία ἠθική, literally "excellence and badness of character") by their relation to
the middle: too large or small an amount is to be
avoided as a vice, and only by remaining between
the extremes can one attain virtue.[20]

Although Aristotle would not reduce moral
behavior to a formula,[21] he is nonetheless able to
apply this doctrine to a wide range of traditionally
named virtues and vices of character (*Nicomachean
Ethics* 1107a33–1108b7):[22]

[19] Among earlier philosophic descriptions of vices are
Plato's account of character types which parallel forms of
government in *Republic* VIII, and the literature of national
characters (Boeotian, Spartan, etc.) based ultimately on
the sort of climatological determinism in the Hippocratic
*Airs, Waters, Places*: see M. Goebel, *Ethnica* (Diss. Breslau
1915).
[20] This in turn is related to Greek popular wisdom that
avoidance of extremes is best: Nisbet-Hubbard on Horace,
*Odes* II.10.5, Hermann Kalchreuter, *Die ΜΕΣΟΤΗΣ bei
und vor Aristoteles* (Diss. Tübingen, 1911), H.-J. Mette,
"ΜΗΔΕΝ ΑΓΑΝ," *Kleine Schriften* (ed. A. Mette and
B. Seidensticker, Frankfurt 1988) 1–38.
[21] See W. F. R. Hardie, "Virtue Is a Mean," chapter 7 in
*Aristotle's Ethical Theory* (second ed. Oxford 1980).
[22] The listing here is based on the *Nicomachean Ethics*;
there is a slightly different list in exactly this format in
*Eudemian Ethics* 1120b38ff. I give the abstract noun
when Aristotle uses one, otherwise the adjective; an asterisk means it is found also in the *Characters*.

| ἔλλειψις (deficiency) | μεσότης (mean) | ὑπερβολή (excess) |
|---|---|---|
| *δειλός (coward) | ἀνδρεία (courage) | θρασύς (rash) |
| *ἀναίσθητος (unable to feel) | σωφροσύνη (temperance) | ἀκολασία (intemperance) |
| *ἀνελευθερία (lack of generosity) | ἐλευθεριότης (generosity) | ἀσωτία (profligacy) |
| μικροπρεπεία (niggardliness) | μεγαλοπρεπεία (magnificence) | βαναυσία (vulgarity) |
| μικροψυχία (pusillanimity) | μεγαλοψυχία (magnanimity) | χαυνότης (vanity) |
| ἀφιλότιμος (unambitious) | φιλότιμος (ambitious-good) | φιλότιμος (ambitious-bad) |
| ἀοργησία (passivity) | πραότης (gentleness) | ὀργιλότης (irascibility) |
| *εἰρωνεία (self-deprecation) | ἀλήθεια (truthfulness) | *ἀλαζονεία (boastfulness) |
| *ἀγροικία (boorishness) | εὐτραπελία (wit) | βωμολοχία (buffoonery) |
| δύσερις (quarrelsomeness) | φιλία (friendliness) | *ἄρεσκος (obsequious) |
| δύσκολος (bad-tempered) | φιλία (friendliness) | *κόλαξ (flatterer) |
| *ἀναίσχυντος (shameless) | αἰδήμων (polite) | κατάπληξ (bashful) |
| ἐπιχαιρεκακία (spitefulness) | νέμεσις (righteous indignation) | φθόνος (enviousness) |

Aristotle goes on in Books 3 and 4 (1115a6–
1128b33) to describe almost all of these virtues and
vices in detail. Although considerably more abstract, his descriptions of individual vices, both here
and in the parallel discussions in the *Eudemian
Ethics* (2.1220b21–1221b3, 3.1228a23–1234b11) and
the Pseudo-Aristotelian *Magna Moralia* (1.1190b9–
1193a37), seem to be precursors of some of the *Characters* (see the Additional Notes on individual characters); it is easy to imagine Theophrastus' work as
inspired by his teacher's approach to vices.

Peripatetic authors after Theophrastus wrote
works in a similar style. A fragment of Satyrus' "On
Characters" condemning profligacy is preserved by
Athenaeus (4.168c). Extensive quotations from Ariston of Keos, "On Relieving Arrogance," are given by
Philodemus, *On Vices* Book 10 (for text and translation see the Appendix); their style and use of detail
show a remarkable resemblance to the *Characters*.
Lycon's description of a drunkard is quoted by
Rutilius Lupus 2.7 (Lycon fr. 26 Wehrli). Other
treatments of vice owe something to character writing as well: Seneca and Plutarch[23] are the most
obvious examples, but also evidently Posidonius (fr.
176 Kidd).

---

[23] He wrote essays *On Garrulity, How to Tell a Flatterer
From a Friend, On Superstition, On Meddling, On the Love
of Money*, and *On Extravagant Self-Praise*.

## INTRODUCTION

### Comedy and Satire

For all their ethical basis, Theophrastus' sketches—
especially in extended scenes like "Idle Chatter"
(3), "Rumor-Mongering" (8), or "Cowardice" (25)—
quite obviously have comic affinities as well. Characterization by type was already an important
feature in Aristophanes,[24] but it was the comedy
of the fourth century which brought stock characters to the fore:[25] the flattering parasite, the greedy
or mistrustful old man, the shameless pimp or
the braggart soldier. The remains of comedies of
this period (or their Roman adaptations) offer in-
structive parallels to the behavior of Theophrastus'
characters,[26] and the titles of fourth-century plays
now lost suggest that traits of character were
sometimes central (those with an asterisk are in
Theophrastus also): *The Boor (Ἄγροικος), *The
Mistrustful Man (Ἄπιστος), The Glutton (Ἄπλη-
στος), The Profligate (Ἄσωτος), *The Superstitious
Man (Δεισιδαίμων), The Grouch (Δύσκολος), *The
Flatterer (Κόλαξ), *The Griper (Μεμψίμοιρος), The
Loner (Μονότροπος), The Meddler (Πολυπράγμων),

[24] W. Süss, "Zur Komposition der altattischen
Komödie," *Rheinisches Museum* 63 (1908) 12–38, R. G.
Ussher, "Old Comedy and 'Character': Some Comments,"
*Greece and Rome* 24 (1977) 71–79.

[25] H.-G. Nesselrath, *Die attische mittlere Komödie* (Berlin 1991) 280–330.

[26] R. L. Hunter, *The New Comedy of Greece and Rome*
(Cambridge 1985) 148–151.

*The Miser* (Φιλάργυρος), *The Busybody* (Φιλο-πράγμων).

Menander, the greatest author of New Comedy, has even been claimed as Theophrastus' student.[27] Not only does he appear to echo several other Theophrastan works in his writing, he manipulates his characters with as much skill as Theophrastus — in fact, even more skill, which prompts caution in assuming any direct influence. His philosophizing passages, impressive in themselves, are often given an ironic turn when put in the mouths of unsuitable characters. His stock characters too (especially soldiers and prostitutes) may often surprise us by transcending their limitations.[28]

Satire and comedy were often linked by ancient theorists,[29] and here too there are occasional resemblances to the *Characters*, especially in the vivid

[27] The imperial writer Pamphile (*FHG* III fr. 10) as quoted by Diogenes Laertius 5.36; for a detailed examination of the tradition of Menander as philosopher see Konrad Gaiser, "Menander und der Peripatos," *Antike und Abendland* 13 (1967) 8–40.

[28] For the "philosophical" passages — note especially the slave Onesimos' garbled psychological theory, *Epitrepontes* 1092–1099 — see Gaiser (preceding note); for the stock characters, Nesselrath (above n. 25) 333, and Wilamowitz' oft-repeated dictum (R. Kassel, *Kleine Schriften* [Berlin 1991], 508 n. 6): "Theophrastus gives us types; Menander gives us people."

[29] Horace, *Satires* 1.4, *Prolegomena* to Comedy p. 3 Koster.

portraits by Hipponax, Herodas, Phoenix, and Cercidas. Other such sketches are found in the poem by Semonides of Amorgos (seventh century B.C.) on types of women: their various vices (e.g., filthiness, cunning, extravagance) are explained by their creation from animals (e.g., the pig, fox, horse) or other elements (the sea). Only the industrious woman, created from the bee, is praiseworthy.[30] Among Roman satirists, Horace discusses greed (1.2, 2.2), and offers an extensive portrait of a bore (1.9); Martial (3.63) defines the *bellus homo* with a Theophrastan eye for detail, and Juvenal skewers the miser (14.126–134). The diatribes of Teles adapt some of the same techniques, and Lucian even shows a direct knowledge of the *Characters*.[31]

## *Rhetoric*[32]

Character sketching could also be an important weapon in court: Aristotle's account of moral traits in the *Ethics* is complemented by a rhetorical discussion of the contrasting traits of the old and young in *Rhetoric* 2.12–14.[33] Just as La Bruyère saw that

[30] Semonides fr. 7 West; H. Lloyd-Jones, *Females of the Species* (London 1975); Walter Marg, *Der Charakter in der Sprache der frühgriechischen Dichtung* (Würzburg 1938).

[31] M. D. MacLeod, *Mnemosyne* 27 (1974) 75–76.

[32] See in general Wilhelm Süss, *Ethos: Studien zur älteren griechischen Rhetorik* (Leipzig 1910).

[33] A. Dyroff, *Der Peripatos über das Greisenalter* (Studien zur Geschichte und Kultur des Altertums 21.3, Paderborn 1939).

fictitious characters could be mixed with the literary portrait of a real individual, so the ancient rhetorical tradition demanded exercises in character drawing as practice for historical portraits from life. Called χαρακτηρισμοί or ἠθολογίαι, these seem to have been standard exercises in all rhetorical training, and are mentioned by Cicero (*Topica* 83), and Quintilian (1.9.3);[34] a fine sample of a braggart is given by the *Rhetorica ad Herennium* 4.50–51.64. They led not only to portraits like Cicero's *In Pisonem*, but also the famous sketches of historical figures in Sallust and Tacitus.[35]

## PURPOSE OF THE *CHARACTERS*

The authenticity of the *Characters* as a work of Theophrastus, although doubted (without argument) by scholars as distinguished as Porson, Haupt, Vettorio, and Valckenaer, is as good as proved, as we have seen, by the frequency and precision of its allusions to Athens ca. 319. Yet it is easy to see why it was suspected: the work's subject

[34] Probably also by Suetonius, *De Grammaticis* 4.

[35] The most detailed introduction (although it slights rhetorical influence) is Christopher Gill, "The Question of Character-Development: Plutarch and Tacitus," *Classical Quarterly* 33 (1983) 469–487. For later parallels see David Nichol Smith, *Characters from the Histories and Memoirs of the Seventeenth Century* (Oxford 1918).

and its execution seem as alien to the philosopher's other work as its style.

Theophrastus' motive for writing the *Characters* might be sought in his ethical works, where several fragments offer connections, for example, the attested title "On Characters" (Περὶ ἠθῶν fr. 436.1); or fr. 465, where he notes how much care is devoted to the choice of a city, friends, even the route for a journey, while the more important choice of a way of life is left to chance; or fr. 449A, on virtue and vice, which closely resembles Aristotle — we have seen that the division of the *Characters* into traits, and even some of their names, recalls the *Nicomachean Ethics* as well.

But the differences between the *Nicomachean Ethics* and the *Characters* are even more obvious. The latter deals only with faults, while Aristotle is far more interested in virtues than in vices; Aristotle develops an argument about virtue as a mean, which is then illustrated with specific examples from spheres like reactions to danger, behavior with money, treatment of other individuals, leading to extended consideration of the virtues of justice and friendship; the *Characters*, on the other hand, are utterly lacking in analysis, their order of presentation apparently random — traits relating to money, friendship, or talk are not treated together, or compared in any way.

Most importantly, the *motives* behind the characters' actions are not discussed.[36] Much of the behavior detailed here — things like charging compound interest and late fees for loans, hiring flute girls for dinner parties, dedicating skulls of sacrificed cows, shirking payments for public service, seeking purification after incurring pollution — is in fact very close to normal, and well-attested for Athens of the fifth and fourth centuries. If the *Characters* are to offer ethical instruction, we need an analysis such as Terence (probably following Menander) puts in the mouth of Micio (*Adelphi* 821–825):

> multa in homine, Demea,
> signa insunt ex quibus coniectura facile fit,
> duo quom idem faciunt, saepe ut possis dicere
> 'hoc licet inpune facere huic, illi non licet.'
> non quo dissimilis res sit, sed quo is qui facit.

> In a person, Demeas, there are many
> clues that lead to an obvious conclusion. Thus
> even though two people behave the same, you can
>     usually say
> "this man can get away with it — that one can't."
> Not because the behavior is different, but because
>     the *person* is.

[36] See especially W. Fortenbaugh, "Die Charaktere Theophrasts," *Rheinisches Museum* 118 (1975) 64. The opening definitions of each character are completely inadequate as indications of motive, and their authenticity is in any case suspect (see pp. 31–33 below).

Thus support is lacking for the idea that the *Characters* is a series of excerpts made from Theophrastus' ethical writings,[37] or was written to illustrate them.

Some have suggested its purpose was not ethical at all. One alternative candidate is comedy.[38] Since there are no examples of virtue in the *Characters*, we are reminded of Aristotle's dictum (*Poetics* 1449a32, cf. 1448a1–5) that the depiction of people we do not take seriously (φαυλότεροι) is the province of comedy. Aristotle and his successors wrote frequently on the techniques and ethical implications of comedy. Their exact views are far from clear, but the so-called "Tractatus Coislinianus," which has peripatetic affinities,[39] lists in section XII three "characters of comedy" (ἤθη κωμῳδίας), the βωμολοχικά, ἀλαζονικά, and εἰρωνικά ("buffoons, braggarts, and tricksters"), two of which appear in the *Characters* (1, 23), the other in Aristotle (*Nicomachean Ethics* 1108a24). Works "On Comedy" and

[37] Formulated by Sonntag (see p. 30 below), but refuted by Gomperz, "Über die Charaktere Theophrasts," 4–8.

[38] R. G. Ussher, "Old Comedy and 'Character'," *Greece and Rome* 24 (1977) 71–79; W. Fortenbaugh, "Theophrast über den komischen Charakter," *Rheinisches Museum* 124 (1981) 245–260.

[39] Most recently and fully R. Janko, *Aristotle on Comedy* (London 1984) and Nesselrath (above n. 25) 102–162.

"On the ridiculous" are ascribed to Theophrastus himself (frs. 709–710), as well as a definition of the genre (fr. 708).

Another suggested purpose is rhetorical instruction.[40] There is no doubt that this is the use to which the work was eventually put; indeed it owes its very survival to its inclusion among the handbooks of the schools; but we have no trace in the rhetorical writings of Theophrastus (fr. 667–707) that he treated characterization, nor in the *Characters* themselves that they have such a purpose; it might indeed seem to be ruled out if the title ἠθικοὶ χαρακτῆρες in Diogenes Laertius 5.47 is correct.

What ultimately defeats any attempt to find an ethical, comic, or rhetorical basis in the *Characters* is the fact that there is no trace in them of structure or analysis at all. Like any other work of fictional literature — and unlike any other work of Theophrastus — the *Characters* are presented as pure entertainment. The question is therefore not the work's purpose so much as its style, and here three scholars have made complementary suggestions: 1) Gomperz (11–13), that the *Characters* bear

[40] O. Immisch, *Philologus* 11 (1898) 193–212, Süss, *Ethos* (above n. 32) 167, A. Rostagni, *Rivista di filologia* 48 (1920) 417–443, D. Furley, *Symbolae Osloenses* 30 (1953) 56–60, S. Trenkner, *The Greek Novella in the Classical Period* (Cambridge 1958) 147–154, Fortenbaugh, "Theophrastus, the *Characters* and Rhetoric," chapter 3 in *Rutgers University Studies in Classical Humanities* 6 (1993).

the same relation to Theophrastus' ethical works as the sketchbook of a painter does to finished paintings — he compared the connection of Aristotle's *Constitution of Athens* to the *Politics*, his *Homeric Problems* to the *Poetics*; in the school of Aristotle, such preliminary collections of materials were published, though they would not be today; 2) Pasquali ("Sui caratteri" 51–3) points to the radically unusual style, which he regards as an experimental publication based on lectures; 3) Gaiser[41] also suggested the lecture hall, as the place where the giving of information, moral instruction, and entertainment intersect.

Indeed Theophrastus' public lectures seem to have been enormously popular and entertaining: Diogenes Laertius 5.37 tells us that he had 2000 students (cf. Theophrastus fr. 15), and Hermippus (fr. 51 Wehrli = Theophrastus fr. 12) that he punctuated his lectures with gestures, citing in particular his mimicry of a glutton. Some other works of Theophrastus, known only from fragments, may have been as lively ("On Marriage," fr. 486), and the peripatetic school after him interested itself in a wide range of popular and practical ethical questions in an anecdotal style.[42]

---

[41] To my knowledge this suggestion was never published; I know it from notes on his Tübingen lectures on the *Characters* lent me by Peter Bing.

[42] Wehrli, "Peripatos" 467–469.

# HISTORY OF THE TEXT

## Medieval Manuscripts

The most valuable individual manuscripts are:[43]

A = *Parisinus graecus* 2977, XI cent.

B = *Parisinus graecus* 1983, X–XI cent.

Both A and B contain *Characters* 1–15, the proem and the table of contents (for 1–15 only); in both manuscripts, the text of *Character* 30.5–16 is wrongly appended to *Character* 11.[44]

V = *Vaticanus graecus* 110, XIII cent., which only begins with *Character* 16, yet it alone continues to the end of *Character* 30 (29–30.5 were first edited from this manuscript by Amaduzzi in 1786).[45]

Since the text of 30.5–16 is (incorrectly) added by AB after *Character* 11, for the final sentences of

---

[43] The clearest and most thorough account of the medieval manuscripts is by Immisch, pp. viii–lii of the Philological Society of Leipzig edition.

[44] For detailed accounts of both these manuscripts see H. Rabe, *Rheinisches Museum* 67 (1912) 323–332, and W. Abraham in Studemund, *Jahrbücher für classische Philologie* 1885 (31) 759–772, E. Matelli, *Scrittura e civiltà* 13 (1989) 329–386.

[45] The writing is indistinct, and heavily abbreviated; see the photograph of fol. 253 r/v (*Characters* 16–21) in R. Merkelbach und H. van Thiel, *Griechisches Leseheft zur Einführung in Paläographie und Textkritik* (Göttingen 1965) no. 5 pp. 15–16.

the work we may compare AB and V, which reveals that at least here (although not necessarily elsewhere) AB gives in many cases a *shorter* text, but often a *better* one than V.

The simplest approach to reconstructing this phase of their transmission is the assumption that an original manuscript α was divided into two parts (1–15, 16–30) and copied separately; the branch of the tradition containing *Characters* 1–15 found a fragment (perhaps the final page detached) containing *Character* 30.5–16 from an abridged text, and re-copied this where it was thought to belong, at the end of *Character* 11.[46] Thus the accompanying stemma (page 26).

All manuscripts *later* than A, B, and V are divided into three groups:[47]

C, consisting of 7 manuscripts (XV–XVI cent.) containing *Characters* 1–28: Immisch pp. ix–xiii.

D, consisting of 6 manuscripts (XIV–XVI cent.) containing *Characters* 1–23: Immisch pp. xiii–xviii

E, consisting of 32 manuscripts (XIII–XVI cent.)

---

[46] On the other hand AB is *not* derived from an abridgment for 1–15, as shown by the papyri (see below).

[47] N. G. Wilson, *Scriptorium* 16 (1962) 96–8, extends this list of manuscripts from published library catalogues: yet among the manuscripts he designates as new, nos. 3, 20, 24, and 55 were already known to Immisch (the first three only in his Teubner edition of 1923); whereas nos. 19, 34, and 63 (none designated "new") have to my knowledge never been mentioned before.

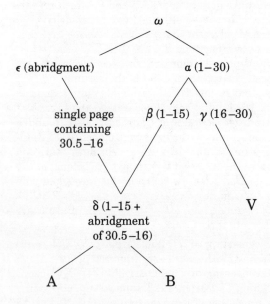

which never contained more than *Characters* 1–15: Immisch pp. xix–xxv.

The transmission of these later families C, D, and E is more complicated: E, containing *Characters* 1–15, appears to derive from A and B, and therefore to have no independent value. The families C and D, however, derive from A and B only for the first 15 characters; after that, they copy 16–23 or 16–28 from another source, which is however not identical with V, since when V was discovered it proved to have a significantly longer text in many passages.[48] Therefore C and D must have derived *Characters* 16ff from an abridged manuscript also, producing the following stemma:

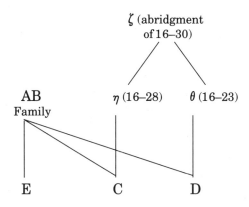

The ultimate source of the abridgment ζ remains in dispute. Diels (followed by Stein, *Definition und*

[48] These so-called "additamenta Vaticana" are printed in bold type in the apparatus of the Philological Society of Leipzig edition and Immisch's 1923 Teubner edition. Steinmetz 38–41 suggested that the abridgments were carried out in the thirteenth century by Maximus Planudes, whom we know to have reworked the rhetorical corpus in A and B (H. Rabe, *Rheinisches Museum* 67 [1912] 332–337).

*Schilderung*, and most modern editors) believed it to be entirely derived from V, so that CD would possess no independent value; Immisch (Leipzig edition pp. xxxvi–lii, Teubner edition pp. iii–iv, followed by Pasquali and Steinmetz) maintained that occasionally C and D preserved an independent tradition.

Finally, there exists an epitome of *Characters* 1–21 in "M" (*Monacensis graecus* 505, XV cent.), which agrees mostly with B in 1–15, mostly with V in 16–21.

## Papyri and Testimonia

The text offered by the medieval manuscripts of the *Characters* may be the most corrupt of any major work of Greek antiquity; yet the fragments found on papyrus suggest that it is more or less that already fixed by the first century B.C.:

P. Hamb. 143 (I B.C., *Characters* 7–8), M. Gronewald *Zeitschrift für Papyrologie und Epigraphik* 35 (1979) 21–2.

P. Herc. 1457 (I B.C., Philodemus *On flattery* citing *Character* 5). For this and other possible citations of Theophrastus among the Herculaneum papyri see Eiko Kondo, "I 'caratteri' di Teofrasto nei papiri ercolanesi," *Cronache ercolanesi* 1 (1971) 73–86, with the corrections reported by T. Dorandi and J. Hammerstaedt in Stein, *Definition und Schilderung*.

P. Oxy. 699 (A. D. III) offers an epitome of *Characters* 25–6.

## INTRODUCTION

In the twelfth century the *Characters* was mentioned (and perhaps imitated, see N. G. Wilson, *Scholars of Byzantium* [London 1983] 200–201) by Eustathius on *Iliad* 12.276 (p. 931.18) and Tzetzes, *Chiliades* 9.941.

### Earliest Transmission

We have seen that the date of the *Characters* is known, while the purpose for which it was written and the earliest stages of its textual history are shrouded in mystery. But it is obvious why the work survived: every single medieval manuscript which contains it is derived from collections of treatises on rhetoric (whose central authors were Hermogenes and Aphthonius), so that it must owe its preservation to a decision to make it part of a rhetorical corpus, doubtless as an aid to the description of character (see p. 22 above). This must have occurred by the ninth century, perhaps considerably earlier.[49]

In the process of being included in rhetorical corpora, the *Characters* was prone to being shortened in transmission: as we have seen, many of the medieval manuscripts of 16–30 are presumed to derive from abridgments, and there exist two epitomes, M and P. Oxy. 699.

Yet at other stages of its history, the work was prey to expansion as well, and here the motive

[49] Immisch, Philological Society of Leipzig edition, xxix–xxxv.

THEOPHRASTUS

seems to have been to adapt the work not to rhetoric, but to moralizing instruction in ethics.[50] The evidence for these expansions is entirely subjective, since even the earliest papyri offer more or less the same sort of text we have today. Yet there can be little doubt that some parts of the *Characters* as we have them are later additions, of three kinds:

*The Proem.* Even beyond its chronological absurdities and fatuous repetitions, the introductory essay now preserved in all manuscripts gives a completely false picture of the work that is to follow. For details see the note *ad loc.* It was first shown to be a later insertion by Carl Gottlieb Sonntag, *Dissertatio in prooemium characterum Theophrasti* (Leipzig 1787).

*Epilogues* are appended to several *Characters* (1.7, 2.13, 3.5, 6.10, 8.10–14, 10.14, 26.6, 28.7, 29.6). The *Characters* themselves, as we have seen, employ a simple and repetitive style to describe the specific actions of a single individual. In these epilogues, by contrast, a florid style and the tendency to moralize and generalize (and consequent use of the plural) betray immediately that they are alien. They are usually considered Byzantine, although not necessarily by the same hand as the proem.[51]

*Definitions* are prefixed to every character: their

[50] Immisch, Philological Society of Leipzig edition, xxxvi.

[51] Gomperz 4; Immisch, Philological Society of Leipzig edition, xxxv; Pasquali, "Sui caratteri" 67–69.

style is uncompromisingly abstract, and they are composed of a limited number of recurring elements;[52] there are often problems in reconciling them with the character description which follows — at worst they flatly contradict it, at best they are irrelevant or offer only a partial introduction to the character described. (It is therefore especially unfortunate that they come first, since they lead the reader to try to match what follows to their formula, rather than reading the description itself.) Most suspicious is the fact that several separate collections of definitions (ethical and otherwise) circulated in antiquity, some of them falsely attributed to famous names: Pseudo-Plato, *Definitions*, Pseudo-Aristotle, *On Virtues and Vices*, and the Stoic definitions of emotions collected in *SVF* III p. 92–102. Some of the definitions in the *Characters* correspond closely either with these collections (*Characters* 5, 7, 9, 12, 16) or with a formula in Aristotelian ethical writings (*Character* 1): since they seem less at home in Theophrastus, it is probable that in at least some cases the *Characters* were "improved" by the addition of definitions from these and other collections.[53]

---

[52] For example, ὡς ὅρῳ / τύπῳ (περι)λαβεῖν in 1, 5, 9, 20, cf. 14; δόξει / δόξειεν ἄν εἶναι in 1, 4, 7, 13, 16, 23, 25, 26, 27.

[53] The first to suggest the definitions were not Theophrastan was Hanow; the case was made more strongly by Gomperz, and more recently by Stein, *Definition und Schilderung*. On the pseudo-platonic and other definitions

On the other hand, there are two strong arguments against athetizing the definitions as a group: 1) the Theophrastan imitations of Ariston of Keos in the third/second century B.C. (see the Appendix) begin with definitions as well (although much more apt ones than in Theophrastus); and 2) three of the definitions (*Char.* 2, 6, 26) are attested in papyri. If *all* the definitions in the *Characters* are post-Theophrastan additions, their interpolation must have taken place extremely early.[54]

## Conclusions

After working backward to investigate the history of the text, we may now speculate at a positive account of its origins and transmission until its republication in the Renaissance.

---

see Ernst A. Schmidt, *Aristoteles über die Tugend* (Berlin 1965 = Aristoteles *Werke*, ed. E. Grumach XVIII.1) 27, 140, who however proceeds from the assumption that the definitions in *Characters* are genuine. Pasquali's suggestion ("Sui caratteri," 85) that Theophrastus himself borrowed from the collections of definitions seems on chronological and intellectual grounds unlikely.

[54] Pasquali ("Sui caratteri" 76) suggests that some of the definitions and titles have been meddled with, others not. As far as titles go (they all end in -ια), there seems reason to be skeptical when they do not match the character, being used elsewhere in a different sense: εἰρωνεία (1), ἀπόνοια (6), ἀναισχυντία (9), ἀναισθησία (14), ἀηδία (20), ὀλιγαρχία (26).

# INTRODUCTION

I. (ca. 319 B.C.) Composition of the *Characters* by Theophrastus, in an experimental style; the publication was perhaps based on lectures. (There is no reason to believe the *Characters* was one of the "lost" works of Theophrastus edited by Andronicus in the first century B.C., on which see Theophrastus fr. 37–41; but it also seems clear that the work never received the kind of scholarly attention in Alexandria that was accorded to Plato or the historians.)

II. (III–II B.C.) At least some definitions added from other sources (Ps-Plato, *Definitions*, Ps-Aristotle, *On Virtues and Vices*. *Characters* known to peripatetics Lykon, Satyros, and Ariston.

III. (I B.C.) *Characters* known to Philodemus.

IV. (Roman empire) Beginnings of use in Roman rhetorical instruction (*Rhetorica ad Herennium*, Cicero, Quintilian): occasional epitomization (P. Oxy. 699).

V. (Later Roman empire) Proem and epilogues added to stress the work's ethical importance.

VI. (Early middle ages) Inclusion of *Characters* in the corpus of rhetorical treatises dominated by Hermogenes and Aphthonius.

VII. (IX–XI cent.) Separation of *Characters* 1–15 from 16–30; major manuscripts produced.

VIII. (Later middle ages) *Characters* mentioned by Tzetzes, Eustathius, Planudes.

## THE *CHARACTERS* AND
## EUROPEAN LITERATURE

The *Characters* had a small but persistent influence on European literature[55] even before the seventeenth century, through the tradition of rhetorical instruction: as we have seen, several ancient rhetorical works include character sketches in the Theophrastan style, and the *Characters* itself owes its very survival into the middle ages solely to its inclusion among the rhetorical treatises of Hermogenes and Aphthonius, doubtless as a model of character depiction. Galleries of such rhetorical portraits can be found already in the prologue to *The Canterbury Tales* or the Seven Deadly Sins in *Piers Plowman*, or Sebastian Brant's *Ship of Fools*.[56]

Although parts of it were edited as early as 1527, it was the great edition and commentary of Isaac Casaubon in 1592[57] that brought the *Characters*

[55] For what follows see especially Smeed, *Theophrastan Character*. There are selections from all these writings in Aldington, *A Book of Characters*.

[56] Smeed, *Theophrastan Character* 6–19.

[57] See Rudolf Pfeiffer, *History of Classical Scholarship* II (Oxford 1976) 120–123. (The detailed and idiosyncratic biography by Mark Pattison, *Isaac Casaubon*, second ed. Oxford 1892, largely ignores Casaubon's scholarship.) Casaubon's commentary remained standard for nearly two centuries. His first edition contained only *Characters* 1–23; 24–28 were added in 1599; 29–30 were first included in the edition by J. C. Amaduzzi, 1786.

wider attention; his multiple corrections of the text, and commentary illustrating the background of the sketches in the life of ancient Athens, made it possible to read it with understanding for the first time. The seed it contained could fall on fertile soil: Rabelais and Cervantes had introduced new literary forms, Erasmus and others had adapted and popularized the writings of Lucian and Juvenal,[58] Montaigne had written in the Senecan manner on the components of character, and Thomas Chapman and Ben Jonson were beginning to exploit the ancient medical theory of humors to produce characters for the comic stage.[59]

The idea of an individual essay devoted to the description of a single psychological type was an instant success. The first to imitate it was Joseph Hall, Bishop of Norwich and later of Exeter, who not surprisingly stressed its moral aspects; his own

[58] Christopher Robinson, *Lucian and His Influence in Europe* (London 1979); Gilbert Highet, *Juvenal the Satirist* (Oxford 1954) 206–218; R. M. Alden, *The Rise of Formal Satire in England Under Classical Influence* (Philadelphia 1899).

[59] Chapman's *A Humorous Days' Mirth* (in 1597) and Jonson's *Every Man in His Humour* (1598) show no direct knowledge of the *Characters*, but the character sketches spoken by Mercury and Cupid in *Cynthia's Revels* (1600) are obviously modeled on Theophrastus; see E. C. Baldwin, "Ben Jonson's Indebtedness to the Greek Character-Sketch," *Modern Language Notes* 16 (1901) 385–396.

*Characters* (first published in London in 1608) were more abstract, moralizing, and rhetorical than Theophrastus, and (following the preface, which he did not know to be spurious) included characters of virtue as well as of vice.

Hall's book itself inspired imitations for the rest of the seventeenth century; but most of these were more interested in vice (and entertainment) than in virtue and moral instruction. Apart from individual sketches issued as pamphlets or incorporated into other books, two other English collections of this period stand out. In 1614 there appeared a book of 21 characters (expanded to 83 in subsequent editions) by the late Sir Thomas Overbury and "other learned gentlemen" (among them Webster, Dekker, and Donne), often employing extravagant wordplay and metaphor, which extend the genre to reflect contemporary English life — there are characters not only of vices and virtues but trades ("The Ostler") and national types ("The Dutchman"). Then in 1628 John Earle's *Microcosmography* retained the wide range of subjects treated in Overbury, but returned to a more relaxed, less mannered style.

Hall, Overbury, and Earle provided the models for innumerable others throughout the seventeenth century in England, where character writing became a standard exercise, as prescribed by Ralph Johnson, *The Scholar's Guide* (1665):[60]

[60] Quoted by Smeed, *Theophrastan Character* 36.

## A Character

A Character is a witty and facetious description of the nature and qualities of some person, or sort of people.

RULES *for making it*

1. Choose a subject, *viz.* such a sort of men as will admit a variety of observation, such be, drunkards, usurers, liars, tailors, excise-men, travellers, peddlers, merchants, tapsters, lawyers, an upstart gentleman, a young Justice, a Constable, an Alderman, and the like.

2. Express their natures, qualities, conditions, practices, tools, desires, aims or ends, by witty Allegories, or Allusions, to things or terms in nature, or art, of like nature and resemblance, still striving for wit and pleasantness, together with tart nipping jerks about their vices or miscarriages.

3. Conclude with some witty and neat passage, leaving them to the effect of their follies or studies.

Among the characters from this period are extensive collections by Samuel Butler and Richard Flecknoe.[61]

In France, Hall's *Characters* had been translated

[61] Aldington, *Book of Characters* 269–333, 390–4.

as early as 1610, but English character-writing had little influence on the great work of Jean de La Bruyère:[62] he began with a translation of Theophrastus, and continued with his own updating, a collection of aphorisms, reflective essays, and character sketches; the latter combine elements of Theophrastus with the then-fashionable literary "portrait": a description (usually flattering) of an unnamed figure from contemporary society, the game being to guess the name, although "keys" were often published separately. Thus La Bruyère's characters have classical names (Menalcas, Theophilus) rather than traits, and while they mostly illustrate moral failings, some of them are clearly based on real individuals as well—his work also attracted the writers of keys. The most original of all modern character writers, La Bruyère offered an ingenious combination: a classical model; a new twist to the genre of the "portrait"; a critical but vivid and entertaining picture of his own contemporaries; and a simplicity and precision of style which matches La Rochefoucauld even more than Theophrastus.

In eighteenth-century England the work of La Bruyère became more influential than the mannered formulas of the Overbury collection, and the character found still another home in the coffee-

[62] *Les Caractères de Thèophraste traduits du grec avec les Caractères ou les Moeurs de ce Siècle*, first edition 1688, subsequently expanded until the ninth edition of 1696. See Smeed, *Theophrastan Character* chapter 2.

house periodical: *The Tatler* and *Spectator* regularly featured sketches by Joseph Addison and Richard Steele, ranging from moralizing abstraction (e.g., Steele's "Women's Men") to accumulations of telling detail for a single individual ("Sir Roger de Coverley," "Will Honeycomb"); in the *Rambler* and *Idler* Samuel Johnson followed suit.[63] The character was further adapted to use in published sermons, and to verse epistles by Alexander Pope.[64]

The writing of characters was never again to be practiced so widely, or with as much originality, as in the seventeenth and eighteenth centuries; but the nineteenth saw its migration — through such preparatory works as Dickens' *Sketches by Boz* (1836) or Thackeray's *The Book of Snobs* (1846) — to the realm of the novel, and collections of sketches were published by George Eliot (*The Impressions of Theophrastus Such*, 1879) and Trollope.[65]

Surveying such a variety of forms, purposes, and styles, we may be inclined to conclude that little remains of Theophrastus' original work apart from its brief scope and a certain concern with typology; that is why the most recent collection of characters, Elias Canetti's *Der Ohrenzeuge: Fünfzig Charaktere*

[63] Aldington, *Book of Characters* 422–476. For the influence of these periodicals on German-language characters see Smeed, *Theophrastan Character* 82–113.

[64] Benjamin Boyce, *The Character-Sketches in Pope's Poems* (Durham, North Carolina 1962).

[65] Smeed, *Theophrastan Character* 225–262.

(*The Earwitness: Fifty Characters*, 1974), is so striking. It contains brief essays, in no particular order, giving details of the behavior of unnamed individuals, each dominated by a single trait. The foibles of Canetti's characters are exaggerated to almost grotesque proportions, e.g. *Der Verlierer* (*The Man Who Loses Things*):

> He manages to lose everything. He starts with small things. He has a lot to lose. There are so many good places to lose things.
>
> Pockets—he has them specially made for losing. Children, running after him on the street—"Hey, Mister!" all around him. He smiles contentedly, never bends down. He must be careful not to find anything again. No matter how many of them run after him, he won't bend down. If it's lost, it's lost. Isn't that why he brought it along? And yet, why does he still have so many things? Shouldn't he be running out of them? Are they inexhaustible? They are, but no one sees that. He seems to have a huge house full of little objects, and it seems impossible to get rid of them all. . . .

The surreal effect is new; but in their simplicity and use of striking detail and his utter silence about these peoples' motives, and his purpose in writing them—there is no preface—Canetti's *Characters* revert almost completely to the Theophrastan form.[66]

[66] Smeed *Theophrastan Character* 130–131, who also gives (367–368) numerous examples of character sketches from popular literature in England of the 1960's and 70's, to which could be added even a popular song: "A Dedicated Follower of Fashion" (The Kinks, 1967).

Modern scholarly literature with an implicit similarity in approach to Theophrastus might be sought in, e.g. the typologies of Jungian psychologists, the trait-theory of Gordon Allport (*Personality*, New York 1937, chapter 3), or sociologists who delineate types (see the essays collected in Lewis A. Coser, ed., *The Pleasures of Sociology*, New York 1980, 232ff).

# BIBLIOGRAPHY

## *Manuscripts*

A = *Parisinus graecus* 2977, XI cent., containing *Characters* 1–15.

B = *Parisinus graecus* 1983, X–XI cent., containing *Characters* 1–15.

V = *Vaticanus graecus* 110, XIII cent., containing *Characters* 16–30.

M = *Monacensis graecus* 505, XV cent., an epitome of *Characters* 1–21.

C = a family of 7 manuscripts (XV–XVI cent.) containing *Characters* 1–28.

D = a family of 6 manuscripts (XIV-XVI cent.) containing *Characters* 1–23.

E = a family of 32 manuscripts (XIII–XVI cent.) which never contained more than *Characters* 1–15.

c, d, e = at least one manuscript of the families C, D, or E.

P. Hamb. 143 (I B.C.), containing *Characters* 7–8

P. Herc. 1457 (I B.C.), Philodemus *On flattery* citing *Character* 5

P. Oxy. 699 (A.D. III), an epitome of *Characters* 25–6.

## *Abbreviations*

FGrHist            *Die Fragmente der griechischen Historiker*, ed. Felix Jacoby, Berlin-Leiden 1922–.

| | |
|---|---|
| *FHG* | *Fragmenta historicorum graecorum*, ed. Carl and Theodor Müller, 5 vols. Paris 1841–1870. |
| LSJ | H. G. Liddell and R. Scott, *A Greek-English Lexicon*, 9th ed. revised by Sir Henry Stuart Jones, Oxford 1925–1940. |
| Menander fr. | A. Koerte, *Menandri quae supersunt* vol. 2, revised ed. by A. Thierfelder, Leipzig 1959. |
| *Paroem. Graec.* | E. Leutsch and F. Schneidewin, *Corpus paroemiographorum graecorum*, 2 vols., Göttingen 1839–1851. |
| *PCG* | R. Kassel and C. Austin, *Poetae comici Graeci*, Berlin 1983–. |
| *RE* | Pauly and Wissowa, *Real-enzyclopädie der classischen Altertumswissenschaft*, Stuttgart 1894–1979. |
| *SVF* | J. von Arnim (ed.), *Stoicorum veterum fragmenta*, 4 vols. Leipzig 1905–1924. |
| Theophr. fr. | W. M. Fortenbaugh, P. M. Huby, R. W. Sharples, D. Gutas, *Theophrastus of Eresus: Sources for His Life, Writings, Thought and Influence*, Philosophia Antiqua 54, 2 vols. Leiden 1992. |
| Wehrli | F. Wehrli, *Die Schule des Aristoteles, Texte und Kommentar*, 10 vols. and 2 supplements, Basel 1967–1978. (Cited for the fragments of peripatetic philosophers.) |

# BIBLIOGRAPHY

## Selected Editions and Commentaries

Casaubon, Isaac *Theophrasti notationes morum*, 3rd ed. Leiden 1617.

Korais, Adamantios *Les caractères de Theophraste*, Paris 1799.

Foss, H. E. *Theophrasti Characteres* (Bibliotheca Teubneriana) Leipzig 1858.

Philological Society of Leipzig (M. Bechert, C. Cichorius, A. Giesecke, R. Holland, J. Ilberg, O. Immisch, R. Meister, W. Ruge), *Theophrasts Charaktere*, edited with translation and commentary, Leipzig 1897.

Diels, Hermann *Theophrasti Characteres* (Oxford Classical Texts) Oxford 1909.

Navarre, Octave *Theophraste, Caractères* (Association Guillaume Budé) Paris 1920.

Immisch, Otto *Theophrasti Characteres* (Bibliotheca Teubneriana) Leipzig 1923.

Edmonds, J. M. *The Characters of Theophrastus* (Loeb Classical Library; with Herodes, Cercidas and the Choliambic Poets) London 1929.

Ussher, R. G. *The Characters of Theophrastus*, edited with an Introduction, Commentary and Index, London 1960.

Steinmetz, Peter *Theophrast, Charaktere*, edited with commentary, 2 vols., Munich 1960–62.

## Selected Books and Articles

Aldington, Richard *A Book of Characters*, New York, 1924.

Fortenbaugh, William "Die Charaktere Theophrasts," *Rheinisches Museum* 118 (1975) 62–82.

Gomperz, Theodor "Über die Charaktere Theophrasts,"

*Sitzungsberichte der kaiserlichen Akademie der Wissenschaften*, Vienna, ph.-hist. Klasse, Vol. 117.10 (1889).

Gordon, G. S. "Theophrastus and His Imitators" 49–86 in Gordon (ed.), *English Literature and the Classics*, Oxford 1912.

Hanow, F. *De Theophrasti characterum libello*, Diss. Bonn, 1858.

Kondo, Eiko "I 'caratteri' di Teofrasto nei papiri ercolanesi," *Cronache ercolanesi* 1 (1971) 73–86.

Pasquali, Giorgio "Sui *caratteri* di Teofrasto," 47–96 in *Scritti filologici*, ed. F. Bornmann, G. Pascucci, S. Timpanaro, with an introduction by A. La Penna, Florence 1986 (originally in *Rassegna italiana di lingue e letterature classiche* 1 [1918] 73–79, 124–150, 2 [1919] 1–21).

Smeed, J. W. *The Theophrastan 'Character': the History of a Literary Genre*, Oxford 1985.

Stein, Markus *Definition und Schilderung in Theophrasts Charaktern* (forthcoming, see the preface to this volume).

Ussher, R. G. "Some Characters of Athens, Rome and England," *Greece and Rome* 13 (1966) 64–78.

Wehrli, F. "Der Peripatos bis zum Beginn der römischen Kaiserzeit," 459–599 in H. Flashar (ed.), *Die Philosophie der Antike* III: *ältere Akademie, Aristoteles, Peripatos* ( = Friedrich Überweg, *Grundriss der Geschichte der Philosophie*, Antike vol. 3, new ed. Basel 1983).

Wilson, N. G. "The Manuscripts of Theophrastus," *Scriptorium* 16 (1962) 96–102.

# ΧΑΡΑΚΤΗΡΕΣ

| ΧΑΡΑΚΤΗΡΕΣ | CHARACTERS[1] |
|---|---|
| 1. ΕΙΡΩΝΕΙΑ | Dissembling[2] |
| 2. ΚΟΛΑΚΕΙΑ | Flattery |
| 3. ΑΔΟΛΕΣΧΙΑ | Idle Chatter |
| 4. ΑΓΡΟΙΚΙΑ | Boorishness |
| 5. ΑΡΕΣΚΕΙΑ | Obsequiousness |
| 6. ΑΠΟΝΟΙΑ | Shamelessness |
| 7. ΛΑΛΙΑ | Garrulity |
| 8. ΛΟΓΟΠΟΙΙΑ | Rumor-Mongering |
| 9. ΑΝΑΙΣΧΥΝΤΙΑ | Sponging |
| 10. ΜΙΚΡΟΛΟΓΙΑ | Pennypinching |
| 11. ΒΔΕΛΥΡΙΑ | Obnoxiousness |
| 12. ΑΚΑΙΡΙΑ | Bad Timing |
| 13. ΠΕΡΙΕΡΓΙΑ | Overzealousness |
| 14. ΑΝΑΙΣΘΗΣΙΑ | Absent-mindedness |
| 15. ΑΥΘΑΔΕΙΑ | Grouchiness |
| 16. ΔΕΙΣΙΔΑΙΜΟΝΙΑ | Superstition |
| 17. ΜΕΜΨΙΜΟΙΡΙΑ | Griping |
| 18. ΑΠΙΣΤΙΑ | Mistrust |

[1] This traditional translation of the title is not accurate: the Greek equivalent for our "character" is ἦθος; a better translation for χαρακτῆρες would be "Traits" (Diogenes Laertius 5.47 gives the title as ἠθικοὶ χαρακτῆρες, "Character traits"). See Introd. p. 11.

[2] The English translations of trait names are meant to match the descriptions rather than the trait names in Greek, which are sometimes suspect (see Introd. n. 54); for the literal meanings of the Greek trait names, see the Additional Notes.

| | | |
|---|---|---|
| 19. | ΔΥΣΧΕΡΕΙΑ | Squalor |
| 20. | ΑΗΔΙΑ | Bad Taste |
| 21. | ΜΙΚΡΟΦΙΛΟΤΙΜΙΑ | Petty Ambition |
| 22. | ΑΝΕΛΕΥΘΕΡΙΑ | Lack of Generosity |
| 23. | ΑΛΑΖΟΝΕΙΑ | Fraudulence |
| 24. | ΥΠΕΡΗΦΑΝΙΑ | Arrogance |
| 25. | ΔΕΙΛΙΑ | Cowardice |
| 26. | ΟΛΙΓΑΡΧΙΑ | Authoritarianism |
| 27. | ΟΨΙΜΑΘΙΑ | Rejuvenation |
| 28. | ΚΑΚΟΛΟΓΙΑ | Slander |
| 29. | ΦΙΛΟΠΟΝΗΡΙΑ | Patronage of Scoundrels |
| 30. | ΑΙΣΧΡΟΚΕΡΔΕΙΑ | Chiseling |

# [ΠΡΟΘΕΩΡΙΑ[1]

(1) ἤδη μὲν καὶ πρότερον πολλάκις ἐπιστήσας τὴν διάνοιαν ἐθαύμασα, ἴσως δὲ οὐδὲ παύσομαι θαυμάζων, τί γὰρ δήποτε, τῆς Ἑλλάδος ὑπὸ τὸν αὐτὸν ἀέρα κειμένης καὶ πάντων τῶν Ἑλλήνων ὁμοίως παιδευομένων, συμβέβηκεν ἡμῖν οὐ τὴν αὐτὴν τάξιν τῶν τρόπων ἔχειν. (2) ἐγὼ γὰρ, ὦ Πολύκλεις, συνθεωρήσας ἐκ πολλοῦ χρόνου τὴν ἀνθρωπίνην φύσιν καὶ βεβιωκὼς ἔτη ἐνενήκοντα ἐννέα, ἔτι δὲ ὡμιληκὼς πολλαῖς τε καὶ παντοδαπαῖς φύσεσι καὶ παρατεθεαμένος ἐξ ἀκριβείας πολλῆς τούς τε ἀγαθοὺς τῶν ἀνθρώπων καὶ τοὺς φαύλους ὑπέλαβον δεῖν συγγράψαι, ἃ ἑκάτεροι αὐτῶν ἐπιτηδεύουσιν ἐν τῷ βίῳ.

(3) ἐκθήσω δέ σοι κατὰ γένος ὅσα τε τυγχάνει γένη τρόπων τούτοις προσκείμενα[2] καὶ ὃν τρόπον τῇ οἰκονομίᾳ χρῶνται· ὑπολαμβάνω γάρ, ὦ Πολύκλεις, τοὺς υἱεῖς ἡμῶν βελτίους ἔσεσθαι καταλειφθέντων αὐτοῖς ὑπομνημάτων τοιούτων, οἷς

---

[1] Prooemium totum del. Sonntag.
[2] e: προκείμενα codd.

## [PREFACE[a]

(1) Before now I've often wondered, when I thought about it, and perhaps will never cease to wonder why, even though Greece lies in the same climate and all Greeks are educated the same way, it happens that we do not have the same composition of character. (2) After a life of ninety-nine years,[b] long observation of human nature, and furthermore an acquaintance with many natures of all types and a detailed study of men both superior and inferior, I have come to believe, Polycles,[c] that I ought to write about how both groups normally behave in their lives.

(3) I shall set forth for you one by one which classes of character are attached to these people and how they manage; for I believe, Polycles, that our sons will be better if such writings are bequeathed to them, which they can use as a guide in choosing

[a] This fatuous and repetitive preface has long been recognized as a later addition to the *Characters* (see Introd.). Steinmetz (volume 2, p. 32) speculates it was composed outside Greece in the fifth century A.D.

[b] In fact, Theophrastus died at 85 (Diogenes Laertius 5.40), and the *Characters* was most likely composed ca. 319 B.C. when he was in his early 50's.

[c] His identity is not known; there was a Macedonian general by this name (Diodorus Siculus 18.38.2).

παραδείγμασι χρώμενοι αἱρήσονται τοῖς εὐσχημο-
νεστάτοις συνεῖναί τε καὶ ὁμιλεῖν, ὅπως μὴ κατα-
δεέστεροι ὦσιν αὐτῶν.

(4) τρέψομαι δὲ ἤδη ἐπὶ τὸν λόγον. σὸν δὲ
παρακολουθῆσαί τε ὀρθῶς τε καὶ εἰδῆσαι, εἰ ὀρθῶς
λέγω. πρῶτον μὲν οὖν ποιήσομαι τὸν λόγον ἀπὸ
τῶν τὴν εἰρωνείαν ἐζηλωκότων, ἀφεὶς τὸ προοι-
μιάζεσθαι καὶ πολλὰ περὶ τοῦ πράγματος λέγειν.
(5) καὶ ἄρξομαι πρῶτον ἀπὸ τῆς εἰρωνείας καὶ
ὁριοῦμαι αὐτήν, εἶθ' οὕτως τὸν εἴρωνα διέξειμι,
ποῖός τίς ἐστι καὶ εἰς τίνα τρόπον κατενήνεκται·
καὶ τὰ ἄλλα δὴ τῶν παθημάτων, ὥσπερ ὑπεθέ-
μην, πειράσομαι κατὰ γένος φανερὰ καθιστάναι.]

## ΕΙΡΩΝΕΙΑΣ Α΄

(1) [ἡ μὲν οὖν εἰρωνεία δόξειεν ἂν εἶναι, ὡς τύπῳ
λαβεῖν, προσποίησις ἐπὶ χεῖρον πράξεων καὶ
λόγων,][1] ὁ δὲ εἴρων (2) τοιοῦτός τις, οἷος προσελθὼν τοῖς ἐχθροῖς ἐθέλειν λαλεῖν [οὐ μισεῖν]·[2] καὶ
ἐπαινεῖν παρόντας οἷς ἐπέθετο λάθρα, καὶ <οἷς
δικάζεται,>[3] τούτοις συλλυπεῖσθαι ἡττωμένοις·
καὶ συγγνώμην δὲ ἔχειν τοῖς αὐτὸν κακῶς λέγουσι

---

[1] del. Hanow, Gomperz, Stein.     [2] del. Ussing.
[3] suppl. Kassel.

to associate with and become close to the finest men, so as not to fall short of their standard.

(4) I shall now turn to my story; it is your task to follow it correctly, and see whether it is told correctly as well. I shall speak first of those who affect dissembling, dispensing with preliminaries and details about the topic. (5) I shall begin with dissembling and define it, then describe the dissembler as to his qualities and how he is inclined; and I will attempt to render clear the rest of the emotions type by type, as I promised.]

## 1. DISSEMBLING

(1) [Dissembling, to put it in outline, would seem to be a false denigration of one's actions and words.]ᵃ The dissembler is the sort (2) who goes up to his enemies and is willing to chat with them. He praises to their faces those whom he has attacked in secret, and commiserates with people he is suing if they lose their case. He is forgiving to those who

ᵃ This introductory definition is derived from Aristotle, *Nicomachean Ethics* 1108a21ff, 1108a11, *Eudemian Ethics* 1233b39–1234a1. Like some other definitions in the *Characters* (see Introd.), it is probably a later addition to the text: it describes well the irony of Socrates (see Additional Notes), but not the character that follows here.

καὶ <γελᾶν>¹ ἐπὶ τοῖς καθ' ἑαυτοῦ λεγομένοις.
καὶ (3) πρὸς τοὺς ἀδικουμένους καὶ ἀγανακτοῦντας
πράως διαλέγεσθαι· καὶ τοῖς ἐντυγχάνειν κατὰ
σπουδὴν βουλομένοις προστάξαι ἐπανελθεῖν.
(4) καὶ μηδὲν ὧν πράττει ὁμολογῆσαι, ἀλλὰ
φῆσαι βουλεύεσθαι καὶ προσποιήσασθαι ἄρτι
παραγεγονέναι [καὶ ὀψὲ γενέσθαι αὐτὸν]² καὶ
μαλακισθῆναι. (5) καὶ πρὸς τοὺς δανειζομένους
καὶ ἐρανίζοντας <φῆσαι ὡς χρημάτων ἀπορεῖ,
καὶ πωλῶν τι φῆσαι>³ ὡς οὐ πωλεῖ καὶ μὴ
πωλῶν φῆσαι πωλεῖν· καὶ ἀκούσας τι μὴ προσ-
ποιεῖσθαι, καὶ ἰδὼν φῆσαι μὴ ἑορακέναι, καὶ
ὁμολογήσας μὴ μεμνῆσθαι· καὶ τὰ μὲν σκέψεσθαι
φάσκειν, τὰ δὲ οὐκ εἰδέναι, τὰ δὲ θαυμάζειν, τὰ δ'
ἤδη ποτὲ καὶ αὐτὸς οὕτως διαλογίσασθαι. (6) καὶ
τὸ ὅλον δεινὸς τῷ τοιούτῳ τρόπῳ τοῦ λόγου χρῆ-
σθαι· "οὐ πιστεύω·" "οὐχ ὑπολαμβάνω·" "ἐκπλήτ-
τομαι·" καὶ "λέγεις αὐτὸν ἕτερον γεγονέναι·" "καὶ
μὴν οὐ ταῦτα πρὸς ἐμὲ διεξῄει·" "παράδοξόν μοι
τὸ πρᾶγμα·" "ἄλλῳ τινὶ λέγε·" "ὅπως δὲ σοὶ

¹ suppl. Darvaris.
² del. Kassel.
³ lacunam statuit Salmasius: φῆσαι ὡς χρημάτων ἀπορεῖ
Kassel, καὶ πωλῶν (τι add. Kassel) φῆσαι Ast.

54

slander him, and laughs at anything said against him. (3) With people who have been wronged and are outraged his conversation is mild,[a] and those who urgently seek a meeting with him he bids to come back later. (4) He admits to nothing that he is actually doing, but says he is thinking it over, and pretends that he just arrived, and behaves like a coward.[b] (5) To those seeking a loan or a contribution[c] he says he's short of cash, and if he is selling something says that he is not, and if he's not, says that he is. If he has heard something, he pretends he hasn't, and says he hasn't seen something when he has, and if he has made an agreement he doesn't remember it. He says about some things that he will look into them, about others that he doesn't know, about others that he is surprised, about others that once in the past he had thought that way himself too.[d] (6) And in general he is apt to employ phrases like this: "I don't believe it." "I don't think so." "I'm astonished." And "you're telling me he's become a different person." "That's by no means what he told me." "The business is a mystery to me." "Save your words for someone else."

[a] That is, he does not share their outrage; cf. Xenophon, *Anabasis* I.5.4.

[b] The text may not be sound; but if it is, the verb is used not of illness (so most translators), but of irresolution in battle (cf. LSJ μαλακίζω).     [c] For ἔρανος see on 15.7.

[d] But does so no longer. Usually translated "he had already come to the same conclusion," which would be an anomaly in this list of responses.

ἀπιστήσω ἢ ἐκείνου καταγνῶ, ἀποροῦμαι·" "ἀλλ'
ὅρα, μὴ σὺ θᾶττον πιστεύεις."

(7) [τοιαύτας φωνὰς καὶ πλοκὰς καὶ παλιλλο-
γίας εὑρεῖν ἔστι τῶν εἰρώνων. τὰ δὴ τῶν ἠθῶν μὴ
ἁπλᾶ ἀλλ' ἐπίβουλα φυλάττεσθαι μᾶλλον δεῖ ἢ
τοὺς ἔχεις.]¹

## ΚΟΛΑΚΕΙΑΣ Β´

(1) [τὴν δὲ κολακείαν ὑπολάβοι ἄν τις ὁμιλίαν
αἰσχρὰν εἶναι, συμφέρουσαν δὲ τῷ κολακεύοντι,]²
τὸν δὲ κόλακα τοιοῦτόν τινα, (2) ὥστε ἅμα πορευό-
μενον εἰπεῖν· "ἐνθυμῇ, ὡς ἀποβλέπουσι πρὸς σὲ οἱ
ἄνθρωποι; τοῦτο δὲ οὐθενὶ τῶν ἐν τῇ πόλει γίνεται πλὴν σοί·" "ηὐδοκίμεις χθὲς ἐν τῇ στοᾷ·"
πλειόνων γὰρ ἢ τριάκοντα ἀνθρώπων καθημένων
καὶ ἐμπεσόντος λόγου, τίς εἴη βέλτιστος, ἀφ'
αὑτοῦ ἀρξαμένους πάντας ἐπὶ τὸ ὄνομα αὐτοῦ
κατενεχθῆναι.

(3) καὶ ἅμα τοιαῦτα λέγων ἀπὸ τοῦ ἱματίου
ἀφελεῖν κροκύδα, καὶ ἐάν τι πρὸς τὸ τρίχωμα τῆς
κεφαλῆς ὑπὸ πνεύματος προσενεχθῇ ἄχυρον,

¹ epilogum del. editores.    ² del. Hanow, Gomperz,
Stein (videtur citare sine nomine auctoris Philodemus in
libro περὶ κολακείας, P. Herc. 222 et 1082, v. T. Gargiulo,
*Cronache ercolanese* 11 (1981) 103–127).

"I do not see how I can doubt you—nor condemn him, either." "Be careful you don't make up your mind too quickly."

(7) [Such are the phrases, dodges and contradictions it is characteristic of dissemblers to invent. When natures are not open, but contriving, one must be more cautious of them than of vipers.]

## 2. FLATTERY

(1) [You might call flattery talk that is shameful, but also profitable to the flatterer.][a] The flatterer is the sort (2) to say, as he walks along, "Do you notice how people are looking at you? This does not happen to anyone in the city except you." "They praised you yesterday in the stoa"; and he explains that when more than thirty people were sitting there and a discussion arose about who was the best, at his own suggestion they settled on his man's name.

(3) While he says more like this, he picks a flock of wool from his man's cloak and, if some chaff in the wind lands on the hair on his head, harvests it, and

[a] The introductory definition, although twice mentioned (without Theophrastus' name) in fragments of Philodemus, *On Flattery*, is probably a later insertion which has partly replaced the original first sentence. The notion that the flatterer's motive is profit is derived from Aristotle, *Nicomachean Ethics* 1108a26, 1127a7, but is irrelevant here.

THEOPHRASTUS

καρφολογῆσαι. καὶ ἐπιγελάσας δὲ εἰπεῖν· "ὁρᾷς;
ὅτι δυοῖν σοι ἡμερῶν οὐκ ἐντετύχηκα, πολιῶν
ἔσχηκας τὸν πώγωνα μεστόν, καίπερ εἴ τις καὶ
ἄλλος πρὸς τὰ ἔτη ἔχεις μέλαιναν τὴν τρίχα."

(4) καὶ λέγοντος δὲ αὐτοῦ τι τοὺς ἄλλους
σιωπᾶν κελεῦσαι καὶ ἐπαινέσαι δὲ ἀκούοντος, καὶ
ἐπισημήνασθαι δέ, εἰ παύεται,[1] "ὀρθῶς," καὶ
σκώψαντι ψυχρῶς ἐπιγελάσαι τό τε ἱμάτιον ὦσαι
εἰς τὸ στόμα ὡς δὴ οὐ δυνάμενος κατασχεῖν τὸν
γέλωτα. (5) καὶ τοὺς ἀπαντῶντας ἐπιστῆναι
κελεῦσαι, ἕως ἂν αὐτὸς παρέλθῃ.

(6) καὶ τοῖς παιδίοις μῆλα καὶ ἀπίους πριάμενος
εἰσενέγκας δοῦναι ὁρῶντος αὐτοῦ, καὶ φιλήσας δὲ
εἰπεῖν· "χρηστοῦ πατρὸς νεόττια." (7) καὶ συνω-
νούμενος ἐπικρηπῖδας τὸν πόδα φῆσαι εἶναι εὐρυ-
θμότερον τοῦ ὑποδήματος. (8) καὶ πορευομένου
πρός τινα τῶν φίλων προδραμὼν εἰπεῖν ὅτι "πρὸς
σὲ ἔρχεται," καὶ ἀναστρέψας ὅτι "προσήγγελκά
σε." (9) ἀμέλει δὲ καὶ τὰ ἐκ γυναικείας ἀγορᾶς δια-
κονῆσαι δυνατὸς ἀπνευστί.

[1] Ast: παύσεται codd.

[a] The flatterer usually plucks the grey hairs from his
patron's beard (cf. *PCG* Aristophanes fr. 416, 689, *Knights*
908).

says with a laugh, "You see! Since I haven't seen you for two days, you've got a beard full of grey hairs—although your hair is black for your years, if anyone's is."[a]

(4) He tells everyone else to keep quiet while his man is saying something, and praises him when he is listening, and if he should pause, adds an approving "You're right!" If he makes a tasteless[b] joke, he laughs at it and pushes his cloak into his mouth to show he can't contain his laughter. (5) He commands everyone who approaches to stand still until his man has passed by.

(6) To his children he brings apples and pears he has bought and, while his man is watching, presents them and kisses the children and says "Chips off the excellent old block!"[c] (7) When he joins him in shopping for overshoes, he says that his foot is more symmetrical than the sandal. (8) When he is going to see one of his friends, he runs ahead and says "He is coming to your house!" Then he runs back and says "I have announced you." (9) You can be sure he is also capable of doing his errands from the women's market[d] without stopping for breath.

[b] Literally "frigid," but cf. *PCG* Eupolis fr. 261 and Timocles fr. 19, Demosthenes 18.256, Theophr. fr. 686.

[c] The proverbial phrase is literally "chicks of their father" (Aristophanes, *Birds* 767), to which the flatterer adds a further complimentary adjective.

[d] Pollux, *Onomasticon* 10.18 says this name is used by Menander (fr. 390) for a place where one could buy household furnishings.

(10) καὶ τῶν ἑστιωμένων πρῶτος ἐπαινέσαι τὸν οἶνον καὶ παραμένων εἰπεῖν· "ὡς μαλακῶς ἐσθίεις," καὶ ἄρας τι τῶν ἀπὸ τῆς τραπέζης φῆσαι "τουτὶ ἄρα ὡς χρηστόν ἐστι·" καὶ ἐρωτῆσαι μὴ ῥιγοῖ, καὶ εἰ ἐπιβάλλεσθαι βούλεται, καὶ εἴ τι[1] περιστείλῃ αὐτόν, καὶ μὴν ταῦτα λέγων πρὸς τὸ οὖς προσκύπτων[2] διαψιθυρίζειν· καὶ εἰς ἐκεῖνον ἀποβλέπων τοῖς ἄλλοις λαλεῖν.

(11) καὶ τοῦ παιδὸς ἐν τῷ θεάτρῳ ἀφελόμενος τὰ προσκεφάλαια αὐτὸς ὑποστρῶσαι. (12) καὶ τὴν οἰκίαν φῆσαι εὖ ἠρχιτεκτονῆσθαι καὶ τὸν ἀγρὸν εὖ πεφυτεῦσθαι καὶ τὴν εἰκόνα ὁμοίαν εἶναι.

(13) [καὶ τὸ κεφάλαιον τὸν κόλακα ἔστι θεάσασθαι πάντα[3] καὶ λέγοντα καὶ πράττοντα ᾧ χαριεῖσθαι ὑπολαμβάνει.][4]

## ΑΔΟΛΕΣΧΙΑΣ Γ´

(1) ἡ δὲ ἀδολεσχία ἐστὶ μὲν διήγησις λόγων μακρῶν καὶ ἀπροβουλεύτων, ὁ δὲ ἀδολέσχης τοιοῦτός ἐστιν, (2) οἷος, ὃν μὴ γινώσκει, τούτῳ

[1] Petersen: ἔτι A, ἔτι B.

[2] Valckenaer: προσπίπτων A^corr. B.

[3] πᾶν Cobet, πάντῃ Diels, sed cf. Xen. Cyr. 8.2.25 (πάντα ὅτου δεῖ), Kühner-Gerth II.1.56.

[4] epilogum del. editores.

(10) He is the first of the dinner guests to praise the wine, and keeps it up by saying "How luxuriously you dine!" He takes up something from the table and says "This is really good!"[a] He asks whether his man is chilly, and whether he wants him to put a blanket on him, and whether he should wrap something around his man's shoulders; and yet he says all this in a whisper, leaning forward toward his ear. He keeps an eye on his man while speaking to others. (11) At the theater he takes the cushions away from the slave, and tucks them under his man personally. (12) He says that his house has been well laid-out, and his farm well cultivated, and his portrait a perfect resemblance.[b]

(13) [And the sum is that the flatterer is on the lookout for everything in word or deed by which he thinks he will curry favor.]

## 3. IDLE CHATTER

(1) Idle chatter is engaging in prolonged and aimless talk. The idle chatterer is the sort (2) who sits right

[a] Cf. *PCG* Alexis fr. 15.8, Antiphanes fr. 238.
[b] Since classical Greek portraits tended toward ideal beauty, this is a handsome compliment.

παρακαθεζόμενος πλησίον πρῶτον μὲν τῆς αὑτοῦ
γυναικὸς εἰπεῖν ἐγκώμιον· εἶτα ὃ τῆς νυκτὸς εἶδεν
ἐνύπνιον, τοῦτο διηγήσασθαι· εἶθ᾽ ὧν εἶχεν ἐπὶ τῷ
δείπνῳ τὰ καθ᾽ ἕκαστα διεξελθεῖν. (3) εἶτα δὴ
προχωροῦντος τοῦ πράγματος λέγειν, ὡς πολὺ
πονηρότεροί εἰσιν οἱ νῦν ἄνθρωποι τῶν ἀρχαίων,
καὶ ὡς ἄξιοι γεγόνασιν οἱ πυροὶ ἐν τῇ ἀγορᾷ, καὶ
ὡς πολλοὶ ἐπιδημοῦσι ξένοι, καὶ τὴν θάλατταν ἐκ
Διονυσίων πλόιμον εἶναι, καὶ εἰ ποιήσειεν ὁ Ζεὺς
ὕδωρ πλεῖον, τὰ ἐν τῇ γῇ βελτίω ἔσεσθαι, καὶ ὅτι
ἀγρὸν εἰς νέωτα γεωργήσει, καὶ ὡς χαλεπόν ἐστι
τὸ ζῆν, καὶ ὡς Δάμιππος μυστηρίοις μεγίστην
δᾷδα ἔστησεν, καὶ "πόσοι εἰσὶ κίονες τοῦ Ὠιδείου,"
καὶ "χθὲς ἤμεσα," καὶ "τίς ἐστιν ἡμέρα τήμερον;"
καὶ ὡς Βοηδρομιῶνος μέν ἐστι τὰ μυστήρια, Πυα-
νοψιῶνος δὲ τἀπατούρια, Ποσιδεῶνος δὲ <τὰ>[1]
κατ᾽ ἀγροὺς Διονύσια. (4) κἂν ὑπομένῃ τις αὐτόν,
μὴ ἀφίστασθαι.[2]

(5) [παρασείσαντα δὴ δεῖ τοὺς τοιούτους τῶν
ἀνθρώπων καὶ διαράμενον ἀπαλλάττεσθαι, ὅστις
ἀπύρευτος βούλεται εἶναι· ἔργον γὰρ συναρκεῖσθαι
τοῖς μήτε σχολὴν μήτε σπουδὴν διαγινώσκουσιν.][3]

[1] suppl. Casaubon.   [2] κἂν . . . ἀφίστασθαι ante καὶ ὡς
Βοηδρομιῶνος codd.: transposuit Schneider.   [3] epilogum del. editores.

down beside someone he doesn't know, and starts out by speaking in praise of his own wife; then he recounts the dream he had the night before; then he relates the details of what he had for dinner. (3) Then, as matters progress, he says that people nowadays are much more wicked than they used to be; that wheat is a bargain in the marketplace; that there are lots of foreigners in town, and that the sea lanes have been open since the festival of Dionysus. And that if it rains more, the soil will be better; that he intends to start a farm next year, and that it's hard to make a living; and that Damippos dedicated the biggest torch at the mysteries.[a] "How many pillars are there in the Odeion?"[b] "Yesterday I threw up!" "What day is it today?" And that the mysteries are in the month Boedromion, and the Apatouria in Pyanepsion, and the country Dionysia in Poseideon. (4) And if you put up with him, he doesn't stop!

(5) [Men like this you must flee at top speed[c] if you want to stay unscathed; it is hard to stand people who don't care whether you are busy or free.]

[a] Initiates carried torches in the procession from Athens to Eleusis, and evidently private individuals could dedicate representations of them in the Eleusinian sanctuary: G. Mylonas, *Eleusis* (Princeton 1961) 204.

[b] An indoor music hall constructed under Pericles, with many interior columns; see Plutarch, *Pericles* 13.9 (with the commentary of Philip Stadter).

[c] Literally "swinging (your arms) and stretching (your legs) wide."

# ΑΓΡΟΙΚΙΑΣ Δ΄

(1) ἡ δὲ ἀγροικία δόξειεν ἂν εἶναι ἀμαθία ἀσχή-
μων, ὁ δὲ ἄγροικος τοιοῦτός τις, (2) οἷος κυκεῶνα
πιὼν εἰς ἐκκλησίαν πορεύεσθαι (3) καὶ τὸ μύρον
φάσκειν οὐδὲν τοῦ θύμου ἥδιον ὄζειν· (4) καὶ μείζω
τοῦ ποδὸς τὰ ὑποδήματα φορεῖν· (5) καὶ μεγάλῃ
τῇ φωνῇ λαλεῖν· (6) καὶ τοῖς μὲν φίλοις καὶ οἰκεί-
οις ἀπιστεῖν, πρὸς δὲ τοὺς αὑτοῦ οἰκέτας ἀνακοινοῦσθαι περὶ τῶν μεγίστων. καὶ τοῖς παρ᾽ αὑτῷ
ἐργαζομένοις μισθωτοῖς ἐν ἀγρῷ πάντα τὰ ἀπὸ
τῆς ἐκκλησίας διηγεῖσθαι. (7) καὶ ἀναβεβλημένος
ἄνω τοῦ γόνατος καθιζάνειν ὥστε τὰ γυμνὰ αὐτοῦ
φαίνεσθαι.[1] (8) καὶ ἐπ᾽ ἄλλῳ μὲν μηδενὶ <μήτε
εὐφραίνεσθαι>[2] μήτε ἐκπλήττεσθαι ἐν ταῖς ὁδοῖς,
ὅταν δὲ ἴδῃ βοῦν ἢ ὄνον ἢ τράγον, ἑστηκὼς θεωρεῖν. (9) καὶ προαιρῶν[3] δέ τι ἐκ τοῦ ταμιείου
δεινὸς φαγεῖν, καὶ ζωρότερον πιεῖν.

[1] ὥστε τὰ γυμνὰ αὐτοῦ φαίνεσθαι del. Darvaris, fortasse
recte, cf. 20.9 [ὥστε εἶναι ψυχρόν].
[2] μήτε suppl. editores, εὐφραίνεσθαι Kassel: θαυμάζειν De.
[3] Casaubon: προαίρων codd.

---

[a] The κυκεών was a mixture of grains, liquids (wine,
milk, water, honey, oil) and spices, drunk by the poorer
classes: N. J. Richardson, *The Homeric Hymn to Demeter*

## 4. BOORISHNESS

(1) Boorishness would seem to be an embarrassing lack of sophistication. The boor is the sort (2) who has some gruel[a] before going to the assembly, (3) and claims that perfume smells no sweeter than thyme. (4) He wears sandals that are too big for his feet. (5) He talks in too loud a voice.[b] (6) He is wary of friends and family, but asks advice from his servants on the most important matters. He describes to hired laborers in the field all the proceedings of the city assembly. (7) He sits down with his cloak hitched up above his knee, thereby revealing his nakedness.[c] (8) He doesn't enjoy or gawk at anything else on the street—yet stands in rapt attention at the sight of a cow, an ass, or a goat. (9) He is apt to eat the food as he is taking it out of the storeroom. He drinks his wine too strong.[d]

[a] (Oxford 1974) 344. The boor does not care how strongly his breath smells of thyme (which in antiquity was a much stronger herb than today; see *PCG* Pherecrates fr. 177).

[b] For a "barnyard voice" cf. *PCG* Cratinus fr. 371.

[c] He isn't wearing anything underneath; cf. *PCG* Philetairus fr. 18, and the illustrations in the Leipzig Edition of the *Characters*, p. 26, and A. Dieterich, *Pulcinella* (Leipzig 1897) 119.

[d] Athenaeus 423d-f cites many parallels to show that ζωρότερον (first in Homer, *Iliad* 9.203) means "with more wine and less water." He also notes that Theophrastus in a treatise *On Drunkenness* (= fr. 574) dissents with an interpretation ("mixed") that cannot be applied here.

(10) καὶ τὴν σιτοποιὸν πειρῶν λαθεῖν, κᾆτ᾽ ἀλέσας μετ᾽ αὐτῆς <μετρεῖν>[1] τοῖς ἔνδον πᾶσι καὶ αὑτῷ τὰ ἐπιτήδεια. (11) καὶ ἀριστῶν δὲ ἅμα τοῖς ὑποζυγίοις ἐμβαλεῖν. (12) καὶ τὴν θύραν ὑπακοῦσαι[2] αὐτός, καὶ τὸν κύνα προσκαλεσάμενος καὶ ἐπιλαβόμενος τοῦ ῥύγχους εἰπεῖν· "οὗτος φυλάττει τὸ χωρίον καὶ τὴν οἰκίαν."

(13) καὶ [τὸ][3] ἀργύριον δὲ παρά του λαβὼν ἀποδοκιμάζειν, λίαν <γὰρ>[4] μολυβρὸν[5] εἶναι, καὶ ἕτερον ἀνταλλάττεσθαι.[6] (14) καὶ εἰ <τῳ>[7] ἄροτρον ἔχρησεν ἢ κόφινον ἢ δρέπανον ἢ θύλακον, ταῦτα τῆς νυκτὸς κατὰ ἀγρυπνίαν ἀναμιμνησκόμενος <ἀπαιτεῖν>.[8] (15) καὶ εἰς ἄστυ καταβαίνων ἐρωτῆσαι τὸν ἀπαντῶντα, πόσου ἦσαν αἱ διφθέραι καὶ τὸ τάριχος καὶ εἰ τήμερον [ὁ ἀγων][9] νουμηνίαν ἄγει, καὶ εἰπεῖν εὐθὺς ὅτι βούλεται καταβὰς ἀποκείρασθαι καὶ ἐν βαλανείῳ δὲ ᾆσαι καὶ εἰς τὰ ὑποδήματα δὲ ἥλους ἐγκροῦσαι καὶ τῆς αὐτῆς ὁδοῦ παριὼν κομίσασθαι παρ᾽ Ἀρχίου τοῦ ταρίχους.[10]

---

[1] suppl. Casaubon.    [2] Casaubon: ἐπακοῦσαι codd.
[3] suspectum habuit Stein (cf. 14.8).    [4] suppl. Eberhard.
[5] Diels: μὲν λυπηρὸν ABce, μὲν λυπηρὸν cDe.    [6] Cobet:
ἅμα ἀλλάττεσθαι codd.    [7] Diels: καὶ εἰ τὸ A, καὶ ὃ CDe,
καὶ τὸ B, καὶ εἰς τὸ e.    [8] suppl. Casaubon.    [9] del.
Edmonds.    [10] Sylburg: τοὺς ταρίχους codd. verba

(10) He seduces his cook without anyone's knowing, but then joins her in grinding up the daily ration of meal and handing it out to himself and the whole household.[a] (11) While he is eating his breakfast, he feeds his plough-animals. (12) He answers the door himself, then calls his dog, grabs his snout and says "This fellow looks out for our property and household."

(13) He rejects a silver coin that he gets from someone because it looks too much like lead, and trades for another.[b] (14) And if he has lent someone a plough, basket, sickle or sack, he asks for it back in the middle of the night, because he just remembered it while he couldn't sleep. (15) And when he is going into town, he asks anyone he meets about the price of hides and salt fish, and whether today is the first of the month,[c] and he says right away that when he reaches town he wants to get a haircut, do some singing at the baths, hammer some nails into his shoes,[d] and while he's going in that direction pick up some salt fish at Archias'.

[a] He is so smitten that he joins her in work the master shouldn't be doing (cf. 30.11).

[b] The text is corrupt; as emended here, the rustic cares more about the appearance than the value of his money, despite the higher value of the older (and less shiny) silver coins. Cf. Aristophanes, *Frogs* 718ff, Plautus, *Casina* 9.

[c] A market-day, Aristophanes, *Knights* 43, *Wasps* 171.

[d] Evidently to stick the soles back on (cf. 22.11).

καὶ ἐν βαλανείῳ — ἐγκροῦσαι fortasse aut post τοῦ ταρίχους ponenda aut secludenda sunt.

## ΑΡΕΣΚΕΙΑΣ Ε΄

(1) [ἡ δὲ ἀρέσκειά ἐστι μέν, ὡς ὅρῳ περιλαβεῖν, ἔντευξις οὐκ ἐπὶ τῷ βελτίστῳ ἡδονῆς παρασκευαστική,]¹ ὁ δὲ ἄρεσκος ἀμέλει τοιοῦτός τις, (2) οἷος πόρρωθεν προσαγορεῦσαι² καὶ ἄνδρα κράτιστον εἴπας³ καὶ θαυμάσας ἱκανῶς, ἀμφοτέραις ταῖς χερσὶν ἁψάμενος⁴ μὴ ἀφιέναι καὶ μικρὸν προπέμψας⁵ καὶ ἐρωτήσας, πότε αὐτὸν ὄψεται, ἐπαινῶν⁶ ἀπαλλάττεσθαι.

(3) καὶ παρακληθεὶς δὲ πρὸς δίαιταν μὴ μόνον ᾧ πάρεστι⁷ βούλεσθαι ἀρέσκειν, ἀλλὰ καὶ τῷ ἀντιδίκῳ, ἵνα κοινὸς εἷς⁸ εἶναι δοκῇ. (4) καὶ <πρὸς>⁹ τοὺς ξένους δὲ εἰπεῖν ὡς δικαιότερα λέγουσι τῶν πολιτῶν.

¹ del. Hanow, Gomperz, Stein.    ² προσαγορεύσας codd. (προαγορεύσας A): ]ρευσαι ut videtur P. Herc. 1457.

³ εἴπα[ς P. Herc. 1457: εἰπὼν codd.

⁴ τα[ῖ]ς χε[ρσ]ὶν [ . . . ]μεν[ . . ] μὴ P. Herc. 1457, ut videtur, supplevit Stein: ταῖς χερσὶ μὴ ἀφιέναι codd.

⁵ μικρ[ὸ]ν [ . ] . . προπέμψας P. Herc. 1457.

⁶ ὄψε]ται ἐπαινῶν P. Herc. 1457 (quod coniecerat Needham): ὄψεται ἔτι αἰνῶν ABCe, ὄψεται ἔτι ἐπαινῶν De.

⁷ δίαιτα[ν μὴ μόνον τούτῳ ᾧ] πάρεστ[ιν P. Herc. 1457, ut videtur, sed de pronomine cf. 13.5, 18.6 (Stein).

⁸ εἷς AB (εἷς om. CDE): τις (quod iam coniecerat Pauw) P. Herc. 1457.

⁹ suppl. Casaubon.

68

## 5. OBSEQUIOUSNESS

(1) [Obsequiousness, to put it in a definition, is a manner of behavior that aims at pleasing, but not with the best intentions.][a] You can be sure that the obsequious man is the sort (2) who greets you from a distance,[b] then, after calling you "your excellency" and expressing great respect, detains you by grabbing you with both hands, walks along a little farther, asks when he will see you again, and calls out compliments as he leaves.

(3) When he is asked to join an arbitration board, he wants to gratify not only the man whose side he is on, but his opponent too, so that he'll be thought the impartial person.[c] (4) He tells foreigners that they have a better case than his fellow-citizens.

[a] Probably adapted from the definition of flattery in Pseudo-Plato, *Definitions* 415e9 (cf. *Gorgias* 465a).

[b] As prescribed in Menander, *Dyskolos* 105. With the whole scene cf. Horace, *Satires* 1.9.4, Plautus, *Aulularia* 114–6.

[c] For a private arbitration one member of the board had to be acceptable to both sides as an impartial tie-breaker, but each disputant could choose any (equal) number of judges. See Douglas M. MacDowell, *Law in Classical Athens* (London 1978) 203–206.

(5) καὶ κεκλημένος δὲ ἐπὶ δεῖπνον κελεῦσαι καλέσαι τὰ παιδία τὸν ἑστιῶντα, καὶ εἰσιόντα φῆσαι σύκου ὁμοιότερα εἶναι τῷ πατρί, καὶ προσαγόμενος φιλῆσαι καὶ παρ᾽ αὐτὸν καθίσασθαι,[1] καὶ τοῖς μὲν συμπαίζειν αὐτὸς λέγων· "ἀσκός, πέλεκυς," τὰ δὲ ἐπὶ τῆς γαστρὸς ἐᾶν καθεύδειν ἅμα θλιβόμενος. <...>[2]


(6) <...> καὶ πλειστάκις δὲ ἀποκείρασθαι καὶ τοὺς ὀδόντας λευκοὺς ἔχειν καὶ τὰ ἱμάτια δὲ χρηστὰ μεταβάλλεσθαι καὶ χρίσματι ἀλείφεσθαι. (7) καὶ τῆς μὲν ἀγορᾶς πρὸς τὰς τραπέζας προσφοιτᾶν, τῶν δὲ γυμνασίων ἐν τούτοις διατρίβειν, οὗ ἂν οἱ[3] ἔφηβοι γυμνάζωνται, τοῦ δὲ θεάτρου καθῆσθαι, ὅταν ᾖ θέα, πλησίον τῶν στρατηγῶν. (8) καὶ ἀγοράζειν αὑτῷ μὲν μηδέν, ξένοις δ᾽ εἰς Βυζάντιον ἐπιστάλματα[4] καὶ Λακωνικὰς κύνας εἰς Κύζικον καὶ μέλι Ὑμήττιον εἰς Ῥόδον, καὶ

[1] Cobet: καθίστασθαι AB, καθίσαι CDe.
[2] lacunam indicavit Casaubon (continuat P. Herc. 1457).
[3] P. Herc. 1457: om. codd.
[4] οἶνον pro ἐπιστάλματα Naber conferens [Dem.] 35.35, alii alia.

(5) When he is invited to dinner, he asks his host to call in the children and, when they come, says "Spittin' image of their dad!"[a] He hugs and kisses them and sits them down beside him; some he joins in a game, himself shouting out "wineskin" and "ax";[b] others he lets fall asleep on his stomach even though they are crushing him ...

*<From a different character (see Additional Notes)>*

(6) ... He gets frequent haircuts and keeps his teeth white,[c] and discards cloaks that are still good, and anoints himself with perfumed oil. (7) In the marketplace he goes frequently to the money-changers; among gymnasia he spends his time at those where the ephebes work out; in the theater, whenever there is a show, he sits next to the generals.[d] (8) He buys nothing for himself, but for foreigners he buys letters of commission[e] for Byzantium, and Laconian dogs for Kyzikos, and Hymettos

---

[a] Literally "more like their father than a fig (is like another)." For the proverb see *Paroem. Graec.* I.293 and Herodas 6.60.

[b] Evidently part of a children's game, no longer known.

[c] Cf. Catullus 39, *Paroem. Graec.* I.159, *PCG* Alexis fr. 103.20.

[d] He is choosing the spots where the greatest crowd will be watching.

[e] The word may be corrupt, but perhaps he sends the equivalent of a "gift-certificate" to a local merchant.

THEOPHRASTUS

ταῦτα ποιῶν τοῖς ἐν τῇ πόλει διηγεῖσθαι.

(9) ἀμέλει δὲ καὶ πίθηκον θρέψαι δεινὸς καὶ
τίτυρον κτήσασθαι καὶ Σικελικὰς περιστερὰς καὶ
δορκαδείους ἀστραγάλους καὶ Θουριακὰς τῶν
στρογγύλων ληκύθους καὶ βακτηρίας τῶν σκολιῶν
ἐκ Λακεδαίμονος καὶ αὐλαίαν Πέρσας ἐνυφασμέ-
νην[1] καὶ παλαιστρίδιον κόνιν ἔχον καὶ σφαιριστή-
ριον. (10) καὶ τοῦτο περιὼν χρηννύναι[2] τοῖς
σοφισταῖς,[3] τοῖς ὁπλομάχοις, τοῖς ἁρμονικοῖς
ἐνεπιδείκνυσθαι·[4] καὶ αὐτὸς ἐν ταῖς ἐπιδείξεσιν
ὕστερον ἐπεισιέναι ἐπὰν συγκαθῶνται ἵν' ἄλλος
ἄλλῳ εἴπῃ τῶν θεωμένων[5] ὅτι "τοῦτον ἐστὶν ἡ
παλαίστρα."

[1] αὐλαίαν ἔχουσαν Πέρσας ἐνυφασμένους codd., α]ὐλαίας
Πέρσας ἐν[υφασ]μέν[ο]υς P. Herc. 1457: corr. Herwerden et
Cobet.

[2] χρηννύναι (quod habet, ut videtur, P. Herc. 1457) Foss:
χρὴ νῦν ἀεί ABe.

[3] τοῖς φιλοσόφοις (quod non habet P. Herc. 1457) ante τοῖς
σοφισταῖς codd.

[4] Cobet (quod habet, ut videtur, P. Herc. 1457): ἐπιδεί-
κνυσθαι codd.

[5] ἔπεισιν ἐπὶ τῶν θεωμένων πρὸς τὸν ἔτερον ὅτι AB, εἰπεῖν ἐπὶ
... πρὸς ἔτερον ὅτι CDe: vestigia P. Herc. 1457 sic interpre-
tatus est Stein: ἐπεισιέναι ἐπὰν] συγκαθῶν[ται ἵ]ν' [ἄλλος
ἄλλῳ εἴ]πῃ τῶν θεω[μ]έν[ω]ν ὅτι.

honey for Rhodes, and as he does so tells everybody in town about it.[a]

(9) You can be sure he is apt to keep a pet monkey, and buys a pheasant,[b] and some Sicilian doves,[c] and dice made from gazelle horns,[d] and oil flasks from Thurii of the rounded sort, and walking sticks from Sparta of the twisted sort,[e] and a tapestry embroidered with pictures of Persian soldiers,[f] and his own little arena (complete with sand) and handball court. (10) The last of these he goes around lending to sophists, military instructors, and musicians to perform in; and during their shows he himself is the last to enter after they are seated, so that the audience will say to each other[g] "That's the man the arena belongs to!"

[a] For the fame of Laconian hunting-dogs cf. Aristotle, *History of Animals* 608a25; for honey from Mt. Hymettos, Gow and Page on *Hellenistic Epigrams: The Garland of Philip* (Cambridge 1968) 2265.

[b] So D'Arcy W. Thompson, *Glossary of Greek Birds* (Cambridge 1936) 282, although other identifications of the *tityros* are possible.

[c] See *PCG* Alexis fr. 58, Thompson, *Glossary of Greek Birds* 285.

[d] See Herodas 3.19; they are mentioned frequently in papyrus-documents as items of great value.

[e] See Aristophanes, *Birds* 1281–3, Plutarch, *Nicias* 19.6.

[f] See *PCG* Hipparchus fr. 1.4.

[g] The text of the medieval manuscripts here is nonsense; the translation is based on a speculative reconstruction of the Herculaneum papyrus.

# ΑΠΟΝΟΙΑΣ ϛ´

(1) ἡ δὲ ἀπόνοιά ἐστιν ὑπομονὴ αἰσχρῶν ἔργων καὶ λόγων, ὁ δὲ ἀπονενοημένος τοιοῦτός τις, (2) οἷος ὀμόσαι ταχύ, κακῶς ἀκοῦσαι, λοιδορηθῆναι δυναμένοις,[1] τῷ ἤθει ἀγοραῖός τις καὶ ἀνασεσυρμένος καὶ παντοποιός. (3) ἀμέλει δυνατὸς καὶ[2] ὀρχεῖσθαι νήφων τὸν κόρδακα καὶ προσωπεῖον ἔχων ἐν κωμικῷ χορῷ.[3]

(4) καὶ ἐν θαύμασι δὲ τοὺς χαλκοῦς ἐκλέγειν καθ᾽ ἕκαστον παριὼν καὶ μάχεσθαι τούτοις τοῖς τὸ σύμβολον φέρουσι, καὶ προῖκα θεωρεῖν ἀξιοῦσι. (5) δεινὸς δὲ καὶ πανδοκεῦσαι καὶ πορνοβοσκῆσαι καὶ τελωνῆσαι καὶ μηδεμίαν αἰσχρὰν ἐργασίαν ἀποδοκιμάσαι, ἀλλὰ κηρύττειν, μαγειρεύειν, κυβεύειν, (6) τὴν μητέρα[4] μὴ τρέφειν, ἀπάγεσθαι κλοπῆς, τὸ δεσμωτήριον πλείω χρόνον οἰκεῖν ἢ τὴν αὑτοῦ οἰκίαν.

---

[1] Foss: δυνάμενος codd.    [2] ὀμόσαι ταχὺ ... δυνατὸς καὶ del. Diels.    [3] καὶ προσωπεῖον ... χορῷ del. Navarre.
[4] κυβεύειν. <δεινὸς δὲ καὶ> τὴν μητέρα Meier.

---

a The definition is alluded to by Philodemus, *On Flattery* (M. Gigante and G. Indelli, *Cronache ercolanesi* 8 [1978] 130), but may still be a post-Theophrastan addition (see Introd.).

## 6. SHAMELESSNESS

(1) Shamelessness is a tolerance for doing and saying unseemly things.[a] The shameless man is the sort (2) who takes an oath too readily, ruins his reputation, vilifies the powerful, in his character is like a market-vendor, coarse and ready for anything.[b] (3) You can be sure he is capable of even dancing the *kordax*[c] while sober, and while wearing a mask in a comic chorus.

(4) At street fairs[d] he goes around and collects coppers from each individual, and fights with those who already have a ticket or claim they can watch without paying. (5) He is apt to keep an inn or run a brothel or be a tax collector, and he rejects no disgraceful occupation, but works as an auctioneer, a cook, a professional gambler. (6) He lets his mother starve, is arrested for theft, and spends more time in jail than at home.

[b] This section and the beginning of the next use an adjectival style alien to the rest of the *Characters*, and may be a later addition.

[c] A lewd dance sometimes included in comedies (see Aristophanes, *Clouds* 540); for the assumption that one danced only when drunk see 12.14. The end of the sentence ("and while wearing ...") offers no sense in this context — it may be a marginal explanation of the dance which has found its way into the text.

[d] Literally "marvels," a mixture of puppet shows, magic tricks, skits, and animal fights; see W. Kroll, *RE* Suppl. VI.1281.

THEOPHRASTUS

(7) [καὶ τοῦτο ἂν εἶναι δόξειε τῶν περισταμέ-
νων τοὺς ὄχλους καὶ προσκαλούντων, μεγάλῃ τῇ
φωνῇ καὶ παερρωγυίᾳ λοιδορουμένων καὶ δια-
λεγομένων πρὸς αὐτούς, καὶ μεταξὺ οἱ μὲν
προσίασιν, οἱ δὲ ἀπίασι πρὶν ἀκοῦσαι αὐτοῦ, ἀλλὰ
τοῖς μὲν τὴν ἀρχήν, τοῖς δὲ συλλαβήν, τοῖς δὲ
μέρος τοῦ πράγματος λέγει, οὐκ ἄλλως θεωρεῖσθαι
ἀξιῶν τὴν ἀπόνοιαν αὐτοῦ ἢ ὅταν ᾖ πανήγυρις.][1]

(8) ἱκανὸς δὲ καὶ δίκας τὰς μὲν φεύγειν, τὰς δὲ
διώκειν, τὰς δὲ ἐξόμνυσθαι, ταῖς δὲ παρεῖναι ἔχων
ἐχῖνον ἐν τῷ προκολπίῳ καὶ ὁρμαθοὺς γραμματι-
δίων ἐν ταῖς χερσίν. (9) οὐκ ἀποδοκιμάζειν[2] δὲ οὐδ᾽
ἅμα πολλῶν ἀγοραίων στρατηγεῖν καὶ εὐθὺς τούτοις δανείζειν καὶ τῆς δραχμῆς τόκον τρία ἡμιω-
βόλια τῆς ἡμέρας πράττεσθαι καὶ ἐφοδεύειν τὰ
μαγειρεῖα, τὰ ἰχθυοπώλια, τὰ ταριχοπώλια, καὶ
τοὺς τόκους ἀπὸ τοῦ ἐμπολήματος εἰς τὴν γνάθον
ἐκλέγειν.

(10) [ἐργώδεις δέ εἰσιν οἱ τὸ στόμα εὔλυτον

---

[1] del. editores.        [2] Meier: ἀποδοκιμάζων codd.

---

[a] I.e., shamelessness; but this whole paragraph is so
different in style (use of the plural, finite verbs instead of

(7) [And this[a] would seem to be the character of those who gather crowds around them and give a harangue, railing in a loud and cracked voice and arguing with them. Meanwhile some of them are coming in, some are leaving before they hear him; yet he manages to say the beginning to some, a word or two to others, a part of his message to others, in the conviction that the only place for his shamelessness to be displayed is among a crowd.]

(8) In court he is capable of being now a defendant, now a plaintiff, now taking an oath for a postponement,[b] now showing up for trial with a potful of evidence[c] in the fold of his cloak and sheaves of memoranda in his hands. (9) He doesn't even have any qualms about being the leader of a group of street vendors, while at the same time giving them quick loans and charging one and a half obols per drachma per day interest,[d] and making the rounds of the stalls where they sell hot food and fresh or smoked fish, and tucking into his cheek[e] the interest he's made from his business.

(10) [They are tiresome, these people who have a

infinitives, rhetorical tone) as to be almost certainly a later addition.

[b] MacDowell, *Law in Classical Athens* 208.

[c] All the documentation in a case was deposited in a pot in the court (Aristotle, *Constitution of Athens* 53.2); this man has brought his own.

[d] Twenty-five percent interest each day.

[e] The poor man's way of carrying money when shopping, see *PCG* Aristophanes fr. 3.

ἔχοντες πρὸς λοιδορίαν καὶ φθεγγόμενοι μεγάλῃ
τῇ φωνῇ, ὡς συνηχεῖν αὐτοῖς τὴν ἀγορὰν καὶ τὰ
ἐργαστήρια.][1]

## ΛΑΛΙΑΣ Ζ΄

(1) [ἡ δὲ λαλιά, εἴ τις αὐτὴν ὁρίζεσθαι βούλοιτο,
εἶναι ἂν δόξειεν ἀκρασία τοῦ λόγου·][2] ὁ δὲ λάλος
τοιοῦτός τις, (2) οἷος τῷ ἐντυγχάνοντι εἰπεῖν, ἂν
ὁτιοῦν πρὸς αὐτὸν φθέγξηται, ὅτι οὐθὲν λέγει καὶ
ὅτι αὐτὸς πάντα οἶδεν καὶ, ἂν ἀκούῃ αὐτοῦ, μαθή-
σεται· καὶ μεταξὺ δὲ ἀποκρινομένῳ ἐπιβάλλειν
εἴπας "σὺ μὴ ἐπιλάθῃ, ὃ μέλλεις λέγειν," καὶ "εὖ
γε, ὅτι με ὑπέμνησας," καὶ "τὸ λαλεῖν ὡς χρήσιμόν
που," καὶ "ὃ παρέλιπον," καὶ "ταχύ γε συνῆκας τὸ
πρᾶγμα," καὶ "πάλαι σε παρετήρουν, εἰ ἐπὶ τὸ
αὐτὸ ἐμοὶ κατενεχθήσῃ·" καὶ ἑτέρας ἀρχὰς τοιαύτας πορίσασθαι, ὥστε μηδὲ ἀναπνεῦσαι τὸν
ἐντυγχάνοντα.

(3) καὶ ὅταν γε τοὺς καθ᾿ ἕνα ἀπογυμνώσῃ,
δεινὸς καὶ ἐπὶ τοὺς ἀθρόους [καὶ][3] συνεστηκότας
πορευθῆναι καὶ φυγεῖν ποιῆσαι μεταξὺ χρηματί-
ζοντας. (4) καὶ εἰς τὰ διδασκαλεῖα δὲ καὶ εἰς τὰς

---

[1] epilogum del. editores.   [2] del. Hanow, Gomperz,
Stein.   [3] del. Meineke.

ready tongue for abuse, and who speak in such a loud voice that the marketplace and workshops resound with them.]

## 7. GARRULITY

(1) [Garrulity, should you like to define it, would seem to be an inability to control one's speech.][a] The garrulous man is the sort (2) who says to anyone he meets that he is talking nonsense — no matter what that man may tell him — and that he knows it all himself, and if he listens, he'll find out about it. And as the other tries to answer, he keeps interrupting and says, "Now don't forget what you intend to say!" and "Good of you to remind me of that!" and "How nice to be able to talk!" "That's something I left out!" and "You're quick to grasp the point!" and "I've been waiting all this time to see whether you would come around to my view!"[b] He tries to give himself more openings like these, so that the man who meets him can't even catch his breath.

(3) Once he has finished off individuals, he is apt to move against whole formations and put them to flight in the midst of their business. (4) He goes into the schools and wrestling grounds and prevents the

[a] The definition seems derived from Pseudo-Plato, *Definitions* 416a23.
[b] Even when he agrees with the other, the talkative man uses these phrases to cut back into the conversation.

THEOPHRASTUS

παλαίστρας εἰσιὼν κωλύειν τοὺς παῖδας προμαν-
θάνειν· [τοσαῦτα καὶ προσλαλεῖ[1] τοῖς παιδοτρί-
βαις καὶ διδασκάλοις.][2]

(5) καὶ τοὺς ἀπιέναι φάσκοντας δεινὸς προπέμ-
ψαι καὶ ἀποκαταστῆσαι εἰς τὰς οἰκίας.[3] (6) καὶ
πυθομένοις[4] <τὰ ἀπὸ>[5] τῆς ἐκκλησίας ἀπαγγέλ-
λειν, προσδιηγήσασθαι δὲ καὶ τὴν ἐπ᾽ Ἀριστο-
φῶντος τότε γενομένην [τοῦ ῥήτορος][6] μάχην καὶ
τὴν Λακεδαιμονίοις ὑπὸ Λυσάνδρου, καὶ οὕς ποτε
λόγους αὐτὸς εἶπας εὐδοκίμησεν ἐν τῷ δήμῳ, καὶ
κατὰ τῶν πληθῶν γε ἅμα διηγούμενος κατηγο-
ρίαν παρεμβαλεῖν, ὥστε τοὺς ἀκούοντας ἤτοι ἐπιλαβέσθαι[7] ἢ νυστάξαι ἢ μεταξὺ καταλιπόντας
ἀπαλλάττεσθαι.

(7) καὶ συνδικάζων δὲ κωλῦσαι κρῖναι καὶ συν-
θεωρῶν θεάσασθαι καὶ συνδειπνῶν φαγεῖν, καὶ
λέγειν ὅτι "χαλεπόν μοι[8] ἐστὶν σιωπᾶν," καὶ ὡς ἐν
ὑγρῷ ἐστιν ἡ γλῶττα, καὶ ὅτι οὐκ ἂν σιωπήσειεν,
οὐδ᾽ εἰ τῶν χελιδόνων δόξειεν εἶναι λαλίστερος.
(8) καὶ σκωπτόμενος ὑπομεῖναι καὶ ὑπὸ τῶν αὑτοῦ
παιδίων, ὅταν αὐτὰ[9] ἤδη καθεύδειν βουλό-

[1] Diels: προσλαλεῖν codd.  [2] del. Diels coll. 8.14
οὕτως καὶ καταπονοῦσι.  [3] Ribbeck: ἐκ τῆς οἰκίας AB.
[4] Foss: πυθόμενος codd.  [5] suppl. Kayser (cf. 4.6).  [6] ut
glossema del. Fischer: τῶν ῥητόρων Casaubon.  [7] Foss:

80

boys from making progress with their studies. [That is how much he talks to their trainers and teachers.]

(5) When people say they must go, he is apt to keep them company, or see them back home. (6) He reports what has happened in the assembly to people who ask him, but adds to his account as well the battle in the year of Aristophon[a] and that of the Spartans under Lysander,[b] and the speeches by which he himself gained a public reputation, and as he tells his story he interjects a condemnation of the masses, so that his hearers interrupt him, or doze off, or go away and leave before he finishes.

(7) When he is among them, he prevents jurors from reaching a verdict, an audience from watching the show, and dinner guests from getting anything to eat, and he remarks "it's hard for me to keep still," and how mobile the tongue is, and that he simply couldn't be quiet, not even if he might appear to chatter more than the swallows.[c] (8) He puts up with being mocked even by his own children when

[a] Aristophon was archon of Athens in 330/29, but no suitable battle is known. Casaubon suggested that this was a political rather than military battle, between Demosthenes and Aeschines in the speeches *On the Crown* and *Against Ctesiphon* in 330; but see Hermann Wankel, *Demosthenes' Kranzrede* (Heidelberg 1976) 29–30.

[b] Again the battle cannot be identified; Lysander was a Spartan general 408–395.

[c] *Paroem. Graec.* II.183.

---

ἐπιλαθέσθαι codd.     [8] Kassel e P. Hamb. 143: τῷ λάλῳ codd.     [9] dubitanter conieci: αὐτὸν codd.

μενον[1] κωλύῃ[2] λέγοντα ταῦτα, "λαλεῖν τι ἡμῖν,
ὅπως ἂν ἡμᾶς ὕπνος λάβῃ."

## ΛΟΓΟΠΟΙΑΣ Η΄

(1) ἡ δὲ λογοποιία ἐστὶ σύνθεσις ψευδῶν λόγων καὶ
πράξεων, ὧν <...>[3] βούλεται ὁ λογοποιῶν, ὁ δὲ
λογοποιὸς τοιοῦτός τις, (2) οἷος ἀπαντήσας τῷ
φίλῳ εὐθὺς καταβαλὼν τὸ ἦθος καὶ μειδιάσας
ἐρωτῆσαι "πόθεν σύ;" καὶ "λέγεις τι;" καὶ "πῶς
ἔχεις;" πρὸ τοῦ δ' εἰπεῖν ἐκεῖνον "καλῶς"[4] ἐπι-
βαλὼν "ἐρωτᾷς[5] μὴ λέγεταί τι καινότερον; καὶ
μὴν ἀγαθά γέ ἐστι τὰ λεγόμενα." (3) καὶ οὐκ ἐάσας
ἀποκρίνασθαι εἰπεῖν· "τί λέγεις; οὐθὲν ἀκήκοας;
δοκῶ μοί σε εὐωχήσειν καινῶν λόγων." (4) καὶ
ἔστιν αὐτῷ ἢ στρατιώτης ἢ παῖς Ἀστείου τοῦ
αὐλητοῦ ἢ Λύκων ὁ ἐργολάβος παραγεγονὼς ἐξ
αὐτῆς τῆς μάχης, οὗ φησιν ἀκηκοέναι· αἱ μὲν οὖν
ἀναφοραὶ τῶν λόγων τοιαῦταί εἰσιν αὐτῷ, ὧν
οὐθεὶς ἂν ἔχοι ἐπιλαβέσθαι.[6] (5) διηγεῖται δὲ τούτους φάσκων λέγειν, ὡς Πολυπέρχων καὶ ὁ βασι-

[1] c: βουλόμενα AB.    [2] Hartung: κελεύῃ codd.
[3] <πιστεύεσθαι> suppl. Diels, <διασπείρων σεμνύνεσθαι>
Navarre.
[4] sic vestigia P. Hamb. 143 interpretatur Gronewald:
περὶ τοῦδε εἰπεῖν καινὸν καὶ ὡς codd.

he wants them to go to bed right now, and they stop him by saying this: "Talk to us a little, so we can get to sleep."[a]

## 8. RUMOR-MONGERING

(1) Rumor-mongering is the invention of untrue reports and events about which the monger wants <...>. The rumor-monger is the sort (2) who, when he meets his friend, immediately relaxes his expression[b] and asks with a laugh, "Where have you been? Do you have anything to tell me? How's it going?" But before the man can say "I'm fine," he interrupts him: "You ask if there's any news? Actually, you know, the reports are rather good." (3) And without allowing an answer, he says "What? You haven't heard *anything*? It looks like I'll be giving you a feast of the latest news." (4) He has got a man he says he's heard just back from the battle itself, a soldier, or a slave of Asteios the flute-player, or Lykon the contractor — he has ways of vouching for his stories that no one can refute. (5) He relates, as he claims these people told him, that Polyperchon and the king were victorious in a battle, and Cas-

[a] The text is uncertain.

[b] For καταβάλλειν in this sense see Van Leeuwen on Aristophanes, *Wasps* 655.

---

[5] Kassel: ἐρωτᾶν codd.

[6] Casaubon: ἐπιλαθέσθαι codd.

λεὺς μάχῃ νενίκηκε, καὶ Κάσανδρος ἐζώγρηται.
(6) καὶ ἂν εἴπῃ τις αὐτῷ, "σὺ δὲ ταῦτα πιστεύεις;"
φήσει· τὸ πρᾶγμα βοᾶσθαι γὰρ ἐν τῇ πόλει, καὶ
τὸν λόγον ἐπεντείνειν, καὶ πάντας[1] συμφωνεῖν,
ταῦτα γὰρ λέγειν περὶ τῆς μάχης, καὶ πολὺν τὸν
ζωμὸν γεγονέναι. (7) εἶναι δ᾽ ἑαυτῷ καὶ σημεῖον
τὰ πρόσωπα τῶν ἐν τοῖς πράγμασιν· ὁρᾶν γὰρ
αὐτῶν πάντων μεταβεβληκότα. λέγει δ᾽, ὡς καὶ
παρακήκοε παρὰ τούτοις κρυπτόμενόν τινα ἐν
οἰκίᾳ, ἤδη πέμπτην ἡμέραν ἥκοντα ἐκ Μακεδονίας, ὃς πάντα ταῦτα οἶδε.

(8) καὶ πάντα διεξιὼν πως[2] οἴεσθαι πιθανῶς
σχετλιάζειν[3] λέγων· "δυστυχὴς Κάσανδρος· ὦ
ταλαίπωρος· ἐνθυμῇ τὸ τῆς τύχης; ἀλλ᾽ οὖν ἰσχυ-
ρὸς γενόμενος·" (9) καὶ "δεῖ δ᾽ αὐτόν σε μόνον
εἰδέναι." πᾶσι δὲ τοῖς ἐν τῇ πόλει προσδεδράμηκε
λέγων.

[1] Casaubon: πάντα codd.
[2] Diels: πῶς codd.
[3] οἴεσθε cDE, σχετλιάζει D.

---

[a] The situation is historical (see Introd. p. 9): the war
between Cassander and Polyperchon lasted 319–309, and
"the king" is most likely Philip Arridaios, half-brother of

sander has been taken prisoner.[a] (6) And if you say
to him "Do *you* believe it?" he will say he does,
because it's the talk of the city, and the discussion is
intensifying; all the people are in unison since they
tell the same story about the battle; it was a huge
bloodbath, (7) and he has proof in the faces of the
political leaders, since he notices they are all
changed.[b] And he says he also overheard that someone who knows the whole story has been kept hidden by them in a private house since he came to
town four days ago from Macedonia.

(8) And as he tells his story, he somehow
believes[c] he is persuasively indignant when he says,
"Miserable Cassander! Poor fellow! You see what
Fortune can do? Well, he had his power once."
(9) and "You must keep it to yourself." But he has
run up to everyone in town with the news.

Alexander the Great. The date is late in 319, just before
the fall of the oligarchic government in Athens supported
by Cassander, and the introduction of a democratic one
encouraged by Polyperchon. But the rumor itself is of
course untrue: Cassander captured Athens two years later.
Note that this is "good news" for democrats, but not
oligarchs (cf. *Character* 26).

[b] Phocion, the leader of the oligarchic government, was
in fact overthrown and executed shortly thereafter.

[c] The rumor-monger abandons his glee at the supposed
fall of Cassander and ends with an evocation of pity. The
text may be corrupt beyond repair; the reading adopted
here assumes that the construction reverts to the typical
string of infinitives begun in § 2 and interrupted with § 6.

(10) [τῶν τοιούτων ἀνθρώπων τεθαύμακα, τί
ποτε βούλονται λογοποιοῦντες· οὐ γὰρ μόνον ψεύ-
δονται, ἀλλὰ καὶ ἀλυσιτελῶς ἀπαλλάττουσι.
(11) πολλάκις γὰρ αὐτῶν οἱ μὲν ἐν τοῖς βαλανείοις
περιστάσεις ποιούμενοι τὰ ἱμάτια ἀποβεβλήκασιν,
οἱ δ' ἐν¹ τῇ στοᾷ πεζομαχίᾳ καὶ ναυμαχίᾳ νικῶν-
τες ἐρήμους δίκας ὠφλήκασιν. (12) εἰσὶ δ' οἳ καὶ
πόλεις τῷ λόγῳ κατὰ κράτος αἱροῦντες παρεδει-
πνήθησαν. (13) πάνυ δὴ ταλαίπωρον αὐτῶν ἐστι
τὸ ἐπιτήδευμα. ποία γὰρ οὐ στοᾷ, ποίῳ δὲ ἐργα-
στηρίῳ, ποίῳ δὲ μέρει τῆς ἀγορᾶς οὐκ ἐνημερεύ-
ουσιν ἀπαυδᾶν ποιοῦντες τοὺς ἀκούοντας;
(14) οὕτως καὶ καταπονοῦσι ταῖς ψευδολογίαις.]²

# ΑΝΑΙΣΧΥΝΤΙΑΣ Θ´

(1) [ἡ δὲ ἀναισχυντία ἐστὶ μέν, ὡς ὅρῳ λαβεῖν,
καταφρόνησις δόξης αἰσχρᾶς³ ἕνεκα κέρδους,]⁴ ὁ
δὲ ἀναίσχυντος τοιοῦτος, (2) οἷος πρῶτον μὲν ὂν
ἀποστερεῖ πρὸς τοῦτον ἀπελθὼν δανείζεσθαι,

---

¹ δ' ἐν CDe: δὲ AB.
² τῶν τοιούτων . . . ταῖς ψευδολογίαις del. editores.
³ Kassel: αἰσχροῦ codd.
⁴ del. Hanow, Gomperz, Stein.

(10) [I wonder what such people hope to gain from their rumor-mongering; not only do they tell lies, they also end up no better off for it. (11) Those who draw a circle of hearers in the baths often have their cloaks stolen, and those who are victorious by land and sea in the stoa lose court-cases forfeited for failure to appear. (12) Some of them capture cities in an all-out talk-fight, but go without their dinner. (13) Their behavior is sad indeed, for in what stoa, or what workshop, or what part of the market do they not pass the day exhausting those who listen to them? (14) That is how they persevere in telling lies.][a]

## 9. SPONGING

(1) [Sponging, to put it in a definition, is a disregard for a bad reputation for the sake of gain.][b] The sponger is the sort (2) who, in the first place, goes back to a man he is holding out on and asks for a loan; second, after performing a sacrifice to the

---

[a] This whole paragraph, beginning in the first person, with tenses and constructions unlikely for fourth-century Greek, and rhetorical questions alien to the *Characters*, is certainly one of the later epilogues.

[b] The definition is too vague to suit the following description, and seems derived from Pseudo-Plato, *Definitiones* 416a14.

εἶτα θύσας τοῖς θεοῖς αὐτὸς μὲν δειπνεῖν παρ᾽ ἑτέρῳ, τὰ δὲ κρέα ἀποτιθέναι ἁλσὶ πάσας, (3) καὶ προσκαλεσάμενος τὸν ἀκόλουθον δοῦναι ἀπὸ τῆς τραπέζης ἄρας κρέας καὶ ἄρτον καὶ εἰπεῖν ἀκουόντων πάντων "εὐωχοῦ, Τίβειε."

(4) καὶ ὀψωνῶν δὲ ὑπομιμνήσκειν τὸν κρεωπώλην, εἴ τι χρήσιμος αὐτῷ γέγονε, καὶ ἑστηκὼς πρὸς τῷ σταθμῷ μάλιστα μὲν κρέας, εἰ δὲ μή, ὀστοῦν εἰς τὸν ζωμὸν ἐμβαλεῖν, καὶ ἐὰν μὲν λάβῃ, εὖ ἔχει, εἰ δὲ μή, ἁρπάσας ἀπὸ τῆς τραπέζης χολίκιον ἅμα γελῶν ἀπαλλάττεσθαι.

(5) καὶ ξένοις δὲ αὐτοῦ θέαν ἀγοράσας μὴ δοὺς τὸ μέρος συνθεωρεῖν,[1] ἄγειν δὲ καὶ τοὺς υἱεῖς εἰς τὴν ὑστεραίαν καὶ τὸν παιδαγωγόν. (6) καὶ ὅσα ἐωνημένος ἄξιά τις φέρει, μεταδοῦναι κελεῦσαι καὶ αὑτῷ. (7) καὶ ἐπὶ τὴν ἀλλοτρίαν οἰκίαν ἐλθὼν δανείζεσθαι κριθάς, ποτὲ δὲ ἄχυρα, καὶ ταῦτα τοὺς χρήσαντας ἀναγκάσαι ἀποφέρειν πρὸς αὑτόν.

---

[1] Cobet: θεωρεῖν codd.

[a] The meat of the sacrifical animal was normally given to guests and the household in a feast on a holy day (W. Burkert, *Homo Necans*, Berkeley 1983, 6–7)—this man goes to another's feast instead.

gods he salts and stores away the meat, and goes to dinner at another's;[a] (3) he invites his slave along too, and gives him meat and bread he takes from the table and says in everyone's hearing "Enjoy yourself, Tibeios."[b]

(4) When he goes shopping, he reminds the butcher of any favor he has done him, then stands by the scale and throws in[c] preferably some meat, otherwise a bone for the soup, and if he gets it, good, otherwise he grabs some tripe from the table with a laugh as he goes away.

(5) When he buys theater tickets for his guests[d] he goes to the show too without paying his share; the next day, he brings along his children and the slave who takes care of them. (6) If anyone makes a purchase at a bargain price, he asks to be given a share too. (7) He goes to other people's houses and borrows barley, sometimes chaff,[e] and makes the lenders deliver it to him besides.

[b] A name of Paphlagonian slaves (Strabo 7.304), often in Menander (*Heros* 21, *Perinthia* 3, fr. 194, 281). For giving slaves a taste, cf. Athenaeus 4.128d–e; but often in such cases the slave's task was to hide the food and take it home for later (Martial 2.37, 3.23, 7.20, 16, *Anth. Pal.* 11.205).

[c] After the weighing: he wants it for nothing.

[d] With money they have given him. Since they make no objection the first time, he is even more brazen for the following day's show.

[e] Used as filling material, or mixed with grain: W. K. Pritchett, *Hesperia* 25 (1956) 182–183.

THEOPHRASTUS

(8) δεινὸς δὲ καὶ πρὸς τὰ χαλκεῖα τὰ ἐν τῷ βαλανείῳ προσελθὼν καὶ βάψας ἀρύταιναν βοῶντος τοῦ βαλανέως αὐτὸς αὑτοῦ καταχέασθαι καὶ εἰπεῖν, ὅτι λέλουται, ἀπιὼν †κἀκεῖ† "οὐδεμία σοι χάρις."

# ΜΙΚΡΟΛΟΓΙΑΣ Ι΄

(1) ἔστι δὲ ἡ μικρολογία φειδωλία τοῦ διαφόρου ὑπὲρ τὸν καιρόν, ὁ δὲ μικρολόγος τοιοῦτός τις, (2) οἷος ἐν τῷ μηνὶ ἡμιωβόλιον ἀπαιτεῖν ἐπὶ τὴν οἰκίαν. (3) καὶ συσσιτῶν ἀριθμεῖν τὰς κύλικας, πόσας ἕκαστος πέπωκε, καὶ ἀπάρχεσθαι ἐλάχιστον τῇ Ἀρτέμιδι τῶν συνδειπνούντων. (4) καὶ ὅσα μικροῦ τις πριάμενος λογίζεται, πάντα φάσκειν εἶναι <...>[1] (5) καὶ οἰκέτου χύτραν[2] ἢ λοπάδα κατάξαντος εἰσπρᾶξαι ἀπὸ τῶν ἐπιτη-

[1] lacunam statuit Holland, e.g. <τιμιώτερα καὶ ἀποδοκιμάζειν> Stein.
[2] post χύτραν add. εἶναι AB.

[a] For the apparatus and procedure see René Ginouvès, Βαλανευτική: *Recherches sur le bain dans l'antiquité grecque*

(8) He is apt to go up to the hot-water tanks at the baths, draw a ladle-full and rinse himself, as the bath attendant screams at him, and say, as he goes away, "I've already had my bath—no thanks to you!"[a]

## 10. PENNYPINCHING

(1) Pennypinching is an immoderate sparing of expense. The pennypincher is the sort (2) who stipulates the repayment of a half-cent "within the month, to his house."[b] (3) When he is sharing a dinner he reckons up how many glasses each has drunk;[c] his initial offering to Artemis[d] is smaller than any other at the table. (4) When someone has bought goods for him at a bargain price and presents his bill, he says they are too expensive, and rejects them.[e] (5) When a servant breaks a clay pot or serving dish, he deducts it from his daily rations.

(Paris 1962) 205, 214. Only the proverbially outspoken (Ginouvès 212) bath attendant (who has lost his fee) has the nerve to object to the sponger's tricks.

[b] The text is very condensed and may be corrupt.

[c] He demands a complete reckoning of each glass before he pays his share of the bill after dinner; cf. *PCG* Alexis fr. 15.

[d] The initial offering was a libation of wine; evidently the dining-group has Artemis as its patron.

[e] Some of the text must be missing; the last part of the sentence translated here is a speculative reconstruction (cf. *PCG* Ephippus fr. 15).

δείων. (6) καὶ τῆς γυναικὸς ἐκβαλούσης τρίχαλκον
οἷος μεταφέρειν τὰ σκεύη καὶ τὰς κλίνας καὶ τὰς
κιβωτοὺς καὶ διφᾶν τὰ καλύμματα. (7) καὶ ἐάν τι
πωλῇ, τοσούτου ἀποδόσθαι, ὥστε μὴ λυσιτελεῖν
τῷ πριαμένῳ.

(8) καὶ οὐκ ἂν ἐᾶσαι οὔτε συκοτραγῆσαι ἐκ τοῦ
αὑτοῦ κήπου οὔτε διὰ τοῦ αὑτοῦ ἀγροῦ πορευθῆναι
οὔτε ἐλαίαν ἢ φοίνικα τῶν χαμαὶ πεπτωκότων
ἀνελέσθαι.

(9) καὶ τοὺς ὅρους δ᾽ ἐπισκοπεῖσθαι ὁσημέραι εἰ
διαμένουσιν οἱ αὐτοί. (10) δεινὸς δὲ καὶ ὑπερημε-
ρίαν πρᾶξαι καὶ τόκον τόκου. (11) καὶ ἑστιῶν
δημότας μικρὰ τὰ κρέα κόψας παραθεῖναι. (12) καὶ
ὀψωνῶν μηθὲν πριάμενος εἰσελθεῖν. (13) καὶ ἀπα-
γορεῦσαι τῇ γυναικὶ μήτε ἅλας χρηννύειν[1] μήτε
ἐλλύχνιον μήτε κύμινον μήτε ὀρίγανον μήτε ὀλὰς
μήτε στέμματα μήτε θυλήματα, ἀλλὰ λέγειν ὅτι
τὰ μικρὰ ταῦτα πολλά ἐστι τοῦ ἐνιαυτοῦ.

(14) [καὶ τὸ ὅλον δὲ τῶν μικρολόγων καὶ τὰς
ἀργυροθήκας ἔστιν ἰδεῖν εὐρωτιώσας καὶ τὰς κλεῖς
ἰωμένας καὶ αὐτοὺς δὲ φοροῦντας ἐλάττω τῶν
μηρῶν[2] τὰ ἱμάτια καὶ ἐκ ληκυθίων μικρῶν πάνυ
ἀλειφομένους καὶ ἐν χρῷ κειρομένους καὶ τὸ μέσον

---

[1] Foss: χρωννύειν codd.

(6) And if his wife drops a three-penny piece, he is capable of moving the dishes, couches, and chests, and searching in the floorboards. (7) If he sells something, he charges so much that the buyer can't recover his price of purchase.

(8) He doesn't allow eating of figs from his own garden, or passage through his field, or picking up of an olive or date that has fallen on the ground.

(9) He inspects his property markers daily to see if they remain the same. (10) He is apt to charge a late fee and compound interest. (11) When he gives a dinner for his precinct,[a] he serves the meat cut into tiny portions. (12) When he goes shopping, he returns home without buying anything. (13) He forbids his wife to lend out salt, or a lampwick, or cumin, or oregano, or barley groats, or garlands, or sacrificial cakes, maintaining that these small items add up to a lot over the course of a year.

(14) [In general, pennypinchers like to see their money boxes moldy and the keys to them rusty, and they themselves wear cloaks that don't cover their thighs, rub themselves down from tiny oil flasks,[b] have their heads shaved,[c] put on their shoes at mid-

---

[a] Lit. "his deme," the members of his local voting-district: David Whitehead, *The Demes of Attica* (Princeton 1986) 152.

[b] At the baths (30.8 note).

[c] To save money on haircuts.

---

[2] A (ante correctionem) et e: μικρῶν A (corr.) et BDe, μετρῶν C.

τῆς ἡμέρας ὑποδουμένους καὶ πρὸς τοὺς γναφεῖς
διατεινομένους ὅπως τὸ ἱμάτιον αὐτοῖς ἕξει
πολλὴν γῆν, ἵνα μὴ ῥυπαίνηται ταχύ.][1]

## ΒΔΕΛΥΡΙΑΣ ΙΑ΄

(1) οὐ χαλεπὸν δέ ἐστι τὴν βδελυρίαν διορίσασθαι·
ἔστι γὰρ παιδιὰ ἐπιφανὴς καὶ ἐπονείδιστος, ὁ δὲ
βδελυρὸς τοιοῦτος, (2) οἷος ἀπαντήσας γυναιξὶν
ἐλευθέραις ἀνασυράμενος δεῖξαι τὸ αἰδοῖον. (3) καὶ
ἐν θεάτρῳ κροτεῖν, ὅταν οἱ ἄλλοι παύωνται, καὶ
συρίττειν, οὓς ἡδέως θεωροῦσιν οἱ λοιποί· καὶ ὅταν
σιωπήσῃ τὸ θέατρον, ἀνακύψας ἐρυγεῖν ἵνα τοὺς
καθημένους ποιήσῃ μεταστραφῆναι. (4) καὶ πλη-
θούσης τῆς ἀγορᾶς προσελθὼν πρὸς τὰ κάρυα ἢ τὰ
μύρτα ἢ τὰ ἀκρόδρυα ἑστηκὼς τραγηματίζεσθαι
ἅμα τῷ πωλοῦντι προσλαλῶν· καὶ καλέσαι δὲ
τῶν παρόντων ὀνομαστί τινα, ᾧ μὴ συνήθης ἐστί·
(5) καὶ σπεύδοντας δέ ποι[2] ὁρῶν περιμεῖναι κελεῦ-
σαι· (6) καὶ ἡττωμένῳ δὲ μεγάλην δίκην ἀπιόντι
ἀπὸ τοῦ δικαστηρίου προσελθὼν[3] συνησθῆναι.

---

[1] epilogum del. editores.
[2] Casaubon: που codd.
[3] Cobet: προσελθεῖν καὶ codd.

day, and insist to the cleaners that their cloaks get a lot of earth[a] so that they won't get dirty again quickly.][b]

## 11. OBNOXIOUSNESS

(1) It is not difficult to define obnoxiousness: it is joking that is obvious and offensive. The obnoxious man is the sort (2) who, when he meets respectable women, raises his cloak and exposes his genitals. (3) In the theater he claps after others have stopped, and hisses the actors whom the others enjoy watching. When the audience is silent he rears back and belches, to make the spectators turn around. (4) When the agora is crowded he goes to the stands for walnuts, myrtleberries, and fruits, and stands there nibbling on them while talking with the vendor. He calls out by name to someone in the crowd with whom he's not acquainted. (5) When he sees people hurrying somewhere he tells them to wait. (6) He goes up to a man who has lost an important case and is leaving the court, and congratulates him.

[a] Fuller's clay: Hugo Blümner, *Technologie und Terminologie der Gewerbe und Künste* (2nd ed. Leipzig 1912) 1.176.

[b] The change in style and the switch to the plural among other things suggest that this closing paragraph is a later addition.

(7) καὶ ὀψωνεῖν ἑαυτῷ[1] καὶ αὐλητρίδας μισθοῦσθαι καὶ δεικνύειν δὲ τοῖς ἀπαντῶσι τὰ ὠψωνημένα καὶ παρακαλεῖν ἐπὶ ταῦτα· (8) καὶ διηγεῖσθαι προσστὰς πρὸς κουρεῖον ἢ μυροπώλιον ὅτι μεθύσκεσθαι μέλλει.

## ΑΚΑΙΡΙΑΣ ΙΒ΄

(1) [ἡ μὲν οὖν ἀκαιρία ἐστὶν ἐπίτευξις <χρόνου>[2] λυποῦσα τοὺς ἐντυγχάνοντας,][3] ὁ δὲ ἄκαιρος τοιοῦτός τις, (2) οἷος ἀσχολουμένῳ προσελθὼν ἀνακοινοῦσθαι. (3) καὶ πρὸς τὴν αὑτοῦ ἐρωμένην κωμάζειν πυρέττουσαν. (4) καὶ δίκην ὠφληκότα ἐγγύης προσελθὼν κελεῦσαι αὑτὸν ἀναδέξασθαι. (5) καὶ μαρτυρήσων παρεῖναι τοῦ πράγματος ἤδη κεκριμένου. (6) καὶ κεκλημένος εἰς γάμους τοῦ γυναικείου γένους κατηγορεῖν. (7) καὶ ἐκ μακρᾶς ὁδοῦ ἥκοντα ἄρτι παρακαλεῖν εἰς περίπατον.

(8) δεινὸς δὲ καὶ προσάγειν ὠνητὴν πλείω διδόντα ἤδη πεπρακότι. (9) καὶ ἀκηκοότας καὶ μεμαθηκότας ἀνίστασθαι ἐξ ἀρχῆς διδάξων.[4] (10) καὶ πρόθυμος δὲ ἐπιμεληθῆναι ἃ μὴ βούλε-

---

[1] Casaubon: ἑαυτὸν codd.
[2] suppl. Ruge.
[3] del. Hanow, Gomperz, Stein.
[4] Korais: διδάσκων codd.

(7) He goes shopping for himself and hires flute girls,[a] and he shows his purchases to anyone he meets and invites them to share. (8) He stands by the barber shop or perfume seller and relates that he intends to get drunk.

## 12. BAD TIMING

(1) [Bad timing is a usage of time which causes pain to those you happen to meet.][b] The man with bad timing is the sort (2) who goes up to someone who is busy and asks his advice. (3) He sings love songs to his girlfriend when she has a fever. (4) He goes up to a man who has just had to forfeit a security deposit in court and asks him to stand bail for him. (5) He shows up to give testimony after the case has already been decided. (6) If he's a guest at a wedding, he launches into a tirade against women.[c] (7) When a man has just returned from a long journey, he invites him to go for a walk.

(8) He is apt to bring in to a man who has already completed a sale a buyer who will pay more. (9) After people have listened and understand, he stands up to explain all over again. (10) He is

[a] Women who were expected to provide music (and sometimes sex) for a dinner party; cf. 20.9 and C. G. Starr, *Parola del passato* 34 (1978) 401–410.

[b] This extremely abstract definition appears to be adapted from the definition of its opposite ("good timing") in Pseudo-Plato, *Definitiones* 413c12.

[c] Cf. the tirade in Theophrastus, *On Marriage* (fr. 486).

ταί τις γενέσθαι, αἰσχύνεται δὲ ἀπείπασθαι.
(11) καὶ θύοντας καὶ ἀναλίσκοντας ἥκειν τόκον
ἀπαιτήσων. (12) καὶ μαστιγουμένου οἰκέτου παρε-
στὼς διηγεῖσθαι ὅτι καὶ αὑτοῦ ποτε παῖς οὕτως
πληγὰς λαβὼν ἀπήγξατο. (13) καὶ παρὼν διαίτῃ
συγκρούειν, ἀμφοτέρων βουλομένων διαλύεσθαι.
(14) καὶ ὀρχησόμενος ἅψασθαι ἑτέρου μηδέπω
μεθύοντος.

## ΠΕΡΙΕΡΓΙΑΣ ΙΓ΄

(1) ἀμέλει <ἡ>[1] περιεργία δόξει εἶναι προσποίησίς
τις λόγων καὶ πράξεων μετὰ εὐνοίας, ὁ δὲ περίερ-
γος τοιοῦτός τις, (2) οἷος ἐπαγγέλλεσθαι ἀναστὰς
ἃ μὴ δυνήσεται. (3) καὶ ὁμολογουμένου τοῦ
πράγματος δικαίου εἶναι ἐντείνας[2] ἐλεγχθῆναι.
(4) καὶ πλείω δὲ ἐπαναγκάσαι τὸν παῖδα κεράσαι
ἢ ὅσα δύνανται οἱ παρόντες ἐκπιεῖν.

(5) καὶ διείργειν τοὺς μαχομένους καὶ οὓς οὐ
γινώσκει. (6) καὶ ἀτραποῦ ἡγήσασθαι, εἶτα μὴ
δύνασθαι εὑρεῖν οἷ[3] πορεύεται. (7) καὶ τὸν στρατη-

[1] suppl. Buecheler.
[2] Immisch: ἔν τινι στάς codd.
[3] Casaubon: οὗ codd.

zealous in seeing to things that you don't desire, but are embarrassed to refuse. (11) When people are consuming a sacrifice, he comes to ask for interest on his loan. (12) When a slave is being beaten he stands watching and tells the story of how a slave of his once hanged himself after being beaten in just this way. (13) When he is on an arbitration board[a] he exacerbates the dispute, when what both sides desire is a reconciliation. (14) When he wants to dance, he grabs a partner who is still sober.[b]

## 13. OVERZEALOUSNESS

(1) You can be sure overzealousness will seem to be a well-intentioned appropriation of words and actions. The overzealous man is the sort (2) who gets up and promises to do things he won't be able to carry out. (3) When people are in agreement that his cause is just, he becomes too intense and loses the case. (4) He forces the servant to mix more wine than the company can drink.

(5) He tries to stop fights even between strangers to him.[c] (6) He leads the way down a path, but then can't find the way to where he is going.[d] (7) He goes

[a] See on 5.3.

[b] Cf. 6.3.

[c] As does the cook in Menander, *Samia* 383ff.

[d] The proverb was "don't take a path when you have a road" (*Paroem. Graec.* I.437).

THEOPHRASTUS

γὸν προσελθὼν ἐρωτῆσαι πότε μέλλει παρατάττε-
σθαι, καὶ τί μετὰ τὴν αὔριον παραγγελεῖ. (8) καὶ
προσελθὼν τῷ πατρὶ εἰπεῖν, ὅτι ἡ μήτηρ ἤδη
καθεύδει ἐν τῷ δωματίῳ. (9) καὶ ἀπαγορεύοντος
τοῦ ἰατροῦ ὅπως μὴ δώσει οἶνον τῷ μαλακιζο-
μένῳ, φήσας βούλεσθαι διάπειραν λαμβάνειν εὖ
ποτίσαι[1] τὸν κακῶς ἔχοντα. (10) καὶ γυναικὸς δὲ
τελευτησάσης ἐπιγράψαι ἐπὶ τὸ μνῆμα τοῦ τε
ἀνδρὸς αὐτῆς καὶ τοῦ πατρὸς καὶ τῆς μητρὸς καὶ
αὐτῆς τῆς γυναικὸς τοὔνομα καὶ ποδαπή ἐστι, καὶ
προσεπιγράψαι ὅτι οὗτοι πάντες χρηστοὶ ἦσαν.

(11) καὶ ὀμνύναι μέλλων εἰπεῖν πρὸς τοὺς περι-
εστηκότας, ὅτι "καὶ πρότερον πολλάκις ὀμώμοκα."

## ΑΝΑΙΣΘΗΣΙΑΣ ΙΔ΄

(1) ἔστι δὲ ἡ ἀναισθησία, ὡς ὅρῳ εἰπεῖν, βραδυτὴς
ψυχῆς ἐν λόγοις καὶ πράξεσιν, ὁ δὲ ἀναίσθητος
τοιοῦτός τις, (2) οἷος λογισάμενος ταῖς ψήφοις καὶ
κεφάλαιον ποιήσας ἐρωτᾶν τὸν παρακαθήμενον·
"τί γίνεται;" (3) καὶ δίκην φεύγων καὶ ταύτην εἰσ-
ιέναι μέλλων ἐπιλαθόμενος εἰς ἀγρὸν πορεύεσθαι.
(4) καὶ θεωρῶν ἐν τῷ θεάτρῳ μόνος καταλείπεσθαι

[1] Foss: εὐτρεπίσαι codd.

up to the general and asks him when he will take the field, and what his orders are going to be the day after tomorrow. (8) He goes up to his father and tells him that his mother is already asleep in their bedroom. (9) Even though the doctor forbids giving any wine to a sick man, he says he wants to do an experiment, and soaks the poor fellow with it. (10) If a woman dies, he inscribes on her tomb the names of her husband, her father and mother, and herself and place of birth, and adds that they were *all* "fine persons."[a]

(11) When he is going to swear an oath he says to the bystanders, "I've sworn oaths many times before."[b]

## 14. ABSENT-MINDEDNESS

(1) Absent-mindedness, to say it in a definition, is slowness of soul in words and deeds. The absent-minded man is the sort (2) who, when he has made a calculation with an abacus and determined the total, asks the person sitting by him, "What's the answer?" (3) If he is a defendant, and intends to appear in court, he forgets and goes to the country. (4) If he's in the audience at the theater, he falls

---

[a] Literally "good" (χρηστός), a term often used of the dead in grave-inscriptions.

[b] Cf. Menander fr. 87. Swearing to the truth of something undocumented (Harrison, *Law of Athens* II, Oxford 1971, 150–152) was a last resort, not to be taken lightly.

καθεύδων. (5) καὶ πολλὰ φαγὼν καὶ τῆς νυκτὸς
ἐπὶ θάκου ἀνιστάμενος[1] ὑπὸ κυνὸς τῆς τοῦ γείτο-
νος δηχθῆναι. (6) καὶ λαβών <τι>[2] καὶ ἀποθεὶς
αὐτός, τοῦτο ζητεῖν καὶ μὴ δύνασθαι εὑρεῖν. (7) καὶ
ἀπαγγέλλοντος αὐτῷ ὅτι τετελεύτηκέ τις αὐτοῦ
τῶν φίλων, ἵνα παραγένηται, σκυθρωπάσας καὶ
δακρύσας εἰπεῖν· "ἀγαθῇ τύχῃ."

(8) δεινὸς δὲ καὶ ἀπολαμβάνων ἀργύριον ὀφει-
λόμενον μάρτυρας παραλαβεῖν. (9) καὶ χειμῶνος
ὄντος μάχεσθαι τῷ παιδί ὅτι σικύους οὐκ ἠγόρα-
σεν. (10) καὶ τὰ παιδία ἑαυτοῦ παλαίειν ἀναγκά-
ζων καὶ τροχάζειν εἰς κόπον ἐμβάλλειν. (11) καὶ ἐν
ἀγρῷ αὐτὸς φακῆν ἕψων δὶς ἅλας εἰς τὴν χύτραν
ἐμβαλὼν ἄβρωτον ποιῆσαι. (12) καὶ ὕοντος τοῦ
Διὸς εἰπεῖν· †ἡδύ γε τῶν ἄστρων νομίζει, ὅτι δὴ
καὶ οἱ ἄλλοι λέγουσι πίσσης† (13) καὶ λέγοντός
τινος· "πόσους οἴει κατὰ τὰς Ἱερὰς πύλας ἐξενη-
νέχθαι νεκρούς;" πρὸς τοῦτον εἰπεῖν· "ὅσοι ἐμοὶ
καὶ σοὶ γένοιντο."

---

[1] post ἀνιστάμενος lacunam statuerunt editores, fortasse
recte (τῆς νυκτὸς καὶ codd., transp. Salmasius).
[2] add. M.

asleep and is left behind alone. (5) If he eats too much and gets up at night to go to the toilet, he is bitten by his neighbor's dog.[a] (6) When he's received something and put it away himself, he looks for it and can't find it. (7) If it's reported to him that one of his friends has died, so he should attend the funeral, he makes a sad face and says weepingly, "Let's hope it's for the best!"

(8) When he receives money that is owed to him, he is apt to ask for a receipt.[b] (9) Despite its being winter he quarrels with his servant because he didn't buy cucumbers. (10) He forces his children to practice wrestling and running until he drives them to exhaustion. (11) When he is cooking himself bean-soup in the field, he adds salt to the pot twice, and makes it inedible. (12) When it rains, he says "He thinks it sweet from the stars," which others in fact say "from pitch."[c] (13) If someone says to him "How many bodies do you suppose have been carried out for burial at the sacred gate?"[d] He says to him, "May you and I have as many!"

[a] The text seems abbreviated: instead of the outhouse he wanders into the watchdog's pen.

[b] Literally "secure witnesses."

[c] The Greek text of this sentence is corrupt beyond repair.

[d] Perhaps in a time of plague, or after a military disaster (for the sacred gate see Plutarch, *Sulla* 14.3). He answers as if he had been asked something like "how much money do you suppose x has?"

THEOPHRASTUS

## ΑΥΘΑΔΕΙΑΣ ΙΕ´

(1) ἡ δὲ αὐθάδειά ἐστιν ἀπήνεια ὁμιλίας ἐν λόγοις,
ὁ δὲ αὐθάδης τοιοῦτός τις, (2) οἷος ἐρωτηθείς· "ὁ
δεῖνα ποῦ ἐστιν;" εἰπεῖν· "πράγματά μοι μὴ
πάρεχε." (3) καὶ προσαγορευθεὶς μὴ ἀντιπροσει-
πεῖν. (4) καὶ πωλῶν τι μὴ λέγειν τοῖς ὠνουμένοις
πόσου ἂν ἀποδοῖτο, ἀλλ᾽ ἐρωτᾶν "τί εὑρίσκει;"
(5) καὶ τοῖς τιμῶσι καὶ πέμπουσιν εἰς τὰς ἑορτὰς
εἰπεῖν, ὅτι οὐκ ἂν γένοιτο διδόμενα. (6) καὶ οὐκ
ἔχειν συγγνώμην οὔτε τῷ ῥυπώσαντι[1] αὐτὸν
ἀκουσίως οὔτε τῷ ὤσαντι οὔτε τῷ ἐμβάντι. (7) καὶ
φίλῳ δὲ ἔρανον κελεύσαντι εἰσενεγκεῖν εἰπών, ὅτι
οὐκ ἂν δοίη, ὕστερον ἥκειν φέρων καὶ λέγειν, ὅτι
ἀπόλλυσι καὶ τοῦτο τὸ ἀργύριον. (8) καὶ προσ-
πταίσας ἐν τῇ ὁδῷ δεινὸς καταράσασθαι τῷ λίθῳ.
(9) καὶ [ἀναμεῖναι][2] οὐκ ἂν ὑπομείναι[3] πολὺν χρόνον οὐθένα. (10) καὶ οὔτε ᾆσαι οὔτε ῥῆσιν εἰπεῖν
οὔτε ὀρχήσασθαι ἂν ἐθελήσειεν·[4] (11) δεινὸς δὲ καὶ
τοῖς θεοῖς μὴ ἐπεύχεσθαι.

---

[1] Foss (cf. Seneca de beneficiis 6.9.1): ἀπώσαντι codd.
[2] del. Reiske.    [3] ὑπομείναι (optativum) Casaubon, Ussing:
ὑπομεῖναι (infinitivum) codd.    [4] Petersen: ἠθέλησε(ν)
AB, θελῆσαι CDe.

104

## 15. GROUCHINESS

(1) Grouchiness is verbal hostility in social contacts. The grouch is the sort (2) who, when asked "Where is so-and-so?" responds "don't bother me." (3) If someone speaks to him he doesn't answer. (4) If he is selling something, he doesn't tell customers how much he would sell it for, but asks "What will it fetch?"[a] (5) If people honor him by sending him some of the food on a festival day,[b] he tells them not to expect anything in return. (6) If anyone splashes him accidentally or jostles him or steps on his foot, he won't forgive him. (7) After first refusing to give to a friend who has asked him to provide a loan,[c] he comes to him later and brings it, but adds that he is throwing his money away again. (8) If he stumbles on the street, he is apt to curse the stone. (9) He isn't likely to wait very long for anyone. (10) He won't sing or recite a speech or dance.[d] (11) He is apt to ask for nothing — even from the gods.

---

[a] For this meaning see LSJ εὑρίσκω V.

[b] For the custom cf. 17.2 below, and Aristophanes, *Acharnians* 1049, Menander, *Samia* 403, *PCG* Ephippus fr. 15.11.

[c] ἔρανος was an interest-free loan from one friend (or several) to another: cf. 1.5, 17.9, 22.9, 23.6 and Paul Millett, *Lending and Borrowing in Ancient Athens* (Cambridge 1991) 153–159.

[d] At a banquet.

## ΔΕΙΣΙΔΑΙΜΟΝΙΑΣ Ιϛ΄

(1) [ἀμέλει ἡ δεισιδαιμονία δόξειεν ἂν εἶναι δειλία πρὸς τὸ δαιμόνιον,][1] ὁ δὲ δεισιδαίμων τοιοῦτός τις, (2) οἷος †ἐπιχρωνῆν[2] ἀπονιψάμενος τὰς χεῖρας καὶ περιρρανάμενος ἀπὸ ἱεροῦ δάφνην εἰς τὸ στόμα λαβὼν οὕτω τὴν ἡμέραν περιπατεῖν. (3) καὶ τὴν ὁδὸν ἐὰν ὑπερδράμῃ γαλῆ, μὴ πρότερον πορευθῆναι ἕως διεξέλθῃ τις ἢ λίθους τρεῖς ὑπὲρ τῆς ὁδοῦ διαβάλῃ. (4) καὶ ἐὰν ἴδῃ ὄφιν ἐν τῇ οἰκίᾳ, ἐὰν παρείαν, Σαβάζιον[3] καλεῖν, ἐὰν δὲ ἱερόν, ἐνταῦθα ἡρῷον[4] εὐθὺς ἱδρύσασθαι.

[1] del. Hanow, Gomperz, Stein.
[2] ἐπὶ Χόων Foss, ἐπιδὼν κορώνην Usener, ἐπιτυχὼν ἐκφορᾷ Bolkestein.
[3] Schneider: Σαβάδιον codd.
[4] Duebner: ἱερῶον (ι in rasura) V, om. CD.

---

[a] The definition resembles one found in Stoic writings (*SVF* III p. 98.42, p. 99.13) and is probably interpolated from another source.

## 16. SUPERSTITION

(1) [You can be sure superstition would seem to be cowardice about divinity.][a] The superstitious man is the sort (2) who < . . . >[b] washes his hands, sprinkles himself with water from a shrine, puts a sprig of laurel in his mouth and walks around that way all day. (3) If a weasel crosses his path[c] he goes no further until someone passes between them, or he throws three stones over the road. (4) If he sees a snake in his house, he invokes Sabazios[d] if it is a cheek snake, but if it is a holy one[e] he immediately founds a hero shrine on the spot.

[b] The word in the text is nonsense, and various changes have been proposed, e.g. "when it is 'Pitchers'" (a festival of the dead, see Burkert, *Homo Necans* 218–222), "when he sees a crow," or "when he meets a funeral procession."

[c] For weasels as bad luck cf. Aristophanes, *Ecclesiazousai* 792, *Paroem. Graec.* I.230.

[d] A Phrygian god often identified with Dionysus, imported to Athens in the fifth century B.C.; Demosthenes gives a detailed account of how he was worshipped in *On The Crown* 18.259–260, and describes handling snakes of the variety mentioned here, which were harmless (Aelian, *Nature of Animals* 8.12).

[e] This variety of snake was poisonous (Aristotle, *History of Animals* 607a30). "Heroes" were potentially harmful spirits of the dead: Walter Burkert, *Greek Religion*, tr. John Raffan (Oxford and Cambridge, Mass. 1985) 206–207. Compare the snake in the fraudulent hero-cult of Heraclides of Pontus, Diog. Laert. 5.89 = fr. 16 Wehrli. Plato, *Laws* X.909e3–910a6 condemns the establishment of private shrines to avert bad luck.

# THEOPHRASTUS

(5) καὶ τῶν λιπαρῶν λίθων τῶν ἐν ταῖς τριόδοις παριὼν ἐκ τῆς ληκύθου ἔλαιον καταχεῖν καὶ ἐπὶ γόνατα πεσὼν καὶ προσκυνήσας ἀπαλλάττεσθαι. (6) καὶ ἐὰν μῦς θύλακον ἀλφίτων διαφάγῃ, πρὸς τὸν ἐξηγητὴν ἐλθὼν ἐρωτᾶν τί χρὴ ποιεῖν, καὶ ἐὰν ἀποκρίνηται αὐτῷ ἐκδοῦναι τῷ σκυτοδέψῃ ἐπιρράψαι, μὴ προσέχειν τούτοις, ἀλλ' ἀποτραπεὶς ἐκθύσασθαι.[1]

(7) καὶ πυκνὰ δὲ τὴν οἰκίαν καθᾶραι δεινὸς Ἑκάτης φάσκων ἐπαγωγὴν γεγονέναι. (8) κἂν γλαῦκες βαδίζοντος αὐτοῦ <ἀνακράγωσι>,[2] ταράττεσθαι καὶ εἴπας "Ἀθηνᾶ κρείττων," παρελθεῖν οὕτω. (9) καὶ οὔτε ἐπιβῆναι μνήματι οὔτ' ἐπὶ νεκρὸν οὔτ' ἐπὶ λεχὼ ἐλθεῖν ἐθελῆσαι, ἀλλὰ τὸ μὴ μιαίνεσθαι συμφέρον αὐτῷ φῆσαι εἶναι.

(10) καὶ ταῖς τετράσι δὲ καὶ ἑβδόμαις προστάξας οἶνον ἕψειν τοῖς ἔνδον, ἐξελθὼν ἀγοράσαι μυρ-

---

[1] Bernard: ἐκλύσασθαι codd.
[2] suppl. Foss: ταράττεται V, corr. Korais.

---

[a] For the anointing of stones see Homer, *Odyssey* 3.406–11; Tibullus I.1.11–12; W. Burkert, *Structure and History in Greek Mythology and Ritual* (Berkeley 1979) 162 n. 20; Frazer on Pausanias 10.24.6. Worshipping them is

(5) When he passes the oiled stones[a] at the crossroads, he drenches them with olive oil from his flask,[b] kneels and prostrates himself before he departs. (6) If a mouse eats a hole in a sack of barley, he visits the theologian and asks what he should do; if the answer is to give it to the tailor to be patched he pays no attention, but hurries off and performs an expiation.

(7) He is apt to purify his house frequently, claiming Hekate has bewitched it.[c] (8) If owls hoot[d] as he passes by he becomes agitated, and says "mighty Athena!" before he goes on. (9) He refuses to step on a gravestone, view a corpse or visit a woman in childbirth, and says it's the best policy for him not to incur pollution.[e]

(10) On the fourth and the seventh of every month he orders his household to boil some wine,[f] then goes out and buys myrtle, frankincense, and

ridiculed by Lucian, *Alexander* 30; Arnobius, *Adv. nationes* I.39; Clement of Alexandria, *Stromateis* 7.4.26.

[b] The one he carries for the baths, see on 30.8.

[c] For an account of a Hekate-exorcism in a mime of Sophron see Robert Parker, *Miasma* (Oxford 1983) 223–224.

[d] Thompson, *Glossary of Greek Birds* 78.

[e] He extends legitimate rules of purity (see West on Hesiod, *Works and Days* 750; Burkert, *Greek Religion* 378 nn. 30–31) to avoid attending funerals, or even seeing his wife after childbirth.

[f] Boiling wine made it sweeter, see MacDowell on Aristophanes, *Wasps* 878, *PCG* Plato Comicus fr. 164.

THEOPHRASTUS

σίνας, λιβανωτόν, πόπανα[1] καὶ εἰσελθὼν εἴσω
στεφανοῦν[2] τοὺς Ἑρμαφροδίτους ὅλην τὴν
ἡμέραν.

(11) καὶ ὅταν ἐνύπνιον ἴδῃ, πορεύεσθαι πρὸς
τοὺς ὀνειροκρίτας, πρὸς τοὺς μάντεις, πρὸς τοὺς
ὀρνιθοσκόπους, ἐρωτήσων, τίνι θεῶν ἢ θεᾷ εὔχε-
σθαι δεῖ. καὶ τελεσθησόμενος πρὸς τοὺς Ὀρφεο-
τελεστὰς κατὰ μῆνα πορεύεσθαι μετὰ τῆς γυναικός, ἐὰν δὲ μὴ σχολάζῃ ἡ γυνή, μετὰ τῆς τίτθης
καὶ τῶν παιδίων. (12) καὶ τῶν περιρραινομένων
ἐπὶ θαλάττης ἐπιμελῶς δόξειεν ἂν εἶναι. (13) κἂν
ποτε ἐπίδῃ σκορόδῳ ἐστεμμένον[3] τῶν ἐπὶ ταῖς
τριόδοις, ἀπελθὼν κατὰ κεφαλῆς λούσασθαι καὶ
ἱερείας καλέσας σκίλλῃ ἢ σκύλακι κελεῦσαι αὐτὸν

[1] Foss: λιβανωτῶν πίνακα V.
[2] Siebenkees: στεφανῶν codd.
[3] Foss: ἐστεμμένων V.

[a] The first is to make wreaths (Aristophanes, *Wasps*
861), the others to burn as a sacrifice (Menander, *Dyskolos*
449–50).

[b] If the text is sound, he seems to spend too much time
and money on a regular household offering. The word
"Hermaphroditos" first occurs here (it is also the title of a
comedy by the third-century writer Posidippus, and found

110

cakes,[a] comes back home and spends all day putting wreaths on the Hermaphrodites.[b]

(11) Whenever he has a dream, he visits the dream analysts or the prophets or the omen-readers to ask to which god or goddess[c] he should pray. He goes to the Initiators of Orpheus[d] every month to be inducted with his wife — if she has no time, he takes his children and their wet-nurse. (12) When people are sprinkling themselves carefully at the seaside,[e] he would seem to be among them. (13) If he ever notices someone at the crossroads wreathed in garlic[f] he goes away, takes a shower, summons priestesses and orders a deluxe purification by sea-

in a votive inscription perhaps of the fourth century B.C.): rather than the androgynous god of later mythology, the plural may designate a variety of the neighborhood portrait-busts known as "herms" with female and male faces on opposite sides. See *Lexicon Iconographicum Mythologiae Classicae* V (Zurich 1991) 269.

[c] A prayer formula: J. Alvar, "Materiaux pour l'étude de la formule *sive deus sive dea*," *Numen* 32 (1985) 236–273.

[d] Itinerant priests, cf. Plato *Republic* 364b–e, W. Burkert, *Ancient Mystery Cults* (Cambridge, Mass. 1987) 33. Evidently the presence of a woman was required.

[e] For the purifying powers of salt water see Robert Parker, *Miasma* 226–227.

[f] Crossroads were repositories of religious pollution, including the bodies of murderers: S. I. Johnston, "Crossroads," *Zeitschrift für Papyrologie und Epigraphik* 88 (1991) 222–224. As it is today, garlic was a protection against evil spirits (cf. Persius 5.188), so that he immediately suspects danger.

περικαθᾶραι. (14) μαινόμενον δὲ[1] ἰδὼν ἢ ἐπίλη-
πτον φρίξας εἰς κόλπον πτύσαι.

## ΜΕΜΨΙΜΟΙΡΙΑΣ ΙΖ΄

(1) ἔστι δὲ ἡ μεμψιμοιρία ἐπιτίμησις παρὰ τὸ
προσῆκον τῶν δεδομένων, ὁ δὲ μεμψίμοιρος τοιόσδε τις, (2) οἷος ἀποστείλαντος μερίδα τοῦ φίλου
εἰπεῖν πρὸς τὸν φέροντα· "ἐφθόνησέν[2] μοι τοῦ
ζωμοῦ καὶ τοῦ οἰναρίου οὐκ ἐπὶ δεῖπνον καλέσας."
(3) καὶ ὑπὸ τῆς ἑταίρας καταφιλούμενος εἰπεῖν·
"θαυμάζω εἰ σὺ καὶ ἀπὸ τῆς ψυχῆς οὕτω με
φιλεῖς." (4) καὶ τῷ Διὶ ἀγανακτεῖν, οὐ διότι ὕει,
ἀλλὰ διότι ὕστερον. (5) καὶ εὑρὼν ἐν τῇ ὁδῷ βαλ-
λάντιον εἰπεῖν· "ἀλλ᾽ οὐ θησαυρὸν εὕρηκα οὐδέποτε." (6) καὶ πριάμενος ἀνδράποδον ἄξιον καὶ
πολλὰ δεηθεὶς τοῦ πωλοῦντος· "θαυμάζω," εἰπεῖν,
"ὅ τι ὑγιὲς οὕτω ἄξιον ἐώνημαι." (7) καὶ πρὸς τὸν
εὐαγγελιζόμενον ὅτι "υἱός σοι γέγονεν" εἰπεῖν ὅτι
"ἂν προσθῇς 'καὶ τῆς οὐσίας τὸ ἥμισυ ἄπεστιν,'

---

[1] Blaydes: τε codd.    [2] Pauw: ἐφθόνησας V.

[a] Also called "squill"; credited with apotropaic powers,
*PCG* Cratinus fr. 250.2; Theophrastus, *Inquiry into Plants*
7.13.4; John Scarborough, "The Pharmacology of Sacred

onion[a] or dog.[b] (14) If he sees a madman or epileptic he shudders, and spits down at his chest.[c]

## 17. GRIPING

(1) Griping is unsuitable criticism of what one has been given. The griper is a type such as this, (2) who, when his friend has sent him part of the meat from a sacrifice,[d] says to the delivery boy, "by not inviting me to the dinner, he did me out of the soup and wine." (3) When he is being kissed by his mistress, he says "I wonder whether you really love me that much in your heart." (4) He is annoyed with Zeus not because it is raining, but because it rained too late. (5) If he finds a wallet in the road, he says, "well, I still haven't ever found a treasure." (6) If he buys a slave at a good price, after much haggling with the seller, he says "I wonder how sound the merchandise can be if I got it so cheap." (7) To the bearer of the good news "you have a son!" he replies, "if you add 'half of your property is gone,' you'll be

Plants, Herbs and Roots," in *Magika Hiera*, ed. C. A. Faraone and D. Obbink (New York 1991) 146–148.

[b] Killed and rubbed around the bodies of those to be purified: Plutarch, *Roman Questions* 280B–C, 290D; N. J. Zaganiaris, "Sacrifices de chiens dans l'antiquité classique," Πλάτων 27 (1975) 322–329; *PCG* Aristophanes fr. 209.

[c] The ancient Greek equivalent of knocking on wood (see Gow on Theocritus 6.39).

[d] Cf. 15.5.

THEOPHRASTUS

ἀληθῆ ἐρεῖς." (8) καὶ δίκην¹ νικήσας καὶ λαβὼν
πάσας τὰς ψήφους ἐγκαλεῖν² τῷ γράψαντι τὸν
λόγον ὡς πολλὰ παραλελοιπότι τῶν δικαίων.
(9) καὶ ἐράνου εἰσενεχθέντος παρὰ τῶν φίλων καὶ
φήσαντός τινος· "ἱλαρὸς ἴσθι," "καὶ πῶς," εἰπεῖν,
"ὅτι δεῖ τἀργύριον ἀποδοῦναι ἑκάστῳ καὶ χωρὶς
τούτων χάριν ὀφείλειν ὡς εὐεργετημένον;"

ΑΠΙΣΤΙΑΣ ΙΗ΄

(1) ἔστιν ἀμέλει ἡ ἀπιστία ὑπόληψίς τις ἀδικίας
κατὰ πάντων, ὁ δὲ ἄπιστος τοιοῦτός τις, (2) οἷος
ἀποστείλας τὸν παῖδα ὀψωνήσοντα ἕτερον παῖδα
πέμπειν τὸν πευσόμενον πόσου ἐπρίατο. (3) καὶ
φέρων αὐτὸς τὸ ἀργύριον [καὶ]³ κατὰ στάδιον
καθίζων ἀριθμεῖν πόσον ἐστίν. (4) καὶ τὴν γυναῖκα
τὴν αὑτοῦ ἐρωτᾶν κατακείμενος εἰ κέκλεικε τὴν
κιβωτόν, καὶ εἰ σεσήμανται τὸ κυλιούχιον, καὶ εἰ ὁ
μοχλὸς εἰς τὴν θύραν τὴν αὐλείαν ἐμβέβληται·
καὶ ἂν ἐκείνη φῇ, μηδὲν ἧττον αὐτὸς ἀναστὰς
γυμνὸς ἐκ τῶν στρωμάτων καὶ ἀνυπόδητος τὸν
λύχνον ἅψας ταῦτα πάντα περιδραμὼν ἐπισκέψα-
σθαι καὶ οὕτω μόλις ὕπνου τυγχάνειν. (5) καὶ τοὺς
ὀφείλοντας αὑτῷ ἀργύριον μετὰ μαρτύρων ἀπαι-

¹ Casaubon: νίκην V.      ² Stephanus: ἐγκαλεῖ V.

114

telling the truth." (8) If he wins a court case, even by a unanimous vote, he criticizes his lawyer for leaving out many valid arguments. (9) If his friends get together a loan for him,[a] and someone says "Congratulations!" he says "Why? Because I've got to pay the money back to each of you, and be grateful besides, as if you'd done me a favor?"

## 18. MISTRUST

(1) You can be sure that mistrust is an assumption that one is being wronged by everyone. The mistrustful man is the sort (2) who, when he has dispatched his slave to do the shopping, sends another one to find out how much he paid. (3) Even though he carries his money himself,[b] he sits down every hundred yards and counts how much he has. (4) When he is lying in bed he asks his wife whether she has locked up the money chest, whether the cupboard has been sealed, and whether the bolt is in place on the front door; and even if she says yes he gets out of bed anyway, naked and barefoot, lights the lamp and runs around checking all these, and only then can he get some sleep. (5) When people owe him money he takes the witnesses with him

[a] See on 15.7.
[b] Normally a slave would carry it (Plautus, *Pseudolus* 170, *Menaechmi* 265), cf. 23.8.

---

[3] del. Needham.

τεῖν τοὺς τόκους, ὅπως μὴ δύνωνται[1] ἔξαρνοι
γενέσθαι. (6) καὶ τὸ ἱμάτιον δὲ ἐκδοῦναι δεινὸς οὐχ
ὃς <ἂν>[2] βέλτιστα ἐργάσηται, ἀλλ' οὗ ἂν ᾖ ἄξιος
ἐγγυητὴς [τοῦ κναφέως].[3] (7) καὶ ὅταν ἥκῃ τις
αἰτησόμενος ἐκπώματα, μάλιστα μὲν μὴ δοῦναι,
ἂν δ' ἄρα τις οἰκεῖος ᾖ καὶ ἀναγκαῖος, μόνον οὐ
πυρώσας καὶ στήσας καὶ σχεδὸν ἐγγυητὴν λαβὼν
χρῆσαι.[4] (8) καὶ τὸν παῖδα δὲ ἀκολουθοῦντα κελεύειν αὑτοῦ ὄπισθεν μὴ βαδίζειν ἀλλ' ἔμπροσθεν,
ἵνα φυλάττῃ αὐτὸν[5] μὴ ἐν τῇ ὁδῷ ἀποδρᾷ.[6] (9) καὶ
τοῖς εἰληφόσι τι παρ' αὑτοῦ καὶ λέγουσι "πόσου,
κατάθου· οὐ γὰρ σχολάζω πω," εἰπεῖν[7] "μηδὲν
πραγματεύου· ἐγὼ γάρ, <ἕως>[8] ἂν σὺ σχολάσῃς,
συνακολουθήσω."

## ΔΥΣΧΕΡΕΙΑΣ ΙΘ΄

(1) ἔστι δὲ ἡ δυσχέρεια ἀθεραπευσία σώματος
λύπης παρασκευαστική, ὁ δὲ δυσχερὴς τοιοῦτός
τις, (2) οἷος λέπραν ἔχων καὶ ἀλφὸν καὶ τοὺς
ὄνυχας μεγάλους περιπατεῖν καὶ φῆσαι ταῦτα
εἶναι αὑτῷ συγγενικὰ ἀρρωστήματα· ἔχειν γὰρ

---

[1] Jebb: δύναιντο codd.
[2] suppl. Diels. (ὃς Salmasius: ὡς codd.)
[3] Ast: ὅταν ᾖ codd.      [4] Schneider: χρήσει codd.

when he collects the interest, so they won't be able to deny the debt. (6) He is apt to give his cloak not to the man who does the best work, but the one whose bondsman is worth the most.[a] (7) Whenever someone comes to him to borrow drinking cups he prefers not to give them at all, but if it is a relative or close friend he makes the loan only after practically testing their composition and weight, and nearly asking for someone to guarantee replacement costs. (8) When his slave is attending him he tells him not to walk behind but in front, so he can watch to make sure he doesn't run away.[b] (9) To those who are buying something from him and say "Add it up and put it down to my account; I don't have time yet," he says "Don't go to any trouble; I'll stay with you until you have time."[c]

## 19. SQUALOR

(1) Squalor is a neglect of one's body which produces distress. The squalid man is the sort (2) who goes around in a leprous and encrusted state, with long fingernails, and says these are all inherited ill-

[a] He assumes his clothing is going to be lost or ruined.

[b] As in Plautus, *Curculio* 487.

[c] The text is uncertain.

[5] Needham: αὐτῷ vel αὑτῷ codd.

[6] φυλάττῃ ... ἀποδρᾷ Hirschig: φυλάττηται ... ἀποδράσῃ codd.　　[7] Madvig: πέμπειν codd.

[8] suppl. Madvig.

αὐτὸν καὶ τὸν πατέρα καὶ τὸν πάππον, καὶ οὐκ
εἶναι ῥᾴδιον αὐτῶν[1] εἰς τὸ γένος ὑποβάλλεσθαι.
(3) ἀμέλει δὲ δεινὸς καὶ ἕλκη ἔχειν ἐν τοῖς ἀντι-
κνημίοις καὶ προσπταίσματα ἐν τοῖς δακτύλοις
καὶ μὴ θεραπεῦσαι ἀλλ' ἐᾶσαι θηριωθῆναι· καὶ
τὰς μασχάλας δὲ θηριώδεις καὶ δασείας ἔχειν ἄχρι
ἐπὶ πολὺ τῶν πλευρῶν, καὶ τοὺς ὀδόντας μέλανας
καὶ ἐσθιομένους [ὥστε δυσέντευκτος εἶναι καὶ
ἀηδής.][2]

(4) καὶ τὰ τοιαῦτα· ἐσθίων ἀπομύττεσθαι· θύων
ἅμ' ἀδαξᾶσθαι·[3] προσλαλῶν ἀπορρίπτειν ἀπὸ τοῦ
στόματος· ἅμα πιὼν ἐρυγγάνειν.[4] (5) ἀναπόνιπ-
τος[5] ἐν τοῖς στρώμασι μετὰ τῆς γυναικὸς αὐτοῦ
κοιμᾶσθαι. (6) ἐλαίῳ σαπρῷ ἐν βαλανείῳ χρώ-
μενος ὄζεσθαι.[6] (7) καὶ χιτωνίσκον παχὺν καὶ ἱμάτιον σφόδρα λεπτὸν καὶ κηλίδων μεστὸν ἀναβαλλόμενος εἰς ἀγορὰν ἐξελθεῖν.

<. . .>[7]

(8) καὶ εἰς ὀρνιθοσκόπου τῆς μητρὸς ἐξελθούσης
βλασφημῆσαι. (9) καὶ εὐχομένων καὶ σπενδόντων

---

[1] Meister: αὐτὸν V.  [2] ut glossema del. Immisch.
[3] Diels: θύων ἅμα δ' ἄρξασθαι V, θύων ἀρξάμενος CD.
[4] Stein: προσερυγγάνειν codd.  [5] Badham: ἀναπίπτοντος V.

nesses; he has them like his father and grandfather before him, so it won't be easy to smuggle an illegitimate child into *their* family! (3) You can be sure he is apt to have sores on his shins, whitlows on his fingers, which he doesn't treat but lets fester. His armpits might belong to an animal, with hair extending most of the way down his sides. His teeth are black and decayed.

(4) And things like this: he wipes his nose while eating, scratches himself while sacrificing, shoots spittle from his mouth while talking, belches while drinking. (5) He sleeps in bed with his wife without washing.[a] (6) Because he uses rancid oil in the baths, he smells.[b] (7) He goes out to the market wearing thick underwear, and a very thin cloak full of stains.

*< From a different character (see Additional Notes) >*

(8) . . . When his mother goes out to the omen reader, he curses.[c] (9) When people are praying and pouring

---

[a] For washing after dinner and before bed cf. Aristophanes, *Ecclesiazousai* 419, *Wasps* 1217, Plato, *Symposium* 223d.

[b] Cf. 30.8.

[c] She is worried about offending the gods (cf. 16.11), but her son deliberately offends them.

---

[6] Petersen: σφύζεσθαι V, χρίεσθαι c, χρᾶσθαι c, χρῆσθαι d.

[7] lacunam stat. edd., qui § 8–11 aliena esse viderunt.

119

ἐκβαλεῖν[1] τὸ ποτήριον καὶ γελάσαι ὡς τεράστιόν
τι πεποιηκώς · (10) καὶ αὐλούμενος δὲ κροτῆσαι
ταῖς χερσὶ μόνος τῶν ἄλλων καὶ συντερετίζειν καὶ
ἐπιτιμᾶν τῇ αὐλητρίδι, τί οὕτω ταχὺ ἐπαύσατο ·[2]
(11) καὶ ἀποπτύσαι δὲ βουλόμενος, ὑπὲρ τῆς τραπέζης προσπτύσαι τῷ οἰνοχόῳ.

## ΑΗΔΙΑΣ Κ´

(1) ἔστι δὲ ἡ ἀηδία, ὡς ὅρῳ περιλαβεῖν, ἔντευξις
λύπης ποιητικὴ ἄνευ βλάβης, ὁ δὲ ἀηδὴς τοιοῦτός
τις, (2) οἷος ἐγείρειν ἄρτι καθεύδοντα εἰσελθών, ἵνα
αὐτῷ λαλῇ. (3) καὶ ἀνάγεσθαι δὴ μέλλοντας
κωλύειν, (4) καὶ[3] προσελθὼν δεῖσθαι ἐπισχεῖν, ἕως
ἂν περιπατήσῃ.

(5) καὶ τὸ παιδίον τῆς τίτθης ἀφελόμενος,
μασώμενος σιτίζειν αὐτὸς καὶ ὑποκορίζεσθαι ποπ-
πύζων καὶ πανουργότερον[4] τοῦ πάππου καλῶν.
(6) καὶ ἐσθίων δὲ ἅμα διηγεῖσθαι ὡς ἐλλέβορον
πιὼν ἄνω καὶ κάτω καθαρθείη καὶ ζωμοῦ τοῦ
παρακειμένου ἐν τοῖς ὑποχωρήμασιν αὐτῷ μελαν-

---

[1] Casaubon: ἐμβαλεῖν codd.
[2] Ribbeck: τί οὐ ταχὺ παύσαιτο V, μὴ ταχὺ παυσαμένη CD.
[3] inter καὶ et προσελθὼν lacunam statuit Stein.
[4] Schneider: πανουργιῶν V.

120

libations, he drops his drinking cup and laughs, thinking he's performed a marvel. (10) When he is listening to a flute performance he is the only one of the group to clap his hands, and he hums along and asks the flute girl accusingly why she stopped so quickly. (11) When he wants to spit, he spits over the table and hits the wine pourer.

## 20. BAD TASTE

(1) Bad taste, to put it in a definition, is a manner of behavior which produces distress without injury. The man with bad taste is the sort (2) who goes in and wakes up a man who is just asleep, to have a chat. (3) He delays people when they are about to set sail, (4) and <...>[a] goes up to a man and asks him to wait until he takes his walk.

(5) He takes his baby from its wet-nurse, chews its food[b] and feeds it himself, gurgles[c] in baby-talk, and says "You're a bigger rascal than your daddy!" (6) While eating he relates that he's drunk some hellebore that cleaned him inside out, and that the bile in his stool was blacker than the soup that is on the

---

[a] Some words may have fallen out of the text in this sentence.

[b] Nurses chewed the baby's food first to soften it (Aristophanes, *Knights* 717, *RE* XVII.1493).

[c] Literally, "says 'pop'" to attract its attention (see Gow on Theocritus 5.89).

τέρα <εἴη>[1] ἡ χολή. (7) καὶ ἐρωτῆσαι δὲ δεινὸς
ἐναντίον τῶν οἰκείων· "εἴπ᾽, ὦ[2] μάμμη, ὅτ᾽
ὤδινες καὶ ἔτικτές με, τίς ἡμέρα;" (8) †καὶ ὑπὲρ
αὐτῆς δὲ λέγειν ὡς ἡδύ ἐστι, καὶ ἀμφότερα δὲ οὐκ
ἔχοντα οὐ ῥᾴδιον ἄνθρωπον λαβεῖν,† (9) καὶ ὅτι
ψυχρὸν ὕδωρ ἐστὶ παρ᾽ αὐτῷ λακκαῖον, καὶ ὡς
κῆπος λάχανα πολλὰ ἔχων καὶ ἁπαλὰ [ὥστε εἶναι
ψυχρὸν][3] καὶ μάγειρος εὖ τὸ ὄψον σκευάζων, καὶ
ὅτι ἡ οἰκία αὐτοῦ πανδοκεῖόν ἐστι· μεστὴ γὰρ ἀεί·
καὶ τοὺς φίλους αὐτοῦ εἶναι τὸν τετρημένον
πίθον· εὖ ποιῶν γὰρ αὐτοὺς οὐ δύνασθαι
ἐμπλῆσαι.

(10) καὶ ξενίζων δὲ δεῖξαι τὸν παράσιτον αὐτοῦ
ποῖός τίς ἐστι τῷ συνδειπνοῦντι· καὶ παρακαλῶν
δὲ ἐπὶ τοῦ ποτηρίου εἰπεῖν, ὅτι "τὸ τέρψον τοὺς
παρόντας παρεσκεύασται," καὶ ὅτι "αὐτήν," ἐὰν
κελεύσωσιν, "ὁ παῖς μέτεισι παρὰ τοῦ πορνοβοσκοῦ
ἤδη, ὅπως[4] πάντες ὑπ᾽ αὐτῆς αὐλώμεθα καὶ
εὐφραινώμεθα."

## ΜΙΚΡΟΦΙΛΟΤΙΜΙΑΣ ΚΑ´

(1) ἡ δὲ μικροφιλοτιμία δόξει εἶναι ὄρεξις τιμῆς
ἀνελεύθερος, ὁ δὲ μικροφιλότιμος τοιοῦτός τις,

[1] suppl. Hanow.    [2] Diels: εἴπου V.

122

table. (7) He is apt to ask in front of the household, "Tell me, mommy, when you were in labor and giving birth to me, what day was it?" (8) He says about her that it is sweet, and that it isn't easy to find a man who doesn't have them both,[a] (9) and that he has a cistern of cold water at his house, and a garden with lots of fresh vegetables, and a cook who prepares dishes well, and that his house is like a hotel, since it's always overflowing, and that his friends are like a pitcher full of holes, since he can never seem to fill them up with his favors.

(10) When he is giving a party he points out to his dinner-companion how impressive his lackey is. While they are drinking he says by way of challenge, "The delight of the guests has been arranged"; if they bid it, "The servant will go and fetch her right now from the pimp, so that she can play for — and gratify — us all."[b]

## 21. PETTY AMBITION

(1) Petty ambition will seem to be an ignoble desire for prestige. The man of petty ambition is the sort

---

[a] The text of this sentence is corrupt beyond repair.
[b] Cf. 11.7.

---

[3] ut glossema del. Bloch.
[4] Siebenkees: πῶς codd.

(2) οἷος σπουδάσαι ἐπὶ δεῖπνον κληθεὶς παρ᾽ αὐτὸν τὸν καλέσαντα κατακείμενος δειπνῆσαι. (3) καὶ τὸν υἱὸν ἀποκεῖραι ἀγαγὼν εἰς Δελφούς, (4) καὶ ἐπιμεληθῆναι δέ, ὅπως αὐτῷ ὁ ἀκόλουθος Αἰθίοψ ἔσται.

(5) καὶ ἀποδιδοὺς μνᾶν ἀργυρίου καινὸν [ποιῆσαι]¹ ἀποδοῦναι. (6) καὶ κολοιῷ δὲ ἔνδον τρεφομένῳ δεινὸς κλιμάκιον πρίασθαι καὶ ἀσπίδιον χαλκοῦν ποιῆσαι, ὃ ἔχων ἐπὶ τοῦ κλιμακίου ὁ κολοιὸς πηδήσεται.

(7) καὶ βοῦν θύσας τὸ προμετωπίδιον ἀπαντικρὺ τῆς εἰσόδου προσπατταλεῦσαι στέμμασι μεγάλοις περιδήσας, ὅπως οἱ εἰσιόντες ἴδωσιν ὅτι βοῦν ἔθυσε. (8) καὶ πομπεύσας δὲ μετὰ τῶν ἱππέων τὰ μὲν ἄλλα πάντα δοῦναι τῷ παιδὶ ἀπενεγκεῖν οἴκαδε, ἀναβαλλόμενος δὲ θοἰμάτιον ἐν τοῖς μύωψι κατὰ τὴν ἀγορὰν περιπατεῖν.

¹ del. Pauw.

(2) who, when invited for dinner, takes care to eat reclining next to the host himself. (3) For the ceremony of cutting his son's hair, he takes him to Delphi.[a] (4) He takes care to have an Ethiopian attendant.

(5) When he pays back a debt of one mina, he does it in brand-new coin. (6) He is apt to keep a jackdaw as a housepet, and buy it a little ladder and make it a tiny bronze shield to hold as the bird hops up the ladder.[b]

(7) When he has sacrificed an ox he nails up its skull facing his front door and wreathes it with large garlands,[c] so that people coming in will see that he's sacrificed an ox. (8) When he has ridden in the cavalry parade[d] he gives his slave everything else to carry home, but walks around the market in his spurs, wearing his riding cloak.

[a] It was customary for youths coming of age to dedicate their hair to a local deity (Burkert, *Greek Religion* 70, 373–374 n. 29); this man has his son imitate Theseus (Plutarch, *Theseus* 5.1).

[b] For vase paintings of pet birds wearing helmets and shields see J. D. Beazley, *Classical Review* 43 (1949) 42–43.

[c] An ox was an expensive sacrifice for an individual (Menander, *Dyskolos* 474; Herodas 4.16; *PCG* Posidippus fr. 28.19; Strato fr. 1.20). For the custom of hanging the wreathed skull of the sacrificial ox (usually in a sanctuary) see Burkert, *Greek Religion* 92, 372 n. 93.

[d] See *RE* XXI.1904ff.

(9) καὶ κυναρίου δὲ Μελιταίου τελευτήσαντος αὐτῷ, μνῆμα [ποιῆσαι]¹ καὶ στηλίδιον ποιήσας ἐπιγράψαι "Κλάδος Μελιταῖος." (10) καὶ ἀναθεὶς δακτυλίδιον χαλκοῦν ἐν τῷ Ἀσκληπιείῳ τοῦτο ἐκτρίβειν, στεφανοῦν, ἀλείφειν ὁσημέραι. (11) ἀμέλει δὲ καὶ διοικήσασθαι παρὰ τῶν συμπρυτάνεων,² ὅπως ἀπαγγείλῃ τῷ δήμῳ τὰ ἱερά, καὶ παρεσκευασμένος λαμπρὸν ἱμάτιον καὶ ἐστεφανωμένος παρελθὼν εἰπεῖν· "ὦ ἄνδρες Ἀθηναῖοι, ἐθύομεν οἱ πρυτάνεις [τὰ ἱερὰ]³ τῇ Μητρὶ τῶν θεῶν τὰ Γαλάξια,⁴ καὶ τὰ ἱερὰ καλά, καὶ ὑμεῖς δέχεσθε τὰ ἀγαθά." καὶ ταῦτα ἀπαγγείλας ἀπιὼν διηγήσασθαι οἴκαδε τῇ ἑαυτοῦ γυναικί ὡς καθ' ὑπερβολὴν εὐημερεῖν.⁵

## ΑΝΕΛΕΥΘΕΡΙΑΣ ΚΒ΄

(1) ἡ δὲ ἀνελευθερία ἐστὶν ἀπουσία τις φιλοτιμίας δαπάνην ἐχούσης,⁶ ὁ δὲ ἀνελεύθερος τοιοῦτός τις, (2) οἷος νικήσας τραγῳδοῖς ταινίαν ξυλίνην

---

¹ del. Pauw.    ² Madvig: συνδιοικήσασθαι (-οικίσασθαι V)... πρυτανέων codd.    ³ del. Schneider.    ⁴ Wilamowitz: τὰ γὰρ ἄξια V, τὰ ἄξια CD.    ⁵ εὐημέρει Needham, sed cf. Kühner-Gerth II.357.3b (Fischer, Stein).    ⁶ Schweighäuser: περιουσία τις ἀπὸ φιλοτιμίας δαπάνην ἔχουσα codd. (definitionem del. Hanow, Gomperz, Stein).

(9) When his Maltese dog[a] dies, he builds it a monument and inscribes on a plaque "Klados of Malta." (10) If he dedicates a bronze ring in the sanctuary of Asclepius, he polishes it, garlands it, and anoints it every day. (11) You can be sure that as council president he obtains from his colleagues the job of reporting the sacrifice, and going to the podium in a white robe and garland and saying "Men of Athens, we presidents of the council have sacrificed the *Galaxia*[b] to the Mother of the gods; the omens are propitious, and we bid you accept their favorable outcome."[c] After making this announcement he goes home and gives a report to his wife of his stupendous success.

## 22. LACK OF GENEROSITY

(1) Lack of generosity is an absence of pride when expense is involved.[d] The ungenerous man is the sort (2) who, if he wins the tragedy competition,

[a] One of the most expensive dogs one could own: Virginia T. Leitch, *The Maltese Dog: A History of the Breed* (2nd ed. D. Carno, New York 1970) 10–22.

[b] Literally "milk-festival," after the mash of barley and milk dedicated then: L. Deubner, *Attische Feste* (Berlin 1932) 216.

[c] A formula attested [Dem.] *Proem* 54, cf. *PCG* Alexis fr. 267.3.

[d] The definition requires extensive emendation, and may in any case be a later addition (see Introd. p. 31–32); it resembles [Aristotle,] *Virtues and Vices* 1251b13.

ἀναθεῖναι τῷ Διονύσῳ ἐπιγράψας μόνον[1] αὑτοῦ τὸ ὄνομα.

(3) καὶ ἐπιδόσεων γινομένων ἐκ τοῦ δήμου, σιωπᾶν ἢ ἀναστὰς[2] ἐκ τοῦ μέσου ἀπελθεῖν. (4) καὶ ἐκδιδοὺς αὑτοῦ θυγατέρα τοῦ μὲν ἱερείου πλὴν τῶν ἱερέων τὰ κρέα ἀποδόσθαι, τοὺς δὲ διακονοῦντας ἐν τοῖς γάμοις οἰκοσίτους μισθώσασθαι.

(5) καὶ τριηραρχῶν τὰ τοῦ κυβερνήτου στρώματα αὑτῷ[3] ἐπὶ τοῦ καταστρώματος ὑποστορέννυσθαι, τὰ δὲ αὑτοῦ ἀποτιθέναι. (6) καὶ τὰ παιδία δὲ δεινὸς μὴ πέμψαι εἰς διδασκάλου ὅταν ἦ Μουσεῖα,[4] ἀλλὰ φῆσαι κακῶς ἔχειν, ἵνα μὴ συμβάλωνται. (7) καὶ ἐξ ἀγορᾶς δὲ ὀψωνήσας τὰ κρέα αὐτὸς

___

[1] anonymus apud Hanow: μὲν V.
[2] Schwarz: ἀναστὰς σιωπᾶν ἢ V (σιωπᾶ cD, σιωπῶν c).
[3] Meier: στρῶμα ταὐτὸν V.
[4] post ὅταν ἦ iterat V τοῦ ἀποτιθέναι καὶ τὰ παιδία: del. Meier.

dedicates to Dionysus a strip of wood with only his own name written on it.[a]

(3) When emergency contributions[b] are announced in an assembly, he either remains silent or gets up and leaves their midst. (4) When he marries off his daughter, he sells the meat from the sacrifice except for the priests' share, and hires staff for the wedding feast who must bring their own dinners.

(5) When he is captaining a ship[c] he spreads his helmsman's bedding on deck for himself, and puts away his own. (6) He is apt not to send his children to the teacher's for the annual pageant,[d] but say they are sick, so they will not have to bring presents. (7) When he goes shopping he carries the

[a] The wealthiest citizens were required to act as *choregus* (producer) and pay for dramatic productions; if the play won the competition, they often dedicated an elaborate monument in a public place (Arthur Pickard-Cambridge, *The Dramatic Festivals of Athens*, revised by John Gould and D. M. Lewis, Oxford 1988, 77–78). The ungenerous man's meager plaque (like some choregic dedications actually preserved) does not even add the customary names of the poet, the play, actors, or the tribe he represented.

[b] In times of crisis the wealthiest citizens were asked to pledge voluntary payments (ἐπιδόσεις) to the government: W. Kendrick Pritchett, *The Greek State at War* II (Berkeley 1974) 110 n. 286.

[c] The wealthy citizen who provided money for a warship became its captain: J. S. Morrison and J. F. Coates, *The Athenian Trireme* (Cambridge 1986) 109, 121–127, 130.

[d] Literally "the festival of the Muses" (cf. Aeschines 1.10).

THEOPHRASTUS

φέρειν <ἐν ταῖς χερσὶν καὶ>[1] τὰ λάχανα ἐν τῷ
προκολπίῳ. (8) καὶ ἔνδον μένειν, ὅταν ἐκδῷ θοἰμάτιον πλῦναι.[2] (9) καὶ φίλου ἔρανον συλλέγοντος
καὶ διειλεγμένου αὐτῷ, προσιόντα προϊδόμενος
ἀποκάμψας ἐκ τῆς ὁδοῦ τὴν κύκλῳ οἴκαδε πορευθῆναι.

(10) καὶ τῇ γυναικὶ δὲ τῇ ἑαυτοῦ προῖκα
εἰσενεγκαμένῃ μὴ πρίασθαι θεράπαιναν, ἀλλὰ
μισθοῦσθαι εἰς τὰς ἐξόδους ἐκ τῆς γυναικείας παιδίον τὸ συνακολουθῆσον.[3] (11) καὶ τὰ ὑποδήματα
παλιμπήξει κεκαττυμένα φορεῖν καὶ λέγειν, ὅτι
"κέρατος οὐδὲν διαφέρει." (12) καὶ ἀναστὰς τὴν
οἰκίαν καλλῦναι καὶ τὰς κλίνας ἐκκορίσαι.[4]
(13) καὶ καθεζόμενος παραστρέψαι τὸν τρίβωνα,
ὃν αὐτὸν[5] φορεῖ.

[1] Navarre (*Revue des études anciennes* 20 [1918] 218).
[2] Hirschig: ἐκπλῦναι V.
[3] Korais, Schneider: συνακολουθῆσαν (-ῆσον perperam Siebenkees) V.
[4] Casaubon: ἐκκορῆσαι V, ἐκκορύσαι CD.
[5] Münsterberg: αὐτός V.

meat home from the market in his hands, with the vegetables in the fold of his cloak.[a] (8) When he is having his cloak cleaned, he doesn't leave the house.[b] (9) If a friend is soliciting a loan[c] and has discussed it with him, he veers out of his path whenever he sees him approaching, and takes a roundabout way home.

(10) Even though his wife brought him a dowry, he doesn't buy her a slave-girl, but rents from the women's market[d] a slave to go along when she leaves the house. (11) He wears shoes with soles that have been stuck back on, and says "They wear like iron."[e] (12) As soon as he wakes up he cleans the house, and picks the fleas off the couches.[f] (13) When he sits down he pulls aside his cheap cloak, even though it's the only thing he's wearing.[g]

[a] Delivery boys (LSJ προὔνεικοι) could be hired cheaply.

[b] He owns only one cloak.

[c] See on 15.7.

[d] See on 2.9.

[e] Literally "they are no different from horn," proverbial for its hardness (Lucian, *True History* I.14, *Alexander* 21).

[f] Instead of having a servant to do it.

[g] That is, he tries to protect his cheapest clothing (τρίβων, see *RE* VIA.2416–17), even when this means sitting on his bare buttocks (cf. 4.7).

## ΑΛΑΖΟΝΕΙΑΣ ΚΓ΄

(1) ἀμέλει δὲ ἡ ἀλαζονεία δόξει εἶναι προσποίησίς[1] τις ἀγαθῶν οὐκ ὄντων, ὁ δὲ ἀλαζὼν τοιοῦτός τις, (2) οἷος ἐν τῷ διαζεύγματι ἑστηκὼς διηγεῖσθαι ξένοις ὡς πολλὰ χρήματα αὐτῷ[2] ἐστιν ἐν τῇ θαλάττῃ· καὶ περὶ τῆς ἐργασίας τῆς δανειστικῆς διεξιέναι ἡλίκη, καὶ αὐτὸς ὅσα εἴληφε καὶ ἀπολώ-λεκε· καὶ ἅμα ταῦτα πλεθρίζων πέμπειν τὸ παιδάριον εἰς τὴν τράπεζαν, δραχμῆς αὐτῷ κειμένης.

(3) καὶ συνοδοιπόρου δὲ ἀπολαῦσαι ἐν τῇ ὁδῷ δεινὸς λέγων, ὡς μετ' Ἀλεξάνδρου[3] ἐστρατεύ-σατο, καὶ ὡς αὐτῷ εἶχε, καὶ ὅσα λιθοκόλλητα ποτήρια ἐκόμισε· καὶ περὶ τῶν τεχνιτῶν τῶν ἐν τῇ Ἀσίᾳ ὅτι βελτίους εἰσὶ τῶν ἐν τῇ Εὐρώπῃ ἀμφισβητῆσαι· καὶ ταῦτα φῆσαι,[4] οὐδεμοῦ ἐκ τῆς πόλεως ἀποδεδημηκώς. (4) καὶ γράμματα δὲ εἰπεῖν ὡς πάρεστι παρ' Ἀντιπάτρου τριττὰ δὴ λέγοντα παραγενέσθαι αὐτὸν εἰς Μακεδονίαν· καὶ διδομένης αὐτῷ ἐξαγωγῆς ξύλων ἀτελοῦς ὅτι ἀπείρηται, ὅπως μηδ' ὑφ' ἑνὸς συκοφαντηθῇ,

---

[1] Auber: προσδοκία codd.
[2] Lycius: αὐτοῖς codd.
[3] Auber: μετὰ Εὐάνδρου codd.

## 23. FRAUDULENCE

(1) You can be sure fraudulence will seem to be a pretence of nonexistent goods. The fraud is the sort (2) who stands on the breakwater[a] and tells strangers how much of his money is invested in shipping; he goes into detail about the extent of his moneylending business, and the size of his profits and losses; and while he exaggerates these, he sends his slave to the bank because a drachma is on deposit for him there.[b]

(3) On a journey he is apt to put one over on a travel companion by relating how he campaigned with Alexander, and how Alexander felt about him, and how many jewel-studded goblets he got, and arguing that the craftsmen in Asia are better than those in Europe (he says all this even though he's never been out of town). (4) He says that he's got no less than three letters from Antipater summoning him to visit Macedonia, and that he has declined a grant to him for the duty-free export of timber, because he refuses to be prey to even one

[a] For the meaning of διάζευγμα see *RE* V.355.
[b] That is, he is actually so poor he must withdraw even the smallest sum immediately.

---

[4] Korais: ψηφῆσαι V.

"περαιτέρω φιλοσοφεῖν προσῆκε τοῖς Μακεδόσι·"
(5) καὶ ἐν τῇ σιτοδείᾳ[1] δὲ ὡς πλείω ἢ πέντε
τάλαντα αὐτῷ γένοιτο τὰ ἀναλώματα διδόντι τοῖς
ἀπόροις τῶν πολιτῶν, ἀνανεύειν γὰρ οὐ δύνασθαι.

(6) καὶ ἀγνώτων δὲ παρακαθημένων κελεῦσαι
θεῖναι τὰς ψήφους ἕνα αὐτῶν καὶ ποσῶν[2] κατὰ
χιλιάδας[3] καὶ κατὰ μίαν καὶ προστιθεὶς πιθανῶς
ἑκάστοις τούτων ὀνόματα ποιῆσαι καὶ δέκα
τάλαντα· καὶ τοῦτο φῆσαι[4] εἰσενηνέχθαι εἰς ἐρά-
νους αὐτῷ[5] καὶ τὰς τριηραρχίας εἰπεῖν ὅτι οὐ τίθη-
σιν οὐδὲ τὰς λειτουργίας ὅσας λελειτούργηκε.

(7) καὶ προσελθὼν δ᾽ εἰς τοὺς ἵππους τοὺς ἀγαθοὺς τοῖς πωλοῦσι προσποιήσασθαι ὠνητιᾶν. (8)
καὶ ἐπὶ τὰς κλίνας ἐλθὼν ἱματισμὸν ζητῆσαι εἰς

---

[1] Casaubon: σποδιᾷ V, σποδία CD.   [2] Goez: πόσων V,
ποσοῦν αὐτὰς CD.   [3] ἑξακοσίας V, ἑξακοσίους CD: χιλίας
Wilamowitz (errorem ratus e compendio X ortum), sed
χιλιάδας correctius esse docet P. Keyser, *Classical Journal*
81 (1986) 231-2.   [4] Lycius: φῆσας codd.   [5] Foss:
αὐτῶν codd.

informer—"The Macedonians should have been smarter than that!"[a] (5) And that during the food shortage[b] his expenses in giving to destitute citizens amounted to more than five talents—he just can't bring himself to say no.

(6) When people he doesn't know are sitting beside him, he asks one of them to move the stones for him, and doing the addition from the thousands column to the ones[c] and convincingly supplying names for each of these sums, he actually reaches ten talents; and says that these are just his loans to friends;[d] he's not counting the warships, nor the public events he's paid for.[e]

(7) He goes up to the high-priced horse market and pretends to the sellers that he wants to buy. (8) Going to the clothing-vendors, he picks out a

[a] I.e., smarter than to think he could be bribed with such a poor gift. He claims to have turned down a lucrative contract, much sought-after by Athenian politicians (Andoc. 2.11, R. Meiggs, *Trees and Timber in the Ancient Mediterranean World*, Oxford 1982, 126) because he feared prosecution for trading with an enemy state (MacDowell, *Law in Classical Athens* 62–63, 158–159).

[b] In Athens, 330–326: see Wankel on Demosthenes *On the Crown* 491, Mikhail Rostovtzeff, *Social and Economic History of the Hellenistic World* (Oxford 1941) 95.

[c] The Greek abacus had columns for counting-stones numbered 1000, 500, 100, 50, 10, 5 and 1: for its use see Mabel Lang, "Herodotus and the Abacus," *Hesperia* 26 (1957) 271–287.

[d] See on 15.7.

[e] See on 26.6.

δύο τάλαντα καὶ τῷ παιδὶ μάχεσθαι, ὅτι τὸ χρυσίον οὐκ ἔχων αὐτῷ ἀκολουθεῖ. (9) καὶ ἐν μισθωτῇ οἰκίᾳ οἰκῶν φῆσαι ταύτην εἶναι τὴν πατρῴαν πρὸς τὸν μὴ εἰδότα, καὶ διότι μέλλει πωλεῖν αὐτὴν διὰ τὸ ἐλάττω εἶναι αὐτῷ πρὸς τὰς ξενοδοχίας.

## ΥΠΕΡΗΦΑΝΙΑΣ ΚΔ΄

(1) ἔστι δὲ ἡ ὑπερηφανία καταφρόνησίς τις πλὴν αὑτοῦ τῶν ἄλλων, ὁ δὲ ὑπερήφανος τοιόσδε τις, (2) οἷος τῷ σπεύδοντι ἀπὸ δείπνου ἐντεύξεσθαι φάσκειν ἐν τῷ περιπατεῖν. (3) καὶ εὖ ποιήσας μεμνῆσθαι φάσκειν. (4) καὶ βιάζεσθαι[1] ἐν ταῖς ὁδοῖς τὰς διαίτας κρίνειν ἐντυχὼν[2] τοῖς ἐπιτρέψασι. (5) καὶ χειροτονούμενος ἐξόμνυσθαι τὰς ἀρχάς, οὐ φάσκων σχολάζειν. (6) καὶ προσελθεῖν πρότερος οὐδενὶ θελῆσαι. (7) καὶ τοὺς πωλοῦντάς τι ἢ μεμισθωμένους δεινὸς κελεῦσαι ἥκειν πρὸς αὑτὸν ἅμ' ἡμέρᾳ. (8) καὶ ἐν ταῖς ὁδοῖς πορευόμενος μὴ λαλεῖν τοῖς ἐντυγχάνουσι, κάτω κεκυφώς, ὅταν δὲ αὐτῷ δόξῃ, ἄνω πάλιν. (9) καὶ ἑστιῶν τοὺς φίλους αὐτὸς μὴ συνδειπνεῖν, ἀλλὰ τῶν ὑφ' αὑτόν τινι συντάξαι αὐτῶν ἐπιμελεῖσθαι.

---

[1] Foss: βιάζειν codd.
[2] Foss: ἐν τοῖς ἐπιτρέψασι codd.

wardrobe totalling two talents, then quarrels with his servant because he came along without bringing any gold coins.[a] (9) When he is living in a rented house, he tells someone who doesn't know that it belongs to his family, and that he intends to sell it because it's too small for him for entertaining.

## 24. ARROGANCE

(1) Arrogance is a sort of contempt for anyone other than oneself. The arrogant man is a type such as this, (2) who says to a man in a hurry that he'll meet him after dinner while he takes his walk. (3) If he does a favor, he says to remember it. (4) If he meets disputants on the street, he forces them to decide their arbitration.[b] (5) If elected to office he takes an oath to avoid serving, claiming lack of time.[c] (6) He won't make the first approach to anyone. (7) He is apt to tell salesmen or employees to come to his house first thing next morning. (8) As he walks down the street he avoids speaking to passers-by by casting his eyes down, then back up again when it suits him. (9) When he entertains his friends he doesn't join them at dinner himself, but orders one of his subordinates to see to them.

[a] Cf. 18.3.

[b] For private arbitrations see on 5.3.

[c] One could avoid office with a sworn statement of ill-health (Demosthenes 19.124).

THEOPHRASTUS

(10) καὶ προαποστέλλειν δέ, ἐπὰν πορεύηται, τὸν ἐροῦντα, ὅτι προσέρχεται.[1] (11) καὶ οὔτε ἐπ' ἀλειφόμενον αὐτὸν οὔτε λουόμενον οὔτε ἐσθίοντα ἐᾶσαι[2] ἂν εἰσελθεῖν.

(12) ἀμέλει δὲ καὶ λογιζόμενος πρός τινα τῷ παιδὶ συντάξαι τὰς ψήφους διωθεῖν[3] καὶ κεφάλαιον ποιήσαντι γράψαι αὐτῷ εἰς λόγον. (13) καὶ ἐπιστέλλων μὴ γράφειν ὅτι "χαρίζοιο ἄν μοι," ἀλλ' ὅτι "βούλομαι γενέσθαι," καὶ "ἀπέσταλκα πρὸς σὲ ληψόμενος," καὶ "ὅπως ἄλλως μὴ ἔσται," καὶ "τὴν ταχίστην."

## ΔΕΙΛΙΑΣ ΚΕ΄

(1) ἀμέλει δὲ ἡ δειλία δόξειεν ἂν εἶναι ὕπειξίς τις ψυχῆς ἔμφοβος, ὁ δὲ δειλὸς τοιοῦτός τις, (2) οἷος πλέων τὰς ἄκρας φάσκειν ἡμιολίας εἶναι· καὶ κλύδωνος γενομένου ἐρωτᾶν εἴ τις μὴ μεμύηται τῶν πλεόντων· καὶ τοῦ κυβερνήτου ἀνακύπτων μὲν πυνθάνεσθαι εἰ μεσοπορεῖ καὶ τί αὐτῷ δοκεῖ τὰ τοῦ θεοῦ, καὶ πρὸς τὸν παρακαθήμενον λέγειν ὅτι

[1] Schneider: προέρχεται V, ἔρχεται C.
[2] Casaubon: ἐάσας codd.
[3] διαθεῖναι Sheppard.

138

(10) When he goes somewhere he sends someone ahead to say that he's on his way. (11) He won't let anyone in when he's oiling himself, bathing, or eating.

(12) You can be sure that when he's reckoning accounts with someone he tells his slave to clear the counters[a] and find the total, and write it in his account. (13) When he sends a commission he doesn't write "would you be so kind as to . . ." but rather "I want this done" and "I've sent to you to pick up . . ." and "no deviations" and "immediately."

## 25. COWARDICE

(1) You can be sure that cowardice would seem to be a sort of fearful yielding of the soul. The coward is the sort (2) who, when at sea, says that the cliffs are pirate ships. When a wave hits, he asks whether anyone on board has not been initiated.[b] Of the helmsman he first pops up and asks whether he is halfway, and how he thinks the heavens look, and says to the man sitting beside him that his fear is

[a] On the abacus see on 23.6. He is so busy that he has his slave perform the whole transaction.

[b] The mysteries at Samothrace promised special protection for seafarers: Burkert, *Ancient Mystery Cults* 15–16.

φοβεῖται ἀπὸ ἐνυπνίου τινός· καὶ ἐκδὺς διδόναι
τῷ παιδὶ τὸν χιτωνίσκον· καὶ δεῖσθαι πρὸς τὴν
γῆν προσάγειν αὐτόν.

(3) καὶ στρατευόμενος δὲ <τοῦ>[1] πεζοῦ ἐκβοη-
θοῦντος προσκαλεῖν πάντας[2] κελεύων πρὸς αὑτὸν
στάντας πρῶτον περιιδεῖν, καὶ λέγειν ὡς ἔργον
διαγνῶναί ἐστι πότεροί εἰσιν οἱ πολέμιοι. (4) καὶ
ἀκούων κραυγῆς καὶ ὁρῶν πίπτοντας εἰπεῖν πρὸς
τοὺς παρεστηκότας ὅτι τὴν σπάθην λαβεῖν ὑπὸ
τῆς σπουδῆς ἐπελάθετο, τρέχειν ἐπὶ τὴν σκηνήν,
τὸν παῖδα ἐκπέμψας κελεύειν προσκοπεῖσθαι ποῦ
εἰσιν οἱ πολέμιοι, ἀποκρύψαι αὐτὴν ὑπὸ τὸ προσ-
κεφάλαιον, εἶτα διατρίβειν πολὺν χρόνον ὡς
ζητῶν.[3] (5) καὶ ἐν τῇ σκηνῇ ὁρῶν τραυματίαν τινὰ
προσφερόμενον τῶν φίλων προσδραμὼν καὶ θαρ-
ρεῖν κελεύσας ὑπολαβὼν φέρειν. καὶ τοῦτον θερα-
πεύειν καὶ περισογγίζειν καὶ παρακαθήμενος ἀπὸ
τοῦ ἕλκους τὰς μυίας σοβεῖν καὶ πᾶν μᾶλλον ἢ
μάχεσθαι τοῖς πολεμίοις. καὶ τοῦ σαλπιστοῦ δὲ τὸ
πολεμικὸν σημήναντος καθήμενος ἐν τῇ σκηνῇ
<εἰπεῖν>·[4] "ἄπαγ' ἐς κόρακας· οὐκ ἐάσει τὸν
ἄνθρωπον ὕπνου λαβεῖν πυκνὰ σημαίνων." (6) καὶ

[1] suppl. Wilamowitz.

the result of some dream. He strips off his shirt and
hands it to his slave;[a] he begs to be put ashore.

(3) When he is on military service and the infan-
try is attacking he calls to everyone and orders them
to stand near him first and reconnoitre, and says
that their task is to discern which ones are the
enemy. (4) When he hears a tumult and sees men
falling, he says to those beside him that in his haste
he forgot to take his sword, and runs to his tent,
sends his attendant out and orders him to spy out
the enemy's location, hides the sword under the pil-
low, then wastes a long time pretending to look for
it. (5) When from his tent he sees one of his friends
brought in wounded, he runs up to him, bids him be
brave, picks him up and carries him; then he takes
care of him, sponges him off, sits at his side shooing
the flies off his wound — anything rather than fight
the enemy. When the trumpeter sounds the charge,
he sits in his tent and says "Go to hell! He won't let
a man get any sleep with his endless signalling!"

[a] To ready himself to swim.

---

[2] sic refinxi: στρατευόμενος δὲ προσκαλεῖν πάντας πρὸς αὐτὸν
καὶ στάντας C, στρατευόμενος δὲ πεζοῦ ἐκβοηθοῦντός τε προσκαλεῖν κελεύων πρὸς αὐτὸν στάντας V.

[3] Schneider: ζητεῖν V.

[4] suppl. Schneider.

αἵματος δὲ ἀνάπλεως ἀπὸ τοῦ ἀλλοτρίου τραύμα
τος ἐντυγχάνειν τοῖς ἐκ τῆς μάχης ἐπανιοῦσι καὶ
διηγεῖσθαι ὡς κινδυνεύσας· "ἕνα σέσωκα τῶν
φίλων." καὶ εἰσάγειν πρὸς τὸν κατακείμενον
σκεψομένους [τοὺς δημότας]¹ τοὺς φυλέτας καὶ
τούτων ἅμ' ἑκάστῳ διηγεῖσθαι, ὡς αὐτὸς αὐτὸν
ταῖς ἑαυτοῦ χερσὶν ἐπὶ σκηνὴν ἐκόμισεν.

## ΟΛΙΓΑΡΧΙΑΣ Κϛ'

(1) δόξειεν δ' ἂν εἶναι ἡ ὀλιγαρχία φιλαρχία τις
ἰσχύος καὶ² κέρδους γλιχομένη, ὁ δὲ ὀλιγαρχικὸς
τοιοῦτος, (2) οἷος τοῦ δήμου βουλευομένου,³ τίνας
τῷ ἄρχοντι προσαιρήσονται⁴ τῆς πομπῆς τοὺς
συνεπιμελησομένους, παρελθὼν ἀποφήνασθαι⁵ ὡς
δεῖ αὐτοκράτορας τούτους εἶναι, κἂν ἄλλοι προ
βάλλωνται δέκα, λέγειν "ἱκανὸς εἷς ἐστι, τοῦτον
δὲ" ὅτι "δεῖ ἄνδρα εἶναι·" καὶ τῶν Ὁμήρου ἐπῶν
τοῦτο ἓν μόνον κατέχειν, ὅτι "οὐκ ἀγαθὸν πολυκοι
ρανίη, εἷς κοίρανος ἔστω," τῶν δὲ ἄλλων μηδὲν
ἐπίστασθαι·

¹ del. Diels.
² P. Oxy. 699: ἰσχυρῶς V, ἰσχυροῦ C.
³ Casaubon: βουλομένου codd.
⁴ Schneider: προαιρήσονται V.
⁵ Schneider: ἀποφήνας ἔχει codd.

(6) Drenched in blood from another man's wound, he meets the men returning from battle and tells the story as if he'd been in danger: "I saved one of our friends." Then he leads the members of his tribe inside to view him lying there, while he tells each one that he personally brought him into the tent with his own hands.

## 26. AUTHORITARIANISM

(1) Authoritarianism would seem to be a desire for office that covets power and profit. The authoritarian is the sort (2) who, when the people are debating which people to choose to assist the chief magistrate with the procession, takes the podium and says they need to have absolute power; if other speakers propose ten of them, he says "One is plenty—but he has to be a real man!" He remembers only one line of Homer—he doesn't know a single thing about the rest: "More than one leader is bad; let one alone be our ruler."[a]

[a] *Iliad* 2.204, Aristotle, *Politics* 1292a13.

# THEOPHRASTUS

(3) ἀμέλει δὲ δεινὸς τοῖς τοιούτοις τῶν λόγων[1] χρήσασθαι, ὅτι "δεῖ αὐτοὺς ἡμᾶς συνελθόντας περὶ τούτων βουλεύσασθαι, καὶ ἐκ τοῦ ὄχλου καὶ τῆς ἀγορᾶς ἀπαλλαγῆναι, καὶ παύσασθαι ἀρχαῖς πλησιάζοντας καὶ ὑπὸ τούτων οὕτως ὑβριζομένους ἢ τιμωμένους," <καὶ>[2] ὅτι "ἢ τούτους δεῖ ἢ ἡμᾶς οἰκεῖν τὴν πόλιν."

(4) καὶ τὸ μέσον δὲ τῆς ἡμέρας ἐξιὼν καὶ τὸ ἱμάτιον ἀναβεβλημένος καὶ μέσην κουρὰν κεκαρμένος καὶ ἀκριβῶς ἀπωνυχισμένος σοβεῖν τοὺς τοιούτους λόγους τραγῳδῶν·[3] (5) "διὰ τοὺς συκοφάντας οὐκ οἰκητόν ἐστιν ἐν τῇ πόλει," καὶ ὡς "ἐν τοῖς δικαστηρίοις δεινὰ πάσχομεν ὑπὸ τῶν δεκαζομένων,"[4] καὶ ὡς "θαυμάζω[5] τῶν πρὸς τὰ κοινὰ προσιόντων τί βούλονται," καὶ ὡς "ἀχάριστόν ἐστι <τὸ πλῆθος καὶ ἀεὶ>[6] τοῦ νέμοντος καὶ διδόντος," καὶ ὡς αἰσχύνεται ἐν τῇ ἐκκλησίᾳ, ὅταν παρακάθηταί τις αὐτῷ λεπτὸς καὶ αὐχμῶν· (6) καὶ εἰπεῖν· "πότε παυσόμεθα ὑπὸ τῶν λειτουργιῶν καὶ τῶν τριηραρχιῶν ἀπολλύμενοι;" καὶ ὡς

---

[1] Casaubon: ὀλίγων V.
[2] suppl. Ussing.
[3] Herwerden: τὴν τοῦ ᾠδίω V (τὴν τοῦ Ὠιδείου Preller).
[4] Meier: δικαζομένων codd.
[5] Schneider: θαυμάζων V.
[6] suppl. Ast.

144

(3) You can be sure he is apt to say things like these: "We ought to get together by ourselves and make decisions about this, and be rid of the rabble and the marketplace, and stop depending on them as we do for reward or rejection when we compete for public offices"; and "Either they must run the city or we must!"

(4) At midday he goes out with his cloak arranged about him, hair cut to a moderate length, fingernails expertly trimmed, and struts along intoning speeches like this: (5) "With the informers, life in the city has become unbearable!" "What the bribe-takers in the courts are doing to us is a crime!" "I wonder what the men getting involved in politics are after." "The common people show no gratitude; they always follow anyone with a handout or a gift." He says that he is ashamed in the assembly when some scrawny, unwashed type sits beside him. (6) And "When will we be delivered from the death-grip of being forced to pay for public events and warships?"[a] "How loathsome the breed of dema-

[a] Literally "liturgies and trierarchies" required of the wealthiest citizens: J. K. Davies, *Athenian Propertied Families* (Oxford 1971) xvii–xxxi.

μισητὸν τὸ τῶν δημαγωγῶν γένος, τὸν Θησέα
πρῶτον φήσας τῶν κακῶν τῇ πόλει γεγονέναι
αἴτιον· τοῦτον γὰρ ἐκ δώδεκα πόλεων εἰς μίαν
καταγαγόντα λῦσαι τὰς¹ βασιλείας· καὶ δίκαια
αὐτὸν παθεῖν· πρῶτον γὰρ αὐτὸν ἀπολέσθαι ὑπ᾽
αὐτῶν·

[καὶ τοιαῦτα ἕτερα πρὸς τοὺς ξένους καὶ τῶν
πολιτῶν τοὺς ὁμοτρόπους καὶ ταὐτὰ προαιρουμέ-
νους.]²

## ΟΨΙΜΑΘΙΑΣ ΚΖ´

(1) [ἡ δὲ ὀψιμαθία φιλοπονία δόξειεν ἂν εἶναι ὑπὲρ
τὴν ἡλικίαν,]³ ὁ δὲ ὀψιμαθὴς τοιοῦτός τις, (2) οἷος
ῥήσεις μανθάνειν ἑξήκοντα ἔτη γεγονὼς καὶ
ταύτας λέγων παρὰ πότον ἐπιλανθάνεσθαι.
(3) καὶ παρὰ τοῦ υἱοῦ μανθάνειν τὸ "ἐπὶ δόρυ"⁴ καὶ
"ἐπὶ ἀσπίδα" καὶ "ἐπ᾽ οὐράν." (4) καὶ εἰς ἡρῷα⁵

---

¹ Kayser: λυθείσας βασιλ᾽ V.
² del. Diels.
³ del. Hanow, Gomperz, Stein.
⁴ τὸ ἐπὶ Schneider: ἐπὶ τὸ codd.
⁵ Schneider: ἥρωα V.

gogues is!" adding that the originator of the city's troubles was Theseus, since he reduced it to a unit instead of twelve cities[a] and broke up the monarchy; but he got what he deserved, since he was the first one they killed.[b]

[He says more of this sort to foreigners, and to those citizens who share his character and political preferences.][c]

## 27. REJUVENATION

(1) [Rejuvenation would seem to be an enthusiasm for work[d] inappropriate to one's age.] The rejuvenated man is the sort (2) who, after turning sixty, memorizes passages, but when he is reciting at a drinking party can not remember them.[e] (3) From his son he learns "right face" and "left face" and "about face."[f] (4) For the hero-festivals, he con-

---

[a] The so-called συνοικισμός of Attika (Thucydides 2.15, *FGrHist* 328 Philochorus F 94, with Jacoby's commentary).

[b] There was a tradition that Theseus was ostracized from Athens, Theophrastus fr. 638.

[c] The epilogue is a later addition; see Introd. p. 30.

[d] φιλοπονία is a quality for which ephebes are often praised (*Inscriptiones Graecae* II$^2$ 900.17, 1039.48–9), but it does not apply to all the behavior described below, and this definition is probably a later addition.

[e] Cf. Philocleon's mangling of the drinking songs in Aristophanes, *Wasps* 1225ff.

[f] Literally "to the spear," "to the shield," and "to the tail" (Pollux 1.129, and frequently in Xenophon), commands from the military training of ephebes.

συμβάλλεσθαι τοῖς μειρακίοις <καὶ>[1] λαμπάδα
τρέχειν. (5) ἀμέλει δὲ κἄν που κληθῇ εἰς Ἡρά-
κλειον, ῥίψας τὸ ἱμάτιον τὸν βοῦν αἴρεσθαι[2] ἵνα
τραχηλίσῃ.

(6) καὶ προσανατρίβεσθαι εἰσιὼν[3] εἰς τὰς
παλαίστρας. (7) καὶ ἐν τοῖς θαύμασι τρία ἢ
τέτταρα πληρώματα ὑπομένειν τὰ ᾄσματα
ἐκμανθάνων. (8) καὶ τελούμενος τῷ Σαβαζίῳ
σπεῦσαι ὅπως καλλιστεύσῃ παρὰ τῷ ἱερεῖ.

(9) καὶ ἐρῶν ἑταίρας[4] καὶ κριοὺς προσβάλλων
ταῖς θύραις πληγὰς εἰληφὼς ὑπ᾽ ἀντεραστοῦ
δικάζεσθαι. (10) καὶ εἰς ἀγρὸν ἐφ᾽ ἵππου ἀλλοτρίου κατοχούμενος ἅμα μελετᾶν ἱππάζεσθαι καὶ
πεσὼν τὴν κεφαλὴν κατεαγέναι.

(11) καὶ ἐν δεκαδισταῖς[5] συνάγειν τοὺς μεθ᾽

[1] suppl. Ast.
[2] Meier: αἱρεῖσθαι V.
[3] Ast: εἰπὼν V.
[4] Schneider: ἱερᾶς V.
[5] Wilhelm: ἕνδεκα λιταῖς V.

[a] Torch races are attested for festivals of Ajax and
Theseus (*Inscriptiones Graecae* I.466.9, II[2].1011.54).

[b] As the ephebes do at some sacrifices (*Inscriptiones
Graecae* I[2] 84.31, II[2] 1028.10, *Supplementum Epigraphi-
cum Graecum* 15 (1958) 104).

tributes to the boys, and runs in the relay races.[a]
(5) If he is invited to a shrine of Heracles somewhere, you can be sure he will throw off his cloak
and try to lift the bull[b] to twist its neck.

(6) He goes into the wrestling schools and chal-
lenges them to a match. (7) At street fairs[c] he sits
through three or four shows, trying to learn the
songs. (8) When he is being inducted into the cult of
Sabazios he wants the priest to judge him the most
handsome.[d]

(9) He becomes infatuated with a prostitute, uses
a battering ram on her door and gets a beating
from her other lover—then takes him to court.[e]
(10) While he is riding on a borrowed horse in the
country he tries to practice fancy horsemanship at
the same time, but falls and hurts his head.

(11) Among the members of a monthly club[f] he

[c] See on 6.4.

[d] The precise context is unknown. For Sabazios see on
16.4.

[e] Fighting over prostitutes is pardoned in the young
(Dem. 54.14, Micio in Terence, *Adelphoe*), but not the old
(Philokleon in *Wasps*): Dover, *Greek Popular Morality*
(Oxford 1974) 103. For the impropriety of older men con-
sorting with prostitutes see *PCG* Pherekrates fr. 77. A
similar court case—except that the prostitute is a young
male—is found in Lysias' 3rd Oration.

[f] Lit. "Tenth-day men," for the day of the month on
which they celebrated. The rest of the sentence remains
unexplained.

αὑτοῦ συναύξοντας. (12) καὶ μακρὸν ἀνδριάντα
παίζειν πρὸς τὸν ἑαυτοῦ ἀκόλουθον. (13) καὶ δια-
τοξεύεσθαι καὶ διακοντίζεσθαι τῷ τῶν παιδίων
παιδαγωγῷ καὶ ἅμα μανθάνειν παρ' αὐτοῦ
<παραινεῖν>,[1] ὡς ἂν καὶ ἐκείνου μὴ ἐπισταμένου.
(14) καὶ παλαίων δ' ἐν τῷ βαλανείῳ πυκνὰ τὴν
ἕδραν στρέφειν, ὅπως πεπαιδεῦσθαι δοκῇ.

(15) καὶ ὅταν ὦσιν ἐγγὺς γυναῖκες,[2] μελετᾶν
ὀρχεῖσθαι αὐτὸς αὑτῷ τερετίζων.

## ΚΑΚΟΛΟΓΙΑΣ ΚΗ΄

(1) ἔστι δὲ ἡ κακολογία ἀγωγὴ ψυχῆς[3] εἰς τὸ
χεῖρον ἐν λόγοις, ὁ δὲ κακολόγος τοιόσδε τις,
(2) οἷος ἐρωτηθείς· "ὁ δεῖνα τίς ἐστιν;" ὀγκοῦσθαι[4]
καθάπερ οἱ γενεαλογοῦντες· "πρῶτον ἀπὸ τοῦ
γένους αὐτοῦ ἄρξομαι. τούτου ὁ μὲν πατὴρ ἐξ
ἀρχῆς Σωσίας ἐκαλεῖτο, ἐγένετο δὲ ἐν τοῖς στρα-
τιώταις Σωσίστρατος, ἐπειδὴ δὲ εἰς τοὺς δημότας
ἐνεγράφη, <Σωσίδημος>.[5] ἡ μέντοι μήτηρ εὐγε-
νὴς Θρᾷττά ἐστι· καλεῖται γοῦν ἡ ψυχὴ Κρινοκό-

---

[1] suppl. Hanow.    [2] ὦσι ... γυναῖκ ... μελετᾶν V:
supplevit Meister.    [3] ἀγὼν τῆς ψυχῆς codd.: ἀγωγὴ
Casaubon, τῆς del. Edmonds.    [4] Diels: οὐκοῦνδε V, om.
C.    [5] suppl. Meier.

plans the attendance of his fellow financial sponsors. (12) He plays "long statue"[a] against his own attendant. (13) He competes in archery and the javelin against his childrens' teacher, and suggests that the teacher, as if he were not an expert, take lessons from him. (14) When he wrestles at the baths, he often twists his hips so that he will look well-trained.[b]

(15) And when women are nearby he practices a chorus-dance, humming to himself.

## 28. SLANDER

(1) Slander is a tendency of the soul toward derogatory talk. The slanderer is the sort (2) who, when asked "Who is such-and-such?" becomes pompous like the genealogers:[c] "Let me begin at the beginning, with his lineage. This man's father was originally named Sosias, but became Sosistratos in the army, and after he had been enrolled as a citizen, Sosidemos. However, his mother was noble — a noble Thracian, that is.[d] The darling[e] is called 'Kri-

---

[a] The game is otherwise unknown.    [b] Hip movements were a specialty of Argive wrestlers: Theocritus 24.111.    [c] Usually a genealogy lists the names of various ancestors: this list gives the aliases of a single man; "Sosias," common in comedies, suggests that he started as a slave.    [d] Considered by the Greeks a wild and uncultured people (Aristophanes, *Acharnians*, 141–171 and Euripides, *Hecuba*).    [e] Literally "soul," a term of endearment suggesting she had many lovers.

THEOPHRASTUS

ρακα· τὰς δὲ τοιαύτας φασὶν ἐν τῇ πατρίδι εὐγε-
νεῖς εἶναι. αὐτὸς δὲ οὗτος ὡς ἐκ τοιούτων γεγονὼς κακὸς καὶ μαστιγίας."

(3) καὶ κακῶς[1] δὲ πρός τινα εἰπεῖν· "ἐγὼ δήπου
τὰ τοιαῦτα οἶδα, ὑπὲρ ὧν σὺ πλανᾷ[2] πρὸς ἐμέ·"
κἀπὶ[3] τούτοις διεξιών· "αὗται αἱ γυναῖκες ἐκ τῆς
ὁδοῦ τοὺς παριόντας συναρπάζουσι," καὶ "οἰκία τις
αὕτη τὰ σκέλη ἠρκυῖα· οὐ γὰρ οἷον λῆρός ἐστι, τὸ
λεγόμενον, ἀλλ' ὥσπερ αἱ κύνες[4] ἐν ταῖς ὁδοῖς
συνέχονται," καὶ "τὸ ὅλον ἀνδρολάλοι τινές," καὶ
"αὐταὶ τὴν θύραν τὴν αὔλειον ὑπακούουσι."

(4) ἀμέλει δὲ καὶ κακῶς λεγόντων ἑτέρων συν-
επιλαμβάνεσθαι εἴπας·[5] "ἐγὼ δὲ τοῦτον τὸν
ἄνθρωπον πλέον πάντων μεμίσηκα· καὶ γὰρ
εἰδεχθής τις ἀπὸ τοῦ προσώπου ἐστίν· ἡ δὲ πονηρία — οὐδὲν ὅμοιον· σημεῖον δέ· τῇ γὰρ ἑαυτοῦ
γυναικὶ τάλαντα εἰσενεγκαμένῃ προῖκα, ἐξ οὗ[6]
παιδίον αὐτῷ γεννᾷ, τρεῖς χαλκοῦς εἰς ὄψον
δίδωσι καὶ τῷ ψυχρῷ λούεσθαι ἀναγκάζει τῇ τοῦ
Ποσειδῶνος ἡμέρᾳ."

[1] Siebenkees: κακῶν V.
[2] Schneider: πλανᾶς V.
[3] Immisch (praeeunte Casaubon): καὶ codd.
[4] anonymus apud Ast: γυναῖκες V.
[5] Cobet: εἴπου V.
[6] Immisch: ἐξ ἧς V.

152

nokoraka — women like that pass for noble where he comes from. As you'd expect coming from such stock, he's a villain and a scoundrel."

(3) He says to someone as an insult, "Of course I know the sort of things for which you are wandering to me."[a] And then beyond this, as he goes into detail: "These women snatch men passing by from the street." And "This house practically has its legs in the air. That's not just a joke, you know, the old saying, they really copulate in the streets like dogs." And "They'll always talk to men." And "These women answer their own front door!"[b]

(4) You can be sure that when others are engaging in slander he will join in, saying "I loathe this man more than anyone; he has a quite hateful-looking face; his wickedness is unequalled, and I'll prove it: his wife brought him thousands in dowry, but ever since she bore him a son, she gets from him three coppers for her shopping, and he makes her bathe in cold water on Poseidon's day."[c]

[a] The text here makes little sense, even with emendations. In what follows, the topic has shifted to the women of a particular family.

[b] Anyone respectable would have had someone to answer the door (cf. 4.12, Aristophanes, *Peace* 979, *Thesm.* 792, Menander fr. 592).

[c] Presumably this was in the cold month Poseideon (December-January).

(5) καὶ συγκαθήμενος δεινὸς περὶ τοῦ ἀναστάντος εἰπεῖν καὶ ἀρχήν γε εἰληφὼς[1] μὴ ἀποσχέσθαι μηδὲ τοὺς οἰκείους αὐτοῦ λοιδορῆσαι. (6) καὶ πλεῖστα περὶ τῶν <αὑτοῦ>[2] φίλων καὶ οἰκείων [κακὰ εἰπεῖν,][3] καὶ περὶ τῶν τετελευτηκότων κακῶς λέγειν, ἀποκαλῶν παρρησίαν καὶ δημοκρατίαν καὶ ἐλευθερίαν καὶ τῶν ἐν τῷ βίῳ ἥδιστα τοῦτο ποιῶν.

(7) [οὕτως ὁ τῆς διδασκαλίας ἐρεθισμὸς μανικοὺς καὶ ἐξεστηκότας ἀνθρώπους τοῖς ἤθεσι ποιεῖ.][4]

## ΦΙΛΟΠΟΝΗΡΙΑΣ ΚΘ΄

(1) ἔστι δὲ ἡ φιλοπονηρία ἐπιθυμία κακίας, ὁ δὲ φιλοπόνηρός ἐστι τοιόσδε τις, (2) οἷος ἐντυγχάνειν τοῖς ἡττημένοις καὶ δημοσίους ἀγῶνας ὠφληκόσι καὶ ὑπολαμβάνειν, ἐὰν τούτοις χρῆται, ἐμπειρότερος γενήσεσθαι καὶ φοβερώτερος.

(3) καὶ ἐπὶ τοῖς χρηστοῖς εἰπεῖν, "ὡς φαίνεται,"[5] καὶ φῆσαι ὡς οὐδείς ἐστι χρηστός, καὶ ὁμοίους πάντας εἶναι, καὶ ἐπισκῶψαι[6] δέ, ὡς χρηστός ἐστι.

---

[1] Schneider: εἰληφότος V.    [2] suppl. Herwerden.
[3] del. Hanow.    [4] epilogum byzantinum capitis prioris

(5) When he is sitting in a group he is apt to start talking about whoever has just left and, once started, not refrain from reviling even his family. (6) He maligns most his own friends and household, and the dead, passing off his slander as free speech, democracy or openness, and taking more pleasure in it than anything in his life.

(7) [That is how the stimulus for learning makes men mad and distraught in their personality.][a]

## 29. PATRONAGE OF SCOUNDRELS

(1) Patronage of scoundrels is a predilection for evil. The patron of scoundrels is a type such as this, (2) who seeks out losers in court and those convicted in public trials, and imagines that with their friendship he will become more experienced and formidable.

(3) About those called "good"[b] he says "apparently," and says "No one is good," and that all people are the same, and ridicules "How good he is."

[a] For the interpolated epilogue (probably displaced from the preceding character) see Introd. p. 30.

[b] E.g., The oligarchic politician Phocion, who received the title χρηστός by public decree (*Suda* s.v. Φρύνων καὶ Φιλοκράτης, Diod. 17.15.2); but the text of this sentence is probably corrupt.

---

(ὀψιμαθία) huc inepte insertum agnovit Hanow.  [5] Diels: γίνεται V.  [6] Nast: ἐπισκῆψαι V.

(4) καὶ τὸν πονηρὸν δὲ εἰπεῖν ἐλεύθερον, ἐὰν βούληταί τις εἰς πεῖραν ἐλθεῖν,[1] καὶ τὰ μὲν ἄλλα ὁμολογεῖν ἀληθῆ ὑπὲρ αὐτοῦ λέγεσθαι ὑπὸ τῶν ἀνθρώπων, ἔνια δὲ ἀγνοεῖν· φῆσαι γὰρ αὐτὸν εὐφυῆ καὶ φιλέταιρον καὶ ἐπιδέξιον· καὶ διατείνεσθαι δὲ ὑπὲρ αὐτοῦ, ὡς οὐκ ἐντετύχηκεν ἀνθρώπῳ ἱκανωτέρῳ·

(4a) καὶ εὔνους δὲ εἶναι αὐτῷ[2] ἐν ἐκκλησίᾳ λέγοντι ἢ ἐπὶ δικαστηρίῳ κρινομένῳ· καὶ πρὸς τοὺς καθημένους[3] δὲ εἰπεῖν δεινός, ὡς οὐ δεῖ τὸν ἄνδρα, ἀλλὰ τὸ πρᾶγμα κρίνεσθαι· καὶ φῆσαι αὐτὸν κύνα εἶναι τοῦ δήμου, φυλάττειν γὰρ αὐτὸν τοὺς ἀδικοῦντας· καὶ εἰπεῖν ὡς "οὐχ ἕξομεν τοὺς ὑπὲρ τῶν κοινῶν συναχθεσθησομένους, ἂν τοὺς τοιούτους προώμεθα." (5) δεινὸς δὲ καὶ προστατῆσαι φαύλων καὶ συνηγορῆσαι[4] ἐν δικαστηρίοις ἐπὶ πονηροῖς πράγμασιν καὶ κρίσιν κρίνων ἐκδέχεσθαι τὰ ὑπὸ τῶν ἀντιδίκων λεγόμενα ἐπὶ τὸ χεῖρον.

(6) [καὶ τὸ ὅλον ἡ φιλοπονηρία ἀδελφή ἐστι τῆς πονηρίας. καὶ ἀληθές ἐστι τὸ τῆς παροιμίας, τὸ ὅμοιον πρὸς τὸ ὅμοιον πορεύεσθαι.][5]

---

[1] supplevit Naber: π . . . . . V.    [2] Meier: τῷ codd.    [3] Meier: προσκαθήμενος V.    [4] Immisch: συνεδρεῦσαι codd.    [5] epilogum del. editores.

(4) About a wicked man, if someone wants to examine him, he says that he is a gentleman, and admits the truth of the rest of what is said about him by people, but some points he does not believe, since he says the man is good at heart, loyal, and fair; he exerts himself on his behalf, stating he's never met a more capable man.

(4a) He supports him when he is speaking in the assembly or a defendant in court, and to the judges he is apt to say: "You must judge the case, and not the man." He claims he is a watchdog for the public,[a] since he is vigilant against wrongdoers. "If we abandon men like this, we won't have anyone left to join in the struggle for the public interest." (5) He is apt to come to the defense of riff-raff, testify for the defence in cases involving the wicked and, when judging a dispute, react negatively to what is said by both parties.

(6) [In general, patronage of scoundrels is evil's close relative. What the proverb says is true: like travels with like.[b]]

[a] Cf. Plutarch, *Demosthenes* 23.4, R. A. Neil on Aristophanes, *Knights* 1017.

[b] Never preserved in quite this form, but cf. Homer, *Od.* 17.218, Aristotle, *Rhet.* 1371b15, *Nicomachean Ethics* 1155a34.

## ΑΙΣΧΡΟΚΕΡΔΕΙΑΣ Λ΄

(1) ἡ δὲ αἰσχροκέρδειά ἐστιν ἐπιθυμία[1] κέρδους
αἰσχροῦ, ἔστι δὲ τοιοῦτος ὁ αἰσχροκερδής, (2) οἷος
ἐστιῶν[2] ἄρτους ἱκανοὺς μὴ παραθεῖναι· (3) καὶ
δανείσασθαι παρὰ ξένου παρ' αὑτῷ καταλύοντος.
(4) καὶ διανέμων μερίδας φῆσαι δίκαιον εἶναι
διμοιρίαν[3] τῷ διανέμοντι δίδοσθαι καὶ εὐθὺς αὑτῷ
νεῖμαι. (5) καὶ οἰνοπωλῶν κεκραμένον τὸν οἶνον τῷ
φίλῳ ἀποδόσθαι. (6) καὶ ἐπὶ θέαν τηνικαῦτα
πορεύεσθαι ἄγων τοὺς υἱεῖς, ἡνίκα προῖκ' ἀφιᾶσιν
οἱ θεατρῶναι.

(7) καὶ ἀποδημῶν δημοσίᾳ τὸ μὲν ἐκ τῆς
πόλεως ἐφόδιον οἴκοι καταλιπεῖν, παρὰ δὲ τῶν
συμπρεσβευτῶν δανείζεσθαι· καὶ τῷ ἀκολούθῳ
μεῖζον φορτίον ἐπιθεῖναι ἢ δύναται φέρειν καὶ
ἐλάχιστα ἐπιτήδεια τῶν ἄλλων παρέχειν· καὶ
ξενίων τὸ μέρος τὸ αὑτοῦ ἀπαιτήσας ἀποδόσθαι.

(8) καὶ ἀλειφόμενος ἐν τῷ βαλανείῳ καὶ εἰπών

---

[1] Cobet: περιουσία V.
[2] Korais: ἐσθίων V.
[3] Petersen: δίμοιρον ("two-thirds") Amaduzzi; διμοίρῳ V.

## 30. CHISELING

(1) Chiseling is a desire for tawdry gain. The chiseler is the sort (2) who doesn't serve enough bread when he gives a feast. (3) He asks for a loan from an out-of-town guest who is staying at his house. (4) When distributing shares[a] he asserts that it is fair for a double share to be given to the distributor, and awards it immediately to himself. (5) If he sells wine, he sells a watered-down wine to his friend.[b] (6) He goes to the theater — and brings his sons — only when the theater managers[c] have remitted the entrance fee.

(7) When traveling abroad at public expense, he leaves his public travel-funds behind at home, and asks for loans from his fellow ambassadors. He burdens his attendant with a greater load than he can carry, and yet gives him fewer provisions than any others. He asks for his own share of the gifts they receive[d] and sells it.

(8) When rubbing himself down in the bath, he

---

[a] The word is vague enough to cover portions of meat at a sacrifice (cf. 17.2), contributions of food to a joint dinner, or even financial returns from a commercial enterprise.

[b] The Greeks mixed water with wine when they drank it, but did not purchase it already watered.

[c] Evidently those who leased rights to produce plays; see Pickard-Cambridge, *The Dramatic Festivals of Athens* 266.

[d] "Guest-gifts" here are presumably those given to the embassy by its foreign hosts.

159

THEOPHRASTUS

"σαπρόν γε τὸ ἔλαιον ἐπρίω, ὦ παιδάριον"[1] τῷ
ἀλλοτρίῳ ἀλείφεσθαι. (9) καὶ τῶν εὑρισκομένων
χαλκῶν ἐν ταῖς ὁδοῖς ὑπὸ τῶν οἰκετῶν δεινὸς
ἀπαιτῆσαι τὸ μέρος, κοινὸν εἶναι φήσας τὸν
Ἑρμῆν. (10) καὶ θοἰμάτιον[2] ἐκδοῦναι πλῦναι καὶ
χρησάμενος παρὰ γνωρίμου ἐφελκύσαι πλείους
ἡμέρας, ἕως ἂν ἀπαιτηθῇ. (11) καὶ τὰ τοιαῦτα·
Φειδωνείῳ μέτρῳ τὸν πύνδακα εἰσκεκρουμένῳ[3]
μετρεῖν αὐτὸς τοῖς ἔνδον τὰ ἐπιτήδεια σφόδρα
ἀποψῶν.

(12) ὑποπρίασθαι φίλου δοκοῦντος πρὸς τρόπου
τι ὠνεῖσθαι, εἶτα λαβὼν ἀποδόσθαι.[4] (13) ἀμέλει δὲ
καὶ χρέος δὲ ἀποδιδοὺς τριάκοντα μνῶν ἔλαττον

[1] Reiske: τῷ παιδαρίῳ AB, παι<sup>δ'ρ</sup> V.
[2] Meineke: ἱμάτιον V.
[3] εἰσ- vel ἐγκεκρουσμένῳ (sic) Casaubon (ad char. 11):
πύνδακα ἐκκεκρουμένῳ AB, π δακ κεκρου μενω V.
[4] locus desperatus: ὑποπριάσθαι φίλου δοκοῦντος πρὸς
τρόπου πωλεῖσθαι V, ὑποπρίασθαι φίλου ἐπιλαβὼν ἀποδόσθαι AB
(τι ὠνεῖσθαι, εἶτα λαβὼν Naber).

a Every visitor to the baths would carry a personal flask
of oil with which to wash himself by rubbing it on and
scraping off again; see Ginouvès, Βαλανευτική 214.

exclaims "Stupid boy, you've bought oil that is rancid!" and uses someone else's.[a] (9) He is apt to ask
for his own share of any coins that are found in the
street by his slaves, citing the proverb "Hermes is
impartial."[b] (10) He sends out his cloak to be
cleaned and, borrowing one from an acquaintance,
hangs onto it[c] for several extra days, until he is
asked for it back. (11) And things like this: he measures out provisions personally to his household staff
in a Pheidonian measure with its bottom hammered
in, levelling it off strictly.[d]

(12) He makes a secret purchase from a friend
who thinks he is buying something on a whim,[e] and
then, once he's got it, resells it. (13) You can be sure
that when he repays a debt of thirty minas, he pays

[b] Lucky finds were called "gifts of Hermes"; for the use
of this phrase to justify sharing them see Menander, *Epitrepontes* 284, 317; Aristotle, *Rhetoric* 1401a22; Lucian,
*Navigium* 12; *Paroem. Graec.* II.483.15.

[c] Literally "drags it behind him," perhaps of rough
wear, but more probably delay (LSJ ἐφέλκω I.4).

[d] He personally oversees the doling out of grain, using a
smaller than average cup (for Pheidonian measures see
Aristotle, *Constitution of Athens* 10.2), made still smaller
by pushing in its base (cf. *PCG* Aristophanes fr. 281,
Pherekrates fr. 110), and scraping off any excess grain on
top (Pollux 4.168).

[e] He dupes his friend into agreeing to a low price by pretending the item is something he aches to own. But the
text is corrupt here, and the version translated is largely
modern conjecture.

τέτταρσι δραχμαῖς ἀποδοῦναι.

(14) καὶ τῶν υἱῶν δὲ μὴ πορευομένων εἰς τὸ διδασκαλεῖον [τὸν μῆνα ὅλον][1] διά τιν᾿[2] ἀρρωστίαν ἀφαιρεῖν τοῦ μισθοῦ κατὰ λόγον· καὶ τὸν Ἀνθεστηριῶνα μῆνα <ὅλον>[3] μὴ πέμπειν αὐτοὺς εἰς τὰ μαθήματα διὰ τὸ θέας εἶναι πολλάς, ἵνα μὴ τὸν μισθὸν ἐκτίνῃ.

(15) καὶ παρὰ παιδὸς κομιζόμενος ἀποφορὰν τοῦ χαλκοῦ τὴν ἐπικαταλλαγὴν προσαπαιτεῖν, καὶ λογισμὸν δὲ λαμβάνων παρὰ τοῦ χειρίζοντος. (16) καὶ φράτορας ἑστιῶν αἰτεῖν τοῖς ἑαυτοῦ παισὶν ἐκ τοῦ κοινοῦ ὄψον, τὰ δὲ καταλειπόμενα ἀπὸ τῆς τραπέζης ἡμίση τῶν ῥαφανίδων ἀπογράφεσθαι, ἵν᾿ οἱ διακονοῦντες παῖδες μὴ λάβωσι. (17) συναποδημῶν δὲ μετὰ γνωρίμων χρήσασθαι τοῖς ἐκείνων παισί, τὸν δὲ ἑαυτοῦ ἔξω μισθῶσαι καὶ μὴ ἀναφέρειν εἰς τὸ κοινὸν τὸν μισθόν. (18) ἀμέλει δὲ καὶ συναγόντων παρ᾿ αὐτῷ[4] ὑποθεῖναι τῶν παρ᾿ ἑαυτοῦ διδομένων ξύλων καὶ φακῶν καὶ ὄξους καὶ ἁλῶν καὶ ἐλαίου τοῦ εἰς τὸν λύχνον.

---

[1] del. Nast.
[2] Unger: τὴν V.
[3] suppl. Bloch.
[4] Korais: ἑαυτῷ V.

four drachmas too little.[a]

(14) If his sons don't go to school because of illness, he makes a deduction proportionally from their fees, and doesn't send them to their lessons for the whole month of Anthesterion because of its numerous shows, to avoid paying the fee.[b]

(15) When he collects tenant-rent from his slave,[c] he demands also the fee to exchange the copper,[d] as also when he settles accounts with his steward. (16) When entertaining his clan,[e] he demands a dinner for his own slaves at joint expense, yet insists that even the radish-halves left over from the meal be inventoried, to prevent the waiters from taking them. (17) When he is travelling with acquaintances he uses their servants, and hires out his own without sharing the proceeds. (18) You can be sure that when people get together at his house he makes a bill for the wood, beans, vinegar, salt

[a] He pretends he is one coin short (the *tetradrachmon* was the largest common silver coin in use in Athens), assuming his creditor will not insist on it.

[b] In the month of Anthesterion (February-March) were celebrated the Anthesteria, the Diasia and the Lesser Mysteries at Eleusis; other months seem to have had more holidays, but our knowledge may be defective.

[c] Masters of slaves often allowed them to work for others, in return for a portion of the wages.

[d] The slave pays in copper coinage, which must be converted to silver at a bank for a fee (see *RE* Suppl. II, "agio").

[e] To celebrate the *Apatouria* (Burkert, *Greek Religion* 255).

(19) καὶ γαμοῦντός τινος τῶν φίλων καὶ ἐκδιδομέ-
νου θυγατέρα πρὸ χρόνου τινὸς ἀποδημῆσαι, ἵνα
<μὴ>[1] προπέμψῃ προσφοράν. (20) καὶ παρὰ τῶν
γνωρίμων τοιαῦτα κίχρασθαι, ἃ μήτ᾽ ἂν ἀπαιτή-
σαι μήτ᾽ ἂν ἀποδιδόντων ταχέως ἄν τις κομί-
σαιτο.

[1] suppl. Amaduzzi.

164

and lamp-oil he's contributed. (19) When one of his friends is getting married, or marrying off a daughter, he leaves town some time before to avoid giving a present. (20) He borrows from acquaintances the sorts of things one wouldn't ask for back, or wouldn't pick up if people offered them back.

# ADDITIONAL NOTES

## 1. DISSEMBLING

The title is literally "irony," a notion with a long and complex history. It consists of saying what one obviously does not mean, and originally εἰρωνεία meant simply "lying" (Aristophanes, *Clouds* 443–451, cf. *Wasps* 174, *Birds* 1227); but it came to be applied specifically to the self-deprecating false modesty of Socrates (e.g., Plato, *Republic* 337A, cf. Aristotle, *Nicomachean Ethics* 1124b; Gregory Vlastos, *Socrates, Ironist and Moral Philosopher* [Ithaca, N.Y., 1991] 21–44). The brothers Schlegel conceived it to be a playful excess of self-confidence (Ernst Behler, *Klassische Ironie, romantische Ironie, tragische Ironie*, Darmstadt 1972); then, by way of reaction, it was viewed as a destructive force (Søren Kierkegaard, *The Concept of Irony*, tr. Lee M. Capel, New York 1965). Modern criticism considers (unconscious) irony to be an important element of tragic drama (beginning with Connop Thirlwall, "On the Irony of Sophocles," *The Philological Museum* 2 (1833) 483–536).

The εἴρων is described also by Ariston of Keos (see the Appendix); he is one of the characters of comedy according to *Tractatus Coislinianus* XII; in Aristotle, *Nicomachean Ethics* 1127a20ff., the εἴρων is opposite to the ἀλαζών (see *Character* 23 below). See in general Otto Ribbeck, "Über den Begriff des εἴρων," *Rheinisches Museum* 31 (1876) 381–400.

Irony as described by Theophrastus is rather different: it is *dissimulation* — avoiding all forthright statements — with the goal of avoiding all involvement in their consequences.

## 2. FLATTERY

Eupolis wrote a comedy *The Flatterers* (PCG fr. 156–191) and there is a play *The Flatterer* by Menander (p. 93 Koerte). Theophrastus himself wrote a book *On Flattery* (fr. 547–8), the peripatetic Klearchos of Soloi did as well (fr. 19 Wehrli), and Plutarch wrote "How to Tell a Flatterer from a Friend" (*Moralia* 48e–75d).

For ancient caricatures of the flatterer see in general Otto Ribbeck, *Kolax: eine ethologische Studie* (Leipzig 1883) and H.-G. Nesselrath, *Lukians Parasitendialog* (Berlin 1985). Another character-trait relating to praising others is "Obsequiousness" (chapter 5); the difference is that the flatterer is totally fixed on the attention of a single patron, for whom he lowers himself to perform tasks usually done by slaves.

## 3. IDLE CHATTER

ἀδολεσχία is mentioned in Aristotle as a vice (*Nicomachean Ethics* 3.1117b35, *Rhetoric* 1390a9) and discussed in Plutarch's "On Garrulity" (*Moralia* 502b–515a). It is listed as one of the "stylistic" techniques for producing laughter in *Tractatus Coislinianus* V (p. 64 line 16 Koster); Lane

# ADDITIONAL NOTES

Cooper, *An Aristotelian Theory of Comedy* (New York 1922) 231–233 gives many examples of long-winded comic characters from Aristophanes to Molière. See also "Garrulity" (*Character* 7).

## 4. BOORISHNESS

Aristotle (*Nicomachean Ethics* 1128a) uses ἀγροικία of an inability to appreciate wit, but here it is closer to its original meaning (that of English "boorish" as well), "like a farmer" (cf. Dikaiopolis or Trygaios in Aristophanes, *Acharnians* and *Peace*, and the plays entitled *Agroikos* by Anaxandrides, Antiphanes, Menander, Philemon and others). See Otto Ribbeck, "Agroikos, eine ethologische Studie," *Abhandlungen der königlichen sächsischen Gesellschaft der Wissenschaften* 23 (1888) 1–68.

It is the first of six characters portraying a general lack of tact — the others are "Shamelessness" (6), "Bad Timing" (12), "Absent-mindedness" (14), "Squalor" (19) and "Bad Taste" (20). This is a more subtle portrait than most of the others, and not entirely unsympathetic.

## 5. OBSEQUIOUSNESS

See the note on "Flattery" (2). Sometimes the distinction is drawn that flattery is for one's advantage, obsequiousness is not (Aristotle, *Nicomachean Ethics* 1108a26, 1127a8), and that is roughly true here, but there are differences as well: "the flatterer [in Theophrastus] ... is the constant, fixed companion of one and the same patron, while the obsequious man is an excessively friendly but basically

169

insecure person, who is driven by the overpowering desire to please everyone" (Nesselrath, *Lukians Parasitendialog* 113).

All the manuscripts (even P. Herc. 1457, of the first century B.C.) make §6–10 follow immediately upon §5. Yet these sections clearly do not describe an obsequious man but an entirely different type, a show-off spendthrift rather like the Aristotelian description of vanity, *Nicomachean Ethics* 1125a27–35, or vulgarity, *Nicomachean Ethics* 1123a19–31, or "Petty Ambition" (21). The only reasonable assumption is that §6–10 belong to a different character, either because they have been displaced from the end of *Character* 21 or — more probably — because a column of text was lost at an early date containing the end of "Obsequiousness" and the beginning of another character. The same thing seems to have happened in *Character* 19.

# 6. SHAMELESSNESS

The title is literally "mindlessness," or "lack of good sense." The term is much rarer than any other trait-name in the *Characters*, and often a virtual synonym for shamelessness: it is applied to a parasite in *PCG* Nicolaos Comicus fr. 1.43, and to a political opponent by Demosthenes *On the Crown* 249 (where see the commentary of Hermann Wankel). R. G. Ussher, *Greece and Rome* 24 (1977) 77, compares the sausage-seller in Aristophanes, *Knights*.

Considering the low reputation of moneylending in antiquity (Paul Millett, *Lending and Borrowing in Ancient Athens*, Cambridge 1991, 179) it is not surprising that his ultimate disgrace is to charge exorbitant interest.

6.4 ("have a ticket *or* claim . . ."): As often in this work (e.g., the next sentence), καί links *alternatives*: see J. D. Denniston, *Greek Particles* (2nd ed. Oxford 1954) 292.

# 7.  GARRULITY

See on ἀδολεσχία (3); there we have a sustained portrait of a single man in one situation, here a series of different characteristic actions.

# 8.  RUMOR-MONGERING

A type of political gossip known to Demosthenes, *In Timocratem* 15 and Aeschines, *De falsa legatione* 153. The historical allusions are precise enough to show that this particular character was composed in 319 B.C. (see Introd. p. 9).

# 9.  SPONGING

Literally "shamelessness," not a term normally applied to the desire for money, although this was a common topic of ancient moralists and satirists: notable are the Pseudo-Platonic *Eryxias*, Plutarch, "On the love of money" (*Moralia* 523c–528b), the comedies entitled Φιλάργυρος (see on *PCG* Dioxippus fr. 4), Plautus' *Aulularia*, and innumerable satirists; see Gilbert Highet, *Juvenal the Satirist* (New York 1954) 282.

    In his discussion of virtues and vices relating to money, Aristotle remarks (*Nicomachean Ethics* 1121b12–1122a3):

"Lack of generosity (ἀνελευθερία) is incurable, since old age and any disability seem to make people ungenerous. It is also more innate in people than is extravagance [the opposite excess]; most people are more inclined to love money than to give it away. It is also widely prevalent, and diverse, since of the lack of generosity there are many varieties. Because it consists of two parts—a deficiency in giving and an excess in taking—it does not occur in its entirety in all [ungenerous people], but is sometimes separated, some being excessive in taking and some deficient in giving. The first group, called things like 'sparing,' 'sticky' or 'skinflint,' are all deficient in giving, but neither desire nor are willing to take others' possessions ... The second are excessive in taking, because they take anything from any source ... what is common to them all is the desire for base profit (αἰσχροκέρδεια), since they all take upon themselves disgrace for the sake of gain."

In this and the other three characters relating to money—μικρολογία (10), ἀνελευθερία (22), αἰσχροκέρδεια (30)—the terminology is differently applied, and the standard names for greed (like φιλαργυρία and φιλοχρηματία) are avoided; but the distinction between taking and keeping is maintained. This particular man is distinguished by his cheerful openness in taking extras for himself: he makes no attempt at concealment, passing off each small depredation as common courtesy or friendship.

## 10. PENNYPINCHING

μικρολογία is "obsession with details," but often applied to one who counts every penny (Menander fr. 97, PCG Ephippus fr. 15.10). On the types of greed in general see the Additional Notes on *Character* 9: this man is not concerned with taking from others, but making sure no others take from him.

## 11. OBNOXIOUSNESS

βδελυρία is literally "hatefulness," a strong term used to describe the most loathsome enemies (e.g., Aeschines 1.31, 189, Demosthenes 25.27). Here it has something in common with Aristotle's "buffoonery" (βωμολοχία, *Nicomachean Ethics* 1128a4), which aims to get a laugh at any price.

## 12. BAD TIMING

καιρός means "the proper time" (see West on Hesiod, *Works and Days* 694). This man's blunders are not always his fault — he simply does not foresee how inopportune are his actions. He might be a comic character in a farce, who manages to do something reasonable in itself at the worst possible time.

## 13. OVERZEALOUSNESS

περιεργία as used here is a synonym of the more common πολυπραγμοσύνη, the meddlesomeness for which Athenians were especially famous: Victor Ehrenberg, "*Polypragmosyne*: A Study in Greek Politics," *Journal of Hellenic Studies* 67 (1947) 46–67. Plutarch wrote a treatise on it (*Moralia* 515b), and πολυπράγμων was the title of comedies by Diphilus, Heniochus, and Timocles. See also

# THEOPHRASTUS

H.-J. Mette, "Die περιεργία bei Menander," *Gymnasium* 69 (1962) 398–406.

## 14. ABSENT-MINDEDNESS

ἀναισθησία is literally "insensitivity," but comes to be used for "stupidity" (Thucydides 6.86, Demosthenes 21.153, Pseudo-Aristotle, *Physiognomica* 3.807b12), and applied especially to Boeotians (see Wankel on Demosthenes, *On the Crown* 43). When Aristotle, *Nicomachean Ethics* 1107b7, applies it to a character-trait, it is the inability to feel pleasure, a meaning not present here.

## 15. GROUCHINESS

The character described here and in *Character* 17 ("Griping") is better-known by the epithet "bad-tempered" (δύσκολος) as described in Aristotle, *Nicomachean Ethics* 1126b11ff, and in Menander's play of that name. In the *Eudemian Ethics* 1221a8, Aristotle actually makes αὐθάδεια the mean between σεμνότης (haughtiness) and ἀρέσκεια (obsequiousness); cf. however *Magna Moralia* 1192b31, Ariston of Keos col. 16–17 (Appendix).

## 16. SUPERSTITION

δεισιδαιμονία is literally "fear of the gods," one of three character-traits relating to fear — "Mistrust" (18) is the fear of being deceived, "Cowardice" (25) is the fear of death.

"Superstition" is in some ways a poor translation, since it ascribes supernatural significance to everyday events or things; but the events listed here *could* have religious meaning in ancient Greece, so that this man merely takes a correct attitude too far. (Xenophon, *Agesilaos* 11.8 and Aristotle, *Politics* 1315a1 actually use the word δεισι-δαίμων in a positive sense.) He attempts to influence the gods on his own behalf, and substitutes personal rituals for public ones. In terms of the Aristotelian mean, his is an excess of piety (εὐσέβεια, on which Theophrastus wrote a treatise, fr. 584A–588), just as atheism is the deficiency of it.

Ancient critiques of superstition in a more modern sense are found in the Hippocratic treatise *On the Sacred Disease*, chapters 1–4, Plato, *Laws* X.909a8–910e4, and Plutarch, "On Superstition" (*Moralia* 164e–171f). Menander wrote a play entitled Δεισιδαίμων (said by an ancient critic to have been modeled on a comedy called "The Reader of Omens" by Antiphanes). For Theophrastus see especially H. Bolkestein, *Theophrastos' Charakter der Deisidaimonia als religionsgeschichtliche Urkunde* (Religionsgeschichtliche Versuche und Vorarbeiten vol. 21.2, Giessen 1929).

## 17. GRIPING

The title means literally "finding fault with one's lot"; see the Additional Notes on 15 (αὐθάδεια). Μεμψίμοιρος was the title of a comedy by Antidotos.

## 18. MISTRUST

Menander wrote a play entitled "The mistrustful man."

# THEOPHRASTUS

## 19. SQUALOR

δυσχέρεια usually indicates "revulsion," i.e. the reaction of the viewer rather than the behavior of the character.

§ 8–11 do not seem to belong to the same character as § 1–7; perhaps they should be placed at the end of another character (e.g. 11, "Obnoxiousness"), or else we must assume a column of text was lost containing the end of "Squalor" and the beginning of this new character, something like "Lack of Cooperation." The same thing appears to have happened in *Character* 5.

## 20. BAD TASTE

ἀηδία is literally "unpleasantness"; the noun and adjective are used of disagreeable or odious people by the orators (Demosthenes 21.153, 47.28, 3.72, 164) and elsewhere (*PCG* Alexis fr. 278). Aristotle uses it simply of a man who gives others no pleasure (*Nicomachean Ethics* 1108a30, 1171b26, *Magna Moralia* 1200a15). This character is more precise than the term used: he offends others like many other characters, but mostly he is a city version of the boor, who is best viewed at home (§ 4–10) and resembles Trimalchio in Petronius' *Satyricon*.

## 21. PETTY AMBITION

μικροφιλοτιμία, a term found only here, is literally "desire for small honor." The corresponding discussion in Aristotle is not on ambition (*Nicomachean Ethics* 1107b27ff, 1125b1–25, where he concludes that the proper mean between ambition and the lack of it has no name) but on the magnanimous man, who "will reject honor that comes from just anyone, or for petty achievements" (*Nicomachean Ethics* 1124a10). With Theophrastus' man it is not the strength of the desire for honor that is in question, but error about the proper kind of it; Aristotle would have called him "vain" (χαῦνος, *Nicomachean Ethics* 1125a27).

## 22. LACK OF GENEROSITY

A wealthy Athenian was expected to be generous to his family, friends and country (Dover, *Greek Popular Morality*, Oxford 1974, 230–231). This man behaves with a shabby parsimony on the very occasions (a dramatic victory, his daughter's wedding, command of a warship, contributions to charity) designed to display generosity, and does not maintain the style of life that suits his prosperity.

A satirist of the third century B.C. mocks the school of Theophrastus for requiring some of the very things the ungenerous man does without: "There [in Theophrastus' school] one needed to have footwear—and it couldn't be re-soled—and further a fancy cloak, a slave to attend you, a large house for dinner parties . . . this way of life was considered 'liberal' (ἐλευθέριος, Teles p. 40.8ff Hense)." Compare also Diogenes Laertius 6.90, Hermippus fr. 51 Wehrli.

## 23. FRAUDULENCE

ἀλαζονεία is literally "boasting"; the word may be taken from the name of a Thracian tribe (Herod. 4.17, 52;

cf. the modern use of "bohemian" or "vandal"). It is defined by Aristotle as the opposite vice to εἰρωνεία (*Nicomachean Ethics* 1108a9–30; in between them is "being truthful"). The ἀλαζών is listed as one of the three "characters of comedy" in the *Tractatus Coislinianus*. It comes to be applied especially to soldiers, like Capitano Spavento in the commedia dell' arte, Bobadill in Jonson's *Every Man in His Humour*, Falstaff and Pistol in Shakespeare's *Henry IV* and *V*, and many characters in ancient comedy. See Walter Hofmann, *Der Bramarbas in der antiken Komödie* (Berlin 1973); J. Arthur Hanson, "The Glorious Military," in T. A. Dorey and D. R. Dudley (eds.), *Roman Drama* (New York, 1965) 51–85.

But its basic sense is "being an impostor," e.g. of a doctor (*De morbo sacro* 2), an ambassador (Aristophanes, *Acharnians* 109, 135), a prophet (Aristophanes, *Peace* 1045, Aristoxenus fr. 1 West), or a philosopher (Aristophanes, *Clouds* 102, *PCG* Eupolis fr. 157). Theophrastus' impostor pretends to have a financial empire, and most closely resembles the *gloriosus* vividly described in *Rhetorica ad Herennium* 4.50–51.64.

Plutarch wrote an essay "On extravagant self-praise" (*Moralia* 539a). On the whole theme see especially Otto Ribbeck, *Alazon: ein Beitrag zur antiken Ethologie* (Leipzig 1886).

## 24. ARROGANCE

For ὑπερήφανος see MacDowell on Demosthenes, *Against Meidias* 83. This man is not really hostile (as is the grouch in 15) but imperious and superior, maintaining a cool distance from everyone he deals with. Cf. Ariston of Keos, col. 20 (Appendix).


## 25. COWARDICE

Aristotle described the coward as one who feared even what he need not (*Eudemian Ethics* 1221a18, cf. *Nicomachean Ethics* 1115b15f, 34f, and Theophrastus fr. 449a). This coward is more developed; he not only fears danger, but attempts to disguise his cowardice with various excuses, and is pictured in two extended scenes.


## 26. AUTHORITARIANISM

ὀλιγαρχία is better known as a form of government than a trait of character; but Plato's sketches of human types who correspond to forms of government in *Republic* VIII include the "oligarchic" man (553a1–554b1), who equates excellence with wealth, and a character is called "oligarchic" when he denigrates large juries in Menander, *Sicyonius* 156.

Theophrastus' "oligarchic" man is a retailer of authoritarian slogans: he could as well be called "antidemocratic," as the word implies in political speeches (Andocides 4.16, Lysias 25.8). He much resembles the anonymous author (sometimes dubbed "the old oligarch") of the treatise *On the Constitution of the Athenians* ascribed (falsely) to Xenophon, but the topic was also fresh: there are reasons for dating the *Characters* to the years around 319 (see Introd.), and from 322 to 318 an oligarchic government of nine thousand led by Phocion replaced the

THEOPHRASTUS

democracy at Athens. See Lawrence A. Trittle, *Phocion the Good* (London 1988) 129–140.

## 27. REJUVENATION

ὀψιμαθία is literally "late learning" (cf. Aulus Gellius 11.7, Cicero, *ad familiares* 9.20.2, Horace, *Satires* 1.10.22), and it is true that a part of this man's oddity consists in going to school at an advanced age; his appearance in military drills and athletic contests is as absurd as Strepsiades' enrolling himself in Socrates' school in *Clouds* (cf. the adjective παιδομαθής "having learned it in childhood," as a term of praise).

But the essential characteristic here is a general enthusiasm and recklessness of behavior that was tolerated in youths (Dover, *Greek Popular Morality* 103) but not their elders: Philokleon's re-education and rejuvenated violence at a symposium in Aristophanes, *Wasps* 1122–end, are closely parallel.

## 28. SLANDER

There were legal sanctions against slander in Athens (for which the more common term was κακηγορία), but this man manages to avoid them, and his techniques are in any case the stock-in-trade of the ancient orator's invective, as itemized by Wilhelm Süss, *Ethos: Studien zur älteren griechischen Rhetorik* (Leipzig 1910) 247ff; see also Severin Koster, *Die Invektive in der griechischen und römischen Literatur* (Beiträge zur klassischen Philologie vol. 99, Meisenheim am Glan, 1980) 14, and Lucian's essay *On Not Being Quick to Believe Slander*.

# ADDITIONAL NOTES

## 29. PATRONAGE OF SCOUNDRELS

φιλοπονηρία is literally "love of wickedness" (πονηρία is often applied to democratic politicians by their enemies), and one of the oddest characters. Although the word is attested (e.g., Aristotle *Nicomachean Ethics* 1165b16, Dinarchus fr. 42, Plutarch, *Alcibiades* 24.5), the type as described here is not: his interests are purely political, and he is a master of slogans, able to cast doubt on claims of virtue (χρηστός, § 3) and misapply aristocratic terms (ἐλεύθερος, εὐφυής, φιλέταιρος, § 4) to a demagogue. On the types of vocabulary used see especially R. A. Neil, "Political Use of Moral Terms," Appendix II (pp. 202–209) in his edition of Aristophanes, *Knights* (Cambridge 1909).

## 30. CHISELING

αἰσχροκέρδεια is literally "base profiteering." The αἰσχροκερδής is an avaricious man in Aristotle, *Nicomachean Ethics* 1122a3; but in Theophrastus' version he is mainly concerned with retaining as much as possible in cash. He buys no oil, accepts (and gives) as little hospitality as possible, always pays the minimum and collects the maximum in every transaction; he surpasses in his greed even the other three misers (9, 10, 22) at every point where he can be compared.

# APPENDIX

## FRAGMENTS OF THE
## CHARACTER SKETCHES
## OF ARISTON OF KEOS (III–II B.C.)

From a work "On Relieving Arrogance" quoted by Philodemus, *On vices* Book 10, edited by Christian Jensen, *Philodemi περὶ κακιῶν liber decimus*, Leipzig 1911.[1] I generally follow the text of F. Wehrli, *Die Schule des Aristoteles* vol. 6: *Lykon und Ariston von Keos* (2nd ed. Basel 1968) fr. 14–16.[2] On Ariston himself[3] see Wehrli in H. Flashar (ed.), *Die Philosophie der Antike* vol. 3: *ältere Akademie, Aristoteles, Peripatos* (Basel 1983) 579–582.

The characters treated are the inconsiderate man (αὐθάδης, col. 16–17), the self-willed man (αὐθέκαστος, col. 17–18), the know-it-all (παντειδήμων, col. 18), and the dissembler or ironic man (εἴρων, col. 21–23). Interspersed with the character descriptions are Philodemus' tedious and contorted analyses of the disadvantages of each trait.

---

[1] Further bibliography in Kondo, "I caratteri."

[2] Note that uncertain letters, or lacunae in the papyrus text which are filled by conjecture, are *not* indicated here: for an exact account of these see the editions of Jensen or Wehrli.

[3] Not to be confused with Ariston of Chios, Stoic and pupil of Zeno (*SVF* vol. 1 p. 75).

# APPENDIX

The sections I think most likely to be from Ariston are italicized in the translation; on their close similarity in form and style to Theophrastus see Pasquali, "Sui caratteri," 59–62.

(XVI.29sqq.) ὁ δ᾽ αὐθάδης λεγόμενος ἔοικε μὲν εἶναι μεικτὸς
ἐξ οἰήσεως καὶ ὑπερηφανίας καὶ ὑπεροψίας, μετέχων δὲ καὶ
πολλῆς εἰκαιότητος. τοιοῦτος γὰρ ἐστιν, φησὶν ὁ Ἀρίστων,
οἷος ἐν τῇ μάκρα θερμὸν ἢ ψυχρὸν αἰτεῖν μὴ προανακρίνας
τὸν συμβεβηκότ᾽, εἰ κἀκείνῳ συναρέσκει, καὶ . . .

(XVII) . . . παῖδα πριάμενος μηδὲ τοὔνομα προσερωτῆσαι
μήτ᾽ αὐτὸς θέσθαι, καλεῖν δὲ "παῖδα" καὶ μηθὲν ἄλλο· καὶ
τὸν συναλείψαντα μὴ ἀντισυναλείφειν· καὶ ξενισθεὶς μὴ
ἀντιξενίσαι· καὶ θύραν ἀλλοτρίαν κόπτων, ἐπερωτήσαντος
τίς ἐστιν, μηδὲν ἀποκρίνεσθαι, μέχρι ἂν ἐξέλθῃ. καὶ ἀρρω-
στοῦντ᾽ αὐτὸν ἐπισκεπτομένου φίλου μὴ λέγειν πῶς ἔχει,
μηδ᾽ αὐτὸς ἐπισκεπτόμενός τινα τοιοῦτό τι προσεπερωτῆ-
σαι. καὶ γράφων ἐπιστολὴν τὸ χαίρειν μὴ προσγράψαι μηδ᾽
ἐρρῶσθαι τελευταῖον.

ὁ δ᾽ αὐθέκαστος οὐ πάνυ μὲν εἰκαῖός ἐστιν οὐδ᾽ ἄλογος
ὥσπερ ὁ αὐθάδης, δι᾽ οἴησιν δὲ τοῦ μόνος φρονεῖν ἰδιογνωμο-
νῶν, καὶ πειθόμενος ἐν ἅπασιν κατορθώσειν, ἁμαρτήσεσθαι
δ᾽ ἂν ἑτέρου κρίσει προσχρήσηται, μετέχων δὲ καὶ ὑπερηφα-
νίας· οἷος μηδενὶ προσαναθέμενος ἀποδημεῖν, ἀγοράζειν,
πωλεῖν, ἀρχὴν μετιέναι, τἆλλα συντελεῖν· κἂν προσερω-
τήσῃ τις τί μέλλει ποιεῖν, "οἶδ᾽ ἐγώ," λέγειν, κἂν μέμφηται
τις, ὑπομειδιῶν, "ἐμὲ σύ;" καὶ παρακληθεὶς ἐπὶ συνεδρείαν
βουλευομένῳ μὴ βούλεσθαι τὸ δοκοῦν εἰπεῖν, εἰ μὴ τοῦτο
μέλλει πράττειν· καὶ πάντ᾽ ἐν ὅσοις ἀποτέτευχε . . .

(XVIII) . . . τελεῖν καὶ μὴ ἐπιτεθυμηκέναι γενέσθαι
φάσκειν· καὶ μὴ δυσωπεῖσθαι τοὔνομα καλούμενος ὡς αὐθέ-

## APPENDIX

(Column 16, line 29 ff.:) *The man called inconsiderate seems to be a blend of conceit, pride and scorn, with a large dose of thoughtlessness. He is the sort,* Ariston says, *who demands hot or cold water in the bath without first asking his fellow-bather whether it is all right, ...*

(Column 17) *... when he buys a slave he doesn't even ask for his name, or give him one himself, but merely calls him "slave." When someone rubs him with oil, he doesn't do the same in return; if he has been invited out, he doesn't return the invitation. When he knocks at another's door and is asked "who is it?" he doesn't answer until the man comes outside. If a friend pays him a visit while he's ill, he won't say how he is feeling, and when he himself visits someone, he won't even ask such a question. When he writes a letter, he doesn't add "greetings," or "best wishes" at the end.*

*The self-willed man is not exactly thoughtless or irrational like the inconsiderate one, but self-opinionated because of his conceit that he alone has any sense, and confident that he will always do the right thing, whereas if he relies on another's judgment he will make a mistake; he also has a dose of arrogance. He is the sort who seeks no one's advice before going on a trip, making a purchase or a sale, running for office, or carrying out other things. If someone asks him what he intends to do, he says "That's for me to know." If someone criticizes, he smirks "Look who's talking!" If he is called to a meeting for a man who seeks advice, he refuses to say what he thinks unless the man is definitely going to follow it. Anything in which he has failed ...*

(Column 18) *... and has no desire to admit it happened. He is not disturbed when you call him self-willed, but says*

κάστος, ἀλλὰ καὶ ἔτι παιδάρια λέγειν εἶναι τοὺς ὡς παιδα-
γωγοῖς ἄλλοις προσανατιθεμένους, καὶ μόνος ἔχειν πώγωνα
καὶ πολιὰς καὶ ζῆν δυνήσεσθαι γενόμενος ἐν ἐρημίᾳ.

τούτου δ' ἔτι χείρων ἐστὶν ὁ παντειδήμων, ἀναπεπεικὼς
ἑαυτὸν ὅτι πάντα γινώσκει, τὰ μὲν μαθὼν παρὰ τῶν
μάλιστ' ἐπισταμένων, τὰ δ' ἰδὼν ποιοῦντας μόνον, τὰ δ'
αὐτὸς ἐπινοήσας ἀφ' αὑτοῦ. κἄστι τοιοῦτος οὐ μόνον οἷον
Ἱππίαν τὸν Ἠλεῖον ἱστορεῖ Πλάτων, ὅσα περὶ τὸ σῶμ' εἶχεν
αὑτῷ πεποιηκέναι λέγειν, ἀλλὰ καὶ κατασκευάζειν οἰκίαν
καὶ πλοῖον δι' αὑτοῦ καὶ χωρὶς ἀρχιτέκτονος· καὶ γράφειν
συνθήκας ἑαυτῷ δεομένας ἐμπειρίας νομικῆς· καὶ δούλους
ἰδίους ἰατρεύειν, μὴ μόνον ἑαυτόν, ἐπιχειρεῖν δὲ καὶ ἄλλους·
καὶ φυτεύειν καὶ φορτίζεσθαι τὰ μάλισθ' ὑπὸ τῶν τεχνικω-
τάτων κατορθούμενα· καὶ ναυαγῶν ἐν ἅπασι μηδ' οὕτω
παύεσθαι τῆς ἀποπληξίας. οἷος δὲ καὶ τῶν μαθημάτων
ἀντιποιούμενος πάντων ἀσχημονεῖν· καὶ τοὺς καταγελῶν-
τας ἀπείρους λέγειν . . .

(XIX) . . . οὐκ ἂν δι . . . δων ἐπιτρέπειν.

τῷ μὲν οὖν αὐθάδει τά τ' ἐκ τῆς οἰήσεως καὶ τῆς ὑπερηφανίας καὶ ὑπεροψίας εἰ μὴ καὶ τῆς ἀλαζονείας δυσχερῆ
παρακολουθεῖ, καὶ ἰδίως τὰ ἐκ τῆς εἰκαιότητος καὶ τὰ διὰ
τῆς ὀργῆς τούτων οἷς οὕτω προσφέρεται, καὶ τὸ τυγχάνειν
ὁμοίων ἢ μηδὲ βουλομένων εἰς ὁτιδήποτε κοινώνημα
συγκαταβαίνειν, δυχρηστεῖσθαι, καὶ τὸ περὶ μαινομένου
πάντας φέρεσθαι καὶ καθαιρεῖν, διότι τὴν κακίαν ἔχειν αὐτὸν
ὑπονοοῦσιν.

τῷ δ' αὐθεκάστῳ τά τε παρὰ τὰς ἀτοπίας ἐξ ὧν μέμεικ-
ται καὶ τὸ μόνον ἀφραίνειν, ὅτι μόνος οἴεται περὶ πάντων
φρονεῖν· διὸ κἂν τοῖς πλείστοις ἀποτυγχάνειν καὶ ἐπιχαίρε-
σθαι μετὰ καταγέλωτος ὑπὸ πάντων καὶ μηδὲ βοηθεῖσθαι·

*those who seek the guidance of others like nursemaids are little children, and that he is the only one with a beard and grey hair, who could survive if left on his own.*

*Still worse than this one is the know-it-all, since he has persuaded himself that his knowledge is complete — some he's learned from experts, some is from merely observing them in action, some he has come up with on his own. He is not only like Plato [Hippias Minor 368B] says Hippias of Elis was, and says that he has made everything he wears, but he also builds a house and boat by himself, without an architect. He draws up contracts for himself that require legal expertise; he acts as physician to his slaves as well as himself, and tries it for others too; he works at the sort of agriculture and merchant shipping which most require experts to be successfully pursued, and if he washes out completely he does not even then stop his madness. He is the sort who makes a fool of himself by laying claim to all subjects; those who laugh at him he calls laymen . . .*

(Column 19) . . . The inconsiderate man is beset by the difficulties arising from conceit, arrogance, and scorn, if not from fraudulence as well, and in particular those from thoughtlessness, and the anger of those to whom he behaves this way, and the fact that he encounters people like him, or who don't want to have anything to do with him at all, that he does not know what to do, and that everyone rushes away and dismisses him for a madman, because they think that vice has him possessed.

The self-willed man is beset by the difficulties attendant on the strange traits of which he is comprised, and the fact that he alone is out of his mind, because of his belief that he alone is sensible about all subjects. That is

THEOPHRASTUS

καὶ μηδὲ τῶν σοφῶν ἀναμαρτήτων εἶναι λεγόντων μηδ'
ἀπροσδέκτων συμβουλίας, τοῦτον ὑπὲρ αὐτοὺς νομίζοντα
φρονεῖν ἐξ ἀνάγκης κακοδαιμονεῖν· ληρεῖν δὲ καὶ διότι τὴν
κοινῶς σύνεσιν οἴεται περιπεποιῆσθαι τὰ τῶν ἰδίας ἐμπειρίας ἐχόντων, καὶ μεταμεμελῆσθαι πολλῶν ἐξ ἀνάγκης
ἐνκυρεῖν, καὶ λοιδορίας καρποῦσθαι καὶ προσκρούσεις ἑτέρων
. . .

(XX) . . . φάσθαι . . . ἄνθρωπον ἄλλων ἀνθρώπων οὐκ ἔχειν
χρείαν.

ὁ δὲ παντειδήμων ἅμα τοῖς εἰρημένοις πᾶσι καὶ μαργιτο-
μανής ἐστιν, εἰ καὶ τὸν ὄντως πολυμαθέστατον προσαγο-
ρευόμενον οἴεται πάντα δύνασθαι γινώσκειν καὶ ποιεῖν, οὐχ
οἷον ἑαυτόν, ὃς ἐνίοτε οὐδέν τι φωρᾶται κατέχων καὶ οὐ συν-
ορῶν· ὅτι πολλὰ δεῖται τριβῆς, ἂν καὶ ἀπὸ τῆς αὐτῆς γίνη-
ται μεθόδου καθάπερ τὰ τῆς ποιητικῆς μέρη, καὶ διότι περὶ
τοὺς πολυμαθεῖς ὀσμαὶ μόνον εἰσὶ πολλῶν, οὐ κατοχαί, καὶ
τἀποτεύγματα περίεστιν τῶν παιδευμάτων, οὐ τὰ κατορθώ-
ματα, καὶ πάνθ' ὅσα τοῖς τοιούτοις συμβαίνειν ἀνελογιζό-
μεθα· καὶ διότι πολλὰ γινώσκειν, ὡς Ἱππίας ἐκαυχᾶτο, καὶ
τὸ παραπλήσιον πᾶν γένος ὀνείδη μᾶλλόν ἐστιν ἤπερ
ἐγκώμια· καί — τί γὰρ δεῖ τἆλλα περὶ ληρούντων λέγειν;
ὡς ὅταν ἀτυχήσωσι, φωρῶνται καταφεύγοντες ἐπὶ τοὺς

188

# APPENDIX

why he fails in most things, and is a source of delight and ridicule for all, and receives no assistance. Whereas not even the wise claim to be without fault or in no need of advice, he, thinking he is more sensible than they, cannot avoid ill-fortune. He talks nonsense, because he imagines his basic intelligence has bestowed on him the talents of those who possess specialized knowledge, and it happens that he must regret many things, and reap the abuse and attacks of others . . .

(Column 20) He says . . . that a man has no need of other men.

The know-it-all, along with everything already said, is also as crazy as Margites,[1] if he thinks that even one truly called the greatest polymath can know and do everything—much less[2] himself, who is sometimes caught with no mastery at all, and no comprehension; the reason is that many things require practice—if they follow the same method as the elements of the art of poetry; and because around the polymaths there is only an aroma of many subjects, not a mastery of them, and what remains is what they have failed to learn, not where they have succeeded, and all the rest of what we have listed as happening to such people; and because multiple knowledge in the way Hippias boasted of it, and every category like it, is more to reproach than to praise. But why say any more about windbags? Since when they fail they are caught run-

[1] The hero of the (now lost) comic epic of whom it was said "he had knowledge of many deeds—and he knew them all badly" (fr. 3 West).

[2] οὐχ οἷον = οὐχ ὅτι (see F. Blass and A. Debrunner, *Grammar of New Testament Greek*, tr. R. Funk, Chicago 1961, § 304).

189

τυχόντας καὶ τῶν ἐλαχίστων ἐλάττους αὑτοὺς εἶναι προσ-
ομολογοῦσιν.

ὁ μὲν οὖν ὑπερήφανος καὶ ὑπερόπτης ἐστίν, ὁ δ᾽
ὑπερόπτης οὐ πάντως καὶ ὑπερηφανεῖ καὶ ἅπαντα διὰ τὸ
... χηρ ... ἔστιν ὅτε τα ... εἶναι· πέφυκε δ᾽ οὐ ...

(XXI) τὸν μὲν σεμνὸν ἐπαινοῦντες ὡς ἀξίαν ἔχοντα μετά
τινος αὐστηρίας, τὸν δὲ σεμνοκόπον καὶ τότε καὶ νῦν
πάντως ψέγοντες ὡς ἐπιφάσκοντα τὸν εἰρημένον καὶ προσ-
ποιούμενον εἶναι τοιοῦτον ἐν τοῖς ὄχλοις καὶ διὰ τῶν λόγων
— ὃν σεμνομυθεῖν ἔλεγον — καὶ τῷ σχήματι τοῦ προσώπου
καὶ τῶν ὀμμάτων καὶ περιβολῇ καὶ κινήσει καὶ ταῖς κατὰ
τὸν βίον ἐνεργείαις. καὶ βρενθύεσθαι δὲ καὶ βρενθυόμενον
ὠνόμαζον καὶ ἔτι νῦν ὀνομάζουσιν — εἴτ᾽ ἀπὸ τοῦ παραδεδο-
μένου θυμιάματος ἢ μύρου τῶν θεῶν βρένθος, ὡς καθ᾽ ἡμᾶς
καὶ μίνθωνος ἀπὸ τῆς μίνθης, εἴτ᾽ ἀφ᾽ ὁτουδήποτε — τὸν
ἀπὸ τῆς εἰρημένης διαθέσεως κατεμβλέποντα πᾶσιν καὶ
παρεμβλέποντα καὶ τῇ κεφαλῇ κατασείοντα καὶ κατασμι-
κρίζοντα τοὺς ἀπαντῶντας ἢ τοὺς ὧν ἄν τις μνημονεύσῃ,
κἂν ὦσι τῶν μεγάλων εἶναι δοκούντων, μετὰ διασυρμοῦ καὶ
μόλις που βραχείας ἀποκρίσεως ὑπεροχὴν ἰδίαν ἐμφαινού-
σης, ἄλλου δ᾽ οὐδενὸς ἀριθμὸν ἐμποιούσης· οἷον ὁ Ἀριστοφάνης "ὅτι βρενθύει τ᾽ ἐν ταῖσιν ὁδοῖς καὶ τὠφθαλμὼ παρα-
βάλλεις" ἐκωμῴδει.

ὁ δ᾽ εἴρων ὡς ἐπὶ τὸ πλεῖστον ἀλαζόνος εἶδος ...

(XXII) διανοεῖ ... ος ... ον, ἀλλὰ καὶ τἀναντία μᾶλλον,
ὥστ᾽ ἐπαινεῖν ὃν ψέγει, ταπεινοῦν δὲ καὶ ψέγειν ἑαυτόν τε

ning to anyone they can find for help, and so they admit they are at the lowest level of all.

The arrogant man is also contemptuous; but the contemptuous man is not necessarily arrogant, and ...

(Column 21) ... since they praised the dignified man as possessing importance combined with some austerity, but the man who makes a show of dignity both then and now alike they mock, as an impersonator of the aforementioned, who for the mob pretends to be like this in his speech (they used to say he "preached"), the cast of his face and eyes, his dress, movements and way of life. And "high-falutin"[1] behavior (*brenthuesthai*) or personality — whether from the well-known incense or perfume of the gods called *brenthos* (just as modern *minthon* from mint), or from whatever else — is what they used to call, and still do call, a man who looks down on everyone, avoids their sight, tosses his head, belittles whoever meets him or whom anyone mentions to him, even from the elite, with ridicule and scarcely even a brief retort to express his own superiority and dismiss everyone else. Just as Aristophanes joked: "Since you act high-falutin on the street, and avert your eyes."[2]

... *The dissembler*[3] *is for the most part a type of fraud* ...

(Col. 22) ... *he intends* ... *but rather the opposite, so that he praises a man he finds fault with, but belittles and faults*

---

[1] An Aristophanic expression for pride, of obscure origin.

[2] *Clouds* 362, of Socrates.

[3] The literal meaning, "ironic man," is better suited to the description here than in *Character* 1 of Theophrastus.

THEOPHRASTUS

καὶ τοὺς <...> οἷός ἐστιν εἰωθέναι πρὸς ὁνδήποτε χρόνον
μετὰ παρεμφάσεως ὧν βούλεται· συνεπινοεῖται δ᾽ αὐτῷ καὶ
δεινότης ἐν τῷ πλάσματι καὶ πιθανότης· ἔστιν δὲ τοιοῦτος
οἷος τὰ πολλὰ μωκᾶσθαι καὶ μορφάζειν καὶ μειδιᾶν καὶ ὑπα-
νίστασθαί τισιν ἐπιστᾶσιν ἄφνω μετ᾽ ἀναπηδήσεως καὶ
ἀποκαλύψεως· μαὶ μέχρι πολλοῦ συνὼν ἐνίοις σιωπᾶν· κἂν
ἐπαινῇ τις αὐτὸν ἢ κελεύῃ τι λέγειν ἢ μνημονευθήσεσθαι
φῶσιν αὐτόν, ἐπιφωνεῖν· "ἐγὼ γὰρ οἶδα τί πλήν γε τούτου,
ὅτι οὐδὲν οἶδα;" καὶ "τίς γὰρ ἡμῶν λόγος;" καὶ "εἰ δή τις
ἡμῶν ἔσται μνεία·" καὶ πολὺς εἶναι τῷ "μακάριοι τῆς
φύσεως εἰ δή τινες" ἢ "τῆς δυνάμεως" ἢ "τῆς τύχης." καὶ μὴ
ψιλῶς ὀνομάζειν, ἀλλὰ "Φαῖδρος ὁ καλός," καὶ "Λυσίας ὁ
σοφός," καὶ ῥήματ᾽ ἀμφίβολα τιθέναι, "χρηστόν," "ἡδύν,"
"ἀφελῆ," "γενναῖον," "ἀνδρεῖον·" καὶ παρεπιδείκνυσθαι μὲν
ὡς σοφά, προσάπτειν δ᾽ ἑτέροις ὡς Ἀσπασίᾳ καὶ Ἰσχομάχῳ
Σωκράτης· καὶ πρὸς τοὺς ἐκ τῶν ἀρχαιρεσιῶν ἀπολυομέ-
νους· "ἐδοκιμ...

(XXIII) ... θεων ... μοι· πάντα γὰρ δεινὸς σὺ κατεργάσα-
σθαι." κἂν συνέλθῃ, τὸν καταπληττόμενον ἐμφαίνειν τό τε
εἶδος καὶ τὴν ἀξίαν καὶ τὸν λόγον πρὸς τοὺς συγκαθημένους
θαυμάζοντα, καὶ προσκαλούμενος εἰς κοινολογίαν φοβεῖσθαι
καὶ τἀλάχιστα φάσκειν ἄπορα καταφαίνεσθ᾽ ἑαυτῷ, καὶ δια-
γελάσαντος· "ὀρθῶς μου καταφρονεῖς τηλικοῦτος ὤν, καὶ

192

*himself and those <...>*[1] *is the sort who is accustomed to do on all occasions, merely hinting at what he desires. In his fabrications one can discern a cleverness and persuasiveness as well. He is the sort who often mocks, grimaces, smiles, and for people in authority he rises to yield his place suddenly, with a leap and uncovering his head. With some people he remains silent, even though he has spent a long time with them. If one praises him or bids him speak or people say that he will be remembered, he responds: "What am I supposed to know, except that I know nothing?" or "Of what importance am I?" or "In the event that anyone remembers me." And he constantly calls people "Blessed, if any are, in their nature," or their "capability," or "fortune." He doesn't call people merely by their names, but "fair Phaedrus," or "wise Lysias," or uses ironic words: "good," "sweet," "simple," "noble," "brave." He shows off thoughts he thinks wise, but attributes them to others as Socrates does with Aspasia and Ischomachus.*[2] *To those who have been eliminated from the elections...*

*(Column 23) ... "You're adept at carrying out everything."*[3] *And if he meets him, to those sitting nearby he reveals himself awestruck with admiration of his appearance, his dignity and speech. When he is asked to share his ideas he is terrified, and says that even the smallest difficulties seem to him impossible, and when the man mocks him he says "A man like you is right to feel contempt for me—I feel it for*

[1] The text is corrupt; probably several words are missing.

[2] In the dialogues *Menexenus* (by Plato) and *Oeconomicus* (by Xenophon).

[3] This paragraph seems to describe the dissembler's ironic treatment of one particular individual.

γὰρ αὐτὸς ἐμαυτοῦ." καὶ "νέος ὤφελον εἶναι καὶ μὴ γέρων,
ἵν' ἐμαυτὸν ὑπέταξά σοι." κἂν τῶν συμπαρόντων του ὁτιδήποτε εἰπόντος ἐκδήλως, ἐκεῖνος εἴπῃ τοιοῦτον· "διὰ τί
λέγεις;" ἐπιφωνεῖν τὰς χεῖρας ἀνατείνας· "ὡς ταχὺ
συνῆκας, ἀλλ' ἀφυὴς ἐγὼ καὶ βραδὺς καὶ δυσαίσθητος." καὶ
προσέχειν μὲν διαλεγομένῳ καὶ ἐγχάσκειν, εἶθ' ὑποκιναιδεῖν
καὶ διανεύειν ἄλλοις, ποτὲ δ' ἀνακαγχάζειν·

οἷος δὲ καὶ πρὸς οὓς ἔτυχεν ὁμιλῶν "διασαφεῖτέ μοι τὰς
ἐμὰς ἀγραμματίας καὶ τὰς ἄλλας ἀστοχίας ὑμεῖς, ὦ φίλοι,
καὶ μὴ περιορᾶτ' ἀσχημονοῦντα." καὶ "οὐ διηγήσεσθέ μοι τὰς
τοῦ δεῖνος εὐημερίας, ἵνα χαίρω, κἂν ἄρα δυνατὸς ὦ μιμῶ-
μαι;" καὶ τί δεῖ τὰ πλείω λέγειν; ἅπαντα γὰρ τὰ Σωκρατικὰ
μνημονεύματα . . .

(XXIV) . . . ὅμοιοι δ' εὐτελιστὴς ἢ ἐξευτελιστὴς καὶ οὐδενω-
τὴς ἢ ἐξουδενωτὴς καὶ ἐπὶ ταὐτὸ φέρονται, διαφέροντες
ἀνέσει καὶ ἐπιτάσει διαβολῆς τοῦ πλησίον· ὁ μὲν γὰρ ἐξευτελιστὴς ἀπόντων τινὰ φαυλότερον δὴ δοκεῖν παρίστησιν, ὁ
δ' ἐξουδενωτὴς ἴσον τῷ μηδενί. λοιπὸν ἔστιν μὲν ὅτε τοι-
οῦτοί τινές εἰσιν ὑπεροχὴν ἐμφαίνοντες ἰδίαν ἢ τῶν <καὶ
τῶν>[1] οὓς ἀποσεμνύουσιν, ἔστιν δ' ὅτε κατατρέχοντες
μόνον ἐνίων· ὥστε τοὺς προτέρους καὶ ὑπερηφάνους εἶναι·
διὸ καὶ δῆλον ὅτι φησὶν ἐπακολουθεῖν αὐτοῖς τὰ δι' ἐκείνην
ἄτοπα καὶ περιττότερόν τι τῇ διαβλητικῇ καὶ βασκαντικῇ
καὶ φθονητικῇ. καὶ τὸν ὑπομνηματισμὸν δὲ τοῦτον αὐτοῦ
καταπαύσομεν, ἐπισυνάψομεν δ' αὐτῷ τὸν περὶ τῶν ἄλλων
κακιῶν ὧν δοκιμάζομεν ποιεῖσθαι λόγον.

---

[1] Supplevi (ἢ τῶν οὓς papyrus).

myself." And "I wish I were young and not old, so I could sit at your feet." When someone in the group makes any sort of obvious comment, if that man says something like "What makes you say that?" he exclaims with upraised hands "How quickly you have grasped it! I've been dull, slow, stupid!" When the man converses he is intent and open-mouthed, then he talks mincingly and nods to others, and sometimes bursts out laughing.

He is the sort who says to whoever he happens to be talking to, "Friends, you must explain to me my ignorance and other blunders, and not let me make a fool of myself"; or "Please tell me about so-and-so's happy state, so that I may have the pleasure of being like him, if I can." Why go on? All the memoirs about Socrates . . .

(Column 24) *The disparager and the utter disparager, and the vilifier and the utter vilifier are the same and amount to the same thing, differing only in whether their slander of their neighbor is relaxed or intense: the utter disparager suggests that a person then absent doesn't seem very significant; the utter vilifier, that he is worthless.* Well, they are sometimes this way because they are hinting at their own superiority, or of this or that group they are praising; sometimes it is only because they run certain people down. The former are therefore arrogant as well; thus it is obvious that he[1] says they are beset by the strange things arrogance produces, and somewhat more abundantly [than the arrogant man] because of slander, malignity and envy.

And here we shall end this excerpt from him [Ariston], and append to it one about the other vices which we are attempting to treat.

[1] Ariston.

# HERODAS

*MIMES*

EDITED AND TRANSLATED BY
I. C. CUNNINGHAM

# INTRODUCTION

In the first half of the fourth century the city-states of Greece continued, as for generations past, their self-destructive warring. Athens, Sparta, Thebes — each in turn achieved and lost brief supremacies. When a new power began to emerge in the north, it was regarded as something to be used, as they had previously used the Persian and other eastern powers, to help defeat whoever was the current chief rival. But Macedonia under Philip II proved to be very different. With a mixture of cunning diplomacy and military might Philip advanced southwards into Thessaly; by the middle of the century he was a power to be reckoned with, a position recognised by his presidency of the Pythian Games in 346. His progress was temporarily impeded by an alliance led by Athens under the orator Demosthenes. But his victory at the battle of Chaeroneia in 339 left him overlord of all Greece. He began to organise it into a confederacy led by Macedonia, with the aim of renewing the age-old struggle with Persia. However in 336 he was assassinated in obscure circumstances, and the kingship and leadership of Greece passed to his son, known to history as Alexander the Great.

After a short period spent in consolidating his position in Greece, in Thrace, and in Illyria, Alexander in 334 turned to Asia. In rapid succession he conquered Asia Minor, defeated the Persian king Darius at Issus, overran Syria and Egypt, advanced into Babylonia, defeated Darius again at Gaugamela, and conquered Persia itself. At the beginning of 330 he rested briefly in the Persian palace, then pursued Darius to Ecbatana; Darius was overthrown in a coup and murdered. Alexander now continued east into modern Afghanistan and the southern Soviet Union, spending some time in Samarkand; then south into Pakistan. He would have gone on but his weary army had had enough. At the end of 324 he returned to Babylon. Six months later he fell ill and died.

Alexander took Greek culture and language with him, but inevitably they evolved in their new surroundings. Greek colonists settled all over the lands of his conquests. Cities called Alexandria were left behind as he marched. He created the first European empire. But it scarcely survived him. In the absence of a recognised successor his generals battled for supremacy and the empire fell apart. India was soon given up. Macedonia, Syria and Egypt emerged as the most powerful kingdoms, which for a century and a half re-enacted the feuding of the old city-states. The rising power of Rome was more and more drawn into their disputes and ended by absorbing all into its empire.

In the fourth century, poetry in Greece was totally overshadowed by the refined and polished prose of orators, philosophers and historians. Only comedy continued a live verse tradition. But in the following century there was a brief revival, mostly centred on the capital of Egypt, Alexandria. Founded by Alexander in 331, it became the capital of the Egyptian kingdom and dynasty of the Ptolemies. In the 280s Ptolemy II, known as Philadelphus, set up both the celebrated Library, into which were collected texts of all Greek literature, and the Museum, a university or research institute rather than a museum in the modern sense. To these were attracted a host of scholars and literary figures, and in this highly intellectual atmosphere flourished the poetry now known as Alexandrian or Hellenistic.

Some authors used traditional genres in a new way, such as Apollonius with his long epic the *Argonautica*. But more typical is the short poem, whether equally traditional in genre like the epyllia of Callimachus and Theocritus; or using old forms for new purposes, like the hymns and iambs of Callimachus; or introducing subjects new to poetry, like the mimiambs of Herodas and the mime-related poems of Theocritus. Common to all is the fact that this is learned poetry, composed by and intended for those who were familiar with earlier literature, recondite myths, obscure words, unusual metres. Poetry was the companion of studies in the Library and the Museum.

## HERODAS AND HIS WORK

No biographical information about the poet has come down from antiquity. Those who quote a few lines of his work (see under Text) variously give his name as Herodas (Ἡρώδας, a later form of Ἡρώιδας), Herodes (Ἡρώδης) or Herondas (Ἡρώνδας). The first and third are Doric, the second presumably a normalisation to the Attic form. The forms with and without the *n* are both possible, but the evidence for the latter is slightly greater.

Pliny the Younger (see end of this section) mentions him in conjunction with Callimachus, in such a way that it is possible that they were contemporaries. This is confirmed by a few internal references. The fourth mimiamb can be dated to between about 280 (as Apelles, mentioned in the past in lines 72–78, must have died before then) and 265 (as the sons of Praxiteles, mentioned in the present in lines 25–26, must have died by then). The first must be after, probably soon after, 272/1 (by which date Ptolemy II and Arsinoe, who have a shrine in line 30, were deified). The second is probably earlier than 266 (by which date the city of Ake, mentioned in line 16, had been renamed Ptolemaïs). Herodas' poetical activity can therefore be assigned to the late 270s and early 260s, exactly the period of Callimachus and of Theocritus, the high point of Hellenistic poetry.

The second mimiamb is undoubtedly set in the

island of Cos in the Dodecanese, and the temple of
Asklepios in the fourth may be that in Cos (though
there is no coincidence between the works of art
mentioned in that poem and those known to have
been in that temple). The connected sixth and
seventh appear to be located in Asia Minor (the
month Taureon in 7.86 suggests that, as does
Kerdon's origin in either Chios or Erythrae, 6.58).
Egypt is highly praised in 1.26–35; and the phrase
'Attic minae' in 2.22 may indicate that this was
written within the Ptolemaic empire (the Attic
silver standard being universal, and the adjective
therefore needless, everywhere else).

The evidence may be summarised: Doric in origin, living in the first half of the third century, connected to a greater or lesser extent with Egypt, Cos
and Asia Minor.

His poems are typical of their place and time in
that they combine the content of one older genre
with the form of another. This is indicated by their
name (recorded by several of the ancient quotations), mimiambs: they are both mimes and iambs.

The Greek mime was a popular entertainment in
which one actor or a small group portrayed a situation from everyday life in the lower levels of society,
concentrating on depiction of character rather than
on plot. Situations were occasionally borrowed from
comedy. Indecency was frequent. Ancient writers
mention a great variety of sub-types, the details of
which are obscure. Some had a musical accompani-

ment; of one such group we are told possible subjects: 'sometimes women who are adulteresses and procuresses, sometimes a man drunk and going on a revel to his lover'.[1] Some performers shared booths in the market-place with conjurers, dancers and the like; others played at private parties. Individual mimes could act several parts in a piece when necessary. The normal vehicle was prose and the spoken language.

A few fragments of or relating to such performances have been found in texts from Egypt dating from the second century B.C. to the fifth A.D.[2] Only one writer is known by name, Sophron of Syracuse, of the late fifth century B.C., whose mimes were introduced to Athens by Plato. But full texts have not survived, and most of the fragments quoted by later writers were selected for grammatical interest, so that we know little of the nature of his work. However it can be said that he wrote in his native Doric dialect and in prose, and his subjects are apparently all realistic.

The iamb was a genre of seventh- and sixth-century Ionia. Named from its characteristic metre,

[1] Athenaeus 14. 621 c (Loeb edition: vol. VI, page 347).

[2] The texts of most of these are in the appendix of the present editor's Teubner edition of Herodas, Leipzig 1987; add P.Oxy. 3700. Several are translated in the Loeb *Select Papyri*, vol. 3, Literary Papyri, Poetry, ed. D. L. Page, 1941 (but note that the obscene beginning of no. 77, P.Oxy. 413 verso, is omitted).

the iambic trimeter, it is personal and realistic, full of immediate loves and hates. Archilochus and Hipponax are the major names, but no complete poems have survived. Archilochus came from the island of Paros, Hipponax from Ephesus; both used their vernacular languages. Hipponax increased the coarse, sneering effect of his verse by using the so-called 'limping iambic' (choliambos), where the second-last element of the line is long instead of short.

Herodas took his subject-matter from the mime. Only in the case of the fifth mimiamb is there an exact parallel in the mime tradition; but the first and second have characters which are known to have figured in the tradition; and the situation of the fourth and subject of the sixth appeared in Sophron. And the treatment is invariably that of the mime: characters from the urban proletariat in realistic settings and situations, and character-depiction more important than plot.

But there is a crucial difference in the form. His language and verse are, as far as we can tell, a slightly imperfect rendering of those of Hipponax. The qualification is necessary because we have so little of the latter's work and because of the possibility of corruption in our texts of both Hipponax and Herodas and in Herodas' text of Hipponax. The imperfections in his rendering consist of a few false Ionic forms and a few non-Ionic (Attic and Doric) words; the not infrequent occurrence of common Greek (Attic) forms is almost certainly due to corruption. The most striking features of the dialect, which differentiate it from most literary Ionic, are the use of κ for π in interrogative and indefinite pronouns and adjectives (κοῦ, κοῖος etc.) and the absence of aspiration at the beginnning of words (psilosis), both of which are sporadically but unmistakably indicated by the papyrus. In his versification Herodas, probably following Hipponax, is far freer than most Greek writers in allowing a long vowel at the end of a word to be followed by one at the beginning of the next, the whole counting as only one long syllable; this may either be indicated in writing (crasis; e.g. μἤλασσον = μὴ ἔλασσον) or not (synaloephe; e.g. μέσωι ἔστω). He resolves long syllables into two shorts (creating anapaests, dactyls or tribrachs in place of iambs) not infrequently, and rarely admits anaclasis (–◡◡– for ◡‒–◡–).

Mimes were recited either by one actor, taking several parts if necessary, or by a small troupe. There has been much discussion as to which method Herodas used. Certainty is unattainable, but it seems unlikely that a troupe with costumes and sets would be assembled for such brief pieces, whose performance is unlikely to have been frequently repeated.[3]

Herodas' work is typically Hellenistic. The

[3] See my review in *Journal of Hellenic Studies* 101 (1981), 161, of G. Mastromarco, *Il Pubblico di Eronda*, 1979 (English translation, *The Public of Herondas*, 1984), who takes the opposite view.

poems are short. The subjects are new to poetry, remote from the experience of the intellectual audience. The language and metre are revivals of obsolete forms. It is clear from the eighth mimiamb that he met with criticism in his own day, but the text is so badly preserved that it cannot be ascertained (if it was clearly stated in the first place) who the critics were or what they objected to.

In the same poem Herodas anticipated fame for himself, but that was not to be. Texts were still to be had in Egypt in the second century A.D., though whether these represent the end of a continuous interest or a revival is unknown. A few sententious lines were taken into the anthological tradition which we know under the name of John of Stoboi (Stobaeus) (see 1.15–16, 67–68; 6.37–39; 10; 12; 13), while one of his many proverbs is in the collection of Zenobius (see 3.10). Grammarians picked up a few unusual words or forms (see 5.32; 8.59–60; 11). But the later Greek literary and biographical sources know nothing of him. The only person known to have read him as literature is Roman: Pliny the Younger about 100 A.D. compliments his friend Arrius Antoninus on his Greek epigrams and mimiambs—'What an amount of elegance and beauty is in them, how sweet they are, and pleasing and bright and correct. I thought I was reading Callimachus or Herodes, or better if such exists.'[4]

---

[4] *Epp.* 4.3.3: *quantum ibi humanitatis, uenustatis, quam dulcia illa, quam amantia, quam arguta, quam*

In the century since he again became known he has excited considerable interest, often for the wrong reasons: despite appearances, he is no 'ancient realist', but a highly literary writer with a similarly elite audience.

## THE MIMIAMBS

1. *A Matchmaker or Procuress.* Metriche, companion of Mandris who has been for some considerable time absent in Egypt, is alone with her slave Threissa. She is visited by her old nurse, Gyllis, the matchmaker of the title. The reason for the visit is approached obliquely: Mandris, tempted by the attractions of Egypt, has gone for good; Metriche will be old before she realises it and should enjoy herself while she can. Then she comes to the point: the athlete Gryllos is desperately in love with Metriche and will not leave Gyllis alone; Metriche should yield to him. Metriche firmly rejects the proposition: she is faithful to Mandris. This little drama is framed by the domestic scene, the arrival and the hospitality before departure.

The characterisation of the matchmaker is the purpose of the piece. This was one of the subjects of the popular mime.

2. *A Brothel-keeper.* Battaros the brothel-keeper

---

*recta. Callimachum me uel Heroden uel si quid melius tenere credebam.*

lives in Cos, a resident alien. He claims that a sea
captain Thales has attacked his house in an attempt
to abduct Myrtale, one of his girls. In Greek courts
complainants and defendants had to represent
themselves, and the mimiamb consists of Battaros'
speech to the jury. He depicts himself as poor and
humble, providing a necessary service to the com-
munity, and grossly abused by Thales. But this is a
charade, and the greed, shamelessness and indecency normally considered typical of his profession
constantly break through. He attempts to follow the
usual pattern of a legal speech (known to us from
the fourth-century Attic orators), but is regularly
diverted from his theme and repeats himself endlessly.

An incoherent orator appeared in Sophron. The
brothel-keeper is a regular character in Middle and
New Comedy.

3. *A Schoolmaster.* Metrotime brings her delin-
quent son Kottalos to the schoolmaster Lampriskos
for punishment. She narrates his wrongdoings:
gambling in bad company, neglect of his studies,
damage to the roof of the building in which they
live, generally leading a lazy and worthless life.
Lampriskos agrees that a beating is required and
with the assistance of other pupils proceeds to inflict
it. The boy pleads for mercy and promises to reform,
but when released is apparently still impudent.
Metriche angrily goes off to get fetters for him.

Despite the title Metriche is the dominant character in the piece, as she obviously is in her household.

4. *Women dedicating and sacrificing to Asklepios.* The two women, with their slaves, come to the temple early in the morning to thank the god for curing an illness. After praying and giving the sacrificial cock to the temple-attendant, they inspect the sculptures and paintings which can be seen. One of them is a stranger and exclaims excitedly at what she sees. The other acts as guide and makes a vigorous defence of the art of the painter Apelles. Finally the success of the sacrifice is announced and arrangements are made for the distribution of the sacrifice—as in 1 the central scene is placed in a frame.

The description of works of art is common in Greek literature, from the shield of Achilles in the *Iliad* on. One of Sophron's mimes was entitled 'Women watching the Isthmian Festival'. Theocritus, *Idyll* 15, roughly contemporary with this poem of Herodas and also related to the mime, includes a description of a tapestry concerning Adonis. Here the observers are poor, unsophisticated women, whose sole criterion of excellence is naturalness.

5. *A Jealous Person.* Bitinna has a sexual relationship with her slave Gastron, whom she accuses in crude terms of infidelity. Rejecting both pleas of innocence and appeals for mercy, she orders that he should be flogged, and on second thoughts tattooed

also. But her anger, though vehemently expressed, is not implacable, and when another slave Kydilla, whom she regards more as a daughter, intercedes on Gastron's behalf, she is prepared to remit his punishment, at least for the present.

The situation is not dissimilar to that of the mime-fragment P.Oxy. 413 verso (see above, note 2), though Bitinna is mild by comparison with the protagonist of that violent piece.

6. *Women in a Friendly or Private Situation.* Metro visits her friend Koritto to enquire who made her the red dildo. Koritto is astonished that she knows of this and asks where she saw it. On learning that Euboule had lent it to Nossis, she complains bitterly of her false friend. Metro consoles her and again asks who made it. Koritto tells her that it was Kerdon and describes him and his skill; she explains why she was unable to get a second dildo from him. Metro further learns that more can be discovered of the cobbler from Artemeis, and departs to see her.

Dildos are at least mentioned in Sophron.

7. *A Cobbler.* Metro brings some other ladies to Kerdon's shop. He shows them his stock, with elaborate praise of his wares. There is some bargaining about prices. Kerdon fits some of the ladies with shoes and tells Metro to come back later. Kerdon has been described as the great craftsman in the previous poem; here he is the consummate salesman.

That Kerdon the cobbler of 6 and 7 is the same

person can hardly be doubted; it is equally certain that the Metro of both is the same, having by the dramatic date of 7 come to know and patronise Kerdon. It is therefore an obvious question if there is not also a continuity of subject; and in fact there are clear indications that Kerdon is still selling dildos as well as shoes, in the very high prices mentioned and in various remarks throughout (especially lines 62–63, 108–112, 127–129).

8. *A Dream.* The speaker, the poet himself, wakens his household and narrates and interprets his dream. It appears that he has participated in some kind of Dionysiac festival, with the sacrifice of a goat, the appearance of the god himself, and a contest in which the participants attempt to stand on an inflated wineskin. He wins this and is threatened by an old man; he replies and calls on a young man. He interprets the dream in relation to his poetry, which is represented by the goat: it is eaten, i.e. attacked by critics; probably he predicts future fame for himself.

The mutilated condition of the text is very unfortunate; if the dream and its interpretation had been better preserved, we should know more of Herodas' view of his own work and perhaps the identity and arguments of his critics. But the damage is so great that no certainty is possible.

9. *Women at Breakfast.* Clearly a domestic scene, perhaps recalling one in Sophron, but the few surviving words give no more detail.

10. *Molpinos.* The surviving fragment advocates avoiding the miseries of old age by death, a not infrequent wish in Greek literature. Here it may well be an aside rather than the subject. Molpinos will have been the main character, Gryllos another.

11. *Women working together.* The only surviving line appears to be erotic.

12 and 13, brief quotations from unknown poems, respectively describe a children's game and repeat a popular commonplace. Nothing is known of their contexts.

## TEXT AND EDITIONS

In 1891 F. G. Kenyon published a papyrus roll which had been discovered in Egypt and purchased by the British Museum.[5] It contains the first seven mimiambs of Herodas more or less complete (though the text is damaged from time to time by abrasions or holes); the eighth and the beginning of the ninth were later put together from fragments of papyrus. Presumably the other two whose names are known from quotations, and quite possibly more, have been totally lost from the end of the roll. The scribe writes a small, clear bookhand which can be ascribed to the early second century A.D. He has the orthographical peculiarity of frequently writing *ι* for *ει*. Words are not usually separated. In some

[5] Now British Library, Pap. 135. It is referred to as P.

difficult passages accents, breathings or punctuation marks are added. Changes of speaker are not marked by names but by the paragraphus, a short line placed under the first few letters of the verse in the middle of or after which the change occurs; this indication is not infrequently omitted. The scribe made or faithfully copied many mistakes; some he corrected himself in the course of writing, many more afterwards, doubtless having looked again at his model. A corrector, probably using a different copy, wrote in about three dozen corrections or variants, mostly in the first three poems. There is a handful of later annotations.

A small fragment of a second roll from later in the second century, discovered at Oxyrhynchus in Egypt, was published by E. Lobel in 1954[6] and recognised a year later by A. Barigazzi as the ends of 8.67–75. Its text is marginally worse than that of P.

Kenyon's first edition was little more than a transcript of P. Shortly afterwards W. G. Rutherford published his, which assigned the lines to their speakers and made some correct emendations (among a host of wild conjectures). Many other scholars made suggestions in periodicals for the reading, supplementing and interpretation of the

[6] *The Oxyrhynchus Papyri*, vol. 22, no. 2326; it is preserved in the Ashmolean Museum, Oxford, and is referred to as O.

new text, including F. Blass, O. Crusius, "F. D." (an unidentified English scholar), O. A. Danielsson, H. Diels, W. Headlam, H. van Herwerden, A. Palmer, H. Richards, and H. Stadtmüller. Editions and commentaries were produced by F. Bücheler (1892), O. Crusius (1892–1914), and R. Meister (1893; fundamental for the dialect). The work of this early period is summarised in the commentary of J. A. Nairn (1904).

Walter Headlam had spent years collecting material for a definitive commentary, but was prevented by his premature death from finally organising and publishing it. This task was undertaken by A. D. Knox, who contributed significantly to the restoration of 8. This edition (1922) is the only one of Herodas which will certainly have a lasting value beyond its immediate sphere, but for that sphere it has major defects, in particular the absence of typographical indications of supplements in the text. P. Groeneboom's French commentary on 1–6 (1922) is also important. Knox and R. Herzog continued to struggle with the problems of 8, and each finished by producing a text with translation: Herzog a revision of Crusius's German one (1926), Knox in the first Loeb edition a very idiosyncratic and unhelpful antique English one (1929). At the same time a French translation in the Budé series was done by H. Laloy, with text by Nairn (1928).

Later editors have followed the modern tendency of keeping the text much freer of uncertain supple-

ments: Q. Cataudella (1948; Italian translation),
G. Puccioni (1950; Italian commentary), L. Massa
Positano (mimiambs 1–4, 1970–3; Italian translation and commentary), I. C. Cunningham (1971;
English commentary), and B. G. Mandilaras (1978
and 1986; Modern Greek translation and commentary). The present editor's Teubner edition (1987)
has a full apparatus, bibliography and index.
Important modern books on the dialect are those of
D. Bo (*La Lingua di Eroda*, 1962) and V. Schmidt
(*Sprachliche Untersuchungen zu Herondas*, 1968);
on the production that of G. Mastromarco (see
above, note 3).

This edition largely repeats the text of the
Teubner one, but is somewhat less austere in print-
ing supplements in damaged passages; these are to
be understood as giving the likely sense, but not
necessarily the exact words lost. The apparatus
records only substantive variations from the
papyrus; corrections by the scribe and orthographical and dialectal modifications are not included.

# MIMES

# 1. ΠΡΟΚΥΚΛΙ[Σ] Η ΜΑΣΤΡΟΠΟΣ

(ΜΗ.)  Θ[ρέισ]ϛ᾽, ἀράσσει τὴν θύρην τις· οὐκ ὄψηι
      μ[ή] τ[ις] παρ᾽ ἡμέων ἐξ ἀγροικίης ἥκει;
(ΘΡ.)  τίς τ[ὴν] θύρην;
&lt;ΓΥ.&gt;             ἐγῶδε.
&lt;ΘΡ.&gt;                    τίς σύ; δειμαίνεις
      ἆσσον προσελθεῖν;
&lt;ΓΥ.&gt;               ἢν ἰδού, πάρειμ᾽ ἆσσον.
&lt;ΘΡ.&gt;  τίς δ᾽ εἶ&lt;ϛ&gt; σύ;
&lt;ΓΥ.&gt;            Γυλλίς, ἡ Φιλαινίδος μήτηρ.     5
      ἄγγειλον ἔνδον Μητρίχηι παρεῦσάν με.
&lt;ΘΡ.&gt;  καλεῖ —
&lt;ΜΗ.&gt;         τίς ἐστιν;

1 Θ[ρέισ]ϛ᾽ Rutherford, Bücheler
2 μ[ή] τ[ις] Blass
3 τ[ὴν] several    ΓΥ. ἐγῶδε (= ἐγὼ ἤδε) Blass
5 φιλαινίου in text, ·νιδος· in margin P
7 So divided by Danielsson: ΜΗ. κάλει ('Invite her in').
τίς ἐστιν; ΘΡ. Γυλλίς, ἀμμίη Γυλλίς Blass (but command and
question should be in the reverse order)

# 1. A MATCHMAKER OR PROCURESS

METRICHE

Th[reis]sa, someone is banging at the door. Go and see [if one] of our people from the country has come.

THREISSA

Who's at [the] door?

<GYLLIS>

It's I.

<THREISSA>

Who are you?  Are you afraid to come nearer?

<GYLLIS>

See, I have come nearer.

<THREISSA>

But who are you?

<GYLLIS>

Gyllis, Philaenis' mother.  Go in and tell Metriche that I am here.

<THREISSA>

There is a visitor —

<METRICHE>

Who is it?

&lt;ΘΡ.&gt;             Γυλλίς.

&lt;ΜΗ.&gt;                     ἀμμίη Γυλλίς.

στρέψον τι, δούλη. τίς σε μοῖρ' ἔπεισ' ἐλθεῖν,
Γυλλίς, πρὸς ἡμέας; τί σὺ θεὸς πρὸς ἀνθρώπους;
ἤδη γάρ εἰσι πέντε κου, δοκέω, μῆνες       10
ἐξ εὖ σε, Γυλλίς, οὐδ' ὄναρ, μὰ τὰς Μοίρας,
πρὸς τὴν θύρην ἐλθοῦσαν εἶδέ τις ταύτην.

(ΓΥ.) μακρὴν ἀποικέω, τέκνον, ἐν δὲ τῆις λαύρηις
ὁ πηλὸς ἄχρις ἰγνύων προσέστηκεν,
ἐγὼ δὲ δραίνω μυῖ' ὅσον· τὸ γὰρ γῆρας       15
ἡμέ‿ας καθέλκει κἠ σκιὴ παρέστηκεν.

[ΜΗ.] σίγη] δὲ καὶ μὴ τοῦ χρόνου καταψεύδεο·
οἵη τ' ἔτ'] εἰ&lt;ς&gt; γάρ, Γυλλί, κἠτέρους ἄγχειν.

(ΓΥ.) σίλλ‿α]‿ε· ταῦτα τῆις νεωτέρηις ὑμιν
πρόσεστιν.

&lt;ΜΗ.&gt;            ἀλλ' οὐ τοῦτο μή σε θερμήνηι.       20

&lt;ΓΥ.&gt; ἀλλ' ὦ τέκνον, κόσον τιν' ἤδη χηραίνεις
χρόνον μόνη τρύχουσα τὴν μίαν κοίτην;
ἐξ εὖ γὰρ εἰς Αἴγυπτον ἐστάλη Μάνδρις

---

15–16 are cited by Stobaeus, *Anth.* 4.50b.52, from
Herodas' Mimiambi, with minor corruptions

    17 σίγη] Bücheler     δὲ Cunningham

    18 οἵη τ' ἔτ'] (ε)ἶ Tucker

    20 Others give the whole line to Gyllis, 'but this will not
keep you warm'.

<THREISSA>

Gyllis.

<METRICHE>

Mama Gyllis! Leave us, slave. What fate has persuaded you, Gyllis, to come to us? Why are you here, a god to men? For it's now, I think, about five months since anyone saw you, Gyllis, coming to this door even in a dream, I swear it by the Fates.

GYLLIS

I live far off, child, and in the lanes the mud comes up to one's knees. And I have the strength of a fly; for old age weighs me down and the shadow is at hand.

[METRICHE]

[Be quiet] and do not bring false charges against your age. For [you are still able] to hug others, Gyllis.

GYLLIS

Joke away; that's typical of you younger ones.

<METRICHE>

Now don't let this heat you.

<GYLLIS>

Well, my child, how long now is it that you've been separated, wearing out your single bed alone? It's ten months since Mandris set off for Egypt, and

δέκ' εἰσὶ μῆνες, κοὐδὲ γράμμα σοι πέμπει,
ἀλλ' ἐκλέλησται καὶ πέπωκεν ἐκ καινῆς.          25
κεῖ δ' ἐστὶν οἶκος τῆς θεοῦ· τὰ γὰρ πάντα,
ὄσσ' ἔστι κου καὶ γίνετ', ἔστ' ἐν Αἰγύπτωι·
πλοῦτος, παλαίστρη, δύναμις, εὐδίη, δόξα,
θέαι, φιλόσοφοι, χρυσίον, νεηνίσκοι,
θεῶν ἀδελφῶν τέμενος, ὁ βασιλεὺς χρηστός,          30
Μουσῆιον, οἶνος, ἀγαθὰ πάντ' ὅσ' ἂν χρήιζηι,
γυναῖκες, ὀκόσους οὐ μὰ τὴν Ἅιδεω Κούρην
ἀστέρας ἐνεγκεῖν οὐραν[ὸ]ς κεκαύχηται,
τὴν δ' ὄψιν οἶαι πρὸς Πάριν κοτ' ὥρμησαν
θ]ε[αὶ κρ]ιθῆναι καλλονήν—λάθοιμ' αὐτάς          35
γρύξασ]α. κο[ί]ην οὖν τάλαιν[α] σὺ ψυχήν
ἔ]χο[υσ]α θάλπεις τὸν δίφρον; κατ' οὖν λήσεις
γηρᾶσα] καί σευ τὸ ὥριον τέφρη κάψει.
πάπτ]ηνον ἄλληι κἠμέρας μετάλλαξον
τὸ]ν νοῦν δύ' ἢ τρεῖς, κἰλαρὴ κατάστηθι          40
( . )......ις ἄλλον· νηῦς μιῆς ἐπ' ἀγκύρης
οὐκ] ἀσφαλὴς ὁρμεῦσα· κεῖνος ἢν ἔλθηι
..........].ν[.] μηδὲ εἷς ἀναστήσηι
ἠ]μέας .... τοδινα δ' ἄγριος χειμών
..[..............].. κοὐδὲ εἷς οἶδεν          45

31 χρήιζη<ις> Bücheler
32 τὴν Δεωκούρην ('daughter of Deo', i.e. of Demeter)
Meister

not a word does he send you; he has forgotten and
drunk from a new cup. The home of the goddess is
there. For everything in the world that exists and is
produced is in Egypt: wealth, wrestling schools,
power, tranquillity, fame, spectacles, philosophers,
gold, youths, the sanctuary of the sibling gods, the
King excellent, the Museum, wine, every good thing
he could desire, women, as many by Hades' Maid as
the stars that heaven boasts of bearing and as lovely
as [the goddesses] who once hastened to Paris to be
[judged] for beauty—may they not notice [what I
say]! What then, poor girl, [is in] your mind that
you are keeping your seat warm?[a] You will [become
old] before you know and ashes will gulp your
beauty. [Glance] elsewhere and for two or three
days change [your] purpose, and become cheerful
[                    ] another: a ship [is not] safe
riding at one anchor. If he comes [                    ]
no one shall raise us, dear, and a wild storm
[                    ], and none of us knows

---

[a] I.e. 'doing nothing'.

---

34 τὴν δ ὄψιν P, with το δ (ε)ἶδος written above by the
corrector

35 θεαὶ κρ]ιθῆναι Bücheler

36 γρύξασ]ᾳ Headlam

37 ἔ]χρ[υσ]ᾳ several

38 γηράσᾳ] Rutherford, Blass

39 πάπτ]ηνον Weil

43 ὁ πορφύρεος] Crusius     [οὐ] μηδὲ Richards

44 -το· δεινὰ seems preferable to · τὸ δεῖνα; but with the
latter φίλη (Bell) may precede

223

τὸ μέλλο]ν ἡμέων· ἄστατος γὰρ ἀνθρώποις
......]..η[.]s. ἀλλὰ μήτις ἔστηκε
σύνεγγυς ἦμιν;

<MH.>                    οὐδὲ ε[ἷ]ς.

<ΓΥ.>                         ἄκουσον δή
ἄ σοι χρε[ί]ζουσ’ ὧδ’ ἔβην ἀπαγγεῖλαι·
ὁ Ματαλίνης τῆς Παταικίου Γρύλλος,          50
ὁ πέντε νικέων ἆθλα, παῖς μὲν ἐν Πυθοῖ,
δὶς δ’ ἐν Κορίνθωι τοὺς ἴουλον ἀνθεῦντας,
ἄνδρας δὲ Πίσηι δὶς καθεῖλε πυκτεύσας,
πλουτέων τὸ καλόν, οὐδὲ κάρφος ἐκ τῆς γῆς
κινέων, ἄθικτος ἐς Κυθηρίην σφρηγίς,          55
ἰδών σε καθόδωι τῆς Μίσης ἐκύμηνε
τὰ σπλάγχν’ ἔρωτι καρδίην ἀνοιστρηθείς,
καί μευ οὔτε νυκτὸς οὔτ’ ἐπ’ ἡμέρην λείπει
τὸ δῶμα, [τέ]κνον, ἀλλά μευ κατακλαίει
καὶ ταταλ[ί]ζει καὶ ποθέων ἀποθνήισκει.      60
ἀλλ’, ὦ τέκνον μοι Μητρίχη, μίαν ταύτην
ἁμαρτίην δὸς τῆι θεῶι· κατάρτησον
σαυτήν, τὸ [γ]ῆρας μὴ λάθηι σε προσβλέψαν.
καὶ δοιὰ πρήξεις· ἡδέω[ν] τε[ύ]ξ[ει] κ[αί σοι
δοθήσεταί τι μέζον ἢ δοκεῖς· σκέψαι,          65

46 τὸ μέλλο]ν several
50 ματακινης P, with λ written above κ by the corrector

224

[the future]; for [          is] unstable for men. But is there anyone near us?

<METRICHE>

No one.

<GYLLIS>

Then listen to what I came here wishing to tell you: Gryllos, son of Pataekion's Mataline, winner of five prizes—as a boy at Pytho, twice at Korinthos over the downy-cheeked youths, while he brought down men twice at Pisa[a]—quite well off, but not moving even a straw from the earth,[b] an untouched seal as far as Kytheria[c] is concerned, on seeing you at the Descent of Mise[d] seethed inside, stung to the heart with love, and neither at night nor throughout the day does he leave my house, child, but wails at me and calls me mama and is dying of desire. Now, Metriche my child, allow the goddess this one fault; dedicate yourself, in case old age sees you unexpectedly. You will gain two benefits: [you will get] pleasure [and] something greater than you expect will be given [to you]. Consider, do as I say;

[a] In the Pythian, Isthmian and Olympic games respectively.

[b] Proverbial expression for a quiet person; also used in 4.67.

[c] Aphrodite.

[d] Festival representing a descent (into Hades) of this minor goddess.

---

64 ἠδέω[ν] τς[ύ]ξ[ει] κ[αί σοι Headlam

πείσθητί μευ· φιλέω σε, να[ὶ] μὰ τὰς Μοίρας.

(ΜΗ.)  Γυλλί, τὰ λευκὰ τῶν τριχῶν ἀπαμβλύνει
τὸν νοῦν· μὰ τὴν γὰρ Μάνδριος κατάπλωσιν
καὶ τὴν φίλην Δήμητρα, ταῦτ' ἐγὼ [ἐ]ξ ἄλλης
γυναικὸς οὐκ ἂν ἡδέως ἐπήκουσα,        70
χωλὴν δ' ἀείδειν χώλ' ἂν ἐξεπαίδευσα
καὶ τῆς θύρης τὸν οὐδὸν ἐχθρὸν ἡγεῖσθαι.
σὺ δ' αὖτις ἔς με μηδὲ ἔν<α>, φίλη, τοῖον
φέρουσα χώρει μῦθον· ὂν δὲ γρήιησι
πρέπει γυναιξὶ τῆις νέηις ἀπάγγελλε·      75
τὴν Πυθέω δὲ Μητρίχην ἔα θάλπειν
τὸν δίφρον· οὐ γὰρ ἐγγελᾶι τις εἰς Μάνδριν.
ἀλλ' οὐχὶ τούτων, φασί, τῶν λόγων Γυλλίς
δεῖται· Θρέισσα, τὴν μελαινίδ' ἔκτριψον
κἠκτημόρους τρεῖς ἐγχέας[α τ]οῦ ἀκρήτου  80
καὶ ὕδωρ ἐπιστάξασα δὸς πιεῖν.

(ΓΥ.)                     καλῶς.

(ΜΗ.)  τῆ, Γυλλί, πῖθι.

<ΓΥ.>           δεῖξον οὐ[.].......πα.[
πείσουσά σ' ἦλθον, ἀλλ' ἔκητι τῶν ἰρῶν.

67–68 are cited by Stobaeus, *Anth.* 4.50b.59, from Herodas' Mimiambi, with γύναι for Γυλλί

73 ἔν<α> Blass

79 In the margin is what appears to be a gloss on μελαινίδα: κυλ(ίκων) γέ(νος) εὐ(τελές)

I love you, I swear it by the Fates.

METRICHE

Gyllis, the whiteness of your hair is blunting
your mind; for by Mandris' return and dear Demeter
I should not have heard this cheerfully from another
woman, but should have taught her to sing her lame
song with a limp and to find the threshold of my
door a hostile place. See that you do not come again
to me, my friend, with any such tale, but repeat to
your young girls one which suits old crones. And let
Metriche, daughter of Pytheas, keep her seat warm;
for no one laughs at Mandris. But it is not these
words, they say, that Gyllis needs; Threissa, wipe
the cup clean and give her a drink, pouring in half of
wine and a splash of water.

GYLLIS

No, thanks.

METRICHE

Here, Gyllis, drink.

<GYLLIS>

Show.[a]   I   did   not   come   to   persuade   you
[                    ], but because of the rites.

[a] The meaning is not clear: perhaps explained by the
lost end of the verse. 'Give it me' (Knox) is an unsupported
rendering.

---

81 ΓΥ. καλῶς Headlam

## HERODAS

&lt;ΜΗ.&gt;  ὦν οὕνεκέν μοι, Γυλλί, ὦνα[

&lt;ΓΥ.&gt;  οσσοῦ γένοιτο, μᾶ, τέκνον π[.]..........  85
ἡδύς γε · ναὶ Δήμητρα, Μητρ[ί]χη, τούτου
ἡδίον᾽ οἶνον Γυλλὶς οὐ πέ[π]ωκέν [κω.
σὺ δ᾽ εὐτύχει μοι, τέκνον, ἀσ[φα]λίζευ [δέ
σαυτήν · ἐμοὶ δὲ Μυρτάλη τε κ[αὶ] Σίμη
νέαι μένοιεν, ἔστ᾽ ἂν ἐμπνέῃ[ι] Γυλλίς.  90

84–85 Division among speakers and readings are
doubtful

## MIME 1

<METRICHE>

On account of which to me, Gyllis, [

].

<GYLLIS>

†        † may be, ah, child, [                              ]
sweet; by Demeter, Metriche, Gyllis has never
before drunk sweeter wine than this. Farewell,
child, [and] look after yourself; but may my Myrtale
and Sime[a] remain young, as long as Gyllis breathes.

[a] Typical names of courtesans.

## 2. ΠΟΡΝΟΒΟΣΚΟΣ

(ΒΑ.) ἄνδρες δικασταί, τῆς γενῆς μ[ὲ]ν οὐκ ἐστέ
ἡμέων κριταὶ δήκουθεν οὐδὲ [τ]ῆς δόξης,
οὐδ' εἰ Θαλῆς μὲν οὗτος ἀξίην τὴ[ν] νηῦν
ἔχει ταλάντων πέντ', ἐγὼ δὲ μ[η]δ' ἄρτους,
....] ὑπερέξει Βάτταρόν [τι π]ημήνας·          5
πολλο]ῦ γε καὶ δ(ε)ῖ· [τ]ὠλυκὸν γὰρ [ἂν] κλαύσαι
....].ιησομαστοσηιασ[..]νχωρη
....].σμε..ι.. ἐστὶ τῆς [πό]λιος κἠγώ,
καὶ ζ]ῶμεν οὐκ ὡς βουλό[με<σ>]θ' ἀλλ' ὡς ἡμέας
ὁ και]ρὸς ἕλκει. προστάτην [ἔχ]ει Μεννῆν,   10
ἐγ]ὼ δ' Ἀριστοφῶντα· πὺξ [νε]νίκηκεν
Μεν]νῆς, ['Αρισ]τοφῶν δὲ κ[ἤτι] νῦν ἄγχει·
κεἰ μ]ή ἐστ' ἀ[λη]θέα ταῦτα, το[ῦ ἡ]λίου δύντος
ἐξε]λθέτω[...]ων ἄνδρες .[..]χε χλαῖναν

5 δίκηι] Crusius
6 πολλο]ῦ γε καὶ δ(ε)ῖ Milne      [τ]ὠλυκὸν γὰρ [ἂν] κλαύσαι
Knox
7 supplements and word-division are quite uncertain
8 κοὖτ]ος μέτοικος F.D.

230

# 2. A BROTHEL-KEEPER

BATTAROS

Gentlemen of the jury, certainly you are not judges of our family or reputation; nor, if the defendant Thales has a ship worth five talents and I not even bread, shall he prevail [          ] and harm Battaros. [Far from it:] for he would weep bitterly [                    ]a of the city, as I am, [and] we live not as we wish but as [the moment] compels us. He [has] Mennes as patron, [I] have Aristophon: Mennes has won with his fists, but Aristophon can [even] now wrestle; [if] this is not true, after sunset (          ) come out,b gentlemen, [     ] cloak [                    ] he will

---

a The meaning of line 7 is quite uncertain. Line 8 may begin 'He too is an alien'.

b This may be said to the jury, 'come out', or of Thales, 'let him come out'.

---

9 καὶ ζ]ῶμεν Headlam     βουλό[με<σ>]θ' Crusius
10 ὁ καὶ]ρὸς Stadtmüller     [ἔχ]ει Milne
12 Μεν]νῆς Crusius     ['Αρισ]τοφῶν Headlam     κ[ῆτι]
Bücheler     13 κεὶ μ]ὴ Blass     ἀ[λη]θέα Blass
14 ἐξέ]λθετ' Blass, ἐξε]λθέτω Knox     ἦ[ν (ε)ῖ]χε Blass,
but the first letter is rather α̣[

231

...] γνώσετ᾽ οἵωι προστάτ[ηι τ]εθώρηγμαι.     15
ἐρεῖ] τάχ᾽ ὑ[μ]ῖν 'ἐξ Ἄκης ἐλήλ[ο]υθα
πυρ]οὺς ἄγων κἤστησα τὴν κακὴν λιμόν',
ἐγὼ δ]ὲ πό[ρ]νας ἐκ Τύρου· τί τῶι δήμωι
........ ; δ]ωρεὴν γὰρ οὔτ᾽ οὗτος πυρούς
........ ]θιν οὔτ᾽ ἐγὼ πάλιν κείνην.     20
εἰ δ᾽ οὕνεκεν πλεῖ τὴν θάλασσαν ἢ χλαῖναν
ἔχει τριῶν μνέων Ἀττικῶν, ἐγὼ δ᾽ οἰκέω
ἐν γῆι τρίβωνα καὶ ἀσκέρας σαπρὰς ἕλκων,
βίηι τιν᾽ ἄξει τῶν ἐμῶν ἔμ᾽ οὐ πείσας,
καὶ ταῦτα νυκτός, οἴχετ᾽ ἧμιν ἡ ἀλεωρή     25
τῆς πόλιος, ἄνδρες, κἀπ᾽ ὅτ<ε>ωι σεμνύνεσθε,
τὴν αὐτονομίην ὑμέων Θαλῆς λύσει.
ὃν χρῆν ἑαυτὸν ὅστις ἐστὶ κἀκ ποίου
πηλοῦ πεφύρητ᾽ εἰδότ᾽ ὡς ἐγὼ ζώειν
τῶν δημοτέων φρίσσοντα καὶ τὸν ἥκιστον.     30
νῦν δ᾽ οἱ μὲν ἐόντες τῆς πόλιος καλυπτῆρες
καὶ τῆι γενῆι φυσῶντες οὐκ ἴσον τούτωι
πρὸς τοὺς νόμους βλέπουσι κἠμὲ τὸν ξεῖνον
οὐδεὶς πολίτης ἠλόησεν οὐδ᾽ ἦλθεν
πρὸς τὰς θύρας μευ νυκτὸς οὐδ᾽ ἔχων δᾶιδας     35
τὴν οἰκίην ὑφῆψεν οὐδὲ τῶν πορνέων

15 γνώσετ᾽ οἵωι Knox     16 ἐρ(ε)ῖ] τάχ᾽ ὑ[μ]ῖν Crusius
17 πυρ]οὺς F.D., Crusius

know by what kind of patron I am protected.
Perhaps [he will say] to you, 'I came from Ake[a] with
[wheat] and checked the bad famine.' [But I] came
from Tyre with girls. What [          ] to the
people? For neither does he [give] the wheat
[          ][b] for nothing, nor again do I give her.[c]
But if because he sails the sea or has a cloak worth
three Attic minas, while I live on land wearing a
rough coat and shuffling along in rotten shoes, he
will by force take one of my girls without my consent, and that at night, the security of your city is
lost, gentlemen, and what you pride yourselves on,
your freedom, will be undone by Thales. Knowing
who he is and from what kind of clay he is mixed, he
ought to live as I do, trembling before even the hum-
blest of the common people. But in fact those who
are the upper-crust of the city, and are puffed with
pride in their family far more than he, respect the
laws; no citizen has thrashed me, the alien, or come
to my doors at night or with torches set my house on

---

[a] The later Acre.
[b] '[to grind]' or something similar.
[c] Or (with κινεῖν) 'give them to screw'.

---

18 ἐγὼ δ]ὲ Headlam
19 τοῦτ' ἔστι; Headlam
20 δίδωσ' ἀλή]θ(ε)ιν F.D., δίδωσιν ἔσ]θ(ε)ιν Crusius
κινῆν P, whence κείνην Hicks, κινεῖν Crusius
28 εχρην αυτον P, corrected by several

βίηι λαβὼν οἴχωκεν· ἀλλ' ὁ Φρὺξ οὗτος,
ὁ νῦν Θαλῆς ἐών, πρόσθε δ', ἄνδρες, Ἀρτίμμης,
ἅπαντα ταῦτ' ἔπρηξε κοὐκ ἐπῃδέσθη
οὔτε νόμον οὔτε προστάτην οὔτ' ἄρχοντα.                    40
καίτοι λαβών μοι, γραμματεῦ, τῆς αἰκείης
τὸν νόμον ἄνειπε, καὶ σὺ τὴν ὀπὴν βῦσον
τῆς κλεψύδρης, βέλτιστε, μέχρις εὖ <'ν>είπηι,
μὴ †προστε† κῦσος φῆι τι κὤ τάπης ἥμιν,
τὸ τοῦ λόγου δὴ τοῦτο, ληίης κύρσηι.                      45

(ΓΡ.)  ἐπὴν δ' ἐλεύθερός τις αἰκίσηι δούλην
ἢ ἔ<λ>κων ἐπίσπηι, τῆς δίκης τὸ τίμημα
διπλοῦν τελείτω.

(ΒΑ.)                    ταῦτ' ἔγραψε Χαιρώνδης,
ἄνδρες δικασταί, καὶ οὐχὶ Βάτταρος χρήιζων
Θαλῆν μετελθεῖν. ἢν θύρην δέ τις κόψηι,             50
μνῆν τινέτω, φησ'· ἢν δὲ πὺξ ἀλοιήσηι,
ἄλλην πάλι μνῆν· ἢν δὲ τὰ οἰκί' ἐμπρήσηι
ἢ ὅρους ὑπερβῆι, χιλίας τὸ τίμημα
ἔνειμε, κἢν βλάψηι τι, διπλόον τίνειν.
ὤικει πόλιν γάρ, ὦ Θάλης, σὺ δ' οὐκ οἶσθας    55

43 <'ν>είπηι Richards
44 πρόσθ' ὁ Piccolomini        φησι P, corrected by Rutherford
47 ἔ<λ>κων Rutherford

fire or forcibly abducted one of my girls. But this Phrygian, who is now called Thales but previously, gentlemen, was Artimmes,[a] has done all this and showed no respect for law or magistrate or ruler. Now, clerk, take and read me the law of assault, and you, my good fellow, stuff the hole of the water-clock until he has spoken, lest bum say †            †[b] and our sheet, as the saying goes, gets the spoil.

CLERK

When a freeman assaults a slave-girl or pulls her about and belabours her, he is to pay double the fine for the crime.

BATTAROS

This was written by Chaerondes,[c] gentlemen of the jury, and not by Battaros wanting to punish Thales. But if someone knocks at a door, he is to be fined a mina, he says; and if he beats someone up, again another mina, and if he burns the house or crosses the boundary, he assessed the penalty at a thousand, and if he causes any injury, to pay double. For he was settling a city, Thales, but you do not

[a] Battaros alleges that Thales has changed his name to conceal his foreign (and possibly servile) origin.

[b] Probably 'lest the bum say something before'. Battaros compares the waterclock, which had a hole and plug in its base, to an anus about to 'speak' (similar vulgarities are found in Aristophanes) and soil the bed (the saying about 'sheet' and 'spoil' is not otherwise known).

[c] A lawgiver.

235

οὔτε πόλιν οὔτε πῶς πόλις διοικεῖται,
οἰκεῖς δὲ σήμερον μὲν ἐν Βρικινδήροις
ἐχθὲς δ' ἐν Ἀβδήροισιν, αὔριον δ' ἤν σοι
ναῦλον διδοῖ τις, ἐς Φασηλίδα πλώσηι.
ἐγὼ δ' ὅκως ἂν μὴ μακρηγορέων ὑμέας,          60
ὦνδρες δικασταί, τῆι παροιμίηι τρύχω,
πέπονθα πρὸς Θάλητος ὅσσα κὴν πίσσηι
μῦς· πὺξ ἐπλήγην, ἢ θύρη κατήρακται
τῆς οἰκίης μευ, τῆς τελέω τρίτην μισθόν,
τὰ ὑπέρθυρ' ὀπτά. δεῦρο, Μυρτάλη, καὶ σύ·     65
δεῖξον σεωυτὴν πᾶσι· μηδέν' αἰσχύνευ·
νόμιζε τούτους οὓς ὁρῆις δικάζοντας
πατέρας ἀδελφοὺς ἐμβλέπειν. ὀρῆτ' ἄνδρες,
τὰ τίλματ' αὐτῆς καὶ κάτωθεν κἄνωθεν
ὡς λεῖα ταῦτ' ἔτιλλεν ὡναγὴς οὗτος,          70
ὅτ' εἶλκεν αὐτὴν κἀβιάζετ' — ὦ γῆρας,
σοὶ θυέτω ἐπ[εὶ] τὸ αἶμ' ἂν ἐξεφύσησεν
ὥσπερ Φίλιστος ἐν Σάμωι κοτ' ὁ Βρέγκος.
γελᾶις; κίνα[ι]δός εἰμι καὶ οὐκ ἀπαρνεῦμαι,
καὶ Βάτταρός μοι τοὔνομ' ἐστὶ κὠ πάππος      75
ἦν μοι Σισυμβρᾶς κὠ πατὴρ Σισυμβρίσκος,
κἠπορνοβόσ[κ]ευν πάντες, ἀλλ' ἔκητ' ἀλκῆς

66 μηδέν' and μηδὲν are both possible
72 ἐπ[εὶ] Blass

236

know a city and how a city is governed: but today
you live in Brikindera, yesterday in Abdera, and
tomorrow if someone gives you the fare you'll sail to
Phaselis.[a] But I, gentlemen of the jury—in order
not with long speeches to wear you out by
digression—I have suffered from Thales what the
mouse did in pitch:[b] I was struck with his fist, the
door of my house, for which I pay a third[c] in rent,
was broken down, the lintel roasted. Myrtale, come
here; show yourself to all—don't be ashamed before
anyone. Consider that in these gentlemen you see
on the jury you are looking on fathers, brothers.
See, gentlemen, her plucked skin, both below and
above, how smooth this "innocent" has plucked it,
when he was dragging and forcing her—Old Age, let
him make you a thank-offering, else he would have
breathed out his blood as Philistos son of Brenx once
did in Samos.[d] You laugh? I am gay and don't deny
it; Battaros is my name and my grandfather was
Sisymbras and my father Sisymbriskos,[e] and all
were brothel-keepers, but for strength I'd boldly

[a] All cities of poor reputation.

[b] Battaros recalls, but very vaguely, the proverbial
mouse which was trapped in pitch and died.

[c] Presumably 1/3 of the value of the house, a large
amount to reflect the dangers to which Battaros' profession
exposed it.

[d] The victim of a boxer falsely accused of softness.

[e] Names suggesting effeminacy.

---

73 φιλιππος corrected to φιλιστος P

θαρσέων λέ<u>ο</u>[ν]τ̣’ ἄ[γχ]οιμ’ ἄν εἰ Θαλῆς εἴη.
ἐρᾶις σὺ μὲν ἴσω[ς] Μυρτάλης; οὐδὲν δεινόν·
ἐγὼ δὲ πυρέων· ταῦτα δοὺς ἐκεῖν’ ἔξεις.               80
ἢ νὴ Δί’, εἴ σευ θ[ά]λπεταί τι τῶν ἔνδον,
ἔμβυσον εἰς τὴν χεῖρα Βαττᾱρίωι τιμήν,
καὐτὸς τὰ σαυτοῦ θλῆ λαβὼν ὅκως χρήιζεις.
ἓν δ’ ἔστιν, ἄνδρες — ταῦτα μὲν γὰρ εἴρηται
πρὸς τοῦτον — ὑμεῖς δ’ ὡς ἀμαρτύρων εὔντων    85
γνώμηι δικαίηι τὴν κρίσιν διαιτᾶτε.
ἢν δ’ οἷον ἐς τὰ δοῦλα σώματα σπεύδηι
κῆς βάσανον αἰτῆι, προσδίδωμι κἀμαυτόν·
λαβών, Θαλῆ, στρέβλου με· μοῦνον ἡ τιμή
ἐν τῶι μέσωι ἔστω· ταῦτα τρυτάνηι Μίνως       90
οὐκ ἂν δικάζων βέλτιον διήιτησε.
τὸ λοιπόν, ἄνδρες, μὴ δοκεῖτε τὴν ψῆφον
τῶι πορνοβοσκῶι Βαττάρωι φέρειν, ἀλλά
ἅπασι τοῖς οἰκεῦσι τὴν πόλιν ξείνοις.
νῦν δείξετ’ ἢ Κῶς κὠ Μέροψ κόσον δραίνει       95
κὠ Θεσσαλὸς τίν’ εἶχε κἠρακλῆς δόξαν,
κὠσκληπιὸς κῶς ἦλθεν ἐνθάδ’ ἐκ Τρίκκης,
κἤτικτε Λητοῦν ὦδε τευ χάριν Φοίβη.

78 λέ<u>ο</u>[ν]τ̣’ ἄ[γχ]οιμ’ ἄν Blass
82 Βαττάρωι Rutherford

238

[choke] a lion, if it were Thales. You love Myrtale perhaps: nothing strange in that; but I love bread: give the one and you will have the other. Or by Zeus, if your passion is roused, stuff the price into little Battaros' hand, and take your own property and bash her as you want. But there is one thing, gentlemen—for this was addressed to him—you must, as there are no witnesses, decide the case with just judgement. But if he is only eager for slaves' bodies and asks them for torture, I offer myself: take me, Thales, and stretch me; only let the value be on hand.[a] Minos judging this with his scales would not have decided it better. For the rest, gentlemen, do not think that you are casting your vote for the brothel-keeper Battaros, but for all the foreigners living in the city. Now you will show to what extent Kos and Merops[b] are strong, and what fame Thessalos had and Herakles,[c] and how Asklepios came here from Trikka,[d] and the reason for Phoebe's giving birth to Leto here.[e] Considering

[a] When a slave was tortured to obtain evidence and the accusation was not upheld, the accuser had to compensate the owner with the value of the slave.

[b] Merops was a legendary king of the island, Kos his daughter.

[c] Herakles, returning from Troy, landed in Kos, and was the father of Thessalos by the king's daughter.

[d] Town in Thessaly, original site of the cult of Asklepios.

[e] Leto, daughter of *Koeos,* is claimed to have been born in *Kos.*

ταῦτα σκοπεῦντες πάντα τὴν δίκην ὀρθῆι
γνώμηι κυβερνᾶτ᾿, ὡς ὁ Φρὺξ τὰ νῦν ὑμιν      100
πληγεὶς ἀμείνων ἔσσετ᾿, εἴ τι μὴ ψεῦδος
ἐκ τῶν παλαιῶν ἡ παροιμίη βάζει.

102 βραζει the corrector

all this, steer the case with straight judgement, and you'll see that the Phrygian will now be better for a beating, unless the saying from men of old speaks false.

## 3. ΔΙΔΑΣΚΑΛΟΣ

(ΜΗ.) οὕτω τί σοι δοίησαν αἱ φίλαι Μοῦσαι,
Λαμπρίσκε, τερπνὸν τῆς ζοῆς τ᾽ ἐπαυρέσθαι,
τοῦτον κατ᾽ ὤμου δεῖρον, ἄχρις ἡ ψυχή
αὐτοῦ ἐπὶ χειλέων μοῦνον ἡ κακὴ λειφθῆι.
ἔκ μευ ταλαίνης τὴν στέγην πεπόρθηκεν        5
χαλκίνδα παίζων· καὶ γὰρ οὐδ᾽ ἀπαρκεῦσιν
αἱ ἀστραγάλαι, Λαμπρίσκε, συμφορῆς δ᾽ ἤδη
ὁρμᾶι ἐπὶ μέζον. κοῦ μὲν ἡ θύρη κεῖται
τοῦ γραμματιστέω — καὶ τριηκὰς ἡ πικρή
τὸν μισθὸν αἰτεῖ κἢν τὰ Ναννάκου κλαύσω —   10
οὐκ ἂν ταχέως λήξειε· τήν γε μὴν παίστρην,
ὅκουπερ οἰκίζουσιν οἵ τε προύνεικοι
κοἰ δρηπέται, σάφ᾽ οἶδε κἠτέρωι δεῖξαι.
κἠ μέν τάλαινα δέλτος, ἣν ἐγὼ κάμνω
κηροῦσ᾽ ἑκάστου μηνός, ὀρφανὴ κεῖται         15
πρὸ τῆς χαμεύνης τοῦ ἐπὶ τοῖχον ἑρμῖνος,

8 κοῦ (i.e. καὶ οὖ) Hicks, Weil
10 The paroemiographer Zenobius, 6.10, says that
Herodes the iambic poet used the proverb

242

# 3. A SCHOOLMASTER

METROTIME

Lampriskos, as the dear Muses may give you
something pleasant, and enjoyment of life, flay this
boy on his shoulder, until his wretched soul is just
left on his lips. He has pillaged my house, poor me,
by spinning coins; for in fact the dice are no longer
enough, Lampriskos, and things are now rushing to
a greater disaster. Where the teacher's door is—
and the woeful thirtieth seeks the fee,[a] even if I
weep the tears of Nannakos[b]—he could not quickly
say: but the gaming house, where the toughs and
runaways live, he knows well enough to show to
someone else. The wretched tablet,[c] which I tire
myself out waxing each month, lies orphaned before

[a] Accounts, including school fees, are paid on the last
day of the month.
[b] A king in Phrygia, said to have attempted to avert the
great flood by tears to the gods.
[c] Wax-tablets are the equivalent of an exercise-book.

---

11 λέξειε many, unnecessarily
12 ὀκλάζουσιν Herwerden

ἢν μήκοτ' αὐτὴν οἷον Ἀίδην βλέψας
γράψηι μὲν οὐδὲν καλόν, ἐκ δ' ὅλην ξύσηι ·
αἱ δορκαλίδες δὲ λιπαρώτεραι πολλόν
ἐν τῆισι φύσηις τοῖς τε δικτύοις κεῖνται          20
τῆς ληκύθου ἡμέων τῆι ἐπὶ παντὶ χρώμεσθα.
ἐπίσταται δ' οὐδ' ἄλφα συλλαβὴν γνῶναι,
ἢν μή τις αὐτῶι ταὐτὰ πεντάκις βώσηι.
τριτημέρηι Μάρωνα γραμματίζοντος
τοῦ πατρὸς αὐτῶι, τὸν Μάρων' ἐποίησεν          25
οὗτος Σίμων' ὁ χρηστός · ὥστ' ἔγωγ' εἶπα
ἄνουν ἐμαυτήν, ἥτις οὐκ ὄνους βόσκειν
αὐτὸν διδάσκω, γραμμάτων δὲ παιδείην,
δοκεῦσ' ἀρωγὸν τῆς ἀωρίης ἕξειν.
ἐπεὰν δὲ δὴ καὶ ῥῆσιν οἷα παιδίσκον          30
ἢ 'γώ μιν εἰπεῖν ἢ ὁ πατὴρ ἀνώγωμεν,
γέρων ἀνὴρ ὠσίν τε κώμμασιν κάμνων,
ἐνταῦθ' ὅκως νιν ἐκ τετρημένης ἠθεῖ
'Ἄπολλον . . . Ἀγρεῦ . . .', 'τοῦτο' φημὶ 'κὴ μάμμη,
τάλης, ἐρεῖ σοι — κὴστὶ γραμμάτων χήρη —          35
κὠ προστυχὼν Φρύξ.' ἢν δὲ δή τι καὶ μέζον
γρῦξαι θέλωμεν, ἢ τριταῖος οὐκ οἶδεν
τῆς οἰκίης τὸν οὐδόν, ἀλλὰ τὴν μάμμην,
γρηῢν γυναῖκα κὠρφανὴν βίου, κείρει,
ἢ τοῦ τέγευς ὕπερθε τὰ σκέλεα τείνας          40

the bed-post next the wall, except when he looks at it as if it were Hades and writes nothing good but scrapes it all smooth. But the dice, much more shiny[a] than our oil-flask which we use constantly, are placed in their skins and nets.[b] He does not even know how to recognise the letter A, if one does not shout the same thing at him five times. Two days ago when his father was teaching him to spell 'Maron', this fine fellow made 'Maron' into 'Simon';[c] so that I said I was a fool, teaching him book-learning instead of to feed asses, thinking I would have a support for bad times. And again when either his father, an old man with sick ears and eyes, or I ask him to recite a speech as one does a youngster, then when he lets it trickle out as if from a holed jug 'Apollo . . . Hunter . . .', 'This' I say 'even your grandmother will recite to you, wretch, and she is devoid of learning, or any passing Phrygian.' And again if we try to speak more forcibly, either for three days he does not know the threshold of the house, but fleeces his grandmother, an old lady destitute of the means of life, or stretching his legs he

[a] With use.

[b] Bags of skin and net.

[c] The name of a throw at dice is substituted for a Homeric name normally used as an example in school.

17 κην P, corrected by Blass, Palmer

κάθητ᾽ ὅκως τις καλλίης κάτω κύπτων.
τί μευ δοκεῖς τὰ σπλάγχνα τῆς κάκης πάσχειν
ἐπεὰν ἴδωμι; κοὐ τόσος λόγος τοῦδε·
ἀλλ᾽ ὁ κέραμος πᾶς ὥσπερ ἴτ<ρ>ια θλῆται,
κἠπὴν ὁ χειμὼν ἐγγὺς ἦι, τρί᾽ ἥμαιθα          45
κλαίουσ᾽ ἑκάστου τοῦ πλατύσματος τίνω·
ἓν γὰρ στόμ᾽ ἐστὶ τῆς συνοικίης πάσης,
'τοῦ Μητροτίμης ἔργα Κοττάλου ταῦτα',
κἀληθίν᾽ ὥστε μηδ᾽ ὀδόντα κινῆσαι.
ὅρη δ᾽ ὁκοίως τὴν ῥάκιν λελέπρηκε          50
πᾶσαν, κατ᾽ ὕλην, οἷα Δήλιος κυρτεύς
ἐν τῆι θαλάσσηι, τὠμβλὺ τῆς ζοῆς τρίβων.
τὰς ἑβδόμας δ᾽ ἄμεινον εἰκάδας τ᾽ οἶδε
τῶν ἀστροδιφέων, κοὐδ᾽ ὕπνος νιν αἱρεῖται
νοεῦντ᾽ ὅτ᾽ ἦμος παιγνίην ἀγινῆτε.          55
ἀλλ᾽ εἴ τί σοι, Λαμπρίσκε, καὶ βίου πρῆξιν
ἐσθλὴν τελοῖεν αἵδε κἀγαθῶν κύρσαις,
μήλασσον αὐτῶι —
(ΛΑ.)                    Μητροτίμη, <μὴ> ἐπεύχεο·
ἕξει γὰρ οὐδὲν μεῖον. Εὐθίης κοῦ μοι,
κοῦ Κόκκαλος, κοῦ Φίλλος; οὐ ταχέως τοῦτον          60
ἀρεῖτ᾽ ἐπ᾽ ὤμου τῆι ᾽Ακέσεω σεληναίηι

42 κάκης Meister, κακῆς most edd.

sits above the roof like a monkey, bending down.
What do you think my heart suffers because of his
wickedness when I see him? My concern is not so
much for him: but all the tiling is broken like
wafers, and when winter is near, I pay in tears three
half-pennies for each tile; for there is one voice in
the whole tenement, that this is the work of Kottalos, Metrotime's son, and it is true, so as not to
move a tooth.[a] See how he has roughened all his
back by dragging out his pointless life in the wood,
like a Delian pot-fisherman[b] at sea. And he knows
the seventh and twentieth of the month[c] better than
the star-watchers; not even sleep overcomes him as
he thinks of when you are on holiday. But if these
ladies[d] are to fulfil for you good success in life and
you are to obtain blessings, no less to him —

LAMPRISKOS

Metrotime, stop praying; for he shall get no less.
Euthies, where are you, and Kokkalos, and Phillos?
Quickly lift him on your shoulders to show him to

[a] Sense uncertain.
[b] Reference uncertain.
[c] Feast days when the school would be closed.
[d] The Muses.

---

44 ἴτ<ρ>ια Rutherford
53 δ' Terzaghi, τ' P
58 <μὴ> several

δείξοντες; αἰνέω τἄργα, Κότταλ', ἃ πρήσσεις·
οὔ σοι ἔτ' ἀπαρκεῖ τῆισι δορκάσιν παίζειν
ἀστράβδ' ὅκωσπερ οἶδε, πρὸς δὲ τὴν παίστρην
ἐν τοῖσι προ<υ>νείκοισι χαλκίζεις φοιτέων;    65
ἐγώ σε θήσω κοσμιώτερον κούρης,
κινεῦντα μηδὲ κάρφος, εἰ τό γ' ἥδιστον.
κοῦ μοι τὸ δριμὺ σκῦτος, ἡ βοὸς κέρκος,
ὧι τοὺς πεδήτας κἀποτάκτους λωβεῦμαι;
δότω τις εἰς τὴν χεῖρα πρὶν χολῆ<ι> βῆξαι.    70

(ΚΟ.) μή μ' ἱκετεύω Λαμπρίσκε, πρός σε τῶν Μουσέων
καὶ τοῦ γενείου τῆς τε Κόττιδος ψυχῆς,
μὴ τῶι με δριμεῖ, τῶι 'τέρωι δὲ λώβησαι.

<ΛΑ.> ἀλλ' εἰς πονηρός, Κότταλ', ὦ<σ>τε καὶ περνάς
οὐδείς σ' ἐπαινέσειεν, οὐδ' ὅκου χώρης    75
οἱ μῦς ὁμοίως τὸν σίδηρον τρώγουσιν.

(ΚΟ.) κόσας, κόσας, Λαμπρίσκε, λίσσομαι, μέλλεις
ἔς μ' ἐμφορῆσαι;

<ΛΑ.>              μὴ 'μέ, τήνδε δ' εἰρώτα.

---

68 σκυλος P, corrected by several
70 χολῆ<ι> Hicks
78 μευ φορησαι P, corrected by Rutherford

---

[a] Akeses, pilot of the ancient hero Neleus, always
waited for the full moon so as not to sail in darkness. His
moon therefore is the time that is ripe for action.

Akeses' moon.[a] I approve of your deeds, Kottalos;
isn't it enough for you any longer to play flashingly
with dice, like these boys, but you go to the gaming
house and spin coins among the toughs? I shall
make you better behaved than a girl, not moving
even a straw,[b] if that is what you want. Where is
my biting strap, the bull's tail, with which I
mutilate those whom I've fettered and set apart?
Put it in my hand before I cough with bile.[c]

KOTTALOS

No, I beseech you, Lampriskos, by the Muses and
your beard and poor Kottalos' life, do not mutilate
me with the piercing one, but with the other.

<LAMPRISKOS>

But you are wicked, Kottalos, so that no one,
even if selling you, would praise you, not even where
mice eat iron equally.[d]

KOTTALOS

How many, how many, Lampriskos, I beg you,
are you going to inflict on me?

<LAMPRISKOS>

Ask her, not me.


[b] Compare 1.54.

[c] He fears his shouting may cause bile to accumulate in
his lungs and make him ill.

[d] I.e. a very barren place whose inhabitants would not
find much fault with potential slaves. The reference of
'equally' is unclear.

&lt;ΚΟ.&gt; τατα&lt;ῖ&gt;, κόσας μοι δώσετ᾽ ;

&lt;ΜΗ.&gt;         εἴ τί σοι ζώιην,
φέρειν ὅσας ἂν ἦ κακὴ σθένηι βύρσα.    80

&lt;ΚΟ.&gt; παῦσαι· ἱκαναί, Λαμπρίσκε.

(ΛΑ.)        καὶ σὺ δὴ παῦσαι
κάκ᾽ ἔργα πρήσσων.

&lt;ΚΟ.&gt;       οὐκέτ᾽ οὐκέτι πρήξω,
ὄμνυμί σοι, Λαμπρίσκε, τὰς φίλας Μούσας.

(ΛΑ.) ὅσσην δὲ καὶ τὴν γλάσσαν, οὗτος, ἔσχηκας·
πρός σοι βαλέω τὸν μῦν τάχ᾽ ἢν πλέω γρύξηις. 85

(ΚΟ.) ἰδού, σιωπῶ· μή με, λίσσομαι, κτείνηις.

(ΛΑ.) μέθεσθε, Κόκκαλ᾽, αὐτόν.

(ΜΗ.)       οὐ δ&lt;εῖ σ᾽&gt; ἐκλῆξαι,
Λαμπρίσκε· δεῖρον ἄχρις ἥλιος δύσηι.

&lt;ΛΑ. ἀλλ᾽ . . . . . . . . . . . . . . . . . . . . . . . . . . . . .&gt;88a

(ΜΗ.) ἀλλ᾽ ἐστὶν ὕδρης ποικιλώτερος πολλῶι
καὶ δεῖ λαβεῖν νιν — κἀπὶ βυβλίωι δήκου,    90

79 τατα&lt;ῖ&gt; Herwerden
82 οὐκέτι Rutherford, οὐχι P
87 δ&lt;εῖ σ᾽&gt; Danielsson, Pearson
88a added by a friend of Headlam

  [a] A line with the general sense 'But he has had enough'
appears to have been lost.
  [b] If he pretends to study.

# MIME 3

<KOTTALOS>

Ow! How many will you give me?

<METROTIME>

As I wish to live, as many as your wicked hide
can bear.

<KOTTALOS>

Stop! Enough, Lampriskos.

LAMPRISKOS

You too stop doing wicked deeds.

<KOTTALOS>

I shall not do any again, I swear to you, Lampriskos, by the dear Muses.

LAMPRISKOS

What a tongue you've acquired; I'll put a gag on
you quickly, if you say any more.

KOTTALOS

See, I'm silent. Don't kill me, I beg you.

LAMPRISKOS

Let him go, Kokkalos.

METROTIME

You ought not to have stopped, Lampriskos; flay
him until the sun sets.

<LAMPRISKOS>

<                                    .>[a]

METROTIME

But he is much more subtle than a water-snake,
and he ought, even over his book,[b] the wretch, to get

251

τὸ μηδέν — ἄλλας εἴκοσίν γε, καὶ ἢν μέλληι
αὐτῆς ἄμεινον τῆς Κλεοῦς ἀναγνῶναι.

&lt;ΚΟ.&gt; ἰσσαῖ.

&lt;ΛΑ.&gt;       λάθοις τὴν γλάσσαν ἐς μέλι πλύνας.

&lt;ΜΗ.&gt; ἐρέω ἐπιμηθέως τῶι γέροντι, Λαμπρίσκε,
ἐλθοῦσ᾽ ἐς οἶκον ταῦτα, καὶ πέδας ἤξω      95
φέρουσ᾽ ὅκως νιν σύμποδ᾽ ὧδε πηδεῦντα
αἱ πότνιαι βλέπωσιν ἃς ἐμίσησεν.

93 ἰσσαῖ is given to Kottalos by Crusius, the rest to
Lampr. by Nairn

another twenty at least, even if he will read better than Kleo[a] herself.

<KOTTALOS>

Ha-ha![b]

<LAMPRISKOS>

May you find your tongue washed in honey.[c]

METROTIME

On second thoughts, Lampriskos, I shall go home and tell the old man this; and I shall come back with fetters, so that the Ladies[d] he has hated may see him jumping here with feet tied together.

[a] One of the Muses.

[b] Rejoicing at his release and his mother's discomfiture.

[c] I.e. be honoured by the Muses (Hesiod, *Theogony*, 83–84), something which is unlikely to happen by his own act.

[d] The Muses.

## 4. ΑΣΚΛΗΠΙΩΙ ΑΝΑΤΙΘΕΙΣΑΙ
## ΚΑΙ ΘΥΣΙΑΖΟΥΣΑΙ

(ΚΥ.) χαίροις, ἄναξ Παίηον, ὃς μέδεις Τρίκκης
καὶ Κῶν γλυκεῖαν κἠπίδαυρον ᾤκηκας,
σὺν καὶ Κορωνὶς ἥ σ᾽ ἔτικτε κὠπόλλων
χαίροιεν, ἧς τε χειρὶ δεξιῆι ψαύεις
Ὑγίεια, κὠνπερ οἵδε τίμιοι βωμοί                          5
Πανάκη τε κἠπιώ τε κἰησὼ χαίροι,
κοἰ Λεωμέδοντος οἰκίην τε καὶ τείχεα
πέρσαντες, ἰητῆρες ἀγρίων νούσων,
Ποδαλείριός τε καὶ Μαχάων χαιρόντων,
κὤσοι θεοὶ σὴν ἑστίην κατοικεῦσιν                         10
καὶ θεαί, πάτερ Παίηον· ἵλεωι δεῦτε
τὠλέκτορος τοῦδ᾽, ὄντιν᾽ οἰκίης †τοίχων†
κήρυκα θύω, τἀπίδορπα δέξαισθε.

The names of the participants and the division of the lines
between them are not certain. One of the women is Kynno,
but the other may be Phile or Kottale (then φίλη = 'dear');
Kokkale and Kydilla are their slaves in either case

5 τε κωνπερ P, corrected by several        [6] Herwerden
transposed χαίροι before κἠπιώ to improve the syntax

254

# 4. WOMEN DEDICATING AND SACRIFICING TO ASKLEPIOS

KYNNO

Greetings, Lord Paeeon,[a] who rulest Trikka and hast settled sweet Kos and Epidauros, and also may Koronis who gave thee birth and Apollo be greeted, and she whom thou touchest with thy right hand Hygieia, and those to whom belong these honoured altars, Panake and Epio and Ieso be greeted, and the sackers of Laomedon's house and walls, curers of cruel diseases, Podaleirios and Machaon be greeted, and whatsoever gods and goddesses live at thy hearth, father Paeeon: may ye graciously come hither and receive this cock which I am sacrificing, herald of the walls of the house,[b] as your dessert.

[a] Epithet of Asklepios, whose parents are Apollo and Koronis, wife Hygieia ('Health'), daughters Panake ('Remedy'), Epio ('Gentleness') and Ieso ('Healing'), and sons Podaleirios and Machaon, both healers, who took part in the siege of Troy (whose walls were built by Laomedon).

[b] It is not clear how the cock is herald of the *walls*. 'Harsh-voiced herald' or 'herald of the labours of the house' would be easier.

---

12 τοιχων P, τρηχὺν Richards, μόχθων Stadtmüller

οὐ γάρ τι πολλὴν οὐδ' ἕτοιμον ἀντλεῦμεν,
ἐπεὶ τάχ' ἂν βοῦν ἢ νενημένην χοῖρον      15
πολλῆς φορίνης, κοὐκ ἀλέκτορ', ἴητρα
νούσων ἐποιεύμεσθα τὰς ἀπέψησας
ἐπ' ἠπίας σὺ χεῖρας, ὦ ἄναξ, τείνας.
ἐκ δεξιῆς τὸν πίνακα, Κοκκάλη, στῆσον
τῆς Ὑγιείης.

<ΦΙ.>              ἆ, καλῶν, φίλη Κυννοῖ,      20
ἀγαλμάτων· τίς ἦρα τὴν λίθον ταύτην
τέκτων ἐπο<ί>ει καὶ τίς ἐστιν ὁ στήσας;

<ΚΥ.> οἰ Πρηξιτέλεω παῖδες· οὐκ ὁρῆις κεῖνα
ἐν τῆι βάσι τὰ γράμματ'; Εὐθίης δ' αὐτήν
ἔστησεν ὁ Πρήξωνος.

<ΦΙ.>            ἵλεως εἴη      25
καὶ τοῖσδ' ὁ Παιὼν καὶ Εὐθίηι καλῶν ἔργων.

<ΚΥ.> ὅρη, Φίλη, τὴν παῖδα τὴν ἄνω κείνην
βλέπουσαν ἐς τὸ μῆλον· οὐκ ἐρεῖς αὐτήν
ἢν μὴ λάβηι τὸ μῆλον ἐκ τάχα ψύξει<ν>;

<ΦΙ.> κεῖνον δέ, Κυννοῖ, τὸν γέροντ' —

24 αυτα P, corrected by Richards
26 ευθιης P, corrected by several
29 ψύξει<ν> Rutherford
30 <ΦΙ.> and <ΚΥ.> Hertling      γεροντά P, divided by
Knox

For our well is far from abundant or ready-flowing, else we should have made an ox or a sow heaped with much crackling, and not a cock, our thank-offering for the diseases which thou hast wiped away, Lord, stretching out thy gentle hands. Kokkale, set the tablet[a] on the right of Hygieia.

<PHILE>

Oh, what lovely statues, dear Kynno; what artist made this sculpture and who is the person who dedicated it?

<KYNNO>

The sons of Praxiteles;[b] don't you see these words on the base? And Euthies son of Prexon dedicated it.

<PHILE>

May Paeon be gracious to them and to Euthies for their lovely works.

<KYNNO>

See, Phile, that girl looking up at the apple: wouldn't you say that if she doesn't get the apple she will quickly expire?

<PHILE>

And that old man, Kynno —

[a] With a description of the cure.
[b] Kephisodotos and Timarchos, artists like their better-known father.

&lt;ΚΥ.&gt;         ἆ πρὸς Μοιρέων   30
τὴν χηναλώπεκ' ὡς τὸ παιδίον πνίγει.
πρὸ τῶν ποδῶν γοῦν εἴ τι μὴ λίθος, τοὔργον,
ἐρεῖς, λαλήσει. μᾶ, χρόνωι κοτ' ὤνθρωποι
κῆς τοὺς λίθους ἔξουσι τὴν ζοὴν θεῖναι.

(ΦΙ.)   τὸν Βατάλης γὰρ τοῦτον οὐκ ὀρῆις, Κυννοῖ,   35
ὅκως βέβηκεν ἀνδρ[ι]άντα τῆς Μυττέω;
εἰ μή τις αὐτὴν εἶδε Βατάλην, βλέψας
ἐς τοῦτο τὸ εἰκόνισμα μὴ ἐτύμης δείσθω.

(ΚΥ.)   ἔπευ, Φίλη, μοι καὶ καλόν τί σοι δείξω
πρῆγμ' οἷον οὐκ ὤρηκας ἐξ ὅτευ ζώεις.   40
Κύδιλλ', ἰοῦσα τὸν νεωκόρον βῶσον.
οὐ σοὶ λέγω, αὕτη, τῆι ὧδε κὦδε χασκεύσηι;
μᾶ, μή τιν' ὤρην ὧν λέγω πεποίηται,
ἔστηκε δ' εἴς μ' ὀρεῦσα καρκίνου μέζον.
ἰοῦσα, φημί, τὸν νεωκόρον βῶσον.   45
λαίμαστρον, οὔτ' ὀργή σε κρηγύην οὔτε
βέβηλος αἰνεῖ, πανταχῆι δ' ἴσῃ κεῖσαι.
μαρτύρομαι, Κύδιλλα, τὸν θεὸν τοῦτον,
ὡς ἔκ με κα&lt;ί&gt;εις οὐ θέλουσαν οἰδῆσαι·
μαρτύρομαι, φήμ'· ἔσσετ' ἡμέρη κείνη   50
ἐν ἧι τὸ βρέγμα τοῦτο †τωυσυρες† κνήσηι.

49 κα&lt;ί&gt;εις Meister
51 τώσυρὲς Blass, Danielsson

# MIME 4

<KYNNO>

Oh, by the Fates, how the child chokes the goose. Certainly if it were not stone before our feet, the work, you'd say, will speak. Ah, in time men will be able to put life even into stones.

## PHILE

Now this statue of Batale, daughter of Myttes, don't you see, Kynno, how it stands? Anyone who has not seen Batale herself, looking at this likeness would not need the real thing.

## KYNNO

Come with me, Phile, and I'll show you a lovely thing such as you have never seen in all your life. Kydilla, go and call the temple-warden. Am I not speaking to *you*, who gape this way and that? Ah, she has paid no heed to what I say, but stands staring at me more than a crab. Go, I say, and call the temple-warden. Glutton, no woman pious or impure praises you as good, but everywhere you are valued equally.[a] I make this god my witness, Kydilla, that you inflame me though I do not wish to swell up. I make him witness, I say: that day will come when you will scratch your filthy head.[b]

[a] I.e. are equally worthless.
[b] Possibly she is to be branded.

259

(ΦΙ.)   μὴ πάντ' ἑτοίμως καρδιηβολεῦ, Κυννοῖ·
       δούλη 'στι, δούλης δ' ὦτα νωθρίη θλίβει.

(ΚΥ.)  ἀλλ' ἡμέρη τε κἠπὶ μέζον ὠθεῖται·
       αὕτη σύ, μεῖνον· ἢ θύρη γὰρ ὤϊκται         55
       κἀνεῖτ' ὁ παστός.

&lt;ΦΙ.&gt;                οὐκ ὁρῆις, φίλη Κυννοῖ;
       οἷ' ἔργα κεῖ 'νην· ταῦτ' ἐρεῖς 'Αθηναίην
       γλύψαι τὰ καλά — χαιρέτω δὲ δέσποινα.
       τὸν παῖδα δὴ &lt;τὸν&gt; γυμνὸν ἢν κνίσω τοῦτον
       οὐκ ἕλκος ἕξει, Κύννα; πρὸς γάρ οἱ κεῖνται    60
       αἱ σάρκες οἶα †θερμα† πηδῶσαι
       ἐν τῆι σανίσκηι. τὠργύρευν δὲ πύραυστρον
       οὐκ ἢν ἴδηι Μύελλος ἢ Παταικίσκος
       ὁ Λαμπρίωνος, ἐκβαλεῦσι τὰς κούρας
       δοκεῦντες ὄντως ἀργύρευν πεποιῆσθαι;    65
       ὁ βοῦς δὲ κὠ ἄγων αὐτὸν ἤ τ' ὁμαρτεῦσα
       κὠ γρυπὸς οὗτος κὠ ἀνάσιλλος ἄνθρωπος
       οὐχὶ ζοὴν βλέπουσι κἠμέρην πάντες;
       εἰ μὴ ἐδόκευν τι μέζον ἢ γυνὴ πρήσσειν,

52 It is not clear if the corrector intended καρδιηβολεῦ or
καρδίηι βαλεῦ: καρδιηβαλλει P
57 κοινην with ι deleted P, explained by Diels, Richards;
κεῖν' ἢν Headlam, καὶ μὴν Verdenius
61 A second θερμὰ is added by a late hand; θερμ&lt;ὸν αἶμ&gt;α
Stadtmüller

## MIME 4

### PHILE

Don't take everything so readily to heart, Kynno;
she is a slave, and a slave's ears are blocked with
sluggishness.

### KYNNO

But it is day and the crush is getting worse. You
there, wait, for the door has been opened and the
curtain unfastened.

### &lt;PHILE&gt;

Don't you see, dear Kynno, what works are here!
You would say that Athene carved these lovely
things—greetings, Lady. This naked boy, if I
scratch him, won't he have a wound, Kynno? For
the flesh is laid on him in the painting, pulsing like
warm springs.[a] And the silver fire-tongs, if Myellos
or Pataekiskos son of Lamprion sees them, won't
they lose their eyes thinking they are really made of
silver? And the ox, and the man leading it, and the
woman following, and this hook-nosed man and the
one with his hair sticking up, don't they all have the
look of life and day? If I did not think I was acting
too boldly for a woman, I should have cried out, in

---

[a] Or, with Stadtmüller's conjecture, 'like warm blood'.

62 πῡρᾰστ͞ον P, explained by Vollgraff
68 βλεπουσιν ημερην P, corrected by Hicks

ἀνηλάλαξ’ ἄν, μή μ’ ὁ βοῦς τι πημήνηι·    70
οὕτω ἐπιλοξοῖ, Κυννί, τῆι ἑτέρηι κούρηι.

(ΚΥ.) ἀληθιναί, Φίλη, γὰρ αἱ Ἐφεσίου χεῖρες
ἐς πάντ’ Ἀπελλέω γράμματ’· οὐδ’ ἐρεῖς ‘κεῖνος
ὤνθρωπος ἒν μὲν εἶδεν, ἓν δ’ ἀπηρνήθη’,
ἀλλ’ ὧι ἐπὶ νοῦν γένοιτο καὶ θέων ψαύειν    75
ἠπείγετ’. ὃς δ’ ἐκεῖνον ἢ ἔργα τὰ ἐκείνου
μὴ παμφαλήσας ἐκ δίκης ὀρώρηκεν,
ποδὸς κρέμαιτ’ ἐκεῖνος ἐν γναφέως οἴκωι.

(ΝΕ.) κάλ’ ὗμιν, ὦ γυναῖκες, ἐντελέως τὰ ἱρά
καὶ ἐς λῶιον ἐμβλέποντα· μεζόνως οὗτις    80
ἠρέσατο τὸν Παιήον’ ἤπερ οὖν ὑμεῖς.
ἰὴ ἰὴ Παίηον, εὐμενὴς εἴης
καλοῖς ἐπ’ ἱροῖς τῆισδε κεἴ τινες τῶνδε
ἔασ’ ὀπυιηταί τε καὶ γενῆς ἆσσον.
ἰὴ ἰὴ Παίηον, ὧδε ταῦτ’ εἴη.    85

<ΚΥ.> εἴη γάρ, ὦ μέγιστε, κὐγίηι πολλῆι
ἔλθοιμεν αὖτις μέζον’ ἴρ’ ἀγινεῦσαι
σὺν ἀνδράσιν καὶ παισί. Κοκκάλη, καλῶς
τεμεῦσα μέμνεο τὸ σκελύδριον δοῦναι
τῶι νεωκόρωι τοὔρνιθος· ἔς τε τὴν τρώγλην    90

75 ὧι = ὃ οἱ explained by Paton     θέων Ellis, θεῶν most
edd.

88 κοτταλη P, corrected by Rutherford

262

case the ox might do me some harm: he glances side-
ways so, Kynno, with the one eye.

KYNNO

Yes, Phile, the hands of the Ephesian Apelles are
truthful in every line, nor would you say 'That man
looked at one thing but rejected another,' but whatever came into his mind he was quick and eager to
attempt; and anyone who has looked on him or his
works without just excitement ought to hang by the
foot in the fuller's house.[a]

TEMPLE-WARDEN

Perfectly fair, ladies, are your offerings, and looking forward to better: no one has found more favour
with Paeeon than you have. Hail hail Paeeon, may-
est thou be well disposed for their fair offerings to
these ladies and to any who are their spouses and
near kin. Hail hail Paeeon; so may it be.

<KYNNO>

May it be, o most mighty, and in good health may
we come again with our husbands and children,
bringing greater offerings. — Kokkale, remember to
cut carefully the bird's little leg and give it to the
temple-warden, and place the batter reverently in

[a] Being hung up by a foot is mentioned as a punishment
in New Comedy. The location in the fuller's adds the
suggestion of being beaten like dirty clothing.

τὸν πελανὸν ἔνθες τοῦ δράκοντος εὐφήμως,
καὶ ψαιστὰ δεῦσον· τἄλλα δ᾽ οἰκίης ἕδρηι
δαισόμεθα, καὶ ἐπὶ μὴ λάθηι φέρειν, αὕτη,
τῆς ὑγιίης †λωι† πρόσοδος· ἦ γαρ ἱροῖσιν
†με.ων αμαρτιησηυγιηστι† τῆς μοίρης.          95

94 δωι P, λωι the corrector; neither is intelligible and no
conjecture is plausible

95 μεθ ων is the likeliest reading at the beginning. The
middle is unmetrical (ὑγῑη). I have conjectured μετ᾽ ὦν
ἀμαρτεῖ (Meister) ἦσ<ίς ἐ>στι (deleting ἡ ὑγίη as a gloss), 'for
certainly at sacrifices after which it (health) follows there
is enjoyment.'

the snake's hole[a] and dip the cakes; the rest we shall feast on at the house's seat—and don't forget, you, to carry some of the health-offering and †       †; surely at sacrifices †                    † of the portion.

[a] The gift to the god's holy animal had by this period been formalised into money placed in a box shaped like a snake, but the old terminology was retained.

## 5. ΖΗΛΟΤΥΠΟΣ

(ΒΙ.) λέγε μοι σύ, Γάστρων, ἤδ᾽ ὑπερκορὴς οὕτω
    ὥστ᾽ οὐκέτ᾽ ἀρκεῖ τἀμά σοι σκέλεα κινεῖν
    ἀλλ᾽ ᾽Αμφυταίηι τῆι Μένωνος ἔγκεισαι;
(ΓΑ.) ἐγὼ ᾽Αμφυταίηι; τὴν λέγεις ὀρώρηκα
    γυναῖκα;
&lt;ΒΙ.&gt;        προφάσις πᾶσαν ἡμέρην ἕλκεις.    5
&lt;ΓΑ.&gt; Βίτιννα, δοῦλός εἰμι· χρῶ ὅτι βούληι &lt;μοι&gt;
    καὶ μὴ τό μευ αἷμα νύκτα κἠμέρην πῖνε.
(ΒΙ.) ὅσην δὲ καὶ τὴν γλάσσαν, οὗτος, ἔσχηκας.
    Κύδιλλα, κοῦ ᾽στι Πυρρίης, κάλει μ᾽ αὐτόν.
(ΠΥ.) τί ἐστι;
&lt;ΒΙ.&gt;       τοῦτον δῆσον — ἀλλ᾽ ἔτ᾽ ἔστηκας; —  10
    τὴν ἱμανήθρην τοῦ κάδου ταχέως λύσας.
    ἢν μὴ κατακίσασα τῆι σ᾽ ὅληι χώρηι

---

1 εἰ δ᾽ Bücheler (if accepted, read εἰς)
4 αμφυταιην P, corrected by Jackson
6 &lt;μοι&gt; Blass, Bücheler

# 5. A JEALOUS PERSON

BITINNA

Tell me, Gastron, is this[a] so over-full that it is no longer enough for you to move my legs, but you are devoted to Menon's Amphytaea?

GASTRON

Amphytaea? Have I seen the woman you speak of?

<BITINNA>

You draw out excuses all day.

<GASTRON>

Bitinna, I am a slave: use me as you wish and do not suck my blood night and day.

BITINNA

What a tongue you've acquired. Kydilla, where is Pyrries? Call him to me.

PYRRIES

What is it?

<BITINNA>

Tie him—are you still standing there?—quickly taking the rope from the bucket. If by my ill-treatment of you I don't make you an example to the

---

[a] His penis, indicated by a gesture.

παράδειγμα θῶ, μᾶ, μή με θῆις γυναῖκ᾽ εἶναι.
ἦρ᾽ οὐχὶ μᾶλλον Φρύξ; ἐγὼ αἰτίη τούτων,
ἐγῶιμι, Γάστρων, ἢ σε θεῖσ᾽ ἐν ἀνθρώποις.      15
ἀλλ᾽ εἰ τότ᾽ ἐξήμαρτον, οὐ τὰ νῦν εὖσαν
μώρην Βίτινναν, ὡς δοκεῖς, ἔτ᾽ εὑρήσεις.
φέρ᾽, εἷς σύ, δῆσον, τὴν ἀπληγίδ᾽ ἐκδύσας.

(ΓΑ.)   μὴ μή, Βίτιννα, τῶν σε γουνάτων δεῦμαι.

(ΒΙ.)   ἔκδυθι, φημί. δεῖ σ᾽ ὀτεύνεκ᾽ εἰ<ς> δοῦλος      20
καὶ τρεῖς ὑπέρ σευ μνᾶς ἔθηκα γινώσκειν.
ὡς μὴ καλῶς γένοιτο τἠμέρηι κείνηι
ἥτις σ᾽ ἐσήγαγ᾽ ὧδε. Πυρρίη, κλαύσηι·
ὁρῶ σε δήκου πάντα μᾶλλον ἢ δεῦντα·
σύσσφιγγε τοὺς ἀγκῶνας, ἔκπρισον δήσας.      25

(ΓΑ.)   Βίτινν᾽, ἄφες μοι τὴν ἀμαρτίην ταύτην.
ἄνθρωπός εἰμ᾽, ἥμαρτον· ἀλλ᾽ ἐπὴν αὖτις
ἕλης τι δρῶντα τῶν σὺ μὴ θέλης, στίξον.

(ΒΙ.)   πρὸς Ἀμφυταίην ταῦτα, μὴ ᾽μὲ πληκτίζευ,
μετ᾽ ἧς ἀλινδῆι καὶ εμ...η ποδόψηστρον.      30

<ΠΥ.>   δέδεται καλῶς σοι.

<ΒΙ.>              μὴ λάθηι λυθεὶς σκέψαι.

30 ἐμέ is likely, but the following verb uncertain: χρὴ can
be read (Milne), then a line must have been omitted

whole country, well, don't count me a woman. Is this not rather a case of the Phrygian?[a] I am the cause of this, Gastron, I am, by having set you among men. But if I was wrong then, you will no longer find Bitinna a fool now, as you expect. Come, you by yourself, take off his cloak and tie him.

GASTRON

No, no, Bitinna, by your knees, I beg you.

BITINNA

Take it off, I say. You must realise that you are a slave and I paid three minas for you. A curse on that day which brought you here! Pyrries, you will regret this: I see you undoubtedly at everything rather than tying him. Bind his elbows tightly; saw them off with the ties.

GASTRON

Bitinna, excuse me this mistake. I am human, I went wrong; but whenever again you catch me doing anything you don't wish, tattoo me.

BITINNA

Don't make up to me like this, but to Amphytaea, with whom you roll about, and [                 ] me a doormat.

<PYRRIES>

He's well tied for you.

<BITINNA>

See that he doesn't slip free. Take him to the

___

[a] Who is the better of a beating (2.100).

HERODAS

ἄγ᾽ αὐτὸν εἰς τὸ ζήτρειον πρὸς Ἕρμωνα
καὶ χιλίας μὲν ἐς τὸ νῶτον ἐγκόψαι
αὐτῶι κέλευσον, χιλίας δὲ τῆι γαστρί.

(ΓΑ.) ἀποκτενεῖς, Βίτιννα, μ᾽ οὐδ᾽ ἐλέγξασα          35
εἶτ᾽ ἔστ᾽ ἀληθέα πρῶτον εἴτε καὶ ψευδέα;

(ΒΙ.) ἃ δ᾽ αὐτὸς εἶπας ἄρτι τῆι ἰδίηι γλάσσηι,
'Βίτινν᾽', ἄφες μοι τὴν ἁμαρτίην ταύτην';

(ΓΑ.) τήν σευ χολὴν γὰρ ἤθελον κατασβῶσαι.

(ΒΙ.) ἕστηκας ἐμβλέπων σύ, κοὐκ ἄγεις αὐτόν          40
ὅκου λέγω σοι; θλῆ, Κύδιλλα, τὸ ῥύγχος
τοῦ παντοέρκτεω τοῦδε. καὶ σύ μοι, Δρήχων,
ἤδη ᾽φαμάρτει <τῆι> σοι ἂν οὗτος ἡγῆται.
δώσεις τι, δούλη, τῶι κατηρήτωι τούτωι
ῥάκος καλύψαι τὴν ἀνώνυμον κέρκον,          45
ὡς μὴ δι᾽ ἀγορῆς γυμνὸς ὢν θεωρῆται.
τὸ δεύτερόν σοι, Πυρρίη, πάλιν φωνέω,
ὅκως ἐρεῖς Ἕρμωνι χιλίας ὧδε
καὶ χιλίας ὧδ᾽ ἐμβαλεῖν· ἀκήκουας;
ὡς ἢν τι τούτων ὧν λέγω παραστείξηις,          50
αὐτὸς σὺ καὶ τἀρχαῖα καὶ τόκους τείσεις.

32 Quoted by the *Etymologicum Magnum,* p. 411.33, for
the scansion ζητρεῖον from 'Herodotus' (i.e. Herodas)

33 τον P, corrected by Rutherford, Blass

41 θλῆ Headlam, Hicks, Ellis: οδη P (ΘΛΗ and ΟΔΗ are
only two strokes apart)

270

executioner's, to Hermon, and order him to hammer
a thousand blows into his back and a thousand to
his belly.

GASTRON

Will you kill me, Bitinna, without proving first
whether this is true or false?

BITINNA

But what about what you just said with your own
tongue: 'Bitinna, excuse me this mistake'?

GASTRON

I wanted to calm you down.[a]

BITINNA

Are you standing there staring, instead of taking
him where I tell you? Bash this knave's snout,
Kydilla. And you, Drechon, follow now where he
leads you. Girl, will you give some rag to this cursed
fellow to hide his unmentionable tail, to avoid his
being seen naked through the market-place. For
the second time, Pyrries, again I tell you, that you
are to instruct Hermon to inflict a thousand here
and a thousand here: have you heard? If you go
astray in any of my orders, you will yourself pay
both principal and interest. Go on, and don't take

---

[a] Lit. 'extinguish your bile'.

---

43 <τῆι> σοι ἄν Danielsson, σοι εαν P

βάδιζε καὶ μὴ παρὰ τὰ Μικκάλης αὐτόν
ἄγ᾽, ἀλλὰ τὴν ἰθεῖαν. εὖ δ᾽ ἐπεμνήσθην —
κάλει, κάλει δραμεῦσα, πρὶν μακρήν, δούλη,
αὐτο<ὐ>ς γενέσθαι.

(ΚΥ.)            Πυρρίης, τάλας, κωφέ,    55
καλεῖ σε. μᾶ, δόξει τις οὐχὶ σύνδουλον
αὐτὸν σπαράσσειν ἀλλὰ σημάτων φῶρα.
ὁρῇις ὅκως νῦν τοῦτον ἐκ βίης ἕλκεις
ἐς τὰς ἀνάγκας, Πυρρίη; <σ>έ, μᾶ, τούτοις
τοῖς δύο Κύδιλλ᾽ ἐπόψετ᾽ ἡμερέων πέντε    60
παρ᾽ Ἀντιδώρωι τὰς Ἀχαϊκὰς κείνας,
ἃς πρῶν ἔθηκας, τοῖς σφυροῖσι τρίβοντα.

(ΒΙ.)  οὗτος σύ, τοῦτον αὖτις ὧδ᾽ ἔχων ἧκε
δεδεμένον οὕτως ὥσπερ ἐξάγεις αὐτόν,
Κόσιν τέ μοι κέλευσον ἐλθεῖν τὸν στίκτην    65
ἔχοντα ῥαφίδας καὶ μέλαν. μιῆι δεῖ σε
ὁδῶι γενέσθαι ποικίλον. κατηρτήσθω
οὕτω κατάμυος ὥσπερ ἡ Δάου τιμή.

(ΚΥ.)  μή, τατί, ἀλλὰ νῦν μὲν αὐτόν — οὕτω σοι
ζώιη Βατυλλὶς κἠπίδοις μιν ἐλθοῦσαν    70
ἐς ἀνδρὸς οἶκον καὶ τέκν᾽ ἀγκάλης ἄραις —

55 αὐτο<ὐ>ς several
59 <σ>έ Blass, Weil
60 τους P, corrected by Blass, Weil

272

him by Mikkale's but the direct road. But I've just remembered! — run and call, girl, call them before they get far.

KYDILLA

Pyrries, you deaf wretch, she is calling you. Ah, you'd think he was dragging a grave-robber rather than a fellow-slave. Do you see how you're now forcibly pulling him to the torture, Pyrries? Ah, it's you that Kydilla will see with these two eyes within five days at Antidoros' rubbing your ankles with those Achaean objects[a] you recently put off.

BITINNA

You there, come back here again with him tied just as you are taking him away, and order Kosis the tattooer to come to me with his needles and ink. At the one go you must become speckled. Let him be hung up gagged as much as His Honour Daos.[b]

KYDILLA

No, mama, but for the moment let him—as Batyllis may live and you may see her going to a husband's house and lift her children in your

[a] Clearly chains, though the reason for the epithet is unclear.

[b] Daos is a common slave-name in New Comedy, and we must suppose that one suffered the fate described.

70 μεν P, corrected by Rutherford, Blass

ἄφες, παραιτεῦμαί σε· τὴν μίαν ταύτην
ἀμαρτίην . . .

(ΒΙ.)            Κύδιλλα, μή με λύπει τι
ἢ φεύξομ' ἐκ τῆς οἰκίης. ἀφέω τοῦτον
τὸν ἑπτάδουλον; καὶ τίς οὐκ ἀπαντῶσα    75
ἔς μευ δικαίως τὸ πρόσωπον ἐμπτύοι;
οὐ τὴν Τύραννον, ἀλλ' ἐπείπερ οὐκ οἶδεν,
ἄνθρωπος ὤν, ἑωυτόν, αὐτίκ' εἰδήσει
ἐν τῶι μετώπωι τὸ ἐπίγραμμ' ἔχων τοῦτο.
(ΚΥ.) ἀλλ' ἔστιν εἰκὰς καὶ Γερήνι' ἐς πέμπτην.    80
(ΒΙ.) νῦν μέν σ' ἀφήσω, καὶ ἔχε τὴν χάριν ταύτηι,
ἣν οὐδὲν ἧσσον ἢ Βατυλλίδα στέργω,
ἐν τῆισι χερσὶ τῆις ἐμῆισι θρέψασα.
ἐπεὰν δὲ τοῖς καμοῦσιν ἐγχυτλώσωμεν
ἄξεις τότ' ἀμελι<τῖ>τιν ἑορτὴν ἐξ ἑορτῆς.    85

73 με λυπεῖ τι Palmer, λυπιτε με P
74–75 ἀφέω ... ἑπτάδουλον is quoted by Eustathius in
his commentary on the *Odyssey* 5.306
85 ἀμελι<τῖ>τιν Headlam

274

arms—let him be excused, I beseech you: this one error —

### BITINNA

Kydilla, do not vex me at all, or I shall rush out of the house! Am I to excuse this sevenfold son of slaves? Would not anyone who met me justly spit on my face? No, by the Queen.[a] But since, though human, he does not know himself, he will soon know when he has this inscription[b] on his forehead.

### KYDILLA

But it is the twentieth, and the Gerenia[c] are in four days —

### BITINNA

For the moment I shall excuse you, and be grateful to her, whom I love no less than Batyllis, as I reared her in my own arms. But when we have poured libations to the dead, you will then keep unhoneyed[d] festival on festival.

[a] Which goddess is meant is not clear.

[b] Probably γνῶθι σαυτόν, 'know yourself'.

[c] An otherwise unknown festival, obviously in honour of the dead (84).

[d] I.e. bitter. Honey was not offered to the dead.

# 6. ΦΙΛΙΑΖΟΥΣΑΙ Η ΙΔΙΑΖΟΥΣΑΙ

(ΚΟ.)   κάθησο, Μητροῖ. τῆι γυναικὶ θὲς δίφρον
       ἀνασταθεῖσα· πάντα δεῖ με προστάσσειν
       αὐτήν· σὺ δ' οὐδὲν ἄν, τάλαινα, ποιήσαις
       αὐτὴ ἀπὸ σαυτῆς· μᾶ, λίθος τις, οὐ δούλη
       ἐν τῆι οἰκίηι <κ>εῖσ'· ἀλλὰ τἄλφιτ' ἢν μετρέω  5
       τὰ κρίμν' ἀμιθρεῖς, κἢ<ν> τοσοῦτ' ἀποστάξηι
       τὴν ἡμέ[ρ]ην ὅλην σε τονθορύζουσαν
       καὶ πρημονῶσαν οὐ φέρουσιν οἱ τοῖχοι.
       νῦν αὐτὸν ἐκμάσσεις τε καὶ ποεῖς λαμπρόν
       ὅτ' ἐστὶ χρ[εί]η, ληιστρί; θῦέ μοι ταύτηι      10
       ἐπεί σ' ἔγευσ' ἂν τῶν ἐμῶν ἐγὼ χειρέων.
(ΜΗ.)   φίλη Κοριττοῖ, ταῦτ' ἐμοὶ ζυγὸν τρίβεις·
       κἠγὼ ἐπιβρύχουσ' ἠμέρην τε καὶ νύκτα
       κύων ὑλακτέω τῆι[ς] ἀνωνύμοις ταύτηις.
       ἀλλ' οὔνεκεν πρός σ' ἦλ[θ]ον — ἐκποδὼν ἡμῖν  15
       φθείρεσθε, νώβυστρ', ὦτ[α] μοῦνον καὶ γλάσσαι,

    5 <κ>εῖσ' Richards     μετρέω, corrected to μετρῆι, P
(the correction, 'when you measure out', loses the nice

276

# 6. WOMEN IN A FRIENDLY OR PRIVATE SITUATION

KORITTO

Be seated, Metro. Stand up and put out a chair
for the lady. I have to give you every instruction
myself: you would do nothing by yourself, you
wretch; ah, you are a stone lying in the house, not a
slave. But if I measure out the meal to you, you
count the crumbs, and if so much should drop the
walls won't contain you as you mutter the whole
day. Are you rubbing it and making it shiny now,
when it's needed, you pirate? Give a thank-offering,
I tell you, to this lady, since I would have made you
taste my hands.

METRO

Dear Koritto, you have the same yoke wearing
you down as I. I too am a barking dog, snapping day
and night at those unmentionable girls. But why
I've come to you—get to hell out of our way, with
your closed minds, only ears and tongues, but

---

point of the characterisation of Koritto as careful, if not
mean, cf. 99 ff.)      6 κη ... αποσταξει P, corrected by
several      10 χρ[(ε)ί]η several      16 ὦτ[α] Hicks

τὰ δ' ἄλλ' ἑορτή — λίσσομαί [σ]ε, μὴ ψεύσηι,
φίλη Κοριττοῖ, τίς κοτ' ἦν ὅ σοι ράψας
τὸν κόκκινον βαυβῶνα;

(ΚΟ.)                    κοῦ δ' ὀρώρηκας,
Μητροῖ, σὺ κεῖνον;

(ΜΗ.)             Νοσσὶς ε[ἶ]χεν ἠρίννης     20
τριτημέρηι νιν· μᾶ, καλόν τι δώρημα.

(ΚΟ.) Νοσσίς; κόθεν λαβοῦσα;

(ΜΗ.)                  διαβαλεῖς ἤν σοι
εἴπω;

(ΚΟ.)       μὰ τούτους τοὺς γλυκέας, φίλη Μητροῖ,
ἐκ τοῦ Κοριττοῦς στόματος οὐδεὶς μὴ ἀκούσηι
ὅσ' ἂν σὺ λέξηις.

(ΜΗ.)          ἡ Βιτᾶδος Εὐβούλη     25
ἔδωκεν αὐτῆι καὶ εἶπε μηδέν' αἰσθέσθαι.

(ΚΟ.) γυναῖκες. αὕτη μ' ἡ γυνή κοτ' ἐκτρίψει.
ἐγὼ μὲν αὐτὴν λιπαρεῦσαν ἠιδέσθην
κἤδωκα, Μητροῖ, πρόσθεν ἢ αὐτὴ χρήσασθαι·
ἢ δ' ὤ<σ>περ εὕρημ' ἁρπάσα<σα> δωρεῖται     30
καὶ τῆισι μὴ δεῖ. χαιρέτω φίλη πολλά
ἐοῦσα τοίη, κἠτέρην τιν' ἀντ' ἡμέων

17 εορτηι P, corrected by Blass, Danielsson

278

otherwise idleness—I beg you, do not lie, dear Koritto: who was it who stitched the scarlet dildo for you?

KORITTO

And where, Metro, did you see that?

METRO

Nossis, daughter of Erinna,[a] had it two days ago; ah, what a fine gift!

KORITTO

Nossis? From whom did she get it?

METRO

Will you disparage me if I tell you?

KORITTO

By these sweet eyes, dear Metro, no one shall hear what you say from Koritto's mouth.

METRO

Bitas' Eubule gave it to her and said that no one should know.

KORITTO

Women! This woman will uproot me yet. I paid respect to her plea, and gave it her, Metro, before I used it myself. But snatching it like a windfall, she passes it on even to those who ought not to have it. Many farewells to a friend who is of such a nature; let her look on some other as her friend in future.

[a] The names of two famous poets, used maliciously.

279

φίλην ἀθρείτω. τὰμὰ Νοσσίδι χρῆσαι
τῆι μὴ δοκέω — μέζον μὲν ἢ δίκη γρύζω,
λάθοιμι δ᾽, Ἀδρήστεια — χιλίων εὔντων     35
ἕν᾽ οὐκ ἂν ὅστις σαπρός ἐστι προσδώσω.

(ΜΗ.) μὴ δή, Κοριττοῖ, τὴν χολὴν ἐπὶ ρινός
ἔχ᾽ εὐθύς, ἤν τι ρῆμα μὴ καλὸν πεύθηι.
γυναικός ἐστι κρηγύης φέρειν πάντα.
ἐγὼ δὲ τούτων αἰτίη λαλεῦσ᾽ εἰμι     40
πόλλ᾽, ἀ<λλὰ> τήν μευ γλάσσαν ἐκτεμεῖν δεῖται.
ἐκεῖνο δ᾽ εὖ σοι καὶ μάλιστ᾽ ἐπεμνήσθην,
τίς ἔστ᾽ ὁ ράψας αὐτόν; εἰ φιλεῖς μ᾽, εἶπον.
τί μ᾽ ἐμβλέπεις γελῶσα; νῦν ὀρώρηκας
Μητροῦν τὸ πρῶτον; ἢ τί τἀβρά σοι ταῦτα;     45
ἐνεύχομαι, Κοριττί, μή μ᾽ ἐπιψεύσηι,
ἀλλ᾽ εἰπὲ τὸν ράψαντα.

(ΚΟ.)                    μᾶ, τί μοι ἐνεύχηι;
Κέρδων ἔραψε.

<ΜΗ.>                    κοῖος, εἰπέ μοι, Κέρδων;
δύ᾽ εἰσὶ γὰρ Κέρδωνες· εἷς μὲν ὁ γλαυκός
ὁ Μυρταλίνης τῆς Κυλαιθίδος γείτων,     50
ἀλλ᾽ οὗτος οὐδ᾽ ἂν πλῆκτρον ἐς λύρην ράψαι·

33 ταλλα P, corrected by Groeneboom    χρησθ̅αι P,
interpreted by others as χρῆσθαι
34 Μηδόκεω Weil wrongly    η γυνη γρυξω P, η δικη γρυ-
ζω the corrector

280

That she should have lent my property to Nossis! To whom I do not think—I speak more strongly than is right, may Adresteia[a] not hear—if I had a thousand, I should not hand over one that was rotten.

METRO

Koritto, don't get bile in your nose as soon as you hear a word not to your liking. It is a good woman's place to bear everything. I am the cause of this by saying too much; <but> my tongue should be cut out. But to return to what I particularly asked you, who is the one who stitched it? If you love me, tell me. Why do you look at me with a smile? Have you just seen Metro for the first time? What is this delicacy of yours? I implore you, Koritto, don't deceive me, but tell me the one who stitched it.

KORITTO

Ah, why do you implore me? Kerdon stitched it.

<METRO>

Tell me, which Kerdon? For there are two Kerdons, one the grey-eyed neighbour of Kylaethis' Myrtaline; but *he* couldn't stitch even a plectrum for

---

[a] Goddess who punished any kind of excess.

36 λεπρος P, σαπρος the corrector    προσδωσω corrected to προσδοιην P

37–39 are cited by Stobaeus, *Anth.* 4.23.14, from Herodas' Mimiambi, with κόρη τὺ for Κοριττοῖ and ῥῖνας

38 σοφον P and Stobaeus, καλον the corrector

41 πόλλ', ἀ<λλὰ> Kaibel

ὁ δ᾽ ἕτερος ἐγγὺς τῆς συνοικίης οἰκέων
τῆς Ἑρμοδώρου τὴν πλατεῖαν ἐκβάντι
ἦν μέν κοτ᾽ ἦν τις, ἀλλὰ νῦν γεγήρακε·
τούτωι Κυλαιθὶς ἡ μακαρῖτις ἐχρῆτο —            55
μνησθεῖεν αὐτῆς οἵτινες προσήκουσι.

(ΚΟ.) οὐδέτερος αὐτῶν ἐστιν, ὡς λέγεις, Μητροῖ·
ἀλλ᾽ οὗτος οὐκ οἶδ᾽ ἢ <᾽κ> Χίου τις ἢ ᾽ρυθρέων
ἥκει, φαλακρός, μικκός· αὐτὸ ἐρεῖς εἶναι
Πρηξῖνον, οὐδ᾽ ἂν σῦκον εἰκάσαι σύκωι            60
ἔχοις ἂν οὕτω· πλὴν ἐπὴν λαλῆι, γνώσηι
Κέρδων ὁτεύνεκ᾽ ἐστὶ καὶ οὐχὶ Πρηξῖνος.
κατ᾽ οἰκίην δ᾽ ἐργάζετ᾽ ἐμπολέων λάθρη,
τοὺς γὰρ τελώνας πᾶσα νῦν θύρη φρίσσει.
ἀλλ᾽ ἔργα, κοῖ᾽ ἐστ᾽ ἔργα· τῆς Ἀθηναίης       65
αὐτῆς ὁρῆν τὰς χεῖρας, οὐχὶ Κέρδωνος,
δόξεις. ἐ[γὼ] μέν — δύο γὰρ ἦλθ᾽ ἔχων, Μητροῖ —
ἰδοῦσ᾽ ἅμ᾽ ἰδμῆι τὤμματ᾽ ἐξεκύμηνα·
τὰ βαλλί᾽ οὕτως ἄνδρες οὐχὶ ποιεῦσι
— αὐταὶ γάρ εἰμεν — ὀρθά· κοὐ μόνον τοῦτο,   70
ἀλλ᾽ ἡ μαλακότης ὕπνος, οἱ δ᾽ ἱμαντίσκοι
ἔρι᾽, οὐκ ἱμάν[τες]. εὐνοέστερον σκυτέα
γυναικ[ὶ] διφῶσ᾽ ἄλλον οὐκ ἀνευρ[ή]σ[εις.

55 τουτωι κυλαιθις or τουτω πυλαιθις P
57 ὦν several, unnecessarily
58 <᾽κ> Kaibel

282

a lyre; and the other, living near Hermodoros' tenement as you go from the main street, he *was* someone once, but now he has grown old; the late
Kylaethis was intimate with him—may her rela-
tions remember her.

It's neither of these, as you say, Metro, but this
one comes from Chios or Erythrae, I don't know
which; bald, small—you'd say he was just Prexinos,
you couldn't liken fig to fig so much; however when
he speaks, you'll know that it is Kerdon and not
Prexinos. He works at home and sells secretly, for
every door now shudders at the tax-collectors—but
his work! What work it is! You would think you
were seeing the handiwork of Athene, not Kerdon;
when I saw them—for he came with two, Metro—
my eyes swelled out at first sight; men do not make
stands—we are alone—so straight; and not only
that, but their smoothness is sleep,[a] and the little
straps are wool, not straps; if you look for another
cobbler better disposed to a woman, you will not find
one.

[a] I.e. they are as smooth as sleep.

---

60 (ε)ικασαις P, corrected by Kenyon
63 κατοικειν P, corrected by Rutherford
65 εργοκοι P, corrected by Herwerden
67 ἐ[γὼ] Bücheler
72 ἱμάν[τες] several
73 ἀνευρ[ή]ς[εις Headlam, Stadtmüller

(ΜΗ.) κῶς οὖν ἀφῆκας τὸν ἔτερον;

&lt;ΚΟ.&gt;　　　　　　　　　　τ[ί] δ' οὔ, Μητροῖ,

ἔπρηξα; κοίην δ' οὐ προσήγαγ[ο]ν πειθοῦν　75
αὐτῶι; φιλεῦσα, τὸ φαλακρὸν κ[α]ταψῶσα,
γλυκὺν πιεῖν ἐγχεῦσα, ταταλίζ[ο]υσα,
τὸ σῶμα μοῦνον οὐχὶ δοῦσα χ[ρ]ήσασθαι.

(ΜΗ.) ἀλλ' εἴ σε καὶ τοῦτ' ἠξίωσ', ἔδει δοῦ[ν]αι.

(ΚΟ.) ἔδει γάρ· ἀλλ' ἄκαιρον οὐ πρέπουτ' εἶναι·　80
ἤληθεν ἡ Βιτᾶδος ἐν μέσωι &lt;Εὐ&gt;βούλη·
αὕτη γὰρ ἡμέων ἡμέρην τε κα[ὶ] νύκτα
τρίβουσα τὸν ὄνον σκωρίην πεποίηκεν,
ὅκως τὸν ωὑτῆς μὴ τετρωβόλου κόψηι.

(ΜΗ.) κῶς δ' οὗτος εὗρε πρός σε τὴν ὁδ[ὸ]ν ταύτην,　85
φίλη Κοριττοῖ; μηδὲ τοῦτό με ψεύσηι.

(ΚΟ.) ἔπεμψεν αὐτὸν Ἀρτεμεὶς ἡ Κανδᾶδος
τοῦ βυρσοδέψεω τὴν στέγην σημήνασα.

(ΜΗ.) ἀιεὶ μὲν Ἀρτεμείς τι καινὸν εὑρίσκει,
πρόσω πιεῦσα τὴν προκυκλίην θα...ν.　90

80 ἀλλ' ἄκαιρον divided by Ellis

81 ηληθεν γαρ P, γὰρ deleted by Wilamowitz　　&lt;Εὐ-&gt;
βούλη Jevons, Kaibel, δουλη P

90 πρό σοι Kaibel　　θάμνην Blass, Θαλλοῦν Meister
(then Rutherford's ποεῦσα must also be read, 'leaving
Thallo behind in pandering'); superscript letters largely
illegible

284

METRO

How then did you let the second go?

<KORITTO>

Metro, what did I not do? What persuasion did I
not bring to bear on him? Kissing him, stroking his
bald head, pouring him a sweet drink, calling him
papa, almost giving him my body to use.

METRO

But if he asked for that too, you should have
given it.

KORITTO

Yes, I should have; but it is not decent to act
unseasonably: Bitas' Eubule was grinding near us.
For by turning our millstone day and night she has
ruined it, to avoid setting her own for four obols.

METRO

But how did this man find his way to you, dear
Koritto? On this too don't deceive me.

KORITTO

The tanner Kandas' Artemis sent him, pointing
out the house.

METRO

Artemis will always find something new, drinking further pander's [      ].[a] But at least, when

[a] Probably '[wine]'.

ἀλλ' οὖν γ' ὅτ' οὐχὶ τοὺς δύ' εἶχες ἐκλῦσαι
ἔδει πυθέσθαι τὸν ἕτερον τίς ἡ ἐκδοῦσα.

(ΚΟ.)　ἐλιπάρεον, ὁ δ' ὤμνυ' οὐκ ἂν εἰπεῖν μοι·
†ταύτηι γὰρ καὶ ἠγάπησεν Μητροῖ.†

&lt;ΜΗ.&gt;　λέγεις ὁδόν μοι· νῦν πρὸς Ἀρτεμεῖν εἶμι,　　　　95
ὅκως ὁ Κέρδων ὅστις ἐστὶν εἰδ[ή]σω.
ὑγίαινέ μο[ι, Κοριτ]τί. λαιμάτ[τε]ι κὤρη
ἡμῖ[ν] ἀφ[έρπειν] ἐστί.

(ΚΟ.)　　　　　　　　τὴν θύρην κλεῖσον,
αὕτη [σ]ύ, ν[εο]σσοπῶλι, κἀξαμίθρησαι
αἱ ἀλεκτο[ρῖ]δες εἰ [σ]όαι εἰσί, τῶν τ' αἱρέων　　　100
αὐτῆισ[ι ρ]ῖψ[ο]ν· οὐ γὰρ ἀλλὰ πορθεῦ[σ]ι
ὠρν[ι]θο[κ]λέ[π]ται, κἢν τρέφηι τις ἐν κόλπωι.

94 is added by a later, cursive hand in the upper margin, with signs indicating its position　　&lt;ἤλω&gt; κἠγάπησέ
ν&lt;ιν&gt; Knox
　　95 εἶμι Rutherford, (ε)ιναι P
　　97 μο[ι, Κοριτ]τί Bücheler　　　λαιμάτ[τε]ι Crusius
　　98 ἀφ[έρπειν] Crusius
　　99 ν[εο]σσοπῶλι Diels
　　100 ἀλεκτο[ρῖ]δες Blass, Crusius　　　[σ]όαι Crusius, Palmer
　　101 αὐτῆισ[ι ρ]ῖψον Blass
　　102 ὠρν[ι]θο[κλ]έπ[τ]αι Headlam

you could not save the two, you should have found
out who it was who ordered the second.

KORITTO

I pleaded, but he swore he would not tell me; for
&lt;he was taken&gt; by her and she loved &lt;him&gt;,
Metro.[a]

&lt;METRO&gt;

Your words mean I must leave: now I shall go to
Artemis, to learn who Kerdon is. Keep well, [Kor-
itto]; it is very hungry[b] and it is time for us [to slip]
away.

KORITTO

Shut the door, you there, [chicken]-seller, and
count if the hens are safe, and [throw] some darnel
to them; for undeniably the bird-thieves raid them,
even if one rears them in one's bosom.

[a] Translating Knox's conjecture for the imperfect line.
[b] I.e., apparently, I need to use the dildo.

287

## 7. [Σ]ΚΥΤ[Ε]ΥΣ

(ΜΗ.)  Κέρδων, ἄγω σοι τάσδε τὰς γ[υνάς, εἴ] τι
τῶν σῶν ἔχεις αὐτῆισιν ἄξιον δεῖξαι
χειρέων νοῆρες ἔργον.

(ΚΕ.)                                  οὐ μάτην, Μητροῖ,
ἐγὼ φ[ι]λ<έ>ω σε.  τῆις γυναιξὶν οὐ θήσεις
τὴν μέζον' ἔξω σανίδα; Δριμύλωι φωνέω·          5
πάλιν καθεύδεις; κόπτε, Πίστε, τὸ ῥύγχος
αὐτοῦ, μέχρις τὸν ὕπνον ἐκχέηι πάντα·
μᾶλλον δὲ τὴν ἄκανθα[ν] ὡς ἔχ[ει ἐ]ν καλῆι
ἐκ τοῦ τραχήλου δῆσο[ν.  εἶ]α δή, [.....]ψ,
κίνει ταχέως τὰ γοῦνα· [μ]έζον [....]..          10
τρίβειν ψοφεῦντα νουθ[ετημάτων] τῶνδε.
νῦν ἔκ μιν αὐτὴν λε[...... λαμπ]ρύνεις
καὶ ψ[ῆι]ς; [ἐγὼ] σευ τη.[..........]ψήσω.
ἔζεσ[θ]ε, Μητροῖ.  Πίστ[ε, ........ ο]ίξας
πυργίδα, μὴ τὴν ὧδ[ε, ..........]ν          15

1 γ[υνάς Diels, γ[έας Crusius      εἴ] Blass, Ellis
8 ἔχει ἐν καλῆι (sc. δέσει) Cunningham, following Crusius
and Edmonds, ἔχ[ω]ν κλάηι Knox ('so that he may weep
with it')

288

# 7. A COBBLER

METRO
Kerdon, I am bringing you these [ladies to see if]
you can show them any skilled work worthy of your
craft.

KERDON
I have good reason, Metro, for loving you. Put
the larger bench outside for the ladies. I'm speaking
to Drimylos: are you asleep again? Pistos, hit his
snout, until he sheds all his sleepiness; or rather tie
the thorn to his neck, as he is, well bound. Come
then, [                    ], move your knees quickly:
[                    ] to rub on objects that make more
noise than these warn[ings?                    , are
you polishing] and [wiping] it now? I'll wipe your
[                    ]. Sit down, Metro. Pistos, open the
[          ] chest, not this one here, [                    ]

---

9 [Κέρκω]ψ Headlam
10 [ἴχην]ας Knox
11 νουθ[ετημάτων] Headlam
12 λε[ιόπυγε, λαμπ]ρύνεις Knox and Headlam, λε[υκόπυγε,
φαιδ]ρύνεις Crusius and Headlam
13 καὶ ψ[ῆι]ς; [ἐγώ] Knox    τὴν [κοχώνην ἐκ]ψήσω Knox
14 τὴν διπλῆν ο]ἴξας Herzog
15 τὴν δ' ἄνω κ(ε)ίνη]ν Headlam, following Crusius

289

τὰ χρήσιμ' ἔργα τοῦ τ.[..........]ος
ταχέως ἔνεγκ' ἄνωθ[εν ......  Μη]τροῖ,
οἶ' ἔργ' ἐπόψεσθ'. ἡσυχῆ [.........]ον
τὴν <σ>αμβαλούχην οἶγ[ε ......] πρῶτον
Μητροῖ, τελέων ἄρη[ρε ......]εων ἴχνος.     20
θηεῖσθε κύμε[ῖ]ς, ὦ γυ[ναῖκες· ἡ πτ]έρνη
ὁρῆτ' ὅπως πέπηγε, .[....]φην.[..]οις
ἐξηρτίωται πᾶσα, κο[ὐ τ]ὰ μὲν κ[αλ]ῶς
τὰ δ' οὐχὶ καλῶς, ἀλλὰ πά[ν]τ' ἴσαι χ[εῖρε]ς.
τὸ χρῶμα δ' οὕτως ὑμ[ι]ν ἡ πα[...] δοίη     25
.[            ].ερ ἰχανᾶσθ' ἐπαυρέσθαι
.[            ἄλ]λο τῶιδ' ἴσον χρῶμα
κ[            ]ωκουδε κηρὸς ἀνθήσει
χ[            ]. τρεῖς ἔδωκε Κανδᾶτ[.].
κ[            ] τοῦτο κἤτερον χρῶμα     30
β.[            ὄμνυ]μι πάντ' ὅσ' ἐστ' ἰρά
κω[            ] τὴν ἀληθ[ε]ί[η]ν βάζειν
            ] οὐδ' ὅσον ῥοπὴν ψεῦδος

16 τρ[ίβωνος Κέρδων]ος Sitzler
17 ἄνωθ[εν Blass, then ὦ μάκαρ Headlam, οὐκ ἐρῶ Stadtmüller
18 [δὲ πρόσμειν]ον Blass, [σύ, λαίμαστρ]ον Knox
19 <σ>αμβαλούχην several      οἶγ[ε· τοῦτ' ὅρη Blass,
· τοῦτό σοι Knox
20 ἐκ μερ]έων Knox
21 γυ[ναῖκες· ἡ πτ]έρνη Rutherford

the serviceable works, bring quickly down from
above [                    ] Metro, what works you shall
see. Quietly [                    ] open the shoe-box.
[                    ] first, Metro, the sole is put together
from perfect [                    ]; look, ladies, you also;
see how the heel is fixed, and it is all fitted
[                    ], and it is not the case that
some parts are well-made and others are not, but all
the [handiwork] is equal. And the colour, as may
[          ] give you [                    ] you wish
to enjoy, [                    other] colour equal to
this. [                    ] beeswax will flower
[                ] gave three [              ] to Kandas
[          ] this and another colour. [          I
swear by] all that is sacred [          ] that I speak
the truth [                    ] nor so much of a lie

---

22 χ[ῶτι σ]φηνί[σκ]οις Kenyon, but the first letter is more
like α̣[

23 κο[ὺ τ]ὰ̣ μὲν κ[αλ]ῶς Blass, Headlam

24 χ[εῖρε]ς Blass

25 Πά[φου] Knox, with μ[εδέουσ' in 26 ('the ruler of
Paphos', i.e. Aphrodite)

26 ὅσων]περ Headlam

27 ἄλ]λο Crusius

28 κοὺδὲ or κοῦ δὲ may be read

29 χ[ρυσοῦ στατῆρα]ς Knox, χ[θὲς οὖν στατῆρα]ς Edmonds
Κανδᾶτ[ο]ς̣ Diels (to be corrected to -ᾶδ-)

31 ὄμνυ]μι Blass

32 κὤ[σια, γυναῖκες,] Crusius, κὤ[σσ' ἐστιν ὅσια] Headlam    βαδιζειν P, corrected by Crusius

291

ἢ] Κέρδωνι μὴ βίου ὄνησις
μ[ηδ᾽      ]ων γίνοιτο κα[ὶ] χάριν πρός με    35
οὐ γ]ὰρ ἀλλὰ μεζόνων ἤδη
      ] κερδέων ὀριγνῶνται
      ]. τὰ ἔργα τῆς τέχνης ἠμ<έ>ων
πί]συγγος δὲ δειλαίην οἰζύν
      ].ναν[..]εων νύκτα κἠμέρην θάλπω    40
      ]. ἠμέων ἄχρι<ς> ἐσπέρης κάπτει
      ]αι πρὸ[ς] ὄρθρον οὐ δοκέω τόσ<σ>ον
τὰ Μικίωνος κηρί᾽ εὐπ[        ]
κοὔπω λέγω, τρισκαιδε[κ...... β]όσκω,
ὁτεύνεκ᾽, ὦ γυναῖκες, ἀργ[.......]ς    45
οἴ, κἢν ὑῃ Ζεύς, τοῦτο μοῦ[νον ἄιδουσ]ι,
φέρ᾽ εἰ φέρεις τι, τἄλλα δ᾽ ἀ[.].[.... ἤ]νται
ὅκως νεοσσο[ὶ] τὰς κοχώνας θά[λ]π[ο]ντες.
ἀλλ᾽ οὐ λόγων γάρ, φασίν, ἡ ἀγορὴ δεῖται
χαλκῶν δέ, τοῦτ᾽ ἢν μὴ ὗμιν ἀνδάνηι, Μητρ[οῖ,    50
τὸ ζεῦγος, ἕτερον κἄτε[ρ]ον μάλ᾽ ἐξοίσει,
ἔστ᾽ ἂν νόωι πεισθῆτε [μὴ λ]έγει[ν] ψευδέα

34 ἢ] Bücheler
35 μ[ηδ᾽ Sitzler
36 οὐ γ]ὰρ Bücheler
37 οἱ βυρσοδέψαι] Crusius
39 πί]συγγος Blass
41 τί]ς Knox, τίς ἔστ᾽ ὅ]ς Edmonds    ἄχρι<ς> Rutherford

292

[                    ] the balance [                 or]
may Kerdon have no profit in life [nor          ]—
and [                 ] thanks to me; for undeniably
[                          ] now grasp at greater gains.
[              ] the works of our craft [            ].
But I the cobbler, [                              ]
wretched woe, heat [                   ] night and day.
[                     ] of us gulps till evening
[                     ] at dawn? I don't think
Mikion's honey is so [              ]. And I
haven't yet said, I feed thirteen [          ], since,
ladies, [                 ] lazy, who, even if Zeus sends
rain, [sing] this alone, 'Bring, if you've anything to
bring'; but otherwise they [sit        ], like chicks
warming their posteriors. But as it's not words,
they say, the market needs but brass,[a] if you don't
like this pair, Metro, he'll bring out another and yet
another, till you are convinced that Kerdon does

[a] Kerdon adapts to his own situation the proverb 'the
market needs not words, but deeds'.

42 ἢ πίετ]αι Knox    τόσ<σ>ον Bücheler
43 μικρωνος P, corrected by Crusius
44 οὓς ἐγὼ Edmonds
45 ἀργ[ίη πάντε]ς Headlam
46 μοῦ[νον ἄιδουσ]ι Crusius
47 ἀ[σ]φ[αλεῖς Herzog    ἦ]νται Headlam
48 κηχωνας P, corrected by Danielsson, Jackson
52 [μὴ λ]έγει[ν] F.D.

Κέρδωνα. τάς μοι σα[μβα]λουχίδας πάσας
ἔνεγκε, Πίστε ... αλισγ̣νηθεισας
ὑμέας ἀπελθεῖν, ὦ γυναῖκες, εἰς οἶκον.　　　　55
θήσεσθε δ᾽ ὑμ[εῖς ·] γένεα ταῦτα πα[ν]τοῖα ·
Σικυώνι᾽, Ἀμβρακίδια, Νοσσίδες, λεῖαι,
ψιττάκια, κανναβίσκα, Βαυκίδες, βλαῦται,
Ἰωνίκ᾽ ἀμφίσφαιρα, νυκτιπήδηκες,
ἀκροσφύρια, καρκίνια, σάμβαλ᾽ Ἀργεῖα,　　　　60
κοκκίδες, ἔφηβοι, διάβαθρ᾽· ὧν ἐρᾶι θυμός
ὑμέων ἑκάστης εἴπατ᾽, ὡς ἂν αἴσθοισθε
σκύτεα γυναῖκες καὶ κύνες τί βρώζουσιν.

(ΜΗ.) 　κόσου χρείζεις κεῖν᾽ ὃ πρόσθεν ἤειρας
ἀπεμπολή<σαι> ζεῦγος; ἀλλὰ μὴ βροντέων　　　65
οὗτος σὺ τρέψηις μέζον εἰς φυγὴν ἡμέας.

(ΚΕ.) 　αὐτὴ σὺ καὶ τίμησον, εἰ θέλεις, αὐτό
καὶ στῆσον ἧς κότ᾽ ἐστιν ἄξιον τιμῆς.
ὀ τοῦτ᾽ ἐῶν γὰρ οὔ σε ρηιδίως ρινᾶι.
ζευγέων, γύναι, τὠληθὲς ἢν θέληις ἔργον,　　　70
ἐρεῖς τι — ναὶ μὰ τήνδε τὴν τεφρὴν κόρσην,

53 σα̣[μβα]λου̣χ̣ίδας Bücheler
54 An unsolved mystery
56 ὑμ[εῖς ·] γένεα Rutherford
57 For λεῖαι Headlam conjectured Χῖαι
58 βλαυ⸀τια P, corrected by Herwerden
65 ἀπεμπολή<σαι> several

[not] tell lies. Bring me all the shoe-boxes, Pistos;
you must, ladies, go back home [                              ]
You will see for yourselves: here are all kinds:
Sikyonians, little Ambrakians, Nossises, plains,
greens, hemps, Baukises,[a] slippers, Ionics with but-
tons, night-walkers, boots, crabs, Argive sandals,
scarlets, youths, flats: say what is the heart's desire
of each one of you; so that thus you may realise why
women and dogs eat leather.[b]

### METRO

For how much do you want to sell that pair which
you lifted up before? But see you, don't put us to
flight with your loud thundering.

### KERDON

Value it yourself if you wish and set what price it
is worth. One who allows this does not readily cheat
you. Lady, if you wish the true craftsmanship of
pairs, you will say something—yes by this ashen

[a] Nossises and Baukises continue the malicious reference of 6.20: for Baukis was the friend of Nossis and subject of her poem 'Distaff'.

[b] Dogs proverbially never forget how to chew their
leather lead; women similarly never give up using a
leather dildo.

---

69 The beginning was read by Meister, the end by
Blass; neither is fully certain

ἐπ' ἦς ἀλώπηξ νοσσιὴν πεποίητα[ι —
τάχ' ἀλφιτηρὸν ἐρ[γ]α[λ]ξῖα κινεῦσι.
Ἑρμῇ τε Κερδέων καὶ σὺ Κερδείη Πειθοῖ,
ὡς, ἤν τι μὴ νῦν ἧμιν ἐς βόλον κύρσῃ,     75
οὐκ οἶδ' ὅκως ἄμεινον ἢ χύτρη πρήξει.

(ΜΗ.) τί τονθορύζεις κοὐκ ἐλευθέρηι γλάσσηι
τὸν τῖμον ὅστις ἐστὶν ἐξεδίφησας;

(ΚΕ.) γύναι, μιῆς μνῆς ἐστιν ἄξιον τοῦτο
τὸ ζεῦγος· ἢ ἄνω 'σ<τ>' ἢ κάτω βλέπειν· χαλκοῦ
ρίνημ' ὂ δήκοτ' ἐστὶ τῆς Ἀθηναίης     81
ὠνευμένης αὐτῆς ἂν οὐκ ἀποστάξαι.

(ΜΗ.) μάλ' εἰκότως σευ τὸ στεγύλλιον, Κέρδων,
πέπληθε δαψιλέων τε καὶ καλῶν ἔργων.
φύλασσε κά[ρτ]α σ' αὐτά· τῆι γὰρ εἰκοστῆι     85
τοῦ Ταυρεῶνος ἡκατῆ γάμον ποιεῖ
τῆς Ἀρτακηνῆς, κὐποδημάτων χρείη·
τάχ' οὖν, τάλης, ἄ<ι>ξουσι σὺν τύχηι πρός σε,
μᾶλλον δὲ πάντως. ἀλλὰ θύλακον ῥάψαι
τὰς μνέας ὅκως σοι μὴ αἱ γαλαῖ διοίσουσι.     90

---

73 ἐρ[γ]α[λ]ξῖα Diels
77 τονθορυξειˢ P, corrected by Rutherford
78 ἐξεφώνησας (Richards) would be easier
80 'σ<τ>' Headlam
85 κά[ρτ]α Blass     σ(οι) αὐτά understood by Bücheler
88 ἄ<ι>ξουσι Crusius

head, on which the fox has made its den[a]—
supplying food quickly to tool-wielders. O Hermes
of profit and profiting Persuasion, if something does
not now chance into the cast of our net, I do not
know how the pot will fare better.

METRO

Why are you muttering instead of having
searched out the price with free tongue?

KERDON

Lady, this pair is worth one mina, you may look
up or down.[b] Not the least shaving of a copper would
come off, if Athene herself were the customer.

METRO

It's not surprising, Kerdon, that your little house
is full of abundant lovely objects. Guard them [care-
fully] for yourself; for on the twentieth of Taureon[c]
Hekate holds the marriage of Artakene, and there is
need of shoes; so, wretch, perhaps with good luck, or
rather certainly, they will rush to you. Have a sack
stitched so that the cats won't plunder your minas.

[a] I.e. which suffers from the disease alopecia, by a pun
with 'alopex', fox.
[b] Probably 'whether you look happy or sad'.
[c] A month in many cities of Asia Minor.

(ΚΕ.) ἤν τ' ἠκατ<ῆ> ἔλθηι, μνῆς ἔλασσον οὐκ οἴσει,
ἤν τ' ἡ 'Αρτακηνή. πρὸς τάδ', εἰ θέλεις, σκέπτευ.

(ΜΗ.) οὔ σοι δίδωσιν ἡ ἀγαθὴ τύχη, Κέρδων,
ψαῦσαι ποδίσκων ὧν Πόθοι τε κῆρωτες
ψαύουσιν; ἀλλ' εἷς κνῦσα καὶ κακὴ λώβη      95
ὥστ' ἐκ μὲν ἡμέων †λιολεοσεω† πρήξεις.
ταύτηι δὲ δώσεις κε[ῖ]νο τὸ ἔτερον ζεῦγος
κόσου; πάλιν πρήμηνον ἀξίην φωνήν
σεωυτοῦ.

<ΚΕ.>          στατῆρας πέντε, ναὶ μὰ θεούς, φο[ι]τᾶι
ἡ ψάλτρι' <Εὐ>ετηρὶς ἡμέρην πᾶσαν      100
λαβεῖν ἀνώγουσ', ἀλλ' ἐγώ μιν ἐχθ[α]ίρω,
κἢν τέσσαράς μοι Δαρικοὺς ὑπόσχηται,
ὀτεύνεκέν μευ τὴν γυναῖκα τωθάζει
κακοῖσι δέννοις · εἰ δ[έ σοί γ' ἐσ]τι χρείη
φερευλαβου<          > τῶν τριῶν [ .... ] δοῦναι      105

91 ἠκατ<ῆ> Rutherford
92 τηι P, corrected by Herwerden
96 Possibly Αἰολέως should be read (taking εω as a correction of εο, added instead of substituted; Αἰολέος Beare), followed by <χεῖρον> or <μεῖον>
100 <Εὐ>ετηρὶς Blass, Rutherford
104 δ[έ σοί γ' ἐσ]τὶ Blass

## MIME 7

### KERDON

Whether Hekate comes, or Artakene, she will not get them for less than a mina; consider this, if you please.

### METRO

Kerdon, does not good fortune grant you to touch the little feet which Desires and Loves touch? But you are an irritation and wicked disgrace; so that from us you will get <              >.[a] But for how much will you give that other pair to this lady? Again blast out a word worthy of yourself.

### <KERDON>

Five staters, by the gods, is what the harpist <Eu>eteris comes each day asking me to take, but I hate her, even if she promises me four Darics, since she jeers at my wife with wicked reproaches. But if [you have] need, †                    † to give

---

[a] The sense must be 'you will get nothing'; with the conjecture suggested, 'you will fare worse than Aeoleus', but the identity of Aeoleus is unknown.

---

105 If the first word is φέρ', one can read with Headlam εὐλαβοῦ <σὺ> τῶν τριῶν [μᾶι] δοῦναι, 'come, beware of giving them to one of the three' (i.e. Hekate, Artakene, Eueteris); if it is φέρευ, then λαβοῦ<σα>· τῶν τριῶν [θέλω] δοῦναι (Blass, Bücheler), 'take them away; I wish to give you them for three Darics'. Knox's placing of a fragment .ον here is uncertain in itself and leads to no good result

καὶ ταῦτα καὶ ταῦτ' ἦι ὗμιν ἐπτὰ Δαρεικῶν
ἔκητι Μητροῦς τῆσδε· μηδὲν ἀντείπηις.
δύ]ναιτό μ' ἐλάσαι σ<ἢ> ἂν [ἰὴ] τὸν πίσ[υγγον
ἐόντα λίθινον ἐς θεοὺς ἀναπτῆναι·
ἔχεις γὰρ οὐχὶ γλάσσαν, ἡδονῆς δ' ἠθμόν.      110
ἆ, θεῶν ἐκεῖνος οὐ μακρὴν ἀπεσ[τ' ὦν]ήρ
ὅτεωι σὺ χείλεα νύκτα κἠμέρην οἴγ[εις.
φέρ' ὧδε τὸν ποδίσκον· εἰς ἴ<χ>νος θῶμεν·
πάξ· μήτε προσθῆις μήτ' ἀπ' οὖν ἕληις μηδέν·
τὰ καλὰ πάντα τῆις καλῆισιν ἁρμόζει·      115
αὐτὴν ἐρεῖς τὸ πέλμα τὴν Ἀθηναίην
τεμεῖν. δὸς αὕτη καὶ σὺ τὸν πόδ'· ἆ, ψωρῆι
ἄρηρεν ὁπλῆι βοῦς ὁ λακτίσας ὑμ<έ>ας.
εἴ τις πρ[ὸ]ς ἴχνος ἠκόνησε τὴν σμίλην,
οὐκ ἄν, μὰ τὴν Κέρδωνος ἑστίην, οὕτω      120
τοὔργον σαφέως ἔκειτ' ἂν ὡς σαφ<έ>ως κεῖται.
αὕτη σύ, δώσεις ἑπτὰ Δαρικοὺς τοῦδε,
ἡ μέζον ἵππου πρὸς θύρην κιχλίζουσα;
γυναῖκες, ἢν ἔχητε κἠτέρων χρείην
ἢ σαμβαλίσκων ἢ ἃ κατ' οἰκίην ἕλκειν      125
εἴθισθε, τήν μοι δουλ[ίδ]' ὧδε <δεῖ> πέμπειν.

108 δύ]ναιτο Bücheler      σ<ἢ> ἂν [ἰὴ] Knox      πίσ[υγ-
γον Knox
109 ληθινον P, corrected by Headlam

[         ] of the three—and this and this may be
yours for seven Darics for the sake of Metro here.
Don't contradict: your [voice] could drive me, the
cobbler, a man of stone, to fly to heaven; for you
have not a tongue but a sieve of pleasure; ah, not far
away from the gods [is the man] to whom you open
your lips night and day. Give me your little foot
here; let's place it on the sole. Right! Neither add
nor remove anything: all lovely things fit lovely
ladies; you would say that Athene herself had cut
the sole. Give me your foot also: ah, the ox that
kicked you was equipped with a scabby hoof. If one
had sharpened one's knife on the sole, by Kerdon's
hearth the work would not have lain so accurately
as it does lie accurately. You there, will you give
seven Darics for this, you who are cackling at the
door more loudly than a horse? Ladies, if you have
need of anything else, small sandals or what you are
in the habit of trailing at home,[a] you <must> send
your slave here to me. But you, Metro, be sure to

---

[a] Loose-fitting house-shoes.

110 ἡδηνης P, corrected by Herwerden      ηθμην or ηθμιν
P, corrected by Bücheler
    111 ἀπες[τ' ὢν]ήρ Blass      112 οἴγ[εις Blass
    113 ἴ<χ>νος Blass      θῶμεν Hicks, better than θῶ μιν
Blass      117 πόδ' ἆ divided by Headlam
    117–118 ψωρη . . . οπλη P, corrected by Rutherford
    126 δουλ[δ'] several      <δεῖ> several

HERODAS

σὺ δ᾽ ἧκε, Μητροῖ, πρός με τῆι ἐνάτηι πάντως
ὅκως λάβηις καρκίνια· τὴν γὰρ οὖν βαίτην
θάλπουσαν εὖ δεῖ ᾽νδον φρονεῦντα καὶ ῥάπτειν.

come to me on the ninth to get your crabs; for in truth a sensible man must stitch inside the skin coat that gives warmth.

# 8. ΕΝΥΠΝΙΟΝ

ἄστηθι, δούλη Ψύλλα· μέχρι τέο κείσηι
ῥέγχουσα; τὴν δὲ χοῖρον αὐονὴ δρύπτει·
ἢ προσμένεις σὺ μέχρις εὖ ἥλιος θάλψηι
τὸ]ν κῦσον ἐσδύς; κῶς δ', ἄτρυτε, κοὐ κάμνεις
τὰ πλ]ευρὰ κνώσσουσ'; αἱ δὲ νύκτες ἐννέωροι.    5
ἄστη]θι, φημί, καὶ ἄψον, εἰ θέλεις, λύχνον,
καὶ τ]ὴν ἄναυλον χοῖρον ἐς νομὴν πέμψ[ο]ν.
τ]όνθρυζε καὶ κνῶ, μέχρις εὖ παραστά[ς σοι
τὸ] βρέγμα τῶι σκίπωνι μαλθακὸν θῶμα[ι.
δει]λὴ Μεγαλλί, κα[ὶ] σὺ Λάτμιον κνώσσεις;    10
οὐ] τὰ ἔριά σε τρύχ[ο]υσιν· ἀλλὰ μὴν στέμμ[α
ἐπ' ἱρὰ διζόμεσ[θ]α· βαιὸς οὐκ ἧμιν
ἐν τῆι οἰκίηι ἔτι μα[λ]λὸς εἰρίων. δειλή,
ἄστηθι. σύ τε μοι τ[οῦ]ναρ, εἰ θέλεις, Ἀννᾶ,
ἄκουσον· οὐ γὰρ νη[πία]ς φρένας βόσκεις.    15

3 θαλψηι, corrected to θαλψ(ε)ι, P
4 τὸ]ν κῦσον Headlam
5 τὰ πλ]ευρὰ Headlam, Palmer
6 ἄστη]θι Diels

304

# 8. A DREAM

Get up, slave Psylla: how long are you going to lie
snoring? Drought is rending the sow. Or are you
waiting till the sun crawls into [your] bum and
warms it? Unwearied one, how have you avoided
tiring [your] ribs with sleeping? The nights are nine
years long. [Get up], I say, and light the lamp,
please, [and] send the unmelodious sow to the
pasture. Mutter and scratch yourself until I stand
beside [you] and make [your] head soft with my
stick. [Wretched] Megallis, are you too in a Latmian
sleep?[a] It is [not] your wool that wears you out:
should we seek a wreath for the rites, there is not
any longer a tiny woollen fleece in the house for us.
Wretch, get up. And you, Annas, please listen to my
dream, for you do not nourish a silly mind. I seemed

[a] Like the mythological sleeper Endymion, who fre-
quented or was buried on Mt Latmos.

---

8 παραστά[ς Vogliano    σοι Sitzler
9 τὸ] Headlam
10 δει]λὴ Palmer
11 οὐ] Palmer
13 μα[λ]λὸς Bücheler
14 τ[οὖ]ναρ Blass

τράγον τιν' ἕλκειν [διὰ] φάραγγος ὠιήθη[ν
μακρῆς, ὁ δ' εὐπώ[γω]ν τε κεύκερως ἦ[εν.
ἐπεὶ δὲ δὴ [.]..[.......]. τῆς βήσσης
ἠο[ῦ]ς φα[ούσης ......] γὰρ ἔσσωμαι
συ[...............].ες αἰπόλοι πλε[                          20
τη[................].ριωντεποιευ[
κἠγὼ οὐκ ἐσύλευν [....].(.)[
καὶ ἄλλης δρυὸς [...].ε[
οἱ δ' ἀμφίκαρτα.[...]τεσ[
τὸν αἶγ' ἐποίευν [....]π[                                    25
καὶ [π]λησίον με.[....]ι.[
κ[.....].νμα.[....].ω[
σχ[.....]κροκωτ[....]φ.[
ω[.....]λεπτῆς ἄ[ν]τυγος ....[
σ.[....]ς δὲ νεβροῦ χλαν[ι]δίω[ι] κατέζω[στ]ο      30
κ[......].ν κύπα[σσι]ν ἀμ[φ]ὶ τοῖς ὤμοις
κο[......] ἀμφὶ κρ[ητὶ κ]ίσσι[ν]' ἔστεπτο
.....κ]οθόρνου[....]η κα[τ]αζώστρηι
.........]ωμεντο [....]σα.[.....] φρίκη[.
.........]ωρηνιχ[...].θι.[        ]                         35
.........]ο λῶπο[ς ...]κον [πε]ποιῆσθαι
...... Ὀδ]υσσέως ο[....] Αἰόλ[ου] δῶρον
..........]φ.[.......]το.[...]α λακτίζειν
..........]εγ[......].εν[..] λῶιστον

to be dragging a goat [through] a long defile, and
it [was] well bearded and well horned; and when
[            ] from the glen, at the [appearance of]
dawn [            ] for I am defeated, [            ]
goatherds [                    ]. And I did not
despoil [                    ] and of another tree
[            ]. And those around [            ] very
[        ] made the goat [        ] and near by
[        ] yellow [        ] of slight curve
[                ]. He was girded with a stole of
[            ] fawnskin, [            ] tunic
about his shoulders, and he was crowned with ivy
[        ] round his head [        ] with the
[            ] lace of a boot.[a] [            ] frost
[            ] cloak [        ] to have been
made [        ] of Odysseus [        ] gift of
Aeolos [            ] to kick [            ] best,

---

[a] Lines 29–35 are clearly a description of Dionysos.

---

16 [διὰ] Crusius
17 εὐπώ[γω]ν Crusius    ἦ[εν Knox, ἦ[ν τις Crusius
18 [ν]ιν Knox    19 ἠ[οῦ]ς φα[ούσης Knox
28 σχ[ιστὸν] κροκωτ[ὸν] Vogliano
30 στ[ικτῆ]ς Knox    κατέζω[στ]ο Herzog
31 κύπα[σσι]ν Crusius
32 κό[ρυμβα δ'] Knox    κρ[ητὶ κ]ίσσι[ν'] Knox
33 -ου or -ους    κα[τ]αζώστρηι Knox
36 λῶπο[ς Bücheler    [πε]ποιῆσθαι Milne
37 Ὀδ]υσσέως Bücheler    Αἰόλ[ου] Knox

307

HERODAS

ὥσπερ τελεῦμεν ἐν χοροῖς Διωνύσου.    40
κοὶ μὲν μετώποις ἐ[ς] κόνιν κολυμβῶ[ντες
ἔκοπτον ἀρνευτῆρ[ε]ς ἐκ βίης οὖδας,
οἱ δ' ὕπτι' ἐρριπτεῦντο· πάντα δ' ἦν, Ἀνν[ᾶ,
εἰς ἓν γέλως τε κἀνίη ['ναμιχθ]έντα.
κἀγὼ δόκεον δὶς μοῦ[νο]ς ἐκ τόσης λείης    45
ἐπ' οὖν ἀλέσθαι, κἠλάλαξαν ἄνθρωπ[οι
ὥς μ' εἶδ[ον .. ]ως τὴν δο[ρὴ]ν πιεζεῦσαν
καὶ φ[                    ]τ[
οιδε [
γρυπ[                         50
ρυπ[
τ.[
τ[
[
[                            55
[
[
τὰ δεινὰ πνεῦσαι λὰξ πατε[
ἔρρ' ἐκ προσώπου μή σε καίπ∟ερ ὢν πρέσβυς
οὔληι κατ' ἰθὺ τῆι βατηρίηι κό[ψω.'    60
κἠγὼ μεταῦτις· 'ὦ παρεόν[τες
θανεῦμ' ὑπὲρ γῆς, εἰ ὁ γέρων μ[
μαρτύρ[ο]μαι δὲ τὸν νεην[ίην

308

as we observe in the choruses of Dionysos.[a]
Some plunging with their foreheads to the dust
forcibly struck the ground like divers, and others
were thrown on their backs; everything, Annas, was
laughter and pain [mingled] in one. And I [alone] of
such a flock seemed to leap on twice, and the men
cried out, as they saw the skin pressing me
[           ] and [           ]. And they [           ] hooked
[           ] dirt [


                                    ] to blow terribly trampling
with the foot [                    ] get out of my sight, lest
although ⌐I am old⌐ I strike you straight down with
my whole stick.' I then [said], 'Spectators, I shall die
for the land if the old man [                    ] and I call
to witness the young man [                              ].' He

[a] A game played at Dionysiac festivals, in which the
participants tried to balance on an inflated wineskin.

---

40 διονυσου P, corrected by Kenyon
44 [’ναμιχθ]έντα Knox
45 μοῦ[νο]ς Herzog
46 ὤνθρωπ[οι Crusius
47 (ε)ῖδ[ον Knox       δο[ρὴ]ν Crusius       πιεζεῦντα Knox
50 πατέ[οντα Crusius, πατέ[ων Herzog
59–60 are cited by the scholiast on Nicander, *Theriaca*,
377, from Herodes the hemiamb (i.e. mimiambic poet) in
his ‘Sleep’ (Ὕπνωι for Ἐνυπνίωι), as evidence for βατηρία =
βακτηρία
59 ερρ P, φ(ε)ύγωμεν schol.
60 κό[ψω Weil, καλύψω or -ηι schol.

309

ὀ δ’ εἶπεν [ἄ]μφω τὸν δορέα . [
καὶ τοῦτ’ ἰ[δ]ὼν ἔληξα. τὸ ἔνδυ[τον     65
’Αν]νᾶ δ[ὸς] ὧδε. τὠναρ ὧδ’ ἰ[
........]ν αἶγα τῆς φ[άραγγος] ἐξεῖλκον
..... κ]αλοῦ δῶρον ἐκ Δ[ιων]ύσου
..... αἰ]πόλοι μιν ἐκ βίης [ἐδ]αιτρεῦντο
τ]ὰ ἔνθεα τελεῦντες καὶ κρεῶ[ν] ἐδαίνυντο,     70
τὰ μέλεα πολλοὶ κάρτα, τοὺς ἐμοὺς μόχθους,
τιλεῦσιν ἐν Μούσῃσιν. ωδεγω[     ]το.
τὸ μὴν ἄεθλον ὡς δόκευν ἔχ[ει]ν μοῦνος
πολλῶν τὸν ἄπνουν κώρυκον πατησάντων,
κἠ τῶι γέροντι ξύν’ ἔπρηξ’ ὀρινθέντι     75
.] κλέος, ναὶ Μοῦσαν, ἤ μ’ ἔπεα κ[
.εγ’ ἐξ ἰάμβων, ἤ με δευτέρη γν[
.μ..ς μετ’ Ἱππώνακτα τὸν παλαι[
τ]ὰ κύλλ’ ἀείδειν Ξουθίδης †επιουσι[

64 [ἄ]μφω Crusius     ξ[ύλωι δῆσαι Herzog, ξ[υνῆι κτῆσθαι Pisani
65 ἔνδυ[τον Crusius
66 ’Αν]νᾶ Sitzler     δὸς] Knox     τὠναρ Knox     (ε)ἰ[κάζειν δεῖ Crusius
67–75 The ends are preserved in O
67 ὡς μὲν τὸ]ν Edmonds     φ[άραγγος] Crusius
68 ἔξω τι κ]αλοῦ Knox     Δ[ιων]ύσου Knox
69 ὡς δ’ οἱ Knox, αἰ]πόλοι Bücheler     [ἐδ]αιτρεῦντο Milne
70 τ]ὰ Crusius     κρεῶ[ν ἐδαί]νυντο Weil, ]αμεδαινυντο O (perhaps corrupt)

said that the flayer [     ] both [                ].
And having seen this I stopped. [Annas, give] my
cloak here. [                ] the dream thus
[                ] I dragged the goat from the
[defile          ] gift from lovely
Dionysos; [          the goat]herds forcibly
butchered it, carrying out their rites of communion,
and feasted on the meat, many among the Muses
will severely pluck the songs, my labours; so
[          ]. However as I seemed alone to have
the prize, though many trod the wind-less bag, and I
shared with the old man in his anger, by the Muse
[          ] my verses [          ] me
[          ] fame from iambics, [          ] a second
[          ] †          † me after
[          ] Hipponax of old to sing limping songs
to [   ] sons of Xuthos.

---

72 ωδεγω[ P, ]το O (ruling out older supplements with
ὦδ' ἐγὼ [ ); I have suggested ὦδέ γ' ὤ[ισ]το or ὤ[λλ]υτο, 'so at
least it presaged' or 'so at least they were destroyed'

73 ἔχ[(ε)ι]ν Knox

74 ἔμπνουν 'full of air' would give better sense

76–79 The grammar and sense of the conclusion are
unfortunately not determinable. The principal verb may
be at the beginning of 76 (ἔξω Vogliano) or at its end (κ[λή-
σει Knox); η ... η may be the feminine relative pronoun or
the disjunctive adverb; εξ may be preposition or numeral;
δευτερη γυ[ωμη (?) may be nominative or dative; the construction of ἀειδειν is unknown    77 μέγ' Knox

78 ἐμοῖς Herzog (but the sense of 'my Ionians' is not
obvious)

## 9. ΑΠΟΝΗΣΤΙΖΟΜΕΝΑΙ

ἔ]ζεσθε πᾶσαι. κοῦ τὸ παιδίον ; δεξ[
.]αιπ[.]ος Εὐέτειραν καὶ Γλύκην . [
.]ιτ[.....]αιδρη τὴν ἕτοιμον ου[
........] .ισμησε[..]ισματων[
........] .ιναπ[.....]νηνυτω[                          5
........] .η[......]αχηπεπο[
......] .. [.......]φερεσκο . [
.ρ[..]οδ̣.[...........]α δειλαίοις βλε[
φερω...[..........] .ακαιτανυ[
αυτησυ.[..........] .εται νο[                         10
ουπροσθα[........]νισηξ[
τίθεσθ' α.[........ ἄ]εθλον ἐξοι[
γλήχ[..............]κεῦσί σ' ἤειρα

1 ἔ]ζεσθε Kenyon
2 κ]αὶ π[ρ]ὸς Crusius
4 μή σε [κν]ισμάτων Crusius
5 ἀ]νηνύτω[ς Knox
10 Apparently P had φρ[εν- corrected to νο[- (Knox)
12 ἐξοι[σ- Crusius
13 το]κεῦσι Knox

## 9. WOMEN AT BREAKFAST

Sit down, all of you. Where is the child? Show
[                    ] Eueteira and Glyke; [                    ],
impudent girl; won't you [                    ] the one that
is ready? Are you [                    ]? Lest [                    ] you of
scratches [                    ] endlessly
[                                                                    ]
bring [                    ] with wretched [                    ].
Bring [                    ] and [                    ]. You there,
[                    ] mind [                    ] not formerly
[                    ] you make [                    ]
will carry off the prize [                    ]
pennyroyal [to your] parents I reared you [

## 10. ΜΟΛΠΙΝΟΣ

ἐπὴν τὸν ἐξηκοστὸν ἥλιον κάμψηις,
ὦ Γρύλλε, Γρύλλε, θνῆισκε καὶ τέφρη γίνευ·
ὡς τυφλὸς οὐπέκεινα τοῦ βίου καμπτήρ·
ἤδη γὰρ αὐγὴ τῆς ζοῆς ἀπήμβλυνται.

Verses 1–3 are cited by Stobaeus, *Anth.* 4.50b.56 from Herodas' 'Molpinos', verse 4 ibid. 55 from Herodas' Mimiambi; linked by Salmasius

1 ἥλιον = 'year' is scarcely possible; perhaps a line has been omitted, e.g. ἐπὴν τὸν ἐξηκοστὸν ἢ λ<ίην πολλὸν / ἥκηις ἔτος χρηστόν τε σὸν β>ίον κάμψηις, 'when you reach your sixtieth or greater year and come to the end of the good part of your life'

3 ὁ ὑπὲρ ἐκεῖνα Stob., corrected by Porson

4 αὕτη . . . ἀπήμβλυντο Stob., corrected by Salmasius

## 11. ΣΨΝΕΡΓΑΖΟΜΕΝΑΙ

προσφὺς ὅκως τις χοιράδων ἀνηρίτης

Cited by Athenaeus, *Deipnosoph.* 86b from Herondas' 'Women Working Together', as an example of ἀναρίτης. The feminine προσφῦσ' (Bücheler) is equally possible

314

## 10. MOLPINOS

Gryllos, Gryllos, when you have turned the post of sixty suns, die and become ashes; for the further lap of existence is blind; then the ray of life has been dimmed.

## 11. WOMEN WORKING TOGETHER

Clinging like a sea-snail to the rocks.[a]

[a] Apparently erotic.

## 12.  From an unknown mimiamb

ἢ χαλκέην μοι μυῖαν ἢ κύθρην παίζει
ἢ τῆισι μηλάνθηισιν ἄμματ᾽ ἐξάπτων
τοῦ κεσκίου μοι τὸν γέροντα λωβᾶται.

Cited by Stobaeus, *Anth.* 4.24d.51 from Herodas' Mimiambi


## 13.  From an unknown mimiamb

ὡς οἰκίην οὐκ ἔστιν εὐμαρέως εὑρεῖν
ἄνευ κακῶν ζώουσαν· ὃς δ᾽ ἔχει μεῖον,
τοῦτόν τι μέζον τοῦ ἐτέρου δόκει πρήσσειν.

Cited by Stobaeus, *Anth.* 4.34.27 from Herodas' Mimiambi
  3 τούτου Stob., corrected by Schneidewin

## 12.

Either he plays brass fly or pot,[a] or fastens ties of my tow to cockchafers and despoils my 'old man'.[b]

[a] Children's games, similar to blind man's buff (the second without blindfold).
[b] Name for a distaff, from the old man's face put on it as ornament.

## 13.

For it isn't possible to find easily a house that lives without troubles; consider him who has less trouble to fare a little better than the other.

# CERCIDAS AND THE
# CHOLIAMBIC POETS

EDITED AND TRANSLATED BY
### A. D. KNOX

## LIST OF ABBREVIATIONS

Bgk. = Bergk
Schnw. = Schneidewin
Cr. = Crusius
Wilam. = Wilamowitz
Kal. = Kalinka
P. = The Papyrus
Mn. = Milne
K. = Kenyon
Hdl. = Headlam

G. = Gerhard
Bi. = Bilabel
K.-Bi.: see page 435
Byz. = Byzantine
   version
Arm. = Armenian
   version
Müll. = Müller (Carolus)

---

[1] His remains were collected by Welcker in a volume easily accessible. Others were added from a British Museum ms. of Tzetzes by Musgrave, by Herwerden and from an Etymologicum by Reitzenstein. The best collection is in Bergk's *Poetae Lyrici Graeci* : and the best abbreviated edition in Hoffmann's *Griechische Dialecte*, iii. p. 135 (including Reitzenstein's addenda). A long but not very able discussion of the fragments is given by ten Brink in early numbers of *Philologus*.

# GENERAL INTRODUCTION

BY common consent one of the greatest of Greek poets was Hipponax,[1] who was the founder of choliambi.[2] Hipponax wrote in a simple adaptation of the Ionic plain iambus of his date, merely substituting a final spondee for the final iambus of Archilochus. The metre has always been misunderstood and confounded with the iambus of Attic tragedy with which it has nothing in common.

The metre was invented to suit the exceptional bitterness of the man. Of his life we are fairly well informed. He was (Suid. *s.v.*) πατρὸς Πύθεω (whence Metriche's parentage in Hrd. Mime I.). His mother was Protis. A native of Ephesus[3] he was expelled by its tyrants and went to Clazomenae.[4] His enmity with the

*Life of*
*HIPPONAX*

---

[2] Greek verse is measured by length of syllables, not by stress (like English). The mark ◡ is for a short, − for a long syllable. Breaks (*i.e.*, end of sense groups) are marked | . The iambic metre of Hipponax' date was ◡̱−◡−◡̱ | −◡ | −◡−◡−, or ◡̱−◡−◡̱ | −◡ | −◡̱− | ◡−. One or both of the first breaks are sufficient. Hipponax' metre is ◡̱−◡−◡̱ | −◡ | −◡−−−, the two breaks being again alternative. There is some evidence for ◡̱−◡−◡̱ | −◡−◡̱ | −−−. The first two syllables are ◡̱−, but there is slight evidence that he may also have permitted himself ◡◡◡ or −◡. Such substitutions are alleged in other places, but the evidence proves worthless. See *Journal of Cambridge Philological Society*, 1927, for a full discussion.

[3] Callim. *Iamb. passim,* Strabo, p. 642, Clem. Al. i. 308.

[4] So Sulpicia, *v. 6.*

321

sculptors Bupalus and Athenis is derived from the insulting statues of him which they made. He must have lived about 550 B.C. (Pliny, *N.H.* xxxvi. 5). He is said by the author of the *Ibis* and a commentator on Horace (*Epod.* 6. 14) to have committed suicide : but their accounts do not tally. In person he was small, thin and ugly (Ael. *V.H.* x. 6), but strong (Ath. 552 c).

Such details are in themselves unimportant Even the scanty fragments show that the quarrel with Bupalus was due not to the studied distortions of the latter's art, but to the natural attractions of his mistress, for whom Hipponax conceived an infatuation. But they are evidence if not of the popularity, at least of the great fame alike of his works and of his very unpleasant character. This fame is further attested by four epitaphs. That of Philippus (*A.P.* vii. 405) scarcely deserves quotation : Alcaeus (of Mitylene), *ib.* vii. 536, gives us little : Theocritus' (in choliambics) is given below. Leonidas (*ib.* vii. 408) adds one detail :—

> Ἀτρέμα τὸν τύμβον παραμείβετε, μὴ τὸν ἐν ὕπνῳ
> πικρὸν ἐγείρητε σφῆκ' ἀναπαυόμενον·
> ἄρτι γὰρ Ἱππώνακτος ὁ καὶ τοκέωνε[1] βαΰξας
> ἄρτι κεκοίμηται θυμὸς ἐν ἡσυχίη.
> ἀλλὰ προμηθήσασθε· τὰ γὰρ πεπυρωμένα κείνου
> ῥήματα πημαίνειν οἶδε καὶ εἰν Ἀίδη.

" Quietly pass by the tomb lest ye rouse the bitter wasp that rests there. For but lately has rest been found and quiet for the soul of Hipponax that barked even at his parents. But beware : even in Hades

---

[1] So W. Headlam for τοκεωνεια.

can his fiery words injure." [1]

The subject of so much curiosity and admiration, who inspired two of the world's greatest poets,
Callimachus and Catullus, has left us a
Fate of mere hundred verses or so. We owe
HIPPONAX' them to the collection of a son of one
works who copied his style (Lysanias, son of
Aeschrion). This book we have not: we only
have some few verses quoted by Athenaeus, sometimes misquoted, often misattributed, and usually
corrupt. Even some grammarians, like those on
whose work Hesychius' dictionary rests, had very
poor texts; though the Etymology has preserved us
one or two fine and vigorous lines. Later Tzetzes,
out of mere passion for the obscure, has preserved
in his commentaries several quotations, haphazard,
inaccurate and corrupt: we can still thank him for
his habit of quoting complete lines and sense which
has preserved for us of the poet far more than we
otherwise might have had.

Beyond the shadowy name of Ananius we know
nothing—perhaps there is nothing to be known of
Hipponax' immediate successors. It may
Disuse be held for certain that for the period
of the when Athens ruled supreme over Greek
metre literary taste the metre and manner was
disused. The development of Greek literature was
entirely in a different direction. There is indeed
one remark in Aristophanes which shows that even
at Athens these two writers had some readers: but

---

[1] The allusion (?) in [Archil.] 80 (D.) is too doubtful and fragmentary.

it is perhaps even more remarkable that the poet makes an error in attribution.

Simultaneously with the fall of Athens as a power, the old styles, subjects, metres and dialects were revived; but with the curious and wholly typical Greek rule that these four ingredients must never be used in the exact and original manner.

The Revival It is true that until the third century A.D. a certain weak reminiscence of the Ephesian sixth-century dialect still flavours the writings of those who employ this metre; and the gradual relapse from this dialect is perhaps the surest test of date. The metre of Hipponax was wholly misunderstood and some writers substituted the rhythms of Attic tragedy, preserving only the final spondaic foot. Even Callimachus, who is the nearest to Hipponax, does not fully represent him: and Catullus, the Latin poet who copies Archilochus faithfully, wholly deserts the Ephesian model. As far as subjects go, it is impossible to draw any lines. The metre was used for short poems on all subjects by Phoenix, for dramatic idylls by Herodes, for mythology or the like by Apollonius Rhodius and Pseudo-Callisthenes, for fables by Babrius,[1] for literary controversy by Callimachus,[1] for the introduction to a moralist anthology by [pseudo-] Cerkidas, and in isolated epigrams by Theocritus and Aeschrion. Of some of these a few words may be said.

Aeschrion is said on doubtful authority to have been a younger contemporary of Alexander. His

[1] Not included here. I hope to help to revise Callimachus' Iambi from the papyrus, a task which has not been attempted since Hunt.

The writers of the revival, AESCHRION son Lysanias may be the same as the author of a book on the writers of choliambics, and this Lysanias a pupil of Eratosthenes : the son then can hardly have been born before 260 B.C. In this case it is a little difficult to accept the statement which Suidas gives on the authority of " Nicander " but is generally supposed to rest only on that of Ptolemaeus Chennus. But there appears to be no good grounds for refusing to place his floruit in the first years of the third century B.C. Some of his writings called *Ephemerides* concerned Alexander and may have been written in hexameters (Tz. *Chil.* viii. 404): others, whether on this or other subjects, were in choliambics and marked by extreme frigidity.

PHOENIX Perhaps a somewhat younger contemporary was Phoenix of Colophon. We are told by Pausanias i. 9. 7, that when Lysimachus destroyed Colophon its dirge was sung by Phoenix. It may be hoped that his dirge did not resemble the plea for Thebes which Pseudo-Callisthenes puts in the mouth of Ismenias the flute-player. He may have written as early as 280 B.C. He made no effort to copy the metre of Hipponax ; his metre depends normally on the Athenian stage writers. But his short poems possess a certain tinkling elegance and follow closely the Alexandrine method of clothing in new garb hackneyed themes. The short moralistic excerpt quoted in the Anthology of [Cercidas] is considered by Gerhard [1] to display cynicizing tendencies :

[1] In his magnificent collection *Phoinix von Kolophon* (Teubner, 1909), which must be consulted for references to the literature on these writers.

but it contains nothing which might not have been prompted by a normal indignation against war profiteers. We cannot conjecture what may have prompted Aeschrion (of Samos or Mitylene) to use this metre : but if Phoenix followed his compatriots to the enlarged city of Ephesus his model was near at hand ; and this accident may well have been the reason which brought the metre into wide prominence. More probable is his intimate connexion with Attica, which is now suggested by a coincidence in his fourth poem. It is, like his other poems, a brief piece of about thirty verses, apparently an elegy on Lynceus. With Professor Crönert we could identify Lynceus with Lynceus of Samos, a contemporary of Menander, mentor of the young Poseidippus (Meineke, *Com. Gr.* i. p. 458) and writer of Attic comedy, and further, identify Poseidippus of frag. 3 with the comic writer and make Phoenix somewhat junior to Menander. We may, I think, go further and identify with certainty the Strassburg papyrus from which this poem is taken as containing some later sheets of the " Cercidean " anthology.

Callimachus (who lived at Alexandria, 260–240), Theocritus (more or less his contemporary) and Apollonius Rhodius, who long out-
Other names lived his instructor Callimachus, need no introduction. Theocritus and Apollonius perhaps wrote hardly anything in this metre. The same may be true of Asclepiades of Samos who ranks in time with the two first-named. Of Diphilus,[1] Parmeno and Hermeias of Curion we *know* nothing

---

[1] Gerhard, *op. cit.* pp. 211 *sqq.*

# GENERAL INTRODUCTION

whatever. Others, like Alcaeus of Messene,[1] have
left nothing in this metre. We may pass on to two
writers for us far more important and more dis-
putable.

The age of Cercidas[2] of Megalopolis, once a matter
of dispute, is now fairly well known. The attack on

CERCIDAS   a disciple of Sphaerus, and the apparent
censure of Stoicism as having degenerated
since Zeno, would encourage us to place Cercidas in
the second half of the third century B.C., when we
know a famous Sphaerus to have been one of the
diadochi of Zeno. In antiquity Cercidas, who had
great weight in the councils of his country, was
famed even above other learned poets for his literary
enthusiasms. He hoped after his death to meet
Pythagoras, Hecataeus, Olympus and Homer: the
first two books of Homer were to be buried with
him. Above all he appears passionately devoted to
the Catalogue (Book II.): and the children of his
city were compelled to learn it by heart. He boasts
of his early devotion to the Muses: and it is no
very wild guess that the anthology of which we have
an introduction in choliambics comes from his selec-
tion. This theme I have developed in a separate
book.[3] Whether he is actually the author of the
sorry verses which formed the introduction thereto
is another question. There is little doubt that

---

[1] *Ib.* p. 226.
[2] *Ib.* p. 206.
[3] *First Greek Anthologist*, Cambridge, 1923. It may
now be dated, on palaeographical grounds, as little later
than 250 B.C. See below on the Strassburg fragment of
Phoenix: also for the metres of Phoenix and [Cercidas].

327

Gregory of Nazianzus attributes them to him : but
equally there is little doubt that the clumsy and
almost random inanities are wholly unworthy of the
skilled and competent metrist of the meliambs. If
they are by him they are merely some juvenile epis-
tolary doggerel preserved by Parnos to whom they
are addressed : if not, they are an anonymous introduction to his collection. Wholly different from these
are the meliambi. For the most part these are
metrically a clever and vigorous combination of the
iambic and hexameter metres, each managed in the
strictest and most graceful fashion. Whatever view
be taken of their contents, in the narrower sense
of the word style they are masterpieces. To our
taste they suffer merely from their Alexandrinism :
that is from the adaptation to one purpose of a form [1]
designed for another use : the bombastic verbiage
proper in a comedian or the writer of a mock cookery-
book appears ill to become the gravity of a quite
serious philosophy of life : and the excellent tech-
nique seems to detract from the seriousness of the
writer.

Among the writers of the third century who used this
metre, hardly any are pure Alexandrines.
There is a far closer connexion with Attica.
Phoenix is the friend of writers of Attic comedy. Aeschrion defends a lady of Athenian ill-fame against an
Athenian attack. Moschine, an Athenian lady (*Philologus,* lxxxi. p. 247), used this metre. Even the use of
the metre for the *short* poem may be due less to Alex-

---

[1] So too the use of Doric dialect (of a conventional kind)
for Ionic metres.

andrine canons than to the practice of Hipponax. Only the use of an old form for new ideas remains typically Alexandrine. Cercidas is a Megapolitan and follower (presumably) of Ananius. So we are left only with Callimachus, whose protests seem to be directed against the Atticism of Hipponax' followers.

The popularity of this metre in the first three centuries A.D.[1]—extending even to the discovery of

Late writers Herodes whom his contemporaries failed to notice—is perhaps partly due to its use by Roman poets. We have (besides Babrius) a few epigrams in quite vulgar style. Again, the choliambic metre, still more the second half of the verse, was commonly used in proverbs : and collectors tended to twist well-known quotations into this form. On the other hand these were again likely to degenerate into pure iambics ; and it is quite unsafe to take any of these as belonging even probably to early writers.

Hipponax perished save as a quarry for the lexicographer and the pedant-poet. Herodes and

The Life of Alexander Phoenix were barely known and little read. The paltry verses of pseudo-Cercidas were known only from their position at the head of a school-thumbed Anthology. Callimachus' Iambi are the least quoted, and now probably the least read of his works. Babrius' fables alone attained a wide public. But those who think of Greek writers as exclusively ' classics,' and ' classics ' as necessarily ' high-brow,' and vaguely picture a

---

[1] From 230 B.C. to about A.D. 100 there is a total eclipse of the metre. The revival is due to the popularity of the metre in Latin.

cultured antiquity which read the private speeches
of Demosthenes without fear of impositions, or the
*Electra* of Sophocles except at the risk of the birch,
should study carefully the doggerel which is the
basis of at least one-third of the pseudo-Callisthenic
life of Alexander. For these are surely the worst
verses, in every respect except that of metre, that
were ever written : bereft of humour, pathos, sense,
truth, style and elegance. Despite considerable
efforts I have been unable in my translation to
avoid flattering them. Yet the work which was
based on them, the life of Alexander, was edited
and re-edited again and again by the Greeks : there
was even a rendering into Byzantine politic verse.
There was a popular Latin version. The Armenian
read a literal translation of the doggerel. Persian
and Syrian, Arabian and Ethiopian knew the book
in their own tongue.[1] Early manuscripts of the more
popular recensions, unread and uncollated, litter the
libraries of Europe. Possessing no other quality
except that they were easy to read, they had a
circulation comparable with that of a modern novel.
It is not inconceivable that these rhetorical inepti-
tudes and childish fables between the third and
twelfth centuries A.D. reached a public as large as
that which was attained by any other book except
those of the New Testament.

[1] For references see Kroll, Introd. p. x.

# HIPPONAX AND ANANIUS

# INTRODUCTION

ONE difficulty in the study of Hipponax is the question of authenticity. Early editions usually contained a number of 'Hipponactean' verses of various length and rhythms having little but this in common that the final foot was a spondee (‒ ‒) or a trochee. But the various metrists who quote these do not profess that they come from the works of Hipponax, and Bergk (*P.L.G.*⁴) though giving the majority of them with asterisks rejected one as 'obviously a mere invention ¹' (p. 491) χαῖρ᾽ ὦ σὺ Λεσβικὰ Σαπφώ, and E. Diehl in his *Anthologia Lyrica* rightly follows Bücheler in omitting many more. For the sake of completeness I give the fragments in the order and with the numeration of Bgk.⁴, but without reference:

(1 inc.) *89 Ἑρμῆ μάκαρ, κάτυπνον οἶδας ἐγρήσσειν (so ten Brink): "Blest Hermes to awake sleepers knowing."

90 εἴ μοι γένοιτο παρθένος καλή τε καὶ τέρεινα. This verse is actually called τοῦ Ἱππώνακτος (Hephaest. 30 *al.*): but there can be little doubt that this is a slip for Ἱππωνάκτειον.

*91 ὁ Κιθαιρὼν Λυδίοισιν ἐν χοροῖσι Βακχῶν (so Gaisford-Bgk.).

¹ But ten Brink may be right in attributing it to Diphilus' play in which Hipponax was a character.

332

\*92 καὶ κνίσῃ τινὰ θυμιήσας.

\*93 ο θεοι τα λοινα τανταλοιο δοντες (Plotius 280) : it is not worth attempting to find an acceptable reading for this or for

\*94 πισηνπασαντες (Plotius 293). Neither give as they stand the metre which Plotius professes to illustrate. Bk. rightly rejects them.

To these may be added without hesitation the example of the ordinary choliambus given by Plotius and Juba (ap. Rufin *de Metr. Com.* p. 386) :

\*13 ἀκούσατ' Ἱππώνακτος οὐ γὰρ ἀλλ' ἥκω. For we know that this is the first verse of Callimachus' iambi. Callimachus perhaps imitates Phoenix *fr.* 1. 15 : but οὐ γὰρ ἀλλά though an Atticism is common in the later choliambists. Clearly it could not have been used by Hipponax. See Callim. *fr.* 92 Schneider. It is never attributed to Hipponax.

With this Bergk gives (2 *Inc.*) ὦ Κλαζομένιοι, Βούπαλος κατεινε or καθινε, *e.g.* τε κάθηνις (P꒐k.) : 'Ye Clazomenians, Bupalus (and Athenis '). It is quite possible that this verse is by Hipponax : but the reading is wholly uncertain and it may well be that Putsch the editor of Plotius was right in supposing it to be a mere variant of Hippon. *fr.* 11. (Bgk.[4]) ὡς οἱ μὲν ἀγεῖ Βουπάλῳ κατηρῶντο. It is quite possible that the two verses quoted by Rufinus both come (as Bergk thought) from the same poet, but that this poet is Callimachus.

Callimachus in his iambi professedly follows Hipponax, saying that all those who wish to write ' lame ' iambi must beg light from Ephesus. And this would justify us if there were no evidence to the contrary in supposing that in simple details the model is the same as the copy. Now Callimachus rigorously

333

avoids the spondee (– –) in the fifth foot, and besides
this we have the direct testimony of Tzetzes and
others. If, therefore, it is true that Hipponax too
did so, Hephaestion the metrist when he was seeking
for an example of the spondee in the fifth foot would
have gone elsewhere; and we need not allow our
judgement to be influenced by the anonymous citation (Bgk. 48* : Hephaest. 31. *Inc.* 3) εἰς ἀκρὸν ἕλκων
ὥσπερ ἀλλᾶντα ψύχων (l. ψήχων: ' as one that strokes
a sausage, drew tipward ')—the more so as ὥσπερ is
doubtful in early Ionic. The writer may be Herodes
since it is easy to take the words *in malam partem.*
No such disability attaches to the other example
quoted of the long fifth foot in Plotius (273) (Bgk. 44 :
*Inc.* 4) αναβιος (l. ἀνὰ δρίος : Simmias *fr.* 20, 15
(so Powell), *Lyr. Adesp.* 7, p. 185 in Powell's *Collectanea Alexandrina*) πλάνητι προσπταίων κώλῳ,
'stumbling about the dell with leg errant'; and
the example might be a mere mistake since the
syllable πται- might be short. Quite possibly it is
from another writer : indeed it would be very
attractive to place it after *v.* 67 of Herodes' Mime
VIII. In fact it will be found on examination that
no satisfactory instance of a certain spondee in the
fifth foot occurs except in proper names : for a fuller
discussion see elsewhere. There is yet another
violation of Porson's law, this time as applied to
the beginning of a trochaic tetrameter in *fr.* 78*
(Hephaest. 34: *Inc.* 5), Μητροτίμῳ[1] δηῦτέ με χρὴ τῷ
σκότῳ δικάζεσθαι, ' with Metrotimus runagate must

---

[1] The flaw could be removed by reading Μητρότιμε ; and
it would be strange were the runaway to possess such an
honourable name.

# INTRODUCTION

I to law once more,' and it may be noticed that
this is again from the metrist Hephaestion (p. 34) :
though ὁ σκότος (*tenebrio* Meineke) is, it is true,
found in an authentic fragment of Hipponax (51
Bgk.⁴). It is probably actually from Hipponax, but
may need alteration. With some misgivings I have
included certain anonymous citations (*e.g.* 61 Bgk.),
since this is attributed to ' one of the old iambists '
by grammarians : and it is certain that many grammarians had easy access to copies of Hipponax'
works and cared little for other writers in this metre.
But for them we should have little or no accurate
knowledge of what the poet did write.

It might be supposed that three citations in the
anthologist Stobaeus might help us. For what he has
preserved for us is, as far as text goes, fairly good.
But by some singular and unfortunate accident all
the passages which he attributes to Hipponax are
from other authors. As to two of these no serious
doubt exists. One is in a plain iambic metre of a
type at this time certainly non-existent. It runs
(Stobaeus lxxii. 5 : 72 Bgk., who agrees with Meineke
in attributing it to Hippothoon) :

> Γάμος κράτιστός ἐστιν ἀνδρὶ σώφρονι
> τρόπον γυναικὸς χρηστὸν ἔνδον λαμβάνειν·
> αὕτη γὰρ ἡ προὶξ οἰκίαν σώζει μόνη.
> ὅστις δὲ †τρυφῶς† τὴν γυναῖκ' ἄγει λαβών
> συνεργὸν οὗτος ἀντὶ δεσποίνης ἔχει,
> εὔνουν, βεβαίαν εἰς ἅπαντα τὸν βίον.

In *v.* 2 Haupt suggested ἔδνον. In *v.* 4 if τρυφῶσαν [1]
be read we must, of course, assume with Meineke a

---

[1] Better ἀτρύφερον perhaps. The first four verses all
contain rhythms impossible in any early Ionic writer.

hiatus, perhaps even allot the last two verses to another author, and the sense is :

> Best marriage is it for a prudent man
> To take as dower a noble character :
> This bridal gift alone can save the house.
> But whoso takes to wife a spendthrift girl
>
> . . . . . . .
>
> He finds a helpmeet, not a mistress stern :
> A kind and true companion to the end."

Nor has another of Stobaeus' attributions found any defenders : *Flor.* xxix. 42 (Bgk. 28 : *Inc.* 6) runs : χρόνος δὲ φευγέτω σε μηδὲ εἷς[1] ἀργός. Apostolius the collector of proverbs gives it as Δημώνακτος. Style and subject are most akin to [Cercidas] : see below. The sense is ' Let not one moment pass thee by idle.' A third again seems equally unsound, and has, like the foregoing, been generally rejected :

> Δύ' ἡμέραι γυναικός εἰσιν ἥδισται[2]
> ὅταν γαμῇ τις κἀκφέρῃ τεθνηκυῖαν (Bgk. 29 : *Inc.* 7),

' Two days in life of woman are sweetest, when she is wed, and when she is buried.' These verses in a Berlin anthology (P. 9773) recently discovered (*Berliner Klassiker Texte* v. 2. 130) are attributed (the lemma is very fragmentary) to . . . λυ . . . ς. Unhappily this does not quite remove all doubt. Professor Schubart has very kindly sent me a sketch of the traces, pointing out that α is as likely as λ. σ as against υ does not seem wholly certain. In the jumbling of citations common to all Anthologies it is possible that these verses were out of order and

---

[1] μηδὲ εἷς is Sicilian Doric, borrowed in Attic Comedy. Hipponax would have divided μὴ δείς.

[2] Compare *Com. Fr. Adesp.* p. 1224.

attributed to τῆς αὐτῆς or τοῦ αὐτοῦ ' by the same.'
At all events we are justified in leaving it out of
account in any generalization we may hope to make.
But there is one fragment which, though possessing
far higher claims than much which Bergk included,
may be relegated (*Inc.* 9, Meineke, *Anon.* 3) perhaps
to a very late date. It is the history of Hipponax'
discovery of the choliamb which I give from schol.
Heph. p. 214 (C.: for other references see Leutsch
and Schneidewin on Apostolius, viii. 59): . . . ἢ ἀπὸ
γραός τινος Ἰάμβης καλουμένης ᾗ πλυνούσῃ συντυχὼν
ὁ Ἱππῶναξ καὶ ἁψάμενος τῆς σκάφης ἐφ' ἧς ἔπλυνεν
ἡ γραῦς τὰ ἔρια ἤκουσε λεγούσης

> Ἄνθρωπ' ἄπελθε· τὴν σκάφην ἀνατρέπεις

(read -τρέψεις, Tricha p. 9 Herm.). ' Another derivation of the word iambus is from an old woman named
Iambé who was washing clothes when Hipponax came
along. He touched the wash-tub in which she was
washing her woollen clothes, and was met with :

> Hence sir ! you'll overbalance my wash-tub.'

To conclude the list of false fragments Suidas attributes to Hipponax the verse rightly assigned by
Meineke to Aristocles (Choerobosc. in *E.M.* 376. 21
says Aristotle).
(*Inc.* 10) εὐνοῦχος ὢν καὶ δοῦλος ἦρχεν Ἑρμίας.
The iota is short (Choerob.) and the fragment need
not delay us.
But perhaps even greater difficulties attach to those
citations, whose genuineness are undoubted, but
which are given by the Byzantine grammarian
Tzetzes. We cannot do better than to examine his
citations from other authors and select, at hap-

# HIPPONAX AND ANANIUS

hazard, a few citations on Lycophron's *Cassandra*. In his citation (*v*. 87) of *Il*. Z 356 εἵνεκ' ἐμεῖο κυνὸς κακομηχάνου the last word really belongs to *v*. 344 (κυν. κακ.), two quotations having been boiled down into one.

On *v*. 39 he quotes ἀνήκεστον λάβεν ἄλγος as ἀν. ἄλγος ἔλαχεν which sheds a curious light on some of the metrical irregularities in his citations of Hipp.

Often his citations are mere rephrasings. On *v*. 175, Pindar's verse (*Pyth*. iv. 436), ὃς πάχει μάκει τε πεντηκόντορον ναῦν κρατεῖ appears as ὅσον π. ναῦς μάκει τε πάχει τε. Just above the same poem *v*. 175 is quoted with two words transposed.

On *v*. 209 Euripides' verse (*Bacch*. 920) is given as καὶ πρόσθε μὲν ἡγεῖσθαι δοκεῖ : Eur. wrote καὶ ταῦρος ἡμῖν πρόσθεν ἡγεῖσθαι δοκεῖς.

On 219-222 Aratus' verses, *vv*. 257-8 and 261-4, are run together and 261 is filled out from . . . ἑπτὰ δὲ κεῖναι to ἑπτὰ δή τοι ταίγε (from 257).

In the very next citation from the first verses of the *Lithica*, οἴζνος ἀτρεκὲς ἄλκαρ is cited as ὁ. ἄλκαρ αἰνῆς.

These verses are selected out of the few citations on Lycophron, 1-225. They are probably due to errors of memory or bad writing clumsily corrected. Another source of error was a habit of glossing, on the part of Tzetzes, as probably as of his copyists. Thus in citing (*l.c.*) Pind. *P*. iv. 149 over ἀταρβάκτοιο he wrote ἀφόβου, which duly appears in two codd. as ἀτὰρ ἀφόβου βάκτοιο. On *v*. 176 he cites a fragment of Hesiod, in which the reading we know from other sources to be τέκεν Αἰακὸν. Unfortunately he wrote (how inanely) υἱὸν over Αἰακὸν. So one ms has τέτοκεν υἱὸν, another τέκεν Αἰακὸν Αἰακὸν, and two leave out Αἰακὸν altogether. But the most striking verse in the narrow limits to which I have confined myself is Ap. Rhod. i. 755 τὸν δὲ μεταδρομάδην ἐπὶ Μυρτίλος ἤλασεν ἵππους, which appears (on *v.* 157) as τῷ δ' ἐπὶ Μυρτίλος (-ῳ) ἐκ στήθους γράφων ἤλασεν ἵππους. As we have a true text we can see that three words are parenthetical. But it is pertinent to ask, when we have no other text, how much of our Hipponax, as editors present it, is really a compound of glosses and parentheses. At any rate when a reading is on two or three accounts unsatisfactory, it is in the highest degree absurd to be satisfied with tinkering at two or three points. We can never be remotely certain of the cause of error. It is clear that in few, if any, of the cases above cited could the original have been restored with the smallest degree of certainty.

There is one hope, although I fear a slight one. It might be that in all these cases Tz., who had presumably no text of Hipp., always copied direct from the source: that is, from older scholia on Lycophron. Up to a point that is true. But these scholia were no doubt cramped and corrupt. Tzetzes had read them, but by no means always did he copy them where they belonged.[1] He was far too cunning and spread his citations over a wide area. Only too often it may be feared he quoted ἐκ στήθους, from memory. Only too often the junctures are invented and words are repeated to fill the gaps in his mnemonic exercises. As he had little metrical ear of his own he often transfers the order of words and gives merely

[1] All quotations including the word πάλμυς are presumably from one source: yet examine and see how they are scattered.

a rough notion of what the author conveyed. With these facts in view we clearly cannot, if we are honest, profess where there is a small difficulty to recover the true text. Such corrections as seem to me absolutely necessary for the sense I give in the text, but for the most part we must never suppose that we possess more than an outside chance of recovering the truth.

For our other resources are slight. Aristophanes, we are told, and certainly Callimachus and Herodes, imitated him. But with writers of such genius we cannot hope to disentangle whole phrases. There is a profusion of words in Hesychius' dictionary: but unfortunately the ms of Hipp. from which some previous Alexandrine scholars took the words was hopelessly corrupt: and the errors have grown in transit. Test this where we have a sound text: what can be made of διοπληητα: ἰσχυροπλήκτην?

Our finest sources, the Etymologica, taking from far older scholars, are liable to the corruption of centuries. Erotian does not quote by verse or preserve the order of the original but subordinates everything to medical interest. Despite the poor character, in parts at least, of our mss of Athenaeus, we might hope much from him. Yet here we are faced by a strange but significant fact. Two citations are admittedly second-hand, one from a critic of Timaeus and one from a work on the (chol)iambographers: a third which gives two (really three) passages is clearly from the same source since it compares a use (of πέλλα) in Hipp. and Phoenix: another is quoted with a parallel from Ananius (*fr.* 18 : see however p. 85): a fifth is more probably from Attic comedy: and we may take leave to

doubt the directness of a sixth[1] which is usually
connected with the second. That so voluminous a
reader should derive at second hand seems to show
that mss of Hipponax at his time were non-existent
or unprocurable. Plutarch appears to have had no
general knowledge of his works. Of other sources
Stobaeus the anthologist gives, as stated, extracts
none of which can conceivably be by Hipp. : and we
are left perhaps with a dozen verses.

To decide questions of dialect and metre on such
evidence is clearly difficult, but fortunately we have
better authority. Callimachus openly professes that
in his iambic he copies the *metre* of Hipponax :
Hephaestion, far our best metrical authority, allows
him great regularity : and even Tzetzes, who disputes
Hephaestion's rulings, can find no evidence against
them worth the name. The solitary dissentient voice
is that of a certain Heliodorus whose total incapacity
may be judged by such of his criticisms on other
authors as Priscian quotes.

It is impossible here to enter into an elaborate
inquiry. Elsewhere I shall show (*a*) that the early
iambus is the most strict of all metres, (*b*) that of
choliambic writers Hipponax alone observes all its
laws in a majority of his verses, (*c*) that of the minority
of verses a large minority are wholly unmetrical on
any standard, and, therefore (*d*) that having cast out
these verses we should not hesitate to remove also
the small minority of cases in which Hipponax appears
to use licences or metrical contrivances not found in

---

[1] There are three single citations, not included in this
collection. One comes to Athenaeus *via* Pamphilus (Bgk.
135), another *via* Hermippus (Bgk. 136), and the third (97)
from Theophrast (p. 87).

other Ionic poets. It is far easier to hold the hypothesis that Hipponax was wholly indifferent to metre than to hold that he foresaw and forestalled contrivances and metres used by Attic poets : especially as during a third of the long time between Hipponax and Tzetzes these licences and contrivances were precisely those which were most likely to creep in. Only after about A.D. 300 is there a probability of corruptions which offend any metrical canon of the iambus.

As we find on close examination [1] that Hipponax obeys subtle rhythmic tests ; that, except on the direct statement of metrists whose conclusions in eight cases out of ten are mistaken, his rhythm is regularity itself ; that he is wholly consistent in his usage of dialectal forms ; and above all that Callimachus in his carefully restricted iambi openly claims to copy the example of Ephesus, we may at least be pardoned if we prefer the testimony of the poet-scholar of the third century B.C. to the ignorant σχολαστικοί of the twelfth or twentieth century A.D. For, as we have said, in reading a text of Hipponax over the second class of citations we are in a curious position : there is no evidence that Tzetzes was successful in disentangling the text of Hipponax from the comments of the scholiast. In *fr.* 68. 6 one might even suppose a predecessor took the comment for text : in *fr.* 61 Tzetzes is probably the culprit : while to complete the chain we may quote the text of Hipponax as elicited from Tzetzes by John Potter (*fr.* 59).

> δὸς χλαῖναν σφύκτουριν Ἱππώνακτι
> καὶ κυπασσίσκον καὶ σαμβάλικα κἀσκέρικα
> καὶ χρυσοῦ μοι στατῆρας ἑξήκοντα
> τοῦ νερτέρου τοίχου.

[1] See my notes *Journal Camb. Ph. S.* 1927 p. xii.

This was precisely the way in which some ancient scholars like the unreliable 'Heliodorus metricus' picked out the text for their metrical criticisms of Hipponax' versification. The sane critic will place as little trust in the discrimination of the pedants of Constantinople as in that of the future Archbishop who was probably a finer Greek scholar. For Tzetzes' metrical criticism, when we may suspect him of writing at first hand, is exceedingly poor. On Lycophron 167 he says that ἴσην is right whether short or long: in the later case it has merely πάθος τὸ λεγόμενον χωλίαμβον! Yet it is, in the main, on the evidence of Tzetzes and on his ability to form an edition of fragments out of obscure and cramped scholia that Hipponax' work is commonly judged.

In closing a long and dull preface some apology for its length and dullness is necessary. But it is manifest that it is wholly impossible to judge of the aims or methods of the later writers who revived this metre unless we have a vague notion of its original character.

[*P.S.*—Much of what has been written above has been rendered superfluous by the discovery of a papyrus fragment printed on pp. 62–63. The thesis of the previous pages that Hipponax was neither an anticipator of metrical licenses used first in the Attic Tragic or Comic Drama, nor an incompetent versifier, is now established beyond the necessity of argument. As all readers of early Greek poetry, for instance of Sappho and Alcaeus, know, " the only correct procedure is to approach the quotations by way of the book texts." Unfortunately this course has not been open to me. Above all we see that there is no similarity between the metres of Hipponax and Herodes.]

# HIPPONAX

## EARLY CITATIONS

### BOOK I

#### GENUINE FRAGMENTS FROM EARLY CITATIONS

$1^{33}_{12}$   τίς ὀμφαλητόμος σε τὸν διοπλῆγα
      ἔψησε κἀπέλουσεν ἀσκαρίζοντα.

(*Et. Vat.* ed. Reitz., *Ind. Lect. Rost.* 1890–91, p. 7.   *E.M.*
154. 27 **ἀσκαρίζειν**· σημαίνει τὸ κινεῖσθαι Ἱππῶναξ (*v.* 2).
Hesych. **ὀμφαλητόμος**· μαῖα. **διοπλῆητα**· ἰσχυροπλήκτην cft.
Reitz.)

$2_{14}$   δοκέων †εκτ†ῖνον τῇ βα[κ]τηρίῃ κόψαι . . .

$3_{14}$   ἡμίεκτον αἰτεῖ τοῦ φάλεω κολαψ†αιε†

(Choerobosc. *Exeg. in Hephaest.* xlviii. 6 (τὰ ἄφωνα)
εὑρέθη ποιοῦντα σπανίως κοινὴν ἐν αὐτοῖς τὸ π̅τ̅ καὶ τὸ κ̅τ̅, οἷον
. . παρὰ Ἱππώνακτι ἐν τῷ πρώτῳ ἰάμβων (2) καὶ πάλιν παρὰ
τῷ αὐτῷ (3).)

1 The upper number 33 is that of the last edition of
Bergk's *Poetae Lyrici Graeci* ; the lower, of Diehl's *Anth.
Lyrica. v.* 1. -λιτομος cod.
2 *l.* τ´ (δ´) ἔκε. I doubt whether either illustration is really
sound. If Hippon. wrote βακτηρίῃ (-ᾳ ms), so must Herodes
have done (viii. 60) : and our choice lies between the two
traditions as to Hipponax' text. 3 ἡμίεκτον may scan ἡμυέκτον.
If φάλης (-εω)=φαλῆς (-ῆτος) as Θαλῆς (-ῆτος, -εω), we might
correct to κολάψασα, ' exsucta mentula,' or place a note of
interrogation after αἰτεῖ and read κολάψαι με. One cod. of
Choerob. has ἐν τῷ τρόπῳ ἴαμβον : corr. Hoffmann.

344

# HIPPONAX

## EARLY CITATIONS

### BOOK I

#### GENUINE FRAGMENTS FROM EARLY CITATIONS

1 What navel snipstress[1] wiped you, dolt blasted,
  And, as you hoofed around yourself, washed you.

('Hoofing around' means 'struggling.' *Hipp. Etymol.*
Navel-snipstress': midwife, *Hesych.* 'Blasted,' strength-
smiter.)

2 Thinking 'twas him I smote with my cudgel.

3 She asks eight obols for her tongue's service.[2]

(Mute consonants seldom allow the preceding syllable to
be of doubtful quantity in the case of pt and kt; *e.g.* . . .
*Hipponax* has băktĕriai in his first book of Iambi (2). So
too the same writer has Hēmiēktŏn(3). *Choeroboscus.*)

---

[1] Midwife. Such allusions were the height of bad
manners. So presumably Theophrast's ἀηδής asks (xx. 7)
εἶπ᾽ ὦ μάμμη ὅτ᾽ ὤδινες καὶ ἔτικτές με τίς ἡ μαῖα (for ἡμέρα);
Hesych's second explanation is corrupt. The real meaning
is ἐμβρόντητος, 'dunderhead.'
[2] Videor mihi fata Aretes videre quae 'nunc in quadriviis
et angiportis glubit magnanimi Remi nepotes.'

345

4$^{38}_{16}$  ἐκ πελλίδος πίνοντες· οὐ γὰρ ἦν αὐτῇ
κύλιξ· ὁ παῖς γὰρ ἐμπεσὼν κατήραξεν.

5$^{39}_{17}$                              ἐκ δὲ τῆς πέλλης
ἔπινον ἄλλοτ' αὐτός, ἄλλοτ' Ἀρήτη
προὔπινεν.

(Ath. xi. 495 c **πέλλα**· ἀγγεῖον σκυφοειδές, πυθμένα ἔχον
πλατύτερον εἰς ὃ ἤμελγον τὸ γάλα . . . τοῦτο δὲ Ἱππ. λέγει
πελλίδα (4), δῆλον, οἶμαι, ποιῶν ὅτι ποτήριον μὲν οὐκ ἦν, δι'
ἀπορίαν δὲ κύλικος ἐχρῶντο τῇ πελλίδι. καὶ πάλιν (5). Φοῖνιξ
δὲ . . Κλείταρχος πελλητῆρα μὲν καλεῖν Θεσσάλους καὶ Αἰολεῖς
τὸν ἀμολγέα πέλλαν δὲ τὸ ποτήριον. Φιλητᾶς δὲ ἐν Ἀτάκτοις
τὴν κύλικα Βοιωτούς.)

6$^{40}_{18}$  σπονδῇ τε καὶ σπλάγχνοισιν ἀγρίης χοίρου

(Ath. ix. 375 c **χοῖρον** δὲ οἱ Ἴωνες καλοῦσι τὴν θήλειαν ὡς
Ἱππ. ἐν ⟨αʹ⟩ (6).)

7$^{41}_{19}$                βακκάρει δὲ τὰς ῥῖνας
ἤλειφον.

(Ath. xv. 690 a παρὰ πολλοῖς δὲ τῶν κωμῳδοποιῶν ὀνομάζεταί
τι μύρον **βάκκαρις**· οὗ μνημονεύει καὶ Ἱππῶναξ διὰ τούτων (7).
ἐσθ' οἵη περ κρόκος.)

8$^{12}_{20}$  τί τῷ τάλαντι Βουπάλῳ συνοίκησας;

(Herodian ii. 301 (Choerobosc. i. 280. 31) ὅτι δὲ καὶ τοῦ
τάλας τάλαντος ἦν ἡ γενική, δηλοῖ ὁ Ἱππ. εἰπὼν (8).)

4. 1 *v.l.* αὐτοῖς.  So Eust. 1561. 37.
5. 2 Perhaps Ἀρήτῃ προὔπινον should be read, or ἔπινεν
. . . Ἀρήτῃ (Schnw.).  I have adopted the former for
purposes of translation.
6 ἀγρίας codd. (em. by Bgk.: ⟨αʹ⟩ ins. id.).
7 ἐσθ' οἵη περ κρόκος] cod. E ἐστὶ δʹ.  Both are corrupt.
The words probably belong to Ath., not Hipp.
8 συνῴκησας plerique codd.

346

# FRAGMENTS 4-8

4 Drank from a paillet : she had no tumbler:
  Her slave had fallen on it and smashed it.
5                                    Now myself
  I drank out of the pail, now Aréte
  Had from me what I left.

(' Pail ' means a vessel shaped like a drinking-cup with
a rather broad bottom into which they used to milk. . .
*Hipponax* calls this paillet (4); and what he says shows
clearly that they had no cup, but in the absence of a tumbler
used the pail. And again (5). But *Phoenix* . . *Cleit-
archus* says that the Thessalians and Aeolians spoke of the
milking utensil as a ' paillier ' but of the cup as ' pail.'
*Philetas* in his *Stray Notes* says that the Boeotians gave the
name ' pail ' to the tumbler. *Athenaeus*.)

6 With drink offerings and a she-boar's entrails

(' Boar ' was used of the female by the Ionians. *Hipponax*
Book I. (6). *Athenaeus*.)

7                          With bakkaris nostrils
  Anointing

(Many of the comedians use the word ' bakkaris ' of a
kind of ointment : *Hipponax* too mentions it in these words
(7). It is rather like saffron. *Athenaeus*.)

8 Why with rogue Bupalus didst cohabit ?

(' τάλας ' too (like μέλας) has the genitive τάλαντος as is
clear from *Hipponax* (8). *Herodian*.)

347

# HIPPONAX

$9^{63}_{21}$    ἐγὼ δὲ δεξιῷ παρ' Ἀρήτην
κνεφαῖος ἐλθὼν ῥωδιῷ κατηυλίσθην.

(Herodian ii. 924. 14 λέγεται δὲ (ἐρωδιός) ἔσθ' ὅτε καὶ
τρισυλλαβῶς ὥσπερ καὶ τὸ παρ' Ἱππώνακτι (9): *id.* i. 116. 25,
ii, 171. 7, 511. 28, *E.M.* 380. 40)

$10^{10}_{22}$    κύψασα γάρ μοι πρὸς τὸ λύχνον Ἀρήτη

(*Et. Vat.* Reitzenstein, *Ind. Lect. Rostoch.* 1891–2, p. 14
λύχνος : λέγεται ἀρσενικῶς καὶ οὐδετέρως ὁ λύχνος καὶ τὸ λύχνον
Ἱππ. (10).)

$10_{B\ 103}$    λίθινον ἀνδρίαντα

(Antiatt. Bekk. *An.* i. 82. 13 ἀνδριάντα τὸν λίθινον ἔφη
ππ. Βούπαλον τὸν ἀγαλματοποιόν.)

$11^{22A}_{30}$    μάκαρς ὅτις . . . θηρεύει †πρήσας†.

$12^{22B}_{31}$    καίτ<ο>ιγ' εὔωνον αὐτὸν εἰ θέλεις δώσω.

$13_{32}$    †ἐκέλευεῖ βάλλειν καὶ λεύειν Ἱππώνακτα.

(Choerobosc. *Exeg. in Hephaest.* ὁμοίως καὶ τὴν ευ εὑρίσκομεν ποιοῦσαν κοινήν, οἷον ἐν τῷ πρώτῳ Ἰάμβῳ (-ων Kal.)
Ἱππώνακτος, ἔνθα φησί (11), τὴν ρευ ἐν τετάρτῳ (?) ποδὶ
συνέστειλε· καὶ πάλιν ὁ αὐτὸς ἐν δευτέρῳ ποδὶ τὴν ευ (12)· εἶτα
πάλιν ὁ αὐτὸς (13) τὴν λευ ἐν τετάρτῳ ποδί· λεύειν δέ φησιν
ἀντὶ τοῦ λιθοβολεῖν.)

9. 1 παρὰ ῥητήρ cod.: em. Schneidewin.
10 Probably the beginning of a tetrameter.
11 The Attic μακάριος ὅστις of two mss is clearly false.
Choeroboscus or his source may be deceived : or *e.g.* θύρετρα
of amatory quarries. μάκηρ' δ τις one cod.
12 'him': since Hipponax appears to use μιν of things.
13 Scan ἐκέλενε, εὔωνον, λεύειν, θηρεύει.

348

# FRAGMENTS 9-13

9 So I with heron favouring[1] at nightfall
Came to Aréte's dwelling and lodged there.

('ἐρῳδιός' is sometimes trisyllabic (ῥῳδιός) as *Hipponax*'
saying shows (9). *Herodian.*)

10 Facing the lamp stooped to me Aréte

(λύχνος and λύχνον are both used (masculine and neuter):
*Hipponax* (10). *Etymologicum Vaticanum.*)

10 B Statue of stone

(Statue of stone was the title given by *Hipponax* to Bupalus
the sculptor. An *antiatticist* in *Bekker's Anecdota.*)

11 Happy is he who hunteth (such quarries).

12 Yet, if you will, I'll give you him dirt-cheap.

13 He bade them pelt and stonecast Hipponax.

(In the same way we find εὖ, as in the first book of the
Iambi of *Hipponax*, where he says (11), he shortens ῥεῦ
in the fourth foot; again he has εὖ in the second foot (12);
again (13) λεῦ in the fourth foot. 'Stonecast' is for
'stone.' *Choeroboscus.*)

---

[1] 'On my right': a favourable omen.

# HIPPONAX

14²³  μ⟨υ⟩δῶντα δὴ καὶ σαπρόν

(Erotian p. 115 σαπρόν : σεσηπότα ὡς Ἱππ. ἐν ᾱ Ἰάμβων
φησί (14).)

## BOOK II

15²⁶₃₃  ἀκήρατον δὲ τὴν ἀπαρτίην ⟨ἴσ⟩χει

(Pollux x. 18 τοὔνομα δὲ ἡ ἀπαρτία ἐστὶ μὲν Ἰωνικὸν
ὠνομασμένων οὕτω παρ' αὐτοῖς τῶν κούφων σκευῶν ἅ ἐστι παρ-
αρτήσασθαι· . . . εἰ μέντοι καὶ ἐν βιβλίῳ τινὶ τὴν ἀπ. εὑρεῖν
ἐθέλοις . . . εὑρήσεις ἔν τε τῷ δευτέρῳ τῶν Ἱππώνακτος ἰάμβων
(15) καὶ παρὰ Θεοφράστῳ . . .)

## UNCERTAIN BOOKS

16³⁴₃₈  συκ⟨έ⟩ην μέλαιναν ἀμπέλου κασιγνήτην

(Ath. iii. 78 b Φερένικος δὲ . . ἀπὸ Συκῆς τῆς Ὀξύλου
θυγατρὸς προσαγορευθῆναι· Ὄξυλον γὰρ . . . γεννῆσαι . . .
Ἄμπελον, Συκῆν . . . ὅθεν καὶ τὸν Ἱππ. φάναι (16).)

17³⁶₃₉  οὐκ ἀτταγᾶς τε καὶ λαγοὺς καταβρύκων,
        οὐ τηγανίτας σησάμοισι φαρμάσσων,
        οὐδ' ἀττανίτας κηρίοισιν ἐμβάπτων

(Ath. xiv. 645 c Πάμφιλος δὲ τὸν ἀττανίτην καλούμενον
ἐπίχυτον φησι καλεῖσθαι.  τοῦ δὲ ἀττανίτου Ἱππῶναξ ἐν τούτοις
μνημονεύει (17).  ix. 388 b μνημονεύει αὐτῶν (ἀτταγῶν) Ἱππ.
οὕτως (17. 1).  Hesych. ὀμπν[ε]ίη δαιτί· ἀντὶ τοῦ πολλῇ.)

14 μαδῶντα corr. by Stephanus.
15 ἀπαρτίαν codd.: -ίην Bgk.  ἔχει codd.
16 συκῆν codd.: corr. Schnw.  Perhaps Aeschriontic.
17. 1 Ath. 645 c ουκατταγε: ? ἀτταγέας.  In both places
λαγώς is given : corr. by Meineke.  καταβρύκων 645 c,
διατρώγων 388 b.  2 τηγανιας mss : corr. by Casaubon.
3 οὐκ Meineke, prob. rightly.

350

14 Clammy and rotten

('Rotten': rotted. *Hipp*. Book I (14).  *Erotian*.)


## BOOK II

15 Untarnished his appendages keeping

(The word 'appendages' is Ionic, the name applying to light articles which may be hung on the belt; . . . if you wish for documentary evidence you may go to the second book of *Hipponax*' Iambi (15) and to *Theophrast* . . . *Pollux*.)


## UNCERTAIN BOOKS

16 (?) The fig-tree black, which is the vine's sister

(*Pherenicus* . . says that the word συκῆ came from Suké, the daughter of Oxylus; he . . . . begat . . . . Ampelos and Suké . . ;  hence *Hipponax*, he says, said (16). *Athenaeus*.)


17 Not partridges and hares galore scrunching,
   Nor flavouring with sesamé pancakes,
   Nor yet with honey drenching fried fritters[1]

(*Pamphilus* speaks of the 'fritter' as a sort of cake.  It is mentioned by *Hipponax* in the following verses (17). Of partridges *Hipp*. speaks as follows (17. 1).  *Athenaeus*. *Here may belong* 'rich feasting': for 'much.'  *Hesych*.)


[1] See on *fr.* 75.

# HIPPONAX

$18^{37}_{40}$ ὁ δ' ἐξολισθὼν ἱκέτευε τὴν κράμβην
τὴν ἑπτάφυλλον ᾗ θύεσκε Πανδώρη
Ταργηλίοισιν ἔγχυτον πρὸ φαρμάκου.

(Ath. ix. 370 a μήποτε δὲ ὁ Νίκανδρος μάντιν κέκληκε τὴν κράμβην ἱερὰν οὖσαν, ἐπεὶ καὶ παρ' Ἱππώνακτι ἐν τοῖς ἰάμβοις ἐστί τι λεγόμενον τοιοῦτον (18). καὶ Ἀνάνιος δέ φησιν . . .)

$19^{46}_{43}$ καὶ τοὺς σολοίκους, ἢν λάβωσι, περνᾶσι
Φρύγας μὲν ἐς Μίλητον ἀλφιτεύσοντας,

(Herodian, de Barbarismo et Soloecismo, Valck. Ammon. p. 193 Σολοίκους δὲ ἔλεγον οἱ παλαιοὶ τοὺς βαρβάρους. ὁ γὰρ Ἀνακρέων φησί . . καὶ Ἱππῶναξ (19). v.l. in Eust. 368. 1.)

$20^{47}_{44}$ οἴκει δ' ὄπισθεν τῆς πόλ‹η›ος ἐν Σμύρνῃ
μεταξὺ Τρηχέ[ι]ης τε καὶ Λέπρης ἀκτῆς.

(Strabo p. 633 καὶ τόπος δέ τις τῆς Ἐφέσου Σμύρνα ἐκαλεῖτο, ὡς δηλοῖ Ἱππ. (20). ἐκαλεῖτο γὰρ Λέπρη μὲν ἀκτὴ ὁ πρηὼν ὁ ὑπερκείμενος τῆς νῦν πόλεως, ἔχων μέρος τοῦ τείχους αὐτῆς· τὰ γοῦν ὄπισθεν τοῦ πρηῶνος κτήματα ἔτι νυνὶ λέγεται ἐν τῇ Ὀπισθολεπρίᾳ· Τραχεῖα δ' ἐκαλεῖτο ἡ περὶ τὸν Κορησσὸν παρώρειος.)

$21^{50}_{46}$ ἔπειτα μάλθῃ τὴν τρόπιν παραχρίσας

(Harpocrat. p. 123 μάλθη· ὁ μεμαλαγμένος κηρός· Ἱππ. (21).)

18. 1 ? ἐξόπισθεν Callim. Iamb. 413 s.v.l. ? ἱκέτευσε since Hrd. seems to shorten ἱκετεύω. But cf. καπηλεύει fr. 70. The forms θύεσκε and perhaps ἱκέτεῦε are not from the vernacular, the dialect being made appropriate to the myth. 3 vv.ll. Θαργ-, Γαργ-: Ταργ- Schnw.
19. 1 ἵν' ἐθέλουσι Eust. 2 vv.ll. ἀλφιτεύσοντας, -σαντας.
20. 1 ᾤκει codd.: corr. Schnw. and ten Brink. πόλιος cod.: corr. Bgk. πρηών also Anton. Lib. xi.
21 v.l. τρόπην.

352

18 So slipping off,[1] adjuréd the cabbage,
  The cabbage seven-leaved, which Pandora
  At the Thargelia gave as cake-off'ring
  Ere she was victim.

(We may suggest that *Nicander* (*fr.* 85) speaks of the
'cabbage' as 'prophetic' because it is holy since we find
in the Iambi of Hipponax something of this sort (18).
And Ananius too says . . . *Athenaeus.*)

19 And the soloeci sell, if they take them,
  The Phrygians to Miletus for mill-work,

(The ancients gave the name soloeci to barbarians.
*Anacreon* says . . And *Hipponax* (19). *Herodian* (explaining the origin of the term solecism. The work is not considered authentic).)

20 Behind the city lived he in Smyrna
  Halfway between Cape Rough and the Crumbles.

(A part of Ephesus used to be called 'Smyrna' as is clear
from *Hipponax* (20); for the Crumbles was the name given
to the cape situate above the present city containing a
part of its wall; the property behind the cape is still
spoken of as 'in the Back Crumbles': 'Rough' was the
name given to the mountain side round Koressos. *Strabo*
(who further tells how Smyrna was founded thence).)

21 Anon the keel along with grease smearing

('Grease': melted wax, *Hipponax* (21). *Harpocration.*)

---

[1] *v.* 1 Presumably off a height. Bergk connects with
the accident to the slave (*fr.* 4 above). On the story see
Schweighäuser. Conceivably the verses are Callimachean.

# HIPPONAX

$22_{48}^{52}$  καί μιν καλύπτει⟨s⟩; μῶν χαραδριὸν πέρνης;

(Schol. Plat. 352 Bekker on *Gorg.* 494 в (χαραδριοῦ βίον λέγεις of the incontinent man) χαραδριὸς ὄρνις τις ὃς ἅμα τῷ ἐσθίειν ἐκκρίνει. εἰς ὃν ἀποβλέψαντες, ὡς λόγος, οἱ ἰκτεριῶντες ῥᾷον ἀπαλλάττονται· ὅθεν καὶ ἐγκρύπτουσιν αὐτὸν οἱ πιπράσκοντες ἵνα μὴ προῖκα ὠφεληθῶσιν οἱ κάμνοντες, (22) ὥς φησιν Ἱππ.)

$23_{49}^{53}$  ἀλλ' αὐτίκ' ἀλλήλοισιν ἐμβιβάξαντες

(*E.M.* 334. 1 ἐμβιβάξαντες : παρ' Ἱππ. (23) ἀντὶ τοῦ ἐμβοήσαντες.)

$24_{50}^{54}$  κριγὴ δὲ νεκρῶν ἄγγελός τε καὶ κῆρυξ

(*E.M.* 539. 1 (on κρίκε) καὶ ῥηματικὸν ὄνομα κριγή· ὡς παρὰ Ἱππώνακτι (24).)

$25_{51}^{55}$  ὤμιξεν αἷμα καὶ χολὴν ἐτίλησεν.

(*E.M.* 624. 4 ὀμιχεῖν· . · ἐστὶ δὲ καὶ . . . ὀμίχω· ὁ μέλλων ὀμίξω ὡς παρ' Ἱππ., οἷον (25).)

$26_{52}^{56}$  σίφωνι λεπτῷ τοὐπίθ⟨η⟩μα τετρήνας

(Pollux vi. 19 καὶ σίφωνα μέν, ὅτῳ ἐγεύοντο, Ἱππ. εἴρηκεν (26).)

$27_{53}^{57}$  στάζουσιν †ὥσπερ ἐς τροπήϊον† σάκ⟨κ⟩ος.

(Pollux x. 75 καὶ ὁ τρύγοιπος καὶ ὁ σάκκος ἐπὶ τοῦ τρυγοίπου εἰρημένος, καὶ ὁ ὑλιστήρ. Ἱππ. δέ φησιν (27).)

22 Corr. Bgk.  μήν for μιν is read in Suid. *s.v.* and Ar. *Av.* 266 schol.  πέρας schol. Ar. (Ven.), -νᾶς cett., ὡς schol. Ar.

23 Also Zonaras, p. 706 Tittmann.

24 Also Zonaras, p. 1258 T., *An. Ox.* i. 268. 12, *Et. Gud.* 347. 27, Choerobosc. ii. 590, 657.

25 Also Zonaras, p. 1451 T., *An. Ox.* iv. 191. 6 (ὤμηξεν), 416. 7 (these have ἐτίλλησεν), schol. Hom. E 531.

26 ἐπίθημα for ἐπίθεμα Welcker.

27 ὥσπερ ἐκ τροπηΐου Bgk., since (Meineke) the wine goes from the vat into the sieve.  Better ὥσπερ ῥεῖ τραπηΐου since ὥσπερ requires a main verb.  σάκος corrected to σάκκος by Salmasius.  τραπη- should probably be read (Hemsterhuys).

354

22 And veilest[1] it ?   Sellest thou a bustard ?

(The ' bustard ' is a bird which evacuates while it eats.
People suffering from jaundice are eased by the sight of it;
so those who sell it wrap it up to prevent patients from being
relieved free of cost (22), as *Hipp.* says.   *Commentator on
Plato, Gorgias,* 494 в, ' life of a bustard.')

23 Anon they shrieked aloud to each other,

(' Shriek to ': in Hipponax (23)=' yell to.'  *Etymologicum Magnum.*)

24 And screech, the ghost-announcer, ghost-herald

(There is also a noun ' screech,' *e.g.* in *Hipponax* (24).   *id.*)

25 Bile in his urin, blood in 's stool brought up.

(Urine . . .; also . . . urin ;  *Hipponax* (25).  (ὀμιχεῖν or
-ίχειν : fut. ὀμίξω.)   *id.*)

26 With a thin tube he bored through the stopper.

(' Tube ' used for tasting mentioned in *Hipp.* (26).   *Pollux.*)

27 They dribble like a winepress-sieve flowing.

(And ' strainer ': and ' sieve ' in the same sense:  and
'filter.'  *Hipponax* says (27).   *id.*)

---

[1] Perhaps καλύπτει could be kept as a middle (καλύπτῃ;)
if ωιν is a part of the body.

# HIPPONAX

28 $^{5}_{5}$ $^{8}_{4}$  κἄλειφα Ῥόδι[ν]ον ἡδὺ καὶ λέκος πυροῦ

(Pollux, x. 87 ἐν δὲ τοῖς Δημοπράτοις **λέκος** εὑρίσκομεν, εἰπόντος Ἱππ. (28).)

29 $^{5}_{5}$ $^{9}_{5}$  πρὸς τὴν μαρίλην τὰς φ<ο>ῖδας †θερμαίνων† οὐ παύεται.

(Erotian p. 134 **φῷδες·** ἐστὶ μὲν ἡ λέξις Δωρική, καλοῦσι δὲ φῷδας τὰ ἐκ τοῦ πυρὸς γινόμενα μάλιστα δὲ ὅταν ἐκ ψύχους ἐν τῷ πυρὶ καθίσωσι στρογγύλα ἐπιφλογίσματα . . .· ὁτὲ δὲ καὶ ἐξανθήματα φοινικᾶ οἷον φῷδες περὶ τὸν θώρακά που γινόμενα. καὶ Ἱππ. δέ φησι (29). Tzetzes on Ar. *Plut.* 535 τὰ ἐκ ψύχους ἐκκαύματα ὡς καὶ Ἱππ. φησί (v. 1).

30 $^{6}_{5}$ $^{6}_{8}$  κύμινδις ἐν λαύρῃ
ἔκρωζεν.

(*Et. Flor.* p. 231 Miller *Mélanges* Οὐδὸν ἐς λαύρην (Hom. χ 128). τὴν δημοσίαν ὁδὸν . . .· τινὲς μὲν ὁδὸν ἀπέδοσαν, τινὲς δὲ τὴν κοπρῶνα, ὡς Ἱππ. (30). στολὴ (στόμα Mill.) δὲ λαύρης τὴν ἔξοδον τὴν εἰς αὐτήν (χ 137). *Cf.* Hesych. **ἐρκανηέντα πυλῶνα** (Dindorf for ἐρχ-)· τὸν πεπυκνωμένον καὶ συνεχόμενον.)

31 $^{6}_{5}$ $^{7}_{9}$  ἐν ταμ[ε]ίῳ τε καὶ χαμευνίῳ γυμνόν

(*Mélanges* p. 402 Mill. **χαμεύνιον·** κραββάτιον καθάπερ καὶ παρ' Ἱππώνακτι (31). p. 307 Ἱππ. ἐν μιῳ τε κτλ. Hesych. **τάμ[ε]ιον·** θάλαμος.)

28 Ῥόδιον I conjecture as Ar. *Av.* 944, where Blaydes' crit. n. is most misleading. See Pape-Benseler *s.v.* Ῥόδος. The converse error in Poll. vi. 104. ἡδὺ with ῥόδινον appears otiose. Scan as Ῥοδγον.

29 See note on opposite page.

31 The initial trochee may be supported from Herodes and is more likely than an initial dactyl, for which there is no good pre-Attic evidence. Corr. Hoffm. *Et. Vat.* has lost several sheets at the end, so that the entry χαμεύνιον is missing.

# FRAGMENTS 28-31

### 28 And Rhodian unguent sweet and a wheat-crock

(In the *Demioprata* (*Goods Sold by Public Auction*) we find ' crock,' used by *Hipp.* (28). *id.*)


### 29 Cease warming at the embers your chilblains.[1]

(' Chilblains ' : the word is Doric and applied to the round inflammations that result from the fire, especially when people sit right in the fire after being out in the cold. . . Sometimes it is applied to crimson eruptions in the region of the chest. *Hipponax* says (29). *Erotian.* Inflammations from cold as *Hipp.* says. *Tzetzes'* note on *Aristophanes' Plutus.*)


### 30            A raven was croaking
   In rear.

(' Passage to the " rear " *Homer* ' : the public way . . . Some explain the word as back-street, others as the privy : *cf. Hipp.* (30).[2] Mouth of the ' rear ' means the exit to it. *Etymologicum Florentinum.* *Cf.* ' Fenced gateway ' : narrow-set or straitened. *Hesychius.*)


### 31 Lay in a room on pallet-bed naked.

(' Pallet-bed ' : a small bed as in *Hipp.* (31). *Didymus Areius* on *Difficult Words in Plato.* So *Et. Flor.*)


[1] A most puzzling quotation. Erotian has τοὺς παῖδας for τὰς φωΐδας (Tzetzes); but Hoffmann, who rightly changes to φοΐδας, is also right in regarding this as a mere error.

The verse . . . ᾱ̆ς | θερμαίνων appears unmetrical. Perhaps it is an injunction, ' up and be doing ' : θερμαίνων | π. τ. μ. τ. φ. οὐ παύσεαι; So I translate. μαρίλην is also cited as -ίλλαν or -ίλλην, here and in 39.

[2] *Et. Flor.* has ἔκρωξεν κ. ἐς λ. *Et. Vat.* Reitz. *Lect. Rost.*, 1891-2, p. 14, gives the true reading, ἐν λαύρῃ.

# HIPPONAX

$32^{6\,5}_{\ 6\,0}$  καὶ νῦν ἀρείᾳ σύκινόν με ποιῆσαι.

(*Et. Flor.* p. 41 Mill. **ἀρειῶ·** τὸ ἀπειλῶ ὡς παρ' 'Ιππ. (32)· τουτεστιν ἀπειλεῖ.  *E.M.* 139. 36 one cod. ἀρειᾶς . . . ἀπειλεῖς, sed ἀρείᾳ *Et. Vat.*)

$33^{4\,5}_{\ 6\,1}$  καὶ Μύσων ὃν ὡπόλλων
ἀνεῖπεν ἀνδρῶν σωφρονέστατον πάντων.

(Diog. L. i. 107.)

$34^{6\,8\,\text{A}}_{\ 2}$  Σινδικὸν διάσφαγμα

(Schol. Ap. Rhod. iv. 321 καὶ 'Ιππῶναξ δὲ μνημονεύει (τῶν Σίνδων) πρὸς τὸ (34).  Hesych. **Σινδικὸν διάσφαγμα·** τὸ τῆς γυναικός.)

$35^{6\,8\,\text{B}}$  σηπίης ὑπόσφαγμα

(Ath. vii. 324 a 'Ιππ. δ' ἐν τοῖς ἰάμβοις εἰπόντος (35) οἱ ἐξηγησάμενοι ἀπέδωκαν τὸ τῆς σηπίας μέλαν.  ἐστὶ δὲ τὸ ὑπόσφαγμα ὡς 'Ερασίστρατός φησιν ἐν 'Οψαρτυτίκῳ ὑπότριμμα.  Eust. *Il.* 1286. 6.)

$36^{6\,9}$  πασπαληφάγον γρόμφιν

(Phot. *Lex.* ii. 67. 12 Naber **πασπάλη·** τὸ τυχόν, οἱ δὲ κέγχρον· οἱ δὲ τὰ κέγχρινα ἄλευρα.  'Ιππ. (36).  *Cf.* Eust. 1752. 121.)

$37^{7\,0\,\text{A}}$  βολβίτου κασιγνήτην

(*E.M.* 204. 28 **βόλιτον·** βόλβιτον δὲ "Ιωνες οἵ τε ἄλλοι καὶ 'Ιππ. οἷον (37).  Bekk. *An.* 186. 10 **βόλβιτον:** 'Ιππ.)

33 Probably Callimachean (ten Brink).
34 In the schol. Meineke reads πρώτῳ for πρὸς τὸ rightly: for a weak caesura would be incredible.  All the same Cr. is very likely right in connecting with *fr.* 43, since Tz. appears to have quoted or meant to quote both verses.
36 πασπάλιν φαγών codd.: corr. Porson.

# FRAGMENTS 32–37

**32** And menaces to render me senseless.

(To 'menace': threaten, as in *Hipp.* (32): *i.e.* threatens. *id.*)


**33**                    Whom Apollo
Declared the wisest man of all, Myson.

(*Diogenes Laertius.* (Probably from *Callimachus.*))


**34**                 Sindian fissure[1]

(*Hipponax* mentions the Sindi in his first book (?) (34). *Commentator* on *Apollonius Rhodius.*)


**35**                 Squid-pudding

(*Hipp.* in his iambi says (35). The interpreters explain it of the ink of the fish. It is really a pudding made of its blood as *Erasistratus* says in his *Cookery.* *Athenaeus.*)


**36**             Middlings-fed porker

(' Middlings': scraps. Others say millet, others millet-flour. *Hipp.* (36). *Photius.* *Hipp.* uses porker either of any sow or of an old one. *Eustathius* on *Homer's Odyssey.*)


**37**             Cow-dung's sister

(Bolitos was called bolbitos in general by the Ionians: and so *Hipp.* (37). *Etymologicum Magnum.*)


---

[1] *i.e.* γυναικεῖον αἰδοῖον Hesych.

# HIPPONAX

38⁷ ⁰ᴮ       ὥσ‹τε . . .› Ἐφεσίη δέλφαξ

(Ath. ix. 375 a καὶ Ἱππ. δὲ ἔφη (38).)

39⁷ ¹    πολλὴν μαρίλην ἀνθράκων

(Erotian p. 96 μᾶλλον δὲ ἡ θερμοσποδιὰ **μαρίλη** λέγεται ὡς
. . . καὶ Ἱππ. φησι (39).)

40⁸ ⁸     ‹τὸν δὲ› ληὸν ἀθρήσας

(Anon. *An. Ox.* i. 265. 6 τὸ λαὸς τῇ μεταγενεστέρᾳ Ἰάδι
τραπέν· (40) Ἱππ.)

41⁷⁷₄₁      κρε‹ῖ›ας ἐκ μολοβρίτ‹εω›
συός

(Eust. *Od.* 1817. 20 Ἀριστοφάνης γοῦν ὁ γραμματικὸς . . .
ἐπάγει ὡς καὶ Ἱππ. τὸν ἴδιον υἱὸν μολοβρίτην που λέγει ἐν τῷ (41).
Ael. *N.H.* vii. 47 ἀκούσαις δ' ἂν καὶ τοῦ Ἱππ. καὶ αὐτὸν τὸν ὗν
μολοβρίτην που λέγοντος.)

42¹ ² ⁷   μεσσηγυδορποχέστα

(Eust. *Od.* 1837. 42 κατὰ δὲ Ἱππ. καὶ ὁ μεσσηγυδορποχέστης
ἤγουν ὃς μεσοῦντος δείπνου πολλάκις ἀποπατεῖ ὡς πάλιν ἐμ-
πίμπλασθαι. Sueton. περὶ βλασφ. is no doubt the source :
Miller's text, p. 425 *Mél.*, gives the same explanation but
does not name *Hipp.*)

42ᴀ¹ ⁰ ⁰ ἄδηκε βουλή.

(Eust. *Od.* 1721. 61 χρήσεως Ἱππώνακτος ἦν Ἡρακλείδης
προφέρει, εἰπόντος (42ᴀ) ἤγουν ἤρεσκε τὸ βούλευμα. Compare
and perhaps add Hesych. Πανθρ‹ό›ῳ δήμῳ · παρρησίαν ἄγοντι
κτλ., Ἀελλῆσι | θυμοῖς ἀνυποστόλοις μετὰ παρρησίας. Τίεσκε
μύθους· ἐτίμα λόγους.)

---

38 *e.g.* ‹δή τις›. Unless the word was pronounced Ἐφεγσίη.
Ἐφεσηῖη ten Brink. Others suggest ἐπιστίη.
40 ‹δὲ› Bgk. invito metro.
41 μολοβριτέω for -ου Schneidewin.

360

38                  Like Ĕphēsĭăn piglet

(*Hipponax* says (38).   *Athenaeus.*)

39  Embers of charcoal many

(Better to say that ' embers ' mean hot ashes as *Hipp.*
. . . says.   *Erotian.*)

40                  Seeing the foulk

(Folk: the vowel is changed in later Ionic.   (40) *Hipp.*
*Grammarian* in *Cramer's Anecdota Oxoniensia.*)

41                  Flesh from a beggar
    Pig

(*Hipponax* calls his own son [1] ' beggar pig,' in the following
(41).   *Aristophanes the grammarian* in *Eustathius* on
*Homer Odyssey* (ρ 219).   You will find *Hipp.* calling even
the pig ' beggar.'   *Aelian.*)

42  In-mid-feast-voiding

(According to *Hipp.* we have also (42), that is one who
in the midst of dinner retires often in order to make room
for more.   *Eustathius* on *Homer* using *Suetonius*' work on
Opprobrious Names.)

42A  (This) counsel pleased.

(A use of Hipponax adduced by Heracleides.   *Hipp.* says
(42A), *i.e.* The proposal met with favour.   *Eustathius* on
*Homer's Odyssey.*   *Cf.* 'Licentious-tongued people': speaking with license, etc.   *Hesych.*  'Flighty of spirit': fearless
in license of speech, *id.*  'His rede did honour ' : honoured
his words, *id.*)

---

[1] There seems to have been some confusion in the text
of a previous grammarian between ῦc pig and υἱóc son.
Aelian's version is clearly right.   It was fashionable to
explain μολοβρός, a Homeric word of doubtful meaning, as
food-seeker.   The Greeks turned their pigs loose early to
find food.   Hrd. Mime viii. init.

42B<sup>109</sup> βεβρενθ‹ονευ›μένον ‹δέ›

(Hesych. (42B)· παρ' Ἱππώνακτι ὀργιζόμενον.)

# LATER CITATIONS, AND CITATIONS
# FROM CORRUPT TEXTS

## BOOK I

43$\frac{3}{2}$ Κοραξικὸν μὲν ἠμφιεσμένη λῶπος

(Tzetz. *Chil.* x. 377 περὶ τῶν Μιλησίων μὲν ἔφαν πολλοὶ ἐρίων, περὶ ἐρίων Κοραξῶν ἐν πρώτῳ δὲ ἰάμβῳ Ἱππῶναξ οὕτως εἴρηκε μέτρῳ χωλῶν ἰάμβων (43). τοὺς Κοραξοὺς δὲ καὶ Σινδοὺς ἔθνη τυγχάνειν νόει. Hesych. **Κοραξοί**· Σκυθῶν γένος καὶ τὸ γυναικεῖον αἰδοῖον.)

44$\frac{1}{4}$ ἔβωσε Μαίης παῖδα Κυλλήνης πάλμυν.

(Schol. Lyc. 219 Μαίας καὶ Διὸς Ἑρμῆς, ὡς . . . ὁ Ἱππ. ἐν τῷ κατὰ Βουπάλου πρώτῳ ἰάμβῳ (44). Tzetz. *ad loc.*)

With this is generally connected:—

45$\frac{1}{4}$ Ἑρμῆ κυνάγχα Μηονιστὶ Κανδαῦλα
φωρῶν ἑταῖρε δεῦρό [τί] μοι σκαπαρδεῦσαι.

(Tzetz. *An. Ox.* iii. 351. 7 τὸ δὲ Κανδαύλης Λυδικῶς τὸν σκυλλοπνίκτην λέγει, ὥσπερ Ἱππῶναξ δείκνυσι γράφων ἰάμβῳ πρώτῳ (45). So Tzetz. *on Iliad* p. 843 B.)

42B βεβρενθυόμενον Hesych. This is the only form which I can find which admits of easy scansion and appears to be sufficiently attested by such corrupt glosses as γρονθονευέται and πραθενεύεσθαι. We might perhaps attribute to Hipponax forms in Hesychius like ἀναγαγγανεύουσι, (κατ)ιμονεύει, λαγγονεύει.

44 *vv.ll.* Κυκλήσιον, Κυκλίης, κυκλίης : βασιλέα πάλμυν almost all codd. ἐβόησε codd.: corr. Schneidewin.

45.2 [τί] bracketed by Bgk. σκαπαρδεῦσαι is explained by συμμαχῆσαι superscribed. **σκαπερδεῦσαι**· λοιδορῆσαι Hesych., who also explains κυνάγχα by κλέπτα. These and other glosses **σκαρπαδεῦσαι** κρίναι and **καπαρδεῦσαι**· μαντεύσασθαι are cited by Bgk.

**42B** With choler puffed

   ((42B): angry in Hipponax. *Hesychius*.)


# LATER CITATIONS, AND CITATIONS
# FROM CORRUPT TEXTS

## BOOK I

**43** Attired in a Koraxian mantle

   (Many writers have mentioned Milesian wool, but *Hipp.*
mentions Koraxian wool in his first book of iambi as follows
in choliambic metre (43). You must know that the Koraxi
and Sindi[1] are tribes. *Tzetzes.* Koraxians: A race of
Scythians, etc. *Hesychius*.)


**44** On Maia's son, Cyllene's tsar, called he.

   (Hermes was son of Maia and Zeus, as . . . *Hipp.* says in
the book of Iambi written against Bupalus (44). *Tzetzes*
and *Commentator* on *Lycophron*.)


**45** Dog-throttling Hermes, thief-mate, whom Maeons
   Kandaules call, come give me a shove up.[2]

   (Kandaules in the Lydian tongue means puppy-throttler,
as Hipponax shows in his first book of iambi (45). *Tzetz.*
in *Cramer's Anecdota Oxoniensia* and on *Homer's Iliad*.)
*Hesychius* translates dog-throttling as 'thief,' and gives
several erroneous translations of 'to my aid come.'


   [1] Hence Cr. is probably right in connecting this with
*fr.* 34.
   [2] *Cf.* λακκοσκάπερδος Hesych.

# HIPPONAX

46$\frac{2}{5}$  Κίκων δ' ὁ †πανδαληκτος†, ἄμμορος καύης,
   τοιόνδε ⟨μο⟩ι κατ⟨εῖπε, κρῆτ'⟩ ἔχων
   ⟨δαῦλον⟩
   δάφν⟨η⟩σ⟨ιν⟩, οὐδὲν δ' αἴσιον προθεσπίζων

(Tzetz. on *Iliad* p. 76. 811 (δάφνη) ἦν οἱ ἱερεῖς τοῦ ἡλίου ἤτοι μάντεις καὶ μάγοι, οἷος ἦν καὶ ὁ Χρύσης, στεφανούμενοι ἐπορεύοντο· καθὼς δηλοῖ καὶ Ἱππ. ἐν τῷ κατὰ Βούπαλον ἰάμβῳ (46. 1) τοιόνδε τι δάφνας κατέχων. id. on Lycophron *Alex.* 424. 5 καύηξ δὲ ὁ λάρος κατὰ Αἰνιᾶνας, ὥς φησι καὶ Ἱππ. (46. 1). Hesych. (added by ten Brink) **Κίκων**· ὁ Κίκων Ἀμυνθάονος ἦν οὐδὲν αἴσιον προθεσπίζων.

47$\frac{4}{6}$  πόλιν καθαίρειν καὶ κράδῃσι †βάλλεσθαι†

48$\frac{5}{7}$  βάλλοντες ἐν λειμῶνι καὶ ῥαπίζοντες
   κράδῃσι καὶ σκίλλῃσιν ὧσ⟨τε⟩ φάρμακον.

49$\frac{6}{8}$  δεῖ δ' αὐτὸν ἐς φάρμακον †ἐκποιήσασθαι†,
50$\frac{7}{9}$  †κἀφῇ παρέξειν† ἰσχάδας τε καὶ μᾶζαν
   καὶ τυρὸν οἷον ἐσθίουσι φάρμακοι·

51$\frac{8}{10}$ παλαὶ γὰρ αὐτοὺς προσ†δέχονται† χάσκοντες
   κράδας ἔχο⟨ντες⟩ . . . . . . . . . . . . . .
   . . . . . ἔχο⟩ντας ὡς ἔχουσι φάρμακοι[ς]

46 The Hesychian gloss, whose language shows that it is *not* a gloss but a quotation, was rightly incorporated by ten Brink. 1 πανδάλητος, πανδαύληκτος, al. Κίκων is glossed ὄνομα μάντεως and καύης λάρος. 2 Supplevi *e.g.*: τοιόνδε τι δάφνης κατέχων Tzetzes. Hereabouts come the words παῖς ὠμυθέωνος.
47 κρ. is glossed by συκαῖς. ?φαρμάσσειν for βάλλεσθαι, as Tz. 48. 2 ὥσπερ codd.
49–51A are probably misquoted in details. It cannot be certain that they were not consecutive. In 49 ἐκπ. must mean 'select': if corrupt it has replaced a passive. In 50. 1 I suspect the truth is πιέξειν (or -εῖν Hrd. viii. 47). On this verse there is a note (ἀφὴ καὶ ἅρμα καὶ τὰ λοιπὰ οἱ Ἴωνες ψιλοῦσιν) whence κἀφῇ must be read. προσδοκεῦσι is probable for προσδεχ.—a slip of memory. The ms. used by Herodes had
364

46 Kikon the hideous, cormorant[1] luckless,
  Amythaon's son, his head with bay-leaves crowned,
  With naught auspicious in his forecast

((Laurel) which the priests of the sun (*i.e.* prophets and
wise-men, like Chryses) wore as a crown when they walked
abroad, as is shown by Hipponax in his book of iambi
against Bupalus (46. 1, 2). *Tzetzes* on *Homer's Iliad.*
'Kikon' was the son of Amythaon (46. 3). *Hesychius.*)

47 Must cleanse the city, and with twigs †pelted†

48 Pelting him in the meadow and beating
  With twigs and squills like unto a scapegoat.

49 He must be chosen[2] from you as scapegoat

50 And in his grip take barley-cakes, dried figs
  And cheese, such cheese as scapegoats may feed
  on.

51 For long have they awaited them gaping
  With twigs in hand ; . . . . . . . . . .
  . . . . . as trembling as scapegoats.[2]

[1] Priests are always represented as greedy. I translate
πανδήλητος : *cf.* πανλώβητος.
[2] If this fragment be not read consecutively it is possible
to explain φάρμακον as in *fr.* 18 and Tzetzes' comment as
equalling καθαρμόν (not -μα): and (with scansion ἐκπὄῃσ.) to
translate 'put him forth for a purification.' Again, if 51 be
not consecutive on 50, we could read :

  πάλαι γὰρ αὐτοῦ προσδέχονται χάσκοντες
  κράδας, ἔχοντες ὡς ἔχουσι φάρμακοι.

'They await there the twigs agape in such (pitiable) state
as scapegoats are in.'

---

χασκεῦντες : *cf.* Hrd. **iv.** 42. In 51. 2 the people who hold
the twigs are those who wait : hence -τες for -τας (Meineke).
But as ὡς ἔχουσι could only mean 'at once' in reference to
the subject of the sentence we need another ἔχοντας (*e.g.*
δέους) to refer to the state of mind of the victims.

# HIPPONAX

52₁₁⁹ λιμῷ γένηται ξηρός, ἐν δὲ τῷ θυμῷ
[ὁ] φάρμακος ἀχθεὶς ἑπτάκις ῥαπισθείη.

(Tzetz. *Chil.* v. 726 ὁ φαρμακὸς τὸ κάθαρμα τοιοῦτον ἦν τὸ
πάλαι. ἂν συμφορὰ κατέλαβε πόλιν θεομηνίᾳ, εἴτ' οὖν λιμός, εἴτε
λοιμός, εἴτε καὶ βλάβος ἄλλο, τῶν (? τὸν) πάντων ἀμορφότερον
ἦγον ὡς πρὸς θυσίαν, εἰς καθαρμὸν καὶ φαρμακὸν πόλεως τῆς
νοσούσης· εἰς τόπον δὲ τὸν πρόσφορον στήσαντες τὴν θυσίαν τυρόν
τε δόντες τῇ χερὶ καὶ μᾶζαν καὶ ἰσχάδας, ἑπτάκις γὰρ ῥαπίσαντες
ἐκεῖνον εἰς τὸ πέος σκίλλαις συκαῖς ἀγρίαις τε καὶ ἄλλοις τῶν
ἀγρίων τέλος πυρὶ κατέκαιον ἐν ξύλοις τοῖς ἀγρίοις. . . ὁ δὲ
Ἱππῶναξ ἄριστα σύμπαν τὸ ἔθος λέγει (47), καὶ ἀλλαχοῦ
δέ πού φησιν πρώτῳ ἰάμβῳ γράφων (48), καὶ πάλιν ἄλλοις
τόποις δὲ ταῦτά φησὶ κατ' ἔπος (49-51), καὶ ἀλλαχοῦ δέ
πού φησιν ἐν τῷ αὐτῷ ἰάμβῳ (52).)

53₁₅¹⁴ τούτοισι θηπ‹έ›ων τοὺς Ἐρυθραίων παῖδας
†οὓς φησὶ† μητροκοίτας Βούπαλος σὺν
Ἀρήτῃ
[κνίζων καὶ] †φέλιζων† τὸν δυσώνυμον
‹χό›ρτον

(Tzetz. on *Posthomerica*, 687 **θήπον**· ἐθαύμαζον· τὸ θέμα
θήπω καὶ Ἱππ. (53). **ἐλλίζων**· τίλλων. *Cf. id.* **ψελιστήν**·
λί‹χ›νον (for λιγ- Mus.) and **χναύων**· περικνίζων, περιτίλλων ;
**χναίει**· λαμβάνει, κνίζει.)


52. 1 θυμός· τὸ ἄρρεν αἰδοῖον Sch. A rightly. Hesych.
confuses with θύμος, thyme. 2 [ὁ] del. Blomfield.
53. 1 θήπων codd.: corr. Bgk. (Hesych. θηπητής· ἀπατεῶν).
2 *l.* τοὺς (ten Brink). 3 ἄρτον codd. κνίζων (in best
cod.) might be an explanation of a participle meaning eat,
gnaw: possibly δρυψελίζων (Bgk.). A simpler correction
would be καὶ κυψελίζων or ἐκυψέλιζε, in which case Hesych.
would be using a corrupt text. We should then further
read κυψελιστήν in gloss above. But there are many other
possibilities, *e.g.* κεῖται (ten Brink) with ψελίζων an otherwise
unknown verb.

52 That he be parched with famine and, led out

    A scapegoat, seven times on 's piece beaten.

(The scapegoat (expiatory offering) in old times was as follows. Did misfortune, by the wrath of heaven, overtake a city, whether famine or plague or other mischief, they led out as to sacrifice the ugliest of all the citizens to be an expiation and scapegoat of the diseased city. And having set the sacrifice at such a spot as seemed fit they placed in his hand cheese and barley-cake and dried figs. For after beating him seven times on the penis with squills and (rods of) wild fig and other wild trees they finally burnt him on a fire of timber of such trees. . .[1] Hipponax describes the custom best (47). Elsewhere he writes in the first book of iambi (48), and again elsewhere in these words (49-51) and elsewhere in the same book (52). *Tzetzes.*)

53 Th' incestuous Erythrean folk fooling

    With these things Bupalus with Aréte

    From day to day scuffled[2] his damned fodder.

θήπον 'they marvelled[3]': pres. θήπω: so Hipp. (53). *Tzetzes.* 'scuffle': tear. *Hesych. Cf. id.* 'scraping': 'scratching round, tearing round'; 'scrapes, gets, scratches.'

---

[1] Tzetzes first cites Lycophron 'as well as he can recall him' and then these passages, which is merely a hypocritical cloak for the fact that he has borrowed them from commentators on Lycophron.

[2] Like a hen, I take it.

[3] θηπ⟨έ⟩ω must, however, be taken transitively.

# HIPPONAX

54¹·⁵  †τε αρεδεύειε† τὴν ἐπὶ Σμύρνης
    †ἴθι† διὰ Λυδῶν παρ[ὰ] τὸν †᾿Αττάλεω†
    τύμβον
    καὶ σῆμα Γύγεω καὶ †μεγαστρυ† στήλην
    καὶ μνῆμα †τωτος μυττάλυτα παλμυδος†,
    πρὸς ἥλιον δύνοντα γαστέρα ⟨σ⟩τρέψας. 5

(Tzetz. in *An. Ox.* iii. 310. 17 στίχοι ῾Ιππ. τρισυλλάβους
ἔχοντες τοὺς παραλήγοντας πόδας . . καὶ †πᾶσαν† (54).  Schol.
Nicander *Ther.* 633 Γύγου δὲ σῆμα τοῦ ἐκεῖ βασιλεύσαντος, ὡς
φησιν ῾Ιππ. ἐν τῷ πρώτῳ τῶν [Λυδίας] ἰάμβων.  μυττάλυτα·
μεγάλου Hesych.)

55⁶·⁹₂₃  [καὶ] τὴν ῥῖνα καὶ τὴν μύξαν ἐξαράξασα

(Tzetz. in *An. Ox.* iii. 308. 20 τὸ μέτρον τὸ Δωρικὸν παρέλειψα
λήθῃ· δέχεται δὲ πλεῖον τῶν ἄλλων ἰάμβ. μ. κατὰ τὴν β' χώραν ἢ
καὶ δ' ἢ ϛ' σπονδεῖον, σπανιάκις δὲ καὶ δάκτυλον ὡς ἰσόχρονον τῷ
σπονδείῳ· Δωρικὸν ῾Ιππ. (55).)

54 In the text of Tzetzes read πάλιν (Meineke) for
πᾶσαν.  In schol. Nicand. Λυδίας (idem) is a gloss on ἐκεῖ.
2 scans ἴθῖ δῠὰ Λ.: but read ἰθύ.  4 μυταλιδι Tz.: Hesych.'s
gloss was connected by Bgk. and M. Schmidt.  For
suggestions on text see notes.  No weight of textual evidence
will induce me to believe that the list contained foreign
dynasts, paramours and bastards.  I fancy there is an
allusion to the conquest of Lydia.  Perhaps begin ὁδὸν
τεωρεύεσκε . . . ἰθύ.  τεωρεύς· . . . κακοῦργος, ληστής (Hesych.).
55 ? μύσπαν : and give μυσπίη (Hesych.) to Hippon.

---

¹ Unfortunately we are helpless here.  There seems no
reason to suppose the corruptions are slight.  Attales (Nicol.
Dam. *fr.* 63) is mentioned as a bastard, Σεσώστριος Bgk.'s
suggestion in *v.* 3 intrudes a foreigner, and any unknown
name or person is improbable.  Perhaps μεγαστρυ is partly

368

# FRAGMENTS 54–55

54 Along the road to Smyrna he ravag'd
　　Through Lydia straight by Alyattes' burrow,
　　By Gyges' grave, and Ardys' tomb mighty
　　And Sadyattes' monument, great tzar,
　　His belly turning, as he went, westward.[1]

(Verses of Hipp. with trisyllabic penultimate feet . . .
Again (54). *Tzetzes* [He mis-scans Ἀττἄλέῶ as Ἀττἄλἐῶ!].
The tomb of Gyges who was king there, as Hipp. says in
the first book of his [Lydian] iambi. *Commentator* on
*Nicander's* Theriaca. μυττάλυτα : ' great.' *Hesychius*.)

55 [And] her nose, and the discharge therefrom
　　knocking

(By a slip of memory I passed over the Dorian metre,
which more than other iambs contains spondees in the second,
fourth or sixth place, or rarely a dactyl as its metrical
equivalent. A Dorian verse of Hipponax (55). *Tzetzes*.)
[Tz.'s next citation suggests that he scanned μυξᾱν : but
I fancy he read τὴν μύξᾱν κᾰτᾰ τῆς ῥινὸς when we need only
read ἐκ for κατὰ to get good sense and metre.] [2]

composed of an old gloss μεγίστου on †μυτταλυτα† (*infra*)
like Hesych.'s μεγάλου. The remainder may be καὶ ⟨παρ'⟩
Ἀρδυος στήλην. In *v.* 2 Ἀλυάττεω Schnw. is the nearest.
　　　　　　　　　　　　　　　　　τοσαδυαττ
In *v.* 4 τωτοσμυττάλυτα might stand for τωλυαττεω. πάλμυδος
is known (Choerob. i. 232) to be an error, and anyhow it
must have ῠ. I suggest *e.g.* καὶ τὸ Σαδυάττεω μνῆμα Λυδίων
πάλμυος or πάλμυ. Ἄτυος (Cr.) is nearer, but A. was never
a ruler (Hdt. i. 34): so παλμ. would have to go into another
verse. On the main point, that we have a list of Lydian
kings, I fancy the version is not misleading.
　[2] Before this may have come ἀποσκαμυνθίζειν : ἀπομυκτηρί-
ζειν Hesych. : *cf.* σκινθαρίζειν ' to strike the nose with the
middle finger,' id.

# HIPPONAX

$56^{17}_{24B}$ δὸς χλαῖναν Ἱππώνακτι· κάρτα γὰρ ῥιγῶ
καὶ βαμβα<λ>ύζω.

(Plutarch *Mor.* 1058 E ὁ δὲ ἐκ τῆς Στοᾶς βοῶν μέγα καὶ
κεκραγώς ‘ἐγὼ μόνος εἰμὶ βασιλεύς, ἐγὼ μόνος εἰμὶ πλούσιος,’ ὁρᾶται
πολλάκις ἐπ’ ἀλλοτρίαις θύραις λέγων (56). The first verse is
quoted with variations of the moral 1068 B and 523 E. See
below. It is possible that the order is *fr.* 57 and *fr.* 56.
1 + ἐπεύχομαι—ῥιγῶ + καὶ β. So I translate. Then follows 59
perhaps with only two words missing.

$57^{16.21A}_{24A}$ ἐρ<έ>ω, φίλ’ Ἑρμῆ, Μαιαδεῦ Κυλλήν<ε>ιε
[ἐπεύχομαί τοι· κάρτα γὰρ κακῶς ῥιγῶ].

(Tzetz. Lycophron 855 ἡ χρεία σοὶ καὶ ἑτέρας μαρτυρίας;
ἄκουσον (57)· καὶ μετά τινά φησιν (59). Priscian *de metr. Com.*
p. 251 L. ‘Hipponactem etiam ostendit Heliodorus iambos
et choliambos confuse protulisse (57) ἐπεύχομαί τοι· κάρτα
γὰρ κακῶς ῥιγῶ. p. 247 L. (21 B Bgk.) Heliodorus metricus
ait: Ἱππ. πολλὰ παρέβη τῶν νενομισμένων ἐν τοῖς ἰάμβοις. . .
Hipp. in primo ἐρέω [γὰρ οὕτω Κυλλήνιε Μαιάδος Ἑρμῆ]. Iste
enim versus cum sit choliambus, in quarto loco et quinto
habuit dactylos, cum in utroque debuerit a brevi incipiens
pes poni. In eodem (58). Iste iambus habet in secundo
loco spondeum et in quarto (*an error for* tertio) dactylum.)

$58^{21B}_{28}$ ἡ δ’ ὀσφυῆγα καὶ ὀδυνοσπάδ’ αἱρεῖται
γέροντα <νωδὸν . . . . . . κἀτερόφθαλμον>

(Plut. *Mor.* 1057 F καὶ κατ’ Αἰσχύλον (an error of memory)
ἐξ ‘ὀσφυαλγοῦς κὠδυνοσπάδος λυγροῦ γέροντος,’ . . . *Lex. de
Spir.* p. 234 Valck. ὀσφυήξ . . . ὡς τὸ ὀσφυῆγος γέροντος.
Priscian (*l.c.*) gives [τοὺς ἄνδρας τούτους] ὀδύνη παλλιρειτ (or π)αε.)

56. 2 βαμβακύζω: corr. Schnw.
57. 1 ὦ φίλ’ Tz. ερμη or εραις Prisc.[1] ἐρέω Prisc.[2] Μαιάδος
Tz. ex gloss. quod integrum in Prisc.[2] habemus. In Prisc.[2]
ἐπεύχομαι is perhaps an explanation of ἐρέω. The words
from γὰρ to Ἑρμῆ are clearly a parallel citation, *e.g.*
Ἀντίμαχος γὰρ οὕτω φησί κτλ. ‘Iste enim versus,’ etc.—not
unnaturally in a citation from Epic. κυλλήνειε Welcker.
58. 2 *e.g.* ὧδε. νωδὸν etc. Plut. *Mor.* 1058 A. The
Lexicon is no doubt quoting from a better ms. of Plutarch
than we possess.

56    I'll say dear son of Maia, Cyllene's
and   Lord, give Hipponax a great coat : chilly
57    I am—I beg you I am right chilly
      And my teeth chatter.

(But the Stoic philosopher, shouting aloud and crying
'I alone am king, I alone am rich,' is often seen at other
men's doors saying (56). *Plutarch* on the *Ultrapoetical
Absurdities of the Stoics* : also *On Common Conceptions*
and *On the Love of Riches.* Inaccurately quoted by *Heliodorus* the metrist as ' Verily I beseech thee : for full chilly
Am I,' and perhaps by *Tzetzes,* ' Give to Hipponax a great
coat, shirtlet,' etc. : see below, 59.)

### 57 See above and *fr.* 56.[1]

(If you need further evidence listen to this (57). Later he
says (59). *Tzetzes. Heliodorus* shows that Hipponax wrote
a mixture of choliambics and iambics (57). *Priscian. Heliodorus* the metrist says ' Hipponax broke many of the iambic
traditions. He says in the first book '' For I will say thus :
son of Maia, Cyllenian Hermes.'' This verse, although
a choliambus, has dactyls in the fourth and fifth place,
although there should be in either place a foot beginning
with a short. In the same book (58). This iambus has
in the second place a spondee, and in the fourth (*he means
'' third* '') a dactyl.' *Priscian.*)

58   ⟨She⟩ a hip-shot old man, pain-racked, chooses,[2]
     ⟨Toothless, one-eyed⟩

(And to be changed from what Aeschylus (? Hipponax)
calls a ' hip-pained sorry old man ' to a beautiful god-like
fair shaped youth. *Plutarch* on *The Stoics say,* etc. ' Hip-
shot': *e.g.* hip-shot old man. *Breathing Dictionary.*)

---

[1] It is clear that Heliodorus drew the verses from a copy
of Hipponax' works interlarded with glosses and marginal
comments. Perhaps these were the first verses.

[2] Priscian gives

Indeed all these men in a pain racked chooses.

Plutarch in the next sentence to that quoted, speaking of
Odysseus in Homer, introduces some details, I suggest from
Hipponax. The reference would be to Arete and Bupalus.

# HIPPONAX

59 $^{18}_{24}$. δὸς χλαῖναν Ἱππώνακτι καὶ κυπασσίσκον
καὶ σαμβαλίσκα κἀσκερίσκα καὶ χρυσοῦ
στατῆρας ἐξήκοντα τούτερου τοίχου.

(Tzetz. Lycophron 855 οὗτος ἀσκέρας τὰ ὑποδήματα οὐ καλῶς
λέγει (59). ἀσκέραι[1] δὲ κυρίως τὰ ἐν τοῖς ποσὶ πιλία ἤτοι ὀρτάρια[1]
λέγονται καὶ χλαῖναν[1] τὸ σφικτουρίον[1] καὶ κυπασσίσκον[1] τὸ
ἐπιλωρικόν.[1] οὗτος δὲ ὁ Λυκόφρων, καίπερ ἀπ' Αἰσχύλου κλέπτων
λέξεις τινάς, ἐξ Ἱππ. δὲ πλέον, ἢ ἐπιλήσμων ὤν, ἢ μὴ νοῶν
ταύτας, ἄλλην ἄλλως ἐκτίθει . . . ἀλλ' ἄκουε πῶς φησιν Ἱππ.
(60). ἔγνως ὅτι διὰ τὸ εἰπεῖν δασείας τὰς ἀσκέρας τὰ ὀρτάριά
φησιν; ἢ . . (57). καὶ μετά τινά φησιν (59).)

60 $^{19}_{25}$. ἐμοὶ γὰρ †οὐκ ἔδωκας οὔτε χλαῖναν†
δασεῖαν, ἐν χειμῶνι φάρμακον ῥίγευς,
οὔτ' ἀσκέρῃσι τοὺς πόδας δασείῃσιν
ἔκρυψας ὡς <μοι μὴ> χίμετλα γί[γ]νηται.

(Tzetz. vide sup.)

61 $^{29}_{20}$. ἐμοὶ δὲ Πλοῦτος, ἔστι γὰρ λίην τυφλός,
ἐς τὠκι' ἐλθὼν οὐδάμ' εἶπεν· Ἱππῶναξ,
δίδωμί <σ>οι μν<έ>ας ἀργύρ[ι]ου τριήκοντα.

(Tzetz. on Ar. Plut. 90 τυφλὸν δὲ τὸν Πλοῦτόν φησιν ἐξ
Ἱππώνακτος τοῦτο σφετερισάμενος· φησὶ γὰρ οὕτως Ἱππ. (61)
καὶ πόλλ' ἔτ' ἄλλα· δείλαιος γὰρ τὰς φρένας.

59 In almost all codd. the text is covered with glosses.
Besides the three explanations above, over τούτερου is
ἰωνικῶς (sc. for Attic θᾶτ.) and μέρους over τοίχου. One
codd. has τοῦ νερτέρου τοίχου (? an error for ἐνδοτέρου). μοι after
χρυσοῦ codd. plur.

60. 1 One cod. has τὰν χλαῖναν. e.g. οὔτε κω Scaliger.
3 δασείῃσι: one cod. φησί. 4 ῥίγνυται one cod.: γίγν. corr.
Hoffmann. μή μοι codd.

61. 3 τοι codd.: σοι Bgk. ἀργυρίου codd.: corr. id.
καὶ πόλλ' κτλ. has falsely been given to Hipponax: cf.
καὶ πολλαχοῦ δυστηνὰ τοιαυτὶ λέγει Aeschrion (fr. 1 q.v.).
Those who insist on giving them to Hipponax should read
δείλᾱγος γὰρ and find a substitute for τὰς φρένας.

## FRAGMENTS 59–61

59 Give to Hipponax a great-coat, shirtlet,
　　Sandals and carpet-slippers ; and sixty
　　Staters of gold by th' inner wall hidden.[1]

(Lycophron wrongly uses the word ' slippers ' for boots
(59). 'Slippers ' properly mean the felt-shoes, that is
*ortaria*, worn on the feet, great-coat the *sphictorium*, and
shirtlet the *epiloricum*. This Lycophron, though stealing
some words from Aeschylus, while preferring Hippon., either
from forgetfulness or ignorance of their sense uses them
anyhow. . . . Listen to what *Hipp.* says (60). You realize
that by calling them ' shaggy ' he means *ortaria*. But *cf.*
(57). Later he says (59). *Tzetzes* on *Lycophron*.)

60 To me thou gavest never (yet) great-coat
　　Shaggy, a cure for ague in winter,
　　Nor hid'st in carpet-slippers right shaggy
　　My feet, to hinder my chillblains growing.

(See above 59 *Tzetzes*.)

61 But never came there Plutus, the blind one,
　　Unto my house, nor spake thus : ' Hipponax
　　Minas of silver give I thee thirty.'
　　[Etcetera : for his intelligence is paltry].[2]

(He calls Plutus blind, borrowing the epithet from
*Hipponax*, who says as follows (61). *Tzetzes* on *Aristophanes'*
Plutus.)

---

[1] τούτέρου τοίχου is of course the inner wall by which the
host sits (Hom. I 219), and the gold is to be there since
the task of the thief who digs under the walls (τοιχωρύχος)
would thereby be rendered more difficult. Refer perhaps to
this passage the word τοιχοδιφήτωρ = τοιχωρύχος cited by
Hesych. ὀρτάρια and σφικτ. are both late mediaeval words.
I note πόδορτα and σφικτ. in Achmes the oneiromancer.

[2] Tzetzes, who presumably borrowed this citation from
an earlier commentator, perhaps on Lycophron (1102 ?),
included the last words (which are really the grammarian's
criticism of L.) in his note. Or they may be Tz.'s own
criticism on Aristophanes' peculations from Hipponax.

# HIPPONAX

## LATE CITATIONS

### From Uncertain Books

$62^{30A}_{34}$ ὦ Ζεῦ πάτερ ⟨Ζεῦ⟩ θεῶν 'Ολυμπίων πάλμυ

(Tzetz. on Lyc. 690 ἡ δὲ λέξις ὁ πάλμυς ἐστὶν 'Ιώνων καὶ χρῆται ταύτῃ 'Ιππ. λέγων (62, 63).)

$63^{30B}_{35}$ τί μ' οὐκ ἔδωκας χρυσόν, ἀργύρου [πάλμυ];

(Vid. supra.)

$64^{31}_{36}$ †ἀπό σ' ὀλέσειεν "Αρτεμις, σὲ δ[ὲ κ]' ὡπόλ-
λων†,
⟨σὲ δ'⟩. . . .

(Tzetz. An. Ox. iii. 310. 17 στίχοι 'Ιππ. τρισυλλάβους ἔχοντες τοὺς παραλήγοντας πόδας (64). Contrast (Bgk.) Hephaestion p. 30 (33 Gaisf.) τὸ δὲ χωλὸν οὐ δέχεται τοὺς παραλ. τρισ. πόδ. id. Exeg. in Il. 797 в.)

$65^{32}_{37}$ παρ' ᾧ σὺ λευκόπεπλον ἡμέρην μείνας
πρὸς μὲν κυνήσει⟨ς⟩ τὸν Φλυησίων'
'Ερμῆν.

(Tzetz. Il. p. 83. 25 H. ἐπὶ μῦθον ἔτελλεν· ὑπερβατόν· ἐστὶ δὲ καὶ τοῦτο 'Ιωνικὸν ὥς φησι καὶ 'Ιππ. (64). καὶ ἀλλαχοῦ (65). Hesych. Φλυήσιος· 'Ερμῆς καὶ μήν τις.

62 ⟨Ζεῦ⟩ rectissime Meineke ex Archil. 88 (Bgk.). v.l. 'Ολ. θεῶν.

63 πάλμυ] v.l. πάλμυν : see opposite.

64 δὲ κὡπ. : corrected by Meineke.

65. 2 κυνήσειν cod. : corr. Welcker. Φλυησίων' Bgk. olim rectissime. Hesych. φλυησί†ο†s is (?) corrupt, for months may end in -ων or -εών (so perhaps -εῶν' here). Nor do they say ὁ Δηλίων 'Απόλλων but ὁ Δήλιος.

## LATE CITATIONS

### From Uncertain Books

62 Zeus, tsar of Gods Olympian, father

(The word ' tsar ' is Ionic and used by *Hipponax* when he says (62, 63).  *Tzetzes* on *Lycophron*.)


63 Why, tsar of silver, me no gold gav'st thou ? [1]

(See above.)


*64 May Artemis destroy thee, [and] Apollo,

(Verses of *Hipp.* (64) with the penultimate foot trisyllabic. *Tzetzes* in *Cramer's Anecdota Oxoniensia*.  Contrast *Hephaestion* : the choliambic does not allow trisyllables in the penultimate foot.)


65 Whereat awaiting day of white raiment
    Phlyesiary Hermes thou 'lt worship.

(' Gave a harsh order ' : transposition (for made good his word); this is Ionic as *Hipponax* too says (64).  And elsewhere (65).  *Tzetzes*.  ' Phlyesian ' : Hermes : also a month.  *Hesych.*[2])


[1] 62 and 63 I have given separately.  But more probably they came together and πάλμυ is mere dittography, ' Why gavest not gold nor mountains of silver,' *e.g.* χρ. ⟨ἤ⟩ (so Lobeck) ἄργυρον πολλόν ;

[2] Hesychius' note ' Phlyesian ' : Hermes, also a month— shows that Phlyesiary is the right reading.

# HIPPONAX

66 ⁴²₄₁ ἐπ' ἁρμάτων τε καὶ Θρ‹ε›ϊκίων πώλων
λευκῶν ὀ‹ρ›ούσ‹ας› ἐγγὺς Ἰλίου πύργων
ἀπηναρίσθη Ῥῆσος Αἰν‹ε›ίων πάλμυς.

(Tzetz. on *Posthomer.* 186 ὁ δὲ Ῥῆσος Αἰνειῶν Θράκης ἦν
βασιλεύς, υἱὸς Στρύμονος ἢ Ἠιονέος καὶ Τερψιχόρης . . . καὶ Ἱππ.
(66). On *Il.* 78. 1 Η. καὶ ἀντὶ τῶν δασέων ψιλὰ ἐξεφώνουν ὡς
ἔχει ἡ ἀρχαία Ἰωνική, ἐπιβρύκων ἀντὶ τοῦ ἐπιβρύχων, καὶ τὸ
(66. 1), καὶ μεταρμόσας. Hesych. **Νεαίρησιν ἵπποις**· τοὺς ἀπὸ
Νεαίρης.

67 ⁴³₄₂ κακοῖσι δώσω τὴν πολύστονον ψυχήν,
ἢν μὴ ἀποπέμψῃς ὡς τάχιστά μοι κριθέων
μέδιμνον ὡς ἂν ἄλφιτον ποιήσωμαι,
κυκεῶνα πίνων, φάρμακον πονηρ[ί]οῖσ‹ι›.

(Tzetz. *An. Ox.* iii. 308 δέχονται καὶ τρισυλλάβους πόδας εἰς (?)
ϛ΄, πλὴν τοὺς ἀπὸ βραχείας ἀρχομένους, τὸν χορεῖον φημὶ καὶ τὸν
ἀνάπαιστον ὡς ὁ Ἱππ. (69) καὶ πάλιν (so Meineke) (68).
Hesych.)

68 ⁴⁹₄₅ Μιμνῆ, †κατωμηχανε†· μηκέτι γράψῃς
ὄφιν τριήρευς ἐν πολυζύγῳ τοίχῳ
ἀπ' ἐμβόλου φεύγοντα πρὸς κυβερνήτην·
αὕτη γὰρ ἔστ‹α›ι συμφορή τε καὶ κληδὼν
†νικύρτα καὶ σαβωνι† τῷ κυβερνήτῃ      5
ἢν αὐτὸν ‹ὁ› ὄφις †ὠντικνήμιον δάκῃ†.

(Tzetz. on Lycophron 425 "**Ἀποθεν**· τὸ π̄ο̄ μικρὸν γράφε.

66. 1 Θρηϊκίων : correxit Fick.   2 ὀείους κάτεγγυς codd.   3
παλάμας one cod.: βασιλεύς cett. Text Schneidewin. Perhaps
there was an incorrect variant ἰόύς, and καὶ ἐγγύς was written
in the margin.   If so ὁ is all that is left of the participle
except that one cod. has an explanation ἰὼν in the margin.
67. 3 Scan πο̄ιήσωμαι or *l.* πονῆσ.   4 πονηρίοις cod. : corr.
Fick.   ? πᾶσι for πίνων with ἀλφίτων in 3.
68. 1 κακῶν μοχλητά ten Brink.   If a vocative, κατωμόδαρτε
is near the traces, but perhaps it is a verb ; *e.g.* κακοῦ μὴ
ἴχαινε or κατ' ὦν μὴ χαῖνε (Hes. **καταχηνη**) which might have
degenerated into ἔχανε.   γράφης one cod. *v.l.* ἔχανε.   4 ἐστι: *v.l.*
αὕτη.   5 *vv.ll.* σινωνι, δαβωνι, σαμαυνι.   6 *vv.ll.* τ' ἀνακείμενον,
τῶν τικνήμων, τῶν τι κνημένον.   See Addenda.

66 On cariot and Thracīan horses
  All white he sallied and near [1] Troy's castles
  There was he slain tsar Aeneian Rhesus.

(Rhesus was king of the Aeneians in Thrace, son of
Strymon or Eioneus and Terpsichore (66). *Tzetzes* on *Posthomerica*.[2] They used smooth consonants instead of aspirated
like old Ionic *souting* instead of *shouting*, and (66. 1), and
*resaping*. *id.* ' Neaerean Horses ': from Neaera. *Hesych*

67 To woe my weeping soul I 'll surrender
  Unless at once you send me a bushel
  Of barley, wherewithal I may find me,
  By drinking groats, of all my ills respite.

(Trisyllables are allowed in the sixth foot except those
beginning with a short vowel, *i.e.* ⌣⌣⌣ and ⌣⌣—: *e.g.*
*Hipp.* (67), and again (68). *Tzetz.* in *Cramer's Anecdota
Oxoniensia*.) [3]

68 Yearn not for mischief, Mimnes.[4] Cease painting
  A snake upon the trireme's benched bulwarks
  Which runs from prow abaft to the helmsman.
  For this brings evil fame and fate evil,
  Thou slave of slaves and yid, to the helmsman,
  If right upon his shin [the] snake bite him.

(ἄποθεν : write *sic* with omicron. Scribes ignorant of

[1] Read either ' straight for ' or ' sallied : hard by.'
[2] Tzetzes purloined this note from a long note by an
earlier editor of Lycophron on the use of πάλμυς ' tsar.'
[3] The criticism (that κριθεῶν is trisyllabic) is erroneous,
as erroneous as the criticism of the next citation ἄπόθεν.
Nor can anyone have written ὄφις in 68. 6, as the snake
has already been mentioned. In view of this, -τῶντῖκνήμιον
and δάκη, the verse may be an early gloss. If the steerer
exposes to the snake the *back* of his leg or calf the sense of
ἀντικν. in Hipp.'s time—' shin ' or the forepart—is somewhat
unsuitable. δάκη has been altered to δάκνη. Σάμορνα,
"God help us," is said to have been another name for
Ephesus from its Semitic inhabitants : Schmidt on Hesych.
*s.v.* Σαμονία.                [4] ? Mimnes thou well-bespankéd.

377

# HIPPONAX

οὗτοι (the ms.?) δὲ ἀγνοήσαντες τὸ μέτρον μέγα τοῦτο γράφουσι. σὺ δὲ τοῦτο γίγνωσκε ὅτι τὸ δασὺ ἐκτείνειν δύναται ὅτε βούλεται ὁ στιχιστὴς ἴσως τοῖς διπλοῖς ὡς ... Τρῶες δ' ἐρρίγησαν ὅπως ἴδον αἰόλον ὄφιν (Hom. Μ 208). εἰ δὲ μείουρον τοῦτον νομίζεις ἄκουσον καὶ τῶν κατὰ Μιμνῆ τοῦ ζωγράφου χωλῶν ἰάμβων Ἱππωνακτείων στίχων (68). ἰδοὺ τοῦ ὄφις τὸ ὃ μακρόν ἐστιν ἐκταθὲν ὑπὸ τοῦ φ̄ δασέος ὄντος. νικύρτας· δουλέκδουλος. Ath. vi. 267 c (cit. ten Brink) σίνδρωνα δὲ τὸν δουλέκδουλον.)

69 ⁷₆ ⁴₇ οὔ μοι δικαίως μοιχὸς †άλῶναι δοκεῖτ
†Κριτίης ὁ Χῖος ἐν τῷ κατωτικῳ δούλωτ

(Tzetz. vid. supra 68. Hesych. δοῦλος· ἡ οἰκία ἢ τὴν ἐπὶ τὸ αὐτὸ συνέλευσιν τῶν γυναικῶν.)

70 ⁵₄ ¹₇ ὁ δ' αὐτίκ' ἐλθὼν σὺν τριοῖσι μάρτυ⟨ρ⟩σιν
ὅκου τὸν ἔρπιν ὁ σκότος καπηλεύει
ἄνθρωπον εὗρε τὴν στέγην ὀφέλλοντα—
οὐ γὰρ παρῆν ὄφελμα—πυθμένι στοιβῆς.

(Tzetz. on Lycophron 579 ἔρπιν· χάλις καὶ ἔρπις ὁ οἶνος. χάλις μὲν παρὰ τὸ χαλᾶν τὴν ἶνα ἤγουν τὴν δύναμιν ἔρπις δὲ κτλ. ὅθεν καὶ οἱ Αἰγύπτιοι τὸν οἶνον ἔρπιν καλοῦσι. Ἱππωνάκτειοι δέ εἰσιν αἱ λέξεις. φησὶ γάρ (72). ἀλλαχοῦ δὲ πάλιν (70. 1-3). On 1165 ὀφελτρεύσωσι: σαρώσωσι· σάρον γὰρ καὶ ὄφελτρον καὶ ὄφελμα καὶ ὄφελμος ἡ σκούπα λέγεται. καὶ τοῦτο Ἱππ. φησίν (70). On Ar. Plut. 435 (v. 2). The second verse is quoted in an older scholium on Lyc. ll.cc. Hesych. Πέρδικος καπηλεῖον· χωλὸς καπηλὸς ὁ Π. ἦν. ἔνθεν ἔνιοι τὴν παροιμίαν φασὶ διαδοθῆναι.)

69. 2 mss give either κατωξ or κτωξ (i.e. κτωικω). See Bast's Commentatio Palaeographica, Tab. vii. 7, 8. Bgk.'s remark, 'Sunt enim iambi (sc. recti)' is inane, since Tz. quotes for trisyllables (exc. ∪∪∪ and ∪∪−) in the final place of choliambi. On 2 see nn.

70. 1 ? αὖτις. μάρτυρσιν Buttmann. 2 ὅπου only schol. Ar. Plut. v.l. σκοπὸς. 3 εὑρών and ὁρῶν vv.ll.

---

[1] See crit. n. Bgk.'s suggestion κασωρ- is excellent. Hesychius' inane note rightly referred here by Ahrens should have provided food for thought for scholars who believe in

FRAGMENTS 68–70

metrical rules write omega. But you, gentle reader, must
realize that an aspirate may at the will of the author count
two letters and lengthen the previous vowel, *e.g.* ὄφις in
Homer, *Il.* (M 208). If you think this verse ' docked '
*cf.* further *Hipp.'s* choliambi attacking Mimnes the painter
(68). Here you have ὄφις before φ aspirate. *Tzetzes* on
*Lycophron.* νικύρτας : slave of slave birth. *Hesychius.*)

69 †Unjust the Chian court that condemned you
   Tamquam adulter in lupanari ¹†

(*Tzetzes* : see on 68. *Slave* : House or a collection of
women in the same place. *Hesychius.*)

70 With three to witness he returned straightway
   To where the runaway his swipes peddles
   And found a man who, having no besom,
   Was besoming the house with a broom-stick.

(' Swipes ' : booze and swipes are names for wine. The
former is derived from brawn and loose, *i.e.* loosening the
strength : the latter (etc.). Hence the Egyptians call wine
swipes. The words are used by *Hipp.*, who says (70).
Again elsewhere (70. 1-3). *Tzetzes* on *Lycophron*, 579).
On 1165 commenting on the unfamiliar verb " besom " *Tz.*
gives various forms for ' sweep,' ' sweeping,' and quotes all
four verses. He quotes *v.* 2 again on Aristophanes' *Plutus*.
They were also given by a previous critic of Lycophron.
' The hostel of Perdix ' : Perdix was a lame innkeeper after
whom some say this proverb became traditional.² *Hesych.*)

the word μαλις and the like. As δοκεῖ is not a trisyllable
with a long vowel it follows that we must end the second
verse ἐν κασωρῑτέῶ : one may therefore write (*e.g.*) with
Ahrens οὔ μοι δικαίως ὥστε μοιχὸς ἀλῶναι δοκέει Κριτίης ὁ
Χῖος ἐν κ., but it is perhaps permissible to suspect that the
whole is a satirical attack on Bupalus : οὔ μοι δικαίως ἐν
κρίτῃσι Χίοισι δοκέεις ἀλῶναι μοιχὸς ἐν κασωρίτεω. This I
translate. There is a further doubt that really we may have
κατωτάτῳ, a favourite word of Tz. in explanation, *e.g.* on
Lyc. 121 ἐν τῷ τοῦ κρυπτοῦ καὶ κατωτάτου τόπου σήραγγι.
² I suggest that there was an older Perdix who gave rise
to this tag if it is choliambic. The famous innkeeper (*Av.*
1292) of this name was, however, an Athenian See Addenda.

# HIPPONAX

71 $^{64}_{56}$                                    ‹’Αθηνα‹ίη››
‹ἰ›λ‹ά›σκο‹μαί σ›ε καί με δεσπότε‹ω›
βεβροῦ
λαχόντα λίσσομαί σε μὴ ῥαπίζεσθαι.

(Tzetz. *An. Ox.* iii. 310. 17 στίχοι Ἱππώνακτος τρισυλλάβους
ἔχοντες τοὺς παραλήγοντας πόδας. . . πᾶσα (*l.* πάλιν Meineke)
(71). Hesych. **βεβρός**· ψυχρός, τετυφωμένος. **βέβροξ**· ἀγαθός,
χρηστός, καλός· and see below.)

# DOUBTFUL FRAGMENTS

72 $^{73}_{66}$ †ὀλιγὰ φρον‹έ›ουσιν οἱ χάλιν πεπωκότες.†

(Tzetz. on Hes. *Op.* 336 ὁ γὰρ οἶνος τὰς φρένας ἐξιστᾷ· ἐνίοτε
καὶ θυμὸν ἐπάγει ὡς καὶ Ἱππ. (72). Sch. Ar. *Plut.* 437, on
Lycophron 579 (see *fr.* 70), Miller, *Mél.* 307). Verses
possibly to be ascribed to Ananius.)

73* $^{55ᴮ}_{26}$ Ἑρμῆς δὲ Σιμώνακτος ἀκολουθήσας

(Miller, *Mél.* 19 **ἀκολουθήσας** (73). ἐκτάσει τοῦ ᾱ· οὕτως
Ἡρωδιανός.)

71. 1 Ἀθηναίη ita Bgk. ? The word Ἀθηνᾶ is a gloss on
the corrupt μάλις : but it is quite probable that Ἀθ. preceded.
Μαλισκονισκε ms. A : κονισκελαιρε cett. $^{χαιρε}$ χαῖρε Bgk. rightly
explained as a gloss. **μαλίς**· Ἀθηνᾶ Hesych. For my
reading *cf.* ἴληθι· χαῖρε Hesych. 2 δεσποτεα βεβροῦ : corr.
Schneidewin. The last word is glossed μα[. . .]οῦ : ? μαλακοῦ
Hoffmann.
72 Very doubtful. Perhaps οἱ . . . πεπώκασιν. *v.l.* πεπτ-.

380

71                                    O Athéne,
I cry thee hail and beg that I gentle
Master may win, and feel not his cudgel.

(Verses of *Hipponax* with trisyllables in the penultimate
feet. . . Again (71). *Tzetzes* in *Cramer's Anecdota Oxoniensia.*)


## DOUBTFUL FRAGMENTS

72 †Full little wit have men who sup on booze.†

(For wine removes wits : occasionally too it induces
passion as *Hipp.* says (72). *Tzetzes* on *Aristophanes' Plutus,
Lycophron.* Also the *Etymologicum*, but without naming
the author.)


73 †Hermes who followed, son of Simonax ¹†

(ἀκολουθήσας. So *Herodian* explains the scansion.)


¹ I am inclined to think the citation spurious and post-
Attic. See on Herodas ii. 47. I read ἀ or ὠκ.

---

73 If Herodian is to be trusted, and his authority is great,
it is perhaps more likely that ᾱκ is some peculiarity of
Ephesian dialect, than that it is an innovation of a later
writer. Lehrs reads Ἑρμῆς δ' ἐς Ἱππώνακτος. But even
Herodian may have been deceived by a false text, and ἀκολ.
is far more fitted to a gloss than to any early Ionic writer.
Even Hrd. eschews it. The real word may have taken the
genitive.

# HIPPONAX

74*[6 1][6 4]      ἀνὴρ ὅδ' ἑσπέρης καθεύδοντα
ἀπ' ‹ὦ›ν ἔδ‹υ›σε †χλούνην.†

(Schol. Hom. I 539 χλούνην: οἱ μὲν ἀφριστήν· χλουδεῖν γὰρ
τὸ ἀφρίζειν τινες Δωριέων ἔλεγον· ἄλλοι δὲ κακοῦργον· καὶ γὰρ
τῶν ἀρχαίων ἰαμβοποιῶν τινα φάναι (74). Ξενοφῶντα δὲ γένος τι
Ἰνδῶν φάναι τὸν χλούνη⁀ εἶναι.)

(See also Introduction and after *fr.* 86.)


75[3 5][3 0 Λ]    See Phoenix *fr.* 8.


76*     ἐκ πελλίδος ‹δὲ› τάργανον κα[ι]τηγυίης
χωλοῖσι δακτύλοισι τήτέρῃ σπένδει
τρέμων οἶόν περ ἐν βορηΐῳ νωδός.

(Ath. 495 c **Πέλλα**· . . . εἰς ὃ ἤμελγον τὸ γάλα. . . Ἱππ.
λέγει πελλίδα (4, 5), Φοῖνιξ δὲ ὁ Κολοφώνιος ἐν τοῖς Ἰάμβοις
ἐπὶ φιάλης τίθησι λέγων οὕτως (Phoenix *fr.* 4). καὶ ἐν ἄλλῳ δὲ
μέρει φησίν (76). Hesych. **τάργανον**· ὄξος, Λυδοί.)


74 Dindorf may be right in placing χλούνην at the end of
*v.* 2, or Meineke in placing it at the beginning. More
probably Bgk. is right in placing χλούνης at the beginning
of *v.* 1. 2 οὖν codd.: corr. Schnw. ἔδησε codd.: corr.
Hermann.
76. 1 ‹δὲ› Schnw. καὶ τηγ. Ath.: corr. Porson.

---

[1] I translate Bergk's conjecture: see crit. n.
[2] Xenoph(anes) and (S)indi: so Hermann and Bergk.
[3] 76 appears to me certainly Hipponactean. (*a*) There

382

# FRAGMENTS 74–76

74 †This rogue[1] here as I was at eve sleeping
    Stripped me.†

(' Rogue ' (of a boar): some explain as ' foaming ' for
certain Dorians spoke of foaming as ' roguing.' Others as
' villain ': for, they say, one of the old (chol)iambic writers
said (74). Xenophanes says that rogue was the name of a
clan of Sindi.)[2]

75 (See Phoenix *fr.* 8.)

76 And tarragon out of a smashed paillet
    With limping fingers of one hand dribbles,
    A-tremble like the toothless in north wind.[3]

(' Pail ': . . . into which they used to milk. . . *Hipp.*
speaks of it as ' paillet ' (4, 5). Phoenix of Colophon in his
Iambi uses it of a cup, as follows (Phoenix, *fr.* 4). And
in another portion of his works he says (76). *Athenaeus.*
'Tarragon': vinegar, a Lydian use. *Hesych.*)

are no difficulties of metre in the ascription. Every other
verse in our *frr.* of Phoenix is metrically impossible for
Hipp. So in *fr.* 1 *v.* 1, 3 ?, 6, 8 (*bis*), 9, 12, 14 (τοῖσι), 15,
17 (see *J. Camb. Phil.* 1927). (*b*) The tone is that of a virulent
lampoonist, not of a plaintive cynic. (*c*) The misery of the
sketch is accentuated if we transfer this paragraph to the
' pail ' illustrations. (*d*) Hipp. certainly *used* not only
πελλίς but also the word τάργανον as the gloss shows. Phoen.
is not very fond of direct imitations, despite λέκος πυρῶν *frr.*
1, 2. If I am right in supposing Plut. had Hipp. in mind
when writing on the ultra-poetical absurdities of the Stoics
νωδός may also be Hipponactean. As against these arguments we may set χωλοῖσι (deb. κυλλ.) and οἷονπερ (deb.
ὅσονπ.). (*f*) They are far too good and concentrated for
Phoenix. Contrast his *fr.* 3. (*g*) What ' other portion '?

# HIPPONAX

## TRIMETER OR TETRAMETER

77 ⁷⁶₆₉ †λαιμώσσει δέ σ‹ε›υ† τὸ χεῖλος ὥσ‹τ›'
ἐρῳδιοῦ.

(Schol. Nicand. *Ther.* 470 μαιμώσσων : ἀντὶ τοῦ ζητῶν καὶ ὁρμῶν. γράφεται δὲ καὶ λαιμώσσων ἀντὶ τοῦ πεινῶν ὡς 'Ιππ. (77). Hesych. λαιμᾷ· εἰς βρῶσιν ὥρμηται.)

## TETRAMETERS

78 ⁸³₇₀ λάβετέ μ‹ε›υ ταἰμάτι‹α›, κόψω Βουπάλου
τὸν ὀφθαλμόν·
ἀμφιδέξιος γάρ εἰμι, κοὐκ ἁμαρτάνω κόπτων.

(Suid. Βούπαλος· ὄνομα. 'Αριστοφάνης· εἰ νὴ Δί[α] ‹ἤδη› [τις] τὰς γνάθους τούτων ‹τις ἢ› δὶς ἢ τρὶς ἔκοψεν ὥσπερ Βουπάλου, φωνὴν ἂν οὐκ ἂν εἶχον. παρὰ τῷ 'Ιππ. (78. 1). *id.* κόπτω· εἰ νὴ Δία ... αὐτῶν ... καὶ αὖθις (78. 1). Erotian p. 43 ἀμφιδέξιος ... ὁ δὲ 'Ιπποκράτης .. ἐπὶ τοῦ εὐχρήστου κατὰ ἀμφότερα τὰ μέρη ... ὁμοίως δὲ καὶ ὁ 'Ιππῶναξ φησίν· (v. 2). Galen, *Gloss. Hippocr.* 430, *Aphorism.* xviii. 1. 148 also quote *v.* 2 but without κόπτων.)

79 ¹⁷₁₃ καὶ δικάζεσθαι Βίαντος τοῦ Πριηνέ‹ο›ς
κρέσσων

(Strabo xiv. 636, Diog. L. i. 84, Suid. *s.vv.* Βίαντος Πριηνέως (one cod. -έος) δίκη and δικάζεσθαι.)

77 The words can easily be arranged, with slight alterations, for a tetrameter. But see n. *v.l.* λαιμῷ. σου codd. Some om. δέ σου.

78. 1 ? τῆτε for λάβετε. μου corr. by Schnw. θαιμάτια Bgk. for θοἰμάτιον: ται. (trisyll.) Hi.-Cr. *v.l.* Βουπάλῳ. 2 The fragments were connected by Bgk. καὶ οὐχ, κοὐχ mss.: corr. ten Brink. Suidas was copying a lost schol. on Arist. *Lys.* 360.

79 ἃ καὶ κτλ. Diog. L.: Meineke cj. πρώτῳ. ἃ καὶ om. Suid. δικάσασθαι Strabo. Πριηνέως codd. omn. κρέσσον Strabo: κρείσσων Suid.: κρεῖσσον Diog. L.

## TRIMETER OR TETRAMETER

77 But thy lip raveneth as a heron's.[1]

('Raving': seeking and hastening. Some write 'ravening,' meaning hungry: *cf. Hipp.* (77). *Commentator* on
*Nicander's Theriaca.*)

## TETRAMETERS

78 Here take my clothes, so in the eye I 'll Bupalus
        pummel;
   For I am ambidexterous and pummelling miss
        not.[2]

('Bupalus': a name. Aristophanes 'In faith if some
one twice or thrice the jaws of these had pummelled, as it
was done to Bupalus, no voice would they have left them.'
In *Hipp.* (78. 1). *Suidas.* 'Pummel.' 'In faith,' etc. And
again (78. 1). *id.* 'Ambidexterous': . . . Hippocrates . .
uses of those whose limbs are equally efficient on both sides
of the body . . . So in *Hipp.* (78. 2). *Erotian.* Also
twice cited by *Galen.*)

79 Than Bias of Priene far a better judge (finding)

(*Strabo, Diogenes Laertius, Suidas* on 'Bias of Priene'
and 'judge.')

---

[1] With the Greeks almost all diving birds and sea birds
are types of gluttony. With us only the cormorant enjoys
that position. Probably read τὸ σεῦ δὲ χεῖλος ὥστε ῥωδιοῦ
λαιμᾷ.
[2] It is by no means certain that these verses are consecutive.

80 $^{8\ 0}_{7\ 4}$ μηδὲ μοιμύλ[α]λειν Λεβεδίην ἰσχάδ' ἐκ
    Καμανδωλοῦ

(Sext. Emp. *adv. Math.* i. 275 Λεβεδίων γοῦν διαφερομένων
πρὸς τοὺς ἀστυγείτονας περὶ Καμανδωλοῦ ὁ γραμματικὸς τὸ Ἱππωνάκτειον παραθέμενος ἑνίκα (80). Hesych. μοιμύλλειν· θηλάζειν,
ἐσθίειν.)

81 $^{8\ 2}_{7\ 5}$ Κυπρίων <λ>έκος φαγοῦσι κἀμαθουσίων
    †πυρῶν†

(Strabo viii. 340 συγκαταλέγειν τὸ μέρος τῷ ὅλῳ φασὶ τὸν
Ὅμηρον. . . χρῶνται δὲ καὶ οἱ νεώτεροι· Ἱππ. μὲν (81). Κύπριοι
γὰρ καὶ οἱ Ἀμαθούσιοι. Eust. *Il.* 305. 23.)

82 $^{6\ 2}_{7\ 1}$         οἱ δέ μευ ὀδόντες
   <οἳ κοτ'> ἐν τοῖσι γναθοῖσι πάντες <ἐκ>-
   κεκινέαται.

(Cram. *An. Ox.* i. 287. 28 μεμετρέαται· . . . Ἰωνικόν· . . .
καὶ παρ' Ἱππώνακτι (82). *Et. Mag.* 499. 41. Miller, *Mél.*
181. 8 (omitting γναθοῖσι.)

83 $^{8\ 4}_{7\ 6}$ †ἑξ†. . . . | τίλλοι τις αὐτοῦ τὴν τράμιν τ'
    ὑποργά<ζο>ι.

(Erotian p. 124 τράμιν· τὸν ὅρρον ὅνπερ καὶ ὑποταύριον
καλοῦμεν ὡς καὶ Ἱππ. φησίν (83). μέμνηται καὶ Ἀρχίλοχος.
Λυσίμαχος δὲ τὸν σφιγκτῆρα.)

80. 1 μοι μύ λαλεῖν codd.: corr. Meineke. Καμανδωδοῦ
most codd. Λεβεδίην trisyll. ?
81 βέκος codd. φαγοῦσι om. Eust. πυρῶν Eust.: πυρόν
Strabo: ? πυρέων Hrd.; *cf.* ii. 80.
82 Metre restored by Ahrens. 2 <ἐκ> ten Brink. οἳ κοτ' I
have inserted *metri gratia.*
83 τράμιν ὑποργάσαι cod.: <τ'> Meineke. Clearly the
difference of tense is indefensible. For the alteration comp.
crit. nn. on 79. I have placed the fragment here following
Bgk. who suggested ἐκ <τρίχας>, but translate ἐξ − − | κτλ.
Certainly the more probable cause of corruption is the loss
of a word after ἐξ. Meineke's ἑξάκις is wholly pointless.
Erotian does not quote by verses, so that a trimeter is more
probable.

FRAGMENTS 80–83

80 Nor mumble figs Lebedian, from far Kaman-
    dolus

(When the Lebedians disputed with their neighbours over
Kamandolus, the scholar won the case by citing *Hipponax'*
verse (80). *Sextus Empiricus.* 'To mumble': chew, eat.
*Hesychius.*)


81 Of Amathusian loaves a crock and Cyprian eating[1]

(They say that Homer mentions together both the whole
and the part. . . So do later writers: *Hipp.* (81). For the
Amathusians are Cyprians. *Eustathius* on *Homer's Iliad.*)


82                                    But my grinders
    [That once] were in my jaws have now been all of
        them knock'd out.[2]

('Number'd': . . . Ionic. . . In Hipponax (82). *Etymologicum Magnum.*)


83                                        His anus
    Let some one pluck withal and knead gently.

('Anus': the rump or hypotaurium: *e.g.* Hipp. (83).
Archilochus too mentions it. Lysimachus says it is the
sphincter muscle. *Erotian.*)


---

[1] I do not believe in the form βέκος in Hdt. ii. 2, in view
of the ms. discrepancies and Aristophanes' βεκκεσέληνος.
Why βέκος Κυπρίων, not Κύπριον, and 'Αμαθουσίων not -ιον?
And why should a Greek in Lydian territory use a Phrygian
word of a Cyprian produce? λέκος removes these difficulties.
[2] Or simply 'have fallen out.' Teeth are thus said
κινεῖσθαι in the medical writers: Aretaeus, p. 17 Kuehn.

# HIPPONAX

84 <sup>2 4 *inc.*</sup>  [ἁ]π<έλ>λα γὰρ τρυγὸς γλυκείης ἦν ἔτικτεν
    ἀνθηδών.

(*Et. Gud.* 57. 33 ἀνθηδών· ἡ μέλισσα παρὰ τὸ τὰ ἄνθη
ἔ[ν]δειν (so *Et. Gen.*) ἐν αὐτῇ ('Ιππ. ἐν πρώτῃ Wilam.) (84).)


[85 <sub>5 7</sub> <sup>8 1</sup>    στέφανον εἶχον κοκκυμήλων . . . καὶ
    μίνθης]

(Ath. ii. 49 e ἐπεὶ δὲ πλεῖστον ἐν τῇ τῶν Δαμασκηνῶν ἐστι χώρᾳ
τὸ **κοκκύμηλον** καλούμενον . . . ἰδίως καλεῖται τὸ ἀκρόδρυον
Δαμασκηνόν. . . κοκκύμηλα μὲν οὖν ἐστι ταῦτα· ὧν ἄλλος
τε μέμνηται καὶ 'Ιππ. (85).)


86 <sup>1 2 0</sup>    καὶ Διὸς κούρ<α>ς Κυβή<β>η<ν> καὶ
    Θρ<ε>ϊκίην Βενδῖν

(Hesych. Κυβήβη· ἡ μήτηρ τῶν θεῶν . . . παρ' ὃ καὶ 'Ιππ.
φησι (86)· ἄλλοι δὲ Ἄρτεμιν.)


(*Inc.* 8)  διὰ †δέρην† ἔκοψε μέσσην καδ δὲ λῶπος
    ἐσχίσθη.


86 Cod. κοῦρος, -ηκη, -ικη : corr. Schmidt.
*Inc.* 8 I include here for convenience.  It is attributed to
Anacreon by writers on Homer, P 542.  It is difficult to
believe that Anacreon wrote scazons, but it is far more
probable that we should read ἔσχισεν than attribute to
Hipponax or Aeschrion.  δέρην is impossible for Hipp. or
Anacreon, hence read δὲ ῥῖν(α).

388

84 A pail there was of honey sweet born of the flower-eater.[1]

('Flower-eater': the bee because it sucks from the flowers. (Hipp.) Book I. (84). *Etymologicum Gudianum.*)

85 A garland wore of damson flower, and mint [full sweet smelling] [2]

(Since the 'damson' . . . grows in profusion in the Damascene district . . . the fruit is specially named 'damascene.' Hipp. among others mentions it (85). *Athenaeus.*)

86 Daughters of Zeus Cybebe hight and Thracian Bendis

('Cybebe': the mother of the Gods. . . Whence Hipp. has (86). Others identify her with Artemis. *Hesychius.*)

(Inc. 8) Clave through the middle of his (nose) and rent was his mantle.[3]

---

[1] The fragment has been allotted to Aeschrion on the ground of the pedantic word. But I find the diction no more tasteless than that (*e.g.*) of *fr.* 15. πέλλα : so Bgk.

[2] In English damson is of course derived from damascene. The Greek words differ. I have given the verse in the only form in which it approaches metre : it is still irregular and probably the attribution is mistaken. In Ionic tetrameters separate words cannot form the first two feet,, and εἶχον is improbable. See however *Journal Camb. Phil. Soc.*, 1927, p. 46. Perhaps read στέφεα μὲν . . . . . -λα καὶ μίνθην.

[3] *Inc.* 8 is really a plain tetrameter ' and rent his mantle wide.'

87* (Anan. 4)       καί σε πολλὸν ἀνθρώπων

ἐγὼ φιλέω μάλιστα ναὶ μὰ τὴν κράμβην.

(Ath. 370 b μήποτε δὲ ὁ Νίκανδρος . . . (see on 18): καὶ
Ἀνάνιος δέ φησι (87*).)

(*Inc.* 9)   καὶ σαῦλα βαίνεις ἵππος ὡς κορωνίτης

(*E.M.* 270. 45 διασα·λούμενος· παρὰ τὸν σαῦλον, τὸν
τρυφερὸν καὶ ἁβρόν. Σιμωνίδης ἐν Ἰάμβοις (*Inc.* 9).)

(*Inc.* 10)     ὥσπερ ἔγχελυς κατὰ γλοιοῦ

(Ath. vii. 299 c Σιμωνίδης δ' ἐν Ἰάμβοις (*Inc.* 10).)

# HEXAMETERS

89$\frac{85}{27}$ Μοῦσά μοι Εὐρυμεδοντιάδε‹ω› τὴν π‹α›ντο-
     χάρυβδιν

τὴν ἐγγαστριμάχαιραν, ὅσ' ἐσθίει οὐ κατὰ
     κόσμον,

ἔννεφ' ὅπως ψηφῖδι κακ‹ῇ› κακὸν οἶτον ὄληται

βουλῇ δημοσίῃ παρὰ θῖν' ἁλὸς ἀτρυγέτοιο.

(Ath. xv. 698 b Πολέμων δ' ἐν τῷ δωδεκάτῳ τῶν πρὸς Τίμαιον
περὶ τῶν τὰς παρῳδίας γεγραφότων ἱστορῶν τάδε γράφει . . .·
εὑρετὴν μὲν οὖν τοῦ γένους Ἱππώνακτα φατέον τὸν ἰαμβοποιόν.
λέγει γὰρ οὗτος ἐν τοῖς ἑξαμέτροις (89). Hesych. **ἐγγαστριμάχαι-
ραν·** τὴν ἐν τῇ γαστρὶ κατατέμνουσαν.)

87* Metre forbids us to accept the attribution to Ananius.
I suspect a dislocation in Ath.'s text or a misunderstanding
of Lysanias. As the rhythm of the first verse is unparalleled
in early Ionic writers, it may belong to Herodes.

*Inc.* 10 ὥσπερ γὰρ A.

89. 1 εὐρυμεδοντιαδεα: corr. Wilam. ποντοχ.: corr. Bgk. ?
2 δς: corr. Kal. 3 κακη (om. tres codd.): corr. quis ? ἔννεπ'
inepte recentiores.

---

[1] If by Hipp. this must be satirical—' I swear on nothing.'
But the metre is late and the author more probably Phoenix
or Herodes. Ananius avoided all choliambi but those which
ended with four long syllables.

87*                              Beyond all men
    I love thee most I swear by this cabbage.[1]

(Perhaps Nicander (. . . see on 18) : and Ananius says
(87).  *Athenaeus*.)

(*Inc.* 9) And treadest proudly like a horse arch-
            necked

(" Proudifying " : from proud = luxuriant, dainty.  Simonides in his Iambi (*Inc.* 9).  *Etymologicum Magnum*.)

(*Inc.* 10)                          Like eel on oil-scrapings [2]

(Simonides in his Iambi (*Inc.* 10).  *Athenaeus*.)


## HEXAMETERS

89 Eurymedontiades his wife with knife in her belly,[3]
    Gulf of all food, sing Muse, and of all her dis-
            orderly eating :
    Sing that by public vote at the side of th' un-
            harvested ocean
    Pebbled with stones she may die, an evil death to
            the evil.

(Polemon in his twelfth book of Criticisms of Timaeus
dealing with parodists writes as follows :  Boeotus and
Euboeus . . surpassed their predecessors.  But the actual
inventor of this class of poetry we must admit to have been
Hipp. the writer of (chol)iambics.  In his hexameters he
says (89).  *Athenaeus*.)

---

[2] *Inc.* 8, 9 and 10 are included here for convenience.
Their true authorship is uncertain and their resemblance to
Choliambi perhaps fortuitous.  ὥσπερ (10) is probably unsound for the old Ionic.  Aeschrion and Simonides are
confused (6).

[3] *v.* 1 That is she bolts her food without slicing it :
Hesychius' explanation appears to be very much abbreviated
and is as hard as the original.

# HIPPONAX

90 $^{8\ 8}_{7\ 8}$        τί με σκιράφοισ' ἀτιτάλλεις;

(Eust. *Od.* 1397. 26 . . . 'Αθηναίοις οἳ καὶ ἐν ἱεροῖς ἀθροιζό-
μενοι ἐκύβευον καὶ μάλιστα ἐν τῷ τῆς Σκιράδος 'Αθηνᾶς τῷ ἐπὶ
Σκίρῳ. ἀφ' οὗ καὶ τὰ ἄλλα κυβευτήρια σκιράφεια ὠνομάζετο. ἐξ
ὧν καὶ πάντα τὰ πανουργήματα διὰ τὴν ἐν σκιραφείοις ῥᾳδιουργίαν
σκίραφοι ἐκαλοῦντο· Ἱππ. (90).)

91 $^{8\ 7}_{7\ 7}$  πῶς παρὰ Κυψοῦν ἦλθε

(*Gramm. Hort. Adonid.* p. 268ᵃ οἱ δὲ Ἴωνες . . . Σαπφοῦν
καὶ Λητοῦν . . . ὁμοίως καὶ παρὰ Ἱππώνακτι (91).)

91 Κυψοῦν is unlikely in an Homeric imitation: read with
Bergk (?) κῶς παρ Καλυψοῦν ἦλθε.


# PAPYRUS FRAGMENT

92    ηὗδα δὲ λυδίζουσα β(ασγ)[ικορλαζε·
      πυγιστὶ τὸν πυγεῶνα παρ[,
      καί μοι τὸν ὄρχιν, τῇ σφαλ[ε
      κ]ράδη συνηλοίησεν ὥσ<τε> [φαρμάκῳ,
      ἐ](ν τ)οῖς διοζίοισιν ἐμπε(δ)[ωθέντι.          5
      καὶ δὴ δυοῖσιν ἐν πόνοισ[ιν              ·
      ἥ τε κράδη με τούτέρωθ[εν
      ἄνωθεν ἐμπίπτουσα· κ[ὦ
      π(αρα)ψιδάζων βολβίτῳ [              ·
      ὦζεν δὲ λαύρη· κάνθαρο[ι δὲ              10
      ἦλθον κατ' ὀσμὴν πλεῦν[ες              ·
      τῶν οἱ μὲν ἐμπίπτοντε[ς
      κατέβαλον· οἱ δὲ τοὺς ὀδό[ντας ὤξυνον·
      οἱ δ' ἐμπέσοντες τἀθυ(ρ)ά[†γ†ματ' ἔγραινον
      τοῦ Πυγέλησι [              15

(For all notes see p. 65.)

392

**90** Why cozenest me with thy dicings? [1]

(... the Athenians who even used to assemble in temples to play dice and most of all in that of Athene Sciras in the quarter Sciron. Hence all other dicing-places were called σκιραφεῖα. Hence too rogueries in general were called σκίραφοι 'dicings' on account of the cheating that went on in the dicing-places. Hipp. (90). *Eustathius* on *Homer's Odyssey*.)

**91** How unto Kypso came he

(The Ionians ... formed the accusative of Sappho and Leto in -oun. ... So in Hipponax <you get Kypsoun> (91). A Grammarian in the *Horn of Amalthea and Gardens of Adonis*, Aldine ed. p. 268 *verso*.)

[1] 'In the quarter Sciron.' So clearly Eust. took it: the derivation of Sciras is disputed.

## PAPYRUS FRAGMENT

**92** Then spoke she foreign wise: [Venez plus vite;
Hereafter I will pluck your foul anus;
Then with a bough [where tripped I lay kicking],
Battered my .... s as though I were scapegoat,
Emprisoned fast in place where twain planks split.
Yes, truly was I [caught] in two evils;          6
On one side fell the rod above on me,
[To my sore pain: below upon th' other]
Befouled my .... dripped with fresh cow-dung.
Then stank the midden; [numberless] beetles   10
Came at the stench [like flies in midsummer].
Whereof some shoved away as they fell on
[Perforce their neighbour]; some their teeth
    whetted;
Some, that had fallen, first devoured th' ordure.
More than Pygelean woes did I suffer.          15

# COMPARISON OF NUMBERS OF FRAGMENTS OF HIPPONAX IN BERGK, *P.L.G.* AND THIS EDITION

| Bgk. | Knox | Bgk. | Knox | Bgk. | Knox |
|------|------|------|------|------|------|
| 1 | 44 and 45 | 32 | 65 | 64 | 71 |
| 2 | 46 | 33 | 1 | 65 | 32 |
| 3 | 43 | 34 | 16 | 66 | 30 |
| 4 | 47 | 35 | 75 | 67 | 31 |
| 5 | 48 | 36 | 17 | 68A | 34 |
| 6 | 49 | 37 | 18 | 68B | 35 |
| 7 | 50 | 38 | 4 | 69 | 36 |
| 8 | 51 | 39 | 5 | 70A | 37 |
| 9 | 52 | 40 | 6 | 70B | 38 |
| 10 | 10 | 41 | 7 | 71 | 39 |
| 11 | 2 Inc. (Introd.) | 42 | 66 | 72 | See p. 5 |
| 12 | 8 | 43 | 67 | 73 | 72 |
| 13 | 2 Inc. | 44 | Inc. 4 | 74 | 69 |
| 14 | 53 | 45 | 33 | 75 | Herodas v. 74 |
| 15 | 54 | 46 | 19 | 76 | 77 |
| 16 | 57 | 47 | 20 | 78 | Inc. 5 Introd. |
| 17 | 56 | 48 | Inc. 3 | 79 | 79 |
| 18 | 59 | 49 | 68 | 80 | 80 |
| 19 | 60 | 50 | 21 | 81 | 85 |
| 20 | 61 | 51 | 70 | 82 | 81 |
| 21 | See 57 | 52 | 22 | 83 | 78 |
| 22A | 11 | 53 | 23 | 84 | 83 |
| 22B | 12 | 54 | 24 | 85 | 89 |
| 23 | 14 | 55A | 25 | 86 | 90 |
| 24 (inc.) | 84 | 55B | 73 | 87 | 91 |
| 25 | om. | 56 | 26 | 88 | 40 |
| 26 | 15 | 57 | 27 | 89 and 91-99 | om |
| 27 | om. | 58 | 28 | 90 | See p. 2 |
| 28 | Inc. 6 | 59 | 29 | 100 | 42A |
| 29 | Inc. 7 | 60 | 55 | 109 | 42B |
| 30A | 62 | 61 | 74 | 120 | 86 |
| 30B | 63 | 62 | 82 | 127 | 42 |
| 31 | 64 | 63 | 9 | | |

NOTE.—So profuse is Hesychius in glosses from Hipponax that I venture to suggest that some of the following anonymous citations may belong to him. Some I have included as illustrations in what *might* be their approximate contexts. In addition most of the Hesychian glosses referred in German texts to Herodes are more probably due to his original.

Words in ἰβυ-, various Lydian glosses, ἄρναν and other

# FRAGMENTS AND NEW DISCOVERIES

Clazomenian glosses, Schmidt *s.v.* αὐριβάτας (Lyd. adv.), λουταρίζημα, μασίγδουπον | βασιλέα, Νεαίρησιν | ἵπποις, ὀδώδυσται, ὀμπνίη δαιτί, †ὀπωφᾶται†, Πέρδικος καπηλεῖον, τοιχοδιφήτωρ, τίεσκε μύθους, Τοξίου βουνός and *e.g.* τομεύουσι, χατεύουσα, φραδεύουσι.

To complete list of addenda to Bergk's edition, I give the following fragment (Diehl addenda): Inscr. Ostrak. Berolin. 12605 ὧρος· ἐνιαυτός . . . . Ἱππώνακτος·

      πονηρὸς [             ]οι πάντας

      Ἀσωποδώρου παῖδα κ[           ]

apparently with the sense ' wicked for all his years beyond the son of Asopodorus.'

Of certain fragments given by Bergk we may guess at metre in *fr.* 133 κύων λιμῷ | σαρκῶν, a dog gnawing In hunger, and *frr.* 110, 111 ἡ βορβορῶπις κἀνασυρτόλις πόρνη, which I do not translate.

Fragment 92 was found at Oxyrrhyncus. Ed. pr. *Rivista di Fil. Class.* 1928, pp. 500 *sqq.* by G. Co[ppola].

1 ξι corr. from ξι P. 6 καιδη ex καινη P. 8 πϊπτ ex πειπτ P. Iotas subscr. om P exc. βολβίτῳ (9). Accents, etc., at 2 πυγεῶνα, 3 καί, 4 ηλοίη, 7 ἡ and τοὐτέρ, 8 εμπϊπτουσα·κ, 9 ἀζῶν, 10 λαύρη, 11 κατ᾿ and πλεῦν, 13 ον· οιδε, 14 οιδ᾿, 15 πυγέλησι, and perhaps 10 ὦξεν. Supplements *v.* 1 Vogliano and Lobel, *v.* 4 Coppola (corr. E. Lobel from ὥσπ[ερ], *v.* 5 (init.) Co., *v.* 10 Lobel, 11, 12, and 13 (ὀδόντας) Co., *v.* 4 . . ]ποις Co., *vv.* 3, 5, 8, 13, 14 (ἔγρ. vel ἔχναυον) supplevi.

I translate *v.* 2 -ις ἐλάκτιζον, *v.* 6 ἡγρευόμην, *v.* 7 ἤλγυνεν, *v.* 9 κατησχύνθη, *v.* 10 τώριθμῷ, *v.* 11 ἢ θέρεος μυῖαι (following Co.), *v.* 12 ἐκ βίης ἄλλους. Only a few letters of the three next verses remain. In *vv.* 2 and 9 the sense is highly controversial. I translate παρτιλῶ σ᾿ αὖθις and φαλῆς καινῷ (vereor ne σπέρμα legendum sit). τὰ διόζια sunt sedes (planks) τῆς λαύρης in quibus Hipponactem aut fraude (*Decameron*, ii. 5) aut casu captum et pronum jacentem Arete spe frustrata tamquam cinaedum (Petron. ch. 138) et impotentem (Burton, *Arabian Nights*, x. 250) contumelia punit. Nescio an cantharorum dapes et titillationes pro viderit mulier. βολβ. de stercore bovino tantum dici potest. In λαύρη ('midden') excrementa omnius generis coacervantur. Pro ἀθυράγματα vid. Hesych. θυραγμ- (extra ordinem): ἀφοδεύματα.

# ANANIUS

1<sup>1</sup> Ἄπολλον ὅς <κ>ου Δῆλον ἢ Πυθῶν' ἔχεις,
ἢ Νάξον ἢ Μίλητον ἢ θεί<η>ν Κλάρον,
ἵκ<ε>υ κα<τ>' ἱ[ε]ρά· †ἢ† Σκύθας ἀ<π>ιξέαι.

(Ar. *Ran.* 659 Dionys. (1. 1). Xanth. ἤλγησεν· οὐκ ἤκουσας ;
Di. οὐκ ἔγωγ' ἐπεὶ ἴαμβον Ἱππώνακτος ἀνεμιμνήσκομεν. Schol.
ἴαμβον 'Ιππ.· ὡς ἀλγήσας καὶ συγκεχυμένος οὐκ οἶδε τί λέγει·
ἐπεὶ οὐκ 'Ιππ. ἀλλ' 'Ανανίου. ἐπιφέρει δὲ ὁ 'Ανανίας αὐτῷ
(1. 2, 3).)


2<sup>2</sup> χρυσὸν λέγει Πύθερμος ὡς οὐδὲν τἆλλα.

(Heraclid. Pont. (Ath. xiv. 625 c) οὗτός ἐστι Πύθερμος οὗ
μνημονεύει 'Ανάνιος ἢ 'Ιππῶναξ ἐν τοῖς ἰάμβοις †ἐν ἄλλῳ†
οὕτως (2).)


1 *που, θείαν, ἴκου, καθ', ἱερά, ἀφιξ-* : corr. Meineke. 3 for
ἢ read καί, the usual error, ' and then you may return
home,' or better τί . . . ;
2 ? χρυσοῦ. On the score of metre Ananius must be the
author. Note that Athenaeus quotes at second hand.

---

<sup>1</sup> The subject seems to be clear. It is an appeal to Apollo
who had a tendency to wander to the north. Himerius
(*Or.* xiv. 10) tells us (from Alcaeus) how on his birth A. was
sent on his swan-car to Delphi by Zeus to give law to the
Greeks. He immediately turned his team to the Hyper-

# ANANIUS

1 Apollo, now at Delos, Pytho town,
  Naxos, Miletus, or Claros divine,
  First to our rites: why Scythiaward must hie?[1]

(*Dionysus* (1. 1). *Xanthias.* It hurt. Didn't you hear?
*Dionysus.* Not it indeed: a verse of Hipponax I hunted
for. *Aristophanes, Frogs,* 659. 'Hipponax': this is said
in his pain and confusion inaccurately, since the verse is
not by Hipp. but by Ananius. The next verses are (2, 3).
*Commentator* on this passage.)

2 Aught else but gold is naught, saith Pythermus.

(This is the Pythermus whom Ananius or Hipponax
mentions in his iambi †. . .†[2] as follows (2). *Heraclides
Ponticus* quoted by *Athenaeus.*)

boreans. He spent a year there before bidding his swans
return (ἐξ Ὑπερβορέων ἐφίπτασθαι). See Wernsdorf *ad loc.*,
J. U. Powell on Simias *fr.* 1 (*Collectanea Alexandrina*,
p. 111). Clearly the address is not that made on this
occasion but merely alludes to Apollo's migratory habits.
  [2] († . . . †) perhaps ἐν ἀδήλῳ βιβλίῳ, 'I cannot say in which
book.

3³  εἴ τις καθείρξαι χρυσὸν ἐν δόμοις †πολὺν†
     καὶ σῦκα βαιὰ καὶ δύ' ἢ τρεῖς ἀνθρώπους
     γνοίη ‹κ›όσον τὰ σῦκα τοῦ χρυσοῦ κρέσσω.

(Ath. iii. 78 d ὅτι δὲ πάντων τῶν καλουμένων ξυλίνων καρπῶν
ὠφελιμώτερά ἐστι τοῖς ἀνθρώποις τὰ σῦκα . . . (f) καὶ Ἀνάνιος
δ' ὁ ἰαμβοποιὸς ἔφη (3).   Stob. iv. 33 Ἱππώνακτος (3).)

4⁴ = Hippon. 87.

5⁵  ἔαρι μὲν χρόμιος ἄριστος, ἀνθί‹η›ς δ' ἐ‹ν›
     χειμῶνι,
    τῶν καλῶν δ' ὄψων ἄριστον καρὶς ἐκ συκέης
     φύλλου,
    ἡδὺ  δ'  ἐσθίειν  χιμαίρης  φθινοπωρισμῷ
     κρε‹ῖ›ας,
    δέλφακος δ' ὅταν τραπ‹έ›ωσι καὶ πατέωσιν
     ἐσθίειν·
    καὶ  κυνῶν  αὕτη  τό‹τ›'  ὥρη  καὶ  λαγῶν
     κἀλωπέκων.                                        5
    ὄϊος αὖτ' ὅ[ε]ταν θέρος τ' ᾖ κηχέται βαβρά-
     ζωσιν.
    εἶτα δ' ἐστὶν ἐκ θαλάσσης θύννος οὐ †κακὸν†
     βρῶμα,
    ἀλλὰ πᾶσιν ἰχθύεσσιν ἐμπρεπὴς ἐν μυ‹σσ›ωτῷ.

**3.** 1 -ξει codd.          πολλὸν edd.   But it is doubtful if
Ananius *ever* used the verse-ending ∪ – – – and the right
reading might be *e.g.* ἅλις.   δόμοις is not Ionic: δόμοισ' is.
3 γνώῃ σχάσοντας Stob.: γνοίη χ' ὅσῳ Ath.   Both writers
(see on Hipp. 75) draw ultimately, I fancy, from Lysanias
on the Choliambists.   This book probably contained a parallel
quotation from Hipp.
**5.** 1 -ίας: corr. Schn.   2 (Cas.) ἐν . . . φύλλοις.   ὄψων
absent in some codd.   3 χιμέρης: corr. Heringa.   5 αὖ τῆμος
398

3 Should any in a room enclose much gold
And a few figs and two or three mortals,
He'd learn that figs than gold are far better.

(That figs are more useful than all so-called orchard fruits
. . . Ananius the iambist says (3). *Athenaeus.* Also
quoted by *Stobaeus* the anthologist in his *Comparison of
Wealth and Poverty.*)

4 See Hippon. 87.

5 For best in spring the salmon[1] is, in winter the
     mack'rel[1];
   And best of dainties is the prawn that peeps from
     green fig-leaves,
   And sweet in autumn 'tis to eat the flesh of a
     young kid,
   And sweet to eat the flesh of pigs the autumn
     grapes treading.
   This is the time to eat of whelps, of hares and
     of foxes.[2]                                          5
   But mutton eat when summer comes and grass-
     hoppers chatter.
   And then the tunny from the sea no paltry food
     renders,
   But set in cheese-cake shineth out among other
     fishes.

[1] 'Salmon,' really umber: see Isaac Walton, *Compleat
Angler* ch. vi. I avoid the familiar English "grayling,"
since the date does not fit. *Our* mackerel is most pleasur-
ably caught in August (in a light wind, sails reefed) off the
Devon coast and eaten within an hour or two, but it keeps
ill in summer.                    [2] See Casaubon.

Meineke is prob. right : τόθ' codd.  6 οἷος: expl. Casaubon.
αυτοεταν : corr. Heringa.  7 ? for κακὸν—*e.g.* δειλὸν.  8 ἐμ-
πρεπεῖς *v.l.*  μυττ.: corr. Bgk. ?

# ANANIUS

βοῦς δὲ πιανθείς, δοκέω μέν, καὶ μεσέων
νυκτῶν ἡδὺς
κἠμέρης.                                              10

(Ath. vii. p. 282 b **ἀνθίας**· κάλλιχθυς.  τούτου μέμνηται
Ἐπίχαρμος ἐν Ἥβας Γάμῳ (fr. 58 Kb.) καὶ σκιφίας χρόμις θ᾽
ὃς ἐν τῷ ἦρι καττὸν Ἀνάνιον ἰχθύων πάντων ἄριστος ἀνθίας δὲ
χείματι.  λέγει δὲ Ἀν. οὕτως (5).)

400

# FRAGMENT 5

A fattened ox, I ween, is sweet o' day and at
    midnight.[1]

('Anthias': beauty-fish. Mentioned by *Epicharmus* in
his *Marriage of Hebe*: 'The sword-fish and the chromis
which in spring Ananius says Is best of fish, as winter brings
the beauty-fish the best.' Ananius' words are (5). *Athenaeus.*)

[1] One would have expected the sense 'when day and
night are equal.'

# CERCIDAS
## MELIAMBS, FRAGMENTS, AND
## CERCIDEA

# INTRODUCTION

THE papyrus of Cercidas is in the British Museum.
For a description see the *editio princeps* (A. S. Hunt,
*P. Oxy.* viii. 1082). Latest edition in *Coll. Alex.* (J. U.
Powell), p. 203. See also Diehl, *Anthologia Lyrica,*
iii. 305. For recent work on the papyrus see articles
by the present writer in *C.R.* xxxviii-xxxix. There
are still a large number of small isolated fragments :
but there is no reason to believe that they were all
once contiguous (Hunt). The general character of
the metre was pointed out by P. Maas and von
Arnim. For references to periodicals see Milne
*Catalogue* 59, p. 45 (where read 1138 for 1158).

# I

col. i

]ε γὰρ ο[.]ξεν.ς εἰδέμεν    1
]νετοι[...] αδ' ἐπ' εἰλαπι-
]αιρω(ν)[.... β]λεννο(το)ι(σ)υ-
πηρί](δ)ας αλ[.....]υσω καὶ δο-
]νυν[....] ..........    5
       ]ρ τον λαμβα[ν ]
       ]μι τοῦτο· (ν)[ ]
           εκτε
       ]συντελῖς τ[ ]
       ]φέρει καὶ γ(α)[ ]
       ]ως μὴ λεγο[ ]    10
       ]ελθε· (δω).[ ]
]⟨ν⟩εσυμ[...]ηνα· καιτ[ ]    12
]⟨ο⟩μιζ[....]υτευσῃ⌈ ]
    ]μ[.....]αρ μοι το[ ]
]ατα .[...]. αλαιος [ ]    15
]ινο[....]τεων· ὤ[ ]
     (νμ)
]των α(ὑτῶ)ν ἁ λαβοῦ[σα ]
    ]Ζεὺς κοιραν[ ]
(σ). .ορειν παρεστιν ε[ ]

Col. i. 1. The placing of ξεν is doubtful: nor can we be
certain how many letters are missing at the beginning of the
lines.    εἰδέμεν P.    **3.** λεννο(τ)οί(ο)υ P (marked as (part
of) one word).    τ(ο)ι not τει (Lobel, Bell): (σ) me

# I

## Col. i

. . . but little in feasting      **2**
               This man delighteth
Child of oily-ragged clothes . . .

               . . . how
     If Zeus be master      **18**
    Never fair result we see?

---

iudice, (possible) Bell : βλεννοτ = βλεννο-νοτ-οισυπ-[. . . .
7. τοῦτο P.    8. as above P.    11. ελθε· P.    12. ηνα·
P.    16. so P.

# CERCIDAS

col. ii κα[. . . . . . . . . . . . . . . . . . . . . . γ]ὰρ ὁ
σχ(ε)[. . . . . . . . . . . . . . . . . . . . ἀλ]λὰ
τι(λλ)
τα(η)[. . . . . . . . . . . . . . . . . . . . .]εν
τ' ού[. . . . . . . . . . . . . . . . . . . .](γ)ας
καιτ[. . . . . . . . . . . . . . . . . . . .]          5
μυε[. . . . . . . . . . . . . . . . . . . .]ν
πιδ[. . . . . . . . . . . . . . . . . . . .]          7
. . . . . . . . . . . . . . . . . . . . . .]α

*fr.* 9       ]η πολιο[                               ? 7
              ]ινακολα[                               ? 8
              ]λεων πυκιν[                             ? 9
              ]χουσι γήρᾳ δ[                           ? 10
              ο]ὐκέτι πάνθ' ὠ[                         ? 11
              ]σᾱπ.[                                   ? 12

                    marg.  σπ]ανιοψιάδᾳ               12
                           ]τος                       13
                           ]καὶ σπυροὶ οἱ πυροί       14

Col. ii. 1. κᾱ P (*e.g.* καλόν). 3, 4. ita P. 3. superscr. ?
τι(ν). 10. (?) ]χου σιγηροὶ H. 12. schol. suppl.
Wilamowitz. Perhaps we have (*fr.* 26) the ends of some

408

# MELIAMB I

## Col. ii (?)

### Fragment 7 (? = 25 *fr.* H. : see crit. n.).

So it appears to me that our 'pot friend' Ulpian, as my Cercidas of Megalopolis says, watches his fellow guests to see if they have overlooked a fish-bone or lumpy piece of gristle in their food before them (Athenaeus).

### ' Child of but frugal repasts '

verses (about 12-14) (δυσ)παλεστωι.[/(ι)λον ἔνθα/(κι)ς καθιζε[ : also below this and just above κ.λ. *fr.* 25 αλ](λ)ους ακα[/]ω παλι . [/]εσσοσι . . ]/. . . (κελευ). This fragment suggests a loose citation in Ath. viii. 347 e οὕτω μοι δοκεῖ καὶ ὁ λεβητοχάρων Οὐλπιανός, κατὰ τὸν ἐμὸν Μεγαλοπολίτην Κερκίδαν, (. . . . .) τηρεῖν (. .) τοὺς ἐσθίοντας εἰ παρεῖδον ἢ "ΑΚΑνθαν ἢ τῶν τραγανῶν ⟨τι⟩ [ἢ] χονδρῶδες τῶν παρατεθέντων, which agrees well enough with the margination just *above* it. In this case *fr.* 26 probably belongs elsewhere, since it is hard to bring this in line with the notes. (λ)ους ακα [. . .) would be 14 fin, (κελευ) [. . .] 17 fin., μέχρι 18 fin., γερπε[ 20 fin., καὐτῶν 22 fin., and λάρον 23 fin. It is not possible to read σπ](ῡ)ριδια in *fr.* 32 nor to place it by the lowest note.

# CERCIDAS

## II

```
. . . . . . . . . . . . . . . . . . . . ]κ.λ.[
. . . . . . . . . . . . . . . . . . . ] μέχρι

. . . . . . . . . . . . . . . . . . . ](β)ριδιατριβα̣[
. . . . . . . . . . . . . . . . . . . ] ΄ γερπε[
. . . . . . . . . . . . . . . . . . . . . . .
```

col. ii.      . . . . . . . . . εἰς [. .]κ᾽ αὐτῶν

fin.      . . . . ὀ]λβοθύλακον

col. iii.

λαρόν | τε καὶ ἀκρασίωνα
θῆκε πενητ(υλίδ)αν
Ξένωνα, ποτάγαγε δ᾽ ἁμίν |          5
ἄργυρον ⟨τὸν                ⟩
⟨εἰς ἀνόνατα⟩ ῥέοντα; |
κα[ὶ] τί τὸ κώλυον ἦς
αἴ τι⟨ς⟩ σφ᾽ ἔρο[ι]το,
(ῥεῖα γάρ ἐστι θεῷ
πᾶν ἐκτελέσ⟨σ⟩αι
χρῆμ᾽ | †ὅκκ᾽ ἐπὶ νοῦν ἴῃ†),
ἢ τ[ὸ]ν ῥυποκιβδοτόκωνα |        10
καὶ τεθνακοχαλκίδαν|,
ἢ τὸν παλινεκχυμενίταν
τῶν κτεάνων ⟨ὄ⟩λεθρον|,
τοῦτον κενῶσαι
τᾶς συοπλουτοσύνας, |

ante 1. ? ἀ]βρίδια, γ᾽ ἕρπε., (εριδια H.).    **1.** εἰσὸκ᾽:
*cf.* μέχρι *supra.*    **2.** ταγὸν (*e.g.*).  Up to this point
I have not attempted to place the words in metrical
setting.  Between γερπε and εισοκ᾽ might be two—three

## II

. . . . . .

Chose out that greedy
    Cormorant, of wealthy purse,
And child of licentiousness, Xeno,
    Turn him to poverty's child,
And gave unto us ⟨who deserve it⟩ [1]        5
    Rivers of silver that now
Are wasted on profitless uses ?
    What should there be to prevent
—Ask God the question,
    Since it is easy for him,
Whate'er he fancy,
    Sure execution to find—,        10
. 10 If one be the ruin of money,
    Pouring out whate'er he has,
Or usurer dross-stain-begrimed,
    Ready to perish for gold,
That God should drain him,
    Void of his swine-befouled wealth,

---

[1] The lacuna may have been ἄργυρον τὸν αὐτόθεν νῦν.

---

verses (or half-verses). (The numeration at the side is that of J. U. Powell, *Coll. Alex.*; the vertical lines mark the lines of the ed. pr.) On Ξένωνα is a note ἀκρατὴς [ὁ Ξένων καὶ ἀπο]/γνωστός τις καὶ (π)ι(κ)ρός (supplevi post Hunt), and on ii fin. ἀ(πό)λαυο(ν) (?).      3. ἀκρασίωνα P.      5. ξένωνα· ποταγαγε δ' P.      7. εροιτο· P.      σ om. P: correxit II. αι ex ει P.   *sqq.* ἴδαν, ἴταν P.      8. τελεσαι P: corr. A(rnim).      9. μ' ὄκ. P.  *e.g.* ἐπὶ νοῦν ὄκ' ἴῃ A.    13. for τῶν perhaps read τὸν with M(aas).    πλεθρον but ολεθρον in margin.    14. -σύνασδομενδ' P.

# CERCIDAS

δόμεν δ' ἐπιταδεοτρώκτα       15
κοινοκρατηροσκύφω |
τὰν ὀλλυμέναν δαπάνυλλαν ; |
μήπο‹κ›' οὖν ὁ τᾶς Δίκας
ὀφθαλμὸς ἀπεσπαλάκωται, |
χὼ Φαέθων μονάδι       20
γλήνᾳ παραυγεῖ, |
(κ)αὶ Θέμις ἁ λιπαρὰ
καταχλύωται ; |
πῶς ἔτι δαίμονες οὖν
τοὶ μήτ' ἀκουὰν
μήτ' ὅπα‹ς› πεπαμένοι ; |
καὶ μὰν τὸ τάλαντον ὁ σεμνὸς |
ἀστεροπαγερέτας       25

col. iv.  μέσσον τ' ‹ἀ›ν' Ὄλυμπον [. . . . .†]
    (ο)ρθον[† . . . . . .|
[κ](α)ὶ νένευκεν οὐδ(α)μῇ· |
καὶ τοῦθ' Ὅμηρος
εἶπεν ἐν Ἰλιάδι· |
ῥέπην, ὅταν αἴσιμον ἆμαρ,       30
ἀνδράσι κυδαλίμοις †ην†|
πῶς οὖν ἐμὶν οὐ ποτέρεψεν
ὀρθὸς ὢν ζυγοστάτας, |
τὰ δ' ἔσχατα Βρύγια Μυσῶν— |
ἅζομαι δέ θην λέγ‹η›ν—       35

15. -τρωκται· (and so often) P.    16. φωι·    17. δα-
πανύλλαν P.    18. μηποτ P.    19. schol. ζῷον δ
τύπους μ(ὲν) ὀφθαλμ(ῶν) ἔχει, ὀφθαλμο(ὺ)ς δ' ο(ὐ), (οὐ)δ(ὲ) βλ[έ]πει
(ita Mn.).    20. ·χω, φαεθων, μονάδι, P.    schol.
ἐνὶ ὀφθαλμῷ π(αρα)βλέπει.    21. αι· πως P.    schol.
                        τοι
ἐπεσκότισ[τ]αι.    22. ὀντοιμη P, but ουνοιμη in margin.
23. οπαν P.    25. Delirant Powell, Wilamowitz, alii
412

15 And give to one frugally feeding,        15
    Dipping cup at common bowl,
The cash that is wasted on trifles?
    Is the eye of Justice then
Beshrunk that a mole might outsee her?
    Phaethon, too, doth he squint      20
With single pupil?
    Themis the bright—doth a mist
Bedim her vision?
    How can man hold them for gods
That neither hearken,
    Nor have any eyes to see?
Yet say they the gath'rer of lightning
    Mighty monarch holds the scales    25
Aloft in the midst of Olympus,
    Nodding not a moment's space.
E'en so doth Homer[1]
    Set in his *Iliad* down :—
' By fate to the mighty of valour
    Sinks the balance of the day.'
Why then doth the balancer even
    Never unto me incline?      30
But Brygians,[2] farthest of mortals,—
    Clearer words I dare not say—    35

---

[1] Θ 72.        [2] Apparently the Macedonians.

---

Homerici στεροπηγερέτα immemores.    26. τον P :
correxi. Between Ὄλυμπον and ὄρθον 5-11 letters missing :
I suggest *metri gratia* ἀνορθοῖ glossed ἀνὰ τὸ ὄρθον ἔχει.
27. suppl. H.    30-31. ρεπειδ P : -ειν A. †την·† del. A. :
fuit verborum ρεπειδ correctio (*cf.* H. praef. 24-5): ῥέπειν
G. Murray : terminationes huiusmodi tacite ⟨η⟩ν⟩ mutavi.
32. εμεν is corrected into εμιν in P.    34. φρυγια
P, while εσχάτᾱ has an accent on ε cancelled : the truth is
given in the margin.    35. ἄξομαι P.

ὅσον [κατά]γει τὸ παρ’ αὐτοῖς |
τῶ Διὸς πλα[στ]ίγγιον. |
ποίους ἐπ’ ἀνάκτορας οὖν τις |
ἢ τίνας οὐρανίδας
κιὼν ἀνεύροι |
πῶς λάβῃ τὰν ἀξίαν,                                    40
ὅθ’ ὁ Κρονίδας, ὁ φυτεύσας |
πάντας ἀμὲ καὶ τεκών, |
τῶν μὲν πατρωός,
τῶν δὲ πέφανε πατήρ; |
λῶον μεθέμεν περὶ τούτων
τοῖς μετεωροκόποις· |                                   45
τούτους γὰρ ἔ(ρ)γον
οὐ‹δὲ› ἓν ἔλπομ’ ἔχην· |
ἀμὶν δὲ Παιάν
καὶ †ἀγαθὰ Μετά[δως μελέτωτ, |
—θεὸς γὰρ αὔτα—
καὶ Νέμεσις κατὰ (γ)ᾶν;
μέσφ’ οὖν ὁ δαίμων |
οὔρια φυσιάει
τιμ‹ῆ›τε ταύταν                                        50
col. v.    φῶ(τ)[ες]· ἐ(λα)[
              κα]ταὶξ
ἀντε(π)[

36. supplevi.    37. suppl. H.       stop after πλα[. .]ιγγιον.
                                                         οι
39. ευρη· P.    40. πῶσλ P.    41. ὁθ P.    42. ἀμε P.
43. πατρώος P.  cited from Cercidas by Poll. iii. 27 as less
414

How far they pull down in their favour
　　　Zeus' scales of equity !
What lords them that lord it above us,
　　　Whom then of Uranos' sons
May any seeking
　　　Merit's retribution find,　　　　　　40
When the offspring of Kronos, our parent
　　　Who begat us one and all,
Some men as father,
　　　Others as stepfather know ?
Fit talk for astrologers truly ;
　　　Let us refer it to them :　　　　　　45
For them to settle
　　　It will be slightest of tasks ;
To us is Paean
　　　Good, and fair-dealing is good—
A very goddess—
　　　Nemesis too, upon earth :
What time the godhead
　　　Blows in our favour astern,
Hold *her* in honour,　　　　　　　　　50
　　　Mortals : though bravely they fare,
A sudden tempest
　　　Swooping down from other airt
Sinks to perdition

---

correct than ἐπιπάτωρ.　　44. ˙λωιον P.　　45. μετεωροκοποις·
is glossed in margin by αστρολογοις.　　46. ουθεν P ?
corr. Wilam.　　εχειν˙ ἁμιν P.　　47. ἀγαθὰ secl. Wilam.
μεταιδως P: corr. Wilam.; schol. has ἐπεὶ δὼς ἀγαθή, whence
it appears that καὶ Μετάδως ἀγαθὰ must have been the reading.　　48. (γ)αν˙ P.　　50. suppl. H.　　51. ]ταῖξ supplevi
et correxi: pessime H., cett. με]τᾴξαντες.　　52. αντ(. π)
vel (. γ): non fuit (εσ).　　*Cf. e.g.* Theod. Presb. *de incarn.*
Dom. p. 245 ἔνθα καὶ ἑτέρας καταιγίδος ἀντιπνευσάσης.

# CERCIDAS

]σητον ὄλ[βον
]τύχα(ς)·
ταῦτ' ε[ . . . .]μιν       55
νείοθεν ἐξεμέσαι;

53. suppl. H.      50-55. I translate ἐλαυνομένως ἄλλος κατᾶῑξ
ἀντέπνευσε ποντιῶν φυσητὸν (-ατὸν) ὄλβον χὐπεραφανεῖς τύχας·
ταῦτ' ἔσθ' ὅς ὑμῖν . . . ; The exact size of the various gaps


## III

Δοιά τις ἅμιν ἔφα       1
γνάθοισι φυσῆν |
τὸν κυανοπτέρυγον
παῖδ' 'Αφροδίτας, |
Δαμόνομ'· οὔτι (γ)[ὰ]ρ εἶ
λίαν ἀπευθής· |
καὶ βροτῶν [ὅτῳ] γὰρ ἂν
πραεῖα καί ⟨πως⟩       5
εὐμενε|δεξιτέρα
πνεύσῃ σιαγών, |
οὗτο(ς) (ἐν) ἀτρεμίᾳ
τὰν ναῦν ἔρωτος |

The new poem is marked by a coronis. It bears no title.

1. schol. δοι[α    ]: δοιάτισᾶμιν P.      3. Δαμονομ'· and
γαρ
ἀπευθης· P.      4. βροτων [?]μεναν πραειακαιευμενὲ[?]δεξιτεραν
416

Puffed-up wealth or fortunes proud :
And who can youward                                      55
    Vomit them back from the deep ?

---

is uncertain.  The meaning of the end is hard to fit: the
nautical metaphor is clear from the schol., and the use of
ἐξεμέω in Hom. μ 237, 437.  On 56 there is a marginal
note ἐκ βαθ(έω)[ν.     54. τύχας· P.     55. ταυτ· P.

## III

Thou, O Damonomus, art
    Not ill instructed :
' Twain are the blasts ' we are told
    ' That Aphrodité's
Offspring doth breathe from his cheeks,
    The azure-wingéd.
Unto whomsoe'er of men
    With gentle mildness
Kindlily-out-of-the-right
    His jaw hath breathéd,
Tranquil the sea of love,
    Whereon that mortal

---

with ν cancelled: supplevi et correxi.  There is no need
(apart from metre) to assume gaps at either point: possibly
⟨ὅτῳ⟩.  [ὅτῳ] Hunt.

# CERCIDAS

σώφρονι πηδαλίῳ
πειθοῦς κυβερνῇ· |
τοῖς δὲ τὰν ἀριστερὰν
λύσας ἐπόρσῃ |
λαίλαπας ἢ λαμυρὰς                    10
πόθων ἀέλλας, |
κυματίας διόλου
τούτοις ὁ πορθμός· |
εὖ λέγων Εὐριπίδας·
†οὑ κάρρον οὖν ἐστὶν
δυ‡ ὄντων |† ἐκλέγ‹η›ν
τὸν οὔριον ἇμιν ἀήταν |
καὶ μετὰ σωφροσύνας          15
οἴακι πειθοῦς |
χρώμενον εὐθυπλο‹ῆ›ν
ὄκ' ἦ κατὰ Κύπριν ὁ πορθμός·
μὴ[                                     18

col. vi.             ]α[         18 a
      ......]στω βι[
fr. 13    .....].κυβερν[
      .....]σω δόξα[
      .....]ν μὲν ἀλλ[
fr. 53    .....]καν Ἰκάρω[
      .......]φ ... πι[

|νομ[                                    19
|δαπ[                                    20
          ]καὶ τ[...(..)           21
..(..)...(τ).(ῥ)ηξεῖ.[
ἀ]στρα(π)[..] (σ)[...](π)λόος·
πᾶν γ[ὰρ] τὸ βι[(αι)οπόν]ηρον
(κ)αὶ προκοθ[η]λυμαν[ἐς

418

Ruddered by discipline calm
　　His ship directeth.
But 'gainst whomsoe'er the boy,
　　His left jaw loosing,
Rouseth the storms or the fierce
　　Typhoons of passion,
These have their voyages fraught
　　With waves unceasing.'
Nobly said, Euripides!
　　Since twain the choice is,
Better far it is for us
　　To choose out the wind in our favour,
So that with calmness of soul,
　　Where leads the goddess,
Voyage we straight on our course
　　And steer us by discipline's tiller.

　　　　Icarus . . . .

　　Lightning besetting his course :　　23
For all that is violent, wicked,
　　Mad in pursuit of its mate,

---

7. ατρεμια P, and 8. πηδαλιωι and κυβερνη· P.　　9. ορση
quae exempla sufficiant.　　10. αελλᾰς P.　　12. ευρι-
πιδας· P.　　οὐκοῦν δύ' ὄντων κάρρον ἐστὶν ἐκλ. recte Maas.
14. ἁμιναηταν· και P.　　16. ευθυπλοειν ὀκῆ P.　　17. πορθμος.
P. schol. ἀφροδίσιος.　　col. vi. fr. 13 huc certe referen-
dum : dubites de columnae lineis. conieceram νομ .. σω/δαπ ..
ν/και τόκ' ἀνίκα : sed refragantur vestigia πι/πλ.　　'Ικάρω
bene Powell.　　21. e.g. τόκα πρὸς ταῦτα ῥηξεῖν.　　ηξεῖ P.
22. στρᾱπ. P.　　? -όβλητος.　　23. supplevi.　　24. προ-
κοθηλ. A.

φέρει ταναβλαψιτέλειαν                    25
(κ)αὶ μεταμελλοδύναν·
ἁ δ᾿ ἐξ ἀγορᾶς Ἀφροδίτα,
καὶ τὸ μη[δε]νὸς μέλ<η>ν
ὁπ[α]νίκα λῇς, ὅκ(α) χρήζῃς,
οὐ φόβος οὐ ταραχά·                       30
τ(α)[ύ]ταν ὀβόλω κατακλίνας
Τ[υν]δαρέοιο δόκει
γαμβ(ρ).[
  |τημεν· κο
  |γα
  |γα
  |ρ(ε)

(Stob. *Fl.* lviii. 10 περὶ ἡσυχίας: Κερκίδα μελιάμβων : (ἡμιάμβων codd.: corr. Meineke) ⟨τ⟩ὸ τᾶς ῥικνᾶς χελώνας †α†μναμονεῦ (em. Meineke)· οἶκος γὰρ ἄριστος κτλ. : *vid. inf.*)

25. λειαν· and δυναν· ἁ P.      28. suppl. H.      29. νι-καλῆσδ P.      30. ταραχα· P.      31. κατακλίνας· P. (There are faint traces of scholia against *vv.* 22, 23, 30, 31.)

32. γαμβρέστατ᾿ ἦμεν potius quam γαμβρὸς το⟨κ⟩? 33. τ<sub>ει</sub>
μεν· νυ P. si huc pertineret fr. 7 (H.) legi non posset quod

Engendereth woe of repentance [1]            25
    And ruin [1] far-spread in the end :
But Venus that paces the market—
    In repletion of desire
Demanding no thought or attention :—
    Here is no fear and no care :            30
One obol will win you a mistress,
    Son-in-law fancy yourself
To Tyndarus (favoured 'mong suitors) :
    (Yet remains one more advice) :—
⟨Remember always
    What the wrinkled tortoise said :
' Both dearest and best, my good masters,
    Truly, of all things, is home.'⟩

---

[1] These Greek words ταναβλ. and μεταμελλ. appear easiest
as two words despite the strange nature of the compounds.
The latter would have to be connected with μεταμέλειν, which
may be compared with, but not excused by, e.g. Nicand.
*Alex.* 81 ξηρὰ δ' ἐπιλλύζων ὀλοῇ χελλύσσεται ἄτη.    μέλος
Ebeling, *Lex. Hom. s.v.*

---

proposui γαμβρες (nam ρ vix aut ne vix quidem possibile):
metri et spatiorum gratia potest e.g. γαμβρ(ὸ)[s χαρι]έσ[τατά] τ'
ἦμεν· . . . [τὸ] τᾶς ῥ[ικνᾶs] γὰ[ρ δὴ χελώναs μναμόν]ευ(ε)· οἶκος γὰρ
[ἄριστος ἀλαθέως] καὶ φίλōs, [⌣]ρε̄[⌣—].    Certe hic poema finem
habet: sub καιφιλοs spatium: e.g. ὦνδρες ἔφα.

# CERCIDAS

## IV

col. vii.                         ά]κις
δμαθεὶς βροτὸς οὔτι ἑκὼν |
ἔκλαξε κανθώς.

τὶν δ' ἀμάλακτον ἔσω |
στέρνων καὶ ἀνί-
κατον κέαρ ἔσκεν |

πιμελοσαρκοφάγων                              5
πάσας μελεδώνας.

†τοιι τὶν διέφευγε†ι†† καλῶν
οὐδέν ποκα· πάντα †δ᾽ ὑπὸ
σπ[λ]άγχνοις τεοῖς†ιι† ἔσκ᾽

(ἀ)βρ(ὰ) Μουσ‹ᾶ›ν κνώδαλα· |

Πιερίδων θ᾽ ἀλ[ι]ευ-
τὰς ἔπλεο, θυμέ, καὶ ἰχν-                     10
(ευτ)ὰς ἄρισ(τ)[ο]ς. |

νῦν δ᾽ †ὅκκα μὲν† ἐκφανέες
λευκαὶ κορυφ[ᾷ] (περι)αι- |
ωρεῦντ᾽ ἐ(θ). . . (ν).

(ἀκαλέῳ) ‹ › λάχνα,
κνα[κ]ὸν δὲ (γένη)-
ον, καί τι ματεύει |

1, 2. metre uncertain.  Above at top of column a schol.
]μενον.  The writer appears to address himself.  In this poem
the metrical divisions do not appear to correspond, as they
do elsewhere, to sense divisions.    1. *e.g.* — ◡◡ μυριάκις.
                                            'ὡς'
2. ἐκλᾶιξε κανθοῦς P.    3. τῦν P.      αμάραντον P : superscr.
(α)·πε᾽(ραντον) : margin ·αμαλακτον·    4. εσκ᾽εν (ἦν εἰς)
Powell : dubito.          ·πῖμελὸσαρκοφαγῶν πασᾶς . . . νᾶς· P.
422

## IV

Many a time
Man loses the fight e'er his orbs
Full loath he closes.

*Thou* hadst a heart in thy breast
Unsoftened and un-
Tamed ever in fighting

'Gainst all the desires of fat flesh
Which gluttons may cherish.

Nothing on earth that was fair
Escaped you : but ever you kept
Within your bosom

All the Muses' cublets young.

Thou wert a fisher my soul
Of all the Pierian maids
And keenest tracker.

But now that there gleam on my head
White hairs but a few at the edge
Around encircling

Still with incipient down,
Still yellow my beard,
And still doth my summer

---

6. *e.g* τὶν διέφευγε(ν) (ex τοιδιεφ). : τιν Wilam.    τοι delen-
dum.    P καλον.    7. ουδένποκα· παντα τεοισιν (ν cancelled)
δυποσπ P.    8. Μουσῶν P.    9. ·πε(cancelled)ιεριδων P.
11. †...† *e.g.* ὅκα τ'.    ·νῦν P.    12. -ωρευνται P.    *e.g.*
ἁμιν.    ἀκαλέφ(ᾳ) is false (?) Doricism for ἠκαλέφ(η).    A
short syllable is missing: *e.g.* ·πὶ.    λαχναι P.    κνα[κ]ον
suppl. H.    γέν(ε)ιον H.

423

κράγυον [ἁ]λικίατστ

⟨χοῖον⟩ κολακεύει⟨ν⟩            15

⟨τῶ⟩ χρόνω τ᾽ ἐπάξιον

δερκομένα βιοτᾶς
εὐρὺν (ποτὶ) (τέ)ρματος οὐδ-
όν· | τᾶμος ἐσλᾶς

14. κάι P (non κάι). superscr. (above (κρ)αγυον) .(τ)[.].
ἁλικία Murray, which I translate.      15 is devoid of metre
and sense. It runs χρ. τ. ἐ. κολακεύει. It seems necessary
to make the⁻ half iambus correspond to ἁβρὰ M. κ.
16. βιοτᾶς P.

## IV (?)

(a) col. viii.       (b) fr. 59 + 11 + 39       (c) col. ix

| μὲν | δ[όμον | ]ον· μὴ νόμιζ[ε | |
| | [ | ]τω ῥευσε[ι | |
| | γ[ | π]όκα· μία πέλ[λα | |
| | νο.[ | ]. μην[..].μι· τουτῶ[ | ]οτ[ |
| | σὶκ   5 | ]οις· .[...]με(ι)[ | ] . ευτω |
| | ἄχαρι(ν) | πολ]λο(ι) [(δ)έ] κ(αὶ)[ | | ]ονμ |
| | ναν, (ο)[ | σοφ]ίας· | πολλᾶ[ν] δ[έ | |
| | μεθα .[ | σό](φ)οις· ἁ δὲ (π)υ[ | |

17. τᾶμος εσλᾶς P with gloss τᾶμος ἔ[πειτα: suppl. H.
     (a) 1. e.g. μὲν δόμον – ⏑⏑ ἐκ κρηπῖδος ... In margin
opposite v. 9 (κνώδαλα): ἀγρεύματα κ(αὶ) ἐνεργήματα ('objects
of chase,' i.e. activities), opp. 14: ἡ[(λικίαν) φ. ματεύ[ει]ν ἀν(τὶ
τοῦ) (τ)[ούτοις] ἤδ[ε](σ)θ[αι ἢ] μέλ(ειν)[ 'Age,' he says,
'seeks': that is, delights in these things or has a care
for them. Opp. 16: (πρ)ο(ορ)ῶν(τι) [δη](λαδὴ) [εἰς] π(ο)[λὺν
τ](ὸ)ν and a much rubbed line: e.g. τοῦ γήρως χρόνον:
'looking forward to a long span of old age.' I give the be-
424

# MELIAMB IV. 14—IV (?). 8

Seek for the thing that is fair
    And able to flatter

Worthy of my riper years

Looking ahead to my life's
Broad threshold of eld at its close,
    Then from foundation
Fair ‹

# IV (?)

Think not

One cup

Mind doth see
And mind doth hearken

‹Poets have said›: can they then
Though standing ‹. . .› at their doors
Behold true wisdom

---

ginnings of col. viii. and ix. (*e.g.*) which it appears hopeless
to combine as viii. init. and fin. Between I give *e.g.* the *frr.*
59 + 11 + 39 and the literary *fr.* 4 connecting παλῶ with Pro-
metheus: for a correction of a previous error of mine my
thanks are due to Hunt. There is of course no certainty
that ix. follows on viii., nor that (*b*) and (*c*) should be
connected. (*b*) 7. πολλᾱ P et cett.; vid. Hunt. 8. metri
gratia σοφοῖς· ἃ δὲ πυνθανόμεσθα, κοὐκ ἀπάτυλλα φάτις.
9. suppl. H. (*c*) *ll.* 4, 5, 6 (οὕτως μέν), 14, 18. are scholl.
The juncture of *fr.* 41 (and 9*) is certain; of 40 probable.

# CERCIDAS

τὶς ἀλα[      ἀ]πα˙ ˙υλλα.[
περ.[    10      ]καλον[
νοω[
ταν[           ]. .δρυ[
ηκὸρυ[φ      ]..[.]υ.[      φῦναι ....
(τ)ας δα[     πα]λῶ˙ πέφ(υ)κε . αλλ᾽ ὀλ.
κτο[    15       ][ ]ρ Προμαθεὺς
πάιλ.[               ](ισαρ)ο
εκτα[             ](τ)άχα ῥη-
στακ.[                (λ)[.]
βεβ[
με.[    20
ἀκτ(ι)[

(Stob. *Fl.* iv. 42, 43 M. (περὶ ἀφροσύνης | : νοῦς ὁρῇ | καὶ νοῦς ἀκούει . ‹–‿‿› πῶς κεν ἴδοι|εν τὰν σοφίαν πέλας ἐστ|ακυῖαν ‹– – | –‿‿–‿‿– | –› ἀνέρες ὧν τὸ κέαρ παλ‹ῶ› σέσακται καὶ δυσεκνίπτω τρυγός (παλος and -τω cod.): corr. Bentley.)

17. τάχαρῆ P.

# V

col. x.    οὐ. [. . . . .]νης πυ[θι ‖          1
            ουτ[. . . .] ἀκάρδιον[          2
            [ . . . ](φ)ρίκαν τ᾽ [᾽Α] πό(λ)[λων ‖ συγ-]   3
            κροτησιγόμφιον ‖             4

The conjunction of the col. which I call (*e.g.*) ix. and x. is certain. I conjecture that no verse is missing and that *fr.* 37 (with coronis) may begin. The spot above, if ink, might be part of a gloss. Metre as poems 2, 3 but without equal correspondence of sense and cola.    1-2. *e.g.* οὐ μάταν ἦς Πύθιος
426

⟨. . . . . ⟩
Those ⟨. . .⟩ mortals whose heart
    With mud is filléd,
Stained with lees that wash not out.

(Cercidas quoted in Stobaeus' *Anthology* : *On Madness.*)

# V

Not in vain the Pythian [1]
Is so entitled :
    Unto each man cowardly blight
Apollo sendeth
    Or cold fear teeth-chattering,

---

[1] The Cynic regarded Apollo and the Muses (music) with as great suspicion as any other patrons of pleasure.

---

βοατὸς οὕτως· ἀλλ' . . . . βλάβαν.    3-4. γόμφ P.    supplevi.
*e.g.* νέμει : gaps [   ] from two to eight letters.    τωι P.

# CERCIDAS

κα]τὰ καιρὸν ἑκάστῳ,                    5
(π)[άντα] θεῖ κἠ(λ)αύνεται
γὰρ (ἀ)[        ]τα
φευξιπόνων ἀν[ὰ γᾶν
φῦλα σκιόθρεπτ'
τάδον[ο]π[λ]άκτων βροτῶν        10
ἀκ[ήρ]ιος ἐγχεσίμωροϛ·              9
καὶ μ[ά]λ' ἐπισταμένως            11
[ὑ]ψ[ι]τράγ[ῳδο]ϛ                      13
(θεὰ) χ(λ)[ι]δᾶγας ὤπας(ας)        12
πί[ειρ]ατϋτ μὲν ὠλεσίκαρπο⟨ϛ⟩     14
[δὲ Φρ]ύγα φυσαλέατϋν               15
(Λ)υδάν [τ' . . . . . . ]ῆ·
νεῦρα δὲ καὶ κρα[δα . .
δι'] ὦτ' ἐλέλιγμα[. . . . . . . . ]ϛ
εὐπα(λ)[αμ

About four lines lost in col. x. and ten in col. xa. The
next ten lines begin ταυτα|γαρου|αθεσ|ναται.|τοσαεικ|ω φιλος
τασι|ησκαι(ν)οοκ.|πενιᾳ ποτιφ|τιμοτάτω δεπ|π[. .](α)μυρο[. There
the poem ends and the remainder of the column is lost.

5. suppl. H.     6. θεῖκἠλαύ P.     e.g. ἀϊόντα.     7. supplevi.
10. suppl. Wilam.     9. supplevi e.g. et transtuli.          φῦλαι

# VI

. . . . . . .

col. xi.   αιο]λόπωλον[        |          |
           βουσόω | μύω[π        |                        2
           ιππον χρέ[ων; |                    |            3

1. suppl. H.          2. σόω P : suppl. Wilam.          fin.
et 3 supplevi.     3. fin. supplevi.
428

Alike unto each in their season.
     See how smoothly all things glide,
For those that hearken,
     Races that live in the shade
Avoiding turmoil,
     Men by stroke of pleasure numbed—
The spear-spurning spiritless godhead :
     Aye, and with cunning intent
The lofty-tragic,
     Fertile dam of sterile stock,
Muse gendereth luxury-shattered
     Phrygian of puffing cheeks
And Lydian wanton :
     Strings and reverberant twang
Of dexterous fingers resounding

.        .        .        .        .        .

P (ι cancelled).           13, 12. ωπασ(ασθεα) χλ. [υ]ψ P.
suppl. et transtuli.       14. ν seclusi.        -καρπον
P : correxi.  Accents on σκιθθ., -ἱμωρος, -ἀκτων, χλιδᾱγας, πῑ.
15. φῡσὰλέαν P: read φυσαλέον.   16. χνδαν might just be read:
                                                          ⏑ – ⏑
not αὐδάν.   17. ἦ·νεῦρα P.   e.g. κραδαλᾰ̀ ... ἐλέλιγμα ......ς
εὐπάλαμός τε λύρα.   schol. ] .. σκρα [ ] (αια)ς.      18. ωτ'
ελέλ P.      19. suppl. Maas.

# VI

.        .        .        .        .        ▪        ▸

What driver of team of four horses
     Brightly sparkling in the sun
Should use to spur them
     Goad that galleth oxen's flanks ?

# CERCIDAS

| τοῦ]το γάρ ἐστ' ἀγάθω     4
τοῦτ' εὐθυδίκω [δελ]εαστᾶ,     5
Στωικὲ Καλλιμέδων·
. . . . . . π[.](σ)[.]στι πονηρὰ
καὶ [. . . . . . . . . . .]μένα·
Σφαίρω γὰρ [αἴ τι
. . . . . .](π)ροβάλης     10
ἢ καί τι [. . . . . . . . .
οὐ]χὶ τὸν εἰς ἀρετὰν
[καὶ . . . . . . . .]δες ἰχνεύεις
ἀλ[λὰ τὸν εἰς . . . . .]
φέροντ' ὀπώραν     15
[. . . . . . . . . . . . . . .]·
κο(ὐ) (το)ῦτ[ο]ν (α)ὐ[τὸν
[       <, ἀλλ>      ]
[               ]

5. τᾶ and δων· P.    1-4. *e.g.* ποτ' αἰολόπωλον ∪ – –ὡμο-
πληξιβουσόῳ μύωπι χρῆσθαι ἀνδρὶ τέθριππον χρέων; πολλοῦ δεήσει.

◆

## VI (?)

col. xii.                 ]ηθρα     1
(*e.g.* 20) σκωπτίλλ(ιο)[. .] αὖ, |
    (λ)η[. . . . . . .]ιδ[ίκ]ως,
    βλαβὰν (ἀκλ)η[
(*e.g.* 25) . . . .]ετρ[. . .]μοφλυακῆν†     5

col. xii. (*e.g.*) probably from same poem and possibly
the next column. See appendix.     ληρολογ. K. F. W.
Schmidt : φόβος, ἀποστομοῖ H.     1. ηθρασκωπτίλλ.ο P.
430

‹Far be it from him.›
>> This is the action of one,
O Stoic Callimedon, seeking
>> To entice the good and just :
Nay, this is the pathway of villains
>> Trodden by the base and ill :
Whoso to Sphaerus
>> Giveth up aught that is dear,
Or aught confideth,
>> It is no guide unto calm
Or virtuous life he pursueth :
>> Nay, it is one who will lead
To madness' harvest

.    .    .    .    .    .    .

---

$\pi$

7. π superscr. *e.g.* τᾷδ' ἀτρακτύς ἐστι.    8. *e.g.* κακοῖς
τετριμμένα : μενᾱ P.    9. supplevi.    10. *e.g.* τῶν ἰδίων.
11. *e.g.* πεισθῇς.    12. supplevi.    13. supplevi *e.g.*
τἀταραχῶδες (ita fere Mayer).    14. supplevi: *e.g* μανίας.
16. *e.g.* κἀσεβῆ διδάσκαλον.    17. supplevi.

## VI (?)

Of idle jestings
>> Pettifogging lawyers they,
Disaster ‹bringing
>> With their sharp and prickly thorns›
To babbling of pitiful nonsense
>> ‹Whetting well their pointed tongue› :

---

2. άυ· P : but corrected to circumflex.  λη is more probably a
gloss. There is a stop after ως.    5-6. ακεῖν τοπος (o is certain)
P : ? κοπος.    αυτο P.    There is not room for Φοῖβος.
see Appendix.

# CERCIDAS

| τόπος ἢ φ[ό]βος αὐτὸ
συ(μ)[πα]|ρὼν [ἀ]ποστ(ο)μ[οῖ];
τᾶς δὴ το[ι]αύτας
σκεπτοσύνας κεν[ὰ] | μὴ
(e.g. 30) σπουδὰν ποιεῖσθ[αι
τῶ] | στρέφ‹η›ν ἄνω κάτω,      10
†(ἀ)[λλ', αἴ] | (τ)[ι]ν' εὕρῃς διὰ (π)ασᾶν
(μ)[ου]|σικῶς ἁρμοσμένον, |
†. ]οτανισοντον πόθον ἕλκ[ε],
(e.g. 35) (κ)αὶ | [(μ)άθ' εὖ τὸν ἵμερον,
τ[ί]s [τ'] ἐστὶ ποτ' ἄρσενας ἄρσ(η)[ν |      15
τίs] τ' ἔ[ρ]ως Ζα(ν)ωνικός.

    Κερκίδα
    κυνός
    με]λίαμβοι

Nor habit of discipline blunteth
  Nor fatigue its bitter edge.
Aspire not therefore
  Into the follies to probe
Of suchlike tenets,
  Turning on from page to page,
But an thou discover a fellow
  Formed in perfect harmony,
To companionship equal of passion
  Take him, finding what desire
Can be for a man of another,
  And what Zeno's love doth mean.

9-10. κενὰ is object of στρέφειν.     11. suppl. Wilam.
for εὕρῃς. *e.g.* ἀθρῇς, ἴδῃς.     διὰ (π)ασαν lucide P: . (θεα)ν H.
hic quidem dormibundus.     12. suppl. H.     14-16. supplevi post H.     13. locus desperatus.  After ἕλκε εἰς πόθον
would be usual.  I suggest ποτὰν ἴσον εἰς πόθον ἕλκε κτλ. (*C.R.*).

# FRAGMENTS

(All fragments of papyrus of over thirty letters have received some adjuncts and been placed in their columns: except those to which I give the name of column xi. (*e.g.*) and col. viii. 9. The remainder, with one possible exception, appear, as long as they remain separate, of little interest. The following meliambic fragments must be added to those read, or cited, above.)

1. (2 Bgk. ii. P.)

οὐ μὰν ὁ πάρος ⟨γα⟩ Σινωπεύς,
τῆνος ὁ βακτροφόρ⟨ο⟩ς,
διπλτοτείματος, αἰθεριβόσκας,
ἀλλ' ἀν' ⟨◡ – ◡⟩ ἔβα
χ⟨ῆ⟩λος ποτ' ὀδόντας ἐρείσας
καὶ τὸ πνεῦμα συνδακών·
⟨Ζανὸς γόνος⟩ ἦς γὰρ ἀλαθέως †Διογένηςt 5
†Ζανὸς γόνοςt οὐράνιός τε κύων.

(Diog. L. vi. 76 οἱ δὲ τὸ πνεῦμα συγκρατήσαντα, ὧν ἐστὶ καὶ Κερκίδας ὁ Μεγαλοπολίτης ἢ Κρὴς (? ἀντίκρυς) λέγων ἐν τοῖς Ἰάμβοις οὕτως (1).) So perhaps *fr.* 19 αταν|(ο)υ(μα) above which is a note which *might* be expanded into ἐκ τούτων ἀκριβ]ῶς γν(ῶ)[ναι . . . . . . . . . ὁποί](αν δ)[ὴ τοῦ βίου τελευτὴν εἶχεν ὁ Διογέν]ης.

2. (5 Bgk., 15 P.) Θέσσαλος δὲ ἅμα τοῖς ἑαυτοῦ σοφισταῖς ἐφ' ὑψηλοῦ θρόνου καθήμενος ἐν κριομύξ⟨α⟩ις ἀνδράσιν, ὡς ὁ Κερκίδας φησίν, εὐδοκιμήσει. Galen (x. 406). C. may have written

ἐν κριομύξ⟨α⟩ις
ἀνδράσιν εὐδοκιμῶν.

434

# FRAGMENTS

1. Others say that he committed suicide by holding his breath : among these is Cercidas of Megalopolis [or Crete ?], who says ⟨plainly ?⟩ as follows in his *Iambi* :—

> Not so did the old Sinopean
>     Famed for the cudgel he bore,
> The double-cloaked liver in ether ;
>     Nay but he rose to the sky
> By clipping his lips with his grinders,
>     Thereby biting off his breath :
> Zeus' son was he rightly entitled,
>     Rightly ' the heavenly dog.' [1]

*(Diogenes Laertius's Lives.)*

2. But Thessalus sitting among his sophists on a lofty seat will, as Cercidas says,

> find favour
> 'mong sheepishly-drivelling [2] folk.

*(Galen.)*

---

[1] From the Dog (κύων) the Cynics took their name.
[2] -μυξης is the common form, *e.g.* Anon. c. Synes. 32 fin. The writer like Synes. may have read Cercidas.

---

1. 1. γεα codd. : corr. Bgk.     2. φορας codd.     3. ο seclusit A.     4. *e.g.* ⟨Ὄλυμπον⟩.     χεῖλος codd. 5-6. Διογένης seclusit et Ζ. γ. transtulit A.
2. 1. κριομύξοις codd.

# CERCIDAS

**3.** (1 Bgk., 15 P.)

$$\mathring{\eta}\nu \ \kappa\alpha\lambda\lambda\iota\pi\acute{v}\gamma\omega\nu \ \zeta\epsilon\mathring{v}\gamma o\varsigma \ \mathring{\epsilon}\nu \ \Sigma\upsilon\rho\alpha\kappa o\acute{v}\sigma\alpha\iota\varsigma.$$

(Ath. xii. 554 d αὗται ὑπὸ τῶν πολιτῶν καλλίπυγοι ἐκαλοῦντο
ὡς καὶ ὁ Μεγαλοπολίτης Κ. ἐν τοῖς ἰάμβοις ἱστορεῖ λέγων (3).)

**4.** (7 Bgk., 16 P.) Greg. Naz. ii. 213 is a mere paraphrase
of portions of [Cercid.] προοιμίον.

**5\*.** (10 P. : Cronert, *Rh. Mus.* lxii. 311.)

$$\tau\hat{\omega} \ \pi\epsilon\rho\iota\langle\sigma\sigma\alpha\nu\rangle\text{-}$$
θηροπέπλου μανίας
ὕβρεός τε περιστάσιμον
στοὰν ἔχοντι
Πυθαγόρου πελάτα                    5

(Ath. iv. 163 e πρὸς ὃν ἐπιστέλλων ὁ Στρατόνικος ἐκέλευσε
τὸν ἀπαίροντα τὸ ῥηθὲν ἀπαγγεῖλαι (5).)

**6.** (28 H.)

αρσε
ῥέθος βλε[π
β]λοσυρομ[ματ

**7.** See above (on col. ii.).

4. See my *First Greek Anthologist*, Cambridge, 1922.
5. 1-2. σσαν inserui (*cf.* Eur. *I.A.* 73).        5. πελαιτᾳ cod.
The metrical agreement of this *fr.* with that of poem iv. is
extraordinary : but it should be remembered that the metre
is also that of Philoxenus and no doubt others.  Chronological considerations preclude the authorship of Cercidas,
unless we suppose that the characters Strat. and Demetrius
Aspendius (πρὸς ὅν) are wrongly given by Athenaeus.

# FRAGMENTS 3–7

**3.** These girls were called ' fair-rumped ' by their fellow-citizens as ⟨pseudo-?⟩Cercidas of Megalopolis narrates in his *Iambi*. Here are his words :—

> There was a fair-rumped pair in Syracuse.
>
> <div align="right">(<i>Athenaeus.</i>)</div>

**4.** (*Fr.* 17 Bgk., 16 Powell from *Gregory of Nazianzus* : see over and n.)

**5.** Stratonicus sent a message to Demetrius of Aspendus and told the messenger dispatched to deliver his words to the

> Pythagorean expert
> Whose portico ever is thronged
> With pride and over-
> Gorgeously-raimented crowds.
>
> <div align="right">(<i>Athenaeus.</i>)</div>

(These verses—older than C.—are interesting as showing that his style and one at least of his metres had previously been applied to kindred topics.)

**6.** (See n.) It is not probable that he will brace himself up and

> with austere eyes

look gold in the face : nay rather would he be struck with awe thereof and yield and finally embrace it. (*Synesius.*)

**7.** (See col. ii.).

---

6. 3. Supp. H. ? ὁ βλοσυρομματίας. I subjoin this fragment which might belong to our second column in order to call attention to a possible adaptation of it in Synesius, *de Regno*, p. 54 Krabinger οὐκ εἰκός γε αὐτὸν διαράμενον βλοσυροῖς ὀφθαλμοῖς ἀντιβλέψαι χρυσίῳ· τοὐναντίον μὲν ⟨οὖν⟩ αἰδεσθῆναί τε καὶ ἐνδοῦναι καὶ τελευτῶντα περιπτύξασθαι.

# APPENDIX

THE last column of the papyrus of Cercidas' *Meliambi*
provides several problems of difficulty : of some of
these I have attempted to provide a solution. But
the gravest difficulties lie in the first few lines.
Scanty as the remains are, they should be sufficient
to guide us as to the general sequence of thought
and metre ; and this they fail to do.

Here are the traces as I see them :

[ ]ηθρασ[ ] κὼπτίλλ. .αῦ·(λη)[
[. . . . . .]ιδ[. . ]ως · βλαβαν(ακλ)η
[. . . . .]ετ.[. . ]μοφλ(υ)ακεῖ(ν)
τοπος ηφ[.] (β)οσαυτοσυ(μ)[. . . . ]
ρων[.]ποστ(ο)μ[.] τας δητο[.] κτλ.                    5

1. αῦ by correction from αὐ.λη or ση.ηθρας may or may not
join κὼ.        2. parts of two letters below ηθρα (ν.) visible.
3. no room for οι after φ. υ(μ) or υ(δ) only.
4. τόπος certain.

Hunt read *v.* 4. τόπ(ο)ς ἢ φόβος. As to the second
*o* of τόπος his doubts are to me unintelligible. The
fragment fits close up not as in the facsimile and *o*
is as certain as any letter in the papyrus (and that
is a high order of certainty). Further Hunt, dis-
regarding ὑπὸ στόμἄ which we know now to be
metrically false, rightly read ἀποστομοῖ.

It may safely be predicted of the metre of this

438

# APPENDIX

poem (especially if *frr.* 5 and 6 belong to it) that it follows the common metre of Cercidas, that is

$$A \begin{cases} -\cup\cup-\cup\cup-\phantom{x}^1 \\ \text{or } -\cup-\underset{\smile}{}-\cup-\phantom{x}^2 \end{cases} \quad +B \begin{cases} \underset{\smile}{}-\cup\cup-\cup\cup-\underset{\smile}{}^1 \\ \text{or } \underset{\smile}{}-\cup-\underset{\smile}{}^2 \end{cases}$$

Whether this is the *whole* law we do not know.

Now these verses flagrantly transgress this rule. At $(\sigma)\nu\mu\ldots$ $\dot{a}\pi o\sigma\tau o\mu o\hat{\iota}$ we are in $A^2$ and at $\tau\hat{a}\varsigma$ $\delta\dot{\eta}$ $\tau o\iota a\acute{\upsilon}\tau a\varsigma$ in $B^2$. Hence at $\tau\acute{o}\pi o\varsigma$ $\mathring{\eta}$ $\phi\acute{o}\beta o\varsigma$ $a\dot{\upsilon}\tau\acute{o}(\varsigma)$ we are at the end of $B^1$. But immediately before this

$\tau \ldots \mu o\phi\lambda$. or $\tau \ldots \ldots \mu o\phi\lambda\upsilon a\kappa\hat{\eta}\nu$ is also an end of $B^1$. In view of the punctuation—for Cercidas always unites

metre and sense in cola—$\iota\delta$ .. $\omega\varsigma \cdot \beta\lambda a\beta a\nu$ is clearly the end of $A^1$ or $A^2$ and beginning of $B^1$ or $B^2$ Line 1 is hopeless.

Of this phenomenon (the complete disappearance of two As running) there can be three solutions :—

(*a*) One A is really B. This is secured in current texts by three errors (or wholly improbable corrections) :—

($a$) Reading $\tau\grave{o}$ $\pi(\hat{\omega})\varsigma$ : this is impossible.
($\beta$) Followed by $\mathring{\eta}$ $\Phi o\hat{\iota}\beta o\varsigma$ : this is impossible.
($\gamma$) By the metre $-\cup\phi\lambda\bar{\upsilon}a\kappa\epsilon\acute{\iota}\nu$ $\tau\grave{o}$ $\pi\hat{\omega}\varsigma$ : this is unheard of.

(*b*) Extensive lacunae. But why should these lacunae be so regular ?

(*c*) The only theory which seems conceivable is that the *Meliambi* of Cercidas in the papyrus from which this is copied ended the roll : that a square piece was torn out : and that the writer simply missed the letters which he did not see. It is a simple calculation that a gap averaging ten syllables

# CERCIDAS

would account for all difficulties after line 1. If the
letters (λη) there are an adscript, there is a certain
improbability, since, *ex hypothesi*, the parent papyrus
had no adscripts here. They would have either to
be text or an adscript (λε)[ίπει . . . .] due to the
actual scribe.

Clearly we must consider on independent grounds
of language whether the view (*a*) with its corrections
of text is more or less probable than (*c*). We have
to choose—since τὸ and even τὸ π[τ can well follow
–φλυακεῖν—between (*c*) τ]όπος ἢ φόβος αὐτὸ (for
H.'s αὐτὸς is meaningless) συμ[ ]ων ἀποστομοῖ, and
(*a*) ἢ Φοῖβος αὐτὸς ὑμ’ [ὁ]ρῶν ἀπ., always remembering
that the papyrus in no way favours this reading.

Now to (*a*) there are three further several objec-
tions.

(i) It appears that here as in *frr.* 5 and 6 only one
person is addressed (*l.* 9 εὕρῃς). Probably H. was
right in reading ποιεῖσθ[αι in 7.

(ii) Phoebus is never spoken of, as far as I know,
as blunting anything or anybody.

(iii) ὁρῶν is wholly pointless.

To (*c*) I can only see one reason why it should fail
here of general acceptance. That is that it falls in
line with a commonplace figure in Greek poetry
which has no exact counterpart in modern languages.
I will take the words singly.

(i) -ος ἢ φόβος. Fear has several companions,
*e.g.* Menand. *fr.* 418 λύπη (so often) φόβος φροντίς,
Callim. *fr. Anon.* 176 αἰδὼς καὶ δέος ἀλλήλων, φόβοι
καὶ πόνοι, Plat. *Legg.* 635 c, Plut. *M.* 128 c (so that
you can go as far back as κ]όπος), Plat. *Symp.* 197 D,
ἐν πόνῳ, ἐν φόβῳ, ἐν πόθῳ, ἐν λόγῳ.

# APPENDIX

(ii) φόβος συμπαρών. In certain writers, especially Xenophon and Plutarch, συμπ. means little more than συνεῖναι (*Thes. s.v.*). Compare *Rep. Lac.* 2. 2 ὥστε πολλὴν μὲν αἰδῶ, πολλὴν δὲ πειθὼ ἐκεῖ συμπαρεῖναι, *Cyrop.* viii. 7. 7 φόβος μοι συμπαρομαρτῶν. But this is of an ever-haunting fear and probably the sense is nearer ' reverence.' For the Greek συνών we use some wholly different metaphor such as ' ingrained.' If κ]όπος be right we should think of some rather strained sense such as ' pain ' : Soph. *Phil.* 880 ἡνίκ' ἂν κόπος μ' ἀπαλλάξῃ ποτέ. Ar. *Plut.* 321 has τῷ κόπῳ ξυνεῖναι.

(iii) Fear blunts. Pind. *Nem.* iii. 39 οὐδέ νιν φόβος ἀνδροδάμας ἔπαυσεν ἀκμὰν φρενῶν—just as in old age αἱ φρένες ἀπαμβλύνονται Hdt. iii. 134. Conversely courage sharpens: so expressly Christodor. *Ecphr.* 295 θάρσεϊ τολμήεντι τεθηγμένος.

(iv) What is blunted ? Clearly anything that has an edge on which fear operates unfavourably. Edged tools are :—

(*a*) The person sharpened : Ar. *Nub.* 1107 εὖ μοι στομώσεις αὐτόν (Blaydes), Poll. ii. 100 Ἀριστοφάνης δὲ στ. εἴρηκε τὸ λάλον ἀπεργάσασθαι.

(*b*) γνάθος : *ibid.*

(*c*) ὀδόντες : Ar. *Ran.* 815 ἡνίκ' ἂν ὀξυλάλου †περὶ† ἴδῃ θήγοντος ὀδόντας.

(*d*) γλῶσσα : Soph. *Aj.* 584, Pindar, *Ol.* vi. 82 δόξαν ἔχω τιν' ἐπὶ γλώσσᾳ ἀκονᾶς λιγυρᾶς, *Trag. Fr. Anon. Adesp.* 423 γλῶσσαν ἠκονημένος.

(*e*) λόγοι : Lucian, ii. 517, Aesch. *P.V.* 327.

(*f*) φρένες : Eur. *Hipp.* 689.

(*g*) ψυχήν : Xen. ; see Index *s.vv.* ἀκονᾶν, θήγειν.

Thus we see that speakers, instruments of speech,

441

or words spoken are most commonly sharpened
whether by courage or anger. But we are seeking
a neuter noun (αὐτό) and the choice lies between
λῆμα Eur. *Or.* 1625, or, what seems more suitable,
στόμα :—

Soph. *O.C.* 794 τὸ σὸν ... στόμα πολλὴν ἔχων στόμωσιν.
    *Trach.* 1176 μὴ 'πιμεῖναι τοὐμὸν ὀξῦναι στόμα.

(v) Can fear blunt the mouth or tongue ? Though
this exact metaphor does not occur we have—

Soph. *Ant.* 180 ὅστις ... ἐκ φόβου του γλῶσσαν
ἐγκλῄσας ἔχει, 505, *Ajax* 171 σιγῇ πτήξειαν ἄφωνοι:
whence it may be questioned whether Sappho's
texts (p. 16 Lobel) had not once ἀλλὰ κἀμ μὲν
γλῶσσα̣ †τέθ›αγε† by error for τέθαπε : if such be
possible in Aeolic.[1] So interlinked are the ideas of
fear, silence, confidence and loquacity.[2]

A case has, I hope, been made out for a lacuna
-μοφλυακὴν τὸ [στόμ᾽ κό]πος ἢ φόβος—the in-
tervening words being *e.g.* εὖ τεθαγμένο— ; τίς ἢ
... For the rest we can hope for little. But βλάβαν
(ἀκλ)η strikes no obvious note and it might be considered whether λη is not part of the same verse
as -φλυακὴν (*e.g.* λήρημα δὲ τρισμοφλυακὴν—with
κι](να)ιδ[ικ]ῶς above), and whether ἀκ does not belong
to βλάβαν. Certainly ἀκ- sharp gives us a wide field
of choice, with ἀκμά, ἀκονά (Pind. *ll.cc.*), ἀκι-, or
even ἄκμων : *P.* i. 86 ἀψευδεῖ δὲ πρὸς ἄκμονι χάλκευε
γλῶσσαν. But I prefer ἀκονα- in view of those two
difficult sayings of Aeschylus :—

---

[1] Hesychius's gloss θάπαν shows that the *root* is not only
found in Ionic.
[2] *E.M. s.v.* βοή· ... ἡ μὲν γὰρ δειλία θραύουσα τὸ πνεῦμα
βραχίστην ἀπεργάζεται τὴν φωνήν. Ach. Tat. ii. 25.

# APPENDIX

*Ag.* 1537 Δίκα δ' ἐπ' ἄλλο πρᾶγμα θήγεται βλάβης
πρὸς ἄλλαις θηγάναισι Μοῖρα,

*Eum.* 861 αἱματηρὰς θηγάνας, σπλάγχνων βλάβας
νέων,

where, however you read or explain, it seems to me
that some subtle and lost connexion between βλάβη
and θηγάνη lies—as if, for instance, βλάβη could bear
the sense of a good or true sharpening surface. As
to the first lines of the column in Cercidas palaeographical difficulties are so grave that it seems idle to
make suggestions : on metrical grounds it would be

desirable to separate (σ)κωπτίλλ ... and αὖ ... But
κ(αὶ ὀ)πτίλλ∪∪ also gives sense and, if the theory of
a considerable gap is right, it is useless to attempt
precision.

# CERCIDEA

THE following verses appear to be continuous and to have been attributed to Cercidas at least as early as the end of the fourth century A.D. The evidence is produced and considered in a work by the present writer (*The First Greek Anthologist*, Cambridge, 1922). They clearly formed the beginning of an Anthology. But it is difficult to believe they actually were by Cercidas, though the anthology may have been due to his efforts. The chief discrepancy lies not so much in style, as Mr. W. E. Barber thinks, but in metre. For style may easily be assumed but, once a metrist as skilful as the writer of the *Meliambi*, always a metrist. Not that the metre is irregular (see on Phoenix *fr.* 4). It is the norm of the moralist, admitting the spondee freely in the fifth foot, and rigidly limiting resolution. But the adaptation of sense to metre is careless and clumsy. As I find it impossible to represent such metrical shortcomings, I translate into prose.

Such an unfavourable verdict could not fairly be given on evidence of the text of the two English papyri [1] which is very unsound : but what remains of the Heidelberg [2] papyrus is excellent. On this

---

[1] Lond. 155 verso, Bodl. ms gr. class. f, 1 (p).
[2] No. 310.

# CERCIDEA

magnificent[1] work was done by Dr. G. A. Gerhard of Heidelberg (*Phoinix von Kolophon*, Teubner, 1909): full illustrations being given of the moral ideas underlying these lines of doggerel verse. Dr. Gerhard's work is also of great bibliographical value for other choliambic writers: but it loses to some extent by a failure to recognize essential metrical differences, and by a theory that the metre was used especially by moralist writers (see on Phoenix). Recently I have visited Heidelberg and with the subsequent aid of Prof. F. Bilabel solved one or two doubtful points. Professor Bilabel has also very kindly examined many doubtful passages. Where he has confirmed my reading I use the symbol (K.-Bi.); where he has detected flaws and helped with sketches to the establishment of a new reading, I use the symbol (Bi.-K.). Where the suggestion is due entirely to him, it is so accredited.

Later leaves of our anthologist may be found at Strassbourg (*Wiss. Ges. Pap.* 304-7: see Phoenix, *fr.* 4).

[1] Dr. Gerhard, however, was not a skilled palaeographer. Among several errors one may especially mention his failure to allow for the form of $\tau$ used by the scribe. The text of the London papyrus is almost entirely due to Milne, assisted, or hindered, by the present writer.

# CERCIDEA

....... ](οὐδ)εὶς οὐ[........ ἀνθ](ρ)ώποις
....... ](ι) κ(ατ)εῖδ(ε)[ν .... ἀ](ν)θρώπων
....... ]σα(ς) οὓς κα(τ)[εῖδεν] ἀνθρώπο(υ)ς
....... ](δ)ὲ (π)ρός (σ)ε χ[ρήσο]μαι πάσῃ
....... ](π)ο[ιή](μ)α(τ)' οὐ μάτ[. .] ἀκούοντα·   5
....... ] . (παρνεσωσπα)[.] ἀνθρώπων
................ ](καιδ)[. .]εν καλὴ κεῖ(ται)
...... κυλλ]όχειρες ὥ[σπ]ερ Ἁρπυῖαι
...... ἄναγ]νον κέρδος ἐκ λίθου παντός
........ ἔ]καστος ἔνθεν ἁρπάξῃ            10
.... κ]υβιστᾷ κἠπινήχεται πᾶς τις
.... ἑ]ταῖρον καὶ (κασί)γν[ητ]ον κ[αὶ] ὧρα
.... ἑ]αυτοῦ τὴν τρισο[ιζύρη]ν ψυχήν
.... οὐ](δὲν) [. . .ἢ] θά[λασσα μὲ]ν πεζή
....... ἀν]θρώποι[σιν ἡ δὲ] (γ)ῆ πλωτή·   15
....... περ]ιφέρουσι τήνδ[ε τ]ὴν ῥῆσιν
κέρδαιν' ἑτα]ῖρε καὶ θέρευς κ(αὶ) χειμῶνος
.... πάντοθε]ν κέρδ(αι)νε· μηδέν' αἰσχύνου
......... α]ἰδοῦ· τοῦτ' ὄνειδ(ι)εῖτα(ί σοι).

---

1. *e.g.* τοῖς νῦν μὲν and καταρᾶται.   2. *e.g.* ὃς κᾂν ὅσον and
ἦθος.   3. *e.g.* ἀποστυγήσας : fin. supplevi.   4. *e.g.* προθυμίῃ
(Πάρνε vix legi potest).     suppl. G(erhard).     5. supplevi.
*e.g.* χρηστῶν and μάτην.     6. *e.g.* ἐὰν διδάξω, Πάρνε σ' ὡς παρ'.
7. *e.g.* οἴχωκεν Αἰδὼς κοὐδ' ἐφ' ἕν.   8. suppl. Hdl.   *e.g.* αὐτοὶ
δὲ.   ὥσπερ Kenyon.   9. suppl. Cr.   *e.g.* ζητοῦσ' *id.*

# CERCIDEA

There is no one who has glanced ⟨for a moment⟩
on the ⟨character⟩ of mankind at present, without
⟨cursing⟩ mankind, and ⟨hating⟩ mankind on whom
he has glanced : but to you I shall display all ⟨zeal⟩,
since you are no idle listener to poems of ⟨worthy⟩
writers, ⟨if, maybe, I might teach⟩ you, Parnos, that
from mankind ⟨Shame has departed⟩ and in no respect is considered fair : while ⟨men themselves⟩
with ⟨crooked⟩ fingers like Harpies seek from every
stone an unholy gain : and each ⟨hunting⟩ for a
stretch to pillage, dives thither and swims to his
prey, ⟨destroying⟩ comrade, brother or wife, but
⟨preserving⟩ his own thrice wretched life. ⟨To them⟩
nothing is ⟨sacred⟩ : ⟨by such⟩ of mankind the sea
is trodden under foot and the land sailed over : all
alike they carry on their lips this saying : ' win
gain, my friend, summer and winter alike : from
everywhere win gain : have no reverence or shame
of any man : he will merely mock you for it.' ' Un-

---

10. *e.g.* διζήμενος δ'.　　11. suppl. Cr.　　*e.g.* ἐκεῖ *id.* or εὐθύς.
12. *e.g.* ὀλλύς.　　　　13. *e.g.* σῴζων δ' cett. ex P Bodl.
14. *e.g.* οὐδὲν ἱρὸν (Mn.), and τοῖς δ'.　　ηθαλλα(σ)α P Bodl. :
corr. *id.*　　15. *e.g.* τοίοισιν Mn.　　(σηδετυ) P Bodl. : corr.
*id.*　16. *e.g.* πάντες δὲ.　　τουτο το ρη P Bodl.　　17. κην
κερους P Bodl. : see Sext. Emp. *adv. Dogm.* v. 122.
18. ἀπαντόθεν Sext. Emp. rightly.　? P habuerit ἀπανταχόθεν.
19. *e.g.* καὶ μηδένα.　See Addenda.

447

. . . . . . . . . . . ](ν) τὴν χεῖρ' ὅκου λαβεῖν δεῖ τι   20
ὅκου [δ]ὲ δοῦναι μηδ' ὅλως φόρει χεῖρα
ἐροῦσι πολλοί· πολλὰ σαυτὸν ἀσπάζου
ἐπὴν ἔχῃς τι· πάντα σοι φίλων πλήρη·   23
πένητα δ' ὄντα χἠ τεκοῦσα μισήσει·   25
πλουτοῦντα γάρ σε χοὶ θεοὶ φιλήσουσι,   24
ἐὰν <δὲ> μὴ ἔχῃς μηδέν, οὐδὲ κηδεσταί.   26
ἐγὼ μὲν οὖν, αἶτα, καὶ καταρῶμαι   27
τοῖς νῦν βίοις καὶ πάντας ἀνθρώπους μισῶ
τοὺς ζῶντας οὕτω, καὶ ἔτι μᾶλλον μισήσω,
ἀνεστρόφαν γὰρ τὴν ζ<ό>ην ἡμῶν οὗτοι·   30
†τῇ γὰρ πάροιθεν ἦν δ' [ἄ]χρ[ι [ν]ῦν (ἐστὶν σεμνή)†
δ]ικαιότης ᾤ(χωκεν) ἔ(νθ)ε[ν ο]ὐχ ἥξει·
ἀπιστίη ζῇ· π(ίστι)s (ε). . . . . . . . . .
ἴσχυκεν ἡ (ἀναίδε)ια (τ)οῦ [Δ]ιὸς μεῖζον·
ὅρκοι τεθ[νήκα]σιωτ· οἱ θ(εο)ὶ δ' (εἰά)κασ(ιν)·   35
ἡ δυσγένεια κριθ(ι)ᾷ κατ' ἀνθρώπους
τῆς δ' εὐγενεί[ας ἁ]λμυρὸν κ(ατ)έπτυσ(ται).
†γῆμαι δ' ἂν οὐ[δεὶ](s) ο[ὐ]δὲ τὴν ("Ηρ)<η>ν θέλοιτ
πτωχὴν (ἐοῦσα)ν τ[. . . . . . ](ε). . .(ο)ντο(s),
μᾶλλον δ' ἕλοι(τ)[ο τὴν ](ἐ)[π](ὶ) [σ](τέ)γους Λυδήν ◁
ἔχων ὀπυίειν (ἔνδ)ο[ν ἢ]ν φέρῃ χαλκοῦς.   41
κα(ὶ) [
οἱ τὰ[
(ἐὰν) [                        ]την
ο. . .[   45
μο.[
αι.[
ε(χ).[
κα(ὶ).[
ὅτα[ν   50

448

fold your hand when you are to receive anything;
but when you are to give have no hand at all,' is
what many will say : ' embrace yourself heartily
when you have anything : then the world is full of
friends for you : but if you are poor even your
mother will hate you. For if you are rich even the
gods will love you : if you have nothing, not even
your relatives will love you.' I then, my comrade,
curse the lives men lead now, and hate all mankind
who live thus, and shall hate them even more. For
these have overturned our life ; for justice, holy
until now, has departed beyond recall. Faithlessness
flourishes, faith ⟨has left the earth⟩ : shamelessness
has won greater strength than Zeus. The sanctity
of oaths has perished, while the gods suffer it. Low
birth runs riot among mankind and men spit salt on
noble birth. And none now would wed even Hera
herself, were she poor, and bereft of all that might
profit him ; rather would he choose to keep in his
house as wife a Lydian harlot, if he[1] get brass
with her.

[1] *Not* ' she bring,' which would be φέρηται.

20. *e.g.* διπλῆν φορεῖ : better perhaps ἀναπέτ(α)σο]ν.
fin. ὅκου (τι) δει λ(αβει)ν P Lond.     ὅκου λαβει[ P Bodl.
which has the middle portions of 22, 23, 26 in this
order. I follow J. U. Powell.     21. suppl. Kenyon.
26. corr. id.   δε om. P Lond.     P Bodl. χεις μηδεν ο(ιη) ab-
surdly.     27. αιτεια P : corr. J. U. Powell.     29. l. καὶ ἐπὶ.
30. ζωην P : corr. C.     31. supplevi.   fin. (lectio vix dubia)
Mn.: *e.g.* del. ην δ Mn.     32. suppl. Mn.     33. *e.g.* ἐκ τῆς
γῆς ἔρρει.     34. suppl. Mn.   l. μέζον.     35. suppl. Mn.
(there are vague traces of (νηκα)).     37. suppl. Mn.   κ(ατ)
επτυσ(. .) P : text Sitzler, dubitante Mn.     38. suppl. Mn.
-αν P.     *e.g.* γ. θ. δ' ἀν. οὐδὲ τ. Ἡ. οὐδείς.     39. εουσαν
K.-Mn.     *e.g.* τοῦ νιν ὠφελήσοντος.     40. suppl. Mn.
(ἀπὸ).     41. supplevi: ἦν Cr.     οπνειν P.

```
κ[                        οὐ](δ)ὲ μαίον[ται
(π)[λὴ]ν                  ]ων
·[                        γα](σ)τρος
··[                       (υ)]σεν
χρ[                                        55
α·[·]ν[

                          ]σων
                          ]α
                          ο](ῦ)τοι
                          ]                60
                          ]φης
····[                     ]
ὁσ·[                      ]
··[                       ]
ὃν ···(α)[                ]                65
κε(ν)····[                ]
```

PHeid ἔοικ’ ἐνεῖναι· π[αντό](θ)εν γὰρ ἕλκουσιν
κοὐκ ἔστιν οὔ[τ]ε [σ]υγγενὴς οὔτε ξεῖνος
ὃ[ς ο]ὐχ[ὶ λα]ιμᾶ τ[οῦδ’] (ὅ)κως ἕξει μέζον·
χ[ω]ρὶς δέατος ὁ (θ)εσ[μὸς ο]ὐδὲ μέμνηται
θεοῦ Δικαίης ἀλλ(ὰ) [···](χλ)ευάζουσιν·   71
ὅκως δὲ χ(ρ)ὴ ζῆν [·]·[···] (ἔγ)ωγε θαυ-
μ(ά)[ζω·
ἐν θηρίοισιν; ἀλλὰ δ·[·]··(ζ)ωαί·
ἀπιστίη γε παντα[···]·[····]·[····]αι[
τὸ τῆς (ἀχ)····[··]†πεν ιατ τ’ ἴσως πάντα[   75
τὸ μειλιχῶδες κ(α)ὶ προσηνὲς δὴ τοῦτο.
ἐκεῖνο μ[ὲ]ν γὰρ ο[ἶδ]α, σὺν θεοῖς εἰπεῖν,
ὅπερ κ(ρά)[τιστ](όν) [ἐ]στιν, οὐ νενίκημ(α)[ι
[···]·[······] καὶ γαστ[ρὸ](ς) ἀλλ’ ἀπ-
(α)ρ[κ]εῦμαι
····] (ἔχε)ις γὰρ πρῆ(ον, ἢ) τ(ί) κερδαί(ν)[εις

450
```
```

⟨51. How well could I have spared, for thee, young swain,
  Enow of such as for their bellies' sake
  Creep and intrude and climb into the fold;
  Of other care they little reckoning make
  Than . . .

MILTON, *Lycidas*, 112 *sqq.*⟩

Such goad ⟨of avarice⟩ is in their souls: they drag
gain from every source: and there is neither kin nor
friend but ventures all in quest of gain. Divine Law
has no terrors, nor are they mindful of the goddess
of justice but mock at her. I wonder only how
one should live among these beasts: nay here life is
unlivable. All around faithlessness overcomes the
cause of spotless faith and all things, perchance,
riot on this comfortable and attractive doctrine.
Nay, but, by heaven's grace, I know that old rule
which is best: I am no slave of pleasures or of my
belly, but am content with little. What[1] civil-

---

[1] One is tempted to *conjecture* πρῆξιν or πλεῖον 'profit,' but
neither can be read.

---

55. A mark of corruption. If the equation with P Heid.
is sound five *vv.* have dropped out. The endings of *vv.* from
P Heid. are *v.* 38 and *v.* 40 ην etc.   55. ? χρόνος δὲ
φευγέτω σε μηδὲ εἶς ἀργός (p. 6).   57-61. ? om. P Lond.,
which marks corruption.   59, 61. So Bi.   66. *e.g.*
κέντρον: or κε(ί)νοις ? (Mn.)   67. . . . κ.ε(ν)[ (optime
quadrat εοικε εν vel εοικ ειν) P Lond.: εοικεν P Heid.
suppl. G.   68. καὶ οὐκ P Heid.: vestigia P Lond. cum
κουκ εστιν quadrant.   suppl. G.   69. non fuit το[λμ]ᾷ
π[άνθ' Bi.-K.: supplevi.   70. θεσμὸς supplevi probante
Bi.: cett. Gerhard.   71. suppl. Hense: praecessit *e.g.*
νιν.   72. supplevimus ego et Powell: *e.g.* τοῖσδε.
73. (K.-Bi.) *e.g.* δ(ύσβιοι).   74. *e.g.* πανταχοῦ πίστεως
νικᾷ.   75. *e.g.* ἀχράντου Sitzler: nullum spatium ante πενία
G.-Bi.: στρηνιᾷ reposui, coll. *v.* 36.   fin. legi rectissime
(iudice Bi.).   77, 78, 79. suppl. G.   79. init. *e.g.*
λαιμαργίης.   80. πρηον Bi.: ad *v.* 73 refero: init. *e.g.* τί
δῆτ'. cett. leg. K.-Bi.

# CERCIDEA

ἰδώ](ν γ)έ πως κάνδ(υλ)ον (ὠ)ς οὕτως εἰ-
π(ώτᾳ†);                                                    81

εἰς] (γ)ὰρ στόμ' ὡς ἔοικ[εν] (ἵ)στ(α)[τ]αι
μο(ῦ)νον

χρό]νον τοσ[οῦ]τον [ὄσσον ἄν] τις ἔσθη [τι],
(ὅτα)ν δ' ἀμείψητα[ι αὐτ](ὸ) καὶ τ(ὸ)[ν ἤκι-
σ](τ)ον

εἰς ζῆν χ(ά)ρυβδ(ιν) [ . . . . . ]. οἴχεται πά[ν-
τ](α)·                                                      85

καὶ ταῦτα τεν[ . . . . ].[ . ]. .ε καὶ ἕτερ(ο)
[ . . . . . ]

ὑπὲρ δὲ τούτων [μ]ὴ πάτει λίνων [ . . . . . . . . .

ἐγὼ μὲν οὖν, ὦ Π[άρ]νε, (τα)ῦτ' οὐχὶ ζ[ηλῶ
ἀλλ' ἐν χαλ[ινοῖς .][.] ἐ(μ)αυτὸν ὠ(ς [ . . . . . . .

γαστρὸς κατ(ί)σ(χ)[ω. .].[ . . . ]βιά[ζ]ομαι τ[οῦ-
τον                                                         90

πρὸς εὐτέλε(ια)ν τ[ὸ]ν [βί](ον) κα(θ)ίστασ(θ)[αι]

καὶ μὴν ὅτ[α]ν γε (θήδ). [. .] σ(π)έν(δ)ειν .[

κάμνω· με[γ]ίσ(τη δ') [. .].[. .]. .[.].(μοι) χό(ν)-
[δρος

τέρπει δέ μ' οὕτως (ο)[ὐ](δ)[ὲ]ν ὡς τὸ κερ-
δ(αί)[νειν

ἐκ] τοῦ δικαίου το[ . . . . . ]. [τ]οῖς ἀν[θ]ρώ-
(π)[οις                                                     95

. .λαμ]βάνειν .[.].[. .].[ . . .] ἐκ τρόπ[ων] α[ἰ-
σχρῶν

. . . . . . .].[.](νενο)ν . .[ . . . .]. ουθεν . .[.].[

. . . . . χρ]όνῳ π[λ]ο(υ)τοῦντας ἐξ ἀ[ . . . . . .

. . . . . . .]. (τ). .(ν). . . (ὤ)σπ(ερ) ουδ(ο). .[

ἔστιν γάρ, ἔστιν, ὃ(ς τ)ά(δε σ)κοπεῖ (δ)αίμων
ὃ(ς ἐ)ν χρόνῳ τὸ θεῖον οὐ καταισχύνει, 101
νέ]μει δ' ἑκάστῳ τὴν καταίσιον μοῖραν.

ization is it, what boots it, to glimpse, so to say, a
*bonne bouche* ? For what is set in the mouth remains
only for the moment of eating : after it has passed
through but a moment, all goes into a live [1] abyss.
Eat then cheerfully just so much as I do and no
more : beyond this walk not as a bird into the
net. These maxims, Parnos, I not only admire, but
keep myself obedient as ⟨a horse⟩ in belly-bands,
and force myself to order my life to simplicity. Aye
and when I must sacrifice to some pleasure I am
weary of it, since a pinch of salt is enough pleasure
for me, and nothing delights me so much as to win
from just dealing that ⟨which never⟩ comes to men
from base courses, ⟨as I now see many⟩ for a short
while enriching themselves by shamelessness,⟨though
their wealth vanishes⟩ as if ⟨it had never come⟩. For
there is indeed a divinity who looks on these things
and in time's course brings not to shame the godhead, but gives to each his due portion. So I,

[1] γαστήρ is derived (*E.M.*) to mean ἡ πάντα τὸν βίον λαμ-
βάνουσα μὴ πληρουμένη.

81. init. leg. Bi.-K.　　supplevi. fin. leg. εἴπω.　　82. supplevi: ἵσταται K.-Bi.　　83. init. supplevi ex Greg. Naz.
(ii. 444).　　ἐσθῃ . . vel ἐσθιῃ Bi.　　supplevi.　　84. supplevi.　　85. suppl. G. init. K.-Bi.　　med. *e.g.* δή τιν'.
86. *e.g.* τένδειν χρή σε καὶ ἑτέρῳ δοῦναι.　　87. πατ. K.-Bi.
[ὄρνις.　　88. suppl. G.　　89. suppl. G.　　*e.g.* νῦν ]
ἐμαυτὸν ὡς (leg. K.-Bi.) [πῶλον.　　90. *e.g.* καὶ ἐκβ. Hense.
τοῦτο G.: τοῦτον Hense.　　91. suppl. G.　　92. suppl. G.
θηδονῇ K.　　σπένδειν K.-Bi.　　93. supplevi *e.g.* ἐσθ' ἁλός γ'
ἐμοί: praecesserit (92) χρήζω.　　94. suppl. Kroll, Powell, ed.
95. suppl. G.　　*e.g.* τοῦθ' ὅπερ.　　96. init. suppl. G.
*e.g.* οὐ, ἔξεστιν.　　fin. supplevi. Cf. *e.g.* Plut. *Mor.* 570
πλουτοῦσιν ἀπὸ πραγμάτων αἰσχρῶν.　　97 sqq. I translate
as *F.G.A.* p. x.　　102, 103. suppl. G.　　102. καταισιαν
P. After this *v.* follows Ἴαμβος Φοίνικος, another citation
(from Phoenix ?), then a comic *fr.*

# CERCIDEA

ἐγ]ὼ μὲν οὖν, ὦ Πά(ρ)νε, βουλοίμην εἶναι
τἀρκεῦντ᾽ ἐμαυτῷ καὶ νομίζεσθαι χρηστός
ἢ πολλὰ πρήσσειν, καί ποτ᾽ εἰπεῖν τοὺς
    ἐχθρούς                                    105
'ἁλῶν δὲ φόρτος ἔνθεν ἦλθεν ἔνθ᾽ ἦλθεν.'

106. αλων ex αλλων.

Parnos, would wish to have just what sufficeth me,
and to be considered worthy, rather than to busy
myself and give my enemies scope for saying ' The
salt cargo returns whence it came.'[1]

[1] A proverb of wasted labour—with a gibe at the Cynic's
diet (*v.* 93).

# FRAGMENTA
# CHOLIAMBICA

# EUPOLIS

'Ανόσια πάσχω ταῦτα ναὶ μὰ τὰς νύμφας.
πολλοῦ μὲν οὖν δίκαια ναὶ μὰ τὰς κράμβας.

(Priscian *de metr. Com.* 415 K. Eupolis Βάπταις . . . hos
. . . posuit in fine habentes spondeos (1, 2).

# PHOENIX

## IAMBOC A.   NINOC

### *fr.* 1 (1 Powell)

'Ανὴρ Νίνος τις ἐγένετ' ὡς ἐγὼ κλύω
'Ασσύριος ὅστις εἶχε χρυσίου πόντον,
τὰ δ' ἄλλα πολλῷ πλε<ῦ>να Κασπίης ψάμμου·
ὃς οὐκ ἴδ' ἀστέρ' οὐ [δίζ]ων ἐδίζητο,

1. ἐγὼ 'κούω Bgk.   3. τάλαντα πολλῷ E : καί τἄλλα πολλὸν
cod. A.   The above reading seems to explain the variants,
but it may be Ph. wrote τὰ δ' ἀγαθά: *cf.* the proverb πόντος
ἀγαθῶν.   4. *e.g.* οὐχ ἄλων.

458

# EUPOLIS

Unholy wrongs I bear by Nymphs swear I !
Nay rightfully by cabbages swear I.

(Eupolis in the *Baptae* wrote the following verses with
spondees at the end (1, 2).  *Priscian* on *Comic Metres*.)

# PHOENIX

## POEM I. NINOS[1]

### 1

There was a man called Ninos, I am told,
Assyrian, who possessed a sea of gold
And all things else more than the Caspian sand :
Who ne'er the stars nor orb of heaven scanned

[1] The song is one of many variants of an alleged inscription
on the tomb of Sardanapallus in the Chaldaean tongue, of
which two translations, one in verse and one in prose, were
current in Greek.  The poise of the fingers of the statue
was interpreted as dismissing everything else as worth no
more than a flick.  I do not think that Phoenix wrote *books*
of Iambi.  This was the first poem in his book.

οὐ παρὰ μάγοισι πῦρ ἱερὸν ἀνέστησεν,　5
ὥσπερ νόμος, ῥάβδοισι τοῦ θεοῦ ψαύων.
οὐ μυθιήτης οὐ δικασπόλος κεῖνος·
οὐ λεωλογεῖν ἐμάνθαν᾽ οὐκ ἀμιθρῆσαι.
ἀλλ᾽ ἦν ἄριστος ἐσθίειν τε καὶ πίνειν　9
κήρᾶν, τὰ δ᾽ ἄλλα πάντα κατὰ πετρῶν ὤθει.
ὡς δ᾽ ἀπέθαν᾽ ὡνήρ, πᾶσι κατέλιπε ῥῆσιν,
ὅκου Νίνος νῦν ἐστί †καὶ τὸ σῆμ᾽ ἀϊδέ‹ς›†·
"Ακουσον εἶτ᾽ 'Ασσύριος εἴτε καὶ Μῆδος
εἶς ἢ Κοραξός, ἢ 'πὸ τῶν ἄνω λιμνῶν
‹Σ›ινδὸς κομήτης· οὐ γὰρ ἀλλὰ κηρύσσω·　15
ἐγὼ Νίνος πάλαι ποτ᾽ ἐγενόμην πνεῦμα,
νῦν δ᾽ οὐκέτ᾽ οὐδέν, ἀλλὰ γῆ πεποίημαι·
ἔχω δ᾽ ὁκόσον ἔδαισα [χὠκόσ᾽ ἤεισα],
χὠκόσ[σ]᾽ ἠράσθην,
τὰ δ᾽ ὄλβι᾽ ἡμέων δήιοι συνελθόντες
φέρουσιν ὥσπερ ὠμὸν ἔριφον αἱ Βάκχαι·　20
ἐγὼ δ᾽ ἐς "Αιδην οὔτε χρυσὸν οὔθ᾽ ἵππον
οὔτ᾽ ἀργυρῆν ἄμαξαν ὠχόμην ἕλκων·
σποδὸς δὲ πολλὴ χὠ μιτρηφόρος κεῖμαι.

(Ath. 530 e Φοῖνιξ δὲ ὁ Κολοφώνιος ποιητὴς περὶ Νίνου λέγων
ἐν τῷ πρώτῳ τῶν 'Ιάμβων γράφει οὕτως (1).)

7. μυθηήτης codd. : corr. Schweighäuser.　　12. is often
regarded as an insertion.　σῆμα (ἰ)δει cod. A.　　15. corr.
by Schweig.　　18. χὠκοσσ᾽ ἐράσθην cod. : corr. Bgk.
Perhaps we should write two verses : so translation.　　Hdl.
read ὁκόσσ᾽ ἔπαισα (Kaibel), χὠκ. ἤεισα, χὠκόσσ᾽ ἔδ‹ωκα γαστρί›,
κτλ. (v.l. ὁκόσσον ἔδ.).　For this I would compare exactly
Greg. Naz. Carm. (ii. 780 Colon) ἔπαιξεν, ἦσε, γαστρὸς ἔπλησεν
νόσον.

# PHOENIX

Nor duly at his magi's side with rod
Stirred up the holy fire and touched his god.
No spokesman was. nor counsellor this man,
No marshal, no reviewer of his clan ;
Wine, food, and lust of all men he adored
The most : aught else but these went by the board :
And when he died he left, to all to say
(Where town and tomb alike are hid to-day)[1] :—
' Assyrian and Median, give ear
Unto my preaching ! hear Koraxian ! hear
Thou long-haired Sindian from the Upper Mere :
I Ninos once of yore was living breath :
And now am nought but common earth in death.
All that I ate ⟨or drank⟩ †and all my song†
And all my lechery to me belong.
But all my goods my foes have ravishéd
And sundered as a Maenad doth a kid.
And I to Hades neither gold did bring
Nor horse, nor car of silver panelling :
I that did wear the diadem on my brow
A far-flung scattering of ash[2] am now.'

(Phoenix the poet of Colophon speaking of Ninos in his
first Iambus says (1). *Athenaeus*.)

---

[1] See Addenda.
[2] πολλή whether " wide-spread " as I take it, or " a heap "
as Mr. J. U. Powell suggests to me, is probably right.    To
my ear it suggests ὥσπερ οἱ πολλοί, which is the point of the
poem.    I have introduced this in *v.* 16 (transl.).    Ninos did
not have the grand burial of the old Assyrian princes, as to
which we are learning new details.    For the earliest burials
with jewelled cars and asses see C. L. Woolley in the *Times*,
p. 11, Jan. 12, 1928.

# FRAGMENTA CHOLIAMBICA

## ΚΟΡΩΝΙCΤΑΙ

### *fr.* 2 (2 Powell)

Ἐσθλοί, κορώνῃ χεῖρα πρόσδοτε κριθέων,
τῇ παιδὶ τὠπόλλωνος, ἢ λέκος πυρῶν
ἢ ἄρτον, ἢ ἤμαιθον, ἢ ὅτι τις χρῄζει.
δότω, 'γαθοί, τις, τῶν ἔκαστος ἐν χερσίν
ἔχει, κορώνῃ. χάλα λήψεται χονδρόν·                    5
φιλεῖ γὰρ αὕτη πάγχυ ταῦτα δαίνυσθαι·
ὁ νῦν ἄλας δοὺς αὖθι κηρίον δώσει.
ὦ παῖ, θύρην ἄγκλινε, Πλοῦτος †ἤκουσε†,
καὶ τῇ κορώνῃ παρθένος φέρ‹ο›ι σῦκα.
θεοί, γένοιτο πάντ' ἄμεμπτος ἡ κούρη                   10
κἀφνειὸν ἄνδρα κὠ‹υ›νομαστὸν ἐξεύροι
καὶ τῷ γέροντι πατρὶ κοῦρον εἰς χεῖρας
καὶ μητρὶ κούρην εἰς τὰ γοῦνα κατθείη,                 13
‹     .     .     .     .     .     .     .     ›     13a
θάλος, τρ‹ό›φ[ε]ιν, γυναῖκα, τοῖς κασιγνήτοις.
ἐγὼ δ' ὅκο‹ι› πόδες φέρ‹ω›σιν, ὀφθαλμούς
τἀμείβτομαι Μούσῃσι, πρὸς θύρῃσ' ᾄδων,                 16
καὶ δοντὶ καὶ μὴ δοντί, πλεῦνα ‹τετ›τίγων.             17

ἀλλ', ὦγαθοί, 'πορέξαθ' ὦν μυχὸς πλουτεῖ·              18
δός, ὦ ‹ἄ›ναξ, δὸς καὶ σὺ πότνα μοι νύμφη·

1 (and 20). ‹ς› χεῖρα?        4. τις after ἔκαστος codd.
Ath.        7. αὖθις codd.        8. *e.g. l.* ἤκει σοι.
9. φέρει codd.: corr. Bgk.        14. τρέφειν codd.
15. ὅκου, φέρουσι codd.: corr. Dind., Bgk.        16. -αισι,
-αις codd.: corr. Cr.        16. See on Herodas (C.E.), p. 395,
where add Opp. *Cyn.* iv. 199, ii. 222.        *e.g.* ἐρείδομαι:
Greg. Naz. *Or.* i. 477 в οἱ μὲν πόδες ἐφέρον[το] ἡ δὲ ὄψις εἶχε
τὴν θάλατταν fixes the sense and punctuation.        17. τωνγεω
codd.        19. so Cr.

462

# PHOENIX

## THE CHOUGH-BEGGARS

### 2

Good sirs, give to Apollo's child the chough
A fist of barley, crock of loaves, enough
Of bread, a farthing.   Each give what he will
Of what he has in hand, kind sirs, to me
The chough.   Coarse salt will not distasteful be.     5
On all these things she loves full well to thrive.
Who now gives salt a honeycomb shall give.
Sir slave ! open the door.   Let wealth come in
What time the girl brings figs from store within.
Pray God the maiden lead a virtuous life              10
And to a famous man and rich be wife.
And set a son upon her father's knee,               12
A daughter on her mother's ; and may she
As child or girl or woman ⟨bring delight,
When forth she ventures⟩ ¹ to her brothers' sight.
I, as I wander over dale and hill,
Keep my eyes fixed upon the Muses still ;             15
And, be ye churl or lavish, at your wicket
More blithely will I sing than any cricket.           17

. . . . . . .

Kind sirs, set forth what cupboard has in store,     18
Kind master give, kind mistress give me more.

---

¹ Clearly a verse is missing.   The sense is secured by
Hom. ζ 154 sqq.τρισμάκαρες μὲν σοί γε πατὴρ καὶ πότνια μήτηρ,
τρισμάκαρες δὲ κασίγνητοι· μάλα πού σφισι θυμὸς αἰὲν εὐφροσύνῃσιν
ἰαίνεται εἵνεκα σεῖο λευσσόντων τοιόνδε θάλος χορὸν εἰσοιχνεῦσαν.
The line lost was something like κῆρ εὐφρανέουσαν ἡνίκ᾽ ἐς
χορὸν φοιτῇ.   The Greeks (in literary tradition) were very fond
of their sisters.   We are not.

463

νόμος κορώνῃ χεῖρα δοῦν' ἐπαιτούσῃ.     20
†τοιαῦτ' εἰδὼς† δός τι καὶ καταχρήσει.

(Ath. viii. 359 e οἶδα δὲ Φοίνικα τὸν Κολοφώνιον ἰαμβοποιὸν
μνημονεύοντά τινων ἀνδρῶν ὡς ἀγειρόντων τῇ κορώνῃ καὶ λέγοντα
(? -ων) ταῦτα (vv. 1-17).   καὶ ἐπὶ τέλει δὲ τοῦ. Ἰάμβου φησίν
(vv. 18-21).)

It is remarkable that these verses differ (metrically) *toto caelo* from those of I and III : perhaps they are written after Callimachus' criticisms in his *Iambi*.   More probably Phoenix varies metre with subject.

21. *e.g.* τοσαῦτ' ἀείδω Bgk.

## ‹ΝΕΟΠΛΟΥΤΟΙ›

### *fr.* 3 (6 Powell)

π(ολ)λοῖς γε θνητῶν τἀγ[ά]θ', ὦ Ποσείδιππε,
οὐ [σύ]μφορ' ἐστίν, ἀλλὰ δεῖ τοιαῦτ' αὐτούς
τ](έμν)ειν, ὁκοῖα καὶ φρονε[ῖ]ν ἐπίστανται·
(νῦν) δ' ο[ἳ] (μ)ὲν [ἡ]μῶν κ(ρή)[γυ]οι καθεστῶτες
(π)ολλὴν ἀ(φ)ειδέως ν(η)[σ](τίην) ἐρεύγοντα[ι     5
(οἳ) δ' οὔτε σῦκα, φασίν, οὔτ' ἐρίν' εὗντες
(π)λουτοῦσι.  τῷ πλούτῳ δὲ πρ(ὸς) τί δεῖ χρῆ[σθ]αι
τοῦτ' αὐτὸ πάντων πρῶτον οὐκ ἐπίστανται,
ἀλ(λ)' (ο)ἰ(κ)[ία]ς μὲν ἐκ λίθου σμαραγδίτου,
εἴ πω[ς] ἀνυστόν ἐστι τοῦτ' αὐτοῖς πρήσσει(ν)     10
πά]το(ν) [τ'] ἐχούσας καὶ στοὰς τετραστύλους
πολλῶ]ν τ(α)λάντων ἀξίας κατακτῶ(ν)ται.
. . . . . .](δ)' ἑαυτῶν τὴν ἀναγκαίην (ψυχ)ὴν
. . . . . .]η σκ[ωρί]η το]ύτων πάντων·
. . . . . . .].ρα [πλοῦ](τ)[ο]ν ἐκπορίζουσιν     15
. . . . λ](ό)γοις χρηστοῖ(σ)ι σωφρονισθεῖσα

1, 2. so Gerhard.     3. suppl. Bi.-K.; *cf.* Poseidippus
*A.P.* ix. 359.   4. νῦν etc. Cr.   κρήγυοι G.   5. νησίην
Bücherer-Cr.   6. ερινα Papyrus.     7, 9, 10. so G.
464

# PHOENIX

So give the chough a fistful as is fit.                        20
So sing I.   Give.   You 'll ne'er repent of it.

(I recall that Phoenix the (chol)iambist of Colophon mentions certain men as collecting for the chough, and says
(saying ?) as follows (1-17).   At the end of the Iambus he
says (18-20).   *Athenaeus.*)

## [THE PROFITEERS]

### 3

Unto full many mortals goods are not
Good, Poseidippos : such should be men's lot
As is their power to stomach.   Now, God wot,
Our nobles belch not save on sorry fare,
Those who nor garden figs nor wild figs are,        5
Are rich.   But how their riches they should spend
They know not.   An they gain their dearest end,
Houses they buy for millions houses bright
With colonnades and floor of malachite.
But for the food whereon their souls should feed,   10
They mix it with the scourings of their greed.
For base are gains when men seek wealth alone
And listen not to words of righteous tone,
To learn precisely what is right and fit.
O Poseidippus let us say of it :                    15
Their houses costly are and fair of note

---

11. . .]($\sigma\tau o\nu$)[.] Heidelb. legere visus sum : sed " besser ]$\tau o\nu$[ "
monet Bi.        12. so G.        13. see G. and read with him
$\psi \upsilon \chi \hat{\eta}$.        Beginning *e.g.* $\tau \rho o \phi \eta \nu$.        14. $\tau o$]$\upsilon \tau \omega \nu$ G.        be-
ginning (for sense) $\breve{\epsilon} \phi \upsilon \rho \epsilon \nu$ $\dot{a} \rho \gamma \eta$.        15. *e.g.* $\kappa \acute{\epsilon} \rho \delta \eta$ $\gamma \grave{a} \rho$ $a \dot{\iota} \sigma \chi \rho \acute{a}$.
$\pi \lambda o \hat{\upsilon} \tau o \nu$ dubium (Bi.).        16. *e.g.* $o \dot{\upsilon}$ $\mu \dot{\eta}$.        $\lambda \acute{o} \gamma o \iota s$ G.

# FRAGMENTA CHOLIAMBICA

. . . . . . ] (τ)ὰ χρηστὰ καὶ τὰ συμφέροντ᾽ εἰδῇ.
[. . . . . . .] τοιούτοις ἀνδράσιν, Ποσείδιππε,
. . σ]υ(μ)βέβηκεν (οἰκ)ίας μὲν κεκτῆσ(θ)α(ι)
κ](α)λὰς καταξίας τε χρημάτων πολλῶν,                    20
α]ὐτοὺς δ᾽ ὑπάρχειν ἀξίους τ[ρι]ῶν χ(α)[λκῶ]ν;
κ]αὶ μάλα δικαίως, ἤν τις ἐνθυμῆτ᾽ [ὀρ]θῶς
. . . . . . . . . . .]ν γὰρ καὶ λίθων φροντίζουσιν.

(In Cercidas' Anthology with lemma Ἴαμβος Φοίνικος (η′).
Follows at once (? τοῦ αὐτοῦ))

### 3*

. . . . . . . . . . . . (μ᾽) [οἴ]κι. [. .] (ἀ)νιστᾶσιν

    .    .    .    .    .    .    .    .

17. *e.g.* ὀρθῶς.      18. *e.g.* τοῖς οὖν G.      19. οὐ συμβ. G.
20, 21, 22, 23. So G.

---

[1] The anthology does not add materially to the reputation
of the poet. Athenaeus would appear to have selected his
two best pieces. But it gives us their scope—say twenty to
fifty lines—and shows us that 1 and 2 may be nearly complete. Moreover, Poseidippus gives us a clue as to date:
that is that this poem may be later than 275, if this (Gerhard)

# PHOENIX

But they themselves are worth not half a groat.[1]
And rightly, too, such verdict may we give,
⟨For stones they are and⟩ unto stones they live.[2]

(The first citation in *Cercidas'* anthology, ' One of *Phoenix'*
*Iambi.*' The citation which follows in the same metre—the
title has been lost—runs :)

### 3*

. . . set up hous. . .

is the Poseidippus who was then studying in Athens under
Zeno and Cleanthes. Another identification (see below) is
with the comic poet who lived later. But again, if my
reading in *v.* 2 is rightly approved by Bilabel, the epi-
grammatist (of the same date as the comic poet) must also
be considered. Indeed the piece might be a commentary on
the epigram ποίην τις βιότοιο τάμοι τρίβον ;

[2] Such seems to be the most apposite ending but it is
somewhat hard to fit in. See Gerhard pp. 134, 140. Perhaps
λίθοι τ' ἔφυν (Pind. *P.* i. 42), written ἔφυσαν.

# PHOENIX (?)

A Papyrus at Strassburg (*W.G.* 304-307)[1] contains
on the recto an anthology of lyrics from tragedy.
On the verso is what appears undoubtedly to be
part of the Cercidas anthology. In general the
metres are iambic and the subjects chosen for their
ethical value. There are no names of authors given.
The date of the hand, according to Bell, Lobel,
and Bilabel, is the middle of the third century B.C.
It can hardly be doubted that the author of the
choliambi given below is Phoenix. The metre is
identical with that used by Phoenix in the Heidelberg fragment; and the loose flowing repetitive
style is typical of all we have of him. Another
reason, observed by W. Crönert, is that the name
Lynceus occurs in this, and Poseidippus in the
Heidelberg fragment. Lynceus is known to have
written letters to Poseidippus, possibly those of an
elder to a pupil. If, as may be, it is Lynceus who
is dead, the verses may have been written about
280 B.C.: for Lynceus is called a contemporary of
Menander, Poseidippus being younger, or at least
younger as a writer : see Suid. *s.vv.*, Ath. viii. 337 d.
The anthology, then, is almost contemporary with the
verses, if these names are those of the well known
writers of Attic comedy.

[1] *Gött. Gel. Nachr.*, 1922, i. 31.

# FRAGMENTA CHOLIAMBICA

This may be a convenient place to note two points : *firstly*, the metre of the fragment. There are two licenses employed by Greek writers as a variant of the rigid form ⏓–◡–◡|–◡–◡–. One is to allow many resolutions. Phoenix adopts this in two pieces. The other is to allow the ending – – – –. This is adopted by Phoenix in two pieces ; also by the author of the anthology whom Gregory calls Cercidas. Callimachus eschews both licences, though occasionally admitting an undivided trochee : Herodes uses both. *Secondly*, we may now place the anthology collector, who contributed the preface, as writing about 250 B.C., and roundly assert that this metre was as far as we know and in all probability not used between 200 B.C. and the Christian era. Earlier columns of the Strassburg portion of the Anthology are not well re-assembled yet. Below this poem we have the verses (already edited by Crönert):

ἀγαπᾶτε τοῦτον πάντες ὃς ἔχει τἀγαθά[1]
ἅπαντ' ἐν αὐτῷ, χρηστός, εὐγενής, ἁπλοῦς,
φιλοβασιλεύς, ἀνδρεῖος, ἐν[2] πίστει μέγας,
σώφρων, φιλέλλην, πρᾶυς, εὐπροσήγορος,
τὰ πανοῦργα μισῶν, τὴν ἀλήθειαν σέβων.

Next column contains three pseudo-Epicharmic verses, ἐπιστα . . . | τιμαν  θεοι . . . | αὐτὸν κυβερ(ν)[ —clearly of ruling the tongue. At the bottom is a fragment of Attic comedy of which I give the beginnings of the last nine verses : Ἄπολλον Ἀ(γρ εὖ ? ?) | οὕτως δ' ἂν ἐμ | ἡμῖν ὑβριζ . . . | καὶ τρίποδες ἁλ . | καὶ μὴν ἀδικεῖται ψ . . . . . . | νῦν μοι διακονουν . . παιδίον | ἀστεῖον οὐχ ὁμ. . . . ἐκ κει. | ἃ δ' ἂν λάβω τοι δεῖ

---

[1] a horrid pun, αγαπα and αγα(θα) πα(ντ).
[2] for εμ.

470

# PHOENIX (?)

διπλό᾽ ἀπο[δοῦναι | τὰ πάτρια γὰρ δὴ τῆς τέχνης |.   In
between are the interesting verses:

> οὕτ(ω) τὰ πρόσθεν[
> κοινῆς τραπ[έζης ἀξίωμ᾽ ἔχων ἴσον,
> ἀκόλαστον ἔσ[χε γλῶσσαν αἰσχίστην νόσον.
> κορυφῆς ὑπε[ρτέλλοντα δειμαίνων πέτρον[1]
> τυχ. . .ετα[
> ἢ που τ[

These I quote, (a) since they give clearly the subject
of this section of the anthology—praise or blame of
the tongue : (b) since, as will be seen, the three
verses taken from the first ten lines of Euripides'
*Orestes may* be choliambic (ἴσον, νοῦσον, πέτρον).

We must consider briefly the subject matter. A
poet is dead. The speaker (Phoenix or, as in the
Ninos poem, another) wishes consolation for the
loss. He longs to see Lynceus, and will render him
famous by iambi at feast of bowls (and in the
country ? ?).   For us there is an unfortunate am-
biguity.   Does Apollo or some representative of
poetry mourn a dead writer, *e.g.* Menander, and
beseech Lynceus to replace him, with promises to
inspire him at the Dionysia in city (see *ap.* Dem.
531) and country ?   Or is the request for the robe
merely an aside to a slave. and is " that which was
my robe " Lynceus, and the iambi those of Phoenix
who speaks ?   On the whole, I believe this is so,
but have no confidence in either interpretation.

[1] *vv.* 2, 3, 4 suppl. E. Lobel.

471

<ANΩNYMOY ΕΠΙΤΥΜΒΙΟC>

*fr.* 4

```
..........]. . ο.[ο .] (ελπ)[. . . .] δεινοῖς
...........] . . (μι)[. .](π)ε[. . . .]ν λέσχῃ
.]. . .[. . . . .]. . (συ).[.](ν) δὲ (λ)αυψηρήν
]. . .[. .]. . . (ι)δαι .[. .] (ἀσφαλ)ῆ 'π(ού)ρ(α)s
.]. . .[.]. . . . ην.(φ). [ἐν]αύεσθαι λύχνον·          5
.]. . . . . .(ε).(αλ)ος, καὶ πα(νοι)κίη θάλλων
ἑτοῖμον †.τον κ(τῆσι)ν ὦ(ν) ἐ(κ)εῖ† τήρει,
καὶ κάε χρείην καὶ π[έν](η)τος ἐμβλέψας.
. . .[. . .]. . ε(s) τ. (θοιλπα) τῆς τύχης κρίνων
. . . . . .] τὸ μηδὲν καὶ κενῷ προσεμβ(α)[. . . .     10
. . . . . . .](ω)δεστ.ν[ε](ξ)αγ. . πάρ σευ
. . . . . . .]. .[. . . . . . . . .]. .[. . . . . . .           12
```

(duo versus desunt)

```
. . . . . . . .ἀ](φν)εα .[. . .] (μηδ)[. . . . . . . . .     15
. . . . . . . .δ]εξιῆς ἤψ(ω) τ' ἡμῶ[ν
. . . . . . . .]τι τ(ῷ) θεῶν ξείνῳ
.](α)[. .].οι(το) (σοὶ) μὲν (Χ)εῖος (ἢ) (ἀ)πὸ τῆς
     Σμύρνης
```

3. *e.g.* σεαυτὸν ἴσθι τὴν τύχην . . .          4. *e.g.* δαίμον'
(init. ἐνταῦθα μίμνε).        5. *e.g.* ἔνθεν έ σ' ἐχρῆν ὀψ'.        6. *e.g.*
πρόφαινε καλός : 1. -οικίη.        7. . . . τον P : ? 1. αὐτοῦ. Dein
suspicor ὡς ἔχει.        8. εβλ. P with μ superscr.: 1. χρείη.
9. *e.g.* τὰ κοινά, τὰ δεινά cett.: init. *e.g.* σὺ δ' ἤλιτες.
472

## ⟨EPITAPH (ON LYNCEUS?)⟩

### 4

Full often would I say in idle] talk,
" Beware of] dangers [if abroad you walk.
Know you are mortal] and swift Fate is not:
Abide at home where] safety is your lot.      4
There are the fires] from which your lamp to light,
Flourish both you and yours, and shining bright
Keep it a ready vessel there [1] with heed
And burn it, apt to serve the poorest's need.
Alas! you] scoffed at Fate's alarms, and found
Faring abroad] your [feet] on hollow ground.    10
No profit is there more of you for me

.    .    .    .    .    .    .    .

.   .   'rich'   .   .   .   .   .   15
.   .   'my right hand clasped' .   .   .   16
.   .   'the host of gods'   .   .   .   17
Praise you in Smyrna, †Crete†, or Chios [2] bred   18

[1] In *v.* 7 I translate αὐτοῦ . . . ὡς ἔχει. P seems to have ωνεκει. There may be an allusion here to Lynceus as a poet: Callim. *Iamb.* 334 Ἔφεσον ὅθεν πῦρ οἱ τὰ μέτρα μέλλοντες τὰ χωλὰ τίκτειν μὴ ἀμαθῶς ἐναύονται. *v.* 8 'Give a light even to the poorest' encourages this interpretation.

[2] Clearly Homer who was born at Smyrna, Chios, Colophon, Salamis, Rhodes, Argos or Athens. The reading 'Crete' is an error, perhaps for ἢ 'Ακτῆς—'from Smyrna or Attica.'

10. *e.g.* εἶναι and προσεμβαίνων.   16. ? ἡμέων.   18 *e.g.* κλήζοιτο.

# FRAGMENTA CHOLIAMBICA

(ἤ) (Κρὴς) ὅ,τ' εἴη καὶ κεν(ὸν κεν)ῷ (β)ἀ(ξ)α(ι)·
ἐγὼ δ' ὑπ' Ἄιδου (δή σε πε)[ί]θομαι γλῶσσαν    20
... .[ . . . . .](τα π)[ερὶ] πασ(ῶ)ν χελιδόνων·
ὅ δ' (εὔκο)[ . . . . . . .](π)[ . . . .](φ)η(μ)[.](μυστα)ισι[.]
(σὺ)ν εὐλαβείη τ(ρι)[ . . . .]. .[ . . . . .].[ . . . . . .
τί πόλλ' ἀείδω; μ(ω)ρίη γὰρ ἡ λέσχη·
στεῖλόν μ(ε χ)λ(αί)νη· κῶς δ' ἔχω ποθέω(ν) βλέψαι
Λυγκεῦ σε; . . . .σύ· νῦ(ν γ)ὰρ ᾧ κατέσταλμαι    26
κατερρύηκε καὶ εἰς τὸν Ἀίδη βαίνει.
ἐγὼ δ' ἰάμβ(οι)ς κἠπὶ Κρητήρων Θοί(ν)η
θήσω σε τιμήεντα καὶ ἐν χώρη παντί.

19. Beginning very uncertain.    (ἄκρως) would fit traces
better.    21. read περὶ χ. π.    25. στειλομ P.    26.
lectio incertissima: μή olim dedi: fort. ἄγρει.    νυγ ex
νῦν?    29. εγ P.

## fr. 5 (3 Powell)

Νίνου κάδοι μάχαιρα καὶ κύλιξ αἰχμή,
κ‹ύ›μ‹β›η δὲ τόξα δήιοι δὲ κρητῆρες,
ἵπποι δ' ἄκρητος κἀλαλὴ ' μύρον ‹χ›εῖτ‹ε›.'

(Ath. x. 421 d καὶ ὁ Κολοφώνιος δὲ Φοῖνίξ φησιν (5).)

5. 2. κόμη corrected by Haupt.    3. κεῖται by Lachmann.

474

# ANECDOTUM ARGENTINENSE

| | |
|---|---|
| Some empty singer to an empty head [1] : | |
| But you have ta'en below, I wot, a tongue | 20 |
| That has all twittering swallows far outsung.[2] | 21 |
| $\cdot$ $\cdot$ $\cdot$ $\cdot$ $\cdot$ $\cdot$ $\cdot$ $\cdot$ | 22 |
| ' with caution ' | 23 |
| Why sing I long ; for idle talk is folly. | 24 |
| Robe me ! How suffer I, who long to see | 25 |
| You, Lynceus, once again ! Come ! robe thou me. | |
| For that which was my robe has vanished quite [3] | |
| And treads the path to Hades out of sight. | |
| But I at country-side and Feast of Bowls [4] | |
| Will win your verses honour from all souls. | 30 |

[1] See *Paroem.* κενοὶ κενὰ βουλεύονται and πρὸς κενὴν (or -ὸν) ψάλλεις.
[2] *vv.* 20 and 21 echo Phoenix *fr.* 1 *v.* 21 and *fr.* 2 *v.* 17 .
[3] See Headlam's note on Herodes ii. 15.
[4] ' Feast of Bowls ': conceivably two mixing-bowls, one for the living and one for the dead. Ionic has no dual. As Phoenix lived at Ephesus, the probable scene for Mime V. of Herodes, this appears as a *possible* name of the feast which Herodes paraphrased with the words ἐπεὰν δὲ τοῖς κα-μοῦσιν ἐγχυτλώσωμεν (84). But see above.

## 5

For casks were Ninus' sword and jugs his spear,
Cups were his arrows, bowls his enemy,
Ho ointment ! his alarm, liqueurs his cavalry.

( And Phoenix of Colophon says (5). *Athenaeus.*)

# FRAGMENTA CHOLIAMBICA

## fr. 6 (4 Powell)

Θαλῆς γὰρ †ὅστις† ἀστέ[ρ]ων ὀνήιστος
καὶ τῶν τότ᾽, ὡς λέγουσι, πολλ‹ὸ›ν ἀνθρώπων
ἐὼν ἄριστος, ἔλαβε πελλίδα χρυσῆν.

(Ath. xi. 495 d Φοῖνιξ δ᾽ ὁ Κολοφώνιος ἐν τοῖς Ἰάμβοις ἐπὶ
φιάλης τίθησι τὴν λέξιν λέγων οὕτως (6). καὶ ἐν ἄλλῳ δὲ μέρει
φησίν (7).)

## fr. 7 (5 Powell)

Hippon. fr. 76*.

## fr. 8

ὁ μὲν γὰρ αὐτῶν ἡσυχῇ τε καὶ ῥύδην
θύνν†οντ τε καὶ μυττωτὸν ἡμέρας πάσας
δαινύμενος ὥσπερ Λαμψακηνὸς εὐνοῦχος
κατέφαγε δὴ τὸν [σ]κλῆρον, †ὥστε χρὴ†
σκάπτειν

6. 1. ὅστις: read e.g. ἀστοῖς. ἀστέων (from false mss. of
Hdt.) : Casaubon's certain correction (quam nemo umquam
dubitavit literarum Graecarum vel minime peritus). Here are
the disjecta membra in Hdt. alone :—τῶν τότε + superlative
i. 23, viii. 8, ix. 72, cf. iii. 125 : ἀνθρώπων + sup. i. 24, 45, iv.
91. viii. 68 : τῶν ἀστῶν + sup. or δόκιμος i. 158, iii. 20, iv. 14,
161, v. 63, 97, 126, vi. 61, 101, vii. 118, viii. 46, ix. 93. It is
true that the expression is intolerably diffuse, but so is all
that we have of Phoenix. Compare Theogn. v. 23. On
ἀστεύς see my First Greek Anthologist, p. 24. 2. -ῶν
A : corr. by Toup. 3. v.l. πελλιάδα.

# PHOENIX (?)

### 6

For Thales, to his townsmen usefullest
Of townsmen, and, say they, by far the best
Of men then living took the paillet gold.

(Phoenix of Colophon in his *Iambi* uses the word (paillet)
of a cup as follows (6). Elsewhere[1] he says (7). *Athenaeus*.)

### 7

Hippon. *fr.* 76.

### 8

One day by day luxuriously dined
In ease on cheese-cake spiced and tunny brined,
Like eunuch Lampsacene : his portion done
He fain would dig 'mid mountain rocks and stone ;

[1] It is clearly impossible to suppose these words are right.
In what other part ? For these are iambi like the others.
But we know of various books of Hipponax, and if we transfer
the text of Athenaeus (or of Lysanias behind it) we get a
natural sequence καὶ πάλιν (495 d) . . . καὶ ἐν ἄλλῳ δὲ μέρει
(495 e). The gravest stylistic argument is that Phoenix was
wholly incapable of such compression as the three verses
show.

---

8. 2. θύνναν A, θύννον C, θυννίδα Meineke.    4. σκληρὸν
cod. Ath.: corr. Dalecamp.        ὥστε χρὴ cod. Ath.: leg.
χρῇ: Soph. *Ant.* 887 (Jebb). So ten Brink.

# FRAGMENTA CHOLIAMBICA

πέτρας [τ'] ὀρείας σῦκα μέτρια τρώγων     5
καὶ κρίθινον κόλλικα δούλιον χόρτον.

(Ath. vii. 303 c θυννίς ... 304 b Ἱππῶναξ δὲ ὡς Λυσανίας ἐν
τοῖς περὶ ⟨τῶν⟩ ἰαμβοποιῶν παρατίθεται, φησίν (8).)

The evidence for attributing this fragment to Hipponax
appears faulty.   On the one hand Athenaeus' attribution is plain, the divisions and the breaks are good,
and the connexion with *fr.* 17 (so most edd.) attractive.
Against this we have (*a*) ῥύδην so typical of later choliambists (ἐμπτύοι Hrd., καταπτῦ (?) Cercid., κλύω Phoenix).
(*b*) The moral tone. (*c*) Three cases of resolution in the first
foot—for Athenaeus seems to have read θυννίδα in *v.* 2.   Of
course his text may have been corrected from better codd.,

# AESCHRION

*fr.* 1. μήνη τὸ καλὸν οὐρανοῦ νέον σίγμα
   2*. στενὸν καθ' Ἑλλήσποντον ἐμπόρων χώρην
      ναῦται θαλάσσης ἐστρέφοντο μύρμηκες.
   3*. ὁ δ' ἐξελὼν ἱμάντα φορτίου ζώνην
   4*. ἶρις δ' ἔλαμψε καλὸν οὐρανοῦ τόξον.
   5*. καὶ πίσσαν ἐφθὴν ἦν θύραι μυρίζονται

(Tzetz. *Rhet. Gr.* iii. 650 Walz ὡς τὴν σελήνην οὐρανοῦ
πάλιν Αἰσχρίων σίγμα· οὕτω γὰρ λέξεσιν αὐταῖς αὐτὸ Αἰσχρίων
λέγει (1)· τὸν λόγον ἐκτραχύνουσι, σκληρύνουσι δὲ πλέον ἢ μᾶλλον
εἰς ψυχρότητα σύρουσι γελαστέαν, ὡς καὶ ὁ γράψας τὰ ψυχρὰ
ταυτὶ τῶν ἰαμβείων (2) καὶ πολλαχοῦ δυστηνὰ τοιαυτὶ λέγει
(3-5).

# AESCHRION

And peck at fodder whereon slaves are fed,
A modicum of figs and barley bread.

(Tunny . . . ; Hipponax, as Lysanias says in his work
on the (chol)iambic poets, remarks (8). *Athenaeus.*)

---

if these were extant. Again, v. 4 is wholly unsatisfactory
though the resolution is not objectionable. (*d*) The fact
that the citation is second-hand. If genuine we should have
to read *e.g.* v. 1 ῥύβδην (Bgk.), v. 2 μυσσωτὸν *id.*, v. 3 ὥστε,
v. 4 κατ᾽ **ὧν** φαγὼν and ὥστε θῆς σκάπτει and in v. 2 keep
θυννόν C (θύνναν A). Even so μέτριᾱ τρώγων is wrong for
Hipponax, but right for Phoenix (2. 1, 6. 3).

# AESCHRION

1. O Moon the heaven's pretty new sigma [1]
2*. Sea-ants the sailors swarmed, where their
    business
    The merchants have in Hellespont's narrows.
3*. So he unloosed a strap, a bale's girdle
4*. A rainbow shone, the heaven's fair iris. [2]
5*. And boiling pitch, a portal's anointment

(Or again as Aeschrion calls the moon the heaven's
pretty sigma. Here are his exact words (1). Thus style is
rendered ' rougher,' I should rather say ' harsher,' or better
still ' diverted to a ridiculous bathos,' as is the case with
the author of these iambi which are typical of bathos (2).
With him these unfortunate effects are common (3-5).
*Tzetzes* in *Rhetores Graeci.*)

[1] C, not Σ.          [2] Transposing the original.

# FRAGMENTA CHOLIAMBICA

## *fr.* 6

ἐγὼ Φιλαινὶς ἡπίβωτος ἀνθρώποις
ἐνταῦθα γήρᾳ τῷ μακρῷ κεκοίμημαι.
μή μ᾽, ὦ μάταιε ναῦτα, τὴν ἄκρην κάμπτων
χλεύην τε ποιεῦ καὶ γέλωτα καὶ λάσθην·
οὐ γὰρ μὰ τὸν Ζῆν᾽, οὐ μὰ τοὺς κάτω Κούρους,   5
οὐκ ἦν ἐς ἄνδρας μάχλος οὐδὲ δημώδης·
Πολυκράτης δὲ τὴν γενὴν Ἀθηναῖος
λόγων τ‹ε› παιπάλημα καὶ κακὴ γλῶσσα
ἔγραψεν ‹ὅ›σσ᾽ ἔγραψ᾽· ἐγὼ γὰρ οὐκ οἶδα.

(Ath. viii. 335 b Φιλαινίδος εἰς ἣν ἀναφέρεται τὸ περὶ
Ἀφροδισίων ἀκόλαστον σύγγραμμα ὅπερ φησὶ ποιῆσαι Αἰσχρίων
ὁ Σάμιος ἰαμβοποιὸς Πολυκράτη τὸν σοφιστὴν ἐπὶ διαβολῇ τῆς
ἀνθρώπου σωφρονεστάτης γενομένης. ἔχει δὲ οὕτως τὰ ἰαμβεῖα (6).
*Α.Ρ.* vii. 345 ἀδέσποτον· οἱ δὲ Σιμωνίδου.)

## *fr.* 7

καὶ θεῶν ‹βρῶσιν›
ἄγρωστιν εὗρες ἣν Κρόνος κατέσπειρεν.

(Ath. vii. 296 e Αἰσχρίων δ᾽ ὁ Σάμιος ἔν τινι τῶν ἰάμβων
Ὕδνης φησὶ τῆς Σκύλλου (*cf. Α.Ρ.* ix. 296)(Hdt. viii. 8) τοῦ
Σκιωναίου κατακολυμβητοῦ θυγατρὸς τὸν θαλάσσιον Γλαῦκον
ἐρασθῆναι. ἰδίως δὲ καὶ περὶ τῆς βοτάνης λέγει ἣν φαγὼν
ἀθάνατος ἐγένετο (7).)

6. *vv. ll.* 4 λάσθνην, 5 Ζεῦν, οὐδὲ, 6 ην, 7 γυνήν, 8 οἶα
and ἄσσα.      8. τι Ath., *Α.Ρ.*
7. 1. so Haupt.

# AESCHRION

## 6

Philaenis I, the whole wide world's byword,
Lie resting here after a long old age.
O idle sailor, rounding the headland,
Spare me your jeers, derisions and mockings,
For so I swear by Zeus, and by Hell's Youths [1]
Ne'er was I common woman, nor lustful.
Polycrates, Athenian native,
Evil of tongue and crafty word-monger,
Wrote of me what he wrote : for I know not.

(Philaenis, to whom is ascribed the obscene work on erotics,
said by Aeschrion of Samos, the writer of iambi, to have
been written by Polycrates the sophist to libel the woman,
who was, in fact, a model of chastity. *Athenaeus.* Also in
the *Palatine Anthology* with lemma "On Philaenis the
courtesan from Elephantiné who painted on a tablet the
famous γυναικείας μίξεις on account of which she is lampooned
by the Athenian wits." A scholiast (*A.P.*) repeats the
charge quoting Lucian (*Amor.* 28).

## 7

### And agrostis
Did'st find, the Gods' repast, sown by Kronos.

(Aeschrion of Samos in one of his iambi says that the
sea deity Glaucus was enamoured of Hydna, daughter of
Scyllus [2] the Scionean diver. And he has an original statement about the food which he ate and became immortal
(7). *Athenaeus.*)

[1] The Dioscuri. For the ellipse of (Dios) compare
Herodes, i. 32.
[2] Scyllus or Scyllies was (Hdt. viii. 8) the famous diver
who deserted to the Greeks before the naval fighting round
Artemisium in connexion with the battle of Thermopylae.
He swam ten miles under sea ! Agrostis is a kind of grass.
Glaucus was originally a fisher of Anthedon.

# FRAGMENTA CHOLIAMBICA

## THEOCRITUS

ὁ μουσοποιὸς ἐνθάδ' Ἱππῶναξ κεῖται·
εἰ μὲν πονηρός, μὴ προσέρχευ τῷ τύμβῳ·
εἰ δ' ἐσσὶ κρήγυός τε καὶ παρὰ χρηστῶν,
θαρσέων καθίζευ, κἢν θέλῃς ἀπόβριξον.

(*A.P.* xiii. 3 and one cod. Theocr.)

2. *A.P.* ποτέρχευ: cod. Med. προσέρχου.     3. χρηστῶ
*A.P.*     4. καθίζου cod. Med.


## DIPHILUS

στρωφᾷς δὲ πώλους ὡς ὁ Μαντινεὺς Σῆμος
ὃς πρῶτος ἅρματ' ἤλασεν παρ' Ἀλφειῷ.

(Scholl. Pind. *Ol.* x. 83 (*a*) παρατίθεται δὲ (Δίδυμος) καὶ τὸν
γράφοντα τὸν Θησηΐδα μαρτυροῦντα τῷ "Ηρωι τὴν τοῦ ἅρματος
ἡνιοχευτικὴν ἀρετήν· τρέψας δὲ πώλους ὡς ὁ Μαντινεὺς "Ηρως.
(*b*) Ἀριστόδημος δέ φησι μὴ δύνασθαι συγχρονεῖν Ἀλιρρόθιον τὸν
κατὰ Κέκροπα Ἡρακλεῖ ἀλλὰ μηδὲ Ἀρκάδα εἶναι ἀλλ' Ἀθηναῖον.
Σῆμον δέ τινα νῦν νενικηκέναι ἅρματι ὥς φησι Δίφιλος ὁ τὴν
Θησηΐδα ποιήσας ἔν τινι ἰάμβῳ οὕτω τρέψας δὲ κτλ. (*vv.* 1-2).

1. *v.l.* τρέψας, "Ηρως schol. (*a*).

# VARIOUS FRAGMENTS

## THEOCRITUS

Stranger, here lies the poet Hipponax :
If thou art wicked, to his tomb come not ;
If thou art goodly and thy sires gentle,
Be bold : sit here : and if thou wilt, slumber

(In the *Anthologia Palatina* and one ms. of *Theocr.*)

## DIPHILUS[1]

And swervest colts like Mantinese Semus
Who won the car race first by Alpheus.

((a) Didymus cites the author of the *Theseis* as witness
to the driving skill of the Hero (*v.* 1). (b) Aristodemus says
that Halirrhothius being contemporary of Cecrops cannot
have been alive with Heracles, nor was he an Arcadian but
an Athenian. In fact the victor in the car race was a certain
Semus, as is stated by Diphilus the author of the *Theseis*
in a (chol)iambic verse as follows (*vv.* 1, 2). Two *Commentators* on an *Olympian Ode* of *Pindar.*)

[1] Of Diphilus nothing is known beyond the statements
above. In the second verse it is not clear whether πρῶτος
means ' was first to ' or ' to victory.' The second schol.
suggests that this was part of a fugitive epigram. Quite
possibly a quotation from the *Theseis* is lost and these
iambi are by another hand. The Diphilus of schol. Ar.
*Nub.* 96 might be the same, but this is improbable.

# FRAGMENTA CHOLIAMBICA

## RHINTHON

(*fr.* 10 Kaibel)

Α. ὁ σὲ Διόνυσος αὐτὸς ἐξώλη θείη.
Β. Ἱππωνά[κ]τ‹ειον› τὸ μέτρον.
Α. οὐδέν μοι μέλει.

(Hephaest. p. 9 Ῥίνθων μὲν γὰρ καὶ ἐν ἰάμβῳ ἐπισημασίας ἠξίωσε τὸ τοιοῦτον. ἐν γὰρ Ὀρέστῃ δράματί φησιν (v. 1), εἶθ' (v. 2). So Choerob. in Theodos. ii. 796 Hillgard πολλάκις εὑρίσκονται καὶ ἐν τοῖς μέτροις ἀποτελοῦντα κοινὴν τὸ κ͞τ καὶ π͞τ, . . . ὡς παρὰ τῷ Ῥ. (v. 2).)

1. θείης ἴθ' cod.
2. Ἱππώνᾰκτος codd.: correxi.
The apparent choliambic fragment in Clement of Alexandria, p. 14 Potter, attributed to Rhinthon, is really a trimeter : see Potter's citations. For another fragment of Rhinthon see my *First Greek Anthologist*, p. 22.

## ASCLEPIADES OF SAMOS

### *fr.* 1

ὃ καὶ κυνὸς καλοῦσι δυσμόρου σῆμα

(Schol. Eur. *Hec.* 1273 περὶ δὲ τοῦ κυνὸς σήματος καὶ Ἀσκληπιάδης φησὶν ὅτι κυνὸς καλοῦσι δυσμόρου σῆμα. Schol. Lyc. 315 σκύλαξ· . . . σκύλακα τὴν Ἑκάβην λέγει, ὅτι κύων ἐγένετο ὥς φησι μυθικῶς Εὐριπίδης (*l.c.*). . . . καὶ Ἀσκληπιάδης περὶ τοῦ τόπου οὗ ἀνῃρέθη (1).)

1. ὃ καὶ om. schol. *Hec.*

# VARIOUS FRAGMENTS

## RHINTHON

A. May Dionysus be thy perdition.
B. A Hipponactean [1] verse !

A. I do not mind.

(Rhinthon in an iambus calls attention to this practice.
In his play *Orestes* he says (*v.* 1) and proceeds (*v.* 2).
*Hephaestion.* *Kt* and *pt* often have the syllable before
them either short or long : *e.g.* Rhinthon (*v.* 2). *Choero-boscus*.)

[1] Rhinthon is satirizing the scansion θείη (Hephaestion)
and ἄκτ- (Choeroboscus). The latter depends on the false
reading βᾱκτηρίῃ in Hipponax (p. 14).

## ASCLEPIADES OF SAMOS

### 1

The luckless ' bitch's tomb ' they now call it.

(About the ' bitch's tomb ' Asclepiades says that (1).
*Commentator* on *Euripides' Hecuba*. ' Whelp ': . . .
Lycophron gives this name to Hecuba since she was turned
into a bitch according to Euripides' legend. Asclepiades
says about the place where she was killed (1).)

# FRAGMENTA CHOLIAMBICA

## fr. 2

κούφῃ κεραί‹ῃ› κεύσταλεῖ παρήνεγκεν

(Plut. *Mor.* 476 A κἄν τις ἔξωθεν ἀρχὴ πάθους ὥσπερ διαδρομὴ γένηται σπιλάδος (ε. καὶ κ. κ. π.) ὥς φησιν ᾿Ασκλ.)


# APOLLONIUS RHODIUS

## CANOBUS

### fr. 1

Κορινθιουργές ἐστι κιόνων σχῆμα.

(Steph. Byz. Κόρινθος· . . . ʼκαὶ σύνθετον Κορινθιουργής ὡς ᾿Αττικουργής. ᾿Απ. ὁ ῾Ρόδιος Κανώ†π†ῳ [δευτέρῳ] (1).)


### fr. 2

†τρέψει δὲ νηὸν† ὁ γλυκύς σε χωρίτης
πλόος κομίζων δῶρα πλουσίου Νείλου.

(Steph. Byz. χώρα· . . . ᾿Απολλώνιος ἐν τῳ Κ. (2).)

1. δευτέρῳ del. Meineke.   In text ?? σῆμα.
2. 1. τρέψει δὲ νηῶν Pinedo, which I translate.   χωρίτης : em. Meineke.   2. Νείλου πλουσίου codd. : em. Gavel.

486

# VARIOUS FRAGMENTS

## 2

Rides out the storm with light and bare yard arm

(And if from outside comes the beginning of any evil like the passage of a storm [1] he as Asclepiades says (2). *Plutarch on Tranquillity.*)

[1] σπιλάς 'storm': see *J.Th.S.* xiv. 56, xvi. 78.   Add Plut. *Dio* 10 τοῦ χειμῶνος παραφερομένου.


# APOLLONIUS OF RHODES

## CANOBUS

### 1

A pillared group Corinthian-fashion

('Corinth': . . . there is a compound 'Corinthian-fashion' like 'Attic-fashion.' Apollonius of Rhodes in his [second] *Canobus.*[1]   *Stephanus of Byzantium.*)

### 2

Thou shalt delight in the ships' sweet passage
That brings the countryfolk rich Nile's presents.

('Country' . . .: compound 'countryfolk.' Apollonius in his *Canobus. Id.*)

[1] Canobus was the steersman of Menelaus who was turned into a star. The Corinthian pillars marked his alleged grave. Out of Helen's tears for him grew, as Apollonius no doubt did not fail to mention, the plant ἐλένειον. *E.M. s.v.* Neither Apollonius nor Asclepiades seem to have written more than one choliambic poem.

# FRAGMENTA CHOLIAMBICA

## PARMENO

*fr.* 1 (1 Powell)

ἀνὴρ γὰρ ἕλκων οἶνον, ὡς ὕδωρ ἵππος,     1
Σκυθιστὶ φωνεῖ                              2
            οὐδὲ κόππα γιγνώσκων          3
κεῖται δ' ἄναυδος ἐν πίθῳ κολυμβήσας       4
κάθυπνος ὡς μήκωνα φάρμακ‹ο›ν πίνων.       5

(Ath. v. 221 a (1) φησὶν ὁ Βυζάντιος Παρμένων.)


*fr.* 2 (2 Powell)

ἦλθον μακρὴν θάλασσαν, οὐκ ἄγων σῦκα
Κα[ι]ν‹αῖ›α φόρτον.

(Ath. iii. 75 f Παρμένων ὁ Βυζάντιος ἐν τοῖς ἰάμβοις τὰ ἀπὸ
Κανῶν τῆς Αἰολικῆς πόλεως ὡς διάφορα ἐπαινῶν φησὶν (2).)


*fr.* 3 (3 Powell)

Αἰγύπτιε Ζεῦ Νεῖλε
(Ath. v. 203 c.    Schol. Pind. *P.* iv. 97.)


*fr.* 4 (8 Powell)

παῖδ' οὔτε γέν‹υσι› πυρρὸν οὔθ' ὑπηνήτην

(Schol. Theocr. vi. 3 πυρρός· ὁ ἀρτίχνους . . . Παρμενίσκος
(-ων Haupt) (4).)


1. 3. κόππα A : κάππα cett.    5. φαρμάκων AC : corr. Cas.
Meineke saw that the order was unsatisfactory.    For
sense lost *e.g.* πρῶτον· εἶτά που πλεῖον πιὼν σεσίγηκ'

2. 2. Καινεα A : corr. Palmerius.        φόρτου A : corr.
Cas.    Sense ἀλλὰ ‿ – πόρνας?

4. γένειον sch. : corr. Bücheler.

488

# VARIOUS FRAGMENTS

## PARMENO

### 1

For one that drinketh wine, as horse water,
First speaks like Scythians : ⟨then when drunk
    deeper⟩
Silent he lies, and cannot say ' Koppa,' [1]
Since he has fallen to a tub's bottom,
As with some opiate, with sleep druggéd.

(Parmeno of Byzantium says (1). *Athenaeus.*)

### 2

⟨Crossing⟩
Far seas I came hither, no figs bringing,
Produce of Canae, ⟨but some fair ladies⟩.

(Parmeno of Byzantium in his iambi praises figs from
Canae the Aeolian city as of superlative quality. *Athenaeus.*)

### 3

O Nile, Egyptian Zeus,

⟨*Athenaeus.* A *Commentator* on a *Pythian* ode of *Pindar.*)

### 4

A boy nor yellow-chinned nor yet downy

(' Yellow ' : used of one whose beard is just beginning to
grow. . . . Parmeniscus (4). *Commentator* on *Theocritus.*)

[1] To the Greeks the northern tongues appeared to have
an undue preponderance of ugly guttural sounds (Hdl. on
Hrd. vi. 34). *ko* is both the ' first ' letter of the Scythian
or as the hiccup of the drunkard's alphabet. The Greeks
said οὐδ᾽ ἄλφα.

# FRAGMENTA CHOLIAMBICA

## HERMEIAS

(p. 237 Powell)

Ἀκούσατ᾽, ὦ Στοίακες, ἔμποροι λήρου,
λόγων ὑποκρ⟨ι⟩τῆρες, οἳ μόνοι πάντα
τἂν τοῖς πίναξι, πρίν ⟨τι⟩ τῷ σοφῷ δοῦναι
αὐτοὶ καταρροφεῖτε, κᾆθ᾽ ἁλίσκεσθε
ἐναντία πράσσοντες οἷς τραγῳδεῖτε.          5

(Ath. xiii. 563 d τούτων τῶν Ἀλέξιδος ἀπομνημονεύσας ὁ
Μυρτίλος κᾆτα ἀποβλέψας εἰς τοὺς τὰ τῆς Στοᾶς αἱρουμένους
τὰ Ἑρμείου τοῦ Κουριέως ἐκ τῶν ἰάμβων προειπών (vv. 1-5),
παιδοπῖπαι ὄντες καὶ τοῦτο μόνον ἐζηλωκότες τὸν ἀρχηγὸν ὑμῶν
τῆς σοφίας Ζήνωνα τὸν Φοίνικα, ὃς οὐδέποτε γυναικὶ ἐχρήσατο
παιδικοῖς δ᾽ αἰεί, ὡς Ἀντίγονος ὁ Καρύστιος ἱστορεῖ ἐν τῷ περὶ
τοῦ βίου αὐτοῦ.)

1. στόακες A : στοίακες (E).          2. ὑποκρητῆρες corr. Mus.
3. πρινή: corr. Porson. Read προεῖπεν in Ath. Perhaps
continue (for otherwise there is no construction), e.g.

> ὡς παιδοπῖπαί τ᾽ ἐστὲ καὶ μόνον τοῦτο
> Ζήνωνα τὸν Φοίνικα ἐοίκατε ζηλοῦν
> ὃς οὐδ᾽ ὄναρ γυναικί, παιδικοῖς δ᾽ αἰεί
> ἐχρήσατ᾽.

## CHARINUS

Ἔρροις πλανῆτι καὶ κακὴ πέτρη Λευκάς·
Χαρῖνον, αἰαῖ, τὴν ἰαμβικὴν Μοῦσαν
κατηθάλωσας ἐλπίδος κενοῖς μύθοις.
τοιαῦτ᾽ Ἔρωτος Εὐπάτωρ ἐρασθείη.

(Ptolemaeus Chennus (Phot. Bibl. p. 153. 5) Χαρῖνος δὲ
ἰαμβογράφος ἡράσθη Ἔρωτος εὐνούχου τοῦ Εὐπάτορος οἰνοχόου, καὶ
πιστεύσας τῷ περὶ τῆς πέτρας λόγῳ κατέβαλεν ἑαυτόν. ἐπεὶ δὲ
καταβαλών τὸ σκέλος κατεάγη καὶ ὑπὸ ὀδύνης ἐτελεύτα ἀπέρριψε
τάδε τὰ ἰαμβεῖα (vv. 1-4).)

490

# VARIOUS FRAGMENTS

## HERMEIAS

Hear me, ye Stoics, merchants of twaddle,
Verbiage-fakers : you yourselves gulp down
All that is in the dishes, ere wise men
Can get a sup or bite : and your actions
Belie your fair pretences :[1] †you're caught out   5
In lust unnatural, herein Zeno
Your founder, and herein alone, aping :
For this Phoenician never knew woman.†

(After quoting these verses of Alexis, Myrtilus stared round
at those of the Stoic persuasion present and quoted the words
of Hermeias of Curium (*vv.* 1-8), as Antigonus the Carystian
states in his *Life.* *Athenaeus.*)

[1] Verses 5-8 are merely paraphrased in Athenaeus : see
crit. n.   Of Hermeias of Curium (in Cyprus) nothing more
is known.

## CHARINUS

Damn thee, Leucadian rock,[1] thou vile truant :
Alas the Muse iambic Charinus
Thou didst burn up with flattering tales empty.
Eupator's love for Love I pray end thus.

(Charinus a (chol)iambic poet fell in love with Love, a
eunuch who was cup-bearer to Eupator, and trusting in the tale
about the rock threw himself over the edge.   In falling
he broke his leg and just as he was dying in agony threw
off these iambic verses (*vv.* 1-4).   *Ptolemaeus Chennus* in
*Photius's Catalogue.*)

[1] Diving over the Leucadian precipice into the sea was
supposed to have the effect of winning the love of a
reluctant loved one.   The whole of the narrative of Ptolemaeus is suspect : but these verses can hardly be later than
A.D. 100 or 200.   πλανῆτις seems to mean ' deceitful.'   See
[Ovid], *Heroid.* xv. 163 *sqq.*

# FRAGMENTA CHOLIAMBICA

## APOLLONIDES (NICAENUS)

Γλῆνιν παρηονῖτις ἀμπέχω χερμάς
πικρῇ κατασπασθέντα κύματος δίνῃ,
ὅτ' ἰχθυάζετ' ἐξ ἀκρῆς ἀπορρῶγος·
χῶσαν δέ μ' ὅσσος λαὸς ἦν συνεργήτης,
Πόσειδον, οὓς σὺ σῷζε καὶ γαληναίην      5
αἰὲν διδοίης ὁρμιηβόλοις θῖνα.

(*A.P.* vii. 693 Ἀπολλωνίδου ἰαμβικόν.)

4. ὅσσος ἦν συνεργάτης λαός conj. Jacobs.

## HERODIANUS

Ἡρωδιανὸς Νι[κί]ου πα[τ]ρὸς [σ]τῆσεν
χαλκεῖον ἀνδρίαντα πατρίδος ψήφῳ
γνώμης τ' ἔκ⟨η⟩τι, μείλιχος γὰρ ἦν [π]ᾶ[σιν]
τερπνῶν τε μ[ί]μων οὓς ἔγραψεν ἀσ[τ]ε[ί]ως.

(Cougny, *A.P.* iii. p. 589, from a grave-stone at Ergissa
(Eski-Zaghra).)

3. τε ἕκατι lapis.

## PARDALAS

Ὁ Σαρδιηνὸς Παρδαλᾶς δὶς ἤκουσα·
μεμνήσομαί σου κἂν ἐμῇσι βύβλοισι.

(Cougny, *A.P.* iii. p. 30. One of a number of inscriptions
on the left leg of the famous statue of Memnon in Egypt.)

2. Num σευ?

492

# VARIOUS FRAGMENTS

## APOLLONIDES (OF NICAEA?)

Here, sea-side cairn, do I embrace Glenis,
In woeful whirl of wave to death sucked down,
What time he sat on rugged cliff fishing.
His mates did pile me here, O Poseidon :
Them save thou : evermore give calm weather
To all who from this sea-board their lines cast.

(In the *Anthologia Palatina*.)

## HERODIAN

Herodianus set this bronze statue
To Nicias his sire by his town's vote
Memorial to his character gentle
And to his pleasant mimes with wit written.

(On a grave-stone : see *Cougny's Appendix to A.P.*)

## PARDALAS OF SARDIS

I, Pardalas of Sardis, twice heard thee
And in my books I promise thee mention.[1]

(*Appendix* to the *Palatine Anthology*.)

[1] Ancient tourists who listened for the sound of Memnon's statue at dawn scrawled their semimetrical testimonies all over the statue and base. Cougny i. 175, 184, 185 are mainly in pure iambi and I omit them despite an occasional choliambus, due to the incompetent author or authoress. Pardalas seems to have had some knowledge of the metre and appropriate dialect.

# FRAGMENTA CHOLIAMBICA

## ANON. I

Ὁ κλεινὸς ἶνις βασιλέως Ἀμάζασπος,
ὁ Μιθριδάτου βασιλέως κασίγνητος,
ᾧ γαῖα πατρὶς Κασπί‹οι›s παρὰ κλήθρ‹οι›s,
Ἴβηρ Ἴβηρος ἐνθαδὶ τετάρχυται
πόλιν παρ' ἱρὴν ἣν ἔδειμε Νικάτωρ                5
ἐλαιόθηλον ἀμφὶ Μυγδόνος νᾶμα.
θάνεν δ' ὀπαδὸς Αὐσόνων †ταγήτορι†
μολὼν ἄνακτι Παρθικὴν ἐφ' ὑσμίνην,
πρίν περ παλάξαι χεῖρα δηΐῳ λύθρῳ,
ἴφθιμον, αἰαῖ, χεῖρα δουρὶ †κανοζωρ†             10
καὶ φασγάνου κνώδοντι, πεζὸς ἱπ‹πεύς τε›.
ὁ δ' αὐτὸς ἶσος παρθένοισιν αἰδοίαις . .

(Cougny, *A.P.* iii. p. 132. In Rome? Non inveni.)

3. -ιας -ρας corr. by Meineke.      7. ? ταγήτορσι and
ἄναξι (8).      10. καὶ τόξῳ M. Haupt.      11. supplied
by Scaliger.

## ANON. II

. . . . . . . . . . .]ιων ἴχνος, εἰ θέλεις γνῶναι
. . . . . . . . . . .]ις τῇδε λαίνῃ στήλῃ.
. . . . . . . . . . .] ἐν φθιτοῖς ἀνὴρ χρηστός,
. . . . . . . . . . .] λέλοιπεν ἡλίου φέγγος,
. . . . . . . . . . .]ων μηδέπω τελειώσας.        5
πάντ' . . . . . . .]ι δέδοκτο, μοῦνος ἀνθρώπων,
καὶ πάντας] ἀρετῇ τοὺς ὁμήλικας προὔχεν
εἰς πᾶν δί]καιος, θεοσεβής, φιλάνθρωπος.
τίς οὐχ ἑ]ταίρων τὸν τεὸν μόρον κλαίει;

1-5. I translate the general sense given by Cagnat (so
7, 9, 10, 12, 13 (δεινὸν) and 14).      3. χρ. ἐν φθ. ἀν. lapis.
6. δέχοιτο lapis : corr. Cagnat.

494

# ANONYMOUS FRAGMENTS

## ANON. I

The famous son of a king, Amazaspus,
And of king Mithridates own brother,
Who by the Caspian gates was born, here lies,
Iberian of Iberian, balméd,
By holy city [1] built by Nicator                    5
On the Mygdonian stream 'neath grey olives.
Unto the Roman emperor [2] fighting
Against the Parthian he went ally,
(And fell his hand not yet in foes' blood steeped,
That hand alas ! both with the bow mighty    10
And with the sword-hilt) horse and foot leading.
Withal he was of modesty maiden . . .

[1] Nisibis.
[2] The emperor seems to have been Trajan.

## ANON. II

⟨Halt passing⟩ if thou wouldest learn, stranger,
⟨Who buried lies⟩ beneath this stone pillar.
Once was he ⟨so and so⟩, a man righteous,
⟨But now hath gone and⟩ left the fair sunlight
And left unfinished ⟨his life's due course⟩.          5
Alone of men was he ⟨in all blameless⟩
⟨And all⟩ his fellows he in worth outdid.
⟨In all things⟩ just, humane, and god-fearing
⟨Which of⟩ thy comrades at thy fate weeps not ?

ἅπας] μὲν ὄχλος οἰκετῶν σε δακρύει,　　10
ἐν παν]τὶ δ' ἦσθα σεμνὸς ὡς δοκεῖν εἶναι
ἔτ' ὄν]τα παῖδα τοῖς νοήμασιν πρέσβυν.
. . . .]ον, ποθητὴ μῆτερ, εὔνασον θρῆνον,
πέ]νθους τιθηνόν, ὃς μάτην σε πημαίνει·
οὐδεὶς γὰρ ἐξήλυξε τὸν μίτον Μοιρῶν,　　15
οὐ θνητός, οὐκ ἀθάνατος· οὐδ' ὁ δεσμώτης
οὐδ' αὖ τύραννος βασιλικὴν λαχὼν τιμήν
θεσμοὺς ἀτρέπτους διαφυγεῖν ποτ' ᾠήθη.
Φαέθοντα Τιτὰν οὐκ ἔκλαυσ' ὅτ' ἐκ δίφρων
ἀπ' οὐρανοῦ κατέπεσεν εἰς πέδον γαίης;　　20
Ἑρμῆς δ' ὁ Μαίας οὐκ ἔκλαυσεν ὃν παῖδα
[Μυρτίλον †ἀπὸ δίφρων† κύμασιν φορούμενον];
οὐδ' αὖ Θέτις τὸν σ⟨θ⟩εναρὸν ἔστενεν παῖδα
ὅτ' ἐκ βελέμνων θνῇσκε τῶν Ἀπόλλωνος;
οὐδ' αὖ βροτῶν τε καὶ θεῶν ἄναξ πάντων 25
Σαρπηδόν' οὐκ ἔκλαυσεν, οὐκ ἐκώκυσεν;
οὐδ' αὖ Μακηδὼν ὁ βασιλεὺς Ἀλέξανδρος
ὃν τίκτεν Ἄμμων θέμενος εἰς ὄφιν μορφήν . . .

(Cougny, *A.P.* iii. p. 123.　In Alexandria.)

16. read οὐδὲ.　　22. is corrupt.　　23. στεναρόν lapis.
25. πάντων ἄναξ lapis.　　28. incomplete.

# ANONYMOUS FRAGMENTS

⟨Aye all⟩ thy household servants are mourners ; 10
And always wast thou dignified, seeming,
Though yet a boy, in intellect man-like.
O yearning [1] mother, thy lament cease thou :
It doth but nurse the grief that hurts idly.
For none have yet escaped from the Fates' thread,
Nor mortal nor immortal : nor pris'ner [2]     16
Nor tyrant borne to consequence kingly
Has ever thought to flee their laws fixéd.
Titan did mourn for Phaethon fallen
Out of his car from heaven to earth's plain.     20
And Hermes Maea's son his own son wept,
Myrtilus, thrown to waves ⟨that his name bear⟩.[3]
Thetis lamented for her son valiant
When by Apollo's darts he lay stricken.
Aye and the king of all gods and all men     25
Bewailéd and lamented Sarpedon.
Aye Alexander, Macedon's ruler,
Whom Ammon did beget disguised snakewise . . .

---

[1] ποθητή must mean weeping.  Read ποθῆτι.

[2] Cf. Ps.-Call. pp. 290 sqq. for these and following verses.
They might actually be by the same writer.

[3] I suppose the author to have written something like
Μυρτίλον ἰαφθέντ' εἰς φερώνυμον κῦμα.  φορηθέντα would suffice.

497

# FRAGMENTA CHOLIAMBICA

## DIOGENES LAERTIUS

### 1 (1 Meineke)

Τί δὴ γέρων ὢν καὶ φάλανθος, ὦ 'ρίστων,
τὸ βρέγμα δῶκας ἡλίῳ κατοπτῆσαι;
τ‹οι›γὰρ τὸ θερμὸν πλεῖον ἢ δέον ζητῶν
τὸν ψυχρὸν ὄντως εὗρες οὐ θέλων Ἅιδην.

(Diog. L. vii. 164 τοῦτον λόγος φαλακρὸν ὄντα ἐγκαυθῆναι
ὑπὸ τοῦ ἡλίου καὶ ὧδε τελευτῆσαι . . . (1).)

### 2 (2 Meineke)

Οὐκ ἄρα μῦθος ἦν ἐκεῖνος εἰκαῖος
ὡς ἀτυχής τις ἐών
τὸν πόδα κολυμβῶν περιέπειρέ ‹πως› ἥλῳ·
καὶ γὰρ ὁ σεμνὸς ἀνήρ,
πρὶν Ἀλφεόν ποτ' ἐκπερᾶν, Ἀλεξῖνος          5
θνῆσκε νυ‹γ›εὶς καλάμῳ.

(Diog. L. ii. 109 ἔπειτα μέντοι νηχόμενον ἐν τῷ Ἀλφειῷ
νυχθῆναι καλάμῳ καὶ οὕτω τελευτῆσαι . . . (2).)

### 3 (3 Meineke)

Εἰ καὶ σέ, Ξενοφῶν, Κραναοῦ Κέκροπός τε πολῖται
φεύγειν κατέγνων τοῦ φίλου χάριν Κύρου,
ἀλλὰ Κόρινθος ἔδεκτο φιλόξενος, ἧ σὺ φιληδῶν
οὕτως ἀρέσκῃ· κεῖθι καὶ μένειν ἔγνως.

(Diog. L. ii. 58 ὡς ἐτελεύτα (3). A.P. vii. 98 (3) ἐκ τῆς
βίβλου τῆς ἐπιγραφομένης Βίων Φιλοσόφων. vv. 3, 4 Suid.
s.v. φιληδῶν from A.P.)

1. 3. τὺ γὰρ corr. Meineke.
2. 3. τὸ cod.: em. Stephanus.      6. νυχθεὶς corr. Hermann.
3. 2. φευγέμεναι A.P.      4. ? ὅκως.

498

# DIOGENES LAERTIUS

## 1

Why, O Ariston old and bald-headed,
Did'st to the sun to bake give thy noddle ?
Withal didst thou, excess of heat seeking,
Discover that cool death which thou shunnédst.

(It is said that Ariston, who was bald, was scorched by
the sun and so died. Here is an epigram of mine (1).
*Diogenes Laertius, Lives of the Philosophers.*)

## 2

That witty jest was no mere jest random
    How an unfortunate wight,
In swimming, on a nail his foot piercéd :
    So did that reverend man
Named Alexinus crossing Alphéus
    Pierced by a bulrush expire.

(Later while swimming in the Alpheus Alexinus was
pierced by a reed and so died. Here is my epitaph (2).
*id.* See Addenda.)

## 3

Xenophon, though by the townsmen of Cecrops
    and Cranaus doóméd
    To exile since thou followedst Cyrus,
Yet did Corinth receive thee hospitable : where
    both in comfort
    Thy life thou passed'st and wast there buried.

(On Xenophon's death *id.* Also in the *Palatine Anthology*
whence *Suidas* quotes the last two verses.)

# FRAGMENTA CHOLIAMBICA

## 4 (om. Meineke)

Καὶ σὲ Πρωταγόρη σοφίης ἴδμεν βέλος ὀξύ
ἀλλ' οὐ τιτρώσκον⟨τ⟩', ⟨ὄντα⟩ δὲ γλυκὺ
⟨χ⟩ρ⟨ῖ⟩μα.

(*A.P.* vii. 132.   Not in our codd. of Diog. L.)

## 5 (om. Meineke)

Ἰλιγγίασε Βάκχον ἐκπιὼν χανδόν
Χρύσιππος, οὐδ' ἐφείσατο
οὐ τῆς Στοᾶς, οὐχ ἧς πάτρης, οὐ τῆς ψυχῆς,
ἀλλ' ἦλθε δῶμ' ἐς Ἀΐδεω.

(Diog. L. vii. 184 τοῦτον ἐν τῷ Ὠιδείῳ σχολάζοντά φησιν
Ἕρμιππος ἐπὶ θυσίαν ὑπὸ τῶν μαθητῶν κληθῆναι· ἔνθα προσ-
ενεγκάμενον γλυκὺν ἄκρατον καὶ ἰλιγγιάσαντα πεμπταῖον ἀπελθεῖν
ἐξ ἀνθρώπων ... (5).   *A.P.* vii. 706.)

4. 2. -ον, -ων corrected by Jacobs.          κρῆμα corrected
by Boissonade.
· 5. 3. οὐχ ἧς *A.P.*: οὐδ' ἧς some codd. D.L. (vitiosissime):
Jacobs οὐ τῆς perhaps rightly.          πάτρας *A.P.*

## 4

Thee too Protagoras do we know, sharp spear-
    point of wisdom,
Not wounding us but sweet as an ointment.

(In the *Palatine Anthology* only.)

## 5

Chrysippus had a fit upon gulping
    A drink, and spared not anyone,
Nor Stoa, nor his land, nor his own self,
    But into Hades passed away.

(Hermippus says that Chrysippus was resting in the
Odeum when he was summoned by his pupils to a sacrifice :
there he took a liqueur and had a fit and five days later
departed this life . . . (5). *Diog. L.* Also in the *Palatine
Anthology.*)

# ANON. AP. PSEUDO-CALLISTHENEM

Poems I and II and those later ones which concern the death of Darius were edited by Kuhlmann, a pupil of W. Kroll (Munster, 1912). Since then Kroll has produced a text of the one best codex, or recension of the life of Alexander (Berlin, 1926). This is codex A (Paris Graec. 1711). Some other codices present quite different versions, B and C (codd. dett.): and I have constantly referred to the Bodleian cod. Barocc. 20, a ms. in the main of type C. Further we have the excellent Armenian version (Arm.) translated into Greek by Richard Raabe [1] (Leipzig, 1896), the Latin translation of Valerius (Val. : printed by Müller-Didot : Arrian etc. 1865), and the Byzantine version (Byz.) into politic verse (W. Wagner,[2] Berlin, 1881), all of which preserve something of value. Of the recensions A (only preserved in one bad codex) is by a stylist more or less faithful to his original : B and C represent a version into the vulgar language. In a way they are more helpful, since wherever a literary metrical phrase peeps out that is necessarily original.

Besides the verses in i. 42 preserved only in the Latin of Julius Valerius, Kuhlmann recognized only three

[1] To whom most of the improvements in the text of i. 46 are due.
[2] *Trois Poèmes grecs du moyen âge.*

choliambic portions : and to these Kroll in his critical notes adds an oracle (which is quite separate) and an account of Darius' appearance when Alexander goes to the Persian camp as his own herald. But, as the verses in i. 46 show, there is far more. For we have no mere song of Ismenias the flute-player : the narrative between his verses and those of Alexander—and indeed, though obscuredly, the narrative before—is all choliambic. Further, in the fable of the mice and wasps, which I give below in verse for the first time,[1] the conclusion is

$$\dot{\omega}s \; \delta \; \epsilon \hat{\iota} \pi \epsilon [\nu \; \dot{\delta}] \; \beta \alpha \sigma \iota \lambda \epsilon \dot{\upsilon}s \; \pi \acute{\alpha} \nu \tau \epsilon s \; \alpha \dot{\upsilon} \tau \grave{\delta} \nu \; \eta \dot{\upsilon} \phi \acute{\eta} \mu o \upsilon \nu$$

and the verses continue. It is clear that for large portions this life of Alexander rests on a choliambic basis : and we may hazard a guess that the whole is based on an anthology of Alexander's deeds in which the choliambic verses (as far as they extended) occupied pride of place. The only known poet who wrote of the fall of Thebes was Soterichus, who lived under Diocletian ; but he seems to have been an epic poet.[2] There are difficulties in placing our choliambist later (when the art of the iambus was beginning to be lost), or earlier (when Soterichus must have merely copied the theme of the fall of Thebes). But the first appears the less unlikely hypothesis. The coincidence of parts of the story with far earlier sources is by no means fatal to this. It is best merely to give what can be found of these verses and leave entirely the question as to when this curious narrative—compound of Egyptian and

[1] So with many other portions.
[2] For another epic poem on this subject introduced into a history see *P. Oxy.* 1798.

# ANON. AP. PSEUDO-CALLISTHENEM

Aethiopian fable, anecdote, forged letters and choliambic verse, with some traces of sound historians as sources—finally took shape. The only certain test of a very late date does not apply to our author, who uses words like the nominative Ἀλέξανδρος in which the accent does not fall on the penultimate.[1]

---

[1] As the verses have to be picked from various sources I use the following signs :—

i. The reading of Codex A is given without mark.

ii. Insertions from codd. dett. are given in round brackets ( ).

iii. Insertions or corrections whether conjectural or from the versions are marked ⟨ ⟩. When they are from the versions the source is given in the crit. app.

iv. Where I indicate omissions (. . .), I give the general sense in italics on the English side. Often one or two isolated traces of metre are omitted. Where no traces of metre occur I give a résumé in English in italics and round brackets.

# I

i. 42. 9 καὶ παραγίνεται εἰς Φρυγίαν καὶ εἰσελθὼν
εἰς αὐτὴν Ἴλιον τὴν πόλιν ἔθυσεν Ἕκτορι καὶ Ἀχιλλεῖ
καὶ τοῖς ἄλλοις ἥρωσιν. praecipue tamen Achillem
veneratur ac rogat uti sibi et ipse faveat et dona
quae ferret dignanter admittat ; haec enim a sese
non ut ab externo ac superstitioso verum ut con-
sanguineo ac religioso dedicari ;

> hinc primus exstat Aeacus Iovis proles,
> atque inde Peleus Phthiae regna possedit,
> quo tu subortus inclyta cluis proles.
> Pyrrhusque post id nobile adserit sanguem,
> quem subsecuta est Pie⟨l⟩i fama non dispar ;　5
> Pie⟨l⟩ique proles Eubius dehinc regnat.
> post Nessus ardens excipit domus nomen,
> Argusque post id, qui potens fuit Xanthi ;
> ex hoc Arete nobilis genus ducit.
> Areta natus Priami nomen accepit,　　　　10
> Tryinus unde et Eurymachus post illum,
> ex quo Lycus fit dives et dehinc Castor.
> Castore natus est Dromon qui dat Phocum ;
> atque hinc suborta est Metrias, quae suscepit
> Neoptolemei nominis vicem dignam,　　　　15
> cui substitutus Charopus.　hic Molossorum

5. Pieri *codd.*: *corr. Mai.*

506

# I

i. 42. 9 [1] Alexander arrived in Phrygia and entered
the city of Ilium itself and sacrificed to Hector and
Achilles and the other heroes. Most of all he
honoured Achilles and asked him to favour him and
deign to accept the gifts he bore. These he dedicated
not as a superstitious stranger, but as a relative and
a religious man.

> Aeacus son of Jove your race founded,
> Next Peleus held the Phthian dominion,
> Whose world-famed progeny you are called.
> Next Pyrrhus vindicates thy blood nobly,
> And Pielus of equal fame follows.                    5
> Thereafter Eubius, Pielus' son, reigns.
> Next glorious Nessus name of thy house bore ;
> Thereafter Argus, master of Xanthus,
> From whom Arete noble her race drew.
> Priamus was the son of Arete,                        10
> Tryinus and Eurymachus next came ;
> Whence wealthy Lycus and anon Castor.
> Dromon was Castor's son and bore Phocus ;
> Hence Metrias was born, and her son bore
> The name Neoptolemeian with full worth ;            15
> Charopus, his successor, the kingdom

---

[1] All our Greek MSS. omit this poem.

FRAGMENTA CHOLIAMBICA

```
regni potitus auctor extitit stirpis
nostrae ‹
              › eritque viscus inclytum matris.
e qua subortus vestro sanguini adnector,            20
quaesoque nomen adseras tuum nobis,
bellisque praestes gloriasque subtexus
velut feracis seminis ‹     › fructum,
quod cuncta late spatia terrae pervadat ;
unaque metis nostra fac Phaethonteis                25
regna explicari mundus adserat cunctus.
```

## II

### (ii. 46. 11)

χεὶρ δὲ Μακεδονικὴ οὐκ ἔκαμε τὸν
    πολυσφαγῆ σίδηρον αἱματώσασα.    1

.   .   .   .   .   .   .

### (46a. 3)

Ἰσμηνίας Θηβαῖος, τῆς αὐλομελῳδίας ἔμπειρος
ἄνθρωπος, . . . . . . τὴν χεῖρα προτείνας
    ἄρχεται λέγειν οὕτως·    2

(Βασιλεῦ μέγιστε, φεῖσαι ἡμῶν εὐτελῶν· μὴ τοιού-

508

Molossian gat, and of our race founder
Became . . .[1]
        will be his mother's famed offspring.
Whose son I, with your race thus connected, 20
Beg that your name by us be asserted,
Given to wars and crowned with glories :
For fruit are we of a seed right fertile,
A seed to range over the whole wide earth.
Grant the whole world declare that our realm be 25
By Phaethontean goals alone bounded.[2]

(*Alexander wins over the cities on the Black Sea, and
enters Greece. The first resistance comes from Thebes.*)

[1] Here should follow the names of Alcetas and Neoptolemus (Kuhlmann).
[2] As we should say, ' the sun should never set on it.'

## II

(*The Thebans close their gates but Alexander forces
an entrance.*)

The hand of Macedon tired not
    Dipping in gore its sword all blood-spattered. 1

  .      .      .      .      .      .

(A certain Ismenias of Thebes, a flute-player,
stretched forth his hand and with many tears)

      did thus begin speaking :— 2

Spare, Alexander of all kings greatest,[1] our sorry

[1] *v.* 1 was *e.g.* φεῖσαι μέγιστε βασιλέων Ἀλέξανδρε. Where
we can see a basic verse I drop into verses in the translation.

# FRAGMENTA CHOLIAMBĬCA

τῳ κινδύνῳ τὴν πόλιν ἡμῶν εἰς τέλος ἀφανίσῃς)·
Ἀλέξανδρε, νῦν πείρᾳ μαθόντες τὸ σὸν (ἰσόθεον)
κράτος σεβόμεθα[a]· ἐπίσχες τὰς ἀνικήτους χεῖρας
ἀπὸ Θηβαίων ⟨ἀγνοίᾳ μήπως ἀσεβεῖν δόξεις
τὰ συγγενῆ σου. Ἡράκλεος, Διόνυσος, οὗτοι
θεοὶ Θηβαῖοι⟩,[b] ἐπιδοξότατοι θεοὶ καὶ προγονικῆς
μίξεως ἀρχέγονον βλάστημα. Διός τε καὶ Σεμέλης
πυριλοχευτὸς Διόνυσος ἐν Θήβαις ⟨ἐτέχθη⟩[b].
Ἡρακλῆς ⟨παρὰ⟩[b] Διός τε καὶ Ἀλκμήνης
⟨ἐσπάρη⟩[c]· οὗτοι[d] πᾶσιν ἀνθρώποις ⟨βοηθοὶ καὶ
εἰρηνικοὶ⟩[e] σωτηρίας φύλακες ἐφάνησαν

                    σοῦ δὲ τυγχάνουσ'[ιν] Ἀλέξανδρε    3
        προπάτορες ὄντες.                               4

τούτ⟨ους⟩[f] σε χρὴ μιμήσασθαι καὶ εὐεργετεῖν,
ὥσπερ ἐκ θεῶν γενόμενος. μὴ ὑπερίδῃς τὰς
Διονύσου καὶ Ἡρακλέους τροφοὺς Θήβας ἀπολ-
λυμένας μηδὲ τὸ βοόκτιστον ἄστυ κατασκάψῃς·
ὄνειδος γὰρ ὕστερον Μακεδόσι γενήσεται.

                    ἀγνοεῖς Ἀλέξανδρε                   5
        ⟨       ⟩ Θηβαῖον [καὶ] οὐχὶ Πελλαῖον·          6

⟨ὅλη⟩[g] σε Θηβαίων χώρα λιτανεύει

⟨θρηνοῦσα⟩, τοὺς σοὺς προπάτορας κομίζουσα        7
θεούς, Λυαῖον                                        8

εὐφροσύνης καὶ χορείης θιασώτ⟨ην⟩,[h] Ἡρακλέα

δίκαιον ἔργοις καὶ βοηθὸν ἀνθρώποις.                 9

---

[a] from σεβόμεθα we have only the versions as a check on
the readings of cod. A.    [b] Byz.    [c] Byz.: κατέσπειραν A.
[d] οὕτω A.    [e] Arm. (Byz.)    [f] Byz.: τούτῳ A.    6. *e.g.*

persons.  Do not in such a disaster destroy our city
completely.

> Taught by experience your divine puissance [1]
> We worship thee : keep off from us Thebans
> Your hands unconquered,

lest you appear in ignorance to wrong your kin.
Heracles and Dionysus are the gods of Thebes,
most glorious gods and ancestral offspring of earliest
union between Zeus and Semele.  Dionysus,[2] with
fire for his midwife, was gotten in Thebes.  In Thebes
was born Heracles, offspring of Zeus and Alcmene.
These appeared to all the world preservers, as helpers
and peaceful guardians of safety.  (3, 4) And they
are your ancestors, Alexander.  As you are born of
gods, you should imitate these and do good.  Do not
allow the continuance of the destruction of Thebes
which nursed Dionysus and Heracles, nor raze the
ox-founded city.  For hereafter it will be a reproach
to the Macedonians.  (5, 6) Do you not know,
Alexander, that you are a Theban and not a citizen
of Pella ?  The whole land of Thebes calls on you
wailing and entreats you through my mouth, (7, 8)
Thebes that displays your ancestral gods, Lyaeus,
god of delight and revel-leader of the dance, and
Heracles

> Righteous of deed and all mankind's helper.      9

---

[1] *e.g.* ἰσόθεον τὸ σὸν κάρτος.
[2] Dionysius Zagreus, distinguished thus by later writers
from D. the late-born.

---

ἔχων γένος      *g* πόλις A : ὅλη Byz. : *e.g.* ὅλη δὲ λιτανεύει σε
Θ. χ.      7. Byz. : διὰ τῆς ἐμῆς φωνῆς A.      Num νομίζουσα ?
8. Byz. : λῦσαι οὓς A.      *h* -as A.

# FRAGMENTA CHOLIAMBICA

ἤδη καὶ μιμητὴς τῶν προγόνων ⟨φαινόμενος⟩,[a]
καλῶν καὶ ἀγαθῶν ὄντων τὸ πλεῖον, εἰς εὐεργεσίαν

μετατρ⟨απεὶς ἐκ⟩ τῆς ὀργῆς,            10
[πρὸς][b] τὸ προχειρότατον ⟨πρὸ⟩[c] τοῦ κολάζειν
τὸ ἐλεεῖν ἔχε.

μὴ θῇς ἐρήμους            11
τούς σε σπείραντας θεούς,

τῶν σῶν γεν[ε]αρχῶν ⟨ἄστυ⟩ μὴ καθαιρήσῃς,
ἰδίαν πατρίδα σου μὴ ἀγνοῶν κατασκάψῃς.
ὁρᾷς τὰ τείχη ταῦτα; ⟨ταῦτα δέδμηνται⟩
Ζῆθός ⟨θ᾽⟩ ὁ ποιμὴν καὶ ὁ λυρῳδὸς Ἀμφίων, 15
οἱ Ζην[ων]ὸς υἱοί, ⟨τ⟩οὺς λάθρᾳ ἔτε⟨κ⟩εν νύμφη
ἡ Νύκτεως ⟨παῖς⟩ ἐν χοροῖς πλανηθεῖσα.
[τὰ] θεμέλια ταῦτα καὶ τὸ πλούσιον δῶμα
πύργωσε Κάδμος. ὧδε λαμβάνει νύμφη⟨ν⟩ 19
⟨τὴν⟩ Ἁρμονίαν ἣν ἔτεκεν ἀφρογενὴς Κύπρις
τῷ κλεψικοίτῃ Θρηκίῳ συνελθοῦσα.
τὴν σὴν ἄρουραν μὴ ἀκρίτως ἐρημώσῃς,
μη⟨δὲ⟩ καταφλέξῃς πάντα Θηβαίων τείχη.
⟨τῇ Λαβδακοῦ⟩ ᾽[ἔ]στι [α]δώμα⟨θ᾽⟩· ὧδε δυσ-
          δαίμων
⟨ὁ⟩ Λάϊο⟨ς⟩ ⟨γυναῖκα λαμβάνει⟩· τίκτει 25
⟨τὸν⟩ πατρο[ς]⟨φ⟩ό[γο]ντην ⟨Οἰδίπουν⟩ λυγρὰ
          μήτηρ.
τοῦ⟨θ᾽⟩ Ἡρακλ⟨ῆ⟩ος τέμενος ἦν, τὸ μὲν πρῶτον
Ἀμφιτρύωνος οἶκος· ⟨ὦ⟩δ᾽ ἐκοιμήθη
τρεῖς νύκτας ὁ Ζεὺς εἰς μί⟨η⟩ν ἀριθμήσας.

[a] ἂν φαίνῃ Byz.    10. Byz.: -τρέπε τὰ A.    [b] del. Kroll.
[c] Müller, Arm.    12. καθ. πόλιν A.    13. σου π. A.
14. δεδομημένα A.    A verse is lost 'with poems, lyre and
lute': Byz., Arm.    15. Kroll.    λοίδορος A; cf. Arm.
512

Do you too imitate your ancestors, persons of
general excellence ;

Turn your anger to benevolence,          10

prefer pity to over-hasty punishment.

Desolate not                        11

the gods that begat you,

The city of your ancestors raze not :     12
Nor thine own land in ignorance ruin.
Seest thou yon walls ? they are the walls builded
By shepherd Zethus, poet Amphion,     15
The sons of Zeus, whom at a feast erring
The child of Nycteus secretly brought forth.
And these foundations here, and the rich house
Were built by Cadmus, who to wife took once
Harmonia nymph, child of foam-born Cypris,  20
By union with ravishér Thracian.
Lay not thine own demesne thus unjudged waste
Nor burn down all the walls of us Thebans.
This is the house of Labdacus : here took
A wife the ill-starred Laius ; here bore     25
Oedipus patricide his poor mother.
Here shrine of Heracles : it was erstwhile
Amphitryon's house : here on a time Zeus slept
Three nights which he did turn to one only.

---

16. Müll., Arm.     ἔτεμεν A.    17. Arm.     χοροῖς Byz.,
Arm.: χρόνοις A.    18. Byz., Arm.: δόγμα A.    19. Kroll
ex Byz. προσεπύργωσε: πύργος καὶ A.    ὧδε Arm.    τὴν ν.
᾽Α. A: corr. Kroll.    21. κλεψοκύτει θρησκείῳ A : corr. Müll
22. ἀκρίτως μὴ A.    24. πλαγιου τε A.    ὅδε A.
25. πλαγίου τε A.    τίκτει: τί δὲ A, which gives one verse:
suppl. et corr. ex Byz., Arm.    26. -ψ- A.    27. Kroll.
-κλέος A.    28. Arm.: ᾽Αμφικτύονος A, Byz.    ὅδε A.
29. εἰς μίαν ἀθροίσας A : ἀριθμήσας Arm., Byz.

# FRAGMENTA CHOLIAMBICA

ὁρᾷς ἐκείνους τοὺς πεφλεγμένους οἴκους    30
ἀκμὴν ἔτ᾽ ἐκ‹στάζ›οντας οὐρανοῦ μῆν‹ι›ν;
ἐκ‹εῖ› κεραυνῶ τὴν ποθουμένην βάλλει
Σεμέλην ποθ᾽ ὁ Ζεύς· ‹ὧ›δε τοῦ πυρὸς μέσ‹σ›ον
τὸν Εἰραφιώτην ἀπεκύησε ‹Ληναῖον›.
‹ὧ›δ᾽ Ἡρακλῆς μέμηνεν· ἔνθεν οἰστρηθεὶς    35
Μεγάραν ἀνεῖλεν τὴν γυναῖκα τοξεύσας.
ὁ βωμὸς οὗτός ἐστιν ὃν βλέπεις Ἥρας,
‹ᾗ τις› λόφου τέτμηκε βῶλον ἀρχαῖον,

    .    .    .    .    .    .    .

ἔνθ᾽ Ἡρακλῆς κιθῶνι σάρκα δαρδάπτων    40
κατηθαλώθη, χερσὶ τῆς Φιλοκτήτου
‹δοὺς τόξα βαφθένθ᾽ αἵματι δρακοντείῳ›.
ταῦτ᾽ ἐστὶ Φοίβου λόγια, Τειρεσίου δῶμα·
ὁ τρισγέρων ‹ἐν τοῖσδε› γίνεται μάντις
ὃν εἰς γυναῖκα μετετύπωσ‹ε› Τριτων‹ίς›.    45
Ἀθάμα‹ς› μανεὶς ἐνταῦθα παῖδα Λε‹ί›αρχον
τόξοις ἀνεῖλεν εἰς νε‹β›ρὸν τυπωθέντα·
ἐνθένδε ‹δ᾽› Ἰνὼ ᾽‹φ›ήλατ᾽ εἰς βυθοῦ κῦμα
σὺν τῷ Μελικέρτῃ τῷ νεογνῷ λυσσώδης.
ἐνθένδε πηρὸς Οἰδίπους ἀπηλάσθη    50
ταγ‹αῖ›ς Κρέοντος· οὗ τὸ βάκτρον Ἰσμήνην
‹ἔπεφνε Τυδεύς· ἧς ἐπώνυμος κρήνη›

---

31. Byz.: -ταξ- A.    -ην A: μῆνιν Arm., Byz.    32. ἐκεῖ
Arm.: ἐκ A.    κεραυνῷ Kroll: -νοῦ A.    33. ὅδε A.    μ. τ. π.
A.    34. ἠρα- A, Byz.    Ληναῖον Byz., Arm.: λινεόχην A.
35. ὅδε A.    38. ᾗ τις inserui: conf. HPHC et HITIC.
λ. τ. β. Byz. fere: ὑψηλὰ κέκμηκεν βῶμον ἀρχαῖον A.    A verse
is missing, e.g. βάθροισιν ὑψηλοῖσι χωρὶς ἱδρύσας; cf. Arm.
40. κιθῶνα A.    δαρδάπτειν A: corr. Maas.    41. καθηλώθη
A: corr. Maas.    42. supplevi e.g. ex Arm.    43. ταύταις τῇ A: corr. Müller.    44. ἐν οἷς Byz.    45. -α -α
A: corr. Müller.    47. Arm.: νεῦρον A.    48. ἐκεῖνο
A: δ᾽ Müll. (Arm.).    49. λυσσότην A: corr. Müll.
514

Beholdest over there those burnt houses,    30
That even now do heaven's wrath ooze out ?
[1] There Semele belovéd did Zeus once
With levin smite ; and in the fire's own midst
Th' Eiraphiot Lenaean from thigh brought forth.
Here was to madness Heracles goaded    35
And Megara his wife slew with arrow.
This altar that thou see'st is of Hera,
Where the hill's ancient sod is by man cut
With lofty steps apart : Heracles here,
In anguish of the shirt his flesh burning,    40
Was burnt on pyre : unto Philoctetes
His arrows steeped in dragon's blood leaving.
See here is Phoebus' pulpit ; three ages
Teiresias living in this house outlived ;
Tritonis changed to woman his manhood.    45
Here Athamas went mad and Leiarchus
His child did shoot with bow a deer deeming.
Hence Ino leapt into the sea's depths down
With Melicertes her young child frenzied.
Hence Oedipus was driven, at Creon's    50
Behest, all lame : his staff, his Ismene,[2]
⟨Did Tydeus slay : from whom this spring gat
    name⟩

[1] *vv.* 14 *sqq.* may be older. Not once is 'O Alexander'
—useful padding in this metre—introduced. The sack is
only mentioned in 22 and 23. The diction is not so late,
the style high-faluting instead of prosaic, the catalogue
straightforward, and the metre excellent. But it is very
poor stuff. *A Midsummer-Night's Dream* provides an easy
model for translation.

[2] Schol. Eur. *Phoen.* 53 Ἰσμήνη ἣν ἀναιρεῖ Τυδεὺς ἐπὶ κρήνης
καὶ ἡ κρήνη ἀπ' αὐτῆς Ἰσμήνη ἐκλήθη.

---

*l. τ. ν. τ.* M.    50. ἀπελάσθην A : corr. Müller.    51. ταγες,
οὔτω A.    52. supplevi ex schol. Eur. *Phoen.*

# FRAGMENTA CHOLIAMBICA

οὗτός ⟨θ'⟩ ὁ ποταμὸς ἐκ μέσου Κιθαιρῶν⟨ο⟩s
Ἰσμηνός ἐστι Βάκχιον φέρων ὕδωρ.
ἐλάτην ὁρᾷς κλάδοισιν ὑψόσ' ἀρθεῖσαν;                    55
ἐν τ⟨ῇ⟩δε Πενθεὺς[ιν] τοὺς χοροὺς κατοπτεύων
πρὸς τῆς τεκούσης δυστυχ⟨ῶ⟩s διεσπάσθη.
πηγὴν ὁρᾷς βρύουσαν αἱμόχρουν ὕδωρ,
ἐξ ἧς βοὸς μύκημα δεινὸν ἠχεῖται;
τοῦτ' ἐστὶν αἷμα τ⟨ῆς⟩ σεσυρμένης Δίρκης.             60
ὁρᾷς ἐκείνην ⟨ὑ⟩στάτην ἀκρώρειαν
τὴν ἐξέχουσαν τῆς ἀταρπιτοῦ ⟨τ⟩αύτης;
ἡ Σφὶγξ ἐπ' αὐτῆς ἔζεθ' ἡ τεραστ⟨ε⟩ία
πρόσταγμα προστάττουσα δημ⟨ό⟩ταις πᾶσιν
ἣν Οἰδίπους ἀνεῖλε πολλὰ μερμήρας.                      65
αὕτη θεῶν πηγή 'στι καὶ ἱερὰ κρήνη,
ἐξ ἧς ἀναβλύζουσ⟨ιν⟩ ἀργυραῖ νύμφαι.
εἰς ⟨ταῦ⟩τα λιβάδι' Ἄρτεμις κατελθοῦσα
φαίδρυν⟨ε⟩ χρῶτας· ὁ δὲ δύσαγνος Ἀκταίων
ἃ μὴ θέμις κατεῖδε λουτρὰ ⟨Λητ⟩ώας.                    70
⟨μετ⟩αλλαγεὶς ⟨δ'⟩ ἐς ἔλαφον ἀκλεῶς σῶμα
κυ⟨σ⟩ὶν ⟨ὠ⟩μοδ[ι]αίτοις διὰ τὸ λουτρὸν ἠγρεύθη.
⟨ὁρ⟩ᾷς ἵν' Ἄρης ἐπολέμησε τὰς Θήβας,
ἐνθὰ Πολυνείκης ἦρξεν Ἀργείου λ⟨ηοῦ⟩,                  74
στράπτων λοχαγὸς ⟨ἑπτὰ⟩ θ⟨ο⟩υρίων λόγχη⟨s⟩;
ἐνταῦθα Κα[μ]πανεὺς παρὰ τὸ χεῖλος ἐφλέχθη.
τὰς μὲν πύλας καλοῦσι ⟨ταύ⟩τας Ἠλέκτρας.

53. οὕτω ἀπότομος A : ποταμ. Kroll.        εἰς μέσον and -νως
A : corr. Müll.        54. -εον φέρον corr. id.        55. εἰς ὕψος
ἀρ. κλ. A.        56. τιδε A.        57. τῇ -σῃ and -χοις A : corr.
Müll.        58. τὴν Ἀγήνορος A : πηγὴν ὁρᾷς Müll. (Arm., Byz.)
ἔμοχθον A : αἱματόεν Arm. : αἷμα χρυσοῦ κτλ. Byz. : ita Kroll.
60. τι A.        61. Müll. : ὑ om. A.        62. σατάρπην· τοῦ
A : corr. Müller, Arm.        αὑτῆς A : ταύτης Sitzler.
63. εἰσφῆξ A : corr. Müll., Arm.        64. -ώταις A.

And eke Ismenus from mid Cithaeron
In his stream bearing Bacchian water.
Dost see that fir with branches aloft borne ?    55
Thence Pentheus Dionysus' rites witnessed
Whom did his mother tear apart sadly.
Dost see the fount whose waters are bloody
And echo up a dreadful bull's bellow ?
This is the blood of Dirce, by bull dragg'd.    60
Dost see that ridge upon the horizon
That juts from out the path of man trodden ?
Upon it sat the Sphinx, that great marvel,
And bade the townsfolk all do her bidding,
Till she was slain by Oedipus crafty.    65
This is the Gods' Well and the spring sacred
From which do silver nymphs gush out water.
Unto these pools did Artemis climb down
To wash her body ; impious Actaeon
Saw the Letoan's bath that none may see.    70
His form uncouthly to a stag's changéd,
Slain by his ravening hounds he paid dearly.[1]
See'st thou, when Ares fought 'gainst Thebes' city,
Where Polynices led the host Argive,
Gleaming of seven spear hosts commander ?    75
There Capaneus was burnt at wall's coping,
Where are the gates men call the Electrae.

---

[1] διὰ τὸ λουτρὸν can hardly be correct. A phrase like δι'
ἀσέβειαν, ' for his impiety,' is needed. I translate λυτρόν.

---

65. μερμήνας A : corr. Müll., Arm.    66. π. θ. ἐστί A :
corr. Müll.    67. -σα A.    69. Byz. : -αι A.    70. Arm. :
διστ· A.    71. ins. Kroll : -αγῆς A.    72. κυριν A : corr.
Müll.    ὁμοδι- A : corr. Sitzler ex Arm.    73. ἐν πᾶσιν
A : παῖδες Arm.    74. λεῶς A (Byz.).    75. Byz. :
ἔνθα A.    -ην A.    77. Kroll.    δε υλοκορας A : corr. Müll.,
Kroll.

# FRAGMENTA CHOLIAMBICA

πύλαις δὲ ταύταις Προίτισιν ⟨τὸν⟩ ἄρρηκτ⟨ον⟩
'Αμφιάραον χαί⟨ν⟩ουσα δέχ⟨νυται⟩ γαῖα.
'Ωγωγίαις πύλ⟨αι⟩σιν ἐν τρίταις κλήθρ⟨ῳ⟩ 80
⟨'Ιπ⟩πομέδοντα ⟨παῖς⟩ Μεγα[νευ]σθέν⟨ους⟩
κτείνει.
ἔπεσε ⟨δὲ⟩ Νηίσταισι παρὰ πύλαις ⟨ταύταις⟩
Παρθενοπαῖος· ὁ δ' 'Ομολωίσιν γαί⟨ων⟩
πύλαισ⟨ι⟩ ⟨Τυδεὺς⟩ μυρί⟨οι⟩σιν ἐ⟨β⟩λήθη. 84
⟨φεύγει δ' "Αδραστος· ἑβδόμαι πύλαι δ' αὗται⟩.

. . . . . . . . . . . .
θάν⟨ο⟩ντα [ἐ]θάψ⟨αι⟩ τὸν λ⟨οχ⟩αγὸν 'Αργείων
[ἡ] διώ⟨ρι⟩σ'[α] ἀγνὰ ⟨πα⟩ῖς ἔτ' εὐσα[ι] Καδ-
με⟨ί⟩α[ν],

. . . . . . . . . . . .
αὗται Λυ⟨αί⟩ου τοῦ φιλευίου Θῆβαι         90
αὐ⟨λ⟩αὶ πέφυκαν ἃς ἐπ⟨έκτ⟩ισ' Αἰσώπῳ,
⟨                    ⟩ Βακχίους ⟨          ⟩    91a
ἃς ⟨νῦν⟩ κελεύεις ἐκ βάθρων ἀναιρεῖσθαι.
ὁρᾷς σὺ σηκὸν 'Ηρακλέους πυρὸ⟨ς μεστόν⟩;
τοῦ σοῦ γεν[ε]άρχου καὶ πατρὸς φιλ⟨ανθρώ⟩που
τεμένη σεαυτὸ⟨ν⟩ ἀγνοῶν θέλεις φλέξαι.    95
τί τοὺς γον⟨ῆ⟩ας τοὺς τεκόντας ὑβρίζεις,
'Ηρακλέους γένος ⟨τε⟩ καὶ κλυτοῦ Βάκχου;
  'Ισμηνίας μὲν ἱκέτευσε τοσ⟨σ⟩αῦτα
πεσὼν παρὰ ποσὶ βασιλέως 'Αλεξάνδρου.

78. προστεθεῖσαις ἡμῖν: corr. Müller, Kroll.         -τες A:
corr. Müll.      79. Arm.: χαιρ- A.          Kroll: δεχοίοιτε
A.      80. -εσιν A.      -ρε A.      81. παῖς Arm.: τὸν A.
ειτ' A: ἀναιρεῖ Arm.      82. ἔπεσε Arm.: εἶπεν τὲ A.      δὲ
suppl. Sitzler.   Νηίσταισι Arm.: κεδίστεσιν A.      83. Arm.:
ὅτε ἦν μόλην A.      γαίης A: cf. θαρρῶν Arm.      84. Arm.
-εσιν A, ἐκλ. A, Arm.      85. supplevi e Byz., Arm.      86.
e.g. ἐνταῦθα πόλεως 'Αντιγονὴ παρὰ γνώμην.      87. -ψε A.

At these the Proetid gates the unshatter'd          78
Amphiaraus was by earth swallow'd.
At third Ogygian gates with the gate-bar [1]       80
Hippomedon Megasthenes' son felled.
Fourth at the Neistean gates perish'd
Parthenopaeus ; at th' Homolóïd
Slain Tydeus was, struck down by darts countless.
Adrastus fled : these are the gates seventh.        85
⟨Here notwithstanding the townsfolk's bidding,⟩
Antigone, unwedded maid Theban,
The leader of the Argive host buried,
⟨And with her love in living tomb perished⟩.
These Thebes upon Asopus are founded                90
Courts of Lyaeus that doth love ' Evoe,'
⟨That⟩ Bacchic ⟨revelry once supported⟩           91a
Which now to be uprooted thou biddest.
Dost see the shrine of Heracles song-famed ?
Homes of thine ancestor and sire, lover
Of all mankind, would'st burn ?   Thyself know'st
          not ?                                                     95
Why dost insult thy parents, thy fathers,
Scion of Heracles and famed Bacchus ?
     Ismenias did supplicate thuswise
Falling at feet of King Alexander.

[1] I translate κλήθρῳ and what the Armenian version
suggests, παῖς Μεγασθένους for slayer of Hippomedon.   But
I find no warrant for either guess.

-έντα and λαυ- A : corr. Müll.        88. λισετευσαι A.   From
this verse to end of speech we have only A.              89. see
translation.        90. Ἀνεου τοῦ φιλέα υἱὸς ὡς οὐ A : corr. Kroll.
91. αὗται A.          ἐσωπω A : corr. Müll.          92. σὺ A :
corr. Kroll.      93. πυρούμενον A.          94. σ ευγενεαρχου A.
Φιλίππου absurde A.      95. σεαυτοῦ τεμ. A.          96. -εας A.
97. Ἡρ. γεν. A : corr. Müll.        98. -τος αὐτὸς μὲν ἱκετεύσας
Ἰσμ. ἔπεσεν π. π. ᾽A. β.

# FRAGMENTA CHOLIAMBICA

ὁ δὲ Μακεδὼν πρὸς αὐτὸν ὄμμα <τρηχ>ύνας 100
καὶ τοὺς ὀδόντας τοῖς ὀδοῦσι συντρίζων
ὀργὴν ἀναπ<ν>έων τοῖον εἶπε τὸν μῦθον·
ὦ παγκάκιστ<ον> ἐκλόχευμα Καδμείων,
ὦ παγκάκιστον ζῷον, <ὦ> θεοῖς μῖσος,
ὦ δήμι<ο>ν βλάστημα βαρβάρου ῥίζης, 105
ὦ τῆς ἐπ᾽ Ἰσμήνῃ σ<ὺ> λείψανον λύπης,
<.                                                    .>,
σοφιστικούς μοι καὶ πεπλασμένους μύθους
εἰπὼν ὑπέλαβες ὅτι πλανᾷς Ἀλέξανδρον;
<ἢν> γὰρ προ[σ]πᾶσαν τὴν πόλιν καθαιρήσω, 110
καὶ πυρὶ τεφρώσω <                                   >,
καὶ πάντας ὑμᾶς μετὰ πάτρας κατασκάψω,
<πῶς> τῶν <γενεαρχῶν ἐξέκοψα τὴν ῥίζαν>;
εἰ γὰρ σὺ πᾶσαν τὴν σπορὰν <ἐ>γίνωσκε[ι]ς
[καὶ] πόθεν <π>έφυ<κ>α, καὶ τίνες λοχεύσαντες,
οὐκ ἦν σε Θηβαίοις<ι> ταῦτα κηρύ<σσ>ειν; 116
ὅτι ἐστὶν ἡμῖν συγγενὴς Ἀλέξανδρος,
μὴ πρὸς πολίτην [α]πο<λέμιοι> καταστῶμεν·
<θ>ῶμεν στρατηγ<ὸ>ν· σύμμαχοι γενηθῶμεν·
ἡμεῖς πολῖται, συγγενεῖς Ἀλεξάνδρου. 120
δόξ᾽ ἐστὶν ἡμῖν τῆς γεραι[ο]τάτης ῥίζης,
<ἢ>ν οἱ Μακεδόνες ἐπιπλακῶσι Θηβαίοις.
ὅτ<ε> δ᾽ εἰς ἄμυναν οὐδὲν †ἀτονησατε†
καὶ τὸ θράσος ὑμῶν τῆς μάχης κατῃσχύνθη,
τότε <δὴ> μεταβολὴ καὶ δέησις ἀγνώμων, 125

100. Kroll?: δ. π. αὐ. A.        μηκύνας A.        102. Byz. :
-πτεων A.        103. Arm., Byz. : -τε A.        104. καὶ A :
(or ἄνθρωπε καὶ θ. Arm. : τῶν κακίστων Byz.).        105. -ων
520

The latter gave at him a glance savage,      100
And gnashing upper teeth upon lower
Spake out as follows his irate answer :
Most evilly begotten of Thebans !
Most evil beast !` Of heaven's hate object !
Of root barbarian a growth common !      105
Last relic of the woe of Isméne !
⟨O dotard of blind mind and of blind eyes⟩ !   107
With barrister-like cunning of false tales
Didst thou expect to cheat Alexander ?     110
Suppose that I destroy the whole city
And burn to ashes ⟨all the walls Theban⟩
And raze you all to earth with your township,
How do I then root out my forefathers ?
If thou hadst known of my descent truly
Whence I was born and who they were gat me,  115
Should'st not have told the Thebans as follows ?—
' Since Alexander is our own kinsman,
Let us not go to war 'gainst our fellow :
Let 's make him general, be his allies :
Kin are we, fellow-citizens are we.      120
To us the honour of the branch eldest
If Macedonians join with us Thebans.'
Now when you 've shown no spirit in combat,
And all your boast of battle disgraced lies,
Now you revert to prayers and pleas idle,   125

A.      106. -νησι A.      107. Arm. : see transl.
110. ἐν A : recte Arm. (Byz.).   111. om. A, Arm., Byz. :
e.g. πάντα Θηβαίων τείχη.   113. τὴν A, Byz. cett.   Byz. :
γονέων A.    114. σύ μου γ. τ. σ. π. A.   115. -σα A.
? κἀκ τίνων -ων.   116. -ττ- A.   118. παραταχθῶμεν Byz. :
πο for ἀπο.   119. δῶμεν -ίαν A.   122. ἐὰν A.   123.
Arm. : ὅτι A.   ηὐτονήσατε Raabe ex Arm. : l. -άντων τὸ
θάρσ.   125. Müller.

⟨οἵ, μὴ δυνάμενοι νο⟩ῦν ἔχοντ⟨ες αἱρεῖσθαι   126
δόξῃ⟩ 'δύνασθε πρὸς μάχην 'Αλεξάνδρ⟨ου⟩.   126a
ἀλλ' οὐδὲ Θηβαίοι[ει]σιν οὐδέ σ⟨οι⟩ πρ⟨ῆξις⟩,
κάκιστα ⟨ἐφ' ὑμᾶς⟩ τοῦ τέλους ⟨ἐπ⟩ελθόντος
Θήβας ⟨μὲν⟩ αὐτ⟨ὰ⟩ς ⟨αὐτόθεν⟩ καταφλέξω.
[καὶ] 'Ισμηνίαν ⟨δ⟩ὲ τὸν κράτιστον αὐλητήν   130
τ⟨ῶ⟩ν ἡμιφλέκτ⟨ω⟩ν δωμάτων ἐφεστῶτα
οὕτω [σε] κελεύω δίδυμ⟨ο⟩ν ὀργάνων ἦχος
βοιωτιά⟨ζει⟩ν ⟨τήν θ'⟩ ἅλωσιν αὐλῆσαι.
⟨οὕτω⟩[ς εἰπὼν ἐ]'κέλευσε τοῖς στράτοις κατα-
        σκάπτειν
ἑπτάπυλα τείχη καὶ πόλισμα Θηβαίων.   135
πάλιν ⟨Κιθ⟩αιρὼν ἐπεχόρευε Θηβαίοις·
'Ισμην[ι]ος αὐτὸς αἱμόφυρτος ⟨ἔρ⟩ρευσ⟨ε·
βέβλητο τείχη καὶ πόλισμα Θηβαίων.
καὶ πᾶσα γαῖα ταῖς σφαγαῖς κοπωθεῖσα,   139
κατα⟨ρ⟩ριφέντων δωμάτων πολυκ⟨λ⟩αύστων,
βαρὺ σ⟨τ⟩ένουσ⟨α τ',⟩ ἀπ' ἐ⟨δαφ⟩ῶν ἐμυκᾶτο·
'Ισμηνίας δὲ δίδυμον ὀργάνων ἦχος
ἦν ἁρμοσάμενος, τ⟨ῶ⟩ν ⟨ἐ⟩ρειπί⟨ω⟩ν ἑστώς
⟨ἧ⟩περ ἐκέλευσεν ὁ Μακεδὼν 'Αλέξανδρος.
ἐπεὶ δὲ τείχη πάντ' ἔπιπτ⟨ε⟩ Καδμείων   145
καὶ μέλαθρα ⟨τὰ⟩ Λύκου καὶ τὸ ⟨Λα⟩βδάκου
        δῶμα,
εἰς εὐσέβειαν τῆς πάροιθε παιδείας
τὴν Πινδάρου ⟨'τήρησεν οἶ⟩κ⟨ί⟩αν ⟨μούνην⟩,

126, 126 a. iniuria desperat Kroll: ita Arm., nisi quod
σωφρονοῦντες et ἠβούλεσθε τὴν δόξαν vertit Raabe: μὴ δυνα-
μένη συνεχόντων ἀναιρῆσαι ὅτι οὐ δύνασθε πρ. μ. 'Αλεξάνδρῳ
A.      127. Arm.: σὺ A.      πρωτο A: συμφέρει
Arm.      128. Byz.: sive ὑμῖν κάκ.      αὐθέντος A: ἐλθ.
Byz.: ἐπιφανέντος Arm.      129. δὲ A: μὲν Byz., Arm.: ὃς
A.          Kroll e Byz. (ἐκ ριζῶν): Arm. ἐν ταύτῃ τῇ ὥρᾳ.

Who, since before you could not choose rightly, 126
Imagined you could fight Alexander.                126a
But neither do the Thebans, nor dost thou
Avail : and now the evil end cometh,
When I will burn the town of Thebes wholesale.
And bid Ismenias, 'best flute-player,'             130
Standing upon the half-consumed houses,
The double harmony of pipes ⟨pouring⟩
Boeotian-wise [1] to play the town's sacking.
Thus did he bid his hosts to earth raze down
The seven-gated walls and fort Theban.             135
Once more Cithaeron raved and Ismenus
With stream of blood did rush on Thebes' city.
Fallen the walls and fort of the Thebans.
And all the earth was by the spade harassed,
As were cast down the houses much wept for,        140
And bellowed from its very foundations.
Ismenias stood there on the ruins,
The harmony of his twin pipes fitting,
Where he was bidden by Alexander.
But as fell all the walls of the Thebans,          145
And Lycus' halls and Labdacus' mansion,
In pious mem'ry of his young training
The house of Pindar did he spare only,

[1] The Boeotian νόμος here alluded to was symbolical of
an unhappy ending.

---

130. σε A.        Arm., Byz. : κάκιστον A.        131. Arm. :
τὴν -ιν A.      132. Byz. : -ων A, Arm.        133. δύο τι ἀναλ.
A : recte Arm., Byz. : sive Βοιώτιον χεῖν.        134. Byz. :
αὐτὸν A.      136. Arm., Byz. : ἐκεῖ χαίρων A.        137. Byz. :
Ἰσμηνίας Arm., ·νιος A.        ρεύσας A.        140. cf. Arm.
141. Arm. : γένους A.        ἀπελθών A.        142. τῆς μηνίας
A : corr. Müll.        143. τὸν ἠρίπιον corr. Müll.        144. ὅπερ A :
ὡς Arm        145. ·ον corr. Müll.        146. Λαβ. Arm.
148. codd. dett. i. 27 (Arm. ἐπῆρεν).        codd. dett. ibid.
μόνην : A κατανα τύμβον, Arm. πύργον : fort. οἰκίας πύργον

ἐν‹θ᾽› ἦλθε παῖς ὢν καὶ μετέσχε ταῖς Μούσαις
πρὸς τὸν λυρ‹ῳ›δὸν τὸν γέροντα φοιτήσας. 150
πολλοὺς μὲν ἄνδρας περὶ πάτραν κατασφάξας
ὀλίγους κατέλιπε παντελῶς ἔτι ζῶντας,
καὶ τοὔνο‹μ›᾽ αὐτῶν τοῦ γένους ἀπήλειψεν.
Θήβας γὰρ εἶπε μή‹τιν᾽› ἔτι ‹κ›αλεῖν Θήβας
ἀλλ᾽ ἄπολιν αὐτῶν τὴν πόλιν γεν[ν]ηθῆναι, 155
ὡς ‹οὐ›νομ‹η›ναι τὸν τοιοῦτον ἄνθρωπον.

(ii. 14. 5.)

ἔξω‹θεν› ἐπὶ λόφου (γὰρ) ἦν ὁ Δαρεῖος
(τάφρους) ὀρύσσων καὶ φάλαγγα[s] συντάσσων
[ὡς] δέ‹ει› [τῶν] Μακεδόνων ‹οὐ μενοῦσαν›
ὑσμίνην.
ὁ δὲ ‹τότ᾽› ἀθρήσας τὸ πολὺ θαῦμα Δαρείου 160
παρ᾽ ὀλίγον αὐτὸν προσεκύνησεν ὡς Μίθραν
θεὸν νομίζων οὐρανοῦ κατελθόντα
τοῖς βαρβάροις πέπλοισιν ἐγκοσμηθέντα.
ἦν γὰρ ‹καθάριον› τῶν τύπων τὸ πρόσχημα·
‹ἀνὴρ μεσῆλιξ›· ‹καὶ› λίθοι πολύτιμοι† 165

149. ἔνθ᾽: ἐν ᾧ A.    παῖς ὢν Arm.: πεσὼν A.    150. -οδὸν
A.    153. Arm.: τοῦ νοῦ A.    154. μηκέτι λαλεῖν A:
recte Arm. καλεῖν.    156. ὡς ἔννομον εἶται A: ἄνομον Arm.
Fuit δs ἂν ὀνομήνῃ vel εἴ τις . . . -ῆναι.    157. Byz.: order
varies in A, B, C: γὰρ C.    158. Byz.: τάφους cod.
Barocc. 20: στράτους cett.    ὑποτάσσων A.    159.
ὡς δὲ ὁ A.    συνεισμηνιοδῷ (i.e. φόβῳ) A: recto propius
Byz.: καὶ φόβῳ συστελλόμενος πολλῷ τῶν M.    160. Arm.
161. θεόν Μίθραν A: Μιθρ. om. cett.  Hic demum usque ad
σῶμα Δαρείου choliambos agnovit Kroll.    163. στολαῖς

Where as a boy he went to learn music—
His master the old lyrical poet.[1]    150
Many he slew around their own city,
And very few indeed he left living,
The very name of all their race rubbed out.
He bade that Thebes should be on no man's lips,
And that their city should be no city,    155
When anyone should speak of such fellows.

(Here the traces of choliambi cease for the time till ii. 13,
when Alexander is in Persia. But, as the last verse shows,
the story of the refounding of Thebes, and much else, was
in this metre once.)

(ii. 13-14. 5 *Alexander sees a vision of Ammon in
guise of Hermes with wand and cloak (and staff) and
Macedonian felt hat and is told to proceed in this disguise
as his own herald. He crosses the frozen Strangas and
tells the outposts of his errand. They take him to
Darius.*)

Apart upon a hill sat Darius    157
Deep ditches digging, and his hosts training
That feared the Macedonian combat.
When he saw Darius, that wonder,    160
He very nearly worshipped him ; Mithras
He thought to see from heaven descended,
Adornéd with barbarian raiment ;
For holy was the monarch's appearance.
He was of middle age. With stones precious    165

[1] Comment is perhaps superfluous.

---

cett.    **164.** Arm. : κατ᾽ αὐτόν **A.**    **165.** Byz. : A
and Arm. paraphrase: ad fin. ἐκ λίθων πολυτίμων dett.

# FRAGMENTA CHOLIAMBICA

διαδήματος [τὸ] κάρηνον ἔσκεπ ⟨ο⟩ν σφιγχθέν[τος]·
πέπλῳ δ' ἐχρῆτο ⟨ὁπ⟩οῖον ἄλλον οὐκ εἶδ⟨ε⟩ν·
Βαβυλωνί⟨ω⟩ν (ὕφασμα) χρυσί⟨ω⟩ν νῆμα
σειραὶ δὲ χρυσ[ει]αῖ καὶ πέδιλα [χρυσέων]
    φοινικ⟨ᾶ⟩,                                    169
⟨σκέποντα⟩ δε⟨ιρ⟩ὴν καὶ δυοῖν ποδοῖν κνήμα[ι].

(χρύσεα δὲ λυχνίδια ἐπάνωθεν αὐτοῦ ἥπτοντο·
ἕτερα δὲ περὶ τοῖς πόσιν αὐτοῦ καὶ κύκλῳ περι-
έστραπτον λυχνία.)

λοχαγέται ⟨δὲ⟩ μυρίοι⟨σι⟩ κηρύκων          171
(σκήπτροισιν) ἑκατέρωθε[ν] μυρίων φωτῶν
κυκληδὸν ἐστέψαντο σῶμα Δαρείου.


σοὶ μηνύω 'γών, (ὡς) παρὼν 'Αλέξανδρος,     174
βασιλεὺς βραδύνων εἰς μάχην ⟨κατέρχεσθαι⟩ 175
ἤδη πρόδηλός ἐστιν ἀσθενῆ ψυχήν
⟨κεκτημένος καὶ δειλός⟩· ὥστε μὴ μέλλε,
⟨πότε δὲ συνάπτεις τὸν πόλεμον⟩, (ἀνάγ-
    γειλον).                                     178


οὐ μὴ [με] ταράξῃς ⟨. . .⟩· ἀλλ' ἐπεὶ δεῖπνον
[τὸ] συνηθὲς [τοῖς] ἀγγέλοισ⟨ι⟩ δεῖ τελειοῦ-
    σθαι,                                        180
καὶ γὰρ αὐτὸς 'Αλέξανδρος (δεῖπνον ἐποίησε τοῖς
ἐμοῖς γραμματοφόροις, συνδείπνησόν μοι. καὶ)

χειρὸς (κρατήσας) δεξιᾶς ('Αλέξανδρον)       181

---

166. A δ. σ. τὸ κ. ἔσκεπεν : φορῶν cett.     167. A (ο)ῖον οὖν οὐκ
εἶδον ἄ.     168. A -ιον (bis) et εὔφασιν.     169. -κων A :
codd. dett. give the colours *vice versa*.     170. σκῆπτρον A.
171. ἀλλ' οἱ λ. A.     172. ἔθνεα ταῖς A : σκῆπτρα (and στίφη)
cett.     174. ἐγώ σοι μηνύω omnes : ὡς om. A.     175.

A diadem his head around girded.
A robe he wore,—the other had ne'er seen
Its like, of Babylonian gold lace :
Necklets of gold he wore and shoes crimson
Cov'ring his neck and calves of his two legs.    170

Golden lamps were alight above him, and larger
lamps shone at his feet and around him.

While generals with countless heraldic          171
Sceptres arrayed on this and on that side
Circled around the form of Dareius.

(*Alexander is brought to Darius and delivers his message* :—)

I tell thee, as I were[1] Alexander,             174
A king who is sloth to enter the combat,         175
At once is shown to have a weak spirit
And cowardliness of heart.  Without halting
Announce to me when combat may open.             178

(*Darius, after commenting on A.'s boldness, says* :—)

Thou shalt not trouble me.  But, since dinner    179
Must be prepared as usual for heralds,           180

for so did Alexander himself give dinner to my envoys,
dine with me.   So

He took the right hand of Alexander              181

---

[1] ὥσπερ ὤν.

---

ὀφείλεις εἰδέναι βασιλεῦ Δαρεῖε ὅτι βρ. ε. μ. β. πρ. ἐ. τῷ ἀντιδίκῳ :
τῷ ἀντιδ. om. Byz. recte.          176. ἀσθενῆ ἔχων τὴν A.
177. κεκτημένος Byz. : καὶ ἄνανδρον Arm.: δειλ- and μαλθακ-
Byz.          178. init. Byz. (exc. δέ): codd. dett. ἀλλὰ ἀνάγ-
γειλόν μοι πότε βούλῃ σύναψαι . . .          180. τὸ σ. δ. τοῖς ἀγ. A :
sim. Byz.          181. τῆς δ. χ. A.

# FRAGMENTA CHOLIAMBICA

[εἰσ]ήνεγκεν αὐτὸν ‹τῶν ἀνακτόρων εἴσω›
ὁ δ᾽[ε ᾽Αλέξανδρος] (ἀγαθὸν) ἔσχ᾽ ἐν καρδίᾳ τὸ
   σημεῖον
ἤδη κρατήσ‹ειν› τῶν τυραννικῶν ‹ἑδρῶν›.
ὁ δὲ ‹οὖν› ἐ[ι]σελθὼν εἰς τὰ μέλαθρα Δαρείου
καὶ †ἐπὶ† τὸ[ν] δεῖπνον εὐθέως ἐκηρύχθη.  186
πρῶτος δ᾽ ἄνω κλιντῆρος ἦν ὁ Δαρεῖο‹ς›,

δεύτερος δὲ ἀδελφὸς ἦν ᾽Οξυάθρης ‹ὁ› Δαρείου,

τρίτος δὲ ‹Δίοχος› σατράπης ᾽Οξυδράκ‹ων›,  188

εἶτα πάλιν ‹᾽Α›δου‹λ›ίτης[a] ὁ ἐπὶ Σούσης,[b] καὶ
Φραόρτης[c] ‹. . .›

μετ᾽ αὐτὸν ‹ἐκλίθη δὲ› Μιθριδάτης ἕκτος  189
καὶ Τιριδάτης τοξοτῶν ‹ὃς ἦν› πρῶτος,   190

ἔτι τε Κανδαύλης ὁ νυκτίχρωος †Μένωπος†,[a] εἶτ᾽
ἀνέκειτο Αἰθιόπων ἄναξ,

καὶ Πολυάρης ἔγγιστ‹ος› ἡγέμων    191
μέγας,[e] ᾽Ορνιράτης, Διόσιος, Καρδερωκέτης, Σουλ-
βάτης, ᾽Αλκίδης,

          τοῖσ‹ι› δ᾽ ἀντίκρυς    192
ἀνέκειτο μο‹ῦ›νος αὐτὸς ἐπὶ μιᾶς κλίνης
ὁ πάντ᾽ ἄριστος ὁ Μακεδὼν ‹᾽Αλέξανδρος›.  194

ch. 15   .    .    .    .    .    .
      .    .    .    .    .    .
      .    .    .    .    .    .

---

182. Byz. (except for ἔσω): ἔνδον τῶν βασιλείων A.   183.
better ‹ἐνὴν δὲ› (καλὸν).   184. -ήσης A.   τόπων Byz.: δε-
σποτῶν absurde Arm.: τὸν τύραννον νικῶν A.   185. οὖν inserui.
186. e.g. πρὸς (πρῶτος codd. dett.).   187. Arm., Byz.: -ου
528

And led him by it into his palace ;
The other treasured up the fair omen,
That he would take the tyrant's throne right soon.
So to Darius' halls did he enter            185
And even unto dinner was summoned.
Now first on couch aloft lay Darius,        187

second came Oxyathres brother of Darius,

Third Diochus the Oxydrak's satrap,         188

then next Adoulites warder of Susa, and Phraortes
‹    .›,

And Mithridates next to him lay sixth        189
And Tiridates chief of the archers,          190

and Menops' son the dusky Candaules, then the king
of the Ethiopians ‹. . .›,

And Polyares nearest great general,          191

Ornirates, Diosius, Carderocetes, Sulbates, Alcides.

                              over          192
Against them lay alone on one divan
Hero of Macedon Alexander.                   194

(*The Persians marvelled at his small size, not knowing
that a drop of heavenly soul resides in a small vessel.
Now the cupbearers plied the cup freely.*)

---

A.        188. Byz.: δὲ ὦχος A.          Kroll : -ησαν A.
*a* δουρίτης A : -λίτης Byz.: Ἀνδ- Arm.     *b* Arm.: ἐκ πισσ- A.
*c* Here and elsewhere the forms differ in our three aut orities
between whom I choose : all miss the description of Ph.
189. συνανεκλ. post ἔκτος A.      190. τόξων τῶν A.      *d* Perhaps ὁ νυκτίχρωος παῖς Μέροπος ὁ Κανδαύλης.          191. ἔγ-
γιστα A.      *e e.g.* δεινός.      193. αὐ. μ. ἀν. A.      194.
Ἀλ. Byz.

# FRAGMENTA CHOLIAMBICA

μεσάσαντος δὲ τοῦ πότου ἐπινοεῖ τι ὁ Ἀλέξανδρος·
  (ὅσους σκύφους ⟨γὰρ⟩ ἔλαβ᾽) ἔσωθεν ἔκρυ⟨π-
  τ⟩εν·                                                                       195

οἱ δὲ [πινεγχύται] βλέποντες ἐνεφάνιζον Δαρείῳ.
ὁ δὲ Δαρεῖος ἐκ τοῦ κλιντῆρος ἀναστὰς εἶπεν· ὦ
γενναῖε

                    πρὸς τί ταῦτ᾽ ἐγκολπίζ[ῃ];          197

(νοήσας δὲ ὁ Ἀλέξανδρος ἀπὸ τοῦ σχήματος τῆς
ψυχῆς ⟨τὴν μωρίαν⟩[a] εἶπε· μέγιστε βασιλεῦ,

οὕτω ⟨γὰρ⟩ (ὁ ἐμὸς δεσπότης Ἀλέξανδρος          198
ὅταν δεῖπνον ποιῇ τοῖς ταξιάρχαις καὶ ὑπερ-
ασπισταῖς)

  τὰ κύπελλ᾽ ⟨ἐν οἷσιν ἂν πίωσι⟩ δωρεῖται       199
  ⟨αὐτοῖσιν⟩· (ὑπενόουν δὲ καί σε τοιοῦτον,       200
καὶ) ὡς παρὰ τῷ ἐμῷ βασιλεῖ ἐνεκολπισάμην . . .

  πρὸς ταῦτα [. . .]ὁρῶντες ⟨τῶν λόγων Ἀλεξ-
                    άνδρου⟩                                          201
  (τὴν πιθανότητα) ⟨πάντες ἦσαν ἔκθαμβοι⟩·
  πλαστὸς (γὰρ) ἀεὶ μῦθος ⟨ἢ⟩ν (ἔ)χῃ πίστιν
  (εἰς ἔκστασιν) πεποίηκε τοὺς ἀκούοντας.
  [. . .] σιγῆς γενομένης ⟨οὖν τις⟩ ἀνεπόλησ[εν]
                    αὐτόν                                            205
  ὄνομα[τι] (Πασάργης), [. . .] ἡγεμὼν γῆς Περ-
  σίδος·

195. ἔκρυβε A.    [a] Arm.    199. ενσιπηνοις A (*i.e.* ἐν ⟨οἷ⟩σι
πίνουσ⟨ι⟩).    200. Arm., Byz.    201. [οἱ Πέρσαι ἀφ] delen-
dum.    fin. Byz., Arm.    202. πιθανότητι (misplaced)
codd. dett.: τῇ π. Arm., Byz.    Byz. (ἄπ-).    203. ἐὰν codd.
σχῇ A.    204. Better ἐξιστάναι πέφυκε.    205. [    ]: πολλῆς

And when the drinking was well started Alexander devised a ruse.

As the cups came to him, in his bosom          195
He hid them : which was shown to Darius.          196

Darius leaping up from his couch said, ' Good sir,

Why put these in your bosom ?          197

Alexander, diagnosing from his appearance the folly of his soul, said, ' O most mighty King,

My master even so, Alexander,[1]          198

if he gives a feast to his own spearmen and colonels

Gives them the cups whereof they have drunken [2] ;
And I supposed you had the same custom,          200

and put them in my bosom as I would at my king's table. (*But if you have not this custom, take them back.*)

Wherefore they when they saw the persuasion          201
Of Alexander's words were astonished.
For ever lying tale if it wins faith
Drives to bewilderment all its hearers.
Silence ensuing, one, the embassy's          205
Chief leader, called Pasarges, remarked him.

---

[1] Om. 'Aλέξ. et lege ὅτ. δ. τ. τ. καὶ ὑ. ποιῇ.
[2] Professor Kroll adds to our difficulties by reading ἐκείνοις for ἐνσιπήνοις. What A copied badly was ἐν οἶσι πίνουσι and the original perhaps κύπελλ' ἐν οἶσιν ἂν πίωσι. See also crit. n.

---

οὖν codd.: ἧς A.          206. A : ὀνόματι ἀσάργης : παράγης C.
[   ]: ὃς ἦν γενόμενος.   Notandum Περσίδος. ἢ τῆς πρεσβείας.

# FRAGMENTA CHOLIAMBICA

ᾔδει γὰρ αὐτὸν κατὰ πρόσωπον, εἰς Πέλλην
ἡνίκα τὸ πρῶτον ἦλθε[ν ὑπὸ] Δαρεί‹ῳ› πεμφθεὶς
Μακεδονίας ‹γ›ῆς (τοὺς) φόρους ἀπαιτῆσαι.
(ἔστη δ᾽ ἐπιστὰς ἀντίκρυς Ἀλεξάνδρου)·      210
καὶ πρὸς ἑαυτὸν ἔλεγεν,

οὐκ ἔστιν οὗτος ὃν λέγουσ᾽[ιν] Ἀλέξανδρον;   211
ἔστιν ‹γε›· δεῖ με τοὺς τύπους ἐπιγνῶναι.   212

καὶ κατανοήσας ἐκ δευτέρου εἶπεν· αὐτός ἐστιν
ἀσφαλῶς·

      ἡ φωνὴ γὰρ αὐτὸν ἤλεγξε         213
‹εἰ καὶ πλανᾷ τύπος με›·              214

(πολλοὶ γὰρ ἄνθρωποι τῇ φωνῇ γινώσκονται κἂν
ἐν σκότει διάγωσιν). . . . παρανακλιθεὶς δὲ τῷ
Δαρείῳ εἶπε·  [μέγιστε]

(βασιλεῦ ‹τε› καὶ δυνάστα ‹Περσικῆς› χώρας)
οὗτός ‹γ᾽› ὁ πρεσβεὺς αὐτὸς ἔστ᾽[ιν] Ἀλέξανδρος
(ὁ παλαὶ Φιλίππου ‹γενόμενος› ἀριστεύων)    217

. . . . . . .
. . . . . . .

ὁ δὲ Ἀλέξανδρος ὑπὸ τοῦ θεοῦ βοηθούμενος

ὤξυνε ([τὸν] πῶλον τὴν ὁδὸν διευθύνων)·     218
νὺξ γὰρ βαθεῖα (καὶ σκότος κατ᾽ Ο‹ὔ›λυμπον)·
‹πλεῖστοι δ᾽ ἐφ᾽ ἵππων βάρβαροι διώκοντες›   220
‹ἴσχυσαν οὐδὲν καταλαβεῖν› ‹Ἀλέξανδρον›·
(ὁ μὲν γὰρ εἶχε τὴν ὁδευτικὴν) πεύκην

207-8. order ἡνίκα . . . ἦλθεν εἰς Πέλλην τῆς Μ. ὑπὸ
Δαρείου π.    209. Better ἀπαιτήσων.    210. so codd.
Barocc. 20 (ἐπιστὰς ἔστη).    212. ἀσφαλῶς ἐστι A.    213. ἔστιν
γάρ?    214. ita fere Byz.: sim. codd. dett.    215. πάσης

532

For by his face he knew him, since erstwhile
He came to Pella town, for Darius
Demanding Macedonian tribute.
He took his stand facing Alexander      210

and said to himself

Is not this he they call Alexander ?      211
'Tis he. I ought to recognize full well.      212

And observing again he said : Certainly it is he ;

His voice so betrays him,      213
Even if his shape trick me.      214

For many people even in the dark are recognized
by their voice. (*Pasarges then concluding certainly
that he was Alexander himself*) lay down beside Darius
and said,

The envoy, King and Lord of all Persia,      215
Is none but Philip's son Alexander
Who among Philip's sons (?) showed most manhood

(*Alexander seeing he is recognized escapes with the
cups and a torch which he snatches from a sentry.*)

And with God's aid      217
He spurred his colt and held on a straight course.
The night was deep, and dark was Olympus.
And many following him on horseback      220
Entirely failed to catch Alexander.
For he held out, unto himself shining,

---

B: Περσ. Byz.     217. γεγονὼς B (num τῶν γόνων ! ?)
Mox τοῦ θεοῦ βοηθοῦντος.     218. δι. τὴν ὁ. αὐτῷ B; cf. Byz.
219. ἦν γὰρ ν. β. A.    Ὄλ. C, Byz.    220. Byz.: πλ.
δὲ τοῦτον β. δ. μεθ' ἵπ. κατ. οὐκ ἴσχ. sim. B.    222. C, Arm.
γῆν C: πεύκην A, Arm.

# FRAGMENTA CHOLIAMBICA

λάμπ‹ων› ἑαυτῷ, (φῶ‹ς› ἄπειρον ἔμπροσθεν)·
(ἦν δ' ὥσπερ ἀστὴρ ‹τῶν ἐν› οὐρανῷ φαιδρός
μόνος τ' ἰὼν εἰς οὐδὲν ἦγε[ιτο] τοὺς Πέρσας),   225
οἱ δ' εἰς φάραγγας ‹ᾗ› ἔτυχον ‹διώλοντο›.   226
ὁ δὲ Δαρεῖος συνεφοράζετο ἐπὶ τοῦ κλιντῆρος
καθεζόμενος· ἐθεάσατο δὲ [τι]<sup>a</sup> ἐξαίφνης

              κρήγυόν τι σημεῖον·   227
‹Ξέρξου› γὰρ εἰκὼν τοῦ ὀρόφου διαστάντος
κατέπεσε‹ν› ἥνπερ ἠγάπ‹ησε› Δαρεῖος.   229

  .   .   .   .   .   .   .<sup>b</sup>

μηδὲν δυνάμενοι τῶν τόπων ἀπέστησαν,   230
ποταμὸς γὰρ οὗτος πᾶσίν ἐστιν ἄπλευστος.   231
καὶ οἱ μὲν Δαρείῳ ἔλεγον

         τὸ εὐτύχημ' Ἀλεξάνδρου.   232
ch. 16   .   .   .   .   .   .

        ἔωθεν τὸν στράτον συναθροίσας   233
(ἐξ ὀνόματος καθώπλισ'), ἐν μέσ‹οις› ἑστώς
ὁποῖος ‹ὁ› Ζεὺς [. . . .] δαίμονας διακρίνων.   235
καὶ πάντας [τοὺς ἑ]αυτοῦ ‹τοὺς στράτους›
       ἀριθμήσας   236
(εὗρεν τὸν ἀριθμὸν χιλιάδας ἑκατὸν εἴκοσι,<sup>c</sup> καὶ
στὰς ἐφ' ὑψηλοῦ τόπου τινὸς παραινεῖ αὐτοὺς
λέγων· ἄνδρες συστρατιῶται,

εἰ καὶ ‹παρ' ἡμῖν›) ὁ ἀριθμὸς βραχὺς λίαν,   237

   223. κατέλαμπεν A.   φῶτ' B, which places this after next
verse.   224. ἐξ codd. dett.   225. ἀνύων τὴν ὁδὸν μόνος C:
ἀνιών B.   226. ᾗ: or ἐν [τῷ] σκότει Byz.: A καὶ οἱ μὲν διώκοντες
εἰς ὃ μέρος ἔτυχον ἐδίωκον· ὁ μὲν γὰρ . . . οἱ δὲ εἰς τὰς φάραγγας

The guiding torch of infinite splendour,
And was as one of heaven's stars radiant,
Lone traveller outwitting the Persians,                    225
Who perished in the dells, as chance led them.    226

Now Darius bemoaned his fate, seated on his divan;
where he

Saw suddenly a trustworthy omen.                           227
The roof cracked and a picture of Xerxes,
By King Darius treasured much, fell down.        229

(*Alexander escapes over the river just before it thaws:
the Persians arrive too late and*)

Retreating from the riverside baffled,                     230
(For this is an impassable river)
Of Alexander's luck told Darius.                          232

(*Alexander next day*)

Full early did assemble his hosts all,                     233
Armed them and called by name, in midst standing,
Like Zeus the heavenly deities counting.           235
And having counted up all his soldiers              236

found there were 120,000. He stood on a high hill,
and harangued them:

Fellow soldiers and friends!
Full small, as well I know, are our numbers,       237

---

κατεκρημνίζοντο.        ᵃ del. Kroll.        228. Arm.: εἰκὼν
γὰρ ἔξω A.        κατ. δι. A.        229. -πα A.        ᵇ There
are only isolated traces of verses in Alexander's escape
across the river, *e.g.* τὸν δ' Ἀλέξανδρον ἔρριψεν· ἐρρύσθη ⟨δὲ⟩
γῆς ἐπὶ στερρᾶς.        230. ἀπ. τῶν τ.· ὁ γὰρ π. οὗ. ἄ. ἐ. π. A.
233. συν. τ. σ.        234. ἐκέλευσεν ἐ. ὁ. καθοπλισθῆναι C, Arm.
μέσῳ A.        235. τοὺς οὐρανίους A, ἐν οὐρανῷ Arm.        ᶜ *e.g.*
δὶς ἑξήκοντα χιλιάδας εὗρεν.        237. A in false place: B
εἰ καὶ β. ὁ ἄ. ἀλλὰ φρ. μεγάλη παρ' ἡμῖν κτλ.

# FRAGMENTA CHOLIAMBICA

ἀλλὰ φρόνησις μεγάλη [παρ' ἡμῖν] καὶ θράσος καὶ
δύναμις

ὑπέρ ⟨γε⟩ Πέρσας τοὺς ἐναντίους ἡμῶν·       238
ἡμῶν δὲ μηδεὶς ἀσθενέστερόν . . .       239

τι λογίσηται

⟨. . . . . . . .⟩ θεωρῶν τὸ ⟨μέγα⟩ βαρβάρων
    πλῆθος·       240
εἷς γάρ τις ἐξ ἡμῶν ⟨γε⟩ χεῖρα γυμνώσας)
†τῶ νῶ θεωρῶν† (χιλίους ἀναιρήσει.       242

μηδεὶς οὖν ὑμῶν δειλιάσῃ·

πολλαὶ γὰρ εἰσὶ μυριάδες ⟨. . . . .⟩ μυιῶν       243
λειμῶνας ⟨. . . . . . . . . . .⟩ θλίβουσαι·
ὁπόταν δὲ ταύταις ἐμπέσωσιν ⟨αἱ⟩ σφῆκες 245
σοβοῦσιν αὐτὰς ταῖς πτέρυξι) κλά⟨ζ⟩οντες·
οὕτω τὸ πλῆθος οὐδέν ἐστι πλὴν πλῆθος·
σφηκῶν γὰρ ὄντων οὐδέν εἰσιν (αἱ μυῖαι).
ὡς δ' εἶπε[ν ὁ] βασιλεύς, πάντες αὐτὸν ηὐφήμουν.
πολλὰς ⟨δὲ⟩ χέρσους καὶ †στόμους† διευθύνας 250
⟨ἦγεν⟩ τὸν ὄχλον ἐπὶ τὰ νῶτα τοῦ Στράγγου.
Δαρεῖος ⟨οὖν⟩ ὡς (εἶδε) τόν ⟨τ'⟩ Ἀλέξανδρο⟨ν⟩
ὀλιγοστὸν ὄντα, (καὶ παγέντα) ⟨. . . . . .⟩
[ ] τὸν ποταμὸν εὑρὼν διεπέρασ'[εν], ἐπιστῆναι
βουλόμενος . . . . . . .τοῖς στράτοις Ἀλεξάνδρου· 255
. . . . . . . . . . . . . . κήρυκας εἰς (μέσον) πέμπει
καλεῖν ⟨ἀνώγων⟩ (εἰς μάχην [τοὺς] ἀριστ⟨ῆ⟩ας)

(ὁ δὲ στράτος Δαρείου

238. τοὺς B.      239. μηδ. οὖν ἡμ. B.      ἀσθενέστερον : -ος
φανείη Byz.: e.g. -ραν ψυχὴν ἔχοι.      240. Byz.: τὸ πλ. τῶν
β. B.      242. τῶν ἀντιμάχων codd. dett. ; verss.: τῶν

536

but we have great resource and courage and personal
strength

Beyond our adversaries the Persians.                    238
Let none of us display the least weakness
Seeing the vast barbarian numbers.                     240
For one of us even with hand empty
Of idle fools like these will slay thousands.
For there are flies ⟨. . .⟩ in thousands
Thronging in days of summer the meadows;
But when the wasps attack them in battle     245
They rout them merely by their wings' whistle.
So numbers count as nothing but numbers.
When there are wasps mere flies count for nothing.
The king spoke and his soldiers all cheered him.
And after many lands and paths traversed      250
He led them to the borders of Strangas.
Darius when he saw the commander
Had few with him, and saw the stream frozen,
Crossed it in haste, desiring to surprise
By stealth the armies of Alexander,           255
Yet heralds sent to summon to combat
The chosen men of all the brave foemen.

Now Darius' host

---

ἀντιδίκων οὕτω τῷ νῷ θεωρῶν (οὕτω τι νωθρῶν Kroll).   Vestigiis
propius τῶν ὧδε μωρῶν, which I translate.            243. e.g. ἀεὶ.
244. ἡμέρᾳ θερινῇ Arm., e.g. -να θερινῆσ' ἡμέρῃσι: θλίβουσαι λειμῶνας B: αἱ σκοποῦσαι τὸν ἀέρα misere cod. A.      246. κλαγόντες
A.      247. πλὴν πλῆθος: πρὸς ἡμᾶς or σύνεσιν codd. dett.
248. codd. omnes?: παρόντων inepte Kroll.            250. οὖν
omnes.      ὁδοὺς καὶ ἄκρα Arm., στίβους Kroll.      251. εὗρεν A.
252. ὁ δὲ Δ. omnes.      ἰδών: ἐθεάσατο A.      στράτον -ρου A.
254. A ἐχλεύασεν ὡς μηδὲν (om. cett.) καὶ εὐ. ἐπιπήκτον τ. π.
255. e.g. ἄφνω: πρῶτος dett.      256. καὶ A: e.g. ὅμως
(Byz.) γε μήν.      ἐκπέμπει A.      257. καλεῖν τὴν μάχην A:
καλοῦντας κτλ. cett.      -εας codd. dett.

<πᾶς ὅπλοις ἐθωρήχθη >.
ὁ δὲ ἅρματος Δαρεῖος ἦν ἐφ᾽ ὑψηλοῦ

καὶ οἱ σατράπαι αὐτοῦ ἐπὶ δρεπανηφόρων ἁρμάτων
ἐκαθέζοντο). τῶν δὲ Μακεδόνων προῆγεν ὁ
᾽Αλέξανδρος ἐγκαθίσας τὸν Βουκέφαλον ἵππον·
προσεγγίσαι δὲ τούτῳ οὐδεὶς ἠδύνατο. . . .

ὡς δ᾽ ἑκατέρους ἔκληζε πολέμιος σάλπιγξ      260
πολὺς δέ τις θροῦς συνεκλονεῖτο καὶ κλαγγ<ή>
στράτων, προθυμίᾳ <γὰρ> ἦλθον εἰς δῆριν,
(οἱ μὲν λίθους ἔβαλλον, οἱ δὲ τόξ. . . . . .      263

ἔπεμπον ὡς ὄμβρον ἀπ᾽ οὐρανοῦ φερόμενον,

ἕτεροι δ᾽) <ἔκρυπτον> βέλεσιν (ἡμέρας φέγγος),
ἄλλοι δ᾽ <ἄρ> ἐξοιστροῦντο <ταῖς> μαχαίραισιν·
[καὶ] ὤλοντο πολλοί, πολὺς ὀδυρμὸς ὠρώρει·
<ὡς> οἱ μὲν ἐσφάζοντο (βέλεσι τρωθέντες),
ἡμισφαγεῖς δ᾽ ἔκειντο . . . . . . . . . (ἄλλοι·      268
γνοφερὸς δὲ ἦν ὁ ἀὴρ καὶ αἱματώδης).

πολλῶν δὲ Περσῶν ὀλεθρίως τελευτώντων,      269
ὁ Δαρεῖος ἔστρεψε τὰς ἡνίας τοῦ ἰδίου ἅρματος,[a]

καὶ πᾶν τὸ Περσῶν πλῆθος εἰς φυγὴν ὦρμα.      270
δρεπανηφόρων <οὖν> ἁρμάτων τροχαζόντων

(ἐθέριζ<ο>ν αὐτο<ὶ> τοὺς πλείστους τῶν Περσῶν
ὄχλους ὡς [ἐπὶ]

258. ἐθωρακίσαντο πανοπλίαν codd. dett.: π. ὅ. ἐθωρακίσθη Byz.
259. ὁ δὲ Δ. ἦν ἐφ᾽ ἅρματος ὑψηλοῦ A.      260. ἔκλαγξε codd.
dett.: οὖν -ους ἔκλιζε A (Kr.).      261. κλαγγείων A: i.e.
κλαγγὴ τῶν Kroll.      262. δὲ A.      263. e.g. οἱ δ᾽ ἐτόξευον
πέμποντες — ὡς ἀπ᾽ οὐρανοῦ ὄμβρον.      264. βολίδας ἐσφεν-
δόνιζον ὥστε ἐπικαλύπτειν codd. dett.: ἐσκέπασαν A.      τὸν
ἀέρα A: ἡμέρας φέγγος codd. dett., Byz. (Arm.).      265. ἅ.
δὲ μ. ἐξ. A.      266. πολλοὶ μ. ὤ., πολὺς δὲ A.      267. καὶ

was all in arms ready.                         258
Darius sat on chariot lofty

and his satraps were seated on scythed chariots.
The Macedonians were led by Alexander on his
horse Bucephalus that none could approach.

Now when the martial trumpet called both sides 260
And mighty din and shouting of armies
Clattered together, eagerly fighting,          262
Some hurled great stones, and others shot arrows,

like rain falling from heaven,

Others with missiles the daylight clouded,     264
Others with swords to frenzy were goaded.      265
Many did fall, and many cries rose up.
As some were slain of wounds from thrown missiles
Or lay half slain . . .

The air was thick and blood-tainted.

When many Persians were by doom taken,

Darius turned the reins of his car,

And the whole Persian host to flight urgéd.    270
Then on their chariots scythed, in haste wheel-
ing,[1]                                        271

the satraps mowed down the common herd of the
Persians like

---

[1] *vv.* 271-2 may be continuous, *e.g.* πεζοὶ ᾽θερίζονθ᾽ ὥσπερ
ὑπ᾽ ἀγροτῶν σῖτος, which is nearer the A version.

---

codd.       268. ἕτεροι δὲ ἡ. ἔ. A, Byz. : ἄλλοι δὲ ἡ. ἔ. codd.
dett.       ᵃ *e.g.* Δ. ἔφυγεν ἡνιοστροφῶν ἅρμα.       270. τὸ πλ.
τῶν II. A.       271. δὲ πολλῶν A.       ᵇ So in general
codd. dett.: -εν -os codd. dett.: *e.g.* ἐθέριζον ὄχλους ὥσπερ
ἐν θέρους ὥρῃ.

# FRAGMENTA CHOLIAMBICA

στάχυας ἀρούρης ἀγρόται ἐπικείροντες).     272

. . . . . . . .

κάτωθε[ν] δ'[ι] ἐλύθη κῦμα καὶ ἥρπασε‹ν› πάντας
οἱ δὲ μὴ φθάσαντες διαπερᾶσαι τὸν ποταμόν
   ὑπὸ τῶν Μακεδόνων (νηλεῶς) ἀνηροῦντο.     274
ὁ δὲ Δαρεῖος φυγὰς γενηθεὶς καὶ εἰσελθὼν εἰς τὰ
βασίλεια[a]

(ῥίψας ἑαυτὸν εἰς [τὸ] ἔδαφος, ἀνοιμώξας,     275
σὺν δάκρυσι ἐθρήνει ἑαυτὸν ἀπολέσας πολὺ πλῆθος
ἀνδρῶν

   καὶ τὴν Περσίδα ὅλην ἐρημώσας).     276

. . . . . . . .

ch. 20     . . . . . . . .


(οἱ δὲ σατράπαι Δαρείου ἔγνωσαν τὸν Ἀλέξανδρον
ἐγγίζοντα ὅ τε Βῆσσος καὶ ὁ Ἀριοβαρζάνης· καὶ
   παρατραπέντες [οὗτοι] τὰς φρενοβλαβεῖς γνώμας
ἐβουλεύσαντο Δαρεῖον ἀναιρῆσαι . . . . . . . .) οὕτως
ἐπήνεγκαν Δαρείῳ

            ἐξιφωμένας [τὰς] χεῖρας.     278
ὁ δὲ τοὺς πονηροὺς ἰδὼν εἶπεν·

      ὦ ἐμοῦ δεσπόται [οἱ] τὸ πρὶν [μου] δοῦλοι,
τί τοσοῦτον ἠδίκησα (βαρβάρῳ τόλμη[ματι])     280

---

272. ἀρούρης στάχυας ἀγρότητι κείροντες cod. Barocc.: first
ἐπὶ rightly omitted by Byz.: ὥσπερ σῖτος ὑπ' ἀρότρῳ, ne mur-
murante quidem Krollio, A : nostrates aratris haud ita utun-
tur: στ. ἀρούρας etiam Byz.     [a] e.g. φ. γ. δ' εἰς δόμους ὁ Δ.
276. e.g. ἑαυτὸν ἐθρήνησεν ἀπολέσας πλῆθος μέγιστον ἀνδρῶν γῆν
θ' ὅλην ἐρημώσας.          280. β. τολ. after ἀνέλητε codd. dett.

The husbandmen the plough-land corn reaping.

(*The Persian host attempt to flee across the Strangas but*)

The ice gave way and the wave engulf'd them.    273

Those who failed to cross in time

Were by the men of Macedon butcher'd.

Darius fled to his palace and

Casting him on the floor, with a loud groan,    275

and floods of tears wept for his loss of so numerous a host,

And desolation of his own country.    276

(*Darius after vain appeals*[1] *flees to Ecbatana and the Caspian gates.  Alexander pursues.*)  Now the satraps of Darius Bessus and Ariobarzanes learnt that Alexander was approaching, and,

By evil stroke from God their hearts smitten,    277

they plotted to kill Darius. . . They attacked Darius,

swords in their hands holding.    278

When he saw the villains he said :

My masters, my slaves once !    279
How have I wronged you that with cruel spirit    280

[1] Darius cites some pure iambic verses : and one letter in his correspondence with Alexander which ensues, unlike the rest of the letters of which this history is full, shows traces of *pure* iambi.  These, like others (i. 33, iii. 24. 3), have no place in this collection.

# FRAGMENTA CHOLIAMBICA

ἵνα με ἀνέλητε;

> (μὴ πλε<ί>ον ὑμεῖς Μακεδόνων τι δράσητε·) 281
> ἐάσατ᾽[ε με] οὕτως ἐπὶ τὰ μέλαθρα ῥιφ<θ>έντα
> ἀναστενάζειν τὴν (ἀνώμαλον <μοῖραν>).
> ἐὰν γὰρ ἐλθὼν ὁ βασιλεὺς Ἀλέξανδρος
> εὕρῃ σφαγέντα †βασιλέα† λῃστρικῇ γνώμῃ, 285
> ἐ<π>εκδικήσει <μ᾽>· οὐ θέμις γὰρ ὀφθῆναι 286

βασιλέα[a] δολοφονηθέντα οἰκτίστω<ς>.[b]

οἱ δὲ ἀσεβεῖς μαθόντες τὴν εἴσοδον (Ἀλεξάνδρου)
... προλείψαντες τὸν Δαρεῖον ἡμίπνουν ἀπο-
φεύγουσιν ... καὶ (εἰσελθὼν πρὸς αὐτὸν Ἀλέξανδρος

> <...> εὗρεν αὐτὸν <αἱμόφυρτον> ἡμίπνουν), 287

καὶ (ἀνοιμώξας

> <ἐλέου γέμοντα> θρῆνον ἄξιον λύπης 288

δάκρυα ἐξέχεεν [καὶ]

> τῇ χλαμύδι <δ᾽> ἐσκέπα<ζ>ε [τὸ] σῶμα
>    Δαρείου), 289
> ἐπιθεὶς δ᾽ ἑαυτοῦ χεῖρας ἐπὶ τὸ Δαρείου 290
> στῆθος τοίους ἔλεξε συμπαθεῖς μύθους·
> ἀνάστα, φησί· τῆς τύχης, ὦ Δαρεῖε,
> καὶ τῶν σεαυτοῦ δεσπότης πάλιν γίνου.
> δέξαι σ[ο]ὺ τὸ διάδημα Περσικοῦ πλήθους,
> ἔχε σοῦ τὸ μέγεθος τῆς τυραννικῆς δόξης. 295
> ὄμνυμί (σοι) Δαρεῖε τοὺς θεοὺς πάντας
> <ὡς ταῦτ᾽> ἀληθῶς καὶ οὐ πεπλασμένως (φράζω).

---

281. δράσηται cod. Barocc. : -σετε codd. dett. ??   283.
ἀνώμαλόν μου (ἀνομαλή cod. Barocc.) τύχην: δυσέκβατον A.

you come to kill me ?

> Excel not Macedon in your actions.                281
> Suffer me thus upon the earth rolling
> To weep aloud at my fate's injustice.
> For if there come the king Alexander,
> And find a king by pirates slain lying,          285
> He will avenge me : Right doth not suffer        286

that a king should be seen slain by guile most pitifully.

*(After a struggle they decamp leaving Darius half dead. Alexander arrives and)*

> found him half alive with blood spatter'd.       287

With a loud groan he uttered

> A lamentable dirge and right piteous,            288

shed tears

> And with his cloak Darius' form veiling,         289
> Upon Darius' breast his hands laid he,           290
> And words of sympathy spoke as follows :—
> Arise, quoth he ; Darius, of fortune
> And of your own be once again master.
> Receive the Persian diadem once more,
> The might of all your kingly fame keeping.       295
> I swear to you, Darius, by heaven,
> I speak this truly with no feigned utt'rance,

---

285. ἄνακτα Kroll.    286. ἐπ- : εὖ A: cett. ἐκδικ. τὸ αἱμά μου·
ᵃ ⟨βασιλεῖ⟩ β. Ausfeld; but sterner measures are needed.
ᵇ -των A.    287. Byz. : ἐκκεχυμένον . . . τὸ . . . αἷμα C.
288. θρ. ἅ. λ. C : ἐλ. γέμ. B later.    289. -ασε C.    290. τὰς
χεῖρας δὲ αὐτοῦ ἐπ. A.    296. σε A.    297. Kroll (ὡς Byz.,
ταῦτα Arm.) : ὅτι ἐγώ A.

FRAGMENTA CHOLIAMBICA

μόνος παρέ‹ξ›ω τὸ διάδημα τῶν σκήπτρων.
μετὰ σοῦ γὰρ αὐτὸς καὶ τροφῆς ἐκοινών‹ουν›
ἐπὶ ‹σ›αῖς τραπέζαις ‹σ›ὴν ἀν᾽ ἑστίαν, χ‹ρεί›αν
ἡνίκα παρήμην ἀγγελ‹ῶν› Ἀλεξάνδρου.      301
ἀλλ᾽ ἐξανάστα καὶ κράτυνε τῆς χώρας.
οὐ δεῖ βασιλέα δυστυχοῦντα λυπεῖσθαι·
ἰσότης γὰρ ἀνθρώποισ‹ι περὶ τέλους μοίρης›.
τίνες δέ σ᾽ οἱ τρώσαντες, εἶπε, Δαρεῖε;      305
μήνυσον αὐτοὺς (ἵνα σε νῦν, ἄνα‹ξ, τί›σω.)
ταῦτα ‹οὖν› λέγοντος [   ] ἐστέναξ[εν] ὁ Δαρεῖος
καὶ ἐπισπασάμενος (τάς ‹τε› χεῖρας ἐκτείνας)
στῆθος φιλήσας ‹τ᾽› εἶπε· τέκνον Ἀλέξανδρε
μη‹δέ›ποτ᾽ ἐπαρθῇς (τῇ τυραννικῇ δόξῃ)·      310
(ὁπότὰν) γὰρ ἔργον ἰσόθεον κατορθώ‹σῃς›,      311
καὶ χερσὶ ταῖς σαῖς οὐραν(οῦ θέλ)ῃς ψαύειν,
σκόπει τὸ μέλλον· ἡ τυχὴ γὰρ οὐκ οἶδεν
‹            › (βασιλέ᾽ οὔτε μὴν πλῆθος),
ἀκρίτῳ δὲ ῥοίζῳ πάντ‹α› (πανταχ)ῶς (ῥέμβε-
   [τα]ι).      315
ὁρᾷ‹s› τίς ἤμην καὶ τίς ἐγενόμην τλήμων·
ὁ τῆς τοσαύτης ἄρτι ‹κύριος γαίης›
νῦν οὐδ᾽ ἐμαυτοῦ δεσπότης ἀποθνήσκω.
θάψον με ταῖς σαῖς εὐσεβεστάτ‹α›ις χερσίν·
κηδευσατώσαν Μακέδονες (με) καὶ Πέρσαι·      320

   .   .   .   .   .   .

μί‹η› γενέσθω συγγένεια Δαρείῳ.      321
τὴν δ᾽ ἐμὲ τεκοῦσαν παρατίθημί σοι τλήμων,

298. -έχω A.      299-300. Kroll: -νουν, ταῖς, τὴν A.      300.
χεῖραν A (χειρὶ Arm.).      301. ἄγγελος A.      304. ἡ π. τ. μύρις
A : corr. Kroll ex Arm.      306. ἀναπαύσω B: ἵνα με ἔκδικον
ἔχῃς A.      307. Ἀλεξάνδρου.      308. καὶ codd. dett., Byz.
544

That you may have again the sole sceptre.
For I myself at meat with you sat once
At table by your hearth, when I came here          300
To bring you message from Alexander.
But now arise and be your land's master :
A king should suffer not nor be wept for.
For all are equal at their last hour's end.
Who are they who did wound you, Darius ?        305
Tell me their names, O King : I 'll avenge you.
As Alexander spake thus, Darius                  307
Groaned, drew him nigh to him, his hands stretch'd
      forth,
And kissed his breast and quoth : Alexander,
Be not elated by your proud kingship :           310
When you have wrought a deed of god worthy
And fancy with your hands to touch heaven
Think of what is to be : for fate knows not
Or king or commoner : all things cruelly
In undistinguished eddy she whirls round.        315
See what I was, and what my fate now is ;
I, who was once of all this land owner,
Am master now not even of myself.
Me with your hands most pious here bury,
Let Macedonians tend me, and Persians : [1]      320
      .        .        .        .        .
Let all as kindred do my kin's functions.
Alack for me, I give you my mother !

[1] Probably the account in C, according to which the king
summons his harem is, for the choliambic writer, original.
But, as usual in this version, traces of metre are few.

---

310. Kroll.        311. -σεις A.        312. οὐρανοὺς A, οὐρανὸν
codd. dett. (φθάσαι).        314. e.g. ὅλως τιν' οὔτε: A βασιλέα
ἢ λῃστὴν οὔτε πλῆθος.        315. παντὶ κακῶς A : πανταχόθεν
cett.        317. Arm. (om. cett.) : κύρον γύης A.        319. -οις
A.        321. μία codd.

καὶ τὴν γυναῖκα ⟨δ'⟩ ὡς σύν⟨αι⟩μον οἴκτειρον·
καὶ τὴν θυγατέρα σοι δίδωμι Ῥωξάνην,
ἵν' εἴ τι κἂν φθιτοῖσι λείπεται γνώμη⟨ς⟩     325
⟨οἱ δύο γονῆες⟩ ἐπὶ τέκνοισ⟨ι⟩ κα(υ)χῶνται.
σ⟨οὶ⟩ μὲν Φίλιππ⟨ος⟩, Ῥωξάνη[ς] δὲ Δαρεῖ⟨ος⟩.
τοσαῦτα λέξας ὁ βασιλεὺς ⟨ὁ⟩ Δαρεῖος
τὸ πνεῦμ' ἔλειψε⟨ν⟩ ἐν χερ⟨οῖ⟩ν Ἀλεξάνδρου.

323. Kroll.     σύνεμὸν A : corr. Raabe ex Arm.     324. Ῥ.
δ. σοι A.     325. γνώμη A.     326. Kroll : σὺ δυὸ
γενεᾶς A.     κάχονται A : καύχ. cett.     327. σὺ, -πῳ,
-ης, -ίῳ codd.: corr. Kroll.     329. ἔ. τὸ π. and χερσὶν A.

Pity my wife here as a kinswoman !
My daughter give I also Roxanes,
That if sense liveth yet among dead men    325
Two parents in their offspring may glory,
Philip in you, and I in Roxanes.
After this utterance King Darius
In Alexander's hands the ghost gave up.[1]

---

[1] Further traces of metre are few : and it is very doubtful whether Book III. containing Alexander's expedition into Judea, his journey to Candace, and his death, owes anything to the versifier. See p. 573.

# FRAGMENTA CHOLIAMBICA

## ORACULUM

*ap. Ps.-Call.* i. 3. 4.

Ἐν δὲ τῷ Αἰγύπτῳ ἀφανοῦς γενομένου
τοῦ Νεκτανεβῶ ἠξίωσαν οἱ Αἰγύπτιοι τὸν προ-
πάτορα τῶν θεῶν Ἥφαιστον τί ἄρα ὁ τῆς Αἰ-
γύπτου βασιλεὺς ἐγένετο. ὁ δὲ ἐπεμψεν αὐτοῖς
χρησμὸν πρὸς τὸν ἀόρατον τοῦ Σεραπείου[a] στῆναι[b]
ὃς χρησμοδοτεῖ αὐτοῖς οὕτως·

> Αἴγυπτον ὁ φυγὼν κρατερὸς ἄλκιμος πρέσβυς
> βασιλεὺς δυνάστης †ἥξει† μετὰ χρόνον νέος,
> τὸ γηράλαιον ἀποβαλὼν τύπων εἶδος,
> κόσμον κυκλεύσας ἐπὶ τὸ πεδίον Αἰγύπτου,
> ἐχθρῶν ⟨ἁπάντων⟩ ὑποταγὴν διδοὺς ἡμῖν. 5

οὕτω δοθέντος . . .

---

[a] Σεραπείου : v.l. Σινωπείου.    [b] στῆσαι A.    iambos no-
tavit W. Kroll.    1. ἐκφυγὼν [cod.] L[eid].    κραταιὸς A :
-ερὸς L.    2. e.g. μ. χ. ν. θ' ἥξει.    3. γεράλαιον A, L.
τύπον εἶδον κόσμου A.    4. Αἰγ. π. A, L (Αἴγυπτον L).
5. ἐλθὼν διδοὺς L.

# ANON. AP. PS.-CALLISTHENEM

## ORACLE

*Ps.-Call.* i. 3. 4

Now in Egypt after Nectanebos' disappearance the Egyptians saw fit to ask Hephaestus the grandsire of the gods what had happened to the king of Egypt. And he sent to them an oracle to go to the recess of the Serapium. And Serapis delivered an oracle to them as follows :—

> The strong, brave sire that has fled Egypt
> Monarch and king will come again youthful,
> Having put off his features old semblance,
> Circling the world to Egypt's plain once more,
> Giving of all our enemies conquest.          5

After this oracle had been thus delivered, [failing to discover its meaning they wrote the verses on the base of Nectanebos' statue, as a memorial against such time as the oracle should come to pass.]

# UNCERTAIN FRAGMENTS

The search for anonymous choliambics has met with but little success. It is very easy for prose passages to appear to belong to such a metre. An excellent instance of this kind appears in Polyb. i. 32 :

τοὺς ἀπολογισμοὺς παρὰ τί νῦν σφαλείησαν
καὶ πῶς δύναιντο τοὺς ἐναντίους νικᾶν;

as quoted by Suidas. Under the heading ' Spuria ' I give a few instances of verses which, it appears to me, are either fortuitous, or belong to another metre. But there is another class, not yet noted by editors, as to which, it seems, some room for doubt exists. The collectors of Greek proverbs normally threw these into the rhythm of the end of a verse, or indeed a whole verse ; and where the choliambic rhythm predominates it seems possible to claim a few of these, not indeed from writers in choliambi, but as conscious choliambi produced by the editor of proverbs. This is why I have ventured to give the late fifteenth-century choliambi of Arsenius, who after the fall of Constantinople augmented Apostolius' (his father's) collection of proverbs ; and drawn attention to a place where a far earlier writer, Synesius, bishop of Cyrene, deliberately casts a proverb into this metre, or uses a metrical authority. Thus Hesiod's δῶρα θεοὺς πείθει degenerates into a verse-end δῶρα

# UNCERTAIN FRAGMENTS

καὶ θεοὺς πείθει and ἡ ἀπὸ Σκυθῶν ῥῆσις assumes an illogical accusative. Since distinction is not always possible I include a certain number of cases where there may actually be a quotation from a choliambic writer (other than a proverb-collector) ; but I do not suppose that there are more than four or five of these. The division into (a) Dicta and (b)[1] is unsatisfactory. It is further possible that of the four or five some like ἀεί με κτλ. and μύωπι κτλ. are from lost fables of Babrius. Where all is so hypothetical detailed discussion is unnecessary ; and this warning must suffice.

[1] Proverbs proper.

# FRAGMENTA INCERTA

## (1-10, vid. pp. 2-7)

### Inc. 11 (Bgk. 25)

ὁ τὸν κυσὸν τρωθείς
ἤδ‹ει›ς ‹ὅ›που μάλιστα τοῦ κράνους χρεί‹η›.

(Photius, ii. 33 Naber.)

### Inc. 12 (Bgk. 26 A)

A. βαύ, βαύ.

　　　B. καὶ κυνὸς φωνὴν ἵεις;

(Joan. Alex. de ton. p. 32. 23 βαύ ... ὀξύνεται (12).)

### Inc. 13

στροβεῖς σεαυτὸν κοχλίου βίον ζώ‹ω›ν.

(Plut. Mor. p. 525 E σὺ δὲ τοσαῦτα πράγματα συγχεῖς καὶ
ταράττεις καὶ (13).)

### Inc. 14 (Bgk. 27)

ἐγὼ μὲν ὦ Λεύκιππ‹ε› δεξίῃ σίττῃ

(Schol. Ar. Av. 704 Δίδυμος δέ, ἐπεὶ ἡ σίττη καὶ εἴ τι
τοιοῦτον ὄρνεον δεξιὰ πρὸς ἔρωτας φαίνεται (14). Suid. ἀεὶ τοῖς
ἐρῶσιν.)

11. 2. ἤδη Αἰσώπου : corr. Dobree.　　　χρεία corr. Bgk.
12. interpunxi.　　13. ζῶν : corr. Crusius.　　　14. ὦ
Suid. : ὡς schol. Ar.　　Λευκίππη corr. Bentley.　　-η -η
corr. Meineke.

552

# UNCERTAIN FRAGMENTS

### (*For* 1-10 *see above*)

## 11

In the rump wounded
Thou knewest where a helmet was needed

(*Photius's Lexicon.*)

## 12

A. Bow !  Wow !

B.  Do'st bark dog-like ?

(*John* of *Alexandria* on *Accents.*)

## 13

You lead a shell-fish life of inquietude.

(You confound all these matters [1] and in your worry (13).
*Plutarch* on *Avarice.*)

## 14

Leucippus, I with favouring parrot

(Didymus' explanation rests on the ground that parrots
and suchlike birds are favourable to lovers (14).  *Commentator* on *Aristophanes' Birds* : also in *Suidas' Lexicon.*)

[1] The reading is uncertain and unsatisfactory.

# FRAGMENTA CHOLIAMBICA

## *Inc.* 15

†ἐπ᾽ ἀνδ†ρὸς ἄνδρα Κερκίδας ἀπέκτεινεν.

(Arist. 673 a 13 τὸ περὶ τὴν κεφαλὴν ὡς ἀποκοπεῖσα φθέγγεται.
. . τοῦ γὰρ ἱερέως τοῦ Ὁπλοσμίου Διὸς ἀποθανόντος . . ἔφασάν
τινες ἀκοῦσαι τῆς κεφάλης ἀποκεκομμένης λεγούσης πολλάκις (15).
διὸ καὶ ζητήσαντες ᾧ ὄνομα ἦν ἐν τῷ τόπῳ Κερκίδας ἔκριναν.)

## *Inc.* 16

ἐγὼ μέντοι ἡ τοσαύτη τρεῖς ἤδη
καθεῖλον ἱστοὺς ἐν βραχεῖ χρόνῳ τούτῳ.

(Strabo, p. 378 μνημονεύεται τις ἑταίρα πρὸς τὴν ὀνειδίζουσαν
ὅτι οὐ φιλεργὸς εἴη οὐδ᾽ ἐρίων ἅπτοιτο εἰπεῖν (16).)

## *Inc.* 17

μὴ πάντοθεν κέρδαινε σαυτὸν αἰσχύνων.

(Greg. Naz. περὶ ἀρετῆς ii. 432. *v.* 387 καὶ ταῦτ᾽ ἐπαινεῖ
τῶν σοφῶς εἰρημένων (17) . . .)

## *Inc.* 18

τέττιγα ⟨μέντοι⟩ τοῦ πτεροῦ συνείληφας.

(Lucian, iii. 162 τὸ δὲ τοῦ Ἀρχιλόχου ἐκεῖνο ἤδη σοι λέγω
ὅτι (18). Apostol. xvi. 32.)

15. I doubt whether there be a verse at all, and whether
the head said more than Κερκίδας ἀπέκτεινεν. The first
two words are anyhow corrupt. The obvious correction
of ΕΠΑΝΔΡΟC is (Ε)ΗΜΙΑΡΟC, which I translate.
17. The verse is expressly attributed by Gregory to an
older writer. However, it may well have been an ordinary
iambus (αἰσχυνῶν). The next citation is from Eur. (*fr.* 20).
See my *F.G.A.* p. 4.

# UNCERTAIN FRAGMENTS

### 15

Foul Cercidas his fellow-man murder'd.[1]

(The story of the head speaking when severed from the
body. . . When the priest of Hoplosmian Zeus was
mysteriously slain, some alleged that the head though cut
off kept on repeating (15). So they hunted out one of this
name there and accused them. *Aristotle.*)


### 16

I at my age three times
In this brief space have undone three pieces.[2]

(A certain courtesan is said to have remarked to a lady
who rebuked her for idleness nor putting her fingers to the
loom (16). *Strabo.*)


### 17

Gain not from every source thyself shaming.

(You must approve the following wise utterances ' (17)
. . .' *Gregory, Bishop of Nazianzus.*)


### 18

You've taken by the wing a grasshopper.

(It is time for me to tell you of Archilochus'[3] dictum (18).
*Lucian's Liar.* Also in *Greek Proverbs.*)


---

[1] Some have actually sought to connect this with Cercidas
(the law-giver of Megalopolis or the cynic) or a relative !
[2] Should probably be classed among paroemiac dicta : it
may not occur in any literary writer.
[3] Pfeiffer has recently shown that Archilochus wrote
τέττιγος ἐδράξω πτεροῦ: so this fragment belongs to p. 347.

# FRAGMENTA CHOLIAMBICA

### Inc. 19

λευκήν

μᾶζαν φυρῶ σοι;

(Diogen. vi. 12 ἐπὶ τῶν μεγάλως ὑπισχνουμένων. Other references *Paroem. Gr.* i. 271.)

### Inc. 20

ζῷον ἐν πυρὶ σκαῖρον

(Cram. *An. Ox.* ii. 371. 19.)

### Inc. 21

⟨τέρψιν⟩ ἦν χαρίζονται νύκτες

(*Ibid.* 483. 3.)

19. *vv. ll.* φύρωσιν, μεγάλους, μεγάλα.  20, 21. indicavit Headlam.

# UNCERTAIN FRAGMENTS

## 19

### May I

A white cake mix you ?

((19) refers to those who make lofty promises. *Greek Proverbs*.)


## 20

### An animal in fire leaping

(*Grammarian* in *Cramer's Anecdota Oxoniensia.*)


## 21

### That pleasure which nights give

(*Ibid.*)

# PAROEMICA

## (a) Dicta

**1.** φιλεῖν ἀκαίρως ἴσον ἐστὶ τῷ μισεῖν.

(*Paroem. Gr.* ii. 778.)

**2.** εἰ τυρὸν εἶχον οὐκ ἂν ἐδεόμην ὄψου.

(Apostol. vi. 76 ἐπὶ τῶν ὀλίγοις ἀρκουμένων καὶ ἐγκρατῶν from Plut. *Mor.* 234 E εἰς πανδοκεῖον (Λάκων τις) καταλύσας καὶ δοὺς ὄψον τῷ πανδοκεῖ σκευάσαι, ὡς ἄτερος τυρὸν ᾔτει καὶ ἔλαιον, ʻ εἶτʼ,ʼ ἔφη (2).)

**3.**                    ζημίαν αἱροῦ μᾶλλον
ἢ κέρδος αἰσχρόν· τὸ μὲν [γὰρ] ἅπαξ σε λυπήσει
τὸ δὲ διὰ παντός.

([Apostol.] viii. 34 b from Stob. *Fl.* **v.** 31 (i. 20 H.). Χίλωνος.)

**4.** ἡ βραχυλογία ἐγγύς ἐστι τοῦ σιγᾶν.

([Apostol.] viii. 41 c from Stob. *Flor.* xxxv. 9 Λυκοῦργος πρὸς τὸν εἰπόντα ʻ διὰ τί Λακεδαιμόνιοι τὴν βρ. ἀσκοῦσιν ;ʼ εἶπεν ὅτι ἐγγὺς κτλ.)

1-5. It is possible that at some period before Plutarch (or Stobaeus) certain dicta may have been given in a metrical choliambic form.     4. *e.g.* τὸ γὰρ βραχυλόγον if the story is adopted from a metrical writer.

558

# PROVERBS

## (a) Sayings (cf. Inc. 16)

**1.** Untimely love 's than hatred no better.

(*Greek Proverbs.*)

**2.** If I had cheese what use to me were meat?

(*Greek Proverbs* from the story in *Plutarch*: A certain Spartan put up at an inn and gave meat to the innkeeper to cook: when the latter asked for cheese and oil, he rejoined (2).)

**3.**                     For loss is far better
  Than gain with shame: the one for one moment,
  The other aye will irk.

(*Greek Proverbs* from *Stobaeus' Anthology*, where it is attributed to *Chilon*.)

**4.** For brevity to silence is next door.

(*Greek Proverbs* from *Stobaeus' Anthology*: Lycurgus when asked why the Spartans practised brevity replied (4).)

559

# FRAGMENTA CHOLIAMBICA

**5.** $$\dot{\epsilon}\xi\ \text{ἴσου}\ \text{δίδου}\ \pi\hat{\alpha}\sigma\iota\nu.$$

(Plut. *Mor.* 208 в (Agesilaus is the speaker) is thus given by Apostol. vii. 51, with the lemma ἐπὶ τῶν ὀρθῶς διανεμόντων καὶ δικαίως κρινόντων.)

## 6. ἀκραῖς ἐπὶ ῥηγμῖσιν Εὐξείνου πόντου

(Plut. *Mor.* 602 A διὸ καὶ Διογένης ὁ Κύων πρὸς τὸν εἰπόντα ' Σινωπεῖς σου φυγὴν ἐκ Πόντου κατέγνωσαν,' ' ἐγὼ δέ,' εἶπεν, ' ἐκείνων ἐν Πόντῳ μονήν ' (6).)

6. Diogenes was well-read but is not likely to have cited Hipponax or Ananius or a contemporary. It is usual to read πόρου.

## (b) [a]

Ἀεί με τοῖ[ουτ]οι πολέμιοι διώκοιεν, Ἀκάνθιος
τέττιξ, Ἅλμη ⟨γὰρ⟩ οὐκ ἔνεστ᾽ αὐτῷ, Ἀκαρπό-
τερος εἶ ⟨τῶν⟩ Ἀδωνίδος κήπων, Ἀκόλω [τὰ]
χείλ⟨έ⟩᾽ οὐ σύκῳ βῦσαι, Ἀπὸ ξύλου καλοῦ[b]
⟨γε⟩ κἂν ἀπάγξασθαι, Ἀρουραία μάντις, Βία
πενήτων πλουσίων παράκλησις, Γῆς ⟨μὲν⟩
οὐκ ἔνεστ᾽ αὐτῷ,[c] Δηλίου κολυμβητοῦ, Δίκτυον
φυσᾷς,[d] Δῶρα καὶ θεοὺς πείθει, Ἐγένετο καὶ Μάν-
δρωνι συκίνη ν⟨ῆ⟩ῦς, Εἴληφεν ἡ παγὶς τὸν μῦν,
Ἐμπεδοκλέους ἔχθρα, Ἐν θέρει [τὴν] χλαῖναν[e]
κατατρίβεις, Ἐξ ἑνὸς πηλοῦ, Ἔχεται δ᾽ ὥσ⟨τε⟩
πο⟨υ⟩λύπους πέτρ⟨η⟩ς, Ἡ τρὶς ἓξ ἢ τρεῖς οἴνας,
Θρᾷκες ὅρκι᾽ οὐκ ἐπίστανται, Κάκιον ἢ Βαβῦς (?)

[a] References will readily be found in the Indexes of Leutsch and Schneidewin, *Paroemiographi Graeci*, Gottingae

# PROVERBS

5          Equal shares all round.

(*Greek Proverbs* : ' applies to fair and just apportionment.'
*Plutarch* is the source where it is part of a saying of *Agesilaus*.)

## 6. Upon the furthest shores of the Euxine

(Hence Diogenes the Cynic when told that the Sinopeans
had condemned him to exile beyond the Euxine sea rejoined
' But I condemn them to remain in Pontus (6).')

## (b)[1]

Such[2] enemies be e'er my pursuers, A hedge-
cricket, Therein is no saltness, Less fruitful than
Adonis (his) gardens, No mere fig but a good mouth-
ful, If hang I must, hang me from strong gallows,
A seer rustic, The poor perforce the rich by persuasion, This plough has no tree to 't, Delian diver's,
A net you 're inflating, Even the gods take bribes,
For Mandron too a ship had—of figwood, The mouse
in trap 's taken, Empedocles' hatred, In summer why
thy overcoat wearest ?, Of one clay founded, Octopus
to rock clinging, Thrice six or three aces, Oaths
in Thrace run not, Than Babys worse player, Than

---

[1] For Πέρδικος καπηλεῖον see on Hippon. **70.**
[2] Greek text corrected by Sauppe.

---

1839, or in Suid. *s.v.*    [b] *cf.* Suid. ἀπο καλοῦ.    [e] Suid.
[d] Suid. *s.v.* δίκτυον.    [e] χλ. ἐν θ.

# FRAGMENTA CHOLIAMBICA

αὐλεῖ, Καλλικυρίων πλείους, Καρικὴ Μοῦσα,
Καρικὸν θῦμα, Κατὰ λίθων σπείρειν, Κατὰ πετρῶν σπείρειν, Κίσσαμις Κῶος, Κρωβύλου ζεῦγος,
Κωδάλου χοῖνιξ, Λίνον λίνῳ κλώθεις, Λυδὸς ἐν
μεσημβρίᾳ παίζει, Λύκου πτερὸν ζητεῖς, Μάρτυς
ἐκ Διὸς δέλτων, Μὴ νεκρῶν θήκας κίνει, Μύωπι
τὸν ‹τ›ρ‹έχ›οντα ‹πῶλον› ἤγειρας, Ὁδοῦ παρούσης τὴν ἀτ‹αρ›πιτὸν ζητεῖς[a]; Οὐ σχολὴ
δούλοις, Παρθένος τὰ πατρῷα, Πρὸς σῆμα μη-
τρυιᾶς κλαίει, Τὰ Σαμίων ὑποπτεύεις, Τὴν ἀπὸ
Σκυθῶν ῥῆσιν, Φάων ὑπάρχεις τῷ κάλλει καὶ
τὸν τρόπον.[b]

[a] Paroem. ἀτραπὸν μὴ ζήτει: Suid. best cod. ἀτραπιτὸν.
[b] e.g. τὸν τρ. καὶ τ. κ.

# PROVERBS

Callicurians are more num'rous, Carian music, Carian
victim, Seed upon stones sowing, Seed upon rocks
sowing, Cissamis Coan, Crobylus' couple, Codalus'
pint-pot, Thread with thread spinning, A Lydian at
noon playing, As one who seeks a wolf's feather,
Witness Zeus' tablets, Let dead men lie quiet, The
willing horse whip not, Seek not the by-way when
thou hast the highway, Slaves have no leisure,
Spends like a virgin, Weeps at the tombstone of
his stepmother, The Samians' fate fearing, The
Scythian saying, As fair of fame and favour as
Phaon.[1]

[1] In cod. Urbin. Gr. 125 a fifteenth-century hand gives on
the fly-leaf δρυὸς πεσούσης ἀκαμάτως ξυλίζεσθαι, 'small search
for fuel when the oak 's fallen.' The alternative version is a
pure iambic.

# SPURIA

1. αἰσχύνομαι μὰ τὴν φιλότητα γηράσκων
   †ἵππος ὑπὸ ζυγὸν θήλειάν τε τροφήν†
   ἔχων ὁρᾶσθαι.

(Diog. ii. 53, [Apostol.] i. 67 d, Prov. Bodl. 171.)


2. Χῖος παραστὰς Κῶον οὐκ ἐᾷ †σῴ⸗ζειν†.

(*App. Prov.* v. 28 gives the right form : this is from
Schol. Plat. p. 320 Bekk., Eust. 1397. 39.)


3. ἄρκτου παρούσης ἴχνη μὴ ζήτει.

(Zenobius, ii. 36 ἐπὶ τῶν δειλῶν κυνήγων. *Paroem. Gr.* i. 42.)


4. ὁ τὸν πάτερα εὑρὼν . . . χαλκοῦ χρείᾳ

(Phot. ii. 33 Naber.)


5. ὑπερδεδίσκευκας πονηρίᾳ πάντας.

(Bekk. *An.* 67. 27.   No choliambic writer entirely neglects
the caesura.   It is clearly from an orator.)


6. ἀνθρωποειδὲς θηρίον ὕδατι συζῶν

(See Nauck, *Tr. Gr. Fragm.* p. 11 : attributed to Aeschylus
by Phrynichus, 5. 21.   Read ὕδ. συζ. θηρ. and attribute to
an Attic comedian.)

## SPURIOUS

**1.**     In friendship's name, it shames me to grow old
         Like horse in harness and to be seen
         Nurtured like woman.

(In the *Proverb-Collections*.)

**2.**     A Chian speaking may a Coan drown.

(*Ibid.*)

**3.**     When bear is near seek not his traces.

(*Ibid.*)

**4.**     Who with no farthing left found his father.

(*Photius' Lexicon*.)

**5.**     You have o'ershot in villainy all men.

(*Harpocration's Lexicon*.)

**6.**     A human form living in water

(Concerning Glaucus appearing from the sea. *Aeschylus* quoted by *Phrynichus* (*Bekk. An.* v. 21).)

---

1. Meineke indicated this: if genuine read τὴν τρ. τε θήλ. v. 2. But probably in all these seven cases the vague resemblance to metre is *wholly* fortuitous. 2, 3 and 5 Sauppe.    2 is really λέγειν.

# FRAGMENTA CHOLIAMBICA

7.                   πολλά[κι] τοι μῦθος
εἰς καιρὸν ‹ἐλθὼν› ῥᾳδίως κατορθοῖ τι
ὅπερ βιαίως ‹οὐκ ἔπραξεν› ἡ ῥώμη.

(Choricius, p. 15, Graux, *Textes inédites*.)

(Diehl, *fr.* 7)

8.          ἀλλ' ἐμοῦ [τοι] τὸ ἐντὸς [ἔφη] σκοπῶν,
ὦ δικαστά, ποικιλωτέραν με τῆσδ' ὄψει.

(Plut. *Mor.* 500 c ἡ μὲν οὖν Αἰσώπειος ἀλώπηξ περὶ ποικιλίας δικαζομένη πρὸς τὴν πάρδαλιν . . . (8).)

7. So Weil.          8. is iambic, *e.g.* δικάστ', ἔμ' ὄψει κτλ. Otherwise omit ὦ and τῆσδ'.

# SYNESIUS

οἱ πάτταλοι γὰρ παττάλοις ἐκκρούονται.

(*Ep.* 45 Ὀλυμπίῳ λυποῦσι τὴν ἐκκλησίαν ἀλλότριοι πονηροί. διάβηθι κατ' αὐτῶν (. . .).)

# SPURIOUS

**7.**                                        For persuasion[1]
Well timed doth often guide aright business
Where strength, employing force, achieves nothing.

(*Choricius* in *Graux' Textes inédites.*)

**8.**                                        But look at my inside,
Good sir juryman : you 'll find me more spotted.[2]

(The fox of Aesop in his case against the pard.   *Plutarch* on *Mental or Bodily Affliction* (8).)

[1] Conceivably, however, this might be from a lost fable of Babrius, or from part of the life of Alexander, or even written in the metre by Choricius.   See on Synesius below.   ἐλθὼν is Graux' suggestion for εἰρημένος.
[2] The word ' spotted ' implied to the Greek both variety of colour and cunningness of disposition.

# SYNESIUS[1]

For wedges must with wedges be knocked out.

(To Olympius.   The church is suffering from evil strangers. Attack them ( . . .).)

[1] Synesius bishop of Cyrene either took this proverb from a collection in which it was adapted to the choliambic metre (see below) or so adapted it.

# FRAGMENTA CHOLIAMBICA

## ARSENIUS

οὕτω σε τανῦν ἑστιῶ τὸν κράτιστον
νηκτοῖς πετεινοῖς, κτήνεσιν ἑρπυστοῖς τε.
αὖθις δέ σοι τράπεζαν, εἰ δοίης, θήσω,
εἰς ἐκτύπωσιν, πορισμὸν τὸν ἀρκοῦντα,
λαμπροῖς στρατηγήμασι τοῦ Πολυαίνου,
οἷς κεῖνος εἰστίασε τῷ βασιλῆε
πάλαι τὸν Οὐῆρόν τε καὶ 'Αντωνῖνον.

Κύων ἐγὼ σὸς καὶ γλυκὺς σὺ δεσπότης·
οὐκοῦν ὑλακτῶ καὶ φαγεῖν ζητῶ βρῶμα.
"Αναξ λεοντόθυμε τὸν κύνα τρέφε·
θρέμματα γὰρ θηρᾶν σε βλέπω βαρβάρου.

(Phile, p. 1 Didot.   These verses end the dedication.)

# ARSENIUS

## ARSENIUS [1]

So now most noble one herein find food.
Herein are birds and fishes, beasts, serpents.
If you will pay enough, I 'll get printed
Later a second course, and Your Highness
Regale with Polyaenus his tactics,
Whereon he once feasted the two rulers
Verus and Antoninus of old Rome.

I am thy dog and thou my master art.
So do I bark and wish for my dog-food.
O lion-hearted king feed thou thy dog.
I see thou huntest the barbarian beasts.

---

[1] Arsenius had lived in Constantinople before its capture and edited his father's collection of proverbs. His choice of metre may be significant.

# ADDENDA

P. 376, *fr.* 68. Add the variants: *v.* 1 κατωμόχαιε, καταμόχανε and κακομήχανε: *v.* 6 τὸν τεκνούμενον and τῶν τικείμενον. The verses are also quoted by Tzetzes on his *Antehomerica, v.* 168. For τῶντικείμενον a good case could be made out, but it has little ms. support.

P. 379, *fr.* 70. In order not to confuse the reader I have given what I believe may have been the Lycophron-Tzetzes view of these verses. It has been suggested to me that πυθμένι στοιβῆς may have been taken as a 'bunch of straw.' But I believe the whole to be nonsense and it is superfluous to trouble much over a patent error. στοιβή means a paving, perhaps as Photius, p. 539. 15 (from Eupolis) explains it, an inlaid paving. ὀφέλλω and ὄφελμα are simply used of raising the ground-level or of adorning. πυθμήν has its natural sense of foundation.

> And found a man adorning the mansion,
> Yet unadorned, with an inlaid pavement.

On the word see also Herwerden, *Lex. Suppl.*

P. 447. The readings of the Bodleian papyrus not noted are as follows:

Above υρην in *v.* 13 at distance of one verse is visible (ημο): certainly not any words in *v.* 11 (Lond). Where εκλιθου should come (*v.* 9) we have ... (τα . αν) πολε. ... In *v.* 13 the του of ἑαυτοῦ is fairly clear. In *v.* 15 fin. πλωιτηρ is clear. In *v.* 22 ολλοι is as easy as αλλοι, and in 26 χεις easier than υεις. In 14 my reading ηθ on which is based Mr. Milne's clever correction is, I think, certain.

Pp. 460–1. There are three main points of difficulty associated with this poem.

In the first place the whole story is associated by all other

571

# ADDENDA

Greek and Latin writers with Sardanapallus, not with Ninos.
As to this I suspect that Phoenix is influenced solely by metrical
considerations. I do not think it credible that -os is throughout corrupt—'son of Ninos,' 'at Nineveh,' ἶνις Νίνου, κτλ.

Secondly, there are two legends as to the inscription, both
given in Athenaeus. According to one, the famous saying,
'Eat, drink, and be merry: the rest is not worth *that*,' is part
of an inscription on Sardanapallus' memorial (not tomb) at
Anchialé, which, with Tarsus, Sardanapallus built in one day.
The other contains the words, 'I drank, I ate, I satisfied my
lust.' This was given to Greece by Choerilus. It was once in-
scribed on a stone pillar on a mound at Nineveh; but the
mound was pulled down by Cyrus. In one account Sardanapallus had no regular tomb but burnt himself with his wives
and concubines, not at Nineveh (Νίνος). In another, he was
murdered in his palace. He was the last of his dynasty.
See Mayor's Juvenal, ii. 178.

The decisive point as to which legend Phoenix followed is
in *v.* 12; but unfortunately this ends with a *vox nihili*, αἰδει.
Editors have generally read ᾀδει which is precisely the one
thing that we cannot read. ἀϊδές which I give is, in a sense,
certain from Hes. *Sc.* 477 τοῦ δὲ τάφον καὶ σῆμ' ἀϊδὲς ποίησεν
Ἄναυρος. We may then either (*a*) regard καὶ . . . ἀϊδές as an
illustrative adscript and read what we will (*e.g.* καὶ τὸ σῆμ'
ἵζει), 'for all men writ Where Ninos on his monument doth
sit.' The σῆμα might be the Anchialé monument and the
quotation given to show that σῆμα is not the same as τάφος.
This seems to me all very unlikely. (*b*) We may suppose
that Phoenix actually scanned the word ᾀδές and that the
diaeresis was put in, as so often in papyrus texts, by editors
to call attention to irregularity. (*c*) We may suppose that
Phoenix wrote (*e.g.*) ὅκου Νίνος νῦν καὶ τὸ σῆμ' ἀϊστωθέν, and
that the adscript gave the same sense as the original. Either
(*b*) or (*c*) seems to me certainly right; but it is quite doubtful
whether Νίνος is Ninos or Nineveh. I prefer the latter, the
destruction of Nineveh (*c.* 600 B.C.) being famous and proverbial. As in the Greek I leave it doubtful in my translation
whether ὅκου is locative or not.

P. 465, 3. 9. Malachite—darkish green, rare, beautiful,
and brittle—would be a suitable extravagance to allege rather
than a sober fact. In the grand hundred-marbled church of
St. Paul outside the Roman walls it appears only in the altars

# ADDENDA

presented by the Emperor of Russia, Nicholas the First. It is given as a material for a palace floor (πάτος: Sophocles *Lex. Byz.*) in the Septuagint version of Esther.

P. 499. 2. To the Greek humourists appropriate misfortune was an enthralling joke. The Greek book of jests called *Philogelos* says: "A drunkard who had bought a vineyard died before vintage." We are not amused. Or rather we use different forms, 'as unlucky as the man who . . .,' 'Why he couldn't even . . . without . . .,' 'Have you heard about poor old X?'

P. 547, *v.* 329. I am inclined to think the choliambic versifier wrote three poems about Alexander, an "Iliad," a "Thebaid," and a "Dareiad." In editing these verses I have made no attempt to estimate how far the Ionic dialect was employed. The writer of cod. A, otherwise our only good guide, atticizes ruthlessly throughout the history. Slight indications would seem to show that the original was in an Ionic dialect at least as strict as that of the Mimes of Herodes.

P. 566, *Adde* 9. Choliambos Scythini ap. Stob. *Ecl.* i. 8. 43 non recte agnovit Meineke.

### CALLIMACHI NOVAE LECTIONES

The following verses of Callimachus have lately been recovered by G. Vitelli (*Bull. Soc. Arch. d'Alex.* No. 24) from scholia. They are verses 99 *sqq.* (see the late Professor Mair's *Callimachus*, p. 272, lines 96 ff.).

They afford an admirable illustration of Callimachus' art in his use of this metre. Essentially lyric in cadence and metre, and strict in their Ionic versification, his verses yet give, as those of no other Greek poet do, the essential illusion of natural speech. A wide and versatile imagination, an use of deft touches to depict the crowd surging round the dead poet Hipponax, who is supposed to be speaking, a breathless but clear and distinct narration—all these mark out the genius of Callimachus as something infinitely higher than that of his rivals.

|  |  |
|---|---|
| ὦ Ἑκάτη πλήθευς ! | 99 |
| ὁ ψιλοκόρσης τὴν πνοὴν ἀναλώσει | 100 |

# ADDENDA

φ σέων ὅκως μὴ τὸν τρίβωνα γυμνώσῃ.
σωπὴ γενέσθω καὶ γράφεσθε τὴν ῥῆσιν.
ἀνὴρ Βαθυκλῆς ᾽Αρκάς—οὐ μακρὴν ἄξω—
ὦ λῷστε, μὴ σίλλαινε, καὶ γὰρ οὐδ᾽ αὐτὸς
μέγα σχολάζ[ων ε]ἰμὶ . . ρμεσ(ον) δινεῖν,          105
(ὦ) Ζεῦ ᾽Αχέροντος !—τῶν πάλαι τις εὐδαίμων
ἐγένετο, πάντα δ᾽ εἶχ᾽ ἐν οἶσιν ἄνθρωποι
θεοί τε λευκὰς ἡμέρας ἐπίστανται.

I translate:

> He'll lose his breath, will my bald-head comrade,
> In panting to keep cloak on his shoulder.
> Let there be silence! write ye my words down!
> In Arcady Bathycles—cease mocking,
> Sirrah! I fly not far: a brief moment
> Have I to spend with you: how stern, great Zeus,
> Is Acheron!—the patriarch thrice blest
> Did live, nor lacked in aught of such riches
> Wherewith endowed men live white days ever.
> (He was about to finish his last lap, etc.)

In *v.* 108 'white days' are 'days of white-raiment,' 'feast days'; see Hippon. *fr.* 65.

*v.* 103 αξω P: correxi.   *v.* 105 non fuit παρμεσον.   *v.* 106 num χάζευ . . . !

574